FREEDOM, NEC
THE KNOWLED
CONVERSATION WITH KARL BARTH
AND THOMAS F. TORRANCE

FREEDOM, NECESSITY, AND THE KNOWLEDGE OF GOD IN CONVERSATION WITH KARL BARTH AND THOMAS F. TORRANCE

By Paul D. Molnar

LONDON • NEW YORK • OXFORD • NEW DELHI • SYDNEY

T&T CLARK
Bloomsbury Publishing Plc
50 Bedford Square, London, WC1B 3DP, UK
1385 Broadway, New York, NY 10018, USA
29 Earlsfort Terrace, Dublin 2, Ireland

BLOOMSBURY, T&T CLARK and the T&T Clark logo are trademarks of Bloomsbury Publishing Plc

First published in Great Britain 2022

Cover design: Terry Woodley

A catalogue record for this book is available from the British Library.

Library of Congress Cataloging-in-Publication Data
Names: Molnar, Paul D., 1946– author.
Title: Freedom, necessity, and the knowledge of God in conversation with
Karl Barth and Thomas F. Torrance / by Paul D. Molnar.
Description: London ; New York : T&T Clark, 2022. |
Includes bibliographical references and index. |
Identifiers: LCCN 2021027898 (print) | LCCN 2021027899 (ebook) | ISBN 9780567700186 (hb) |
ISBN 9780567700223 (pb) | ISBN 9780567700162 (epdf) | ISBN 9780567700179 (epub)
Subjects: LCSH: Theology. | Theology, Doctrinal. | Barth, Karl, 1886–1968. |
Torrance, Thomas F. (Thomas Forsyth), 1913–2007. | LCGFT: Essays.
Classification: LCC BR118 .M56 2022 (print) | LCC BR118 (ebook) |
DDC 230–dc23
LC record available at https://lccn.loc.gov/2021027898
LC ebook record available at https://lccn.loc.gov/2021027899

ISBN: HB: 978-0-5677-0018-6
PB: 978-0-5677-0022-3
ePDF: 978-0-5677-0016-2
ePUB: 978-0-5677-0017-9

Typeset by Newgen KnowledgeWorks Pvt. Ltd., Chennai, India
Printed and bound in Great Britain

To find out more about our authors and books visit www.bloomsbury.com
and sign up for our newsletters.

CONTENTS

PREFACE

This is a book that I have been thinking about for a long time! My primary consideration in this work concerns the fact that I have come to believe that everything in theology really looks different when Jesus Christ, the Word of God incarnate, is allowed to be both the *first* and the *final* Word in theology. Of course, all Christians can find a place for Christ. But, whenever we have to find a place for Christ, I believe it is already too late, because, unless theological reflection begins with him, it has already bypassed God himself in an effort to speak about God as our Creator, Reconciler, and Redeemer. So, one might say that the whole point of this book is to illustrate the difference Jesus himself makes for all forms of theology including theological method, the doctrine of God, Christology, soteriology, liberation theology, interreligious dialogue, language for God, as well as specific theological issues such as the issues of universalism and "nonconceptual" knowledge of God, which Anselm for one, firmly rejected.

In the first chapter, I discuss the specific subject of God, Freedom, and Necessity with a view toward explaining why it is problematic to ascribe any sort of dialectical freedom and necessity to God in his eternal being and act as Father, Son, and Holy Spirit. I explain that whenever that is done, then it is thought that creation is in some sense necessary for God since God is love. I address this issue arguing, with the help of Karl Barth, that God is the One who loves in freedom and is not subject to any inner or outer necessities because he does not even need his existence to be who he is inasmuch as God simply *is* the Trinity from and to all eternity. And God certainly does not need us, even though in his free grace he has decided to have us as his covenant partners from eternity, and God remains faithful to us in and through his actions in his incarnate Word and the Holy Spirit.

However, that relationship is a relationship grounded in the freedom of God's grace and love, and therefore I argue that whenever that freedom is compromised with ideas that God is somehow becoming who he will be in relation to us, or realizing his eternal being by relating with us, then the power of God's saving actions actualized and demonstrated on the cross and in the resurrection of Christ himself is lost to view with important theological implications. Several key points in relation to divine freedom and the doctrine of the immanent Trinity which I have previously treated are reintroduced. But this time they are introduced with a view toward seeing what happens to the thinking of those who confuse the eternal generation of the Son from the Father with God's actions *ad extra* as Creator, Reconciler, and Redeemer. When that happens, one confuses the fact that God is indeed selfless in his love of us with the idea that because God is selfless toward us that must mean that God cannot find happiness in his eternal love without us. Such thinking I contend follows from a panentheistic view of the Creator/creature relationship that is unable to distinguish God's free actions of love for us from the processes of creation itself, to the detriment of both divine and human freedom.

Preface

Among the important issues discussed in this chapter is the issue concerning how to think about divine possibility and impassibility in ways that avoid Nestorian separation of Christ's divinity and humanity as well as the errors of *Patripassianism*. God can and does take our suffering and pain to himself in the incarnation and in doing so does what corresponds to his free and compassionate love of us. But God does not need to suffer in order to love since his free love expresses his eternal perfection as well as his mercy and righteousness. Also discussed is the question concerning whether or not God chooses to be dependent on the world so that God is somehow in need of the world for all eternity and thus in need of us in order to fulfil his purposes of love for us.

In Chapter 2, I offer a discussion of Karl Barth's theology in relation to two well-known Roman Catholic theologians, Walter Kasper and Elizabeth Johnson. Both Kasper and Johnson present their theologies in dialogue with Karl Rahner in an effort to advance beyond neo-scholastic views that were considered to be extrinsicist and unhelpful. While Kasper raised some questions to Rahner's thinking, Johnson relies heavily on Rahner's transcendental method to advance her own theology. I place their perspectives in dialogue with the views of Karl Barth focusing on the issue of the *analogia entis* in relation to the *analogia fidei*, and I argue that, while there is some agreement between Barth and his Catholic dialogue partners, their basic disagreement still stems from the fact that both Kasper and Johnson remain indebted to a version of the analogy of being which by definition begins with our religious experiences instead of with Jesus Christ, while Barth consistently was committed to allowing Jesus Christ as the Word of God incarnate to be the *first* and the *final* Word in his theology. In this chapter, I show what things look like when theology allows Jesus himself to be the *first* and *final* Word with a view toward possible agreement between Reformed and Roman Catholic theology that centers on a properly functioning Christology.

In the third chapter, I take up the difficult question of natural theology once again by focusing on Thomas F. Torrance's espousal of what he called a "new natural theology." After presenting a brief statement of what traditional natural theology upholds, I discuss a recent attempt to defend Torrance's "new natural theology" by illustrating why I think there were serious problems with Torrance's own position because he firmly insisted that natural theology must function within revelation in order to be scientific. By that he meant that theology needs to be shaped by the unique object of its reflection, namely, God, Christ, and the Spirit, in order to be objectively true. I compare Torrance's thinking to the views of Karl Barth arguing that both theologians wanted to apply the doctrine of justification to our knowledge of God and that they were right to do so. After a careful analysis of Torrance's view that our knowledge of God, which could only take place when the reconciliation accomplished for us in Christ is actualized in us by the Holy Spirit, I conclude by arguing that what Torrance really offered in his efforts to present his "new natural theology" was a theology of reconciled human nature as understood in light of grace, faith, and revelation. Notwithstanding that, I also point out that there were elements of the old natural theology Torrance consistently rejected still present in his work but chiefly when he was considering the relationship between theology and science. I raise the question about whether he might have been misled

viii

in his analysis by relying on Einstein's view of the relationship between geometry and physics.

Chapter 4 is a crucial chapter because in it I illustrate the enormous difference it makes if and when theologians espouse a scientific theology which Torrance rightly claims must be controlled *cognitively* by our relation with God in obedience to his reality and self-giving in his Word and Spirit. That means faith is not just a virtue that we cultivate in an effort to find God and live good Christian lives. Rather, faith really means knowledge of the truth which comes to us from God in our encounter with Jesus himself here and now as the risen, ascended and coming Lord through the power of his Holy Spirit. That means certainly one cannot know who God is without a conceptual relation with his incarnate Son who alone enables our knowledge of God the Father here and now. This chapter demonstrates with some power how different Torrance's view of grace, faith, and revelation is by contrasting his understanding of these theological categories with the views of Karl Rahner.

Rahner is an ideal conversation partner for Torrance on this issue because his entire theology is structured by his view that all knowledge of God, grace, and revelation can be understood best when understood from our unthematic and thus from our nonconceptual knowledge of God, grace, faith, and revelation. I argue that as long as God, revelation, grace, and faith are understood in that way, then in some sense the Holy Spirit becomes confused with the human spirit, and theology loses its objective grounding in acts of God himself who interacts with us in history in his Word and Spirit. Part of the difficulty regarding this issue is that Rahner thinks there is *continuity* between our transcendental experiences and God, grace, and revelation while Torrance argues that Jesus himself, as the grace and revelation of God in history, discloses to us that because of sin, which was clearly manifest in human rejection of Christ, there is *no continuity* between us and God that can be found in human experience, whether it be religious or not. That continuity can only be found in and through the Holy Spirit uniting us to Christ as our reconciler and redeemer and thus to the Father in faith. For Torrance, in other words, our minds really need healing so that we might have the mind of Christ and thus know both our sin and our salvation as these are disclosed in the very person and work of Christ himself. But that can only occur through conceptual union with God the Father through faith in his Son which also means through conceptual union with Christ. Therefore, Torrance would certainly reject Rahner's notion of anonymous Christianity as an attempt to present a Christianity without Christ that is akin to the way Paul Tillich attempted the very same thing by confusing knowledge of God with our experiences of depth and our ultimate concerns. This chapter illustrates that if Catholic and Protestant theologians could agree on the importance of conceptual knowledge of God, grace, faith, and revelation, then there could be widespread practical agreement among Christians who then would find their union not directly in magisterial statements of the church or in sets of universal nonconceptual experiences but in Christ himself as the Lord of the church which is his body on earth united to its heavenly head.

Preface

Following upon my argument in Chapter 4 for the importance of a properly understood scientific theology, I then analyze some recent views of liberation theology with a view toward demonstrating that whenever theological knowledge, including Christian ethics, is understood from experiences of liberation rather than exclusively from Christ who liberates us from the self-will that causes enmity between us and God and us and each other, then and there theology has lost its true and proper source of liberation. It is argued in Chapter 5 that when Christ is at the center of the discussion about political, theological, and religious liberation, then it will be seen that any attempt to identify the Holy Spirit by focusing on human acts of liberation and compassion always leads to versions of self-justification and thus to more estrangement from God's love and the freedom which is ours in Christ, and thus can only be found in him and not directly in our attempts to work for a better world. Christians do, of course, always work for a better world. But when it is thought that true liberation in the Christian sense can be seen, understood, and lived only by first working against oppression, then Christianity is reduced to moralistic attempts at self-justification. Such an approach will always fail just because in ourselves we are sinners who stand in need of Christ's reconciling grace and love as the enabling factor of our love of our neighbors. From this it follows that our working against what oppresses others spiritually and politically must be grounded in the fact that, while we were still sinners, God loved us in Christ and freed us to love him and on that basis to love our neighbors. In this chapter, I explain why serious mistakes are made in understanding Christian freedom and liberation by those who think that the truth of the Christian faith must be judged by people's ethical behavior.

Chapter 6 continues by explaining that while I strongly agree with those who think women and men should live their equality in the church and in the world, I do so because the sin that leads to patriarchalism has already been overcome in Christ's own life history for the human race. Since that is the case, I explain that the very idea that language for God must be changed for women to have equality with men in the church is seriously misguided for three important reasons. First, if men and women actually lived the freedom that is already theirs in Christ, since in him our self-will which expresses our enmity to God and others is already overcome for us, then women would not be subordinated to men within the church or anywhere else for that matter. Second, because this is the case, there is no need to attempt to redefine who God is for women to have equality in the church or elsewhere. Indeed, it is argued that the very idea that we have the power to define and redefine who God is indicates an immense confusion about theology since the truth of theology simply cannot be detached from Jesus himself who really is the way, the truth, and the life (Jn 14:6). Third, since any trained Christian theologian knows that there is no gender in God and that the Fatherhood of God is defined by the Father's unique relation with the Son and Spirit in eternity and not by anything within the realm of creation, the truth of who God is must never be thought of as coming *from* us. I explain in detail the difference this makes for those who think that conversion means women must tap into their own power in order to know God and the true meaning of what it means to be human today. In reality, conversion for Christians means tapping into the power of Jesus Christ through union with him in faith so that people can live from and in him as friends of God and as those who therefore love their neighbors by working against oppression. Since there is no gender in God, it makes no sense trying to find gender-neutral language for God. Any attempt to do so, I argue, leads to an impersonal idea of God that subverts God's personal acts of love toward us in Christ and within us by his Holy Spirit. Indeed, any attempt to do so suggests that we have the ability to define and redefine who God is when in reality we have no such ability since God alone names himself to us as the eternal Father, Son, and Spirit in his self-revelation.

In Chapter 7, I return to a discussion of the problem of universalism. I say this because in a 2015 article discussing Thomas F. Torrance's view of universalism published in the *Scottish Journal of Theology*, I explained exactly why he viewed a doctrine of universalism as a "menace to the Gospel." His point was that, while we may hope God will save everyone in the end, any attempt to make that a dogmatic statement will introduce a deterministic view of God's relations with us. The problem with this is that we cannot say exactly what will happen at the end since that will not occur until Christ actually returns to judge the living and the dead. Also, such a view does not take seriously the problems of sin and evil and presents a view of God such that if it was thought all would not be saved, then God's act of salvation for us would be considered a failure. Such a view would express our misguided and hopeless human attempt to limit who God is to what he does or might do for us.

Here I place Torrance's views in conversation with the views of David Bentley Hart in his recent book, *That All Shall Be Saved*. I explore Hart's view that if Christianity is taken as a whole then "the universalist understanding of its message is the only possible one." Hart is a particularly interesting dialogue partner for Torrance because his views illustrate with great clarity just how universalism, as a logical conclusion to one's view of Christian faith, results from an attempt to combine natural theology with a theology based on grace and revelation. What I show is that if one's view of sin and evil is developed apart from the fact that a proper view of both can only be achieved in light of Christ's forgiving grace, then it might follow that the idea of an eternal hell would mean a failure on God's part. In reality, an eternal hell is not a creation of God but the final alienation from God brought about by a final and inexplicable rejection of the love of God for us in Christ himself. While Torrance opposes universalism and limited atonement, the point in this chapter is that wherever universalism becomes the logical conclusion of one's reflections, then in reality both divine and human freedom have been compromised in crucial ways.

In the final chapter, I address the important question of whether Christians worship the same God as those from other Abrahamic faiths. This is an interesting and timely subject since it concerns a pressing issue. That issue concerns how we know the truth of the Christian religion and how that knowledge affects Christian relations with Jews and Muslims. I rely on Karl Barth's view of religion as our capricious and arbitrary attempt to reach God so that, in his view, all religions, including the Christian religion, need God's own reconciling grace if they are to be considered true. However, since the truth of the Christian religion is in no way grounded in Christians but in Christ alone, it is argued that any attempt to solve this problem religiously will only result in conflict among the three faiths which will never be settled because the truth of Christianity and the truth of Christianity in its unique and indispensable relation to Israel will never be understood apart from the revelation of God to Moses as the God of Abraham, Isaac, and Jacob. In other words, since truth is grounded in the God of the covenant and not at all in anyone's religious viewpoint or religious practice, Christianity cannot be understood at all as one religion among others. When that is attempted, then it is thought that we can find an idea or religious ideal that unites us. The point of the chapter, however, is that since all three faiths appeal to the God of Abraham, Isaac, and Jacob, then to that extent they all claim to worship the same God. But, as Muslims, Jews, and Christians explain their understanding of God from a religious perspective rather than from the revelation of God attested in the Old and New Testaments, then serious problems arise.

To explore this predicament, I consider the views of a Muslim scholar, a Jewish scholar, and a Christian scholar and show that while it may seem reasonable to claim all three faiths are united in a common monotheism, nothing separates them so radically as their commitment to their own version of monotheism. In the end, my argument is that what unites us is the God who acted as the savior of the human race in Jesus Christ himself such that Jews and Muslims are just as dependent on the grace of God at work in Christ for the whole world as Christians are. Thus, any attempt by Christians to claim that theirs is the true religion in itself in comparison with Islam and Judaism, and even in opposition to Islam and Judaism, have missed the point that Christianity's truth is grounded exclusively in grace so that the Church is the locus of true religion only to the extent that Christians live by grace alone. That means they are in no position to think that they are better than either Jews or Muslims since, apart from Christ's forgiving grace, all stand in need of reconciliation that can only come from God the Father through his Son and in the power of his Holy Spirit. Inasmuch as all three faiths appeal to the fact that they should be in solidarity because Jesus taught that we should love God above all and our neighbors as ourselves, there is hope in that the command to love God and neighbor is a command grounded in revelation and not in religion!

ACKNOWLEDGMENTS

I would like to thank Anna Turton, senior editor at Bloomsbury T&T Clark, for being consistently supportive and helpful in bringing this book to publication and in many other ways as well. She is a superb editor. I would also like to thank Sinead O'Connor of Bloomsbury T&T Clark for her assistance with the many technical details related to the publication of this volume. In addition, I am grateful to Iain R. Torrance for reading and commenting on a draft of Chapter 4, for his consistent friendship over many years and his willingness to discuss key theological issues and provide invaluable insight. I am also grateful to Todd Speidell for his interaction and discussion of many important issues related to the theology of Thomas F. Torrance as well as for his support and friendship. I would like to express my gratitude to Alex Irving for his interactions and discussion of Torrance's "new" natural theology. I am grateful to the journal of the Thomas F. Torrance Theological Fellowship, *Participatio*, for permission to reprint a previously published article entitled "Natural Theology: An Impossible Possibility?," supplemental volume 4: "Torrance and the Wesleyan Tradition" (2018): 148–83 in revised form in what is now Chapter 3. In addition, I wish to acknowledge Paul T. Nimmo and Paul Dafydd Jones for their helpful interactions with regard to a previous and shorter version of what is now Chapter 2. I am grateful to Oxford University Press for permission to reprint the following previously published material: Paul D. Molnar, chapter 42, "Barth and Roman Catholic Theology," *The Oxford Handbook of Karl Barth*, ed. Paul Dafydd Jones and Paul T. Nimmo (Oxford: Oxford University Press, 2019), 670–86. I must also thank the Karl Barth Society of North America for inviting me to speak on the subject of liberation theology in connection with Rubén Rosario Rodríguez's book, *Dogmatics after Babel: Beyond the Theologies of Word and Culture* at their meeting held in conjunction with the American Academy of Religion in San Diego, California, on November 24, 2019. That brief lecture has developed into what is now Chapter 5. Thanks are also due to the Thomas F. Torrance Theological Fellowship for inviting me to speak on the topic of T. F. Torrance's view of Universalism at its meeting held in conjunction with the Annual Meeting of the American Academy of Religion held in San Francisco, California, on November 18, 2011. That is a previous version of what is now an expanded discussion of Torrance's view of Universalism in Chapter 7 which includes a lengthy discussion of David Bentley Hart's recent book, *That All May Be Saved*. A revised version of that lecture was first published with the title "Thomas F. Torrance and the problem of universalism," in *The Scottish Journal of Theology* 68 (2) (2015): 154–86 and is here reprinted with permission. The original lecture given in San Francisco was recorded and later offered as a video on the website of Grace Communion International. Finally, I am grateful to the Journal *Cultural Encounters* for permission to reprint the following previously published material: Paul D. Molnar, "Do Christians Worship the Same God as Those from Other

Abrahamic Faiths?," in 15 (2) (2020): 39–71 as what is now Chapter 8. That chapter originated as a lecture at the American Academy of Religion given at the Evangelical Theology Session in San Antonio, Texas, on November 22, 2016. Additionally, I need to thank my good friend Paul Metzger for his support and interaction in connection with the material in Chapter 8.

I would also like to thank George Hunsinger for reading and commenting on a previous version of Chapter 1 and for his consistent friendship and support over many years. Thanks are also due to my good friend Myk Habets for his reading of a previous version of this book and for his excellent suggestion to add a chapter on language for God. That suggestion greatly enhances the quality of this book. In addition, I need to thank John J. McCormick for generously giving his time and expertise in reading through more than one version of this work and making editorial and substantive suggestions for improving the work along the way. Finally, I would also like express my gratitude to Tatiana I. Belanich, my graduate assistant at St. John's, for proofreading the entire manuscript during the spring semester of 2021. It goes without saying that the sole responsibility for any errors that remain is mine.

CHAPTER 1
GOD, FREEDOM, AND NECESSITY: KARL BARTH AND THE CURRENT DISCUSSION

The question of whether creation is necessary to God has long been an issue for Christian theologians in light of the traditional understanding of the *creatio ex nihilo*. Christian theologians traditionally have rejected the idea that the world is coeternal with God ever since that notion was identified and rejected in Origen's understanding of God's relation with the world.[1] Theologians realized that to presume creation is in any sense necessary for God or coeternal with God would blur the distinction between Creator and creature. This, in turn, would obliterate God's freedom in such a way that one might then conceptually confuse and reverse the roles of Creator and creature by somehow reducing God to his creative function. According to Thomas F. Torrance, it became increasingly evident in the fourth century that without a clear distinction between the eternal generation of the Son from the being of the Father and the creation of the world by the will of God bringing something into existence from nonexistence, "the Church would finally lapse back into paganism."[2]

In essence, the problem to be considered here concerns the fact that the Christian understanding of creation was, as Georges Florovsky held, "alien and even unintelligible to the Greek mind."[3] The reason for this is that "the Greek mind was firmly addicted to the conception of an Eternal Cosmos, permanent and immutable in its essential structure and composition. This Cosmos simply existed. Its existence was 'necessary,' it was an ultimate or first *datum*, beyond which neither thought nor imagination could

---

[1] See Georges Florovsky, "St Athanasius' Concept of Creation," *Studia Patristica*, vol. VI, ed. F. L. Cross (Berlin: *Akademie Verlag; Texte und Untersuchungen zur Geschichte der altchristlichen Literatur, Band 81,* 1962), 36–57. Reprinted at https://afkimel.wordpress.com/2014/11/07/florovsky-on-st-athanasius-and-the-doctrine-of-creation/, 1–13, 1–6.

[2] Thomas F. Torrance, *The Trinitarian Faith: The Evangelical Theology of the Ancient Catholic Church* (hereafter: *The Trinitarian Faith*) (Edinburgh: T&T Clark, 1988), 84. Torrance helpfully explains that Athanasius believed that Origen failed "to distinguish between the eternal generation of the Son and the creation of the world, between ontological and cosmological dimensions" and that this failure "is not unlike ... what is found today in process theology according to which the external relations of God are held in some measure to be *constitutive* of what he is as God." Thomas F. Torrance, *The Christian Doctrine of God, One Being Three Persons* (Edinburgh: T&T Clark, 1996), 208, emphasis mine. Torrance affirms that in creation and incarnation "the mighty living God who reveals himself to us through his Son and in his Spirit is absolutely free to do what he had never done before, and free to be other than he was eternally: to be Almighty Creator, and even to become incarnate as a creature within his creation, while nevertheless remaining eternally the God that he always was" (ibid.).

[3] Florovsky, "St Athanasius' Concept of Creation," 1.

penetrate."[4] While the shape of the cosmos was in flux, it nonetheless was thought to exist necessarily since "its very existence was perennial."[5] Florovsky went on to explain that for Christians, "the Creation of the world was conceived as a sovereign and 'free' act of God, and not as something which was 'necessarily' implied or inherent in God's own Being."[6] To make his point, Florovsky cited Gilson's well-known remark that "it is quite true that a Creator is an eminently Christian God, but a God whose very essence is to be a creator is not a Christian God at all."[7] His point was simply that "the very existence of the world was regarded by the Christians as a mystery and miracle of Divine Freedom."[8]

If Florovsky is right, and I believe he is, then it is crucial to recognize that whenever the world is thought to be necessary to God, God's freedom in himself and his freedom to act effectively as savior and redeemer for us become unrecognizable as acts of God in creation since they cannot be distinguished from creation itself. This chapter will address this theme by focusing on exactly what difficulties arise in the thinking of a number of contemporary theologians who either claim to follow Barth's thinking or critique it in order to advance views of God's relations with us that ascribe *both* necessity *and* freedom to God. Relying on Barth's view that while God's eternal being is necessary in that he could not be other than the triune God and still be God, I will argue that he nevertheless rightly held that God does not act out of need just because he is free as the one who loves in himself, and therefore God can and does love us in freedom on that basis.[9] Failure to recognize this leads to views that God needs the world and needs to be perfected and such views tend to undermine the freedom of grace with the idea that God is somehow dependent on creation, as we shall see.

Necessity and Divine Freedom

Karl Barth maintains that in connection with the Father's eternal begetting of his Son, God has freedom to will or not to will creation, but that

> He does not have this freedom in respect of His being God. God cannot *not* be God. Therefore—and this is the same thing—He cannot *not* be Father and cannot be

---

[4]Ibid.

[5]Ibid.

[6]Ibid., 2.

[7]Ibid. Florovsky was citing Etienne Gilson, *God and Philosophy* (New Haven, CT: Yale University Press, 1979), 88.

[8]Ibid.

[9]According to Florovsky God's triune being can be described as necessary in St. Athanasius' thinking, even though Athanasius never directly did so. But this did not imply "that God is subject to certain 'constraint' or fatalistic determinism." Rather, it meant that "God does not 'choose' His own Being. He simply is." Florovsky, "St Athanasius' Concept of Creation," 8. Barth's thinking echoes that of St. Athanasius as when he speaks of "the God who knows no necessity, who, not needing His own being, simply has being as a matter of empirical fact … as the One who is." Karl Barth, *Church Dogmatics*, 4 vols. in 13 pts., vol. II, *The Doctrine of God*, pt. 1, ed. G. W. Bromiley and T. F. Torrance, trans. T. H. L. Parker, W. B. Johnston, Harold Knight, and J. L. M. Haire (hereafter: CD) (Edinburgh: T&T Clark, 1975), 307.

without the Son. His freedom or aseity in respect of Himself consists in His freedom, not determined by anything but Himself, to be God, and that means to be the Father of the Son. A freedom to be able not to be this would be an abrogation of His freedom.[10]

Nonetheless, Barth insists that God's acts of creation and incarnation are not at all demanded by his essence because God's actions are free in the sense that God does not even need his being to be who he is since as God, he already and always simply is who he is as the triune God who loves in freedom: "The freedom in which God exists means that He does not need His own being in order to be who He is: because He already has His own being and is Himself."[11]

Having said this, Barth therefore insisted that it is appropriate to consider what God "might have done" when thinking about the fact that God did not and does not need us but nonetheless freely chose to love us. Thus, Barth maintained that

> it is only in this antithesis that we can really understand what He has done. In this light one can also see how dubious it is to set the doctrine of the Word of God in the framework of an anthropology. In that case the freedom of the divine purpose for man can be asserted only at a later stage, while it is really denied by the starting-point.[12]

These remarks by Barth rule out any idea that in electing us God could be thought to give himself his being as triune. In fact, they rule out any idea at all that God gives himself his being since, as God, he already and eternally is who he is in the freedom and perfection of his act as Father, Son, and Holy Spirit and thus as the one who loves.[13] Accordingly, for Barth,

> in the intertrinitarian life of God the eternal generation of the Son or Logos is, of course the expression of God's love, of His will not to be alone. But it does not follow from this that God could not be God without speaking to us. We undoubtedly understand God's love for man, or in the first instance for any reality distinct from Himself, only when we understand it as free and unmerited love not resting on any need. God would be no less God if He had created no world and no man … Only when we are clear about this can we estimate what it means that God has actually, though not necessarily, created a world and us, that His love actually, though not necessarily, applies to us.[14]

---

[10]Barth, CD I/1, 434, emphasis mine.
[11]Barth, CD II/1, 306. For a discussion of the implications of this insight, see Paul D. Molnar, *Divine Freedom and the Doctrine of the Immanent Trinity: In Dialogue with Karl Barth and Contemporary Theology*, 2nd edition (hereafter: *Divine Freedom*) (London: T&T Clark, 2017) 172–7.
[12]Barth, CD I/1, 140.
[13]This is one reason Barth held that "the God who takes His origin from himself or is *constituted* by Himself is in a certain sense limited by the possibility of His non-being and therefore He is not the free God." CD II/1, 305, emphasis mine.
[14]Barth, CD I/1, 139–40.

Importantly, Barth very clearly avoided the error of Origen by asserting that "the eternal generation of the Son by the Father tells us first and supremely that God is not at all lonely even without the world and us. His love has its object in Himself. And so we cannot say that our existence as that of the recipients of God's Word is constitutive for the concept of the Word."[15] This series of statements should not pass without explaining that the position for which I am arguing in this chapter, which takes Barth's stated position on freedom and necessity seriously, is diametrically opposed to the views of Bruce McCormack and some of his followers who think that God did indeed give himself his eternal being in electing to be God in relationship with us. McCormack claims that there was an important change in Barth's thinking between CD I/1 and IV/1 such that in CD II/1, for instance, Barth could describe "the work of reconciliation and redemption as a 'fundamentally new work' "[16] while in CD IV/1 Barth rejected this idea.[17] Therefore, he alleges that in CD IV/1 Barth does not think of the incarnation as "a new event in God when it happens in time."[18] While it is new to us as the revelation of what had been a hidden mystery up to that point in time, McCormack claims that

> it is not new to God because it is the outworking in time of the eternal event in which God gave to himself the being he would have for all eternity. We have before us here another piece of significant evidence demonstrating that an important change has taken place within the bounds of the *Church Dogmatics*. In I/1 … Barth insisted that the incarnation was a new event in God's life. In IV/1, he denies it.[19]

However, the text that McCormack cites in support of his view (CD IV/1, 193) does not actually support his claims here since Barth never says that God gives himself his being. In fact, Barth argues that the mystery which is revealed in Jesus is offensive because in Jesus Christ what is revealed is that "for God it is just as natural to be lowly as it is to be high, to be near as it is to be far, to be little as it is to be great, to be abroad as to be at

---

[15]Ibid., 140.

[16]Bruce L. McCormack, "The Actuality of God: Karl Barth in Conversation with Open Theism," in *Engaging the Doctrine of God: Contemporary Protestant Perspectives*, ed. Bruce L. McCormack (Grand Rapids, MI: Baker Academic, 2008), 185–242, 234.

[17]Bruce L. McCormack, "The Doctrine of the Trinity after Barth: An Attempt to Reconstruct Barth's Doctrine in the Light of His Later Christology," in *Trinitarian Theology after Barth*, ed. Myk Habets and Phillip Tolliday (Eugene, OR: Pickwick, 2011), 108.

[18]Ibid.

[19]Ibid. This idea that God gives himself his eternal being in election is repeated more than once by McCormack. Thus, "God's gracious decision is an eternal one and that means that the triunity of God cannot follow this decision in some kind of temporal sequence of events. The two things belong together because God is a Subject insofar as he gives himself (by an eternal act) his own being." Bruce McCormack, "Grace and being: The role of God's gracious election in Karl Barth's theological ontology," in *The Cambridge Companion to Karl Barth*, ed. John Webster (Cambridge: Cambridge University Press, 2000), 104. The problem here is that Barth rejects that idea all along the line because he claims that if God had to give himself the being he already and eternally has as triune, then God would be limited by the fact that he might not have been eternally the triune God.

home."[20] Following this, he holds that because God chooses to become present to us in the world created by him and yet characterized by sin,

> He chooses to go into the far country, to conceal His form of lordship in the form of this world and therefore in the form of a servant. He is not untrue to Himself but genuinely true to Himself, to the freedom which is that of his love. He does not have to choose and do this. He is free in relation to it. We are therefore dealing with the genuine article when He does choose and do this.[21]

So, while Barth does indeed claim that God's humility in the incarnation is a new mystery to us and is not a mystery for him, he intends to say that "in the condescension in which he gives Himself to us in Jesus Christ He exists and speaks and acts as the One He was from all eternity and will be to all eternity." And who he was and is happens to be the eternal Father, Son, and Holy Spirit.[22] Thus, "it is His sovereign grace that He wills to be and is amongst us in humility, our God, God for us, as that which He is in Himself, in the most inward depth of His Godhead. He does not become another God … The One who reconciles the world with God is necessarily the one God Himself in His true Godhead."[23] Barth's point here is that there is "a humility grounded in the being of God" so that the obedience of the man Jesus is not a capricious act but "a free choice made in recognition of an appointed order … which was intended to be obeyed."[24]

From here Barth argues that God's freedom for us as reconciler in Jesus means that

> the freedom in which God can be lowly as well as exalted, abroad as well as at home, our God in the hidden form of One who is accused and judged as well as in Himself (and known only to Himself) the Lord of Glory—this freedom of which God makes use in His action as the Reconciler of the world is not simply an arbitrary ability.[25]

Enough has been said here to illustrate that Barth nowhere claims that in these free acts of condescension for us or in God's choice to act in these ways, God gives himself his being. He does of course go on to argue that "there is in God Himself an above and a below, a *prius* and a *posterius*, a superiority and a subordination" so that "it belongs to the inner life of God that there should take place within it obedience."[26] While Barth certainly wished to avoid both modalism and subordinationism with this viewpoint, there were

---

[20]Barth, CD IV/1, 192.
[21]Ibid., 193.
[22]This is why he says of God that "the one name of the one God is the threefold name of Father, Son and Holy Spirit" and that God "does not exist as such outside or behind or above these modes of being. He does not exist otherwise than as Father, Son and Holy Spirit" (CD IV/1, 205).
[23]Barth, CD IV/1, 193.
[24]Ibid.
[25]Ibid., 194.
[26]Ibid., 200–1.

unfortunately difficulties in his reading the obedience of the Son in his economic condescension for us back into the eternal Trinity as a basis for God's actions *ad extra*. Nonetheless, even with the difficulties in his thought here, Barth never abandoned the notion that God's condescension was a free action of the triune God as an act of grace. Thus, it was in no sense constitutive of the divine being but an expression of it. I will not discuss this matter here in detail since I have done that elsewhere.[27]

Inasmuch as McCormack mistakenly thinks that for Barth election should be considered the ground of God's triunity, he believes that Barth should have logically reversed the doctrines of election and the Trinity, even though Barth never did. On that basis, he maintains that God gives himself his triune being in deciding for election. Many statements of McCormack's can be adduced to express the basic confusion that follows these assumptions. But the main confusion can be very simply expressed by noting that in his thinking he has basically reduced the eternal Trinity to God's actions of creation, reconciliation, and redemption. Just consider the following statement: "If the eternal being of God is constituted by His eternal act of turning towards the human race—if that is what God is 'essentially'—then God's essence is not hidden to human perception. It is knowable because it is constituted by the fact of turning towards us. God in himself *is* God 'for us.'"[28] Barth never actually espoused any such view at all.[29] In fact, Barth consistently opposed such thinking because God's essence is not constituted by his turning towards us since, as noted above, Barth maintained that "one cannot say that our existence as that of the recipients of God's Word is constitutive for the concept of the Word" and since the eternal generation of the Son tells us that "God is not at all lonely even without the world and us" Barth also believed that God's love "has its object in Himself."[30] Instead, it is precisely as the eternal Father, Son, and Spirit that God freely turns toward us. However, God does so in free grace without surrendering his deity but in exercising it for us. Therefore, any espousal of the view that God's eternal being is constituted by his turning toward us leads not only to the false idea of a dependent deity but also to the false idea that God's being and act are reduced to his actions *ad extra*. In the words of George Hunsinger,

> The Father does not eternally generate the Son for the purpose of pre-temporal election. If election were the purpose of the Son's eternal generation by the Father ... The Trinity would *necessarily* be dependent on the world ... the Son would

---

[27]See Paul D. Molnar, "The obedience of the Son in the Theology of Karl Barth and of Thomas F. Torrance," *Scottish Journal of Theology* 67 (1) (2014): 50–69.

[28]McCormack, "Grace and Being," 99.

[29]This has been discussed at length in Molnar, *Divine Freedom*; Paul D. Molnar, *Faith, Freedom and the Spirit: The Economic Trinity in Barth, Torrance and Contemporary Theology* (Downers Grove, IL: IVP Academic, 2015); George Hunsinger, *Reading Barth with Charity: A Hermeneutical Proposal* (Grand Rapids, MI: Baker Academic, 2015); and *Trinity and Election in Contemporary Theology*, ed. Michael T. Dempsey (Grand Rapids, MI: Eerdmans, 2011).

[30]Barth, CD I/1, 139–40.

be subordinated to an external end; and … the Son would be object but not the subject of election.[31]

Divine Freedom and the Immanent Trinity

Here it is worth considering for a moment the fact that in the 1920s Barth was criticized by Erich Przywara for a supposed "sinister reduction running through [his] whole work" such that "the Trinity supposedly dissolves into that of revealer, revealing and being revealed, the incarnation is only a concretion of this process of revelation, and grace is simply the subjective possibility of revelation."[32] From this, Przywara concluded, according to Barth's own assessment, that "all the fulness of the divine life is thus reduced to the one address, and in the last resort the final pantheistic correlation-theology of Protestant Liberalism is simply reversed in me. The 'from below upwards' is changed into a 'from above downwards.'"[33] Barth concluded that "this is certainly not a correct estimation of [his] intentions nor of what [he] actually said."[34] And in response to this misreading of his theology, Barth asserted that he did not want to hold a view in which "God becomes a predicate of man" or in which "man becomes a requisite in God's nature."[35]

Decisively, then, in order to avoid this mistaken theology, Barth powerfully contended that "we must not think away the free basis that this correlation [between God and us] has in God" as Wobbermin, Winckler and then Bultmann did.[36] How could this be avoided? According to Barth it could only be avoided if "we make a deliberate and sharp distinction between the Trinity of God as we may know it in the Word of God revealed, written and proclaimed, and God's immanent Trinity … between the 'eternal history of God' and His temporal acts."[37] From this he concluded that " 'God for us' does not arise as a matter of course out of the 'God in Himself,' " since this is not "a state of God which we can fix and assert on the basis of the concept of man participating in His revelation, but that it is true as an act of God, as a step which God takes towards man and by which man becomes the man that participates in His revelation."[38] It must be forcefully noted here that what Barth was rejecting was precisely the kind of logical necessity that McCormack has read back into the Trinity. Instead, Barth consistently insisted that "in the strict doctrine of the Trinity as the presupposition of Christology, it must speak of God in Himself, in isolation from man" instead of assuming that the "correlation" of

---

[31]George Hunsinger, "Election and the Trinity: Twenty-Five Theses on the Theology of Karl Barth," *Modern Theology* 24 (2) (April 2008): 179–83, 192, emphasis mine.
[32]Barth, CD I/1, 172.
[33]Ibid.
[34]Ibid.
[35]Ibid.
[36]Ibid.
[37]Ibid.
[38]Ibid.

God and us is "conditioned from without, by man." Against Gogarten, Barth therefore wrote that when we know ourselves as addressed by the Word of God, then we will know God "as the One who addresses us in freedom, as the Lord, who does not exist only as he addresses us, but exists as the One who establishes and ratifies this relation and correlation, who is also God before it, in Himself, in His eternal history."[39]

Importantly, then, these remarks in response to Przywara's misunderstanding of Barth's view of God's freedom, appear again in CD IV/1 when Barth once more insisted upon God's freedom. He did so not by absolutely rejecting the *logos asarkos*, but by asserting that in the doctrine of reconciliation one could not retreat to the *logos asarkos* as a way of avoiding the fact that we only know God in himself through the incarnate Word and not directly. Any attempt to avoid the incarnate Word in those circumstances would inevitably use the idea of the *logos asarkos* to speak of God without actually relying on the revelation of God in Christ. That is impossible. However, Barth also claimed that

> the second "person" of the Godhead in Himself and as such is not God the Reconciler. In Himself and as such he is not revealed to us. In Himself and as such He is not *Deus pro nobis*, either ontologically or epistemologically. He is the content of a necessary and important concept in trinitarian doctrine when we have to understand the revelation and dealings of God in the light of their free basis in the inner being and essence of God. But since we are now concerned with the revelation and dealings of God, and particularly with the atonement, with the person and work of the Mediator, it is pointless, as it is impermissible, to return to the inner being and essence of God and especially to the second person of the Trinity as such, in such a way that we ascribe to this person another form than that which God Himself has given in willing to reveal Himself and to act outwards.[40]

In other words, for Barth one could not separate the form of revelation (the humanity of the Word) from the content, which is the act of God speaking, reconciling, and redeeming us as the incarnate Word.[41] With these words, Barth certainly was not

---

[39]Ibid. This is why Barth insists that in our knowing God on the basis of his revelation "the possibility and necessity on the basis of which this is so are grounded only on the fact that He wills to have these dealings with us ... so there is in itself neither a necessity nor even a possibility that God must or can be present as the object of our viewing and conceiving. God is the One who is to and by and in Himself ... God does not have to be the object of our cognition ... If, in spite of this, He is, what is revealed in this fact is only the exuberant freedom of the love in which He is who He is; not a necessity, on the basis of which He has to be this, or even the possibility, on the basis of which He can be. In His self-revelation as Father, Son and Holy Spirit we can see the fact that He is the object of our cognition ... But ... it does not mean that we can see why and how, on the basis of what necessity and possibility, He is this One. We know Him very badly in his revelation, in His emergence from his self-sufficient glory, if we do not accept this emergence and His love as free love or if we try to regard His objectivity for us as necessary or even possible. His objectivity is always grace even in His revelation" (Barth, CD II/1, 206). This is why Barth insists that when God actually is an object of our knowledge this is due to the miraculous action of God alone acting in freedom for us.

[40]Barth, CD IV/1, 52.

[41]Thus, Barth claims that the revelation of God the Father who "can be our Father because He is Father in Himself, because fatherhood is an eternal mode of being of the divine essence," is imparted to us "in the

rejecting the existence of the eternal Word within the immanent Trinity as *logos asarkos*. Instead, he was asserting that this existence of the eternal Son or Word of God must be acknowledged in a proper doctrine of the Trinity in order to recognize the freedom of God's grace in God's actions *ad extra*. This is what McCormack lost the ability to recognize and to state in his logical reversal of election and the Trinity. And because he lost this, he could make no sense of Barth's assertion of God's freedom here.

So he responded to these comments by Barth by asking, "Why is it 'in *this* context' that we must not refer to the second 'person' of the Trinity as such? What context could there possibly be which would justify speaking in this way?"[42] Barth just gave the answer to that question. But from within the logic espoused by McCormack, namely, that it is in God's election of us that God constitutes his triunity, there can be no justification for recognizing the fact that God's freedom refers to his eternal triune being and act in which God loves before loving us and without having to love us. Without that acknowledgment, God's eternal being as the triune God is always reduced to his actions *ad extra*. So the context for those assertions was a strict doctrine of the Trinity.

In his commentary on this passage, McCormack claims that if Barth had stopped at simply speaking of the *logos asarkos*, then this might have represented a "lapse in concentration." But because he went on to assert that this statement was necessary to recognize God's freedom, McCormack concludes that "Barth either did not fully realize the profound implications of his doctrine of election for the doctrine of the Trinity, or he shied away from drawing them for reasons known only to himself."[43] However, it must be said here, as forcefully as possible, that Barth really knew what he was doing when he made those assertions which appear once again in a different form in CD IV/2. He stated as clearly as anyone could that these assertions are necessary in order to recognize the freedom of God. McCormack lost that ability with his further claim that "there is no longer any room left here [in IV/1] for an abstract doctrine of the Trinity. There is a triune being of God—only in the covenant of grace."[44] This is exactly what Barth wished to avoid all along the line! If the triune being of God only exists within the economy as McCormack claims here, then there is in reality no preexistent immanent Trinity prior to the covenant. Beyond that, Barth's view of the Trinity was never abstract in any case since it was always specifically shaped by the eternal being and act of God the Father, Son, and Holy Spirit.

Listen for a moment to Barth's words from CD IV/2 on this point.

---

person of the Revealer Jesus of Nazareth. Its content cannot be abstracted from this form. There can be no question here of distinguishing between content and form as though the content could be regarded as divine and necessary and the form as human and contingent ... The form here is essential to the content, i.e., God is unknown as our Father, the Creator, to the degree that He is not made known by Jesus." Barth, CD I/1, 390.
[42] McCormack, "Grace and Being," 102.
[43] Ibid.
[44] Bruce McCormack "Election and the Trinity: Theses in Response to George Hunsinger," *Trinity and Election in Contemporary Theology*, ed. Michael T. Dempsey, 115–37 (Grand Rapids, MI: Eerdmans, 2011), 128.

The statements "God is" and "God loves" are synonymous. They explain and confirm one another. It is in this way, in this identity of being and love, that God reveals Himself to us as He loves us. He reveals Himself as the One who, even though He did not love us and were not revealed to us, even though we did not exist at all, still loves in and for Himself as surely as He is and is God; who loves us by reason and in consequence of the fact that *He is the One who loves in His freedom in and for Himself*, and is God as such. It is only of God that it can be said that He is in the fact that He loves and loves in the fact that He is.[45]

Following his own view, McCormack claims that "the *decision* for the covenant of grace is the ground of God's triunity and, therefore of the eternal generation of the Son and of the eternal procession of the Holy Spirit from the Father and Son."[46] This position is diametrically opposed to Barth's view that the eternal generation of the Son was "the ground of God's free election of us."[47] It is on the basis of this misreading of Barth, that McCormack then criticizes him for opening a gap between the immanent and economic Trinity with his quite proper insistence that God's omnipotence cannot be reduced to his omnicausality. Thus, Barth rightly maintained that God "is omnipotent in his work" but that

He has not lost His omnipotence in this work [creation, reconciliation and redemption]. It has not changed into his omnicausality in this work ... The love with which He turns to us in this work, and in which He has made Himself our

---

[45]Barth, CD IV/2, 755, emphasis mine.

[46]McCormack, "Grace and Being," 103. Lest anyone think that McCormack actually upheld God's freedom as Barth understood it, this statement certainly did not, since for Barth the eternal generation of the Son was the ground of God's free election of us; it was not the other way around. Thus, "the triune life of God which is free life in the fact that it is Spirit, is the basis of His whole will and action even *ad extra*, as the living act which He directs to us. It is the basis ... of the election of man to covenant with Himself" (Barth, CD IV/2, 345). And McCormack's thinking here logically led him to claim in a later article on impassibility that "an attempt has been made here to think together divine immutability with divine passibility based on the view that *the second trinitarian person is eternally generated as divine-human relation*, which accounts for the inseparability of natures in the incarnated Christ." Alexandra Pârvan and Bruce L. McCormack, "Immutability, (Im)passibility and Suffering: Steps towards a 'Psychological' Ontology of God," in *Neue Zeitschrift für Systematische Theologie und Religionsphilosophie* (March, 2017; 59 (1): 1–25, 25). The idea that the second trinitarian person is eternally generated as a divine-human relation obliterates God's freedom as Barth understood it because he invariably insisted that God's Word would "still be His Word apart from this becoming [incarnate], just as Father, Son and Holy Spirit would be none the less eternal God, if no world had been created" (CD I/2, 135). If the second person of the Trinity is generated as a divine-human relation then Jesus' true humanity and true divinity are undermined because he was eternally generated as the Son who is *homoousios* with the Father and his humanity, as true humanity, only came into being in the actual event of incarnation. This thinking embodies a clear confusion of the immanent and economic Trinity since the second trinitarian person within the immanent Trinity is not a "divine-human relation" but the eternal Son of the Father. Not only does McCormack's thinking in this instance impersonalize the eternal Son in relation to the Father, but it once more obliterates the unique and exclusive relation of the Son to the Father in pretemporal eternity by espousing a view which substitutes a "divine-human relation" for the eternal Son. This repeats Origen's failure to distinguish the eternal generation of the Son from creation and incarnation as noted in n. 2.

[47]Barth, CD IV/2, 345.

God, has not made Him in the least degree poorer or smaller. It has its power and its reality as love for us too in the fact that it continues to be free love ... He is wholly our God, but He is so in the fact that He is not our God only.[48]

However, ignoring Barth's proper idea that while God is wholly our God, "He is so in the fact that He is not our God only," McCormack claims this thinking by Barth is dangerous and goes "against the very core of [Barth's] methodological commitments" by opening the door "to speculation with regard to what God could have done—thereby looking away from the limits set for us by God's self-revelation in Jesus Christ."[49]

In these statements McCormack fails to acknowledge the freedom of God that Barth affirmed and which was noted above. Barth held together two critical insights, namely, (1) that the eternal generation of the Son expresses the fact that in his own eternal being and act as the one who loves, God's will is not to be alone and (2) that "it does not follow from this that God could not be God without us ... God would be no less God if He had created no world and no man ... Only when we are clear about this can we estimate what it means that God has actually, though not necessarily, created a world and us, that His love actually, though not necessarily, applies to us."[50] Far from espousing a dangerous idea here by supposedly looking away from Jesus Christ, Barth actually was thinking of the fact that unless we acknowledge this freedom of God in creation and reconciliation, we would not be thinking about the Trinity or the covenant precisely as a covenant of grace.

Barth on Freedom and Necessity

Having clarified what I am arguing for and against in this chapter, I now return to Barth's own understanding of God's freedom and necessity. For Barth, when we say that God is *a se*

we do not say that God creates, produces or originates Himself. On the contrary, we say that (as manifest and eternally actual in the relationship of Father, Son and Holy Ghost) He is the One who already has and is in Himself everything which would have to be the object of his creation and causation if He were not He, God.[51]

Moreover, for Barth, "God acts with inward freedom and not in fulfilment of a law to which He is supposedly subject."[52] Importantly then for Barth, God "cannot 'need' His

---

[48]Barth, CD II/1, 547.
[49]McCormack, *Engaging the Doctrine of God*, 236.
[50]Barth, CD I/1, 139–40.
[51]Barth, CD II/1, 306.
[52]Barth, CD I/2, 135.

own being because He affirms it in being who He is" so that "what can need existence, is not God Himself, or His reality, but the reality which is distinct from Himself."[53] This is why Barth insisted that if we seek the "necessity" of God's being as the triune God on any other basis than the "empirical decision" in which God freely reaffirms himself as Father, Son, and Holy Spirit and indeed as the one who loves as such, then we might well have referred to "a God who in his need to be is not God but the postulated apotheosis of our creaturely existence."[54] This remark is clearly in harmony with the views of Florovsky and Gilson insofar as they both opposed reducing God to his creative function. For Barth, God is not conditioned by anything within his own nature and certainly not by anything outside himself. Thus, he held that "the creature which conditions God is no longer God's creature, and the God who is conditioned by the creature is no longer God."[55]

God's Free Act of Creation

For Barth, this view of God's freedom and love means that to speak of the Christian God as Creator of the world has a "double content," that is, "it speaks of the *freedom* of God … over against the world, and of His *relationship* … to the world."[56] Thus, God's relationship to the world is not one of parity, Barth says, "but that in this relationship God has absolute *primacy*" such that "heaven and earth are what they are *through* God and *only* through God."[57] It follows then that "heaven and earth are *not themselves God*, are not anything in the nature of a divine generation or emanation, are not, as the Gnostics or mystics would … have it … identical with the Son or Word of God."[58]

This is an extremely important point, as we shall see, because those theologians who ascribe necessity to God's eternal being and act in the sense rejected here by Barth inevitably confuse the Father's eternal generation of the Son with his actions as Creator in relation to us. There is, in other words, a connection between mistakenly identifying God with creation in some sense and thinking of creation as an emanation from the divine being so that God's free choice in creating is eradicated. To avoid such thinking Barth insisted that "the creation of the world is not a movement of God in Himself, but

---

[53]Barth, CD II/1, 306.
[54]Ibid., 307. The fact that "no other being is absolutely its own, conscious, willed and executed decision" (CD II/1, 271) must not be taken to mean that God's being as Father, Son, and Spirit results from his decision to reaffirm himself, as we have just seen. Rather it means that God really loves in freedom in himself, and therefore God can love us effectively, without needing us, as only God can. This follows from the positive fact that God is the only "self-moved being" who loves as such but is also free of necessity in "His own inner being" (CD II/1, 268–70, 303).
[55]Barth, CD II/1, 580.
[56]Karl Barth, *Credo: A Presentation of the Chief Problems of Dogmatics with Reference to the Apostles' Creed* (Sixteen lectures delivered at the University of Utrecht in February and March, 1935), trans. J. Strathearn McNab (hereafter: *Credo*) (London: Hodder & Stoughton, 1936), 30.
[57]Ibid., 30–1.
[58]Ibid., 31.

a free *opus ad extra*, finding its necessity only in His love" without "casting any doubt on His self-sufficiency: the world cannot exist without God, but if God were not love … He could exist very well without the world."[59]

With this last remark, it is vital not to misconstrue what Barth is saying here. This last statement should not be taken to mean that because God is love, therefore he must love another outside himself, given what was already said above. Such a false interpretation of Barth would suggest that in some sense God needs the world to be God. That idea, as noted above, would compromise God's self-sufficiency and also the effectiveness of God's actions for us as reconciler and redeemer. Barth insisted that God's "freedom in Himself," that is, "His primary absoluteness,"

> has its truth and reality in the inner Trinitarian life of the Father with the Son by the Holy Spirit. It is here, and especially in the divine mode as the Son who is the "image of the invisible God" (Col. 1:15), in God Himself that the divine freedom in its aspect of communion with the other, i.e., the secondary absoluteness of God, has its original truth. Here it is not yet relationship and fellowship with the other that is outside God, with the created world. We should be repeating the error of Philo and Gnosticism, which was unhesitatingly repudiated by the Early Church, if we tried to identify the Son of God with the world, and therefore *to introduce the world in some sense as a necessary element*, a divine mode, into the life of the Godhead. There could not then be any question of God's freedom in regard to it … *The existence of the world is not needed in order that there should be otherness for Him [God]*. Before all worlds, in His Son He has otherness in Himself from eternity to eternity.[60]

It is also crucial to recognize here that for Barth it is not God's act of relating with us that constitutes his eternal freedom as the one who loves but simply the fact that God's eternal act is the act of the Father, Son, and Holy Spirit who freely and in grace seeks and creates fellowship with us, a fellowship that is already and eternally his as Father, Son, and Holy Spirit.[61] Hence, "this essence of God [His innermost hidden essence] which is seen in His revealed name is His being and therefore His act as Father, Son and Holy Spirit" and because in this being and act, God is God

> in Himself without us, and therefore without this [fellowship with us], He has that which He seeks and creates between Himself and us. It implies so to speak an overflow of His essence that He turns to us … this overflow … is an overflow

---

[59]Ibid., 31–2.
[60]Barth, CD II/1, 317, emphasis mine. It should be noted that these very words repeat what Barth said in CD I/1, 139–40, as presented above.
[61]Ibid., 273.

which is not demanded or presupposed by *any necessity*, constraint, or obligation, least of all from outside, from our side, or by *any law by which God Himself is bound and obliged*.[62]

This last remark is in direct conflict with the idea, discussed below, that since God has become bound by his own love-desire for creation, he then allows his life to be determined by creatures as a kind of freely chosen necessity. It also rules out all ideas of "volitional necessity" because these notions also function by ascribing necessity to God in the manner just mentioned.[63] T. F. Torrance's important belief that any thought that there is a "law in the Divine nature which makes God love, is to misunderstand it quite as much as to think of something in man which demands that God love him."[64] This is in harmony with Barth's thinking. For Torrance this distinguishes the Christian religion from all others.

---

[62]Barth, CD II/1, 273, emphasis mine. This is a point that Matthew J. Aragon Bruce seems to have misunderstood when he claimed that my statement that God's love in himself and for us is not subject to a principle of love. I certainly did not mean what he thinks I meant when he says that my denial that God's love is subject to a principle of love "is the exact opposite of Barth's view." Matthew J. Aragon Bruce, "Election" in *The Oxford Handbook of Karl Barth*, ed. Paul Dafydd Jones and Paul T. Nimmo (Oxford: Oxford University Press, 2019), 320. I meant exactly what Barth says here, namely, that as the one who loves in freedom, God's loving us and God's eternal love within the immanent Trinity are not subject to any principle of love or of freedom (any law for that matter), because God is the subject of his loving and is thus free in his love and not constrained by any law or principle. I meant to affirm that God's love cannot be understood from any general definition of love since as Barth says, "God loves because he loves; because this act is His being, his essence and His nature. He loves without and before realising these purposes [fellowship with us]. He loves to eternity. Even in realising them, He loves because He loves. And the point of this realisation is not grounded in itself, but in His love as such, in the love of the Father, the Son and the Holy Spirit" (Barth, CD II/1, 279). The point then was that since God's love is his free love "He loves us and the world as He who would still be One who loves without us and without the world" (ibid., 280). That is why, as we shall see below, Barth insisted, against the pious blasphemies of Angelus Silesius, that "we do not speak of His, the divine love, if we try to deny to it the movement that is proper to it in itself, even though it is not an attitude to us" (ibid., 282). As noted above, Barth was consistent in arguing that "God acts with inward freedom and *not in fulfilment of a law* to which He is supposedly subject" (CD I/1, 135, emphasis mine). When Bruce says that "God determines from eternity to affirm who God is (essentially) and the result is the overflowing of intra-Trinitarian love to the other who is not God," he misses Barth's often repeated point that "we do not speak of His, the divine love, if we try to deny it the movement that is proper to it in itself, even though it is not an attitude to us" (CD II/1, 282). For Barth God's actions *ad extra* are free actions that cannot simply be equated with his free affirmation of his triune existence within the immanent Trinity as the one who loves. To claim that the overflowing of God's love toward us as Creator, Reconciler, and Redeemer is the result of his free and eternal self-affirmation within the eternal Trinity is in fact to make creation necessary to God in exactly the way Barth rejected. This is also why Barth said that he was required to take God's freedom just as seriously as his love (ibid., 440). And he also insisted that God's free love toward us did not mean "that His being necessitated Him to do it [to act as Creator and reconciler]. In that case, where would there be freedom in His love?" (ibid., 514).

[63]For some problems with ideas of "volitional necessity" as applied to God, see Molnar, *Divine Freedom*, 180–2, 187.

[64]Thomas F. Torrance, *The Doctrine of Jesus Christ* (Eugene, OR: Wipf and Stock, 2002), 87.

Freedom and Necessity in Contemporary Discussion

Curiously, it is becoming routine for theologians today to ascribe both freedom *and* necessity to God in exactly the way Barth methodically resisted. Jürgen Moltmann does it with problematic results. For instance, Moltmann argues that "the distinction between the immanent and economic Trinity would be necessary if, in the concept of God, there were really only the alternative between liberty and necessity."[65] He then claims, in a way that clearly does not distinguish between God's eternal love within the immanent Trinity and God's free love of us, that "if God *is* love, then his liberty cannot consist of loving or of not loving,"[66] implying that since God is love he cannot but love us.[67] Indeed that is exactly where the panentheistic thinking he embraces leads him when he explains that a "non-creative God would be imperfect ... if God's eternal being is love, then the divine love is also more blessed in giving than in receiving. *God cannot find bliss in eternal self-love if selflessness is part of love's very nature.*"[68] While Moltmann rightly claims that God is not compelled by some inner or outer necessity,[69] his thinking is shaped by his desire to unite *freedom* and *necessity* in God.[70] Moltmann's intention was to take up "panentheistic ideas from the Jewish and the Christian traditions" so that he could "try to think *ecologically* about God, man and the world in their relationships and indwellings."[71]

In his consideration of the doctrine of creation, Moltmann notes that one crucial consideration concerns the world's contingency. He thus asks, "Is the creation of the world necessary for God himself, or is it merely fortuitous? Does it proceed from God's nature, or from his will? Is it eternal, or temporal?"[72] Moltmann begins to answer these questions by first noting that traditional Christian theism held that "God need not have created the world" since "God is self-sufficient. His bliss is self-complete. He is perfect and needs neither his own creative expression of himself, nor a creation."[73] Nonetheless, he says, according to this view, "it was his good pleasure to create a world with which he could be 'well pleased.' "[74] According to Moltmann, Christian theism had to "fall back on *God's essential nature* in order to avoid the impression of divine arbitrariness" because for such theism creation was solely based on "the decree of God's free will."[75] Since God's

---

[65]Jürgen Moltmann, *The Trinity and the Kingdom, the Doctrine of God* (hereafter: *Trinity and Kingdom*), trans. Margaret Kohl (New York: Harper & Row, 1981), 151.
[66]Ibid., 151.
[67]This kind of thinking emerges in Jesse Couenhoven's contention in "The Necessities of Perfect Freedom," *International Journal of Systematic Theology* 14 (4) (October 2012): 398–419, that "for God not to create would be a deficiency that undermines the greatness necessary to God ... saying that God need not create sells triune love short" (411).
[68]Moltmann, *Trinity and Kingdom*, 106, emphasis mine.
[69]Ibid., 151.
[70]Ibid., 107–8.
[71]Ibid., 19.
[72]Ibid., 105.
[73]Ibid.
[74]Ibid.
[75]Ibid.

nature is "perfect goodness," God "cannot create evil." Thus, one could only reconcile chance and necessity and exclude arbitrariness or compulsion by understanding the world "as a play of his divine good pleasure."[76] In Moltmann's opinion, "the fictitious suggestion of arbitrariness in God leaves behind it a residue of despotism in the concept of God" because the love which God "had in view when he created free men and women is not in accord with the absolutism of pure power; for power is replaced by mutual friendship."[77] It is in this context that Moltmann then sets out his view of panentheism, reasoning that

> *Christian panentheism* .... started from the divine essence: Creation is the fruit of God's longing for "his Other" and for that Other's free response to the divine love. That is why the idea of the world is inherent in the nature of God himself from eternity. For it is impossible to conceive of a God who is not a creative God. A noncreative God would be imperfect.[78]

This approach leads Moltmann to conclude that since God is love, God cannot just as well exist without us: "God 'needs' the world and man. If God is love, then he neither will nor can be without the one who is beloved."[79] From this he reckons that "creation is a part of the eternal love affair between the Father and the Son."[80] These ideas clearly introduce the necessity associated with created being directly into the immanent Trinity exactly because in the first instance Moltmann did not clearly distinguish between the eternal Father's *free* love of the Son in a mutual but free relation of love taking place in the unity of the Holy Spirit and his free love of us, as Barth did.[81] Moltmann's claim that creation is the "fruit of God's longing for his 'Other' "[82] neglects the crucial point that creation is the result of a free choice and a free act of God in seeking and creating fellowship with another outside himself, as Barth so clearly indicated. By contrast Moltmann held that since "God has desired not only himself but the world too" from eternity, that would explain "why the idea of the world is already inherent in the Father's love for the Son. The eternal Son of God is closely related to God's idea of the World."[83] With this notion and the ideas that a noncreative God would be imperfect, and that God needs the world and creatures, it is clear that Moltmann has conceptualized creation as in some sense

---

[76]Ibid., 106.

[77]Ibid.

[78]Ibid.

[79]Ibid., 58.

[80]Ibid., 59.

[81]For Barth, "as and before God seeks and creates fellowship with us, He wills and completes this fellowship in Himself. In Himself ... He is Father, Son and Holy Spirit and therefore alive in His unique being with and for another" (CD II/1, 275). It is no secret that Moltmann not only embraced Rahner's "axiom" that the immanent Trinity is identical with the economic and vice versa, but he explicitly moved beyond this claiming that "the economic Trinity not only reveals the immanent Trinity, it also has a retroactive effect on it" (*Trinity and Kingdom*, 160).

[82]Moltmann, *Trinity and Kingdom*, 106; see also below, 25–30, 49–55.

[83]Ibid., 108.

necessary for God. So, while Moltmann certainly wishes to avoid a pantheistic confusion of Creator and creatures,[84] his panentheistic perspective prevents that because with that perspective he attempts to unite freedom and necessity in God. Regarding such panentheistic thinking, George Hunsinger correctly judges that

> the great problem with panentheism, from the standpoint of Christian theology, has always been either that it seems to make God ultimately responsible for whatever evil there is in the world, or else that it seems to regard God and the world as somehow inherently conditioned by one another, thereby obliterating the divine freedom implicit in the biblical witness to God as Creator and Lord. In working out his new position, which he openly acknowledges as "panentheism," Moltmann unfortunately manages to escape neither of these liabilities.[85]

Attempting to Reconcile Freedom and Necessity in God

Moltmann of course is not the only contemporary theologian to cross this line by ascribing necessity to God. We will return to Moltmann's thinking later. For now, I would like to consider a recent argument that attempts to answer an atheistic question concerning the origin of sin and evil by explaining who is responsible for these. In his consideration of the passion of God, Bruce McCormack explains that God's "life-act" as one who is "self-knowing and self-willing" is "an act of self-love which is the source of all things in its superabundance." As such that "life-act" is "'person-forming' both as it looks inward (toward the processions) and outward toward that which will be created." Accordingly, "*necessarily* to will himself as self-giving, self-donating, self-emptying love contains in itself a relation to another. And since that which is other than the Maker of heaven and earth can only be 'finite,' the love of God for himself as self-giving love *necessitates* the existence of the finite."[86]

Notice first that these remarks fail to distinguish God's eternal self-sufficient love within the immanent Trinity from God's free expression of that love toward us in the economy. This clearly indicates a key difference between Barth and McCormack as discussed above. Second, notice how similar these remarks are to Moltmann's understanding of Christian panentheism. McCormack's conception of God's self-giving love here presents that love only in relation to another outside of God. As with Moltmann, it can be seen thirdly that in this remark the kind of distinction for which Barth argued

---

[84]Jürgen Moltmann, *God in Creation: A New Theology of Creation and the Spirit of God*, trans. Margaret Kohl (New York: Harper & Row, 1985), 89. Thus, for Moltmann "there is no external necessity which occasions his creativity, and no inner compulsion which could determine it" (ibid., 74). Moltmann explicitly rejects what he takes to be Tillich's pantheistic view of creation (ibid., 84).
[85]George Hunsinger, "Review of *Trinity and Kingdom*," *The Thomist* 47 (1983): 129–39, 133.
[86]Bruce L. McCormack, "The Passion of God Himself: *Barth on Jesus's Cry of Dereliction*" *Reading the Gospels with Karl Barth*, ed. Daniel L. Migliore (Grand Rapids, MI: Eerdmans, 2017), 155–72, 171, some emphasis mine.

is missing. Barth insists that God is related to another within the immanent Trinity since Father, Son, and Holy Spirit are eternally and perichoretically or coinherently related before and apart from creation and *without needing* creation or another outside himself. Nothing in God or outside of God necessitates his creating, reconciling, and redeeming the world because God's creating, reconciling, and redeeming are free acts of his love for us. Having deliberately moved beyond Barth with this thinking, Bruce McCormack then asserts that "the finite understood only in its 'otherness' includes its extreme limit, which is death. So physical 'death' at least is … the necessary outworking of the love of God for the self-giving love that God is."[87]

Aside from implying that the outworking of God's love requires the finite, this viewpoint also seems to suggest that death is necessary for God because of the nature of his self-giving love. This thinking, however, eradicates the fact that God relates with creation in a free contingent act or choice which cannot simply be equated with his own self-knowledge and love. Marginalizing both these ideas, McCormack concludes that "if God already knows what he is 'going to will' in knowing himself, then it has been willed in his self-willing and there can be no second act in pretemporal eternity."[88] From this it follows that "God has a *necessary relation* to the finite."[89] Moreover, "if God is indeed self-emptying love, then the love of God 'necessarily' overflows."[90] Here we are told that this thinking does not make God dependent on creation; it does not mean that God acts out of need or that there is a deficiency in God's being that needs to be realized by God's acting in time for us. This is the case, it is said, because "we are already there, in the self-emptying love which realizes itself in overflowing. But the fact that we are there, in our finitude and sinfulness, means that the love of God contains, in its very nature, the seeds of death, sin, and misery."[91]

Such a conclusion may well follow once someone confuses the eternal act and being of God within the immanent Trinity and his temporal actions in the economy by arguing that God's self-emptying love *realizes itself* in overflowing. However, since God's love is free love as discussed above, that love does not need to realize itself at all since God eternally exists as Father, Son, and Spirit in perfect freedom and love without any need whatsoever to overflow beyond himself as in loving us and establishing fellowship with us. That this occurs is, according to Barth, and the classical tradition, the result of God's eternal choice; but it is a free and contingent eternal choice of his love for us. Moreover,

---

[87] Ibid., 171.

[88] Ibid., 172.

[89] Ibid.

[90] Ibid. Notice how far away from Barth's actual thinking this is when compared to Barth's insistence that God's overflowing love is a free choice that God did not need to make. For Barth, as noted above, this is "an overflow of His essence … which is not demanded or presupposed by *any necessity*, constraint, or obligation, least of all from outside, from our side, or by *any law by which God Himself is bound and obliged*" (CD II/1, 273, emphasis mine). Notice also that McCormack additionally argues that willing in its highest form cannot involve choice among options (171). This view coheres with Moltmann's thinking more than with Barth's, as Moltmann thinks God's loving us is never open to choice at any time, as will be discussed below.

[91] Ibid., 172.

any argument at all that finitude and sinfulness are already contained in the very nature of God's eternal love and that the seeds of death, sin, and misery are there as well clearly introduces the specter of a God who is himself the author of sin, death, and misery. That is certainly not the Christian God. And it definitely is not the God that Karl Barth had in view when he spoke of sin as an impossible possibility, and death and misery as consequences of our human disruption of our relationship with God because of our self-will and unbelief.[92]

This outcome suggests that George Hunsinger was right to claim that panentheistic views of the Creator/creature relation ultimately make God responsible for sin and evil, when in reality, God is not responsible for them. God indeed makes himself responsible for us in Christ by taking these to himself in forgiving our sins and experiencing our God-forsakenness on our behalf in order to overcome sin, suffering, evil, and death itself for us. Hunsinger was also right to argue that panentheistic thinking introduces the kind of mutual necessity and conditioning into the Creator/creature relationship that Barth rightly argued was excluded precisely because there is no necessity in the divine being; necessity can be discussed in relation to the immanent Trinity only in the sense that God cannot *not* be Father, Son, and Holy Spirit and still be God.

Hunsinger also helpfully explains the proper way to understand "Rahner's Rule," namely, that the immanent Trinity is identical with the economic Trinity, which he thinks is "systematically ambiguous" and "has led to a great deal of confusion."[93] Hunsinger asserts that a

> Barthian interpretation would run as follows. The Rule is correct in so far as there is only one Holy Trinity existing in two distinct forms. It is incorrect, however, in so far as it suggests that the distinction between the forms can be collapsed. If the Trinity's "immanent" form is eternal, while its "economic" form is temporal or historical, then to collapse the two forms would be to collapse the distinction between time and eternity, and thus between God and the world.[94]

He goes on to explain that the proper view of the two forms, and thus of eternity and history, "is one of 'correspondence'" and not one of "dialectical identity" because "the two forms of the one Holy Trinity comprise a 'unity-in-distinction.'" Dialectical identity would make it seem "as if when looked at in one way the Trinity was eternal but in another way it was historical, or as if eternity and history were merely two sides of a single process."[95] Hunsinger helpfully concludes that

---

[92]For a discussion of Karl Barth's view of sin in relation to his understanding of God, see Paul D. Molnar, "What Difference Does One's View of God Make in Understanding Sin and Salvation? Some Suggestions from Karl Barth," forthcoming in the *Scottish Journal of Theology*.

[93]George Hunsinger, "Karl Barth's Doctrine of the Trinity, and Some Protestant Doctrines after Barth," *The Oxford Handbook of the Trinity*, ed. Gilles Emery, O.P., and Matthew Levering (Oxford: Oxford University Press, 2011), 294–313, 309.

[94]Ibid., 310.

[95]Ibid.

for Barth, the Trinity's temporal form is secondary and dependent, while its eternal form is primary and constitutive. The eternal Trinity is distinguished, among other things, by the simplicity, perfection and a-seity (or self-sufficiency) of its essence (*ousia*). For Barth, with the main catholic tradition, East and West, God just is the Holy Trinity. As a self-sufficient communion of love and freedom, joy and peace, God's identity would be triune whether the world had been created or not.[96]

We are about to see what happens when these carefully nuanced statements are not followed.

Alan Lewis: Between Cross and Resurrection

Having said this, one can at least understand why those theologians who rely on Moltmann's thinking find themselves not only in direct conflict with Barth's more traditional view of the freedom of God's love, but they inevitably espouse the idea, unanimously rejected by the tradition, namely, that creation is somehow necessary for God. Thus, for example, while Alan Lewis wonders whether or not Moltmann risks "Arian subordination of the Son," "the heresy of Marcellus of Ancyra, who denied that the incarnation, and therefore the glorification of Christ's humanity and ours, is permanent"; and the idea that the Son's reign "is not eternal, for at the end he surrenders his lordship to the Father," he still makes a number of attempts to defend Moltmann's position.[97]

Important here is the idea that what God does in history for us is thought to be in some sense constitutive of who God is in eternity. This thinking, which is intrinsic to panentheistic conceptuality, is the thinking that I am targeting as necessarily undermining the freedom of God *in se* and *ad extra*. Lewis recognizes that

> Moltmann not only identified the economic with the immanent Trinity more closely than Barth, but even suggested that it is the economic acts, including the handing over of the kingdom, but especially the cross, which *shape and constitute* the immanent Trinity, rather than the reverse, where the economy merely reveals in time God's independent, eternal life and nature.[98]

---

[96]Ibid. These ideas are clearly supported by Barth's insistence that God's love for us and our "being taken up into the fellowship of His eternal love" suggest that "it is not part of God's being and action that as love it must have an object in another who is different from Him. God is sufficient in Himself as object and therefore as object of His love. He is no less the One who loves if He loves no object different from Himself ... While He could be everything only for Himself (and His life would not on that account be pointless, motionless and unmotivated, nor would it be any less majestic or any less the life of love), He wills—and this is for us the ever-wonderful twofold dynamic of His love—to have it not only for Himself, but also for us" (CD II/1, 280–1).

[97]Alan E. Lewis, *Between Cross and Resurrection: A Theology of Holy Saturday* (hereafter: *Between Cross and Resurrection*) (Grand Rapids, MI: Eerdmans, 2001), 221.

[98]Ibid., 221–2, emphasis mine. This is certainly an accurate interpretation of Moltmann's position as noted above in n. 81.

Relying on this misguided perspective, Lewis criticizes Barth for not just distinguishing without separating the immanent and economic Trinity but for opening a gap between them such that there is a God hidden behind the God revealed in and through Christ's death and resurrection.

While Lewis helpfully says that the idea that Barth thinks of God in his innermost being as "an individualistic monad" is incorrect, he nonetheless objects to Barth's "classical distinction" between the immanent and economic Trinity.[99] Lewis claims this distinction threatens "to render the temporal acts of creation and redemption finally inconsequential for the *constitution* of the immanent, eternal Godhead."[100] By advocating a "deliberate and sharp" distinction, Lewis contends that Barth "unwittingly" perpetuates "Augustine's dualism" and creates "a gap so large between eternity and time, internal and external, that we can no longer be sure, even in CD, IV, that the humanity and death of Christ truly reflect and affect the heart of God's own being."[101] Here we reach the core of the issues under discussion in this chapter. How exactly should we conceptualize God's freedom *in se* and *ad extra*? Regarding Barth's view of God's sovereign freedom as the one who loves, Lewis asks, "Does this sovereign freedom mean that behind God's actual decision to love, elect, and assume our humanness there stands an open choice, a freedom *not* to love us, a possibility in God's immanence to be other than the loving, self-humiliating God revealed in the economy?"[102]

Distinguishing the Immanent and Economic Trinity and Understanding Grace as Grace

Here we can see Lewis's failure to grasp Barth's understanding of the Trinity which stressed that what God is toward us in the economy, he is eternally in himself. However, Barth never countenanced the idea that what happens in the economy *constitutes* who God is in eternity. Therefore, he was not opening a gap between the immanent and economic Trinity, since for him, there is only one Trinity active in eternity and temporally. Hence, the Trinity active in Christ's life, death, and resurrection and in the outpouring of the Holy Spirit at Pentecost is the very same eternal Father, Son, and Holy Spirit he is and would have been even if he never decided to create, reconcile, and redeem us.

So, what we have in Lewis's criticism of Barth is the following misunderstanding: Lewis thinks that because Barth distinguishes God's essence from his work *ad extra*, as he should have, therefore his view of God's freedom must mean that "God's love toward us" must be "contingent and capricious—a possibility actually chosen, but which might not have been."[103] The mistake embedded in this assertion is the idea that because God's act

---

[99] Ibid., 208–9.
[100] Ibid., 209, emphasis mine.
[101] Ibid.
[102] Ibid.
[103] Ibid.

of election and God's subsequent acts as Creator, Reconciler, and Redeemer are free acts of grace, unconstrained by God's own nature since God is not subject to a principle of love or law of love, but corresponding to that nature as the one who loves in freedom, consequently his actions *ad extra* must have been "capricious." Lewis concludes that Barth's view risks advancing an "arbitrary grace as the price of safeguarding God's own freedom."[104]

Barth, however, never espoused such a view and in fact argued against it. The difference between Barth's actual position and the characterization offered by Lewis is enormous. Lewis, Moltmann, and others want to eliminate the possibility of choice in God by arguing that creation and redemption are necessary for God to be God. Barth argued that God's eternal choice to elect us and then to relate with us is grounded in who he is as Father, Son, and Spirit, but is neither constitutive of who he is nor is it constrained by his nature as the one who loves in perfect love and freedom from eternity to eternity. For if it were constitutive of who God is or constrained by God's nature as the one who loves, then God would indeed be dependent on history and could not act effectively within history for our benefit. Put bluntly, such a view would obliterate grace as grace. This is why Barth insisted that

> God's work is His essence in its relation to the reality which is distinct from Him and which is to be created or is created by Him. The work of God is the essence of God as the essence of Him who (N.B. in a *free decision* grounded in His essence *but not constrained by His essence*) is … Creator, Reconciler and Redeemer … Though the work of God is the essence of God, it is necessary and important to distinguish His essence as such from his work, remembering that this work is grace, a *free divine decision*, and also remembering that we can know about God only because and to the extent that He gives Himself to us to be known … God gives Himself entirely to man in His revelation, but not in such a way as to make Himself man's prisoner. He remains free in His working, in giving Himself.[105]

The difference between these two views is stark. Lewis has embraced Moltmann's train of thought that advances the idea that what happens in the economy *constitutes* the immanent Trinity by having a retroactive effect upon it. Because of this he argues that it is a mistake to embrace Barth's ideas that God is and remains free such that "there

---

[104]Ibid. Of course, Barth's view of God's free love specifically opposes any sort of arbitrariness or caprice because he rightly insists that in himself and in his actions *ad extra* God himself is wise, that is, God acts with "reason, meaning and order" so that our own freedom, which comes from knowing God, "comes only from the recognition of reason, meaning and order, and not from the consideration of chaos, chance or caprice" (CD II/1, 425). And this all depends upon "how far we recognise God as wisdom. God is wise in so far as His whole activity, as willed by Him, is also thought out by Him … with correctness and completeness, so that it is an intelligent and to that extent a reliable and liberating activity. We have to say of His activity in His works and also of His inner activity, of the essential actuality of His divine being, that God is wise, that in Him is wisdom. God Himself is wisdom" (CD II/1, 425–6).

[105]Barth, CD I/1, 371, emphasis mine.

is in God's own inner being a perfect *independence*" since "this God has no need of us. This God is self-sufficient."[106] Having said this, Lewis claims that "the outward God" becomes "empty, vulnerable, and needy in the incarnation" while "there is an inner, self-contained, invulnerable deity who has no need of us."[107] And this must mean that "the cross and grave do not after all determine or even correspond to the inmost truth of God's identity."[108] Thus, following Paul Fiddes's thinking which is both panentheistic and makes God's acts of love toward us conditional upon our responses,[109] Lewis claims that Barth's position leaves us with " 'an untouched hinterland in the immanent being of God' " such that there is now "a dualistic gap" which becomes a "wedge, between 'the passion of God' and a residual element of impassibility."[110]

Divine Passibility and Impassibility

None of this actually represents Barth's position accurately. For Barth, as for Torrance,[111] God himself is both passible and impassible because God is not subject to suffering and death but chooses, as our savior, helper, and friend to subject himself to these in the exercise of his impassible deity precisely in order to overcome them as threats to us. George Hunsinger offers a particularly clear and accurate account of Barth's view when he writes that "Barth maintained that through the incarnation of the eternal Son, God suffered in his divine nature without ceasing to be essentially impassible. God suffered in one sense without ceasing to be impassible in another."[112] For Barth

> divine impassibility does not exist "above and behind [God's] living activity within the universe" (II/2, 79) … it exists in and with that living activity as something present and operative even though concealed. In the cross of Christ, divine impassibility is hidden under the form of its opposite without ceasing to be what it is. Its concealment does not detract from its reality.[113]

That is why Barth maintains that

> we know him even in this concealment. He is our Lord and Hero, the Shepherd of the whole world and our Deliverer, even in this lowliness. He has acted as the true Son of God even in His suffering of death on the cross. And we are made alive and

---

[106]Lewis, *Between Cross and Resurrection*, 210, citing CD IV/2, 346 and II/1, 307–8.
[107]Ibid.
[108]Ibid.
[109]See Paul Fiddes, *Two Views on the Doctrine of the Trinity* (Grand Rapids, MI: Zondervan Academic, 2014), 108.
[110]Lewis, *Between Cross and Resurrection*, 210.
[111]See Torrance, *The Trinitarian Faith*, 184–5.
[112]Hunsinger, *Reading Barth with Charity*, 147.
[113]Ibid., 152.

justified and sanctified and exalted to the status of the children of God and made heirs of eternal life in His execution. For it was in His humiliation that there took place the fulfilment of the covenant, the reconciliation of the world with God. It is in Him that we have our peace, and from Him our confidence and hope for ourselves and all men.[114]

Thomas F. Torrance

This thinking coheres with T. F. Torrance's view that if we approach the question of whether God is passible or impassible logically, then the ideas cancel each other out so that one must say that if God is passible then God cannot be impassible and vice versa.[115] But Torrance argues that we must not read logical necessities back into who God is and what God does for us as savior and concludes that in light of the incarnation and Christ's atoning actions for us as Mediator,

> There is certainly a sense in which we must think of God as impassible (ἀπαθής), for he is not subject to the passions that characterise human and creaturely existence, but that is not to say that he is not afflicted in all the afflictions of his people or that he is untouched by their sufferings.[116]

Clearly, in Torrance's view, one does not have to hold that God is not afflicted by our afflictions in maintaining his impassibility, as Lewis thinks. This is because, with Barth, he conceptualizes passibility and impassibility "dynamically and soteriologically on the ground of what has actually taken place in the vicarious life and passion of God's incarnate Son."[117] Of course both Torrance and Barth do not wish to think about God's impassibility in the Greek or Stoic sense, but only in the sense that God "stooped down to take upon himself our passion, our hurt and suffering, and to exhaust it in his divine impassibility."[118] In sharing our passion, Jesus Christ "makes us share in his own imperturbability (ἀπάθεια)."[119] Importantly, this thinking does not in any way neutralize Torrance's often repeated assertions that what God is toward us he is eternally in himself and that there is no God behind the back of Jesus Christ. This in itself illustrates how mistaken Lewis's view of the matter really is, since Torrance himself is able to hold together both these important insights only because he, with Barth, made a proper distinction without separation of the eternal and temporal actions of the Trinity.[120]

---

[114]Barth, CD IV/2, 350.
[115]See Torrance, *The Trinitarian Faith*, 185.
[116]Ibid., 184–5.
[117]Ibid., 185.
[118]Ibid., 185–6. See also Torrance, *Christian Doctrine of God*, 251.
[119]Torrance, *The Trinitarian Faith*, 186.
[120]See Torrance, *Christian Doctrine of God*, 4–7, 92, 108–9, 198–9.

In a similar way Karl Barth claimed that "if God had not remained impassible in his sufferings and eternally alive in his [Christ's] death, neither sin nor death would have been destroyed."[121] Both Torrance and Barth would agree that to understand Christ's redemptive suffering properly one must realize that "when the Son of God became incarnate in Jesus Christ, he did not cease to be God, and when he became man within the conditions of our limited existence in space and time, he did not leave the throne of the universe."[122] Barth's thinking is in harmony with Torrance's:

> The fact that Jesus Christ is very God and very man means that in this oneness of His with the creature God does not cease for a moment or in any regard to be the one, true God. And the strength and blessedness and comfort of His work of creation as of reconciliation and revelation consists in the fact that in these works of His too He is never less than wholly Himself.[123]

In the suffering and death of Jesus Christ, Barth asks whether or not in experiencing death as the Judge judged in our place, God has "renounced and lost Himself as God, whether in capitulating to the folly and wickedness of His creature He has not abdicated from His deity … whether He can really die and be dead?"[124] His answer is that "in this humiliation God is supremely God, that in this death He is supremely alive, that He has maintained and revealed His deity in the passion of this man as His eternal Son."[125] Here Barth insists this is not just a human happening but an act of the Son of God who in this act has reconciled the world with God. It is vital to recognize that those theologians who choose to argue for God's passibility at the expense of his impassibility invariably undercut the all-important fact that God does not cease to be God in his actions for us in history. And that means that God never becomes dependent upon us precisely because he does not need us but freely chooses to place himself at our service in his grace, mercy, and freedom.

Against Lewis's thinking then, both Barth and Torrance claim that God can and does experience our suffering and is afflicted by our suffering *as* God, but he does so without ceasing to be impassible, and in the exercise of his impassible deity in order to extinguish our suffering, pain, and death itself.[126] Therefore Lewis's entire analysis and critique of Barth falters because he believes that what happens in the crucifixion of Jesus Christ is not an act of free choice on God's part for our benefit but an inner necessity "grounded in God's own free but unswerving decision to be God, *this* God, of boundless, self-exposing grace." Hence, "God is free, not as one who could do otherwise, but as *the* one above all

[121]Hunsinger, *Reading Barth with Charity*, 155, referring to CD II/1, 400.
[122]Torrance, *The Trinitarian Faith*, 184.
[123]Barth, CD II/1, 446.
[124]Barth, CD IV/1, 246.
[125]Ibid., 246–7.
[126]See also Torrance, *Christian Doctrine of God*, 246–54.

who can do *no* other. Self-bound to the sole way of being, God is committed, necessarily but thus freely, to the cognate course of action."[127]

The difference here is clear: Barth invariably insisted that God could have been God without us but chose not to be so and that God did not and does not need us or need to love us. By contrast Lewis argues that "the ineffable love which takes God down that path [of suffering and death] is free and sovereign, even if there is *no* possibility for God to be or act otherwise, no choice to be made internally between this love and some alternative."[128] This thinking more closely resembles Moltmann's position than Barth's. Lewis therefore believes that

> God's lordship in bowing to the contradiction of the godless cross and godforsaken grace does not reside, as Barth occasionally and illogically asserts, in a prior self-sufficiency and secure immutability, but—as he more often understood and later followers more emphatically underscored—in the uncoerced impulse to self-consistency: love's determination not to be deflected from its purposes but to flourish and perfect itself through willing self-surrender.[129]

Here Lewis's crucial mistake is to suppose that God's love needs perfecting. For Barth, it is only because God's love is perfect in itself that God can effectively act for us. Hence,

> God's being consists in the fact that he is the One who loves in freedom. In this he is the perfect being: the being which is itself perfection and so the standard of all perfection; the being, that is, which is self-sufficient and thus adequate to meet every real need; the being which suffers no lack in itself and by its very essence fills every real lack. Such a being is God.[130]

For Lewis, this thinking illustrates the gap that Barth opened between the immanent and economic Trinity because he thinks "the Trinity, historically active in the cross, will bring to final fulfillment its own still-unfinished life."[131]

For Barth, however, the fact that God's being is in becoming did not signify that his divine being needed fulfilment because it was in any sense unfinished, as Lewis states; what needs fulfilment is God's love for us in perfecting our sinful lives in and through Christ's suffering, death, and resurrection. George Hunsinger once again offers a more accurate view of Barth's theology arguing that "God freely determines his perfect being as a being in compassion."[132] Thus, "God does not have to, but he can, take to himself the suffering of another" and God's "entry into suffering is not improper for him" since "in

---

[127]Lewis, *Between Cross and Resurrection*, 211.
[128]Ibid.
[129]Ibid., 211–12.
[130]Barth, CD II/1, 322.
[131]Lewis, *Between Cross and Resurrection*, 213.
[132]Hunsinger, *Reading Barth with Charity*, 150.

doing so … he does what corresponds to his worth."[133] Here Hunsinger captures Barth's thinking in a way that understands God's freedom does not imply that he acts arbitrarily, but in accordance with his freedom to be both sovereign and meek because "He can be and wills to be God not only in the height but also in the depth—in the depth of human creatureliness, sinfulness and mortality."[134] This thinking coheres with the views of Barth and Torrance since for them God's eternal impassibility and his passibility through the humanity of Christ is part of the mystery of the incarnation and therefore is not "illogical."

Hunsinger's views correspond with important insights from Barth. Barth argues, for instance, that God's omnipotence is of such kind that God "can assume the form of weakness and impotence and do so as omnipotence, triumphing in this form."[135] That is why Barth could speak of the element of truth in the early Patripassian position in spite of its otherwise mistaken way of ascribing suffering to the divine nature. That element of truth is that it is "God the Father who suffers in the offering and sending of His Son, in His abasement. The suffering is not His own, but the alien suffering of the creature, of man, which He takes to Himself in Him."[136] With his carefully nuanced view of this matter, Barth does not make suffering part of God's nature as Moltmann later seemed to do because Barth is clear that the suffering is our suffering brought on by sin and death which God takes to himself in Christ to overcome these. So Barth can say that God in his "innermost being" is moved and stirred to compassion for us in our suffering— not in "powerlessness" like us but simply because God is "open, ready, inclined … to compassion with another's suffering and therefore to assistance." Nevertheless, it still must be recalled that "God finds no suffering in Himself."[137] Torrance follows Barth and argues that "the Christian doctrine of salvation depends" upon "the fact that it is *God*, really *God in Christ* who suffers and bears the sin of the world—that is the particle of truth, the *particular veri*, as Karl Barth once said in the Patripassian heresy."[138] Since the Holy Trinity is one, he concludes that "we cannot but think of the suffering or passion of

---

[133]Ibid., 150, citing Barth CD II/1, 375.

[134]Ibid., and Barth CD IV/1, 134.

[135]Barth, CD IV/1, 187.

[136]Barth, CD IV/2, 357. T. F. Torrance cites this text from Barth more fully to make it clear that while God is impassible in the sense that he does not surrender his deity, he became passible by taking our suffering to himself in Christ so that we might share in "his own peace and imperturbability" (*Christian Doctrine of God*, 249, 251). Suffering, Torrance says, does not belong to God by nature but through the incarnate Word suffering for our benefit God himself actively suffered *as* God for us and made it "serve the purpose of his love for the world" (ibid., 249). In that sense Christ experienced God's judgment, which reached its pinnacle at the Cross, and this disclosed "the active suffering of God" (ibid.). For Torrance, "what Christ felt, did and suffered in himself in his body and soul for our forgiveness was felt, done, and suffered by God in his innermost Being for our sake … the self-sacrifice of the Son is the correlate of the self-sacrifice of the Father" (ibid.). See also, Torrance, *The Doctrine of Jesus Christ*, 146, where Torrance says, "The vicarious suffering of Jesus on the cross reveals and points to the pain in the eternal heart of God the Father himself … He who spared not his own Son, but delivered him up for us all, how shall he not with him also freely give us all things? (Rom. 8:31-2). There is a Cross, the Cross, in the very heart of God the Father" (ibid.).

[137]Barth, CD II/1, 370.

[138]Torrance, *The Doctrine of Jesus Christ*, 146.

the incarnate Son as in a completely inexplicable way as grounded in and upheld by the Father and the one Eternal Spirit of the Father and of the Son."[139]

By contrast, following the thinking of Moltmann and Robert Jenson, Lewis mistakenly argues that a theology of Easter Saturday must hold that this was a "terminal event which ruptures God's own life" so that

> our conceiving of the Trinity must move on from the willingness of … the Son [to be for us through eternal sacrifice], to a loving community which endures death in the radical separating of the Father and the Son, and which, through the life-giving Spirit, *is still perfecting its being and its act in the slow triumph over evil*, until the end of history when the world will be made new and God at last be all in all.[140]

Here, once again, we see the two critical errors that follow from introducing necessity into the Trinity. First, Lewis mistakenly thinks there was a radical separation of the Father from the Son in Christ's death for us, when in reality Christ experienced our God-forsakenness without his oneness in being with the Father and Spirit being broken or separated. For that reason, the union between divinity and humanity achieved in the hypostatic union also held even in his death, as this was disclosed in his resurrection.[141] Second, Lewis incorrectly thinks that the being and act of the eternal Trinity is still perfecting itself in triumphing over evil. However, God's act of love for us in the incarnation, death, and resurrection of Christ has already triumphed over evil and that

---

[139]Ibid.

[140]Lewis, *Between Cross and Resurrection*, 214, emphasis mine. Importantly, Torrance speaks of God's being in becoming but insists that this only indicates the dynamic nature of God's being and act. It certainly cannot mean that God is "perfecting" his being by overcoming evil for us. God is exercising his sovereign grace for our benefit in that action. Thus, Torrance writes, "His Becoming is not a becoming on the way toward being or toward a fullness of being, but is the eternal fullness and the overflowing of his eternal unlimited Being. Becoming expresses the dynamic nature of his Being" (*Christian Doctrine of God*, 242).

[141]Unlike Lewis and Moltmann, T. F. Torrance gets this exactly right. He says of the hypostatic union of the divine and human natures in the one Person of Christ understood dynamically and not statically that this "was a living and dynamic union which ran throughout the whole of his life, in which he maintained union and communion with the Father in the steadfastness of the Father toward the Son and in the steadfastness of the Son toward the Father. The resurrection means that this union did not give way but held under the strain imposed not only by the forces that sought to divide Jesus from God, but the strain imposed through the infliction of the righteous judgment of the Father upon our rebellious humanity which Christ had made his own—and it held under the strain imposed by both in the crucifixion: the hypostatic union survived the descent into hell and Christ arose still in unbroken communion with the Father. The resurrection is thus the resurrection of the union forged between man and God in Jesus or of the damned and lost condition of men into which Christ entered in order to share their lot and redeem them from doom" (*Space, Time and Resurrection* (Edinburgh: T&T Clark, 1998; reissued Cornerstones Edition, 2019), 54). Torrance refers to this again in *Incarnation: The Person and Life of Christ*, ed. Robert T. Walker (Downers Grove, IL: IVP Academic, 2008) by speaking of the hypostatic union referring to the inseparability of Christ's divine and human natures so that "it is precisely in the impossibility of their separation that our redemption lies, for it is redemption into the unbreakable union and communion with the Father, and the once and for all exaltation of our human nature in Christ, into the life of eternal God. It is because the incarnate Son and the Father are one, and cannot be divided or separated from one another, that our salvation in Christ is eternally secure in the hand of the Father, for no one can snatch us out of his hand" (208–9).

completed event in the history of Jesus Christ himself is what will be disclosed when Christ returns to complete the redemption.

Any idea that the Trinity needs perfecting must mean that God is somehow dependent on creation to achieve his purposes, and this would undercut the fact that God's grace is truly effective in itself for our benefit. There can be little doubt that it is Moltmann's attempt to ascribe both freedom *and* necessity to the life of the immanent Trinity that has misled Lewis here as Lewis himself spells out Moltmann's thinking in contrast to Barth's. He stresses that for Moltmann, who he says learned from Barth that God's being is in becoming,

> this becoming is marked … even more by temporality, happening and futurity than in Barth. For it is less that God *is*, through motion and change, than that God "is" not yet. God will be who God will be … so that only in the future, becoming what God not yet is, will the divine identity be finally fulfilled … God's eternal life and being will not be complete until the end of time.[142]

Accordingly, for Moltmann, Lewis claims "the temporal adds to and enriches the eternal."[143] Here, unfortunately, we have the results of a panentheistic view of the Trinity, that is, an impoverished God who needs time and history to enrich his eternal life and who is not yet who he will supposedly still become. The problem with this reasoning is not just that it conflicts with Barth's more accurate view of the Trinity, revelation, and reconciliation, but that such an impoverished God himself needs redemption. There is little doubt that Moltmann did truly believe that God makes himself in need of redemption.[144] The problem with this thinking, however, is that such a view raises the unanswerable question about who then can redeem a God who needs redemption![145]

In light of what was said above, my point here is this: whenever it is thought that there is "necessity" in God in the sense that God needs his own being or needs us, such thinking results from projecting the necessity associated with all human experiences of love (since for us to love we need another outside ourselves) back into God's free and

---

[142]Lewis, *Between Cross and Resurrection*, 218.
[143]Ibid., 218–19. Compare this to Barth: "While this event [incarnation] as a happening in and on the created world makes, magnifies and enhances the glory of God outwardly, inwardly it neither increases nor diminishes His glory, His divine being" (CD II/1, 513). See also n. 140 where Torrance stresses that God's becoming is not on the way to being because obviously God is eternally and sovereignly the one who loves as Father, Son, and Holy Spirit and thus does not need any fulfilment of his divine being to act as God for us.
[144]Following the thought of Franz Rosenzweig Moltmann conceptualizes the "Shekinah" as God's descent "to man and his dwelling among them" such that there is "a divorce which takes place in God himself. God himself cuts himself off from himself, he gives himself away to his people, he suffers with their sufferings, he goes with them into the misery of the foreign land … God … makes himself in need of redemption. In this way, in this suffering, the relationship between God and the remnant [of Israel] points beyond itself" (*Trinity and Kingdom*, 29). Thus, Moltmann claims that as God "enters into his finite creation … he also participates in its evolution" so that "God and the world are then involved in a common redemptive process" with the result that "we need God's compassion and God needs ours" and "God himself becomes free in the process … even God himself will only be free when our souls are free" (ibid., 39).
[145]See Molnar, *Divine Freedom*, 394–5, 408–18 for more on this.

eternal love. This then leads to the confusion of nature and grace, reason and revelation, and to ideas that God needs the world, that God is somehow dependent on the world, that God's own being needs fulfilment, and that consequently God needs our cooperation in order to save us. Such thinking therefore undermines the freedom and effectiveness of God's gracious actions toward us in his Word and Spirit. Let us explore this point a bit further reflecting on several arguments made in a recent book discussing freedom and necessity in relation to trinitarian theology.

Freedom and Necessity in Modern Trinitarian Theology

In a recent study of freedom and necessity in trinitarian theology, Brandon Gallaher certainly recognizes God's freedom and wishes to maintain that freedom in relation to creation.[146] Gallaher analyzes the theology of Sergeii Bulgakov, Karl Barth, and Hans Urs von Balthasar to explain his own view of freedom and necessity with respect to the Trinity following his own vision of the dialectic of freedom and necessity within God and in God's relations with us. He thus also relies on the thinking of John of the Cross and Paul Fiddes to explain divine freedom. Part of that explanation includes the idea that God "freely becomes the 'prisoner' of the soul and he 'is surrendered to all her desires … those who act with love and friendship toward him will make him do all they desire

---

[146]Thus, Brandon Gallaher quite rightly maintains that the God of Christian revelation calls us in his grace, "but yet is in no way impelled to create and redeem the world … and, indeed, as some have claimed, might have been satisfied with His own life of love" (Brandon Gallaher, *Freedom and Necessity in Modern Trinitarian Theology* (Oxford: Oxford University Press, 2016), 6). He also maintains that the "predominant Christian tradition asserts that [God] does not necessarily will these created things, because He would attain His goodness regardless of their creation" because "the divine will is perfectly free, having no necessary relation to any particular created end" (ibid., 18). The context of these remarks, however, includes the problematic assertion by Balthasar that "God wills things other than Himself in willing Himself—creatures—since their end is his goodness" (ibid.). The problem with that remark is that there is no clear distinction between God willing himself and then willing creatures. If God wills the existence of creatures in willing himself, then the distinction between the eternal generation of the Son and the creation of the world is in danger of being lost as it certainly was lost in the perspective advanced by Bruce McCormack as discussed above. This problematic element is also present in Gallaher's own thinking since he also argues that since God is "uncontainable," he "becomes subject to the parameters of flesh and temporality through emptying Himself and taking on the form of a slave (Phil. 2:5ff)" such that he (Gallaher) is led to "the admittedly hard conclusion that the created world seems inseparable from the Trinity" (ibid., 6). He concludes that since the triune God has "*eternally* chosen to be God for us in Christ" therefore "through this eternal self-determination" Christ "has become part of God's own self-identity" with the implication that "if there was no world, there could be no Christ, so there is a tension or dialectic at work in this divine love for creation between God's absolute freedom and, in the incarnation, the necessity of the world for Him as God for us in Jesus Christ" (ibid.). In line with this problematic thinking is the overt confusion we find, for example, in Bulgakov when he writes, "'By the very act of this creation [God] gives birth also to God'" (ibid., 84). Bulgakov asserts that this does not obviate God's freedom. But it does. Gallaher notes that this thinking results from a kenotic view of the intratrinitarian relations and "appears to fulfil the theological ideal of a balance of divine freedom and necessity towards the world we set forth in our Introduction" (ibid.). It is easy to see here that Gallaher is attempting to think out God's freedom and love in relation to the contemporary debate in Barth studies about the relation between election and the Trinity. More on that later.

… by love they bind him with one hair.'"[147] Yet, he says, "no credit is due to the soul in attracting the ecstatic desire of God in Christ through its love. The soul cannot of its own power 'capture this divine bird of heights.' God's love is free and He was 'captivated by the flight of the hair' because He first gazed at us, loved, and came down to arouse our desire in taking flesh. The love that John speaks of is the desire of the soul for the Son of God, Jesus Christ."[148] From this Gallaher concludes that "the Word, the Son of God, together with the Father and Spirit is hidden by His essence, which is love itself, and therefore is present 'in the innermost Being of the soul.'"[149]

There can be little doubt that Karl Barth would have great difficulty with the ideas presented here because for him, as for Torrance, God loves simply because he loves. Thus, as we shall see in detail below, in loving us God does not love us because he finds something in us to love;[150] in fact since we are sinners in need of Christ's reconciling grace, he loves us while we are still sinners and enemies of grace. For Barth and Torrance that means God never becomes the prisoner of anyone's soul, and no one can make God do all they desire, no matter how much they love. Most importantly, God did not love us because he was captivated by the flight of the hair. In Barth's understanding, as in Torrance's, that very idea ends up making God in some way dependent upon us and finally indistinguishable from us in our actions of love. In any case if one supposes that God is present in the innermost being of the soul, then one could look at us to find the meaning of God's love. That is the very last thing that Barth and Torrance would ever want to do because they both insist that God's love can only be found outside of us in the incarnate Son who freely loved us and loves us by coming to us as our revealer and reconciler. The problems here will unfold as we proceed. How did Gallaher come to embrace this perspective? Let me briefly explain his view of what he calls the dialectic of freedom and necessity as he thinks this can be ascribed to God and to God's relations with us.

Gallaher presents several different types of freedom and necessity, which he designates as F1-F3 (freedom) and N1-N3 (necessity). Then he attempts to understand the triune God in a way that will respect his freedom in himself while holding that certain aspects of God's freedom are determined by necessity because he holds that "one needs to give both F3 with N3 their full force by seeing them in a dialectic."[151] So he argues that "divine desire for the world is not arbitrary. It is the external but free expression of God's own intra-dependent eternal but irrevocable desire for Himself, where each hypostasis freely gives its all to the Other (F3)."[152] Thus, he further claims that "such love, ecstatically

---

[147]Gallaher, *Freedom and Necessity*, 4.

[148]Ibid.

[149]Ibid.

[150]That is why Barth insists that "God's loving is concerned with a seeking and creation of fellowship without any reference to an existing aptitude or worthiness on the part of the loved. God's love is not merely not conditioned by any reciprocity of love. It is also not conditioned by any worthiness to be loved on the part of the loved, by any existing capacity for union or fellowship on his side. If he has such a thing, it is itself the prior creation of the love of God. It is not and does not become the condition of that love" (Barth, CD II/1, 278).

[151]Gallaher, *Freedom and Necessity*, 38.

[152]Ibid., 37.

desires to make itself vulnerable in the world (F3) by freely making itself captive to its creation even unto death on a cross (N3)" so that one could speak of the Trinity "as a 'heavenly Cross of love' which is the foundation of the cross of Christ: 'The love of the Father is the crucifying one. The Love of the Son is the crucified one. The love of the Holy Spirit is the one triumphing in the power of the cross. So has God loved the world!' God is freely captive on the cross because *His own law of love always already freely binds Him*."[153] With these ideas in place, Gallaher asserts that Christology and God's freedom can only be properly understood "where Absolute Freedom embraces *in itself*, in a perfect tension, F3 and N3 because it has always already freely chosen out of love (F2) to be God as God for us in Christ (N2) even unto '*servitutis extremum summumque supplicium*' (N1) which will not turn back from its love (N3)."[154]

Because he sees this dialectic at work in both the immanent and the economic Trinity, his "theological ideal" is to strike a balance between freedom and necessity in order to "make a case for its application to God both in Himself and in His relationship to the world" and also to "argue for the coherence of a form of divine self-determination focused on Jesus Christ."[155] It is on this basis that he offers his critical correction of Fiddes's thinking, that is (his quasi-Barthian insight), which will be presented below because he says F3 cannot simply be identified with N3 without collapsing the immanent into the economic Trinity. By giving these two forms of freedom and necessity their full dialectical weight, Gallaher thinks that it is possible to hold a "theology of divine self-determination" in which "the divine economy both 'could have been otherwise' (F3) and 'could not have been otherwise' (N3). Absolute Freedom as a concept embraces both notions, and once one emphasizes one position, then one must immediately correct it with the other."[156] Following upon these insights, Gallaher then relies on Heidegger to maintain that " 'Man and Being are appropriated [*sind übereignet*] to each other. They belong to [*gehören*] each other.' "[157] Conceptualizing this theologically Gallaher then claims that "God and the world are enowned one to the other in Jesus Christ and exist in Him in a loving tension of unity in difference, albeit initiated entirely by God." What this means to Gallaher is that in relation to Barth in particular he will pursue a dialectic of freedom and necessity to understand God and the world "and freedom and necessity where they exist in an identity-in-difference in Christ."[158] Finally, Gallaher constructs his position following David Tracy with a concept of analogy that was developed by Balthasar which adapts "the Balthasarian idea of Christ as the 'concrete analogy of Being.' "[159] Gallaher's book then is mainly constructive and aims to show that different forms of freedom and necessity are different conceptual aspects "of what we shall call Absolute

---

[153]Ibid., 37–8, emphasis mine.
[154]Ibid., 38, emphasis mine.
[155]Ibid.
[156]Ibid., 38–9.
[157]Ibid., 40.
[158]Ibid.
[159]Ibid.

Freedom, by which is meant the eternal divine movement of love which is Father, Son, and Holy Spirit, both in Himself (immanent) and for the world (economic)."[160]

What I am arguing in this chapter, following Barth and Torrance, is that God really is eternally free as the one who loves and is not subject to *any* internal or external necessities. Most especially God is not subject to any law of love as depicted above. If that were even remotely so, then love would be the subject and God the predicate in precisely the way that Gallaher claims he wants to avoid, namely, God would need the world and the two (God and the world) would exist in a mutually conditioning relationship. That is precisely what Barth was continually at pains to reject with his view of the freedom of God's love within the immanent Trinity as discussed above. God, Barth said, does not even need his own being to be who he is because he simply is the triune God from all eternity. And God is always the free subject both of his inner life and his actions in the economy. This can be decisively seen in Barth's remark that

> it is not, [of] course, to satisfy a law of love, nor because love is a reality even God must obey, that He must be the Father of the Son … Love is God the supreme law and ultimate reality, because God is love and not *vice versa*. And God is love, love proceeds from Him as His love, as the Spirit He Himself is, because He posits Himself as the Father and therefore posits Himself as the Son. In the Son of His love, i.e., in the Son in and with whom He brings forth Himself as love, He then brings forth in the *opus ad extra* too, in creation, the creaturely reality which is distinct from himself … The love which meets us in reconciliation, and then retrospectively in creation, is real love, supreme law and ultimate reality, because God is antecedently love in Himself; not just a supreme principle of the relation of separateness and fellowship, but love which even in fellowship wills and affirms and seeks and finds the other or Other in its distinction … Because God is antecedently love in Himself, love is and holds good as the reality of God in the work of reconciliation and in the work of creation.[161]

I am claiming that because Gallaher attempts to preserve God's freedom by ascribing a dialectic of freedom and necessity to God's being via Christology, he finally collapses the immanent into the economic Trinity, against his own intentions. And the basis of that collapse is already resident in his interpretation of Barth which is built upon McCormack's unfortunate reading of Barth. This is because he claims that "Absolute Freedom embraces *in itself*, in a perfect tension, F3 and N3 because it has always already freely chosen out of love (F2) to be God as God for us in Christ."[162] This statement represents the confusion introduced by McCormack into the eternal divine relations of the Trinity by equating election and the Trinity and failing to see that while election is an eternal divine act, it is a contingent act and not a necessary act.

---

[160]Ibid., 12.
[161]Barth CD I/1, 483–4.
[162]Gallaher, *Freedom and Necessity*, 38.

Its only proper necessity is based on the fact that once God becomes incarnate in history in Jesus Christ in accordance with his eternal but contingent decision to elect us as covenant partners, then he will not go back on that event and all that this implies. Thus, when Barth does speak of necessity with respect to the Trinity or even creation, he is referring to factual necessities, namely, to the fact that God simply is the triune God and could not be other than that without ceasing to be God. And one could even say creation and incarnation are necessary insofar as they are what they are because God has in fact freely acted to create the world and to reconcile the world in his incarnate Son. Their necessity lies in the fact that they are what they are as works enacted by God. But, as Barth maintained "we certainly can and should utter a warning against the inference, which is not ruled out to full satisfaction in Augustine or even Anselm, that the creation of the world was as essential to God as the begetting of the Son, that it was not the result of a *nova voluntas* (as Augustine says, *Conf.* XII, 15, 18), that the existence of the world was necessarily included in God's Word ... that the world is thus an essential predicate of God."[163]

A key problem in Gallaher's thinking, as I see it, is that he attempts to apply what he calls (F3), a third type of freedom to God and that creates a situation in which one could conceptualize the relations between God and us as relations of mutual conditioning. That is the kind of freedom consistently and rightly rejected by both Barth and Torrance because it undermines the freedom of God's grace and love in relation to us. The issue that I hope to bring to light is that while Gallaher can speak of (F3) by referring to the Trinity, that very attempt causes him to undermine God's actual freedom for us in his Word and Spirit. Thus, for instance, he can say things that Barth and Torrance would never say. Of course, the fact that they would never say something is not a final criterion of truth. But I think the reason they would not say these things is because of their quite proper view of God's freedom and love. For them, God loves in freedom in such a way that he really does not need us and also does not even need to save us from sin; that he did so and does so is an expression of his free spontaneous love which is not subject to any law of love because if that were so, then some idea of mutual conditioning along the lines espoused by Angelus Silesius would threaten. So, Gallaher says that (F3) involves both kenosis, as kenosis of (F1) and (F2) so that this also involves "their ultimate fulfilment and flowering."[164]

First, the eternal Trinity exists in freedom and love such that the persons of the Trinity do not need each other, are not dependent on each other, but exist coinherently or perichoretically in free relations of love. Second, since God is eternally free and loving, God does not need fulfillment or flowering because the triune God is already, always, and eternally who he is and needs nothing internally or externally to be God. This "kenotic" thinking stems from Gallaher's view that the three theologians he considers in his book all "draw on nineteenth-century kenoticism" and thus use the language

---

[163]Barth, CD I/1, 443.
[164]Gallaher, *Freedom and Necessity*, 19.

of "self-emptying for the Trinitarian relations, thereby wedding revelation with God himself."[165] Gallaher then claims that "Jürgen Moltmann puts this approach neatly: 'The content of the doctrine of the Trinity is the real cross of Christ Himself. The form of the crucified Christ is the Trinity.' "[166] He says that all three theologians he will consider offer an "intratrinitarian kenoticism."[167] This very thinking, however, completely contradicts the important assertion by Karl Barth that "the content of the doctrine of the Trinity ... is not that God in His relation to man is Creator, Mediator and Redeemer, but that God in Himself is eternally God the Father, Son and Holy Spirit ... [God acting as Emmanuel] cannot be dissolved into His work and activity."[168] And, contrary to this kenotic view of the inner trinitarian relations, Barth insisted that "to the unity of Father, Son and Spirit among themselves corresponds their unity *ad extra*, God's essence and work are not twofold but one, God's work is His essence in its relation to the reality which is distinct from Him and which is to be created or is created by Him. The work of God is the essence of God as the essence of Him who (N.B. in a free decision grounded in His essence *but not constrained by His essence*), is revealer, revelation and being revealed, or Creator, Reconciler and Redeemer."[169] To put the matter pointedly, when one says that God has always already chosen to be God for us in Christ and that this is so because God is captive of a law of love, this freedom of God is lost and so also is a proper concept of the freedom of God's grace.

Interestingly, Gallaher mentions that Barth met Bulgakov and was scathing in his critique of Russian religious philosophy and theology saying that these "obliterat[e] the frontiers of philosophy and theology, of reason and revelation, of Scripture, tradition and direct illumination, of spirit and nature, of pistis and Sophia (but also the distinction between the economic Trinity and the immanent Trinity)."[170] So, it is obvious that Barth thought he was maintaining a distinction in union of the immanent and economic Trinity in a way that Bulgakov did not. And that is not surprising given some of Bulgakov's remarks such as when he claimed "it is necessary to include the world's creation in God's own life, coposit the creation with God's life, correlate God's world-creating act with the act of His self-determination."[171]

To be clear, then, Gallaher defines F3 as freedom which "includes 'necessity' within it as an element of dependence, neediness, vulnerability, or the freedom to be wounded by love, a divine-human nexus of desire."[172] This view of freedom "assumes a form of self-limitation, a curbing of F1-2, by freely entering into relation and even putting itself in need of another."[173] While F1 and F2 involve the freedom of the will, F3 involves

---

[165]Ibid., 8.
[166]Ibid.
[167]Ibid.
[168]Barth, CD I/2, 878–9.
[169]Barth, CD I/1, 371, emphasis mine.
[170]Gallaher, *Freedom and Necessity*, 10.
[171]Ibid., 91.
[172]Ibid., 18.
[173]Ibid., 19.

"sacrifice of the will ... self-assertion through self-giving." It is with the formulation of F3 that Gallaher's work builds on the so-called quasi-Barthian insight of Fiddes.

My point here is that because Gallaher has built these ideas into his discussion of freedom and necessity, he then deliberately "builds on the fundamental quasi-Barthian insight of Paul Fiddes that 'God freely chooses to be in need,'" while offering "greater clarification" to this idea which was noted above.[174] Hence, he believes that "if God has an everlasting love for us in Christ and He is eternally Father, Son and Holy Spirit, then it would seem that God is God as Trinity only as God for us in Christ."[175] From this it follows that

> God out of a free ecstatic self-giving and self-receiving love, an ordered outward-going desire (marrying *eros* and *agape*="love-desire") which is both Trinitarian and Christoform, has become bound by His own desire for creation, allowing His life to be determined by the creature as a certain freely willed necessity for Him creating a divine-human joint captivation of love.[176]

Let me be as clear as I can possibly be here once again. Karl Barth would never accept this mutually conditioned view of our relationship with God. Any statement that "God is God as Trinity *only* as God for us in Christ" manifestly reduces the immanent to the economic Trinity and obliterates God's freedom for us as an act of pure grace. God's life may be determined by our life for Paul Fiddes, Jürgen Moltmann, Bruce McCormack, and others such as Bulgakov, but it is not for Karl Barth. For Barth therefore, as we shall see in detail below and have already suggested above, such a view blurs the distinction between Creator and creature at the outset, ignores the problem of sin and the need for reconciliation, and makes the profoundly mistaken assumption that God's life is somehow determined or conditioned by our life.

The most important point to be noted here, then, is that Gallaher follows Balthasar and argues for a type of *analogia entis* which posits a dialectic of freedom and necessity in all being, including divine being and action which, among other things, leads him to ask, "Do we not *need* to exist in order that God might be lovingly (albeit freely)

---

[174]Ibid.

[175]Ibid., 5. This remark is comparable to McCormack's statement that there is a triune God only in the covenant of grace, as noted above. A similar statement appears later in the book when Gallaher says, in defense of Bulgakov, that "it is an unreal case to talk about what God might have done, who He might have been. God as God is only what is revealed to us" (ibid., 99). This corresponds with Bulgakov's problematic assertion that "God ... kenotically withdraws His omnipotence to allow man in Christ a role in His own creation and redemption and therefore creation is shown to be necessary for God as He freely allows Himself in Christ to be *dependent* on it for its own creation and redemption" (ibid., 113). This follows from his idea that "from the perspective of Christ, that which is pre-accomplished in the pre-eternal divine counsel is actually dependent on His temporal divine-human decision" (ibid.). It really is not.

[176]Ibid., 4. Contrast this view, which appears to be the fruit of a panentheistic view of God and creatures, with Barth's astute remarks: "God is not the prisoner of His own power. He is not conditioned by possessing it. But He Himself conditions it. He is not bound to use it. He controls it. He is its Lord" (Barth, CD II/1, 566). God "is not bound by the essence or the existence of what has been willed by Him" (ibid., 562).

captivated by us in Christ?"[177] Note that the element of necessity in this remark stems from Gallaher's presupposition, taken from John of the Cross and Paul Fiddes, that God somehow needs creation in order to love us in Christ. While, for Barth, creation was indeed the external basis of the covenant, that never meant that God needed creation in order to establish the covenant of grace since God's actions as Creator and reconciler are free and unconstrained by any inner or outer necessity.

In any case, Gallaher refers to Moltmann as one who exhibits the view that in some sense the world is necessary to God and notes that for Moltmann " 'it is impossible to conceive of a God who is not a creative God' " so that "one can even say God 'needs' the world" since "necessity and freedom coincide" in God's "free love-desire."[178] Embedded in this thinking is Gallaher's depiction of the Platonic view that "the world, therefore, acts after all in some way as an external necessity (N1) on God/the One, given His own internal necessity (N2) in forming it as the Good who must flow out of Himself."[179] However, my point in this chapter is that this very thinking could never apply to the Christian God who is subject to no internal or external necessities according to Barth's view of God's freedom as the one who loves. In any case, this thinking is precisely what leads Gallaher to argue that God's self-determination to love us in Christ is

> a sort of freely chosen (F2) internal necessity (N2) for God, because *by His own free choice* He can become constrained from acting otherwise than as a God who has determined to be God for the world in Christ. In order for Him to be this particular man, Jesus of Nazareth, an internal necessity, though freely chosen, seems to compel Him to create a world in which this man exists.[180]

From this, Gallaher concludes that "the world, therefore, acts as a sort of external necessity (N1) on God, given His own freely chosen (F2) internal necessity (N2) to be out of His own free will dependent on the world (F3) in taking flesh."[181]

All of this reasoning unfortunately is built upon Gallaher's having read a logical necessity back into God's eternal being and action as the one who loves in freedom. First, for Barth the world is not an external necessity for God in any sense because the world is utterly contingent (which means it might never have existed or might have existed differently). Second, God's free choice to create the world through his Word and in his Spirit does not become an "internal necessity" which God himself must obey because the freedom of God's love means that God is free and not constrained in the sense that he must continue to love us. That he does so is simply a sign of his faithfulness to his covenant promises; but these do not create an internal necessity which God then must obey. Third, for Barth, as for Torrance, God never becomes dependent on the world;

---

[177]Gallaher, *Freedom and Necessity*, 5.
[178]Ibid., 35.
[179]Ibid.
[180]Ibid.
[181]Ibid.

such an idea could only arise from a confusion and reversal of the roles of Creator and creature. Consider how different Barth's view of God's trinitarian life actually is from what Gallaher espouses:

> What was and is and will be primarily in God Himself, and not primarily in the form in which we know or think we know it, is history in partnership … God was never solitary … God was always a Partner. The Father was the partner of the Son, and the Son of the Father. And what was and is and will be primarily in God Himself is history in this partnership: the closed circle of the knowing of the Son by the Father and the Father by the Son which according to Mt. 11:27 can be penetrated only from within as the Son causes a man to participate in this knowledge by His revelation … There is only the being of God as the Father and the Son with the Holy Spirit who is the Spirit of both and in whose eternal procession they are both actively united. This history in partnership is the life of God before and above all creaturely life … His inner union is marked off from the circular course of a natural process as His own free act, an act of majesty … *it is not subject to any necessity*. The Father and the Son are not two prisoners. They are not two mutually conditioning factors in reciprocal operation. As the common source of the Spirit, who Himself is also God, they are the Lord of this occurrence. *God is the free Lord of His inner union.*[182]

Clearly, then for Barth nothing in God's inner trinitarian life is subject to "any necessity" since God lives and loves in an eternal partnership, an eternal history of which he is the divine subject. Thus, "the triune life of God, which is free life in the fact that it is Spirit, is the basis of His whole will and action even *ad extra*, as the living act which He directs to us."[183] Importantly, however, and against the views of Gallaher and Fiddes, Barth maintains that "God is not under any obligation to will and do all this [elect us in Christ, establish his covenant with us, determine to become incarnate in his Son and fulfil the covenant, to create us, to overcome sin in atoning reconciliation]."[184] Barth insists that "in the triune God there is no stillness in which He desires and must seek movement, or movement in which He desires and must seek stillness. This God has no need of us. This God is self-sufficient. This God knows perfect beatitude in Himself. He is not under any need or constraint. It takes place in an inconceivably free overflowing of His goodness if He determines to co-exist with a reality distinct from Himself."[185]

While Gallaher is properly critical of Bulgakov's panentheistic approach with its tendencies toward pantheism,[186] he still believes that there are resources in Bulgakov's

---

[182]Barth, CD IV/2, 344–5, emphasis mine.
[183]Ibid., 345.
[184]Ibid.
[185]Ibid., 346.
[186]It is hard to avoid the conclusion that Bulgakov's views are pantheistic when he claims that even though creation is both created and temporal "in being based on His own divine nature of love-desire, it is also uncreated and pre-eternal in its foundation" (Gallaher, *Freedom and Necessity*, 91).

thinking that will help explain the dialectic of freedom and necessity in appropriate ways.[187] With Barth, Gallaher clearly recognizes and repeatedly asserts the importance of acknowledging that God could have existed without the world but freely chose not to. He properly maintains that Barth argues for factual necessities but not for logical necessities with respect to God's actions in history. However, his thinking appears to be unstable as already noted just because he, like Moltmann, ascribes both freedom *and* necessity to the eternal Trinity in ways that Barth, as seen above, did not and would not.

This leads him to misinterpret Barth in a number of crucial ways. First, he asserts that "if divine election is only actualized in time, then for God to be God for us He would seem to be freely dependent on man (F3), insofar as man's attesting of his own election by God in faith, as an election of God, is freely necessary (N3) for God's own self-determination as God for us in Jesus Christ."[188] This is certainly not an accurate view of election in Barth's thought because in Barth's theology, for God to be God for us does not require that we freely respond to his loving actions in Christ for those divine actions to be effective for us. Also, election in the first instance refers to Jesus Christ as electing God and elected and electing man in whom the covenant is fulfilled. Thus, his free human response to God the Father as the incarnate Son is free because it is his human action in hypostatic union with his divine being. As such it is not necessary for God's self-determination to be for us; it is rather an expression of the freedom of God for us in his human actions of obedience to God for our benefit. Second, Gallaher then claims that Barth supposedly held that "God, although He is absolutely free, becomes freely dependent on His creation in order to be God for us in Christ, which, following our problematic [concerning freedom and necessity], gives creation a certain necessity for God."[189] As explained above, however, both of these ideas are utterly foreign to Barth's understanding of God's freedom.[190] If, as Gallaher claims, Barth ever held that God was freely dependent on his creation or that creation is in some sense necessary for God, such a view would be in complete conflict with Barth's view of the kingdom of God. For Barth,

> in its coming as the act of God himself, the kingdom of God escapes all intellectual systematizing. It must be known as a unique reality and truth with its own nature and power. It is thus independent of human will and act and different from all the human works and achievements into whose sphere it enters. It is God's own independent action which limits all human history from outside, which is sovereign in relation to it, and which thus determines and controls it … This kingdom and its righteousness are certainly to be sought. They are to be sought above all the other

---

[187]Gallaher, *Freedom and Necessity*, 92.
[188]Ibid., 128.
[189]Ibid.
[190]It will be recalled that for Barth, God never becomes dependent on creation since he does not cease to be the impassible God in the incarnation, and for Barth creation is in no sense necessary for God since its necessity is entirely dependent upon God's free grace of election.

things that man may seek … But like the treasure in the field (Mt. 13:44), it is there even before it is sought or found by anybody … The kingdom would still be what it is even if there were never any such following and response anywhere.[191]

Third, this questionable line of interpretation offered by Gallaher is connected with two other doubtful presuppositions. The first is that Gallaher interprets Barth to hold that all concepts "from 'God' through to 'atonement' derive their significance from Jesus Christ and His history so that (at least methodologically) election precedes and grounds the Trinity rather than the Trinity founding election."[192] While it is quite true that for Barth all concepts from God to atonement do indeed derive their significance from Jesus Christ, that assertion is a far cry from claiming that election precedes and grounds the Trinity. This is the case because we can only know God as well as atonement from Jesus Christ since he himself is the eternal Son of the Father who through his Holy Spirit enables us to participate in the closed circle of God's eternal self-knowledge as Father and Son. But the fact that we know God truly only in Jesus Christ and know of our reconciliation with God only in Christ is ultimately grounded in God's freely choosing to elect us in his Son Jesus Christ to be his covenant partners. Since that election is the act of the eternal Father, Son, and Holy Spirit, election is clearly grounded in the Trinity, not the other way around. That is precisely why, as noted above, Barth firmly claimed that "the triune life of God, which is free life in the fact that it is Spirit, is the basis of His whole will and action even *ad extra*, as the living act which He directs to us."[193]

The second doubtful interpretation of Barth offered by Gallaher concerns Gallaher's statement that Barth used "substance/essence language" and "even presupposes it by assuming an eternal divine Being/love which to be itself necessarily loves. Nevertheless, God's eternal choice and act of becoming man in time *constitute* His Being as God, since 'precisely as the One He is, He acts.' "[194] There are two key errors embedded in these statements. First, Barth was much more careful than Gallaher when he said that "God's loving is necessary, for it is the being, the essence and the nature of God."[195] I say this because Barth goes on to assert that God "loves us and the world as He who would still be the One who loves without us and without the world" since God "needs no other to form the prior ground of His existence as the One who loves and as God … It is not part of God's being and action that as love it must have an object in another who is different from Him."[196] In other words, for Barth, God's eternal being and act as Father, Son, and Holy Spirit is complete in itself and did not and does not need an object outside this eternal being and act to be the eternal triune God that he is. Second, the only way one

---

[191]Barth, CD IV/4 Lecture Fragments, 240.
[192]Ibid., 126. Gallaher refers to CD IV/1, 16–17, to support this view. However, on those pages Barth never says that "election precedes and grounds the Trinity." For a full discussion of the fact that this is not Barth's actual position, see Molnar, *Divine Freedom*; and Hunsinger, *Reading Barth with Charity*.
[193]Barth, CD IV/2, 345.
[194]Gallaher, *Freedom and Necessity*, 128, emphasis mine.
[195]Barth, CD II/1, 280.
[196]Ibid.

could draw the conclusion here, as Gallaher did, that God's eternal choice to become man *constitutes* his being as God, is if one failed to distinguish God's eternal freedom as the one who loves, from his free actions of love *ad extra*. That is precisely what Gallaher failed to do here because he simply said that God necessarily loves and then concluded that God's eternal choice and acts for us constitute his eternal being. In drawing that conclusion, he undermined Barth's emphatic assertions that God's love of us is free love of another who is different from him. Hence, for Barth,

in the fact that He determines to love such another, His love overflows. But it is not exhausted in it nor confined or conditioned by it. On the contrary, this overflowing is conditioned by the fact that although it could satisfy itself, it has no satisfaction in this self-satisfaction, but as love for another it can and will be more than that which could satisfy itself.[197]

What is more, even though Barth explicitly and strongly rejected the thinking of Angelus Silesius and Rainer Maria Rilke, Gallaher is compelled by his own presuppositions to marginalize Barth's opposition to their thinking, claiming that one of his central tasks "is to argue that there exists an explicitly Christoform problematic of divine freedom and necessity which is that God acts on the basis of love and He has determined to be Himself as love for us *in Christ*."[198] From this it follows for Gallaher that

in order for Him to be this particular man, Jesus of Nazareth, an internal necessity, though freely chosen, seems to compel Him to create a world in which this man exists. The world, therefore acts as a sort of external necessity (N1) on God, given His own freely chosen (F2) internal necessity (N2) to be out of His own free will dependent on the world (F3) in taking flesh.[199]

This leads Gallaher to claim that "God graciously condescends to become man for our sake even to the point of becoming dependent on His creation and by this free divine humanization, man is made God by divinization."[200] Embracing this perspective, Gallaher then claims that

---

[197] Ibid.
[198] Gallaher, *Freedom and Necessity*, 35.
[199] Ibid.
[200] Ibid. Against the perspective advanced by Gallaher here, Thomas F. Torrance follows Barth in insisting that "we cannot think of the ontological Trinity as if it were constituted by or *dependent* on the economic Trinity" (*Christian Doctrine of God*, 108–9). He also maintained with clarity that "just as there is no necessary relation between God and the world which he has freely created, for God does not need the world to be God, so the Fatherhood of God is in *no way dependent* on or constituted by relation to what he has created outwith himself" (ibid., 207, emphasis mine). It is also no accident then that Torrance criticizes Basil and his brother Gregory Nyssen for conceptualizing "the relations between the Father and the Son and the Spirit as constituting a structure of a causal series or, as it were 'a chain of dependence'" (ibid., 178). This problematic thinking leads to the idea that "it is the *Person* of the Father who causes, deifies and personalises the Being of the Son and of the Spirit and even the existence of the Godhead!" (ibid.). Torrance follows Dydimus to insist that "the generation of the Son and the procession of the Spirit from the *Person* of the Father ... is not

Angelus Silesius (1624-77) is typical of the radical Christocentrism of such theology, which looks towards Barth, in arguing that God is necessitated to love by His own eternal self-determination to be God as man for us in Christ, since "Love rules o'er everything; even the Trinity/ Itself has been her subject throughout eternity."[201]

These assertions are in conflict with Barth's clear opposition to the idea that God's love is subject to a law of love, and they really are ludicrous when you consider what Barth said about Angelus Silesius. It is worth listening to Barth himself for a moment. For Barth, "the eternal correlation between God and us, as shown in God's revelation, is grounded in God alone, and not partly in God and partly in us. It means that we are tied to God, but not God to us."[202] This statement is diametrically opposed to the idea that God becomes dependent on history or that there is a mutually conditioned and mutually conditioning relationship between God and us. Then Barth writes that we simply cannot have a proper view of God's love if it is drawn from a "common concept of love" which "we can produce and presuppose."[203]

Accordingly, Barth insists that "we must beware of an unreflecting inversion and therefore of a definition of the divine love on the basis of a common concept of love. If we are not careful at this point we shall inevitably rob God of His deity."[204] It is in connection with these views that Barth refers to Angelus Silesius saying that what must be avoided can be seen "in a crude form" in his thinking. Here are just four statements that Barth unequivocally rejected: (1) "I know that without me God cannot an instant be. He needs must perish at once were death to come to me." (2) "God owes as much to me as the debt that I must pay, I give my help to Him, He keeps me in my way." (3) "The blessedness of God, His life without desire, He doth as much from me, as I from Him acquire." (4) "God loveth me alone, He holdeth me so dear, That if I love him not, He dieth of anxious fear."[205] Barth concludes by dubbing these remarks as "pious blasphemies" which are similar to the views of Rainer Maria Rilke, and which were published "with the imprimatur of a Roman Catholic bishop" and says "we may well ask whether this bishop was an imbecile or whether he had a secret understanding with the modern rogue."[206] Once again, Barth's understanding of God's freedom is as far away from the views suggested by Gallaher as they could possibly be. And once again the reason is because in loving us God cannot be reduced to his love for us as happened in the statements cited from Silesius. So, Barth

---

to be equated with the *causation of their being*" because the eternal being of the Son and Spirit must not be understood as "derived" from the deity of the Father as that idea is inherently subordinationist (ibid., 178–9).
[201]Gallaher, *Freedom and Necessity*, 35–6. Gallaher cites Angelus Silesius and is aware of Barth's rejection of Silesius's thinking. Nonetheless, he embraces this supposedly Christocentric viewpoint "despite Barth's criticism of Angelus Silesius: CD, II/1, 281-2" (ibid., 35).
[202]Barth, CD II/1, 281.
[203]Ibid.
[204]Ibid.
[205]Ibid., 281–2.
[206]Ibid., 282.

always emphasizes that God loves us in his Son and his loving is "his own being and essence" which he gives to us in Christ. However, as always, he adds that

> we must not allow the completeness of His being in love for us to blind us to the fact that we do not speak of His, the divine love, if we try to deny it the movement that is proper to it in itself even though it is not an attitude to us ... God's act is His loving ... in so far as it is His essence even apart from us ... He does not need us and yet He finds no enjoyment in His self-enjoyment ... He turns to us in the overflow of the perfection of His essence and therefore of His loving, and shares with us, in and with His love, its blessedness. This blessedness of the love of God is founded on the fact that he is Father, Son and Holy Spirit and as such loves us ... as the One who loves eternally.[207]

With Barth's forceful rejection of the thinking of Silesius and any idea that God is dependent on us, it is difficult to fathom how Gallaher could claim that such theology looked toward Barth. It will be noticed here that while we saw above that Barth insisted God did not even need his own being to be who he is because he already was the triune God who loves in freedom, Gallaher can say that

> God, one might say, who is absolutely free in Himself as love (F2), yet utterly dependent upon Himself, gives Himself to the world in free love by choosing (F3) to be Himself as the God of divine desire for us in Christ (N2). He lays upon Himself an external necessity of the world in His love for it in Christ (N1). This love ... has put itself in need to the world (N3). Divine desire for the world is not arbitrary. It is the external but free expression of God's own intra-dependent eternal but irrevocable desire for Himself.[208]

From this he concludes that God not only desires to make himself vulnerable to the world but that he makes himself "captive to its creation even unto death on a cross."[209] Therefore "God is freely captive on the cross because His own law of love always already freely binds Him."[210] Here we simply must note that for Barth, God was not a captive on the cross but there freely condescended to be one with us in order to reconcile the world to himself on the cross. And since God is the free subject of his own inner life, he therefore is not subject to a law of love. Such a view would make love the subject and God the predicate. And that is precisely what Barth always rejected.

From these reflections, Gallaher incorrectly maintains that Barth blurred the lines between God's willing himself and willing the world and that Barth risks pantheism since for him freedom and necessity necessarily coincide.[211] He thus incorrectly claims

---

[207]Ibid., 282–3.
[208]Gallaher, *Freedom and Necessity*, 37.
[209]Ibid.
[210]Ibid., 38.
[211]Ibid., 138.

that "in identifying the act of election with the inner life of God as Trinity, Barth ends up arguing that God's willing of all things *ad extra* in willing to be God for us in Christ is *also* necessary."[212] He thus interprets Barth to be saying that "God's freedom and necessity coincide in willing creation in Christ. God then wills Himself and creation in a synthesis of freedom and necessity."[213] According to Gallaher,

> the necessity for God to be Creator, for Barth, seems to give creation an external necessity (N1) which is internalized in the eternal loving decision (F2) to be God in Christ (N2). Here we have a Barthian way of expressing the fact that God freely gives Himself to us in dependence in Christ (F3) and this dependence is irrevocable, as God has bound Himself to us for eternity (N3).[214]

Accordingly, he thinks that for Barth "it becomes divinely necessary for God to be Creator."[215]

In light of Barth's position discussed above, however, it should be clear that Barth would utterly reject each of these ideas: (1) As already noted, God's love of us in Christ cannot be said to imply that "God is God as Trinity only as God for us in Christ" as Gallaher claims,[216] because, as noted above, such a remark reduces God to his actions for us in history in exactly the way Barth tenaciously opposed. For Barth, "God's being and nature are not *exhausted* in the encroachment in which He is God among us and for us, nor is His truth in the truth of His grace and mercy."[217] Barth thus held that God acting as reconciler

> makes a completely new start as the freest possible subject … He acts to maintain and defend His own glory. But no one and nothing outside Himself could ordain for Him that this should be a matter of His glory. He acts with a view to the goal to which He wills to bring man, but there is not really *any necessity* which constrains Him to do this.[218]

For Barth, God "loved the world of men, but He did not need to continue to love the sinful world of men. We can only say that He has actually done so."[219] Gallaher's reasoning also flies in the face of Barth's view that God's being "does not need any origination and

---

[212]Ibid., 139.
[213]Ibid.
[214]Ibid.
[215]Ibid., 155.
[216]Ibid., 5. That remark clearly reflects the fact that Gallaher has misread Barth in light of McCormack's collapse of the immanent into the economic Trinity with his statement that there is a triune God *only* in the covenant of grace, as noted above.
[217]Barth, CD II/1, 75, emphasis mine. See also CD II/1, 280 where Barth repeats this idea. For Barth, "in the fact that He determines to love such another, His love overflows. But it is not exhausted in it nor confined or conditioned by it."
[218]Barth, CD IV/1, 79, emphasis mine.
[219]Ibid., 80.

constitution. He cannot 'need' His own being because He affirms it in being who He is
… And what He creates, produces and causes, what needs origination and constitution
in order to be, what can need existence, is not God Himself, or His reality, but the reality
which is distinct from Himself."[220]

Moreover, Barth maintains that

> when we say that God is free to exist, we do not say that God lifts Himself, as it
> were, out of non-existence into existence, that He makes Himself free to exist.
> What we say is that the mode of existence is proper to Him which is exempt from
> any limitation by the possibility of its non-existence. He is the One who is in
> Himself the Existent. By existing in this way He is not subject to any necessity, as
> though He must first exist in order to be who He is. But by His existence He simply
> reaffirms Himself. It is not that He needs to reaffirm Himself, but that, being who
> He is, He does in fact reaffirm Himself and His existence.[221]

From this Barth concludes that "it is not that His being needs this confirmation, but that
the very fact of His being, *free from all need*, is in fact this confirmation. This is the first
primary meaning of God's being in freedom, in aseity."[222]

Therefore, for Barth, the triune God exists as the one who loves in freedom just
because his love is "free from all need" as the "Existent."[223] Importantly, then Barth
concludes that since God really is free in himself, therefore "he is the One who is free
from all origination, conditioning or determination from without, by that which is not
Himself."[224] Barth means what he says and therefore he does not think that God makes
himself dependent on creation or upon history as Creator, Reconciler, or Redeemer.
Barth stresses that we first have to grasp God's freedom in himself *before* attempting
to understand his freedom in relation to creation, that is, his freedom from all external
conditioning. That is precisely why he argues that "the absoluteness of God—that which
makes it a genuine absoluteness—does not derive primarily from the mode of His
relationship with the latter [the world]. For this very reason, He can enter into a real
relationship with the latter."[225] Finally, our existence and freedom as God's creatures, who
are utterly dependent upon God for our existence, is real because God in his freedom
has conferred that upon us. However, and this is the crucial point blurred in Gallaher's
thinking, we have our being

> not because He was obliged to do so, or because His purpose was influenced by
> [our] being and nature, but because [our] being and nature is conditioned by His

---

[220]Barth, CD II/1, 306.
[221]Ibid.
[222]Ibid., emphasis mine.
[223]Ibid.
[224]Ibid., 307.
[225]Ibid., 309.

being and nature. If [we] belong to Him and He to [us], this dual relationship does not spring from any need of His eternal being. This would remain the same even if there were no such relationship. If there is a connexion and relatedness between [us] and Him, God is who He is in independence of [us] even in this relatedness … He does not mingle and blend Himself with [us] … He remains who He is. He creates and sustains this relationship.[226]

These are the crucial elements of Barth's theology that have been contradicted and marginalized by Gallaher's attempt to incorporate the dialectic of freedom and necessity into the life of the Trinity. Barth's thinking repeatedly excludes any such attempt as I have been showing. Furthermore, the idea that in the incarnation God is subject to an internal necessity contradicts Barth's persistent claim that God's love is not subject to *any* internal or external necessities. For Barth, "God acts with inward freedom and not in fulfilment of a law to which He is supposedly subject."[227] Here, I suspect Gallaher has been misled by Paul Fiddes's view that for Barth, God supposedly has made himself dependent on creation. Let me repeat what for Barth was a most basic insight from which he never wavered:

Every relationship into which God enters with that which is not Himself must be interpreted—however much this may disturb or correct our preconceived ideas of connexion and relationship—as eventuating between two utterly unequal partners, the sheer inequality consisting in the fact that no self-determination of the second partner can influence the first, whereas the self-determination of the first, while not cancelling the self-determination of the second, is the sovereign predetermination which precedes it absolutely.[228]

Having said all of this, it is also important to realize that for Barth, God is free for us in Jesus Christ and "can allow this other which is so utterly distinct from Himself to live and move and have its being within Himself … God can in fact be nearer to it than it is to itself."[229] However, these statements cannot be understood in the panentheistic sense employed by so many today because panentheism always collapses back into pantheistic confusion of God and creatures. Barth insists that God can spontaneously bind himself "in a certain way to the world" but that "He remains unbound from the point of view of the world and its specific determinations … His presence in the life and being of the world is His personal and therefore actual presence expressed in continually new forms according to His sovereign decisions."[230] Everything here, however, hinges upon exactly

---

[226]Ibid., 311.

[227]Barth, CD I/2, 135.

[228]Barth, CD II/1, 312.

[229]Ibid., 314.

[230]Ibid. It is within this context that Barth says, "God is free to be and operate in the created world either as unconditioned or as conditioned. God is free to perform His work either within the framework of what we call the laws of nature or outside it in the shape of miracle" because that is how God meets us in Christ (Barth, CD II/1, 314).

what Barth might have meant when he wrote that "God is free to be and operate in the created world either as unconditioned or as conditioned. God is free to perform His work either within the framework of what we call the laws of nature or outside it in the shape of miracle."[231] Is Barth arguing for the kind of mutual conditioning embraced by Fiddes, Moltmann, Bulgakov, and Gallaher—a mutual conditioning that is endemic to panentheistic perspectives? I think the answer is a definite NO because Barth's point here simply is that God is genuinely free to act as he has in Jesus Christ in such a way that God "is free to be wholly inward to the creature and at the same time as Himself wholly outward." Moreover, God can be "eternal also in our finitude."[232] Furthermore, for Barth, "we do not speak of His, the divine love, if we try to deny it the movement that is proper to it in itself, even though it is not an attitude to us."[233] Thus,

> God loves us, and loves the world, in accordance with His revelation. But He loves us and the world as He who would still be One who loves without us and without the world; as He, therefore, who needs no other to form the prior ground of His existence as the One who loves and as God.[234]

Here it is imperative to maintain God's self-sufficiency as the basis of all his actions *ad extra*. For Barth,

> it is not part of God's being and action that as love it must have an object in another who is different from Him. God is sufficient in Himself as object and therefore as object of His love. He is no less the One who loves if He loves no object different from Himself.[235]

When Barth asserts that in loving us God's love "overflows," he does not embrace any sort of emanationist perspective, and so he says, "In the fact that He determines to love such another, His love overflows."[236] Notice that this determination is a free choice on the part of the triune God; it is not something that constitutes his triunity. God's love "is not exhausted in it [his love for us], nor confined or *conditioned* by it."[237] This overflowing of God's love then is an act of grace and not nature because "God does not owe us either our being, or in our being His love."[238] Consequently, "the eternal correlation between God and us, as shown in God's revelation, is grounded in God alone, and not partly in God and partly in us. It means that we are tied to God, but not God to us."[239] In making these vital assertions, Barth maintains that "God's love surpasses and

---

231 Ibid.
232 Ibid., 315.
233 Ibid., 282.
234 Ibid., 280.
235 Ibid.
236 Ibid.
237 Ibid., emphasis mine.
238 Ibid., 281, 513–14.
239 Ibid.

oversteps the common concept of love that we ourselves can produce and presuppose."[240] Unfortunately, Gallaher's own attempt to move even further than Barth in his view of God's overflowing love has more than a tinge of emanationism attached to it. He claims that God's "excessive love for creation" is "a divine desire spilling out beyond God's Triune life" which "in some sense … could not be otherwise and must express itself in creation as a free dependence."[241]

Having accepted the perspective of Angelus Silesius, Gallaher explained that, for Bulgakov, God is understood both as "Absolute" and as "Absolute-Relative." As "Absolute," Gallaher says, God could have refrained from creating the world. But for God as "Absolute-Relative" such a view would be "unbefitting to the divine essence." Consequently, "God could not have refrained from creating the world, since it flowed from His very life as love."[242] This, he claims, is not a need for God himself "but for the world itself as a sort of freely chosen … internal necessity … of the world. Such a need— and in what follows, Bulgakov is adapting a concept found from Plotinus to Moltmann and Fiddes—is the need of divine love-desire."[243]

The necessity Bulgakov has in mind, according to Gallaher, "is the *necessity of love*, which cannot *not* love and which manifests and realizes in itself *the identity* and *indistinguishability of freedom and necessity*."[244] According to Gallaher, this thinking about "divine 'need' might be characterized" by saying that "God freely chooses to be dependent on the world (F3), to be in need to it, and this dependence is an eternal reality that God cannot simply undo (N3)."[245] Gallaher makes much of the fact that Barth supposedly united freedom and necessity in God dialectically so that in his view Moltmann offered the right interpretation of God's free love within his panentheistic perspective. This leads Gallaher to maintain that, in accordance with his own version of the *analogia entis*, there is both freedom and necessity in God so that God in some sense must create and must be seen as dependent on creation in some way. But the fact is that when Barth spoke of necessity and contingency within the divine being,[246] he was referring to the factual necessity that he believed was grounded in God's free eternal election which itself was contingent and not necessary for God to be God. He never held that creation was in any sense necessary for God.[247]

---

[240]Ibid.

[241]Gallaher, *Freedom and Necessity*, 136.

[242]Ibid., 97.

[243]Ibid.

[244]Ibid.

[245]Ibid.

[246]See, e.g., Barth, CD II/1, 547–8.

[247]Creation's necessity lay in the eternal divine "decree and will" of the God who "loved man and man's whole world from all eternity, even before it was created … He created it because He loved it in his Son who because of its transgressions stood before Him eternally as the Rejected and Crucified" (Barth, CD III/1, 50–1). As the second person of the Trinity who became incarnate for us, Jesus Christ existed in the counsel of God and that eternally contingent choice of God is the only basis of the necessity that God is in fact the Creator: "The fact that God has regard to his Son—the Son of Man, the Word made flesh—is the true and genuine basis of creation" (ibid., 51).

Barth, Moltmann, and Necessity

In this context, Gallaher specifically refers to the thinking of Moltmann to underscore what he wishes to express. Moltmann cites three statements from Barth indicating that God could have been God without us just because the God who is for us has no need of us since God is "self-sufficient."[248] After explaining this, Moltmann then asks, "Does God really not need those whom in the suffering of his love he loves unendingly?"[249] And Moltmann's answer is that for God not to reveal himself "and to be contented with his untouched glory would be a contradiction of himself" because if God is love, then God cannot be without us. This is where he explicitly disagrees with Barth's concept of God's freedom, claiming that Barth's view is nominalistic because Barth thought God existed in perfect love and freedom without us and did not and does not need us even as God chooses to love us in freedom.[250]

In this thinking Barth followed Athanasius in part inasmuch as Athanasius held that "God is not patterned after human beings, but rather human beings after God, who is truly and pre-eminently the one Father of His own Son, and from this human beings are named fathers of their own children."[251] Implied here is Barth's belief that God is free both in himself as the one who loves since Father, Son, and Holy Spirit are fully *homoousios* and in relation to the world since God did not and does not need the world, but nevertheless freely created it and loves it. I say that Barth followed Athanasius in part because Barth was critical of both Athanasius and of Anselm for introducing necessity unwittingly into the divine being. After arguing that the Word becoming flesh took place "in the divine freedom of the Word" so that the miracle of the incarnation could not be explained "in terms of the world-process," Barth concludes by saying, "It does not rest upon *any necessity* in the divine nature or upon the relation between Father, Son and Spirit, that God becomes man" even though he also says that God's love to us is "originally grounded upon the eternal relation of God, Father and Son."[252] However, here once again, Barth stresses the fact that God's freedom excludes ascribing a dialectic of freedom *and* necessity to the divine being, maintaining that since God's love to us "is already free and unconstrained in God Himself, so, too, and only then rightly, is it free in its realisation towards man."[253]

In his doctrine of Providence, Barth is no nominalist but insists, against the kind of views offered by Gallaher and Moltmann, that God's

---

[248]Moltmann, *Trinity and Kingdom*, 52–3.

[249]Ibid., 53.

[250]Ibid., 53–4. Such a criticism fails to account for Barth's important statements that "God is not first the One who loves, and then somewhere and somehow, in contradistinction to that, the One who is also free. And when He loves He does not surrender His freedom, but exercises it … The principle of division which we recognise at this point cannot mean that out of the distinction suggested but also overcome in revelation we have to establish a separation between a God in Himself and a God for us" (Barth, CD II/1, 344–5).

[251]Barth, CD I/1, 393. Barth's citation in the text is in Greek.

[252]Barth, CD I/2, 135, emphasis mine.

[253]Ibid.

love is free or it is not love. Therefore when God accompanies the creature He gives Himself. In so doing He is not the prisoner either of Himself or of the creature. He still acts according to His good-pleasure. When the love of God overflows in creating, the preserving and now the accompanying of the creature, this means that it is revealed in its freedom. And it is in this freedom that it is necessary to God.[254]

Barth is most definitely not arguing here on the basis of a dialectic of freedom and necessity that is supposedly present in all being because in this volume he continually rejects any idea that God's cooperation with creation is even remotely conditioned by creaturely activity. He invariably insists that the relationship between the triune God and creatures is irreversible saying that

the god of all synergistic systems is always the absolute, the general, the digit 1, the concept. And it is clear that the operation of this god and that of the creature (the relative, the particular, the multiplied or divided part, the perception) have necessarily to be thought of as reciprocal. But this god is not God. Between this god and the creature all kinds of reversals are possible, and the devious dialectical mind of man has constantly made them.[255]

Barth goes on to say that God "cannot encounter any limits in the creaturely sphere which can and must compel Him to conform … allowing Himself to be determined and conditioned by it. He is absolutely sovereign in relation to all the different possibilities of the creature."[256] Barth insists that while God works with us and even cooperates with us, God's work in this and his revelation

---

[254]Barth, CD III/3, 110.

[255]Ibid., 139.

[256]Ibid. Barth explains that on the creaturely level all relations are "reversible" but that "the relation between the divine and creaturely activity cannot be reversed as the relation between the individual activity and the totality of creaturely activity can be reversed. And this is what distinguishes the divine activity from the totality of creaturely activity" (ibid., 122). Barth explicitly rejects any idea of "a conditioning and determining and to that extent a limiting of the activity of God by the activity of the creature" (ibid., 114). Because God's love is free love, it is based on God's own good-pleasure and "is an act of sovereignty the honour of which is God's honour" so that God's will "is not limited by the 'givenness' or determination of the creature, nor is it conditioned by any act of the creature. On the contrary, it is the will which conditions these acts. The concept of *concursus* is itself irreversible. God 'concurs' with the creature, but the creature does not 'concur' with God. That is, the activity of the creature does not impose any conditions upon the activity of God" (ibid., 113). Barth insists that "we must think of the divine activity as first and foremost a free activity—free in the sense that it is a work which God does not owe either to Himself or to the creature" (ibid., 109). Barth even says that God does this with an "inward necessity." But that does not mean God is subject to some principle other than his own free good-pleasure; so he says that "this involves an unbreakable order in the work of the creature, for in that the creature exists God exists with it in the supremacy of His own work … to preserve it in its reality … But the necessity with which God does hold to this and do it is the necessity of His love. And love is free or it is not love. Therefore when God accompanies the creature He gives Himself. In so doing He is not the prisoner either of Himself or of the creature. He still acts according to His good-pleasure. When the love of God overflows in the creating, the preserving and now the accompanying of the creature, this means that it is revealed in its freedom. And it is in this freedom that it is necessary to God" (ibid., 109–10).

in the revealing of the creature, can never be ascribed to the creature, but only and always to God Himself. That which works is His co-operating love. That which speaks is His co-operating Word. And for that … the creature on its side has no capacity. It is not, then, the creature which works in God's working, but God Himself who works on and in His own working. God alone is and remains eternal love. The creature can only be loved by Him, or at the very best love Him in return. The freedom of God cannot be violated. An awareness of the supremacy of God over all the power of the creature, of the qualitative distinction between divine and creaturely potency, of the irreversibility of the order of precedence in divine and creaturely activity, must be brought into place and relentlessly kept in place at this juncture.[257]

This thinking is in harmony with Barth's statement, noted above, that "God acts with inward freedom and not in fulfilment of a law to which He is supposedly subject."[258] Because this is a miracle (a special new direct act of God within history that cannot be explained by observing history itself), this act of God "does not follow of necessity from this or that attribute of God," and it is for this reason and not because Barth embraces any kind of nominalism that he then asserts that "His Word will still be His Word apart from this becoming, just as Father, Son and Holy Spirit would be none the less eternal God, if no world had ever been created."[259] Additionally, Barth asserts that God was not "in duty bound to [creation] or to Himself to command a halt to its destruction through sin by a fresh creation. If He has actually done this, we have to recognise His free good will in doing so, and nothing else."[260] It is in this context that Barth asks if Athanasius "has sufficiently thought out the matter" when in his consideration of the incarnation he writes

that the actual victory of death in consequence of sin would have been ἄτοπον ὁμοῦ καὶ ἀπρεπές [nevertheless out of place and unseemly], that the extinction of an intelligent being participating in the Logos would have been unseemly, that the destruction of this creation would have been incompatible with the goodness of God, that the undoing of the divine work of art would have been τῶν ἀπρεπεστάτων [among the most unseemly of things]. Since such an undoing of reality threatened to take place, τί τὸν θεὸν ἔδει ποιεῖν ἀγαθὸν ὄντα; … Οὐκοῦν ἔδει τοὺς ἀνθρώπους μὴ ἀφιέναι φέρεσθαι τῇ φθορᾷ διὰ τὸ ἀπρεπὲς καὶ ἀνάξιον εἶναι τοῦτο τῆς τοῦ θεοῦ ἀγαθότητος [What was necessary for God to do, since He is good? … Therefore it was necessary that he not allow men to be carried off in destruction, because this would be unseemly and unworthy of the goodness of God].[261]

---

[257]Ibid., 111.
[258]Barth, CD I/2, 135.
[259]Ibid.
[260]Ibid.
[261]Ibid.

Barth raised similar concerns about Anselm's statements about the necessity of the incarnation saying that "there is a wrong note in all this, as everyone must admit."[262] Nonetheless, he did say that Anselm's intention was "not as wrong as it sounds" since for him "*necessitas* is not a last word either noetically (in the recognition of the object of faith) or ontically (in this object's existence prior to faith's recognition)."[263] In light of these statements by Barth, we can see quite clearly that Moltmann, Lewis, Gallaher, and all who ascribe necessity to God in his eternal being and act as Father, Son, and Holy Spirit in the way they do end up claiming that because God is love he needed to create, reconcile, and redeem the world. This conclusion unfortunately follows from reading necessities associated with our limited and sinful experience of love and freedom into God thus compromising the nature of God's free love and grace by claiming that God is bound to us in a way that God is not.

It is here that Moltmann's panentheism leads him astray as noted above so that he claims that "it is impossible to conceive of a God who is not a creative God. A non-creative God would be imperfect."[264] Moltmann believes that the "distinction between immanent and economic Trinity would be necessary if, in the concept of God, there were really only the alternative between liberty and necessity. But if God *is* love, then his liberty cannot consist of loving or not loving."[265] These remarks illustrate that Moltmann's thinking becomes doubtful just because he confuses the immanent and economic Trinity. He argues that "God by no means has the choice between mutually exclusive possibilities. For he cannot deny himself. So he does not have that choice between being love and *not* being love."[266] This statement is true insofar as it refers to the immanent Trinity. But God is free as the one who loves and would have suffered no lack even if he never chose to love us. The difference here between Barth and Moltmann is that Barth distinguishes without separating the immanent and economic Trinity in his thinking and Moltmann confuses the two because he builds his trinitarian theology on a kind of panentheistic view of love and freedom. By contrast, as we shall see in a moment, Barth rejects panentheism as worse than pantheism because he does not think God had to love us but that he loves us according to his good-pleasure.

So Moltmann concludes that "if he [God] is love, then in loving the world he is by no means 'his own prisoner'; on the contrary, in loving the world he is entirely free because he is entirely himself."[267] From this it follows that "love is a self-evident, unquestionable 'overflowing of goodness' which is therefore never open to choice at any time"[268] and that "when we say 'God *is* love,' then we mean that he is in eternity this process of self-differentiation and self-identification; a process which contains the whole pain of the

---

[262]Ibid.
[263]Ibid.
[264]Moltmann, *Trinity and Kingdom*, 106.
[265]Ibid., 151.
[266]Ibid., 54–5.
[267]Ibid., 55.
[268]Ibid.

negative in itself."[269] Consequently, "God 'needs' the world and man. If God is love, then he neither will nor can be without the one who is his beloved."[270] Indeed, he argues that "creation is part of the eternal love affair between the Father and the Son."[271] Following this line of thinking then, it is not at all surprising that, as seen above, Moltmann finally concludes that "it is impossible to conceive of a God who is not a creative God" and "God cannot find bliss in eternal self-love if selflessness is part of love's very nature."[272]

Each of these statements unfortunately reflect Moltmann's confusion of the immanent and economic Trinity. Having denied God's freedom of choice in loving us, his thinking quite logically leads him to conclude that God cannot exist without us since God is selfless in his love. Certainly, God is selfless in his love of us; but God does not on that account need us because, as we noted above, what can need existence is not God but the reality distinct from God. Moltmann has confused the two and thus claims that God cannot exist without us if he is love. But that is precisely wrong because God is love and yet God's love is indeed self-sufficient and free and for that very reason it can be and is effective love for us.

It is this logic that drives Gallaher's discussion of what he calls God's "free love-desire."[273] From this he concludes that "in order for Him [God] to be this particular man, Jesus of Nazareth, an internal necessity, though freely chosen, seems to compel Him to create a world in which this man exists."[274] It is clear at this point that the whole idea of "love-desire" illuminates the fact that with that notion, a logical necessity has been introduced into the divine being. This line of thinking leads to some bizarre notions such as that God can be surprised by us with the result that God can discover "new ways of coaxing the world back to God through His Spirit";[275] that "creation can by grace give

---

[269]Ibid., 57.

[270]Ibid., 58.

[271]Ibid., 59.

[272]Ibid., 106.

[273]Gallaher, *Freedom and Necessity*, 35.

[274]Ibid.

[275]Ibid., 248. This leads Gallaher to say that "when God finds out that the Son of Man affirms Him as His God, it is as if the curtain covering the ultimate decision of the Son of Man, the 'space' of creatureliness in God's self-knowledge, as to whether He would put aside His human will for the sake of His divine will, and by which God voluntarily blinded Himself, is torn in two from top to bottom" (ibid.). It really cannot be said, as Gallaher does here, that there ever was a curtain covering God's eternal self-knowledge so that the very idea that the Son of Man might go against the Father's will and his own divine will as the eternal Son would indeed compromise the divine freedom of God's own knowledge and love. Gallaher can speak of a "synergy" of the Spirit with the man Jesus while Barth and Torrance rejected any and all synergistic conceptions of divine/human relations, even in Christ. Then Gallaher says, "The Spirit in effecting divine-human unity manages to surprise even God Himself" (ibid.). However, since the divine/human unity in Christ is and remains a miraculous action of God for us, the outcome does not surprise God since it occurs precisely in accordance with his will, good-pleasure, and power to love us from all eternity. There are a few other confusing remarks. For instance, we are told that "creation, which is external and not proper to God, is made God's very own by this divine enownment. When God enowns divine-human election, making it proper to Him like His own primordial election, then creation can truly be said to become a 'portion of God'" (ibid.). For Gallaher this means that God gifts creation in such a way that "by grace in Christ" creation has "the very same synthesis of freedom and necessity that He has by nature" (ibid., 249). For Barth and for Torrance, creation never becomes a "portion of God" because we must consistently distinguish between God's eternal being and act within the immanent Trinity in which God is free

something back to God";[276] and that God has gifted creation with the very same freedom and necessity God supposedly has by nature.[277] Further, Gallaher asserts that

> God has chosen that the necessity of the world should be a part of the actualization of divine freedom, both together constituting Absolute Freedom or the divine life of love-desire. He has chosen that any divine action eternally exists within the compass of Christ Himself and, therefore, to be free, it must of necessity be not merely a divine action but a divine-human action. One can no longer climb back up to some modality of a divine act that is purely divine.[278]

In this thinking, unfortunately, the immanent Trinity has been completely collapsed into the economic Trinity just because the ideal of a dialectical necessity *and* freedom was ascribed to the immanent Trinity at the outset. Finally, Gallaher carries through his mistaken idea that election grounds the Trinity with the idea that God's eternal being as Father, Son, and Holy Spirit is itself discretionary:

> In the case of primordial election, God the Father eternally and necessarily … chooses His Son in begetting Him and the Son in obedient Eucharistic thanksgiving elects Him in turn by freely receiving … His own begottenness as a necessity. This is an act which could have been "otherwise," since He need not so affirm His natural Being.[279]

---

as the one who loves, without being subjected to any internal or external necessity, and his eternal contingent act of electing us to be in covenant fellowship with him. Torrance calls attention to the danger of *vertigo* when conceptualizing ourselves as "exalted in Christ to partake of the divine nature" (*Space, Time and Resurrection*, 136). Torrance notes that "one finds a form of this vertigo also in some mystics and pantheists who tend to identify their own ultimate being with the divine Being" (ibid.). One of the indicators that Gallaher has succumbed to the danger of vertigo can be seen in his statements that "we can say, audaciously, that God to be a God of love had to love beyond Himself in creation and redemption. Creation can by grace in Christ give something back to God which is its own creaturely participation in God's self-generation as Father, Son, and Holy Spirit" (Gallaher, *Freedom and Necessity*, 249). Gallaher continues by saying that "in needing creation, God cannot but love it since His free self-giving in Christ cannot be otherwise (N3)." All of this is what I am rejecting in this chapter because such thinking blurs the distinction between the freedom of God's grace and our fellowship with God in grace—a fellowship in which we do not participate in the eternal generation of the Father, Son, and Spirit. Rather, through union with Jesus in his divine/human unity as the ascended Lord we participate in the eternal knowledge and love of the Trinity precisely as creatures in distinction from God in his eternal "self-generation." Our union with God in his eternal being is through union with the human Jesus who is hypostatically one with God and us. This means that God does not need creation, but creation needs God's reconciling and redeeming grace to be what it is in Christ. Therefore our participation in God's nature is one in which we have nothing to give back to God that is not his already. Such an idea manifests the kind of reversibility between divine and human relations that Barth and Torrance consistently, forcefully, and rightly rejected.

[276]Gallaher, *Freedom and Necessity*, 249.
[277]Ibid.
[278]Ibid., 240. Again, these remarks clearly fall into the vertigo Torrance rightly rejected, as noted in n. 275.
[279]Ibid., 246. Thus, "in the case of primordial election, God the Father eternally and necessarily (N3) chooses His Son in begetting Himself and the Son in obedient Eucharistic thanksgiving elects Him in turn by freely receiving (F3) His own begottenness as a necessity. This is an act which could have been 'otherwise', since He need not so affirm His natural being" (ibid.). Just this thinking opens the door to Arianism with the suggestion

Here the failure to note that God's being as Father, Son, and Spirit is eternally necessary while God's eternal election to be God for us is eternally contingent, leads Gallaher to confuse election with God's triunity by equating "primordial election" with the begetting of the Son by the Father. Indeed, while claiming that this is a necessity, he simultaneously maintains that this eternal begetting could have been otherwise. Such thinking, however, unwittingly opens the door to Arianism since the Son might not have been one in being with the Father from all eternity if that was his choice.

The underlying difficulty here concerns the fact that some theologians today are reading necessities associated with the common concept of love back into the immanent Trinity and then mistakenly claiming that creation is in some sense necessary for God. It is not. That is why Barth rejected panentheism as worse than pantheism.[280] Panentheists erroneously think they overcome the pantheist failure to distinguish God from the world, along with the concomitant espousal of a mutually conditioning relationship between God and the world, but in reality, they do not. In Barth's words,

> The right understanding of the freedom of God's will excludes all those views which seek to represent the relation between God and the reality distinct from Himself as a relation of mutual limitation and necessity. In the first instance this includes all pantheistic and panentheistic systems according to which the existence of this other reality belongs in some way to the essence and existence of God Himself.[281]

The all-important point that is questionable in Moltmann's thinking and those who have followed him in one way or another by ascribing freedom *and* necessity to the divine being and in closing the supposed gap that they mistakenly claimed Barth opened between the immanent and economic Trinity is that divine love is free and that God never loses his free ability to decide and act. All that is problematic in Moltmann's approach is in reality crystal clear in Barth's approach, namely, that God freely permits his creatures to exist in relation to him with a real being of their own as objects of his knowledge and will. He even cooperates with them as noted above. Still, "He is not conditioned by them. They are conditioned by Him. They have not proceeded from his essence."[282] This is not a minor theological quibble, but an essential, perhaps even the central, issue without which theology can never be a theology of freedom and of grace in the truest sense of those words.

---

that the Son's eternal generation from the Father might have been other than it was and is. Beyond this, another serious error which we will not discuss here is that Gallaher thinks that in the Father's generation of the Son there is something of a causation of the Son's being as God: "The Father, when He begets the Son with a necessary (but tacitly free) will, gives Him all that he is, His divine Being" (ibid.). As noted above, Torrance flatly and rightly rejects any such notion of causality as leading to some form of subordinationism (*The Trinitarian Faith*, 238). See also Paul D. Molnar, "Theological Issues Involved in the *Filioque*," chapter 3, *Ecumenical Perspectives on the* Filioque *for the Twenty-First Century*, ed. Myk Habets (London: T&T Clark, 2015), 26.

[280]Barth, CD II/1, 312.
[281]Ibid., 562.
[282]Ibid.

CHAPTER 2
BARTH AND ROMAN CATHOLIC THEOLOGY

Ever since Hans Urs von Balthasar wrote his groundbreaking book on Karl Barth in 1951, Catholic theologians have shown great interest in Barth's theology, most especially because of his Christocentrism.[1] Theologians like Balthasar and Rahner were looking for ways to escape the "extrinsicism" of neoscholastic theology, and Balthasar in particular wanted to prevent a return to such theology, which he labeled "sawdust Thomism,"[2] and preferred to pursue theology in an ecumenical way that might lead toward unity between Catholics and Protestants as they focused on Christ as the center. Hence, it has been said recently that "Balthasar was a Catholic Barthian who offers to Protestant Christianity a 'form' that could provide a counter to its 'formlessness,' which as he warned, could only 'prove disastrous for Christianity.'"[3] Balthasar of course believed that as Barth's theology developed from its earlier dialectical version to its later analogical version, his thinking approached more closely to Catholicism such that "he retrieved elements Catholics themselves neglected, such as the Triune rendering of God's perfections ... Balthasar saw in Barth the proper 'form' theology should take."[4] But, Balthasar found Barth's thinking "too narrowly constricted," and thus in his view it "failed to recognize the true difficulty in modern Catholic theology. It was never the *analogia entis*. Instead it was the innovative doctrine of pure nature in the late medieval and early modern eras."[5] Unlike Rahner, Balthasar opposed any sort of anthropological or philosophical starting point, which could end with the idea that we might affirm God "by affirming ourselves."[6] Joseph Cardinal Ratzinger also decisively criticized Rahner for resolving the particularity of Christian revelation into the universal by reducing "Christian liberation into pseudoliberation ... Self-acceptance—just being human—is all that is required [to be a Christian]."[7] Bruce D. Marshall criticizes Rahner's interpretation of Christ's resurrection for failing "to be a characterization of Jesus' resurrection as a specific event

---

[1]D. Stephen Long, *Saving Karl Barth: Hans Urs von Balthasar's Preoccupation* (Minneapolis, MN: Fortress Press, 2014), 174. See also Dominic Robinson, *Understanding the "Imago Dei": the Thought of Barth, von Balthasar and Moltmann* (Farnham, UK: Ashgate, 2011), 166–7.
[2]Long, *Saving Karl Barth*, 11–12.
[3]Ibid., 88.
[4]Ibid., 87.
[5]Ibid.
[6]Ibid., 277.
[7]Joseph Cardinal Ratzinger, *Principles of Catholic Theology: Building Stones for a Fundamental Theology*, trans. Sister Mary Frances McCarthy, S.N.D. (San Francisco: Ignatius Press, 1987), 167. See also Paul D. Molnar, "Can Theology Be Contemporary and True? A Review Discussion," of Joseph Cardinal Ratzinger's *Principles of Catholic Theology*, *The Thomist* 52 (3) (July 1988): 513–37.

... in which his particular identity is most clear"[8] because it is not the particular man Jesus who rose from the dead who conveys soteriological intelligibility in Rahner's reflections, but instead the "transcendental experience of the expectation of one's own resurrection."[9] The result is a vague reference to Jesus' "eternal validity" and to our own. Ratzinger and Marshall are both rightly concerned that Jesus himself as attested in the New Testament had to be the starting point for a properly Christian theology.

While Karl Barth took a strong interest in Vatican II with the hope that genuine ecumenical unity might result from the Council's move toward a more Christocentric understanding of the church and theology, he did not fail to point out that even in its important document on revelation (*Dei verbum*) he saw some difficulties. Positively, he noted scripture was given a firm place as the norm for grasping Christian revelation in a way that did not take place at Vatican I. Negatively, Barth noted that the second chapter was "the great fit of weakness which befell the Council" by the way "holy tradition" and "teaching office" were "placed alongside the Holy Scriptures" since this obscured "the unmistakable declaration of chapter I in reference to revelation itself" and of later chapters referring to Scripture.[10] In a letter to Pope Paul VI in September 1968, Barth discussed the "problem of church authority" with respect to the Pope's encyclical *Humanae vitae* and its reception. He mentioned the encyclical's "estimate of natural law as a kind of second source of revelation" together with critics who ascribed "a similar function to the conscience of the individual" noting that "the fine constitution *Dei verbum*" said nothing about these as "sources of revelation."[11]

Cardinal Cicognani responded to Barth's letter on behalf of the Pope in November 1968 saying that strictly speaking Barth was right and that "it is obvious that natural law and conscience are not, in the strict sense, sources of revelation."[12] But he then added that conscience and natural law are ways of finding God and that for Christians "revelation does not suppress natural law, which is equally divine."[13] In his response to the cardinal, Barth noted that in spite of the possibility of agreeing on a number of issues, especially the fact that revelation is to be truly found "only in holy scripture ... with due respect to tradition," there could be no consensus that it is right or possible to "set nature and conscience alongside revelation as equally divine."[14]

In this chapter, I have chosen Walter Kasper and Elizabeth Johnson as dialogue partners for Karl Barth, first because Kasper's thinking is a faithful explication of

---

[8]Bruce D. Marshall, *Christology in Conflict: The Identity of a Saviour in Rahner and Barth* (Oxford: Basil Blackwell, 1987), 96.

[9]Ibid., 95. For further analysis of Rahner's view of the resurrection and of Christology, see Paul D. Molnar, *Incarnation and Resurrection: Toward a Contemporary Understanding* (Grand Rapids, MI: Eerdmans, 2007), 53–68.

[10]Karl Barth, *Ad Limina Apostolorum: An Appraisal of Vatican II*, trans. Keith R. Crim (Richmond, VA: John Knox Press, 1967), 47–8.

[11]Jürgen Fangmeier and Hinrich Stoevesandt, eds., *Karl Barth Letters 1961– 1968*, trans. and ed. Geoffrey Bromiley (Grand Rapids, MI: Eerdmans, 1981), 314.

[12]Ibid., 357.

[13]Ibid.

[14]Ibid., 334.

post-Vatican II Catholic theology that is aware of Balthasar's important appropriation of Barth and also cognizant of Rahner's major contributions to contemporary Catholic theology. Like Ratzinger, Balthasar, and Marshall, however, Kasper is not uncritical of Rahner or Barth. Still, like Balthasar, Rahner, and Marshall and against Barth, Kasper thinks he can retain an important role for natural theology and certain insights that flow from that belief. With respect to Marshall, one might notice a similar procedure in the way he deals with the Catholic and Protestant debates about whether analogy is a "gift of divine wisdom" or "the invention of Antichrist" as Barth once put it,[15] by turning to Thomas Aquinas to suggest that Thomas rejected analogy on Christological grounds in favor of univocity (by ascribing all that Jesus does humanly to God) while yet finding a role for analogy which acknowledges that all our naming of God as creatures must respect the fact that in "the order of being … perfections belong first to God, and only derivatively to creatures."[16] Nonetheless he follows Thomas's "austere" view of analogy and maintains that we think of God "most perfectly in this life by knowing that he is beyond all that our intellect can conceive. For this reason we are joined to him as to one unknown."[17] Hence, for Marshall, "even though faith, as well as natural knowledge, leaves the divine nature unknown to us in this life, 'nevertheless we know God more fully' by faith than by natural reason, since 'in the revelation of grace … more, and more excellent, effects of God are shown to us.'"[18] We shall see that both of these assertions are problematic for Barth and why as the chapter develops.

Second, I have chosen Elizabeth Johnson because, among progressive Roman Catholics, she is perhaps one of the most widely recognized and acclaimed Catholic theologians in the United States today. She also relies heavily on Rahner's theology to make her case for a feminist retrieval of doctrine in light of her post-Vatican II reading of Scripture and tradition. Still, she embraces a kind of natural theology that, when compared to Barth's thinking, causes great difficulty both in connection with the doctrine of the Trinity and the doctrine of revelation.[19] By exploring these two prominent theologians, I hope to show exactly why it is impossible to offer the kind of Christ-centered theology that Balthasar and Ratzinger sought to offer as long as it is supposed that analogies for speaking about God can be drawn from our supposed innate movement toward the divine as well as from the revelation of God attested in the Old and New Testaments. The question I plan to address in this discussion is whether or not the real problem still dividing Roman Catholic and Reformed theologians remains the *analogia entis*.

Balthasar thought that Barth eventually embraced the Catholic view. But he criticized Barth for his "christological constriction." Barth himself wondered about this charge and suggested that the criticism stemmed from Balthasar's failure to allow Jesus Christ to be

---

[15]See Barth, CD I/1, xiii.
[16]Bruce D. Marshall, "Christ the End of Analogy," in *The Analogy of Being: Invention of the Antichrist or the Wisdom of God?* ed. Thomas Joseph White, OP, 280–313 (Grand Rapids, MI: Eerdmans, 2011), 295.
[17]Ibid., 302.
[18]Ibid., 311.
[19]Johnson's theology will be considered again in Chapter 6 which discusses language for God.

the sole starting point and norm for his theology, contrary to Balthasar's own intentions.[20] At this point, one might legitimately wonder whether or not the real difficulty after all might have been the *analogia entis* (and not simply the idea of "pure nature" as has been suggested) since, in Barth's understanding, this category encompassed any view that did not allow Jesus the *first* and *final* Word in theological or ethical reflection. This is tellingly reflected in D. Stephen Long's statement that for Balthasar the *analogia fidei* "must be understood within the *analogia entis*"[21] while for Barth it is clearly the other way around. I intend to show exactly how and why this problem is still with us today by asking whether or not it is really possible to be faithful to revelation without always allowing Christ the *first* and *final* Word both in the doctrine of God and thus also in all other dogmatic reflections. I hope to show that the problem that divides Catholics and Protestants in this regard can be seen most clearly in the fact that Barth insists that our knowledge of God in faith is begun, upheld, and completed by the Holy Spirit uniting us to Christ and thus to the Father; that is why his understanding of analogy is essentially dictated by his view of the doctrine of justification by faith and by grace in a way that it does not for most post-Vatican II Catholic theologians. Proper unity between Catholics and Protestants, I believe, will remain elusive as long as this problem remains unaddressed and unresolved. This chapter is an attempt to address this issue and to point toward a possible resolution.

Understanding God in Faith

What is the root of the doctrine of the Trinity? For Karl Barth the answer was simple and clear, but with profound implications both for theological method and for the knowledge

---

[20]Barth, CD IV/1, 768–9. After praising Balthasar for his focus on Christ in his book on Barth which he thought was "incomparably more powerful than that of most of the books which have clustered around [him]," Barth also noted that Balthasar had with him "and under him quite a chorus of German and especially French friends who in different ways and with varying emphases all seem to wish to look again to the centre, to the 'author and finisher of our faith' (Heb. 12:2), who alone can make possible either theology itself or any attempt at ecumenical agreement" (ibid., 768). Then, however, Barth notes that Balthasar focused on Theresa of Lisieux and others who might be understood to represent Christ so that the saints and those who achieve a measure of sanctity might be understood to repeat and even reenact Jesus' "being and activity" with the result that "the One whose being and activity is supposedly reproduced obviously fades into the background as compared with His saints" (ibid.). It is in light of this context that Barth then explained that he now understood what Balthasar meant by criticizing him for his "christological constriction." To that Barth responded, "We must bring against him the counter-question, whether in all the spiritual splendour of the saints who are supposed to represent and repeat Him Jesus Christ has not ceased—not in theory but in practice—to be the object and origin of Christian faith" (ibid.). Barth then suggested that the promising new beginning by Roman Catholics by starting from Jesus Christ was "in danger of returning to" or perhaps "may be has never left, the well-worn track on which the doctrine of justification is absorbed into that of sanctification—understood as the pious work of self-sanctification which man can undertake and accomplish in his own strength" (ibid.). Barth then suggested that if he were a Roman Catholic, he would focus on the Christological center and from there cautiously offer an appraisal of the saints "which would be more subdued—and probably less impressive, but all the more truthful because it gives more honour to the Holy One" (ibid.). He concluded saying that he wished all could agree that "the redemptive act of God" must not be confused with "our response to it." When that happens then "everything is jeopardized" (ibid.).
[21]Long, *Saving Karl Barth*, 129.

of God; it was the revelation of God attested in Scripture. In this chapter, I shall explore Barth's starting point and some of his key conclusions regarding our knowledge of God and of God's relations with us in history in order to place him in dialogue with Walter Kasper and Elizabeth Johnson as proposed above. By comparing and contrasting these three approaches, I hope to explain positively what it is about the doctrine of the Trinity that both invites Christian unity and yet illustrates where certain divisions still lie. Among other things, this chapter will include a discussion of the problem of natural theology,[22] the nature of God as triune, the relation between the immanent and economic Trinity, the possibility and limitations of analogy, the role of Jesus Christ and the Spirit, and finally how to conceptualize the relations between Creator and creature.

Trinity and Barth's Dogmatics

What is the chief reason Barth gives for holding that there can be only one root for the doctrine of the Trinity? The answer to this question will illustrate Barth's method which itself is dictated by who God is in revelation, namely, by the living Jesus Christ himself who is the unique object of Christian faith and not a theory, doctrine, or theology.[23] Thus, he was quite clear that there could be no knowledge of God without experience of God, but knowledge of God is not based on experience or upon human knowledge. At the beginning of CD II/2, Barth summed up his major findings in CD II/1:

> We have tried to learn the lofty but simple lesson that it is by God that God is known, and that He is the living God as the One who loves in freedom; living both in the unity and also in the wealth of His perfections. Our starting-point in that first part of the doctrine of God was neither an axiom of reason nor a datum of experience. In the measure that a doctrine of God draws on these sources, it betrays the fact that its subject is not really God but a hypostatised reflection of man.[24]

Barth made this statement for the same reason that he insisted that the sole root for the doctrine of the Trinity was God's particular act of revelation in the history of Jesus as attested in Scripture.

Being and Act

Because he held that God's being as Father, Son, and Holy Spirit was self-sufficient as his being in act, Barth also maintained that Jesus Christ as God's act or Word of revelation is

---

[22]The problem of natural theology will be taken up again in Chapter 3 by analyzing and responding to Alexander Irving's recent discussion of Thomas F. Torrance's "new" natural theology.
[23]Barth, CD IV/1, 760–1.
[24]Barth, CD II/2, 3; II/1, 183.

one in essence with the Father and also with the Spirit. But, as the root of the doctrine of the Trinity, what is revealed in Jesus Christ cannot be separated for a moment from Jesus himself because "God's revelation has its reality and truth wholly and in every respect— both ontically and noetically—within itself";[25] hence, revelation "is an absolute ground in itself, and therefore for man a court from which there can be no possible appeal to a higher court."[26]

Barth is not thinking of just any revelation but of revelation in its identity with Jesus in his uniqueness as the one Word of God incarnate in history and acting as revealer and reconciler; thus, this is not a revelation "alongside which there are or may be others."[27] In Jesus the form and content of revelation cannot be separated. Because "what God reveals in Jesus and how He reveals it, namely, in Jesus must not be separated from one another according to the New Testament,"[28] Barth insists "God is unknown as our Father, as the Creator, to the degree that He is not made known by Jesus."[29] This means that if we bypass Jesus, then we make impossible any true and certain knowledge of the triune God because such an approach represents an attempt to know God without God. That, for Barth, was the main difficulty with the *analogia entis*. This, as noted above and as we shall see as the chapter develops, will be one of the key issues, perhaps the key issue, that divides Barth from the Roman Catholic approach to knowing God offered by Walter Kasper and Elizabeth Johnson. It is the issue of natural theology. While all three theologians would formally agree that the doctrine of the Trinity is what unites all Christians, material difficulties still arise over the issue of natural theology.

Barth and Roman Catholic Trinitarian Doctrine

Barth happily acknowledged that his own explication of the doctrine of the Trinity was "very close to the Roman Catholic doctrine"[30] and that Roman Catholics would likely accept most of his doctrine. He followed Thomas Aquinas and Bernhard Bartmann in explaining his view of appropriation according to which certain works of God are assigned to different persons of the Trinity, since they all agreed that such appropriations should neither be arbitrary nor exclusive.[31] But Barth stipulated that "Evangelical dogmatics" needed to add a "third and decisive rule that appropriations must not be invented freely" since they must be taken from the Bible "literally or materially."[32] It is in that last stipulation that Barth believed there would still be some disagreement. Nonetheless, Barth was "glad to have found such a basic point of agreement with the Roman Church"

---

[25]Barth, CD I/1, 305.
[26]Ibid.
[27]Barth, CD I/1, 295.
[28]Ibid., 399.
[29]Ibid., 390.
[30]John D. Godsey, ed. *Karl Barth's Table Talk* (Richmond, VA: John Knox Press, 1962), 50.
[31]Barth, CD I/1, 374.
[32]Ibid.

and believed that on that basis they could at least "talk with each other"[33] in a way that Protestant Modernism could not since in Barth's view "Modernism has no Doctrine of the Trinity. The notion of a 'Social Trinity' is fantastic [bizarre]!"[34]

While it is worth pondering how Barth might have reacted to his student Jürgen Moltmann's attempt "to develop a social doctrine of the Trinity" precisely by taking up "panentheistic ideas from the Jewish and the Christian traditions,"[35] I think it is safe to say that Barth would object to Moltmann's panentheistic approach to God's relations with us since Barth regarded panentheism as worse than pantheism.[36] I have documented the difficulties in Moltmann's presentation which include, among other things, his view that "God 'needs' the world and man. If God is love, then he neither will nor can be without the one who is beloved."[37] Barth would surely regard such statements as possible only to the extent that the freedom of God *in se* and therefore also *ad extra* had been compromised. In the words of George Hunsinger, "Having espoused the panentheistic notion that God inherently needs the world, Moltmann's ambivalent attempt to Christianize it is simply not convincing."[38] Hunsinger astutely maintains that "for Barth, with the main catholic tradition, East and West, God just is the Holy Trinity … God's identity would be triune whether the world had been created or not"[39] while for Moltmann "time and eternity were objectively constituted by their mutual relations in 'dialectical identity.' "[40] Over against Barth's view that God would have been no less God if he never created the world since God is not "lonely even without the world and us,"[41] for Moltmann "God would not be one in and for himself until he was also one with the world and the world with him."[42]

Indeed, Moltmann's social doctrine of the Trinity also has been frequently criticized for either coming very close to a type of tritheism or perhaps even directly espousing such a view.[43] Hence, while Moltmann claims there has never been a Christian tritheist, George Hunsinger asserts that "if this is true then one can only conclude that Moltmann is vying to be the first. Despite the evident scorn with which he anticipates such a charge, *The Trinity and the Kingdom* is about the closest thing to tritheism that any of us are ever likely to see."[44] Walter Kasper also noted the danger of tritheism in Moltmann's view of the Trinity.[45]

---

[33]Godsey, *Table Talk*, 50.
[34]Ibid.
[35]Moltmann, *Trinity and Kingdom*, 19.
[36]Barth, CD II/1, 312, 562.
[37]Moltmann, *Trinity and Kingdom*, 58. See also Molnar, *Divine Freedom*, 379–428, 384.
[38]Hunsinger, "Review of Jürgen Moltmann, *The Trinity and the Kingdom*," 124–39, 135.
[39]George Hunsinger, "Karl Barth's Doctrine of the Trinity, and Some Protestant Doctrines after Barth," in *The Oxford Handbook of the Trinity*, ed. Gilles Emery, OP, and Matthew Levering (New York: Oxford University Press, 2011), 310.
[40]Ibid., 311.
[41]Barth, CD I/1, 140.
[42]Hunsinger, "Karl Barth's Doctrine of the Trinity," 311.
[43]Molnar, *Divine Freedom*, 418–19.
[44]Hunsinger, "Review of Jürgen Moltmann, *The Trinity and the Kingdom*," 131.
[45]Walter Kasper, *The God of Jesus Christ*, trans. Matthew J. O'Connell (New York: Crossroad, 1986), 379, n. 183.

Returning to Barth's view of the Trinity, he insisted that because Jesus is the *novum* beyond which one could not appeal when coming to know God, one could either obey him or not. One could not provide "motives or grounds for this [sharing in revelation]" because one who was confronted by revelation "was not instructed or persuaded, he followed neither his own reason or conscience nor the reason or conscience of other men—all this might also happen, but the Bible has little to say about it and it is not the important thing in this matter." Barth maintained that all of this could be summed up with the statement that "God reveals Himself as the Lord."[46] This means primarily that there is no court of appeal beyond Jesus Christ as God's revelation in history to know God in truth. God's freedom is God's "ontic and noetic autonomy" in the sense that God alone is self-sufficient and "reveals what only He can reveal, Himself." God is with us as the man Jesus is with us, namely, "as the One He is, as the Lord, as He who is free";[47] thus, "there is in revelation a fellowship in which not only is God there for man but in very truth—this is the *donum Spiritus sancti*—man is also there for God."[48]

Barth carries through this thinking in CD II/1, IV/1, IV/2, and IV/3, consistently arguing that God is the One who loves in freedom and is free in his love and that God therefore seeks and creates fellowship with us and enables us to know him with "apodictic" certainty by overcoming our enmity with God and thus our sin and uniting us to himself. But this certainty is lost the moment we look in any direction other than to Jesus Christ in whom we are reconciled to God and thus in whom we have true knowledge of God.[49] Consequently, one could not move from some general understanding of being, act, or love and then hope to understand the specific love of God revealed in the history of Jesus himself who, as the incarnate Word was the very love of God given to the world so that anyone who believed in him should not perish, but have eternal life (Jn 3:16).[50] This is why Barth specifically argued that no idea of lordship could lead to the truth of God's Lordship revealed in Jesus Christ[51] and that no analogies are true in themselves but become true as God miraculously enables it.[52] This can only be seen and understood by the power of his Holy Spirit and in faith.[53]

What God Is in Revelation God Is in Eternity

Barth held that all statements about the immanent Trinity were "reached simply as confirmations or underlinings or, materially, as the indispensable premises of the economic Trinity."[54] On this basis Barth argued that "the reality of God in His revelation

---

[46]Barth, CD I/1, 306.
[47]Ibid., 307.
[48]Ibid., 480.
[49]Barth, CD II/1, 162.
[50]Ibid., 275–85.
[51]Ibid., 75–6.
[52]Ibid., 182, 194, 226.
[53]Ibid., 157–8.
[54]Barth, CD I/1, 479.

cannot be bracketed by an 'only,' as though somewhere behind His revelation there stood another reality of God; the reality of God which encounters us in His revelation is His reality in all the depths of eternity."[55] This means that the Holy Spirit "is the Spirit of both the Father and the Son not just in His work *ad extra* and upon us, but that to all eternity—no limit or reservation is possible here—He is none other than the Spirit of both the Father and the Son."[56] Hence Barth distinguished without separating or confusing the immanent and economic Trinity and consistently refused to reduce the immanent Trinity to God's actions within history. Thus, he held that "[God] is not, therefore, who He is only in His works. Yet in Himself He is not another than He is in His works."[57] This remains a burning issue today and it is why Barth insisted that

> the content of the doctrine of the Trinity … is not that God in his relation to man is Creator, Mediator and Redeemer, but that God in Himself is eternally God the Father, Son and Holy Spirit … [God acting as Emmanuel] cannot be dissolved into His work and activity.[58]

While Barth agreed that a correlation between us and God takes place in revelation, he rejected "a theology in which God swings up or down in His relation to us, either from below upwards so that God becomes a predicate of man, or from above downwards so that man becomes a requisite in God's nature … we must not think away the free basis that this correlation has in God."[59] From this it follows that for Barth there is nothing higher or better in God than that God is the one who lives and loves in freedom precisely *as* the eternal Father, Son, and Holy Spirit. Because that is who God eternally is, the name of God cannot be understood as a freely chosen symbol or metaphor that can be changed for religious, social, or political reasons. Thinking of God as Father and Son does indeed take place using our very limited human concepts or metaphors, but for Barth "correctness belongs exclusively to that about which we have thought and spoken, not to what we have thought and spoken."[60]

Does this mean that the "metaphor of father and son," since it involves human conceptuality with all its limitations, does not say who God really is? It might be helpful here to note that the way one answers this question will depend on where one begins to think about God; here is one of the difficulties I intended to discuss when I mentioned above that it is the *analogia entis* that still is the problem that divides much contemporary Catholic theology from Protestant theology as represented by Karl Barth. Hence, we may note that here Barth makes a crucial distinction that is noticeably absent, for instance, from Elizabeth Johnson's understanding of metaphors. He insists that "if we call what is

---

[55]Ibid.
[56]Ibid., 479–80; CD IV/2, 360.
[57]Barth, CD II/1, 260.
[58]Barth, CD I/2, 878–9.
[59]Barth, CD I/1, 172.
[60]Ibid., 432.

said about Father and Son figurative, it should be remembered that this can apply only to our human speech as such but not to its object."[61] Johnson would certainly agree that our language about Father and Son is figurative. But she would not agree that it only applies to our speech and not also to God. That is where the difficulty arises. Following his own presuppositions, Barth insists, "It is not true that in some hidden depth of His essence God is something other than Father and Son" because "these names" are not "just freely chosen and in the last analysis meaningless symbols, symbols whose original and proper non-symbolical content lies in that creaturely reality … it is in God that the father-son relation, like all creaturely relations, has its original and proper reality."[62] As we shall see below, and in Chapter Six discussing language for God, Elizabeth Johnson's view of analogy develops by negating our experience of fatherhood at its best, instead of exclusively from the nature of God revealed in Jesus Christ and through the Spirit. Instead of making the subtle distinction with Barth, that our human speech about God is not determined by that speech or by us in any way at all but by the God who reveals himself to us through our speech, Johnson insists we cannot "literally" refer to who God is without confusing God with our concepts.[63] From this she concludes that if such confusion occurs then "the church has no option in the light of women's pressing experience but to continue to repeat the pattern of language about God in the metaphor of ruling men."[64] In this way, she thinks "'Revelation then becomes a brake on the articulation of divine mystery in the light of women's dignity."[65]

Here the disagreement is clear: for Barth women's dignity is grounded in the reconciliation of God accomplished in the history of Jesus Christ since God was in Christ reconciling the world to himself; hence women's dignity as a "pressing experience" could never become the basis for conceptualizing God's eternal being since knowledge of God must be grounded in God and God's revelation of his being and nature in and through his Word and Spirit in the economy. And in Barth's understanding, who God is as Father and Son has nothing to do with ruling males since such a view would be based on projection of human gender and human power into God, thus reversing the irreversible relation between God and creatures established and maintained in Christ.

Following her own methodology then, instead of allowing revelation in its identity with Christ to shape her view of God, Johnson conceptualizes God as "holy mystery," which never can be named by "one straight-as-an-arrow name," so that God can never be understood "literally";[66] "no name or image or concept that human beings use to speak of the divine mystery ever arrives at its goal: God is essentially incomprehensible."[67] It

---

[61]Ibid., 432, 392–3.
[62]Ibid., 432.
[63]Elizabeth A. Johnson, *She Who Is: The Mystery of God in Feminist Theological Discourse* (New York: Crossroad, 1992; reissued in 2002 as a tenth anniversary edition and in 2017 as a twenty-fifth anniversary edition), 75–82.
[64]Ibid., 77.
[65]Ibid.
[66]Ibid., 116–19; and Elizabeth A. Johnson, *Quest for the Living God: Mapping Frontiers in the Theology of God* (New York: Continuum, 2008), 19–21, 41, 214–15.
[67]Johnson, *She Who Is*, 117.

is important to note here that while Johnson and Barth agree that our "symbols" are human expressions and thus are limited, Johnson takes this to mean that when we speak of the Father and Son in the Trinity we are not actually referring to God as God eternally exists since this, to use a Thomistic expression, remains essentially unknown to us. By contrast, incomprehensibility for Barth refers specifically to the mystery of God as Father, Son, and Spirit. For Johnson, however, it represents a shorthand expression for a type of agnosticism that allows her to ground her metaphors, analogies, and symbols in the experience of women who struggle to extricate themselves from what she calls the "white male symbol of the divine."[68]

Unfortunately, the very idea that when Christians named God Father and Son they were thinking of a "white male" represents just the kind of thinking Barth rightly rejected; one cannot know the eternal Father and Son revealed in, from and by Jesus himself as the incarnate Son by projecting gender or race back into God. That is what Athanasius accused the Arians of doing when they thought of the Father as the Spirit's grandfather. More importantly, however, Barth insists that we do have a straight-as-an-arrow name that discloses who the eternal God really is, that is, Jesus Christ himself. That difference between them displays the profound difference between Barth and Johnson. Barth insists that Jesus himself must be allowed to be both the *first* and *final* Word to us just because what God is toward us in him, he is in all the depths of eternity; it follows then that this is not just a symbolic reference *from* our religious experiences, but a statement of who God really is in all his incomprehensibility based on revelation. By contrast, Johnson thinks that our naming God is a symbolic reference *from* the experiences of women and men with the result that one cannot literally and exclusively think of God as Father and Son without introducing gender and patriarchal subordination of women into the equation. This is because she believes the conflicts that break out over naming God "He" or "She" "indicate that, however subliminally, maleness *is* intended when we say God."[69] Of course, maleness is exactly what was not intended when the Nicene fathers referred to God as Father, Son, and Spirit. More will be said about this later.

Kasper, Rahner, and Barth

Having considered Barth's view of the Trinity in dialogue with Elizabeth Johnson and Jürgen Moltmann in the context of post-Vatican II theology, we begin this section noting that Walter Kasper, like most Catholic theologians today, wrestles with the theology of Karl Rahner who is certainly regarded as one of the most significant Catholic theologians of the twentieth century. As noted above, Rahner wanted to overcome the "extrinsicism" of neoscholastic theology. He wanted to make the connection between doctrine and experience so he could show that a proper view of the Trinity, for instance, would have

---

[68]Ibid., 117; Molnar, *Divine Freedom*, 20–44.
[69]Johnson, *Quest for the Living God*, 98.

an impact on our experiences of faith and thus on our knowledge of God and ourselves. Rahner's famous axiom that "the immanent Trinity is strictly identical with the economic Trinity and vice versa,"[70] however, lent itself to various interpretations.

According to George Hunsinger this axiom is "systematically ambiguous" and "has led to a great deal of confusion."[71] This axiom can have a perfectly noncontroversial meaning, with which almost all contemporary Catholic and Protestant theologians would agree, if it is interpreted to mean only that what God is toward us, God is eternally in himself. But difficulties arise in Rahner's own thought just because he does not begin his reflections on God and God's relations with us exclusively with the economic trinitarian self-revelation since he intends to avoid a "*too narrowly Christological approach* ... [because] a too narrow concentration of the foundational course on Jesus Christ as the key and the solution to all existential problems and as the total foundation of faith would be too simple a conception."[72] This difficulty once again, I think, concerns the *analogia entis* in the sense that Rahner does indeed attempt to understand revelation, grace, and indeed God himself by offering a transcendental analysis of human experience and not by allowing Jesus to be the first and the final Word informing his views.

It will be remembered that Barth's *analogia fidei* meant, above all, that one simply could not bypass Jesus himself to know God or the meaning of grace and revelation because he was God himself acting for us in the economy. Rahner, however, begins with "a knowledge of God which is not mediated completely by an encounter with Jesus Christ."[73] This knowledge starts with our transcendental experience which he claims mediates an "unthematic and anonymous ... knowledge of God" such that knowledge of God is always present unthematically to anyone reflecting on themselves so that all talk about God "always only points to this transcendental experience as such, an experience in which he whom we call 'God' encounters man in silence ... as the absolute and the incomprehensible, as the term of his transcendence."[74] This term of "transcendence" Rahner eventually calls a "holy mystery" because he believes that whenever this experience of transcendence is an experience of love, its term or goal is the God of Christian revelation.

From this it follows for Rahner in his landmark piece on the "Concept of Mystery in Catholic Theology" that he will "inquire therefore into man, as the being who is oriented to the mystery as such, this orientation being a constitutive part of his being both in its natural state and in his supernatural elevation."[75] Rahner thus searches for a "more original unity" among natural theology, revealed theology, and knowledge

---

[70]Karl Rahner, *Theological Investigations*, vol. 9, *Writings of 1965-1967*, trans. Graham Harrison (hereafter: TI) (New York: Herder and Herder, 1972), 32.

[71]Hunsinger, "Karl Barth's Doctrine of the Trinity," 309.

[72]Karl Rahner, *Foundations of Christian Faith: An Introduction to the Idea of Christianity*, trans. William V. Dych (New York: A Crossroad Book, Seabury Press, 1978), 13.

[73]Ibid.

[74]Ibid., 21.

[75]Rahner, TI 4, 49.

of God that comes from "experience of existence."[76] In his famous article on mystery, Rahner claims that "all conceptual expressions about God … always stem from the unobjectivated experience of transcendence as such: the concept from the pre-conception, the name from the experience of the nameless."[77] Here I believe I have said enough to illustrate that it is precisely Rahner's peculiar natural theology which clearly shaped his conception of our knowledge of God. In part, this is because he believes "the revealed Word and natural knowledge of God mutually condition each other."[78] From this thinking, Rahner then can say of revelation and grace that revelation is "a modification of our transcendental consciousness produced permanently by God in grace. But such a modification is really an original and permanent element in our consciousness as the basic and original luminosity of our existence. And as an element in our transcendentality … it is already revelation in the proper sense."[79] Because revelation is conceptualized in this way, Rahner and those who follow his approach believe we can look to our own experiences for the meaning of revelation, even though Rahner then tries to connect this so-called transcendental revelation with what he calls "categorical revelation" which attempts to confirm those experiences by referring to the events of salvation history.

The problem with this reasoning of course is that from Barth's perspective the idea that revelation is an element in our consciousness does not describe revelation at all since for him revelation meant that "the Word became flesh" in Jesus Christ.[80] Indeed, if revelation is an element in our transcendentality, then revelation has also been detached from the revealer and confused with our experience of ourselves; that of course is what opens the door to Rahner's idea that we have an obediential potency which is our openness to being as spirit in the world, which is thought to be part of our human nature as such, since "we are by nature possible recipients of God's self-communication."[81] By nature, we are "listeners for a possible divine word."[82] It also leads to his idea of a supernatural existential, namely,

> a basic structure which permeates the whole of human existence … Our being in the world, or our being with others could serve as examples … this existential is not given automatically with human nature, but is rather the result of the gratuitous gift of God … Because of the supernatural existential, grace is always a part of our actual existence.[83]

---

[76]Rahner, *Foundations*, 55.
[77]Rahner, TI 4, 57.
[78]Rahner, TI 1, 98.
[79]Rahner, *Foundations*, 149.
[80]Barth, CD I/1, 119.
[81]John P. Galvin, "The Invitation of Grace," in *A World of Grace: An Introduction to the Themes and Foundations of Karl Rahner's Theology*, ed. Leo J. O'Donovan (New York: Crossroad, 1981), 64–75, 72.
[82]Ibid.
[83]Ibid., 71–3.

Needless to say, Barth would unequivocally reject such thinking since in view of God's grace and revelation such ideas confuse nature and grace and reason and revelation. Such thinking fails to realize that what was revealed in Christ's atoning death for us and in his resurrection was precisely the fact that any capacity for God that we now have since the fall of Adam is newly created by the Holy Spirit. As such, the Spirit enables us to hear the Word of God spoken and enacted by Christ himself through our union with Christ in faith. Thus, our focus would have to be on Christ himself as the grace of God revealing God to us and enabling our knowledge of God through the Spirit.

Rahner's thinking leads him to think God's offer of grace is given in our transcendental experiences so that if we accept ourselves, we are already accepting Christ without necessarily knowing him. Barth would never accept this thinking simply because Christ himself reveals to us the fact that in ourselves we are not in reality open to God but closed to God and need to be made open by a specific act of God in his Word and Spirit so that we are open to God in truth. That is why Barth specifically argued that grace and the Word of God must come to us from outside ourselves. Thus, Barth says that "man as such," even "believing man," is one who is "closed to the readiness of God" and can only be opened "from without," that is, a person's human reality must

> be rooted and grounded in Someone quite other outside himself; so rooted and grounded that it lives entirely by Him, and derives its whole reality from Him. If we disregard this and understand it as his own inner reality, we have to say of it that in it this closedness [to grace] is not destroyed by a long way, that, on the contrary, it is confirmed in it. The very existence of man considered in its reality, i.e., its reality as disclosed by the grace of God, shows us man in himself and as such not at peace but at war with grace.[84]

This is an extremely important point because Barth is here arguing that one can speak of grace, affirm grace but not live by grace as long as one attempts to think about God's grace by referring to themselves even themselves in their Christian life. So, Barth maintains that "the reality of the life of real Christians ... and the reality of the life of the Church as such, nowhere bears witness to an openness of man for grace."[85] Yet it is this very idea that we are in ourselves open to grace that supposes "God is knowable to [us] otherwise than from and through [God] Himself," and this means to Barth that such a view presumes that "the truth can be had without the truth itself."[86]

Importantly, then, since for Barth God's grace is identical with God's self-revelation in Christ, it literally cannot be envisioned as a possibility chosen by us.[87] But this means that revelation simply cannot under any circumstances be conceptualized with Rahner

---

[84]Barth, CD II/1, 133.
[85]Ibid., 134.
[86]Ibid., 135.
[87]Ibid., 139.

as something present in our consciousness and in our transcendental experiences; it cannot be identified with a possibility we might choose; it most certainly cannot be equated with the idea that self-acceptance is the same as accepting Christ. This is the case because in Barth's view,

> God's real revelation simply cannot be chosen by man and, as his own possibility, put beside another, and integrated with it into a system. God's real revelation is the possibility which man does not have to choose, but by which he must regard himself as chosen without having space and time to come to an arrangement with it within the sphere and according to the method of other possibilities.[88]

For Barth this is what happens "when from an object of faith the Gospel becomes the object of our own experience of faith; when from a gift of God it becomes an element in our own real existence."[89]

The hallmark of a theology which has not really recognized grace as grace and revelation as the revelation of God himself is that such a theology will not recognize that the grace of God that meets us in Christ meets us in judgment and in that way places us "under grace."[90] However, even when this is experienced, it will not allow us to look to ourselves at all to know God in truth just because our openness to God in Christ can only be known in and from him and not from ourselves at all. That is why Barth insists that "it is not in his reality as such that we find the human readiness enclosed in the readiness of God … His reality as such is the conflict against grace, his attempt to preserve himself and hold his own."[91] In light of God's judgment and therefore God's grace, "in the last resort man is always to be understood as the enemy of grace"[92] and the friend of God only in Christ himself who is the grace and revelation of God in and through which we really and truly know God and ourselves. For these reasons Barth insists that "no anthropological or ecclesiological assertion is true in itself and as such. Its truth subsists in the assertions of Christology, or rather in the reality of Jesus Christ alone."[93] In him we are judged and in Christ alone we become part of the new creation. But this can be seen and attested solely

> in a seeing and attesting of Jesus Christ the only begotten Son of God, who is come in our flesh and as whose brethren alone we can become the children of God. If we look past Jesus Christ, if we speak of anyone else but Him, if our praise of man is not at once praise of Jesus Christ, the romance and the illusions begin again.[94]

---

[88] Ibid.
[89] Ibid., 141.
[90] Ibid., 142.
[91] Ibid.
[92] Ibid., 145.
[93] Ibid., 149.
[94] Ibid.

It is not necessary here to offer a full analysis and critique of Rahner's thinking, which I do offer elsewhere.[95] I simply note that for Barth a theology that begins with Christ would never claim for Christians an anonymous or nonconceptual knowledge of God since God has a name (Jesus Christ), and God is no nameless reality but the reality of the eternal Father, Son, and Holy Spirit. So Barth would never claim, as Rahner does, that all concepts of God stem from an experience of the nameless; instead, a proper concept of God would have to arise from an encounter with God as he meets us in Jesus Christ himself as we have just explained. Thus, for Barth true knowledge of God comes from the Holy Spirit enabling us to know God the Father through union with his Son. It is quite specific. For Rahner, knowledge of God is found preconceptually in everyone because grace is an original element in their consciousness since grace is "an inner, objectless though conscious dynamism directed toward the beatific vision."[96] Indeed, for Rahner, "grace, therefore, is experienced, though not as grace, for it is psychologically indistinguishable from the stirrings of human transcendentality," and "God and self are the objective and subjective poles of the original experience of transcendence, wherein God is given objectively though not as an object."[97] But for Barth these very ideas confuse nature and grace, make objective knowledge of God impossible, and fail to recognize that revelation means reconciliation such that we simply cannot move from natural theology to revealed theology as Rahner does, because such movement is the movement of those who do not yet know of God's reconciling grace in Christ. Nor do they know the true meaning of sin since that can only be known from Christ's actual victory over sin and death. So, the idea that natural theology and revealed theology are mutually conditioning may be necessary for Rahner's thinking, grounded as it is in our transcendental experiences, but it is an impossibility in Barth's thinking because grace is and always remains identical with the Giver of grace, namely, Christ himself who comes to us in the power of his resurrection as the Holy Spirit enables our true knowledge of God as an object who can be known with our views and concepts precisely as God enables this in his judgment and grace as described above. So, Barth will never identify revelation or grace with our transcendentality as Rahner does.

Here, I submit that the real problem that still divides Catholic theology as represented by Karl Rahner and Protestant theology as represented by Karl Barth is indeed the problem of natural theology (the *analogia entis*) and the attempt to unite the results of such a theological reflection with the God of Christian revelation. It leads Rahner to ascribe grace and revelation directly to us in our transcendental experiences. And then it leads him to argue that we can have an anonymous experience of the resurrection (which would have been an anomaly to Barth and to St. Paul),[98] that there is a mutually

---

[95]See Molnar, *Divine Freedom*, 207–62.
[96]Rahner, TI 4, 61. I will offer an in-depth analysis of Rahner's nonconceptual knowledge of God in Chapter 4.
[97]Stephen J. Duffy, "Experience of Grace," in *The Cambridge Companion to Karl Rahner*, ed. Declan Marmion and Mary E. Hines (Cambridge: Cambridge University Press, 2007), 48.
[98]See Karl Rahner and Karl-Heinz Weger, *Our Christian Faith Answers for the Future*, trans. Francis McDonagh (New York: Crossroad, 1981), 113. Rahner writes, 'Whenever we experience the unshakeableness of our own hope of a final victory of our existence, there takes place, perhaps anonymously, that is, without reference to

conditioned relation between Christology and anthropology,[99] between knower and known,[100] and between natural theology and revealed theology.[101] For Rahner, "anyone therefore, no matter how remote from any revelation formulated in words, who accepts his existence, that is, his humanity … has accepted the son of Man."[102] Rahner believes this because he thinks God's self-communication is "as a matter of course, given in [our] spiritual reality. And this is the most fundamental, the most original element of what we call revelation."[103]

Having discussed some of Rahner's key concepts, we may now look at some of what Kasper says about Barth and Rahner. Kasper recognizes that Barth starts with revelation as the root of the doctrine of the Trinity, while he believes Rahner's starting point is "the subjectivity not of God but of man";[104] for Rahner, "the doctrine of the Trinity emerges from this concept of self-communication by way of a kind of transcendental reflection on the conditions of its possibility. The Trinity is thus the condition for the possibility of human subjectivity."[105] According to Kasper, while Barth and Rahner "proceed in quite different ways," both theologians have in common the idea that God is not to be understood "as substance" as in "one substance, three persons … but as subject of a self-revelation (K. Barth) or as subject of a self-communication (K. Rahner)."[106] And while Kasper generally praises Rahner's approach as an excellent contribution to Christian theology, he also offers a few interesting criticisms. He argues that Rahner's approach in his *Foundations of Christian Faith* "has handed over" the "structuring role" of the doctrine to "theological anthropology" so that it "is now studied only as a condition of

---

the name of Jesus, an experience that he is risen." For Barth of course one would have to know about the risen Lord conceptually and thus really, to have an experience of him. But since, for Rahner, that which drives his thought here is our human experience of hope and not the risen Lord himself, one could have an experience that he is risen without any reference to him at all.

[99]Rahner, TI 9, 28. That is why Rahner thinks he can explore anthropology to establish the truth of Christology while Barth invariably insists that the "necessity of faith does not lie in man. It does not lie even in the good nature of man as created for God, let alone in his being as the sinner who in denial and perversion of his good nature has turned away from God and in so doing deprived himself already of the possibility of faith. It does not even lie in faith in itself and as such. It is to be found rather in the object of faith. It is this object which forces itself necessarily on man and is in that way the basis of his faith. This object is the living Lord Jesus Christ" (CD IV/1, 747).

[100]Rahner, TI 11, 87.

[101]Rahner, TI 1, 98.

[102]Rahner, TI 4, 119.

[103]*Karl Rahner in Dialogue: Conversations and Interviews 1965–1982*, ed. Paul Imhof and Hubert Biallowons, trans. Harvey D. Egan (New York: Crossroad, 1986), 75. For Rahner, revelation emerges when grace, which refers to "the self-communication of God in the depth of the person's spiritual existence," and our historical experience of Jesus "meet each other and confirm each other" so that in that way we have revelation "accepted in faith in the full sense of the word" (ibid., 75, 77). This mutually conditioned view of revelation is precisely what Barth rejects because he understands revelation as "the condition which conditions all things without itself being conditioned" since it is identical with God speaking his Word in Jesus Christ himself who is the Word of God and the reconciler (CD I/1, 119). Grace simply cannot in any sense be equated with the depth of a person's spiritual experience for Barth.

[104]Kasper, *The God of Jesus Christ*, 300.

[105]Ibid., 301.

[106]Ibid., 300.

the possibility of the doctrine of grace."[107] This, Kasper says, affects the meaning of the doctrine by shifting the ground entirely to soteriology and away from doxology so that

> while the subjectivity of man is in danger of being lost in Barth's thematizing of God as absolute subject in his theology of the Trinity, it is the Thou of God that is in danger of being lost in Rahner's thematizing of the subjectivity of man in his theology of the Trinity.[108]

Kasper's criticism of Barth is more than a little problematic, since, in his doctrine of the Trinity, Barth's theology actually builds on the fact that because God's being and act are one, therefore God's own act in his Word and Spirit *ad extra* is the foundation and enabling condition of human subjectivity since human freedom is and remains grounded solely in Christ as enabled by the Holy Spirit.[109] So Barth holds that

---

[107]Ibid., 302.

[108]Ibid.

[109]Barth, CD IV/1, 748–9; IV/3.1, 446–7. Barth's stress on Christology and therefore on Jesus Christ as the one from whom we know the true meaning of human freedom comes through when Barth says that "the man Jesus is not a mere puppet moved this way and that by God. He is not a mere reed used by God as the instrument of His Word. The man Jesus prays. He speaks and acts. And as He does so He makes an unheard of claim, a claim which makes Him appear the victim of delusion and finally brings down upon Him the charge of blasphemy. He thinks of himself as the Messiah, the Son of God. He allows Himself to be called *Kyrios*, and, in fact conducts Himself as such. He speaks of His suffering, not as a necessity laid upon Him from without, but as something which He Himself wills … In His wholehearted obedience in His electing of God alone, He is wholly free … The truly astounding feature about this person of Jesus Christ is this, that here is a man who not only testified to God's rule by His Word and deeds. In the last analysis all the prophets had done that. Jesus did that, too, but in doing it He did more. He actually claimed and exercised lordship, even the lordship of God. The perfection of God's giving of Himself to man in the person of Jesus Christ consists in the fact that far from merely playing with man, far from merely moving or using him, far from merely dealing with him as an object, *this self-giving sets man up as a subject, awakens him to genuine individuality and autonomy, frees him, makes him a king, so that in his rule the kingly rule of God himself attains form and revelation*" (CD II/2, 179, emphasis mine). Barth continues by saying that what Jesus' Jewish contemporaries saw in Jesus led them to condemn him "in the name of the offended God. They did so because in the King who stood before them they did not recognise the servant of God. They did so because in the form of the servant they did not recognise the King. They did so because they did not recognise in Jesus Christ either very God or very man. They did so because the will of God was hidden from them. For what took place in Jesus Christ … was not merely a temporal event, but the eternal will of God temporally actualised and revealed in that event. God's eternal will is man: man who is the wholehearted witness to God's kingdom and enjoys as such a kingly freedom—the Lamb of God which taketh away the sin of the world … On man's side this election becomes actual in man's own electing of God, by which he is made free to do the will of God, and achieves and possesses individuality and autonomy before God" (ibid., 179–80). Barth connects this divine decision for us which frees us with the Holy Spirit when he speaks of faith as the "Yes of the free act which corresponds to [the awakening power of the Holy Spirit]." He says, "The divine decision is not made and cannot be made in him, in his spirit. It can only be repeated" because we cannot finally free ourselves from the "old man" of sin. It is the act of faith, Barth says, that "is the doing of the self-evident—just because it takes place in the free choice beside which man has no other choice, so that it is his genuinely free choice. The Holy Spirit is the power in which Jesus Christ the Son of God makes a man free, makes him genuinely free for this choice and therefore for faith … faith can know and confess itself only as His work and gift, as the human decision for this object, the human participation in it which he makes in his own free act but which he can only receive, which he can understand only as something which is received, which he can continually look for as something which is received again and which has to be confirmed in a new act. It is not that he is strong when he believes. But the One in whom he believes shows Himself to be strong over him when he believes—strong

with the divine No and Yes spoken in Jesus Christ the root of human unbelief, the man of sin, is pulled out. In its place there is put the root of faith, the new man of obedience. For this reason unbelief has become an objective, real and ontological impossibility and faith an objective, real and ontological necessity for all men and for every man.[110]

Hence, for Barth,

the Holy Spirit is the power in which Jesus Christ the Son of God makes a man free, makes him genuinely free for this choice and therefore for faith. He is the power in which the object of faith is also its origin and basis, so that faith can know and confess itself only as His work and gift, as the human decision for this object, the human participation in it which he makes in his own free act but which he can only receive.[111]

Barth concludes that as faith is based on Christ as its object,

there takes place in it the constitution of the Christian subject … it becomes and is this subject only in this action: not on the basis of a creaturely character of this action as such, but in virtue of the fact that as it is oriented so it is also based on Jesus Christ. Yet it is also true, and we must say it expressly, that in this action there begins and takes place a new and particular being of man.[112]

Interestingly, however, for our purposes here, it is worth noting that Kasper objects to Rahner's "radical rejection of the modern concept of person" since we cannot "adore and glorify 'distinct manners of subsisting.' We can only fall silent before Rahner's ultimately nameless mystery of God."[113] This is an important criticism, because if God

---

as the One who is raised again from the dead to awaken him first from the death of unbelief to the life of faith" (CD IV/1, 748). So, for Barth, the existence of Christians as those who believe in Jesus Christ through his Holy Spirit consists in the knowledge that "the night has passed and the day dawned; that there is peace between God and sinful man, revealed truth, full and present salvation. This simple thing [faith], and this mystery, constitute the being of the Christian, his being by the One in whom he believes" (ibid., 748–9). Barth goes on to maintain that as faith is tied to Jesus Christ by being "orientated and based on Him as its object, there takes place in it the constitution of the Christian subject … it becomes and is this subject only in this action: not on the basis of a creaturely character of this action as such, but in virtue of the fact that as it is orientated so it is also based on Jesus Christ … in this action there begins and takes place a new and particular being of man" (ibid., 749). God thus acts upon us in "an unconditioned and irresistible work" as the triune God objectively in his Word and subjectively in his Spirit precisely in a way that "does not prejudice the autonomy, the *freedom*, the responsibility, the individual being and life and activity of the creature, or the genuineness of its own activity, but confirms and *establishes* them … the rights and honour and dignity and freedom of the creature are not suppressed and extinguished but vindicated and revealed" (Barth, CD III/3, 144–5, emphasis mine).
[110]Barth, CD IV/1, 747.
[111]Ibid., 748.
[112]Ibid., 749.
[113]Kasper, *The God of Jesus Christ*, 302.

is ultimately nameless then who God is in eternity would differ according to the names we choose to use based on our transcendental anthropology, which would open the door to projection, to the possibility of agnosticism, pantheism, and even dualism, all of which Kasper rightly rejects. Kasper pushes his point further claiming that Rahner's anthropological approach leaves

> no room … for the relations and unity of the trinitarian persons themselves. They are moments in the economic self-communication of God to man, but not subjects of an immanent self-communication … His trinitarian speculation thus stops short of the goal; it is unable to show clearly in what the special character and difference of each hypostasis consists and what comprehensible meaning each has.[114]

Even if Barth might not agree with the tritheistic sounding reference to "subjects" rather than the three "modes" or persons acting in self-communication as a single subject, he might approve the extremely important Christological question Kasper raises to Rahner's approach:

> It is not so clear in Rahner that [Jesus'] human I subsists in the hypostasis of the Logos, so that in Jesus Christ the Logos himself speaks and acts; it is not so clear that in the man Jesus Christ God is not only present in a unique and unsurpassable way but that in addition Jesus Christ *is* the Son of God.[115]

Kasper's own development of the doctrine is an explicit attempt to avoid these weaknesses in Rahner's approach by specifically uniting a doxological approach with a soteriological approach. Still, Kasper thinks, "there is no need to choose between the approaches of Barth and of Rahner."[116]

These criticisms of Rahner by Kasper may seem a bit off the mark. But when one considers the fact noted above that for Rahner "anyone who accepts his own humanity in full … has accepted the son of Man";[117] that one can have an "anonymous" experience of the risen Lord[118] since anyone who accepts his or her life as meaningful is already an "anonymous Christian" with "anonymous faith";[119] that what Rahner calls revelation is not always and exclusively understood to be identical with the incarnate Word, that is, with Jesus himself but rather is also present in our own transcendental experiences of ourselves such that revelation can be described as "modification of our transcendental consciousness produced permanently in grace" and that this is a "permanent element

---

[114]Ibid.

[115]Ibid., 303.

[116]Ibid., 304.

[117]Rahner, TI 4, 119.

[118]Rahner and Weger, *Our Christian Faith Answers for the Future*, 113.

[119]Rahner, TI 16, 58.

in our consciousness as the basic and original luminosity of our existence" in such way that "it is already revelation in the proper sense,"[120] then perhaps one can see that, while Rahner surely wished to maintain Christ's uniqueness as God become man for us and for our salvation, his thinking at crucial points tended to undermine the fact that Jesus himself *is* God acting for us because he detached revelation from Jesus and located it also in us. I am suggesting that the culprit is Rahner's attempt to unite natural and revealed theology in his laudable attempt to reunite the treatises on the one God and the triune God and overcome the perceived extrinsicism of neo-scholasticism.

Analogia Entis/Analogia Fidei

Despite his criticisms of Rahner and while Kasper's assertion that we do not need to choose between Barth and Rahner is beguiling, this assertion seems based on an inaccurate assessment of the *analogia entis*. Any analogy of being between Creator and creatures which attempts to construct a bridge between us and God in his transcendence by exploring general concepts of love, freedom, or mystery for instance would, in Barth's estimation, amount to an attempt to know the one true God without actually relying on God himself as he made himself known to us in Christ and through his Spirit and thus through faith and by grace.[121] For Barth, the *analogia fidei* fundamentally means that all analogies used to speak of the triune God, who alone is the true God, must begin and end with revelation in its identity with Jesus Christ the revealer and reconciler.[122]

But, as we shall see, to the extent that both Kasper and Johnson begin their theological considerations with general reflections on human experiences of transcendence and immanence and then argue that Jesus Christ is the ultimate fulfilment of human desires for justice and freedom and the like, they demonstrate the inherent problem Barth saw with the *analogia entis* and consistently attempted to avoid. Consider, for example, this perplexing remark by Kasper: "What the Bible says about the Father could be taken as an answer (for which philosophy itself paved the way) to the basic question asked in philosophy."[123] From this Kasper claimed that there is "an internal correspondence between" what he terms "philosophical inquiry into the ultimate ground ... of all reality" and "the biblical message about God as Father."[124] Given Barth's statement above that God as Father and Creator remains unknown to us to the extent that he is not made known by Jesus, it is clear that Barth would question these remarks. Indeed, Barth is firm that "true and certain faith" must correspond "to the death and resurrection of Jesus Christ" such that in answer to the question of how we participate in Christ, Barth

[120]Rahner, *Foundations*, 149.
[121]Barth, CD I/1, 334; CD II/1, 280–97, 299–321.
[122]Barth, CD II/1, 251–4.
[123]Kasper, *The God of Jesus Christ*, 146.
[124]Ibid., 147.

stresses that a proper answer "does not start from the believing man but from Jesus Christ as the object and foundation of faith."[125]

As already noted, Rahner self-consciously begins his theology with human experience as Kasper and Johnson both agree. Johnson follows Rahner claiming rather explicitly that God is experienced "as the ultimate depth and radical essence of every personal experience such as love, fidelity, loneliness, and death" such that in our experience of ourselves we "are grasped by the holy mystery of God as the very context of our own self-presence. In fact the silent, nonverbal encounter with infinite mystery constitutes the enabling condition of any experience of self at all."[126] Moreover, following Rahner, Johnson claims that "the personal history of the experience of the self is in its total extent the history of the ultimate experience of God also"[127] and concludes that "surrendering to the incomprehensible mystery at the core of our life, however, allows the liberating grace of God to be at work … Consequently, Rahner reasons, this 'actually postulates thereby a history of our own concept of God that can never be concluded' … new attempts at envisioning and articulating this mystery should be expected and even welcomed."[128] Barth, as already noted, claims that any theology that begins with our experience of ourselves has lost its ability to think about the Christian God. Indeed, for Barth, it is not our surrendering to some incomprehensible mystery that could be newly envisioned by us that "allows the liberating grace of God to be at work" simply because God's liberating grace in his Word and by his Spirit is the enabling condition of our knowledge of God in the first place. And Barth conceptualizes this God by insisting that

> the eternal riches of God are the riches of His trinitarian life as Father, Son, and Holy Spirit. And for this reason His operation by Word and Spirit is the demonstration of a life which is eternally rich … there is no reason whatever why the activity of the creature should be destroyed or suppressed by His omnipotent operation. On the contrary, it is necessarily the case that the omnipotent operation of God not merely leaves the activity of the creature free, but continually makes it free … the effect of their operation is not bondage but freedom.[129]

Kasper believes Barth moved away from his original vociferous rejection of the *analogia entis* as the "Antichrist"[130] toward a position more in accord with the Catholic

---

[125]Barth, CD II/1, 155–6. See also CD IV/1, 741 where Barth flatly rejects any idea that the possibility of Christian faith "can be demonstrated and explained in the light of general anthropology … the possibilities which can be demonstrated and explained in light of anthropology may perhaps be religious, but they are not those of Christian faith" because faith in the Christian sense "cannot in any sense think of itself as grounded in itself."

[126]Johnson, *She Who Is*, 65; Johnson, *Quest for the Living God*, 25–47.

[127]Johnson, *She Who Is*, 66.

[128]Johnson, *Quest for the Living God*, 45–7.

[129]Barth, CD III/3, 150. Importantly, however, Barth insists that we must honor, respect, and love the actual freedom of this God who is our Lord because this "is not a God who is unknown to us, but the God who is our Father in Jesus Christ, the eternal Father of all His creatures" (ibid., 154).

[130]Kasper, *The God of Jesus Christ*, 97.

understanding of analogy.[131] Kasper believes that "structurally" Barth's view is not much different from the Franciscan view (Bonaventure in particular), according to which "knowledge of God is possible only on the basis of revelation and of the analogy of faith which revelation establishes."[132] Now, if Rahner, Kasper, Johnson, and Barth really held this view in common, we would have a far-reaching agreement of monumental theological significance.

If, however, Kasper is right in his assertion that the later Barth had moved closer to the Catholic position, then one would expect that Barth must have abandoned his strict idea that the object of faith *alone* and *always* dictates both the shape of one's method and one's conclusions. Unfortunately, it is precisely the approach of natural theology, which, according to both Kasper and Johnson, cannot be based on an idea of "pure nature"[133] but only upon a theological view of nature that includes grace, that leads to the idea that somehow "the *analogia fidei* presupposes the *analogia entis* or *libertatis* and brings the latter to its fulfillment."[134] That of course is the sense in which they, following Rahner, believe that Jesus Christ is the ultimate fulfilment of human desires for justice, love, and freedom.

The question then is this: if the *analogia fidei* presupposes the *analogia entis*, does that not have to mean that theology can first begin with being in general and human experiences of self-transcendence as generally understood and then understand the *analogia fidei* and grace itself as the fulfillment of what is first discovered in those presupposed sets of reflection? If this is in any sense the case, then in relation to Barth's position, it would follow contra Kasper, that (1) one must make a choice between Barth's approach to the Trinity and Rahner's because such a view would preclude at the outset that Jesus himself must be the *first* and *final* Word of theology and (2) one cannot begin with a general understanding of love, hope, freedom, or even of God as mystery and then move to the particular understanding disclosed in revelation without distorting the meaning of revelation, faith, grace, and God himself, as Barth understood these categories. Rather, one must begin and end in faith precisely because revelation and not human experience or understanding dictates truth in this matter. Because the triune God, and not some general infinite mystery knowable without faith in Christ, is the object of faith, the relationship between faith and its object is unequivocally irreversible. That is the primary assertion that Barth wished to make in rejecting the *analogia entis*, and he never wavered on that point.

Natural Theology

While Barth, Kasper, and Johnson would all agree that what God is toward us, he is eternally in himself, they clearly differ in the way they understand that statement. Kasper

---

[131]Ibid., 98.
[132]Ibid., 97.
[133]Ibid., 74.
[134]Ibid., 99.

and Johnson accept Rahner's axiom that "the immanent Trinity is strictly identical with the economic Trinity and vice versa"[135] even though, as noted, Kasper posed a few pertinent questions to Rahner's understanding of that axiom. And Johnson places such an emphasis on our experience of faith, that she frequently loses sight of what for Barth was the sole object of faith. Difficulties arise because while all three theologians think revelation is central to understanding the Trinity, Kasper and Johnson do not consistently begin and end their thinking *exclusively* with Jesus Christ himself as attested in Scripture. I say consistently because at times, Kasper especially, due to what Barth once called a happy inconsistency,[136] allows Jesus Christ in his uniqueness to shape what he has to say—as when he turns to John's Gospel in order to speak of the unity of God as specifically God's unity as Father, Son, and Spirit and as love.[137] He also asserts that "a Christian doctrine of God cannot be concerned with 'just any' God but only with the one God of Abraham, Isaac and Jacob, the God of Jesus Christ."[138] When Johnson turns her attention to Christ, she asserts his uniqueness but consistently portrays him as either an "envoy"[139] or a Spirit endowed human being claiming that "while Jesus is named the Christ in a paradigmatic way, multiple redemptive role models are available within the community."[140] From this it follows for her that the "symbol Christ ... cannot be restricted to the historical person of Jesus."[141] This thinking allows her to separate the Spirit from the Word in order to find the Spirit's presence in communities that do not recognize Jesus in his uniqueness.[142] It also allows her to argue, as seen above, that any experience of love or freedom is an experience of God so that her thinking is not necessarily and always bound to Jesus Christ himself when she speaks of the "divine" or "holy mystery."[143]

Kasper's inconsistency consists in the fact that in this instance he overtly and rightly places revelation at the center to speak of the "deepest and utterly hidden nature of the unity and oneness of God [as Father, Son, and Spirit]"[144] instead of referring to God as the "nameless" with Rahner. Then, however, inconsistently he analyzes the meaning of love by analyzing human love claiming that human persons exist "only in co-existence with other persons ... The human person is possible only in the plural; it can exist only in reciprocal acknowledgment, and it finds fulfillment only in the communion of love. Persons thus exist only in mutual giving and receiving."[145] In accordance with his belief

---

[135]Rahner, TI 9, 32.
[136]Barth, CD II/1, 242, 457.
[137]Kasper, *The God of Jesus Christ*, 305.
[138]Ibid., 121.
[139]Johnson, *She Who Is*, 168–9.
[140]Ibid., 162.
[141]Ibid.
[142]Johnson, *Quest for the Living God*, 162–3.
[143]Ibid., 45. In Chapter 6 we shall see how this thinking affects her view of language for God, the Trinity, and her view of conversion all in a problematic way which could only be avoided by allowing Christ himself in his uniqueness to shape our understanding of these concepts.
[144]Kasper, *The God of Jesus Christ*, 305.
[145]Ibid., 306.

that natural theology explores the presuppositions of faith, without being constantly bound by the object of that faith, Kasper claims to have developed a "preapprehension that enables us to understand the unity in love which according to the Gospel of John exists in God and is the very being of God."[146] But the question I am raising in this chapter is: can any "preapprehension" ever "enable" us to understand the love that only Christ reveals? For Barth, the answer was a definitive "no" while for Kasper it is a qualified "yes." Here I am suggesting we are presented with a "happy inconsistency." Kasper explains that this "preapprehension" can only be applied analogically to God because unlike God, human beings depend upon one another, need one another, are finite, and "no single person is wholly identical with himself; none exhausts the nature of humanity and all of its possibilities," and human love is also erotic in that it always "seeks fulfillment."[147]

Here Kasper's thinking is not consistently being shaped by his "preapprehension" of love discussed in relation to human love; rather it is clearly being formed at least in part by the love of God referred to in John's Gospel. I say this because he proceeds to explain that all of what was just described is "excluded from God by his very nature. God does not possess being; he *is* Being in the absolute perfection that has no slightest trace of neediness. He is therefore absolute oneness, perfect self-identity and complete self-possession, personal unity in the most perfect sense."[148] Furthermore, God cannot be understood to be dependent "on the world or man" because God is "co-existent within himself."[149] Referring to John's Gospel, Kasper also maintains that "within the unity and simplicity of his being he must be a communion in love, and this love cannot be a love marked by need but only a love that gives out of the overflowing fulness of his being."[150] God, Kasper says, is a communion of love but not a "communion of separate beings, as it is among men, but a communion with a single nature."[151] In these remarks, there are genuine grounds for unity between Catholic and Protestant theology. Thinking along these lines, Kasper explicitly appeals to Barth's understanding of God as One who loves in freedom to explicate his view that God remains free in his love of us and that we must always clearly distinguish Creator and creature.[152] Thus, he concludes with Augustine, in a way that Barth would surely approve, that "the Trinity is the one and only God, and the one and only God is the Trinity."[153] Let me explain how this problem of inconsistency arises just because of the kind of natural theology which is adopted by Walter Kasper and why Karl Barth consistently rejected such a procedure.

---

[146]Ibid.
[147]Ibid.
[148]Ibid.
[149]Ibid.
[150]Ibid.
[151]Ibid.
[152]Ibid., 144, 155–7, 195, 266, 293–4.
[153]Ibid., 306–7.

Presuppositions for the Understanding of Faith

Kasper thinks of natural theology as "reflection on the presuppositions for the understanding of faith."[154] So he claims that the real issue today "is no longer primarily this or that truth but the very ability to believe" because, he says, "We have to a large extent lost the dimension of faith."[155] In this context, Kasper makes no effort to trace the "dimension of faith" or the "ability to believe" to the miraculous action of the Holy Spirit as Barth regularly did and claims instead that the Bible practices natural theology because there is recourse in the Bible to the religious ideas and experiences of everyday life and from these the Bible derives "images for use in religious statements."[156]

Kasper cites a number of biblical texts in support of natural theology. His consideration of Johannine theology is particularly instructive because it leads him to believe that John takes the questions human beings ask "in order then to proclaim Jesus Christ as the definitive answer to these questions."[157] Accordingly, John starts "with the assumption that the lives of human beings are inspired by the quest for salvation and that in this way men and women have a preunderstanding of salvation."[158] This leads Kasper to compare Philo's Logos with the Logos of John's Gospel and then conclude that "the Logos at work in creation is no other than the Logos who in the fullness of time became a human being in Jesus Christ."[159] Here it is crucially important to contrast this approach of natural theology to Barth's approach which never moves outside the specific revelation of God in his incarnate Word. Thus, for Barth one could never assume that we have any sort of preunderstanding of salvation which results from the human quest for salvation since the very meaning of salvation can and was disclosed only in the act of God in the history of Israel and uniquely in the incarnation. So Barth insisted that "it is not because we have already sought Him that we find Him in faith, but, it is because He has first of all found us that we seek Him—now really *Him*—in faith" precisely by seeking him in Jesus Christ.[160]

Knowledge of God

Here we have a fundamental disagreement between Barth and Kasper. For Barth, the Logos incarnate in Jesus Christ is the one and only Son or Word of the Father—it is this particular Logos in its identity with Jesus Christ who commands our obedience. In Barth's view, the moment Jesus is seen as the answer to a set of questions which set the ground for

---

[154]Ibid., 65.
[155]Ibid.
[156]Ibid., 66.
[157]Ibid., 67.
[158]Ibid.
[159]Ibid.
[160]Barth, *Credo*, 13.

understanding the answer, he is stripped of his uniqueness. Such an approach cannot allow Jesus himself to be the starting point *and* the exclusive criterion of theological truth. For Barth, when Jn 14:6 says Jesus is the truth, that assertion is not the result of a general inquiry after the truth but of an acknowledgment, recognition, and confession of Jesus as the Lord based on the revelation of the Father in and through Jesus himself precisely as enabled by the Spirit; this is therefore a recognition that could only come from faith in Jesus himself and thus from union with him in the Spirit.[161] This is the weakness of natural theology for Barth.

Natural theology does not and cannot begin and end with revelation in its identity with Jesus Christ. This disagreement is no minor quibble, because it leads Kasper to think that in some sense the doctrine of the Trinity is the answer to the human quest to understand the problem of the one and the many[162] and it leads him to argue, as many social trinitarians do, that the modern concepts of person and freedom can be used to understand divine relationality.[163] Thus, he thinks that all human knowledge "presupposes a pre-apprehension of the infinite" and that "there is always present in human freedom and understanding an implicit and latent knowledge of the unconditioned and infinite."[164] Since Kasper thinks the early church fathers believed God could be known "both from visible things and from the human soul,"[165] he also claims that knowledge of God can be derived both from nature and from reflection on the human soul. This allows him to follow the "modern approach [to God] through subjectivity"[166] and argue for "the presence in the human conscience of a real apprehension of God."[167] In this thinking, Kasper is surely closer to Rahner than to Barth.

These claims unfortunately weaken Kasper's ability to maintain the priority of Jesus Christ as he also wishes to do when he writes that the "proof of the reasonableness of faith has for its starting point the fact that in Jesus Christ the definitive truth about God, man and the world has made its appearance."[168] Kasper thinks experience can never be the criterion "for what is accepted as the word of God; rather, the word of God is meant to, and must, make known to us what true experience is as compared with illusory appearances."[169] Yet, he still begins his theological analysis from general human experience, then religious experience, claiming that human beings experience themselves as a mystery which they can never master and, on that basis, concludes that such experience can be interpreted both theistically and pantheistically or even atheistically.[170]

So, after noting that Vatican I intended to reject both fideism and traditionalism with its affirmation that "by the natural light of reason man can know God with certainty from

---

[161]Barth, CD II/1, 3, 181, 205; and Molnar, *Faith, Freedom and the Spirit*, 37–58.
[162]Kasper, *The God of Jesus Christ*, 241.
[163]Ibid., 97–9.
[164]Ibid., 98.
[165]Ibid., 68.
[166]Ibid., 104.
[167]Ibid., 105.
[168]Ibid., 78.
[169]Ibid., 80.
[170]Ibid., 86.

created reality,"[171] Kasper claims that the Council "deliberately says nothing about whether such a natural knowledge of God actually exists"[172] and maintains that the issue simply was "the openness, in principle, of reason to God."[173] Hence, for Kasper the theological concept of nature understands nature in relation to grace: "man [is] a being endowed with intellectual knowledge and with freedom, a being who as such is capable of encountering and receiving grace" because "spirit and freedom … are the transcendental presuppositions for faith and … grace."[174] Again, however, there is a vast difference between the thinking of Barth and Kasper on this issue just because Barth consistently allows Jesus Christ himself to reveal the possibilities and limitations of human reason. For Barth, we learn from revelation that we are God's enemies as those who brought Jesus to the cross and are there forgiven;[175] thus it is only because God became incarnate in his Son Jesus Christ and reconciled the world to himself, that we can come to know God as he is in himself only as the Holy Spirit unites us to Christ and thus to the Father. Consequently, for Barth, openness to the infinite cannot be equated with openness to the God of Christian faith.

Human Reason/Grace/Vatican II

Both Kasper and Barth reject fideism because they think that faith involves knowledge of the truth and thus understanding of who God is and who we are. But for Kasper that understanding comes, at least in part, *from* human reason, while for Barth it comes *to* human reason from revelation and thus by grace alone so that "although the knowledge of God certainly does not come about without our work, it also does not come about through our work, or as the fruit of our work."[176] The key difference between them can be seen in Barth's unequivocal rejection of any notion of an obediential potency in human being for revelation and Kasper's belief that such a potency is part of human nature and indeed the presupposition for understanding revelation as the revelation of God in the first place.[177]

According to Kasper, Vatican II integrated the abstract approach of Vatican I into a historical and salvation-historical perspective noting on the one hand the difficulties

---

[171]Ibid., 69.

[172]Ibid.

[173]Ibid.

[174]Ibid., 77.

[175]Thus, Barth writes, "About man as such, about autonomous man, existing otherwise than in Jesus Christ, the only thing we need to know is that he has brought Jesus Christ to the cross and that in this same cross his sins are forgiven; that in his independence he is judged and removed, really removed, i.e., moved and taken up into fellowship with the life of the Son of God" (Barth, CD II/1, 162).

[176]Barth, CD II/1, 182–3. This is the case because for Barth we have no innate capacity for knowing God or for fellowship with God. So he says "Our viewing and conceiving are not at all capable of grasping God" because it is only through God that God is known and when we actually do know God, that knowledge takes place in "pure discipleship and gratitude. At this very point we are finally dissuaded from trusting and confiding in our own capacity and strength" (ibid., 183).

[177]Kasper, *The God of Jesus Christ*, 61, 343, n. 79.

"contemporary man has with the natural knowledge of God, and the resultant forms of modern atheism." On the other hand, Vatican II "brings out the fact that the answer to the question which man is for himself is given, in the final analysis, not through the natural knowledge of God but only through Jesus Christ."[178] This assertion, however, illustrates the predicament with natural theology from Barth's perspective. Because it is supposed that our human questions guide us toward the proper answer, even this assertion that in the final analysis we can only arrive at knowledge of that answer through Jesus Christ has already lost its force. In Barth's estimation, it is Jesus Christ himself who questions us and thus who sets the questions for us and not the general human quest for meaning. Claiming only this finality for Jesus without allowing him to be the starting point and criterion for the quest itself makes a claim that ultimately ascribes the possibility for knowledge of the triune God to us and not exclusively to the reconciling action of God himself in his Word and Spirit, to nature rather than exclusively to grace.

Elizabeth Johnson

We have already discussed some key issues related to Elizabeth Johnson's thinking. Here, we resume that discussion in more detail. Those familiar with Johnson's landmark book, *She Who Is*, will recall that she explicitly follows the thinking of Gordon Kaufman[179] and Sallie McFague.[180] That would raise a red flag for anyone thinking about the Trinity in relation to the theology of Karl Barth since Kaufman understood theology to be *essentially imaginative construction*,[181] and McFague thought her models of God as mother, lover, and friend did not describe God since she did "not *know* who God is," but could only speak of God based on those experiences that mattered most to her.[182] Interestingly, McFague argued that "the Christian insistence on relationality … received dogmatic status in the doctrine of the trinity"[183] claiming that "emphasis on relationships among the persons of the immanent trinity negates the very point the doctrine should make— that God as intrinsically relational is, as, are we, the *imago dei*, interrelational with other forms of life."[184] In a similar manner, Johnson argues that "the metaphors of Word and Son … signify not maleness in God but a certain divine relationality that can be superbly

[178]Ibid., 69–70.
[179]Johnson, *She Who Is*, 4, 276, n. 3
[180]Ibid., 7, 132.
[181]Gordon D. Kaufman, *Theology for a Nuclear Age* (Philadelphia, PA: Westminster Press, 1985), 26.
[182]Sallie McFague, *Models of God: Theology for an Ecological, Nuclear Age* (Philadelphia, PA: Fortress Press, 1987), 192, n. 7.
[183]Ibid., 166.
[184]Ibid., 167. Here of course she misses the actual point of grounding theology within the immanent Trinity since it is that very God who is eternally rich in himself who enables us to relate with him in his Word and Spirit in an effective way that could never occur if God were simply understood as "interrelational with other forms of life." That latter idea would make relationality the subject with God as the predicate and reduce God to the relations visible in creation.

reprised in the symbol of Sophia"[185] whereas for Barth and the tradition, Jesus *is* the Son or Word of God in his unique relation of being with the Father and the Spirit in eternity and for us in history. Barth considered theology to involve the imagination, but only insofar as one's imagination was utilized in faithfulness to revelation in its identity with Jesus Christ.

By contrast, McFague explicitly claims that Jesus was not ontologically different from anyone who loved God and neighbor since for her he is "paradigmatic of God the lover but is not unique,"[186] and Kaufman openly rejected the idea that Jesus was utterly unique in the Nicene sense.[187] For Kaufman and McFague, God was understood to be a pliable symbol that human beings needed to define and redefine in order to create a more peaceful and loving society. Johnson uses Kaufman's terminology to describe God as *our* ultimate point of reference.[188] In a way similar to the approach of Kaufman, Johnson argues that we must change the symbol today to make it function in order for women to achieve full equality in the church and in society. This leads her to argue that we must name God mother as well as father and Jesus as Sophia in order for women to experience liberation from patriarchalism today.

In Johnson's view, women today are rightly "engaged in creative 'naming toward God,' as Mary Daly so carefully calls it, from the matrix of their own experience."[189] Here is

---

[185]Johnson, *She Who Is*, 166, 214.

[186]McFague, *Models*, 136. She directly asserts that his means that "Jesus is not ontologically different from other paradigmatic figures … who manifest in word and deed the love of God for the world. He is special to us as our foundational figure: he is our historical choice as the premier paradigm of God's love." It is precisely this assertion that is in conflict with the grace of God and revelation of God in Jesus Christ from Barth's perspective for at least two key reasons. First, for Barth, Jesus Christ simply cannot be understood in his uniqueness as attested in Scripture if he is understood in any sense as an ideal case of someone who loves God and others because in reality "every word of the biblical witness about Him so binds us to Him that He stands above, while we come to stand beneath. In this irreversible order he is the One He is" (CD II/1, 150). But that means that he is not "man as such" who is at enmity with God. Scripture tells us that "whatever position we may take up towards it, that we are here concerned with the Lord: with the only begotten, unique and eternal Son of God, and therefore with God Himself; and therefore always with the One who is ready and open for God and to whom God is knowable. For this reason, when and because we are concerned with Jesus Christ, we stand in the mystery and at the same time in the revelation of God, in His innermost reality. God is knowable to Himself; the Son to the Father, but also the Father to the Son" so that it is only in him that we truly know God's inner being and ourselves as God's children (ibid., 151). Second, while McFague thinks Jesus is foundational for Christians because they chose to make him so, Barth insists that Jesus, as the grace of God and the revelation of God in history, and our knowledge of him as Lord of history, is simply not a possibility we can choose at all. For Barth "God's real revelation simply cannot be chosen by man and, as his own possibility, put beside another, and integrated with it into a system. God's real revelation is the possibility which man does not have to choose, but by which he must regard himself as chosen" (ibid.) so that we must respect the uniqueness of the one who chooses us. This means that we cannot "come to an arrangement with it [revelation as grace and miracle] within the sphere and according to the method of other possibilities. By treating it as if it does not do the choosing but is something to be chosen, not the unique but just one possibility, Christian natural theology very respectfully and in all humility re-casts revelation into a new form of its own devising" (ibid.).

[187]Gordon D. Kaufman, *In Face of Mystery: A Constructive Theology* (Cambridge, MA: Harvard University Press, 1993), 390–1.

[188]Johnson, *She Who Is*, 4.

[189]Ibid., 5.

where a theology based on revelation in its identity with Jesus Christ the revealer offers a very different view: for Barth, because Jesus *is* God acting *as* man for us in history, when we know God in himself through Jesus as enabled by his Spirit, then we know that there is nothing higher or better in God than that God is the eternal Father, Son, and Holy Spirit.[190] Theology certainly uses human terms, but their meaning is determined not by us or the way we choose to use them. This is where there is disagreement: these terms have their truth only in and from God who *is* the eternal Father, Son, and Holy Spirit and who is open to us in Christ and knowable only in him and thus only through faith and by grace. What this means above all is that our knowledge of God has a very definite certainty. But it has this only as such knowledge is begun, upheld, and completed by God himself in and through our obedient use of language.[191]

Johnson's Trinitarian Position

Unlike McFague, who explicitly claimed that statements about the immanent Trinity simply could not be made at all,[192] Johnson argues that "the concrete ways that God is given to us in history point to three interrelated ways of existing within God's own being. God really corresponds to the way we have encountered the divine mystery in time."[193] Johnson rightly rejects thinking that eschews anchoring who God is for us in the immanent Trinity. But the question that Barth's theology might raise to her is whether and to what extent her basic starting point and her view of analogy keep her from achieving her goal. While Johnson insists that "we would lose a great deal if we ceased speaking altogether of the immanent triune God,"[194] her view of analogy begins by negating our human experiences of paternity "at its best in this world" to affirm that God is father in an eminent way beyond what we experience.[195]

There is a fundamental issue of extraordinary importance at stake here. Johnson maintains that no one doubts that Jesus did indeed "speak to and about God using the paternal metaphor."[196] However, she questions whether this should be done exclusively.

---

[190]Barth, CD I/2, 377. Because of this, one cannot simply substitute the idea of relationality for the three distinct persons of the Trinity, namely, the eternal Father, Son, and Holy Spirit as McFague and Johnson do. We shall see how this problem arises in more detail in Chapter 6 when we consider language for God.

[191]Barth, CD II/1, 181, 204; CD II/1, 152–4.

[192]McFague, *Models*, 224. Thus, she writes, "It should be obvious that the trinitarian view I am supporting is a functional one, focused on God's activity in relationship to the world and our talk about that activity. It makes no claims about the so-called immanent or intrinsic trinity, for I see no way that assumptions concerning the inner nature of God are possible." For Barth, as long as our talk about the trinity is not grounded in the inner nature of God himself as the eternal Father, Son, and Spirit, we have no true and certain knowledge of God at all. And for Barth we do not have to leave the sphere of human history to know God's inner being because God has made himself knowable in the incarnation, that is, in Christ himself within human history.

[193]Johnson, *She Who Is*, 200.

[194]Ibid.

[195]Ibid., 173.

[196]Ibid., 80.

Nevertheless, the problem I am raising at this point concerns the fact that Jesus did not just speak *to* and *about* God with a freely chosen metaphor; he was in reality the eternal Son or Word speaking to us about his Father with whom he was uniquely related since he alone was *homoousios* with the Father and the Spirit. Johnson thinks that if we "select this one metaphor and grant it sole rights," then we would not be following "the pattern of Jesus' speech" but that such speech would likely be governed by "a subtle endorsement of the priority of the father in social arrangements."[197] I am claiming here that this is a faulty theological assumption because when Jesus is spoken of as Son of the Father, that speech is not governed by any human social arrangements at all and should not be so governed precisely because its meaning is governed by the Father/Son relation within the immanent Trinity made known by Jesus himself.[198]

Johnson's problem comes to a head with her idea that Jesus should be spoken of as Sophia incarnate. This change in language forces her thought into a modalist caste even though she intends to speak of relations within the Trinity. Hence, instead of thinking of the three persons of the Trinity as eternally inherent within the being of the one God, Johnson speaks of Jesus' "rootedness in God" using the "female figure of personified Wisdom so influential in biblical Christology" even though some biblical scholars utterly reject the idea that Paul, for instance, thought of the preexistent Son as "personified Wisdom"[199] and linguistic scholars acknowledge that just because a Greek word like Sophia has a feminine ending, that hardly means that those who used the word were thinking of a "female figure" as Johnson does.[200] From this she concludes that the person "Jesus-Sophia" is "constituted by these two fundamental relations [Sophia's relation with the "unoriginate God" and "her ... solidarity with human beings whom she makes into friends of God"]."[201]

Unable to think accurately about the eternal relation of the Son to the Father within the Trinity when conceptualizing Jesus as Sophia incarnate, Johnson thinks the person of Jesus Christ is constituted both by his human relation to the unoriginate God and by this unoriginated God's relations with us when in reality, according to traditional Christology, his human nature was grounded in the person of the Son who was constituted in and by his relations with the Father and the Spirit within the immanent Trinity. Moreover, she refers to Jesus, speaking of "the story of the liberating mission of this prophet and child of Sophia."[202] If Jesus really is Sophia incarnate and this is supposed to be a faithful recognition of his true and eternal deity, then it makes no sense to speak of him as the child of Sophia unless one is thinking of Jesus in subordinationist terms. How could the man Jesus, whose humanity is *enhypostatic*

[197]Ibid., 81.
[198]We will discuss this issue at length in Chapter 6.
[199]Gordon D. Fee, *Pauline Christology: An Exegetical-Theological Study* (Peabody, MA: Hendrickson, 2007), 93, 102–5, 501, n. 2.
[200]Johnson, *She Who Is*, 165; and Molnar, *Divine Freedom*, 34–5.
[201]Johnson, *She Who Is*, 165.
[202]Ibid., 167.

within the eternal Word, with no independent existence of his own (*anhypostasis*), be a child of himself? This problematic way of speaking, with its subordinationist and modalist overtones, cannot refer to a real eternal and personal relation between the Son and the Father in the Spirit just because God has been conceptualized as Sophia instead of as Father, Son, and Holy Spirit. And since she thinks of God simply as the "unoriginate," she, perhaps unwittingly, depersonalizes the eternal Trinity. Additionally, it should be noted here that some theologians argue that the use of Sophia connects with Gnostic and Arian thinking and, in that way, introduces gender and sex into the divine being.[203]

In any case, Johnson follows Rahner's thinking and conceptualizes God as "holy mystery" in such a way that her reflections are not structured (to use the language of Walter Kasper) by who God eternally is as the One who loves in freedom, that is, as the eternal Father, Son, and Holy Spirit.[204] Rather, since "this language is not a literal description of the inner being of God who is in any event beyond human understanding,"[205] it must be understood as "a pointer to holy mystery in trust that God really is the compassionate, liberating God encountered through Jesus in the Spirit."[206] But God is not just encountered *through* Jesus. Were that the case one might claim to encounter God in the same way through others, as Johnson indeed does, as noted above.[207] Instead, Jesus really is God himself actively revealing God to us *as* Jesus and now, as his Holy Spirit unites us to Christ and thus to the Father, he acts as our eternal high priest seeing to it that our knowledge of God is true.[208] Put another way, one cannot separate the form of revelation (Jesus' human history) from the content of revelation (the fact that he alone is the one Word or Son of the Father) acting as our reconciler, who, through his Spirit, now enables such knowledge.

---

[203]See Molnar, *Divine Freedom*, 34–5. The issue of gender with respect to the terms Father and Son will be discussed in detail in Chapter 6.

[204]Cherith Fee Nordling, *Knowing God by Name: A Conversation between Elizabeth A. Johnson and Karl Barth* (New York: Peter Lang, 2010), 187.

[205]Johnson, *She Who Is*, 200; and Johnson, *Quest for the Living God*, 98–100.

[206]Johnson, *She Who Is*, 200.

[207]Ibid., 162–3. It will be recalled that she claimed that Jesus was called Christ in a paradigmatic way but that there are other role models within the community.

[208]Barth, CD II/1, 156–7. Since Christian faith is not just a matter of faith for Barth, but a matter of true and certain faith, he insists that to speak rightly of our knowledge of God the answer that must be given "does not start from the believing man but from Jesus Christ as the object and foundation of faith" so that "the right answer can only be that as the one and only man ready for God, Jesus Christ has not only lived, died and risen for us once in time, so that the abounding grace of God might be an event and at the same time revelation among us, but that as this same One He stands before His Father now in eternity for us, and lives for us in God Himself as the Son of God He was and is and will be. Thus our appropriation of what he has won for us has not first to be executed by us. By the fact that He is for us in eternity in God Himself the man who is ready for God, it is executed in eternity, in God Himself, by Him, in the eternal continuation of His high-priestly office" (ibid., 156). That then means that "Jesus Christ Himself sees to it that in Him and by Him we are not outside but inside … this representing of Jesus Christ is an eternal representing and therefore one which is contemporary to all time" (ibid.).

God is Like a Trinity

Johnson's starting point for the knowledge of the triune God leads her ultimately to claim that "God is *like* a Trinity, *like* a threefoldness of relation."[209] This is entirely consistent with her belief that Father/Son language refers only to a certain "divine relationality" and not to the inner being of the Godhead, as in Barth's thinking. If, however, God is only "*like* a Trinity or *like* a threefoldness of relation," then God cannot be conceptualized *as* the eternal Father, Son, and Holy Spirit behind and beyond whom there is no other God. The point is captured nicely in Barth's statement already alluded to that

> we cannot say anything higher or better of the "inwardness of God" than that God is Father, Son, and Holy Spirit, and therefore that He is love in Himself without and before loving us, and without being forced to love us. And we can say this only in the light of the "outwardness" of God to us, the occurrence of His revelation.[210]

While Barth and Johnson certainly agree that we can only speak of God's inner being from within the economy and by analogy, this statement firmly suggests that the truth of theological analogies is bound to who God IS as the eternal Father, Son, and Spirit and that we cannot know that apart from his incarnate Son or the Holy Spirit uniting us to the Father through the Son.[211]

Instead of moving from the particular revelation of God in Jesus Christ to an understanding of who God eternally was and is, Johnson's thought, following Rahner, moves from a more general conception of divinity based on religious experience as "holy mystery," and then on to a description of relationality and finally speaks of God as mother and Sophia without realizing that such terminological changes fundamentally end up changing who God is, so that we can only say that God is *like* a Trinity because of our threefold experience of "holy mystery." For Barth, our experience of God is anchored in the fact that God is not just *a* Trinity but the eternal Father, Son, and Spirit. For Johnson, relationality based on women's experience of relationality shapes her understanding of the Trinity while her equation of God's incomprehensibility with an agnostic view of God's eternal being allows her to name God in a myriad of ways which are not dictated by who God actually and exclusively is for us in Jesus Christ and through his Holy Spirit. Indeed, her notion of mystery allows her to move "beyond the narrow notion of God as the deity of the Christian tribe alone by affirming the universality of God's gracious presence to each and every human being."[212]

For Barth, God is indeed graciously present to each and every human being as well. But God is present in his Word and Spirit. However, for Johnson this gracious presence is not necessarily mediated by Christ and his Holy Spirit at all because "holy mystery graciously

---

[209]Johnson, *She Who Is*, 205.
[210]Barth, CD I/2, 377.
[211]Barth, CD IV/2, 361–2.
[212]Johnson, *Quest for the Living God*, 43.

offers the gift of divine life to everyone, everywhere, and at all times."[213] And that offer in Johnson's view is not exclusively made in Christ alone but in our relation to "the silent immensity that surrounds us as something infinitely distant and yet ineffably near" so that if

> we have the courage to accept our own life in all its concreteness and yearning, which is possible only by grace, then we have the mystical experience of faith. Accepting our life means letting ourselves fall into this unfathomable mystery at the heart of our existence … people who courageously accept themselves … in point of fact accept holy mystery.[214]

There is no need to repeat here that for Barth accepting God in faith means believing in Jesus Christ through the power of his Spirit and thus in the Father of Jesus Christ. That is why grace for Barth cannot be equated with self-experience or with what we think God is by conceptualizing "holy mystery" as the silent term of our transcendental experiences. One simply cannot equate acceptance of ourselves with acceptance of and knowledge of God.

Female Experience/Panentheism

Johnson argues that we must reconceptualize not only who God is but how God relates with the world based on "female experience" because "to be so structured that you have room inside yourself for another to dwell is quintessentially a female experience."[215] Accordingly, the fact that everyone "yet born has lived and moved and had their being inside a woman" becomes for Johnson "the paradigm without equal for the panentheistic notion of the coinherence of God and the world."[216]

That, however, is the problem: the persons of the Trinity exist in an eternal *perichoresis* of mutual coinherence; but we have our relation with God only by grace and thus it is not an eternal relation and there is no mutual dependence or coinherence between God and us. This is one reason Barth rejected panentheism as worse than pantheism.[217] Even though Johnson quite rightly intends to uphold the idea that there is an "asymmetrical reciprocity" between God and the world so that it is theologically legitimate to focus "solely on God," the very way she conceptualizes the relation of God and history becomes fuzzy because she immediately speaks of God "who is never not related to the world."[218] If God is never not related to the world, then we

---

[213]Ibid., 44.
[214]Ibid., 45.
[215]Johnson, *She Who Is*, 234.
[216]Ibid.
[217]Barth, CD II/1, 312, 562. We will see below in Chapter 6 that Catherine LaCugna's misunderstanding of *perichoresis* also leads her to a panentheistic view of God's relations with us that finally collapses into a kind of pantheism.
[218]Johnson, *She Who Is*, 236.

not only have in this panentheistic vision a relation of mutual dependence between God and the world, but we have a vision that portrays God and creation as coeternal. The outcome of reconceiving God as *She Who Is* leads to such problematic ideas as the following: (1) "the world then, although not necessary in a hypothetical sense, does make a difference to God. She would not be creator, vivifier, redeemer, liberator, companion and future without it."[219] This idea is problematic because if God could not be the Creator without the world, then in that sense, the world would be necessary for God; God would be reduced to his creative function. But God creates out of the freedom and superabundance of his love and needs nothing outside himself to act *ad intra* or *ad extra*; (2) there is an "intrinsic relatedness between God and the world."[220] However, God is not intrinsically related to the world, but he relates to the world in free grace. An intrinsic relation is a necessary one. God's relatedness to the world is contingent.

For Johnson, however, pregnancy gives us the image that " 'I' am the 'other' and the 'other' is 'me' … we are essentially interrelated to one another."[221] Moreover, Sophia's essence, we are told, "might well be called connectedness, for in play with the world she is a breath, an emanation";[222] (3) while Johnson realizes that Jesus' maleness is part of his historical being, she also argues that the "exclusive use of father and son metaphors" exacerbates the patriarchal perspective so that "such language is thought to be not 'mere metaphor' but is taken literally to mean that the man Jesus is the revealer of a male Father-God" with the result that "maleness appears to be of the essence of the God made known in Christ."[223] This would only be true, of course, if someone mistakenly projected Jesus' maleness into God, which would amount to a confusion of divinity and humanity, which Johnson rightly recognizes in her appeal to the Chalcedonian distinction of natures in Christ. But the problem here concerns her assumption that exclusive use of father and son language for God is what leads to this misunderstanding. The misunderstanding, however, does not come from that but from those who refuse to acknowledge that God is Father and Son in an utterly unique sense as disclosed in revelation in its identity with Jesus, the incarnate Word.[224]

Thus, taking the metaphor literally does not have to mean that one would think of God as a "male Father-God." In fact, it would prevent that idea. Taking that language literally would mean that any reference to Jesus as the Son and God as his Father was not in reality a reference to the human Jesus in himself and as such, but to his being as the Son who, as the eternally begotten Son, is one in being with the Father. Johnson mistakenly assumes that if the metaphor of father and son is exclusively used, it would

---

[219]Ibid., 232.

[220]Ibid., 185.

[221]Ibid., 298. As we shall see in Chapter 6, this is why T. F. Torrance so firmly insisted that we cannot simply use images taken from human relations to speak correctly about God and God's relations with us. Those concepts must be transformed to refer "imagelessly" to God and to God's relations with us.

[222]Ibid., 168.

[223]Ibid., 152.

[224]More will be said about this problem in Chapter 6.

inevitably refer only to maleness[225] when in reality, since very early in church history, this has always been governed by the truth propounded in Mt. 11:27 which refers not to maleness but to the closed circle of knowing between Father and Son into which we are drawn by grace and through faith in our relations with Jesus in and through the Spirit; (4) we can only "hope that it is the livingness of *God* who is with us in the suffering of history" without *literally* knowing the God who acted for us in the suffering and death of Jesus himself.[226] But we do not just hope that God is with us in the suffering of history. We really know that God *is* with us in the particular suffering and death of his Son for the salvation of history in its suffering; (5) images of mother and Sophia encourage a panentheistic view of God's relations with us. However, as already noted, these images make it impossible to maintain conceptually the asymmetrical relation of Creator and creation that Johnson intended to maintain. Instead of allowing God, who *is* the Father of Jesus Christ to determine her thinking, Johnson uses the "symbol" God to think inclusively in a way that allows women to use their own experiences as metaphors for the divine being.[227] In sum, for Karl Barth the truth of our metaphors for divine being does not come *from* the experience of women *or* from the experience of men; it comes *to* them as a revelation of God in Jesus Christ and through his Spirit and is known only in faith.

Concluding Comments

Given the constraints of space, I could never do total justice to all of the insights of Barth, Kasper, and Johnson. But I believe that I have demonstrated moments when their respective approaches carry on important dialogue with each other's positions. Clearly, there are many questions which yet must be addressed: how can trinitarian doctrine better illustrate the unity of Christians in a way that respects both divine and human freedom and affirms the mission of the church to teach the good news to the world in a way that is thoroughly inclusive of all and respects the dignity of women in their equality with men already realized by the God who reconciled the world to himself in his Son?[228] What needs to be done to avoid the errors of a poorly elaborated *analogia entis* in relation to natural theology?[229] How should we conceptualize revelation in a way that allows Jesus in his uniqueness to be the starting point and criterion of true faith, since without him we have no access to the triune God at all?[230] Why is it of critical importance

---

[225]Johnson, *Quest for the Living God*, 98–100.

[226]Johnson, *She Who Is*, 201.

[227]Johnson, *Quest for the Living God*, 99.

[228]This question will be taken up in Chapter 6 when we discuss language for God in relation to the thinking of Thomas F. Torrance by specifically arguing that since patriarchalism as sin was overcome for the world in and through Jesus' life of perfect obedience, there really is no need to change the name for God in order for women to have equality with men in the church and in the world. That is what God himself accomplished for us as our Reconciler.

[229]This issue is taken up in Chapter 3 on natural theology and Torrance's "new" natural theology.

[230]This is the central question taken up in each chapter of this book with different implications in relation to each topic.

never to separate the Holy Spirit from the Father and Son?[231] Where does feminist religious experience have something to say to trinitarian development, and where does trinitarian theology have something to say to feminist religious experience? It is hoped that this chapter whets the appetite of readers to pursue greater understanding of the fact that all human beings have already been united with God in and through what God has accomplished in the life, death, and resurrection of his Son, so that this can best be understood when God is truly recognized and praised as the eternal Father, Son, and Holy Spirit who loves in freedom.

Given what was said above, it is clear that both Barth and Roman Catholics today think that Christ is and must be at the center of how they think about God and our relations with God. Especially since Vatican II, Catholic theologians have focused on Scripture as the primary source of revelation. They have also placed Christ at the center of theology in important ways. Yet, it is also clear that what still divides Catholics and Protestants is a version of the *analogia entis* which allows the Catholic theologians discussed here to reflect on who God is and who they are without first beginning with the revelation of God in its specificity with Jesus Christ and his Holy Spirit. Until that happens, our unity will at best be only partial and theoretical. That we all may be one is still something for which we must pray. That would be the primary question Barth might raise to today's post Vatican II Catholic approach to theology. Of course, from the feminist side, one key question to Barth might be whether or not, when he spoke of an eternal subordination or obedience of the Son as he did in CD IV, he had not read his own problematic view of the subordination of women to men back into the Godhead. But that would have to be a study for another day.

---

[231] This will be seen to be a critical issue in relation to our discussion of liberation theology in Chapter 5.

CHAPTER 3
KARL BARTH, THOMAS F. TORRANCE, AND THE "NEW" NATURAL THEOLOGY

When I originally wrote my article "Natural Theology Revisited,"[1] I drew a sharp contrast between Karl Barth's interpretation of natural theology and Thomas F. Torrance's view, which Torrance presented as his "new natural theology." After reading Alexander J. D. Irving's interpretation of Torrance's natural theology and his critique of my take on Torrance, I began to wonder whether I did not draw the contrast between them sharply enough! This chapter which appeared in a previous form as an article in *Participatio*, the *Journal of the Thomas F. Torrance Theological Fellowship*, will advance three key theses. First, I will interact with Alex Irving's articles responding to my interpretation of Torrance's "new" natural theology in order to demonstrate why I think Torrance's "new" natural theology is not in any sense a natural theology at all in spite of the fact that there are indeed residual elements of the natural theology Torrance explicitly rejects. Second, I will explain that in his response to my initial article comparing Barth and Torrance on natural theology Irving did not acknowledge the inconsistency in Torrance's own thought on the subject that I clearly demonstrated. Here I will clarify the problem by analyzing Torrance's analogy from geometry which I think misled him since that analogy functioned without taking into account the problem of sin and the need for reconciliation which permeates the rest of Torrance's thinking. Third, I will illustrate exactly why I think what Torrance actually presented with his "new" natural theology was a theology of reconciled human nature because his thinking finally is dictated by revelation as grace in its identity with Jesus Christ who overcomes our sin by enabling us to have the mind of Christ through the power of his Holy Spirit in faith. It should be noted at the outset that after I responded to Alex Irving with the article in *Participatio*, we had a number of discussions and came to some agreement that it was unhelpful for Torrance to call his approach to knowledge of God a "new" natural theology.

According to Irving, "theological science is … found to be constituted by a synthetic structure in which natural theology and revealed theology combine to the end of theological knowledge that is determined by God's self-revelation."[2] In other words,

---

[1] Paul D. Molnar, "Natural Theology Revisited: A Comparison of T. F. Torrance and Karl Barth," *Zeitschrift Für Dialektische Theologie* 20 (1) (2005): 53–83.

[2] Alexander J. D. Irving, "Natural Theology as the Intra-structure of Theological Science: T. F. Torrance's Proposals for Natural Theology in the Context of the Synthesis of Rational Structure and Material Content," *Participatio*, *The Journal of the Thomas F. Torrance Theological Fellowship* 7 (December 2017): 99–124, 99. In this quotation, as written, the claim made is that natural theology is somehow combined with revealed

"for Torrance, theology is a synthesis of natural theology as rational structure and the material content of our knowledge of God's self-revelation" such that "it is upon the natural co-operation of these two components that thought may be determined by reality."[3] How could one possibly reconcile this view with Barth's insistence that "what is 'God' to the natural man, and what he also certainly calls his 'God' is a false god"?[4] Indeed, according to Barth, "we cannot allow that it [natural theology] says anything about God at all, or that it is one of the assertions which have to be made in the Christian doctrine of God."[5] Moreover, in Barth's view, the logic of natural theology in whatever form "demands that, even if we only lend our little finger to natural theology, there necessarily follows the denial of the revelation of God in Jesus Christ. A natural theology which does not strive to be the only master is not a natural theology."[6] The answer concerning how the definition of theological science offered above and Barth's unequivocal rejection of natural theology with the idea that natural theology ceases to be natural theology when it functions within revelation clearly has to do with how one defines natural theology.

---

theology and is determined by God's self-revelation. One key point that I will make in this chapter is that this very assertion is problematic because by definition natural theology is an attempt to know God without revealed theology and without being determined by God's self-revelation. Accordingly, the moment natural theology is in fact determined by God's self-revelation, it ceases to be natural theology and becomes a theology of revelation. It may also be noted that in his book *Theology in Reconstruction* (London: SCM Press, 1965), Torrance viewed natural theology in a rather different way when he wrote, "We come now to the problem of natural theology, and here, too, it must be emphasized, Reformed theology takes its stand only within the inference from grace. When we come to know God in the Face of Jesus Christ, we know that we have not seen that Face elsewhere, and could not see it elsehow. Christ is the Way, the Truth, and the Life, and there is no door, nor way leading to the Father but by him. And so the natural wisdom of the world about God is made foolishness at the Cross, and our natural knowledge is completely set aside by the new creation" (109).

[3]Irving, "Natural Theology as the Intra-structure of Theological Science," 107.

[4]Barth, CD II/1, 86.

[5]Ibid., 84.

[6]Ibid., 173. In a podium discussion in Chicago in 1962, Barth responded to a Father Cooke who said that while there was an "essential difference between the knowledge of God arrived at in faith and that knowledge about God attained in natural theology (i.e., a philosophical approach to a transcendent being), is it not possible to bring these two knowledges to bear on one another and so enter into an integrated act of theologizing?" Eberhard Busch, ed., *Barth in Conversation: Volume 1, 1959–1962*, trans. The Translation Fellows of the Center for Barth Studies Princeton Theological Seminary, Karlfried Froehlich, German editor, Darrell L. Guder, English editor, David C. Chao, project manager (Louisville, KY: Westminster John Knox Press, 2017), 175. Barth noted Cooke's stress that there was an *essential* difference between the knowledge *of* God in faith and *about* God via natural theology, saying that was not accidental and that he loved him for that. He then said, "Yet you presuppose the identity of the Gods perceived by these two methods. My counterquestion is [this]: Are they identical?" If so, then why is there conflict between "knowledge of gods, deities … and so forth, and the revealed and faithful knowledge of those to whom God has spoken as the God of Abraham, Isaac, and Jacob … who is not the god of the philosophers?" (ibid.). Interestingly, Barth went on to say that since there is this distinction "it excludes identity" and that means "natural theology (as it is called and as you call it) and Christian theology cannot be integrated in one system" because one cannot attempt to serve Yahweh and Baal at the same time (ibid., 176).

Natural Theology Defined

To my knowledge, natural theology has always been defined in one way or another as referring to "a theology based on the natural light of reason, the dictates of conscience, or purported evidences of God in the processes of nature or the events of history. Natural theology is independent of God's revelation attested in Scripture and God's decisive self-communication in Jesus Christ."[7] This is certainly how Karl Barth understood it when he wrote that "natural theology is the doctrine of a union of humanity with God existing outside God's revelation in Jesus Christ."[8] It is "a theology which grounds itself on a knowability of God distinct from the grace of God, i.e., on a knowability of another God than Him knowable only in his grace."[9] According to the *Catechism of the Catholic Church*, natural theology is described as follows: "starting from movement, becoming, contingency, and the world's order and beauty, one can come to a knowledge of God as the origin and the end of the universe."[10] Indeed, it is said that "the Church teaches that the one true God, our Creator and Lord, can be known with certainty from his works, by the natural light of human reason (DS 3026)."[11] In their *Theological Dictionary*, Karl Rahner and Herbert Vorgrimler claim that natural theology is "a term applied to metaphysical ontology insofar as the general doctrine of being necessarily includes some statement about the absolute being of God."[12] What all these statements have in common is that they present natural theology as an activity of human reason, untouched by explicit faith in revelation as attested by the church in its confession of the Nicene faith, that is capable of understanding God by virtue of its own power, at least as the origin and end of the universe or as absolute being, however understood. Thomas F. Torrance seemed to understand natural theology this way as well when he wrote that "grace reveals that the natural man in the very motion of his mind is enmity to God. He is unable to know God, not only because he himself perverts the truth when it confronts him, but because God, who cannot be known against his will, that is, against his gracious self-revelation, will not reveal himself to human self-will and perversity."[13]

---

[7]Daniel L. Migliore, *Faith Seeking Understanding: An Introduction to Christian Theology*, 3rd edition (Grand Rapids, MI: Eerdmans, 2014), 459. See also James Barr, *Biblical Faith and Natural Theology: The Gifford Lectures for 1991 Delivered in the University of Edinburgh* (Oxford: Clarendon Press, 1993), who writes, "Traditionally, 'natural theology' has commonly meant something like this: that 'by nature,' that is just by being human beings, men and women have a certain degree of knowledge of God and awareness of him, or at least the capacity for such an awareness; and this knowledge or awareness exists anterior to the special revelation of God made through Jesus Christ, through the Church, through the Bible … it is this pre-existing natural knowledge of God that makes it possible for humanity to receive the additional 'special' revelation. The two fit snugly together" (1).
[8]Barth, CD II/1, 168.
[9]Ibid., 143.
[10]*Catechism of the Catholic Church* (Mahwah, NJ: Paulist Press, 1994), 15.
[11]Ibid., 18.
[12]Karl Rahner and Herbert Vorgrimler, *Theological Dictionary*, ed. Cornelius Ernst OP, trans. Richard Strachan (New York: Herder and Herder, 1965), 307.
[13]Torrance, *Theology in Reconstruction*, 110.

Torrance's "New" Natural Theology

So, the question that faces us here is this: did Torrance embrace such a knowledge of God in any sense at all, even with his "new" natural theology? If he did, then even his "new" natural theology contains a residue of this more traditional understanding which he was at pains to reject on scientific grounds, as Irving rightly contends. If he did not, then in reality, his theology is exclusively shaped by the revelation of God in Jesus Christ and not at all by some naturally known God understood apart from revelation and faith. In that case, it would be confusing and indeed mistaken for him to describe human knowledge of God determined by revelation as natural theology since, even in his own understanding, theology based on revelation needs God's reconciling grace to be rightly ordered to its unique object (which of course is the triune God who meets us in his Word and Spirit).

Put another way, natural theology, even according to Torrance's own understanding of theological science, cannot properly claim to know the one true God of Christian faith because he states, "We are prevented by the whole cast of our natural mind from apprehending God without exchanging His glory for that of a creature or turning His truth into a lie."[14] This leads him to argue that the Gospel requires of us a "radical change even in the inner slant of our mind, and in the structural capacities of our reason."[15] And, importantly, in his dogmatic work, he regularly cited Athanasius's statement that " 'it would be more godly and true to signify God from the Son and call him Father, than to name God from his works alone and call him Unoriginate' "[16] in order to stress that

> the possibility of our knowing God is grounded in His divine freedom to cross the boundary between Himself and us and to give Himself to be known by us within the conditions of our frailty on earth ... in an adaptation of humanity to God in which man is lifted up to know God above and beyond his natural powers.[17]

This takes place for us in the incarnation so that any attempt to know God that proceeds from his works alone will never acknowledge the unique deity and humanity of the Son and indeed will bypass God himself as he comes to us in the incarnation to reconcile us to himself from the divine and human side in Christ himself. It will, in other words, engage in an unscientific theology precisely because its thinking will not be "appropriate and adequate to the nature of the object of his knowledge."[18] Moreover, the incarnation itself, Torrance insists, "reveals that as a matter of fact man stands outside that relation with God in which true knowledge of Him is actualized, and cannot get

---

[14]Thomas F. Torrance, *Theological Science* (Oxford: Oxford University Press, 1978), 49. This same view is clearly presented in *Theology in Reconstruction* as the proper Reformed view of the matter (109–15).
[15]Torrance, *Theological Science*, 49.
[16]Torrance, *The Christian Doctrine of God, One Being Three Persons* 117; and Torrance, *The Trinitarian Faith: The Evangelical Theology of the Ancient Catholic Church* (Edinburgh: T&T Clark, 1988), 49.
[17]Torrance, *Theological Science*, 49–50.
[18]Ibid., 50.

inside it because in his very existence he is imprisoned in the closed circle of his own estrangement and self-will."[19] That is why Torrance claimed that "no self-willed or self-propelled motion by unrepentant man can make the slightest progress toward knowing God."[20]

Natural Theology: Natural to Its Object?

Given these assertions, it is at the very least confusing for Torrance to claim we need a natural theology that is natural to its object (God) since according to his belief that a proper natural theology can only function within revelation this cannot happen except on the basis of our justification by grace and faith. What he really presents us with therefore is not a natural theology at all but very definitely a theology of human nature based on grace and revelation and therefore an understanding of nature as it appears in light of our reconciliation in Christ and as that theology is actualized in us through the Holy Spirit.[21] Hence,

> in Him [Jesus Christ] there has already been fulfilled what we are unable to achieve, the reconciliation and adaptation and union of man with God, without which there is no true knowledge of God, so that in Him, in His true and obedient humanity, the Truth of God has been given and received for all men.[22]

Of course, Torrance's goal is to show that when nature is indeed perfected by grace it is not destroyed but rightly related with God,[23] without destroying but rightly empowering our human reasoning. Indeed, he quite properly argues that faith itself is "the orientation of the reason toward God's self-revelation, the rational response of man to the Word of God."[24] "Faith," he says, "is the behaviour of the reason in accordance with the nature of its divine Object."[25] But, as soon as faith and revelation are brought into the discussion as they must be, in order to do scientific theology, then that theology ceases to be a natural

---

[19]Ibid.

[20]Torrance, *Theology in Reconstruction*, 110.

[21]This is one reason why I agree with Colin Gunton that, while there may be parallel rationalities in the sciences of God and created realities and that "created and uncreated intelligibility" may be viewed together, it is preferable to speak in this context of a theology of nature rather than a transformed natural theology (Colin E. Gunton, *A Brief Theology of Revelation* [Edinburgh: T&T Clark, 1995], 63).

[22]Torrance, *Theological Science*, 51.

[23]Torrance cites Barth in this regard who held that when natural theology "is included and brought into clear light in the theology of revelation (*theologia revelata*); in the reality of divine grace is included the truth of the divine creation. In this sense it is true that 'Grace does not destroy nature but completes it' (*Gratia non tollit naturam sed perfecit*). The meaning of the Word of God becomes manifest as it brings into full light the buried and forgotten truth of the creation" (Karl Barth, *Theology and Church: Shorter Writings 1920–1928*, trans. Louise Pettibone Smith, introduction by Thomas F. Torrance [New York: Harper & Row, 1962], 342).

[24]Torrance, *Theological Science*, 33.

[25]Ibid.

theology and becomes instead a theology of revelation which includes human nature now living its reconciliation in Christ, as this is actualized in us through the power of the Holy Spirit.

Difficulties in Torrance's "New" Natural Theology

It was my contention in that original article and later to say simply that there were at least three difficulties present in Torrance's effort to develop what he calls his "new" natural theology: the first, as just noted, is that it is confusing because natural theology by definition is a theology that functions without necessarily relying exclusively on revelation and grace; second, natural theology, relying as it does on what can be known of God without revelation, knows nothing of the need for the radical repentance that Torrance also believes is necessary to rightly understand God and ourselves; and third, even Torrance's "new" natural theology, which is supposed to function exclusively within revelation, contains residual elements of "traditional" natural theology; and this opens the door to inconsistency because he thinks that it is possible to bracket natural theology from its proper object (revelation) for purposes of clarity. This possibility follows his use of the analogy of geometry which leads him to a view of natural theology that is benign in the sense that it could be characterized as being merely incomplete without four dimensional geometry;[26] the implication then is that natural theology is merely

---

[26]See Molnar, "Natural Theology Revisited," 60, where I noted that Torrance thinks geometry can function independently of physics in a certain limited way and that he uses the analogy that our human understanding of God "apart from the divine side of the bi-polar relationship which knowledge of God involves" amounts to an artificial methodological separation akin to "converting four-dimensional geometry back into three-dimensional Euclidean geometry, or physical geometry back into *a priori* geometry" (Thomas F. Torrance, *Reality and Scientific Theology* [Eugene, OR: Wipf and Stock, 2001], 59). Torrance claims this approach can only have a "quasi-validity" because of these artificially imposed limits (ibid., 60). On this basis Torrance argues that geometry when properly understood would not function independently of physics but instead would function as the "epistemological structure in the heart of physics, although considered in itself it would be *incomplete* without physics" (Thomas F. Torrance, *Reality and Evangelical Theology* [Philadelphia: Westminster Press, 1982], 33; and Torrance, *Reality and Scientific Theology*, 39, emphasis mine). It is this analogy, adapted from the thinking of Einstein, that leads to Torrance's inconsistency because on the one hand he claims (rightly) that our natural knowledge is twisted and inturned and cannot function accurately at all without reconciliation and grace. On the other hand, however, with his "new" natural theology, he thinks it is incomplete without revelation and only needs to be completed beyond itself to be accurate theology. That is the inconsistency. His entire theology of nature, which is built upon the doctrine of justification by grace and faith, demands that we see that we are self-willed and always use our natural reasoning in opposition to God. Furthermore, he insists that this cannot change unless and until we live as part of the new creation in and from Christ through the power of his Holy Spirit. My point then and now was and remains that a definite choice between these two opposing options is required, even according to Torrance's own scientific theology, and his new natural theology is an example of an approach that suggests, epistemologically, that choice is not absolutely necessary because natural theology does have a "quasi-validity" in spite of our self-will and sin. I contend that it does not, and that while both Barth and Torrance clearly saw this, Barth's thinking was more consistent on this point than was Torrance's. So, by introducing his "new" natural theology, I would say that far from this providing the "necessary but insufficient infrastructure of theology" (Alexander J. D. Irving, "Does the Epistemological Relevance of the Holy Spirit Mean the End for Natural Theology? A Response to Paul Molnar

incomplete without revelation and grace when in fact he also believes that our natural knowledge is not just incomplete but that it is "diseased," "twisted," and "in-turned" and needs God's grace to be put right.[27] For Torrance "we cannot truly know God without being reconciled and renewed in Jesus Christ. Thus the objectivity of our theological knowledge is immutably soteriological in nature."[28] In light of these views, it is problematic for Torrance to then claim that natural theology can be properly viewed only as the "space-time structure ... embedded in a ... realist theology"[29] because in fact natural theology, without the soteriological aspect that includes our need to be reconciled and renewed in Christ to know God, truly is in conflict with this benign view of it simply as a "space-time structure" of human thought.

It should be noted here that Torrance uses the analogy from geometry as a way to explain that Barth's objection to natural theology was only to an independent natural theology, that is, one that develops "in abstraction from the active self-disclosure of the living Triune God—for that can only split the knowledge of God into two parts, natural knowledge of the One God and revealed knowledge of the Triune God, which

---

with Reference to Thomas F. Torrance's Reconstruction of Natural Theology," *Trinity Journal* [2107]: 225–45, 243), Torrance has damaged his own pivotal insight that that "intrastructure" is itself damaged and cannot function rightly except through the power of the Holy Spirit. So at the crucial moment where grace would actually rule, Irving insists that "God's self-revelation must be cognized by us through the development of an appropriate rational structure through which the inherent Trinitarian structure of God's self-revelation is cognized. In this sense, it can be seen that Torrance's natural theology is about bringing human modes of thought and speech into coordination with God's self-revelation" (ibid., 244). While this may sound right to the untrained ear, what is said here is problematic because even according to Torrance's own theology, the only way we can "cognize" God's self-revelation is when, through grace, God himself enables that; it is not by developing an appropriate rational structure. That development *follows* an acknowledgement of grace as grace—it cannot provide the basis for that recognition at all since God alone in his reconciling movement towards us in the incarnation is the only basis for that. Thus, natural theology is not necessary here, and in reality it must give up this self-willed attempt to be the necessary but not sufficient presupposition of theology proper. Otherwise, the door is opened for a scientific theology that is not exclusively faithful to the unique object which is the triune God himself. Irving tellingly speaks of a "collaboration of divine act and human act" in this regard while paying lip service to the idea that the human act is "subordinate to and dependent upon the divine act" (ibid., 244). But, to the extent that natural theology can still function with any "quasi-validity" at all, then according to Torrance's trinitarian theology as it is based on reconciliation, as this has occurred for us in Christ, God's self-revelation simply cannot be the exclusive starting point and criterion for theology.
[27]Hence, Torrance writes, "Face to face with Christ our humanity is revealed to be diseased and in-turned, and our subjectivities to be rooted in self-will" (*Theological Science*, 310). Indeed, Torrance insists, "it was our diseased *mind* that our Lord assumed for our sakes. In assuming it, however, far from sinning himself or being estranged and alienated from the Father, even when he penetrated into the fearful depths of our alienation—'My God, my God, why have you forsaken me?'—he converted it from the very bottom of our disobedient human being, from the roots of our estranged mental existence, into perfect oneness with the mind of God—'Father, into thy hands I commit my spirit'" (*Atonement: The Person and Work of Christ*, ed. Robert T. Walker [Downers Grove, IL: IVP Academic, 2009], 441). This is why Torrance speaks of modern persons as afflicted by a deep-seated mental disease which leads them into subjectivism and false objectivism as well (see Paul D. Molnar, *Thomas F. Torrance Theologian of the Trinity* [Farnham: Ashgate, 2009], 191) referring to Torrance, "The Relevance of the Doctrine of the Spirit," *Theology in Reconstruction*, 231. This compares exactly to Barth's view that the cross and resurrection disclose us as enemies of grace and friends only in Christ's having overcome this enmity in relation to God (CD II/1, 140–57).
[28]Torrance, *Theological Science*, 41.
[29]See n. 36 below.

is scientifically as well as theologically intolerable."[30] Torrance is certainly right to argue against splitting knowledge of God into two parts, as he indicates. However, the moment he claims that natural theology must function within the revelation of the triune God, then natural theology ceases, to the extent that one's thought actually is functioning exclusively within revelation. That is the problem. Barth did not just reject an independent natural theology; he rejected all natural theology because, by definition, it did not begin and end its reflections exclusively with the revelation of God in Jesus Christ, thus allowing Christ to be the first and final Word in theology.

What Torrance was attempting to do, at least in part, was to pursue Athanasius's view in his *Contra Gentes* where "he showed that as we let our minds tune in to the rational order that pervades the universe, they are already on the way that leads to the really existent God."[31] However, Torrance says Athanasius made no attempt to reach God by "logical reasoning, but rather to point out a way of communing with the regulative and providential activity of God in the rational order of the universe, in which our minds come under the force of the truth of God as it bears upon us in its own self-evidence and shines through in its own light." And that, for Torrance, means that one learns of God not from some "cosmological reason, or *logos*," but "from the uncreated and creative *Logos* of God … so that as we contemplate the rational order in the creation, we are directed above and beyond ourselves to the one God, the Lord of creation."[32] Torrance connects Athanasius's *Contra Gentes* with his *De Incarnatione* which he calls its twin and concludes that "it is within the compass of that integrated theological understanding of creation and incarnation that we have embedded the argumentation that some would regard as 'natural theology.'"[33] Torrance claims that what Athanasius did here was to "show that knowledge of God and knowledge of the world share the same ultimate foundations in the *Logos*, or Rationality, of God the Creator."[34] His major point then is that "the knowledge of the world … cannot be abstracted and made to stand on its own" because such knowledge functions "only in a deep and unbreakable polarity with our actual knowledge of God revealed in and through Jesus Christ."[35]

This reasoning confirms my point in this chapter. When Torrance speaks of natural theology and of "new" natural theology, he is simply presenting a view of nature and its intelligibility from the vantage of revelation. And that then is a theology based on revelation; it is a theology of nature as reconciled by God in Christ. It simply is not natural theology in any traditional sense. But it is very evident in his reasoning here that his pervasive stress on the fact that our natural minds are twisted, diseased, and inturned without God's grace and revelation is almost invisible in his treatment of natural theology

---

[30]Thomas F. Torrance, *The Ground and Grammar of Theology* (Charlottesville, VA: University Press of Virginia, 1980), 90–1.
[31]Ibid., 76.
[32]Ibid., 76–7.
[33]Ibid., 77.
[34]Ibid.
[35]Ibid., 78.

in connection with his analysis of science and theology. Indeed, it is completely invisible when he applies his analogy from geometry. And that is not surprising since one does not need to have the mind of Christ to do geometry, either in its inadequate Euclidean form or in its proper form when united with physics. Moreover, if our minds really are twisted, inturned, and diseased as Torrance rightly claims apart from the grace of reconciliation, then what sense would it make to ascribe to the view he attributes to Athanasius that when we perceive the intelligibility of creation our minds are on the way toward God? It makes no sense at all because it is not the intelligibility of nature that directs us to the true God. Rather, according to his own often repeated view, it is the Holy Spirit uniting us to Christ and thus to the Father in faith who alone can and does do that.[36]

Enemies of Grace by Nature

The key point then in this context is that, as Barth repeatedly asserted, and as I think Torrance would agree, we are shown to be enemies of grace by nature in light of revelation. As Barth put it, in light of our "real determination by the judgment and grace of God, the fact is that finally and in the last resort man is always to be understood as the enemy of grace."[37] That of course is not the end of the story here, because Barth also

---

[36]Hence, when in relation to Barth's supposed rejection only of the independent nature of natural theology, Torrance claims that "as natural geometry is the space-time structure embedded in a dynamic and realist physics, so natural theology is the space-time structure embedded in a dynamic and realist theology. Looked at in this light Barth's exclusion of an independent natural theology assumes a formidable character" because no real "scientific inquiry" can allow itself to be controlled "by an independent logical structure" as "an indispensable precondition or a prior understanding for the inquiry in question" (Torrance, *Ground and Grammar*, 93). Here's the problem: natural geometry may be the space-time structure embedded in a realist physics. But natural theology simply cannot be regarded as the space-time structure embedded in a realist theology, even according to Torrance's own repeated insights, simply because it must be transformed through an encounter with God's grace and revelation to become true knowledge of the one true God! That is precisely why Torrance insists that in knowing God "the Word of God seizes our minds, sets up within their conceiving the force of its own rationality, and thus opens them to conceptual understanding of God" (Thomas F. Torrance, *God and Rationality* [London: Oxford University Press, 1971; reissued Edinburgh: T&T Clark, 1997], 22–3). Hence while "Knowledge of God in the Spirit is profoundly conceptual, rational knowledge in its own right, knowledge in which we are carried right over to what transcends us, yet which is apposite to the nature of God as *Spirit*," it must also be recalled that when God personally addresses us in his Word through his Spirit, God "opens us out toward Himself, and calls forth from us the response of faith and love, [and] He rehabilitates the *human subject*, sustaining him in his personal relations with God and his fellow creatures" (ibid., 188). It is the Spirit who emancipates us "from the prison-house of [our] own in-turned subjectivity" and makes us "free for genuinely objective experience" since we are thus "made open for God in [our] thinking and knowing and loving" through the personalizing work of the Holy Spirit (ibid., 189). Through our justification by faith, Torrance maintains that we are enabled "to share in the righteousness of God in Christ. Thus we are made to live in union with him and in the communion of the Holy Spirit who sheds the love of God into our hearts, and informs our life with the very mind of Christ the obedient Son of the Father" (Torrance, "The Atonement: The Singularity of Christ and the Finality of the Cross: The Atonement and the Moral Order," in *Universalism and the Doctrine of Hell: Papers Presented at the Fourth Edinburgh Conference in Christian Dogmatics, 1991*, ed. Nigel M. de S. Cameron [Carlisle, UK: Paternoster Press; Grand Rapids, MI: Baker Book House, 1992], 225–56, 254).
[37]Barth, CD II/1, 145.

claimed that our life of faith, which is enabled by the Holy Spirit since "the Holy Spirit is the temporal presence of Jesus Christ who intercedes for us eternally in full truth," refers to our "new birth from God."[38] Thus,

> faith extinguishes our enmity against God by seeing that this enmity is made a lie … expiated and overcome by Jesus Christ … and destroyed. Our truth is not the being which we find in ourselves as our own. The being which we find in ourselves as our own will always be the being in enmity against God. But this very being is a lie. It is the lie which is seen to be a lie in faith. Our truth is our being in the Son of God, in whom we are not enemies but friends of God, in whom we do not hate grace but cling to grace alone, in whom therefore God is knowable to us.[39]

Torrance's understanding of our knowledge of God is quite similar to this:

> God's Truth is His Person turning to us and condescending to become one with us that He may turn us to God in revelation and reconciliation. God does not have to do this. He is entirely free to live His own Life apart from us, but in His freedom He chooses to turn to us and give Himself to us to be known and loved … It is out of pure Grace that He gives Himself to us to know and think as the Truth … This communicating of the Truth in Jesus is not for God's sake, but for our sake … Therefore in all our knowledge of the Truth we have to look beyond ourselves, to appeal to what transcends us for justification … the Truth reveals that we are not in the Truth and delivers us from the vicious circle of our own untruth, reconciling us to the Truth and putting us in the right with it beyond us. That is the movement of God's Truth as Grace … which is the ultimate secret of the truth of our knowledge of God. It is because the Truth of God is His Grace that justification by Grace alone belongs to true knowledge of God—that is to say, the verification of theological statements is to be undertaken in terms of justification by Grace alone.[40]

In Torrance's view then,

> theological truth … has its essential *form* in the Life of Jesus in which He laid hold upon our mind and will and bent them back in Himself to perfect love and confidence in the Father … Unless theological statements participate in that glorification of the Father in Jesus, and so take the form of humble inquiry… they cannot be credited or sealed with a genuine *Amen*.[41]

---

[38]Ibid., 158.

[39]Ibid., 158–9.

[40]Torrance, *Theological Science*, 157–8.

[41]Ibid., 161. Indeed, "in Jesus Christ the Son of God entered into our rebellious humanity, laid hold of the human nature which we had alienated from the Father in disobedience and sin, and by living out from within it the life of the perfectly obedient Son he bent our human nature in himself back into obedience to the Father" (Torrance, *Theology in Reconstruction*, 126).

Thinking along these lines, Barth insisted that

> we cannot ascribe to man as such any readiness corresponding to the readiness of
> God ... If we try to presuppose any such thing we are treading on air. Man does
> not lend himself to the fulfilling of this presupposition. The knowability of God is
> not, therefore, to be made intelligible as the predicate of man as such.[42]

It is for this reason that Barth rejected the idea that there could be some sort of cooperation
with grace from the human side,[43] as is certainly implied in the above statement from
Irving that "natural theology and revealed theology combine to the end of theological
knowledge that is determined by God's self-revelation." In Barth's words,

> Though God could compete and co-operate with the creature—if He did not do
> this he would not be its Creator—there could not be even the remotest possibility
> of the creature competing and co-operating with God ... The reason is this. God
> is God and the creature is creature ... there can only be God's competition and
> co-operation with the creature, but not the reverse. An inversion would compromise

---

[42]Barth, CD II/1, 145. In his response to Brunner, Barth wrote, "Freedom to know the true God is a miracle,
a freedom of God, not one of our freedoms. Faith in the revelation of God makes this negation inevitable. To
contradict it would be unbelief ... How can man ever in any sense know 'of himself' what has to be known
here? He may know it *himself, yes!* But 'of himself,' never!" (Karl Barth, *Natural Theology: Comprising "Nature
and Grace" by Professor Dr. Emil Brunner and the Reply "No!" by Dr. Karl Barth*, trans. Peter Fraenkel, intro.
John Baillie (Eugene, OR: Wipf and Stock, 2002), 117).
[43]Referring to the coming of the kingdom of God for which we pray in the second petition of the Lord's prayer,
Barth makes two decisive remarks: (1) "As it is prayed for in the second petition, the kingdom is not a kind of
continuing, prolonging, excelling, and completing of what people may, as commanded, attempt and undertake
in a more or less rich understanding" (CD IV/4, *Lecture Fragments*, 240); (2) "The Lord does not reason or
discuss or debate with either demons or the men to whose help he hastens in doing what he does here. He
does not have to explain himself to them or justify himself before them. *He does not link up with their own
achievements. He does not concur or collaborate with them.* He simply goes his own way, the way of his own
honor and our salvation. That he should and will act thus is the promise that is given to Christians and it is as
such the summons and command to call upon him and to pray 'Thy kingdom come' " (ibid., 235, emphasis
mine). This thinking surely excludes any idea that knowledge of God's kingdom rests upon some sort of natural
cooperation between empirical and theoretical components of knowledge since the truth of our knowledge of
the kingdom rests exclusively upon God's grace and thus God's promise and command. Thus, while Irving is
correct to say that for Torrance knowledge is "devoted to and bound up with its object" (Irving, *Participatio*
[December 2017], 107) and that "to know objectively is to allow the structure of the object to determine the
structure of human thought" (ibid., 108), he neglects to mention that for Torrance we are incapable of knowing
God as he truly is apart from God's own *atoning action* in his Holy Spirit as the Spirit actualizing the atonement
completed in Christ's own life, death, and resurrection, thus enabling this knowledge on our part. That means
of course that true knowledge of God is not the result of our human cooperation and God's revelation, but
only the result of a knowledge that takes place in obedience to Christ himself. In his discussion of "ontologic,"
all that is mentioned is how human logic relates to empirical reality within creation—he leaves out Torrance's
all-important discussion of the logic of grace. That is the central problem that separates his view of Torrance's
"new" natural theology from mine. It is worth noting here, that in discussion of these issues, Alex Irving and
I have come closer because we both now are in agreement that this is an important point that must be taken
into account when considering Torrance's "new" natural theology.

and abrogate the very presupposition of the relationship: the character of God as God, and of the creature as creature.[44]

Complementarity? Natural Theology/Revealed Theology

The real issue here concerns the question of whether or not one can maintain that there is a "complementarity between the synthesis of natural and revealed theology and the synthesis of the logic of empirical form and the logic of systematic form" without fundamentally subverting Torrance's own insistence on the priority of the "Logic of Grace" which, according to Torrance, refers to

> the unconditional priority of the Truth as Grace and the irreversibility of the relationship established between the Truth and us. The Logic of Grace is the way the Truth has taken in His disclosure to us. Because He does not cease to be Grace in our knowing Him, all our thoughts and their interrelations must reflect the movement of Grace.[45]

Because there is what Torrance calls an "epistemological inversion of our relation to God,"[46] he insists that there is "no formal-logical relation between the death of Jesus

---

[44]Barth, CD II/1, 580.

[45]Torrance, *Theological Science*, 214. This is why Torrance insists that "I cannot love God through loving my neighbour. I can love my neighbour truly and only through loving God. To love God through loving my neighbour is to assert that the Incarnation is not a reality, the reality it is, that relation to God is still a mediated one. To love God through my love to my neighbour is to move toward God. It does not know a movement of God toward man" (*The Doctrine of Jesus Christ*, 88–9). For more on this, see Chapter 4 where Torrance's view of nonconceptual knowledge is placed in dialogue with Rahner's nonconceptual view of God. Torrance also helpfully links the logic of grace to analogy arguing for a dynamic rather than a static view of analogy and of the image of God in a way that avoids viewing these two important concepts in the manner of Augustine as "already lodged in the being of man" (*Theology in Reconstruction*, 114). Since both concepts are grounded in the motion of grace, they must be understood from "the hypostatic union … that is, upon the central relation and union of God and Man of which every other relation must partake" (ibid.). So, he naturally wanted to avoid an analogy of being that would support a static and "a logical (ontic-noetic) relation" that could be read directly from created being and a problematic view of grace as "a transferrable quality infused into and adhering in finite being, raising it to a different gradation where it can grasp God by a connatural proportion of being" (ibid.). For Torrance, "analogy must correspond with the essential motion of grace," and thus it cannot be grounded at all "upon the self-asserting or self-explanation of man" (ibid., 115). In Torrance's view, "all our natural theology is built upon this inverted analogy of grace" which moves from us instead of from a center in God provided for us in the incarnation (ibid.). Torrance follows Calvin and argues that Christian *metanoia* occurs "when the believer, transformed by the renewing of his mind, knows that he has not chosen Christ, but that Christ has chosen him; that his knowing of God is grounded on his being known of God; and that every analogy of men, such as fatherhood, is grounded reflexively upon the action and love of the heavenly Father, after whom every fatherhood in heaven and earth is named" (ibid., 116). But this means that all theological knowledge must be grounded in "the *ordo essendi* (order of being) conceived entirely as grace" so that "the *ordo essendi* reaches its true destiny in the *ordo cognoscendi*" (the order of knowledge). Apart from grace, "the truth of God is inevitably turned into a lie" (ibid.).

[46]Torrance, *Theological Science*, 215. This thinking illustrates Torrance's own approach which always moves from a center in God provided in the incarnation and outpouring of the Holy Spirit. Hence, he says, "the

Christ on the Cross and the forgiveness of our sins"[47] even though there certainly is a relation. But that relation "is established by divine action and discerned through faith."[48] Thus, our knowledge of God is grounded in God's knowing us such that "our act of faith is grounded on God's decision of Grace to give Himself to us and to choose us for Himself."[49]

For Torrance, then, our decisions for God are rooted in "election" which for him means "the prevenient movement of God's love that is so incarnated in Jesus Christ that in Him we have both the pure act of divine Grace toward man and the perfect act of man in obedient response toward God's Grace."[50] In other words, because Christ lived a life of perfect obedience, appropriating God's grace for our benefit by standing in for us before God the Father, he "actualised in Himself the Truth of God translating it into His human life, that we may know the Truth in and through Jesus Christ."[51] For this reason, Torrance can say that "every theological doctrine must reflect in its way, directly or indirectly, the unconditional priority of the Grace of God if it is to be faithful to the Truth."[52] That of course must mean that in reality in light of a proper theology of human nature, there is no "quasi-validity" to any independent natural theology, as Torrance claimed there was based on his analogy between natural theology and geometry.

The key question then that arises in connection with Irving's thought-provoking but problematical article concerns whether or not Torrance's reconstructed natural theology is natural theology in the traditional sense described above at all. According to Irving, the answer seems to be no because Torrance insists that natural theology must be natural to its proper object, namely, the God who has revealed himself in Jesus Christ. But, as noted above, if theology begins and ends with faith in Christ as God's self-revelation, then in reality it is a theology of revelation based on grace and not nature; it is a theology that is determined exclusively by the unique object of Christian faith and not by any naturally known God either as absolute being or as the origin and end of the

---

Incarnation, as culminating in the Cross and the Resurrection, is the great act of God in which he entered our perverted order of nature, and wrought the basic soteriological inversion by which we are reconciled to God. But that basic soteriological inversion must be pushed through the whole region of the mind, inasmuch as we are alienated from God, as Calvin said, 'in the whole of our mental system'" (Torrance, *Theology in Reconstruction*, 115–16). Torrance argues that "the inner life of the Holy Trinity which is private to God alone is extended to include human nature in and through Jesus … because of the atonement that took place in him, for now that the enmity between God and man has been abolished, God the Holy Spirit may dwell in the midst of mortal sinful man. That is the way that the divine love has taken to redeem man, by making him share in the holy power in which God lives his own divine life" (ibid., 241). It is the Holy Spirit then who comes to us only in the name of Jesus (ibid., 247) and is "the immediate Agent of our worship" and "of its renewal, he who realizes in us the recreative power of the risen and glorified Humanity of Christ" (ibid., 250). This means of course that the Spirit does not just continue a work begun by Christ which he left off at some point but that it is "through the Spirit, in and with his coming" that "Christ himself returns to be present among us" (ibid., 253).
[47]Torrance, *Theological Science*, 214–15.
[48]Ibid., 215.
[49]Ibid.
[50]Ibid.
[51]Ibid.
[52]Ibid., 215–16.

universe or perhaps as an "imperious constraint from beyond" as Torrance himself once claimed. We will return to this in a moment.

Either/Or Choice

For now, it seems clear that an either/or choice is required here. But, just as certainly, it seems from this presentation that Torrance's "new" natural theology can still be called natural theology because it is supposed to be seen as the "infra-structure"[53] or, as Torrance also called it, the "intrastructure" of revealed theology. This means that Torrance "had in view a rational structure that had been transposed into the material content of theology."[54] But, if that is true, then by his own definition, this is no longer natural theology as traditionally understood. It is a theology based upon and shaped exclusively by revelation and grace.[55] The problem we are concerned with here then is that either a theology is based on revelation and grace or it is based on some sort of natural knowledge that is confirmed by and then clarified by revelation; in which case

---

[53]Irving, *Participatio*, 105.

[54]Ibid.

[55]Here, it seems, we are very close to what Torrance really seemed to be after in his pursuit of a "new" natural theology. So he said that he did not want to "deny natural theology, as such, for that would mean a denial of the natural man in his actual existence, but it does mean that a Christian theology cannot be built upon a carnal foundation: to do that would be to open the flood-gates of naturalism and to inundate the Church with paganism" (Torrance, *Theology in Reconstruction*, 112). If we connect these remarks with what Torrance also says when he claims that "justification by the grace of Christ alone, does not mean that there is no natural knowledge—what natural man is there who does not know something of God even if he holds it down in unrighteousness or turns the truth into a lie? But it does mean that the whole of that natural knowledge is called in question by Christ who when he comes to us says: 'If any man will come after me, let him deny himself, take up his cross and follow me'" (ibid., 162-3). So it seems that Torrance, like Barth, did not want to eliminate natural theology from the face of the earth since that is all the "natural man" has who does not yet or no longer recognizes God's grace and revelation in its identity with Jesus Christ. That is why Barth said that "natural theology is the only comfort of the natural man in life and death. A captious, untenable, false, pernicious comfort no doubt—but this is the very thing which cannot be seen by the man who has shunned the possibility of real comfort" (CD II/1, 169). But Barth simply would not allow that natural theology said anything that is true about the true God at all because it was essentially built on the human self-expression of someone who is essentially engaged in the process of self-justification and who, in that way, "makes himself equal to God" (CD II/1, 168). Additionally, however, for Torrance the important point he wanted to stress in his pursuit of a "proper" natural theology is that "there is a proper place for rational argumentation in what is traditionally known as 'natural theology'" (Torrance, *Space, Time and Resurrection* [London: T&T Clark, 2019], 1). He identified a "proper natural theology" as one "in which form and content, method and subject-matter, are not torn apart—that is, not a 'natural theology' as an *independent* conceptual system, *antecedent* to actual empirical knowledge of God" (ibid.). Torrance's view of a "proper natural theology" is one that allows for the fact that God as Creator is "intelligibly accessible to our understanding" and "actively at work within the world in revealing himself in cognitive ways to those whom he has made for communion with himself. Divine revelation and intelligible content belong inseparably together" (ibid., 1–2). However, it is just in these reflections that the problem I have identified with Torrance's "new natural theology" is evident. The moment Torrance brings revelation into the picture, as he must, since he thinks natural theology has to function within revelation, he is no longer doing natural theology at all but a theology in which knowledge God is achieved through revelation, grace, and faith.

the exclusive criterion of truth ceases to be grace and, in some sense, becomes nature which, according to both Barth and Torrance, needs to be reconciled and was indeed reconciled in Christ, but now must live from and in that "new" humanity that is ours in Christ, *before* we can think theologically.

This is an exceptionally important and often overlooked issue. Can we view natural theology benignly simply by thinking of it as incomplete (as Torrance sometimes does) apart from revelation, so that it is completed in revelation? Or must we think of natural theology as the attempt by sinful human beings to know God without actually relying on revelation as grace from start to finish, as Torrance also does? This is made all the more difficult by the fact that natural theology, even as the "new" natural theology envisioned by Torrance, might claim to be subordinate to revelation, but notwithstanding that claim, it would not in reality be truly subordinate to the revelation of God in Christ to the extent that it could still be described as natural theology.

In reality, I am arguing that natural theology is not the necessary presupposition of revealed theology; rather that presupposition is our "new" humanity that has been restored in the humanity of the incarnate Word so that the infrastructure of a theology of grace itself can only be seen and described in faith as it is tied to Christ and enabled by the miraculous action of the Holy Spirit. Undoubtedly, Torrance also affirms this when, in his important book *Space, Time and Resurrection*, he rightly claims that we would have no objective knowledge of the true God without Christ's own resurrection from the dead. Thus,

> the resurrection is therefore our pledge that statements about God in Jesus Christ have an objective reference in God, and are not just projections out of the human heart and imagination … The resurrection demonstrates not only that all division has been removed in atoning reconciliation, but that atoning reconciliation has achieved its end in the new creation in which God and man are brought into such communion with one another that the relations of man with God in being and knowing are healed and fully established.[56]

In this chapter, I am contending that when anyone depicts scientific theology as cooperating with revelation and thus suggests that natural and revealed theology *together* make up what Torrance called theological science, then the heart of theology as a creaturely act within the *new* creation is compromised.

It is Torrance's somewhat inconsistent answer to these questions that has led some who embrace his "new" natural theology to think that "the human mind possesses the capacity to recognize this work of creation as such [which all would of course agree with], and to draw at least some reliable conclusions concerning the nature and character of God from the created order [which Barth firmly and consistently rejects and Torrance firmly rejects, except on occasion, when relating theological and natural science to each

---

[56]Torrance, *Space, Time and Resurrection*, 72–3.

other]."[57] In his consideration of "natural revelation," Barth freely admitted that God had made himself objectively known in creation but because of sin and self-will human beings could not actually understand that natural revelation except through Christ and the Spirit. This view by Barth may also have been what Torrance was after with his "new" natural theology; but again, for both theologians the fact is that even this "natural revelation" is not natural theology in any recognizably traditional sense.

Alister McGrath

Consider also the following statement from Alister McGrath, who claims to be developing his thought on the basis of Torrance's "new" natural theology within the ambit of revelation:

> There is an essential harmony between the Christian vision of the world, and what may actually be known of it. In developing this point, we would argue that Christian theology provides an ontological foundation which confirms and consolidates otherwise fleeting, fragmentary glimpses of a greater reality, gained from the exploration of nature without an attending theoretical framework. A traditional natural theology can be thought of as drawing aside a veil briefly, partially, and tantalizingly, eliciting an awareness of potential insight, and creating a longing to be able to grasp and possess whatever is being intimated. What is transient and fragmentary is clarified and consolidated from within the standpoint of the Christian tradition, which is able to affirm whatever can be known in this tantalizing manner, while clarifying it and placing it upon a firmer foundation in the divine *logos*.[58]

---

[57]Alister E. McGrath, *Scientific Theology: Volume I Nature* (Grand Rapids, MI: Eerdmans, 2001), 299. Also, Alister E. McGrath, *A Fine-Tuned Universe: The Quest for God in Science and Theology: The 2009 Gifford Lectures* (Louisville, KY: Westminster John Knox Press, 2009) where instead of realizing that when Colin Gunton said everything looks different in light of the Trinity he meant to offer a proper theology of nature, McGrath mistakenly assumes he was supporting his (McGrath's) view of natural theology. Thus, McGrath concludes, with Moltmann, that "we must learn to think of the 'world of nature as bearing the prints of the Triune God'" (70). Of course if this is in any sense true, then we can look to nature as well as to revelation to understand the mystery of the Trinity. And that is exactly what Barth, Gunton, and Torrance all vigorously rejected!

[58]Alister E. McGrath, *The Open Secret: A New Vision for Natural Theology* (Oxford: Blackwell, 2008), 248. Strangely, while this position clearly depicts Christian theology as affirming what can be known of God through natural theology in the traditional sense, and carrying it forward, in another context, he recognizes that this approach could be questioned in light of a proper trinitarian theology. See McGrath, *A Fine-Tuned Universe*, 63. Yet, even that does not stop McGrath from proposing a "Trinitarian natural theology" in which he claims to be following Barth and says "Revelation is thus not limited to the divine self-disclosure, but to the matrix of actions and frameworks which enable this self-disclosure to be recognized as such and appropriated as revelation" (ibid., 72). Accordingly, this "matrix" includes "social embodiments ... such as worship, the recital of creeds, and the public reading of Scripture—and the influence of God" (ibid., 72). For Barth, the only one who could enable God's self-disclosure to be recognized is God himself and not any framework. Thinking this way, however, McGrath claims that nature can indeed "render the character of God to a limited

There can be little doubt that Irving's inadequate reading of my analysis and critique of Torrance's "new" natural theology will further the confusion embodied in Alister McGrath's problematic construction of his own natural theology. Here it should be noted that McGrath's thinking goes beyond anything that Torrance himself would countenance with his apologetic intent to appeal to those with or without faith in the Christian God. He argues that the apologetic value of a "legitimate natural theology" will allow us to see that "the Christian evangelist will have a number of 'points of contact' for the gospel within the created order."[59] This assertion is directly antithetical to the view of Torrance and Barth that there is in reality only one point of contact for the Gospel and that is Jesus Christ himself. That is why Torrance insisted that "the Humanity of Christ is thus crucially significant for the saving knowledge of God by man ... It is the human form and reality of Jesus of Nazareth which is the necessary 'point of contact' or *Anknüpfungspunkt* for our Salvation, the necessary ... bridge between God and man, and man and God."[60]

McGrath also believes that all acts of understanding are based upon some pre-understanding. Thus, he claims that "nature has to be seen in a certain way before it has revelatory potential," and this "depends upon the assumptions which the observer brings to the act of observation." Therefore, "the act of the interpreter is based upon a *Vorverständnis*, a 'pre-understanding' which is brought to this act by the observer on account of his or her standing within a tradition of discourse."[61] While certain interpretative frameworks do not allow "any significant connection between the world as we observe it and the nature of God," McGrath alleges that a connection can be asserted

---

extent" and maintains, following Gerard Manley Hopkins, that created entities have the "capacity to signify their creator" and from this he embraces Emil Brunner's idea that "God has bestowed upon his works 'a permanent capacity for revelation...' which can be discerned through human contemplation of the 'traces of his own nature which [God] has expressed and made known in them' " (ibid., 74). All of this is what Barth explicitly rejected in rejecting natural theology. But it is this kind of problematic thinking that ensues when one supposes that Torrance's "new" natural theology authorizes this type of understanding of revelation. This is why Torrance's "new" natural theology is so problematic: it leads those who think he was embracing a "benign" natural theology to ignore a major theme of his theology which, with Barth, forcefully asserted that the only way to truly know God is through God himself and not through reflection on nature. It leads McGrath to state that his more modest and realistic natural theology is "based on the idea of a resonance or 'empirical fit' between the Christian worldview and what is actually observed. The Christian faith, grounded ultimately in divine self-revelation, illuminates and interprets the natural world; the 'Book of Scripture' enables a closer and more fruitful reading of the 'Book of Nature' " (ibid., 218). Here it is worth noting that for Barth the creation of worldviews is just another indication of what happens when our actual reconciliation in Christ himself is ignored or marginalized. Creating worldviews represents an active human attempt to come to terms with revelation and reconciliation by incorporating God's act of grace into a view of reality which then becomes the criterion for grace itself. Barth says, "a world-view is the glorious possibility of evading" the offensive nature of revelation as grace which comes to us as a "radical, warm and unconditional Yes" which strikes us "from without and from a superior height." He says, "So long as man, viewing the world, is observer, constructor and manager, he is safe, or at any rate thinks he is safe from this offence [namely, that someone can only say yes to himself or herself, but only] as "an answer to the Yes said to him [by God in Jesus Christ]" (CD IV/3.1, 257).
[59]McGrath, *Scientific Theology*, 299.
[60]Torrance, *The Doctrine of Jesus Christ*, 136–7.
[61]McGrath, *Scientific Theology*, 298.

only if three conditions are met. First, "the created order is held to be the work of the Christian God, not any other entity"; second, "the act of creation was not determined or significantly influenced by the quality of the material which was ordered through this act"; and third "that the human mind possess the capacity to recognize this work of creation as such, and to draw at least some reliable conclusions concerning the nature and character of God from the created order."[62] He then claims that these three insights were "secured through the Christian revelation."[63]

But that is exactly the problem. Neither Torrance nor Barth are willing to admit that any pre-understanding that we bring to the encounter with God in Christ can be allowed any determinative function here at all since it is only God who can heal our minds such that they may know the truth.[64] When that happens, they claim, it is the result of God's forgiving grace actualized through the Holy Spirit in us enabling our freedom and is not at all the result of any capacity of ours to draw conclusions about God from the world. Here is where McGrath has introduced a version of traditional natural theology that is clearly at variance with the thinking of both Barth and Torrance. McGrath mistakenly believes that it "is wrong to treat natural theology and revealed theology as being opposed to each other, *provided* that nature is construed in a trinitarian manner as the creation of the self-revealing God."[65]

But according to both Barth and Torrance we know from God's self-revelation, as seen above, that we are enemies of grace, that our minds are diseased and twisted apart from Christ the reconciler. And human nature is what it is as fallen and as justified by grace alone whether we construe it in a trinitarian or some other manner. In other words, our construal of nature does not make our vision of nature true to what it actually is. That our vision is true depends entirely upon the nature of creation as created by God and as fallen, justified, and sanctified by God in Christ and through his Spirit.[66] McGrath thinks, "Natural theology cannot become a *totally* autonomous discipline, independent of revelation, in that it depends for its credibility upon the revealed insight that God is creator of the natural order."[67] But Barth and Torrance based their entire theologies on

---

[62]Ibid., 299.

[63]Ibid.

[64]Thus, Torrance insisted that the objective presence of the Holy Spirit "opening us up within our subjectivities for Christ … is the objectivity that will not allow us to confuse the Holy Spirit with our own spirits … It is an objectivity that demands the renunciation of ourselves, with all their pre-understanding … It is precisely by taking in all its terrible seriousness the objection of God to our sin, and the fulfilment of that objection in the Incarnation and Atonement … that we are healed of the mental and spiritual disease in which we fail to distinguish our own subjective conditions from objective realities" (*Theology in Reconstruction*, 238–9). See also Torrance, *Christian Doctrine of God*, 153–4.

[65]McGrath, *Scientific Theology*, 296.

[66]That is why Torrance insists that "we have to think of this triumph of the Kingdom of God [over sin, darkness, and evil] merged with the Person of the crucified and risen Lord Jesus as a triumph not just over a difference, vast as it is, between the created realm, to which we belong, and God, but a triumph over a fallen, twisted and alienated world which exists in direct *opposition* to God, while nevertheless being continuously sustained by his omnipotent grace" *Christian Doctrine of God*, 225.

[67]McGrath, *Systematic Theology*, 296, emphasis mine. This assertion once again illuminates the problem being discussed in this chapter because McGrath presumes that natural theology depends upon what he calls a revealed insight that God is the Creator of the natural order. However, since it is God the Father almighty who

the fact that natural theology has *no* autonomy at all because, as Barth bluntly put it, "if we look past Jesus Christ, if we speak of anyone else but Him, if our praise of man is not at once praise of Jesus Christ, the romance and the illusions begin again."[68] Then

> we fall back again into the aspect under which it is impossible to see, or with a good conscience to speak about, the man who is ready for God in life and truth … in the doctrine of the knowledge and knowability of God, we have always to take in blind seriousness the basic Pauline perception of Colossians 3:3 which is that of all Scripture—that our life is our life hid with Christ in God. With Christ: never at all apart from Him, never at all independently of Him, never at all in and for itself. Man never at all exists in himself … Man exists in Jesus Christ and in Him alone; as he also finds God in Christ and in Him alone. The being and nature of man in and for themselves as independent bearers of an independent predicate, have, by the revelation of Jesus Christ, become an abstraction which can be destined only to disappear.[69]

There is not one word here of what Barth says that Torrance would disagree with, and thus I believe he himself would respond to McGrath's affirmation that "there is an intrinsic capacity within the created order to disclose God" rather negatively. McGrath claims that this capacity within the created order is somehow grounded in the covenant and thus is not an assertion of an *analogia entis*. He even cites Torrance's view that creation

> cannot be interpreted or understood out of itself, as if it had an inherent likeness or being to the Truth, but only in light of the history of the covenant of grace … Reformed theology certainly holds that God reveals himself in creation, but not by some so-called "light of nature," and it certainly holds that God's revelation makes use of and is mediated through a creaturely objectivity, but it does not hold that an examination of this creaturely objectivity of itself can yield knowledge of God.[70]

And yet McGrath's basic thesis for his new natural theology that supposedly functions exclusively within revelation hinges on his assertion "that the human mind possesses the capacity to recognize this work of creation as such, and to draw at least some reliable conclusions concerning the nature and character of God from the created order."[71]

---

alone is that creator of the natural order, therefore if one is faithful to the fact that we only know the Father through his Son, then once again such insights result from revelation through faith and not at all from natural theology of any kind.

[68]Barth, CD II/1, 149.

[69]Ibid. There is no doubt that Torrance would agree with this as he also asserts that the Holy Spirit opens us for Christ "in such a radical way that we find our life *not in ourselves but out of ourselves, objectively in him*" (*Theology in Reconstruction*, 238). See also Torrance, *The Trinitarian Faith*, 19, 47, 52–3, 69, 73, and 78.

[70]Torrance, *The School of Faith*, cited in McGrath, *Scientific Theology*, 297.

[71]McGrath, *Scientific Theology*, 299.

To put this matter rather decisively, the issue that I am raising here concerns the consistency of Torrance's own belief that God himself is the only one who can make us aware of who he truly is; and this happens only as God himself through his Holy Spirit and thus through union with Christ and on the basis of reconciliation itself enables our proper knowledge of who he is and who we are in Christ. Can traditional natural theology actually draw aside the veil and elicit an awareness of the triune God, as McGrath thinks? Can revealed theology be correctly grasped if it is conceptualized as simply clarifying some sort of fragmentary knowledge of God which McGrath thinks is available to us in our natural theology and then placing it on a firmer foundation as McGrath believes?

Barth's answer to these questions was an unequivocal No because he very consistently maintained that all of our knowledge of God was enabled by the grace of God in its identity with God's act of revelation and reconciliation in the person and work of Jesus Christ. Torrance clearly followed Barth in this since both argued that true knowledge of God could only occur on the basis of our justification and sanctification by grace and through faith. Those who embrace Torrance's "new" natural theology also espouse the seemingly innocuous statement that this natural theology must function within revelation. But perhaps this is not so innocuous after all. For even on Torrance's own reckoning, there is no way from human logic to the logic of grace (which is never mentioned by Irving but which is decisive in Torrance's book *Theological Science* in a way which places his theological perspective much closer to Barth's at that point, as indicated above). According to Torrance, our minds need to be reconciled through the action of the Holy Spirit (which is also not featured in Irving's articles) *before* we can truly know God from a center in God and not from a center in ourselves.[72] He spells this out in his *Theological Science* and in *God and Rationality*. The question that Barth raised is whether natural theology in *any form* (new or old) really can allow revelation to be its *exclusive* source for understanding who God is. We have just seen that McGrath's thinking also demonstrates that a choice is required here. Therefore, I would say things are not as clear as Irving makes them out to be in the articles referred to above.

Artificially Separating Revealed and Natural Theology

While Irving mistakenly claims that I have misinterpreted Torrance for bracketing his "new" natural theology from revelation for purposes of clarification, the fact is that I have understood exactly what he was attempting to do; he was attempting to hold that the "logic of empirical form has a nascent coherence owing to its determination by the material context of reality," as Irving puts it, so that "natural theology 'still retains the imprint of its empirical origins and foundations.'" Thus, natural theology's propositions can be properly evaluated "by artificially separating revealed and natural theology."[73]

---

[72]See also Torrance, *Ground and Grammar*, 154–5; and Torrance, *The Trinitarian Faith*, 19, 47–58 and 69–75.
[73]Irving, *Participatio*, 106–7.

We are thus told that this artificial and temporary separation will allow us to "test its coherency and verify the connection between natural theology and revelation."[74]

Yet, according to Torrance's own theology as it is shaped by revelation, he claims, together with Barth, that no analogies or concepts are true in themselves and that theological propositions simply cannot be verified except through revelation and grace, as discussed above. In Torrance's words,

> Justification by putting us in the right with the Truth of God calls in question all that claims to be knowledge of the truth on our part and calls into question our theological statements in so far as they claim to have truth in themselves, and directs them away from themselves to Christ as the one Truth of God ... in so doing justification establishes us in certainty [by grounding all our knowledge and action upon] the divine Reality in Christ.[75]

This is why he insists that Jesus is an "ultimate." This means that who he is and the truth that he reveals cannot be verified on any other ground than that which he himself provides. But that ground, in Torrance's view, is the revelation of God attested in Scripture and given in the deposit of faith. It is not to be found in natural theology at all. Here then once again is the real problem that is never adequately addressed by Irving: how can natural theology possibly be considered as a cooperative feature of our knowledge of revelation without actually reversing what Barth and Torrance considered to be an irreversible relationship, that is, the relationship between nature and grace as discussed above?

An example of the difficulty being discussed here can be seen in the following statements once made by Torrance:

> Justification by the grace of Christ alone, does not mean that there is no natural knowledge—what natural man is there who does not know something of God even if he holds it down in unrighteousness or turns the truth into a lie? But it does mean that the whole of that natural knowledge is called into question by Christ who when he comes to us says: "If any man will come after me, let him deny himself, take up his cross and follow me." The whole man with his natural knowledge is therefore questioned down to the root of his being, for man is summoned to look away from all that he is and knows or thinks he knows to Christ who is the Way the Truth and the Life; no one goes to the Father but by him.[76]

---

[74]Ibid., 107.

[75]Torrance, *Theological Science*, 201. In fact, Torrance insists that "our ideas and conceptions and analogies and words are twisted in untruth and are resistant to the Truth" (ibid., 49). See also Torrance, *Theology in Reconstruction*, 55, 90–1, 163, and 270, as well as *Christian Doctrine of God*, 43, 73, and 76. In *Karl Barth, Biblical and Evangelical Theologian* (Edinburgh: T&T Clark, 1990), Torrance writes, "Theology by its very nature must renounce any claim to possess truth in its own theological statements" (59).

[76]Torrance, *Theology in Reconstruction*, 162–3. Karl Barth's understanding of "natural revelation" as depicted by George Hunsinger comes close to what Torrance is saying here. But by designating this "natural revelation," the confusion that follows from designating it "natural theology" is avoided. And the point is made clear. For Barth,

Here, two comments are in order. First, Torrance is certainly claiming some sort of natural knowledge of God here in the traditional sense while also acknowledging that as sinners we cut ourselves off from the Truth.[77] Could this perhaps explain why he can also say that created intelligibility points beyond itself "with a mute cry for sufficient reason"[78] so that "the fact that the universe is intrinsically rational means that it is capable of or open to, rational explanation—from beyond itself"?[79] While this may be so, one wonders how the universe can offer a mute cry as nature since, as Torrance insists, nature in itself is dumb and needs us as priests of creation to bring to light its intelligibility.[80] In any case,

---

"natural revelation was not absolutely ruled out, but it was reinterpreted from a center in Christ" (*Evangelical, Catholic and Reformed: Doctrinal Essays on Barth and Related Themes* [Grand Rapids, MI: Eerdmans, 2015], 99). Importantly, however, for Barth "God could not be known, even through natural revelation, without God's bringing the human subject into living union with himself (II/1, 105)" (ibid.). That bringing into living union is what is marginalized by all worldviews.

[77]McGrath himself sidesteps this issue claiming that the "extent to which the human mind and will have been affected by sin is contested within the Christian tradition" (*Scientific Theology*, 292). But he argues that "there is widespread agreement that the human situation is characterized by some such diminution in the human epistemic capacity to discern, and subsequently to respond appropriately to, God" (ibid., 293). By contrast, Barth and Torrance are both claiming that, in light of revelation, we know that our ability to know God in truth apart from Christ is not just diminished but is impossible. Of course, McGrath speaks of atonement in *A Fine-Tuned Universe*, but for him that means a transformed vision in which we see things differently (39, 218) while for Torrance and Barth it means recognizing our utter dependence on the living Christ to empower us to know the Father through the power of his Holy Spirit.

[78]This statement of course conflicts with Torrance's own remark that creation as such is dumb and needs us as priests of creation to bring to light its intelligibility. See Torrance, *God and Rationality*, 41; and Torrance, *Reality and Evangelical Theology*, 26–7. See also Torrance, *Ground and Grammar*, 5–6.

[79]Torrance, *Reality and Scientific Theology*, 52.

[80]See Molnar, *ZDTh*, 55, n. 11. Torrance writes, "Nature after all is dumb; she cannot talk back to us. Hence we must not only frame the questions we put to nature but also put into the mouth of nature the answers she is to give back to us" (*God and Rationality*, 41). These important remarks are, to say the least, not easily reconcilable with the following remarks made by Torrance in another setting: "in listening to nature or giving ear to what it has to say, the hearer is summoned to respond to a word or communication from what Walter Thorson has called 'the objective other'" (Thomas F. Torrance, *The Christian Frame of Mind: Reason, Order, and Openness in Theology and Natural Science* [Colorado Springs: Helmers & Howard, 1989], 80). This certainly would make sense in connection with Torrance's idea that auditive knowing "is most marked in communication between persons when the objective other is not just an object but a subject" (ibid.). And, when applied to knowledge of God, this leads Torrance to say that "the unqualified weight of the emphasis is upon God" (ibid., 80–1). The point here, however, is that if nature is indeed dumb and cannot talk back to us, what sense does it make to claim that we should give ear to what nature has to say? Again, it is in the context of his relating science and theology that these inconsistencies seem to arise. Indeed it is again in the context of this very discussion that another indication of the residue of the old natural theology that Torrance rejects seems present as when he says, "The mysterious imperative that bears upon him [the scientist] from the fundamental nature of things in the universe, of which he is implicitly aware in his desire to understand *why* things are what they actually are and how they *ought* to be what they are or are still to become, will resonate with the creative *purpose* of God disclosed through his Word in such a way that an ultimate belief in the *goodness of the created order* will take its place in the controlling framework of his inquiries" (ibid., 82). However, both Barth and Torrance insist that we really do not know God's creative purposes properly apart from the incarnation through which we know God the Father almighty as Creator in the first place. Moreover, we do not recognize properly the goodness of creation apart from knowing that goodness in light of the covenant which was fulfilled in Christ himself.

Torrance reasons that since the universe is intrinsically rational and open to explanation from beyond, therefore this

> *suggests*, or directs us to, a transcendent ground of rationality as its explanation. It is the objective depth of comprehensibility in the universe that projects our thought beyond it in this way … To be inherently reasonable the universe requires a sufficient reason for being what it is as an intelligible whole.[81]

An Imperious Constraint from Beyond/An Active Agency

Therefore, in the process of reasoning, Torrance claims that "we are aware of coming under an imperious constraint from beyond"[82] with the result that this "would seem to *suggest* that there is an *active agency* other than the inherent intelligibility and harmony of the universe, unifying and structuring it, and providing it with its ground of being."[83]

However, the critical question raised by Torrance's own understanding that theology can only be done within revelation and by the power of grace itself leads me to wonder exactly how he can transfer that power to the objective depth of comprehensibility in the universe that is supposed to be able to project our thought beyond it so as to suggest an active agency or an imperious constraint from beyond. More importantly, however, the ideas of an active agency or imperious constraint from beyond can only lead us to a god of our own making and have no power to lead us to the true God.

Here another problem surfaces. Whereas Barth rightly insisted that we either know God in his entirety as Father, Son, and Holy Spirit or not at all,[84] this thinking implies that some knowledge of that one true God is attained as the intelligibility of the universe drives our thought toward these twin ideas. This is confirmed by Torrance's question: "Does it [an independent natural theology] not really miss the mark, by abstracting his [God's] existence from his act, and so by considering one aspect of his being apart from other aspects?"[85] When and if through faith we actually acknowledge the truth of God's grace

---

[81]Torrance, *Reality and Scientific Theology*, 53.

[82]Ibid., 54; and Torrance, *Reality and Evangelical Theology*, 26.

[83]Torrance, *Reality and Scientific Theology*, 55.

[84]Thus, "God is who He is, the Father, Son and Holy Spirit, Creator, Reconciler and Redeemer, supreme, the one true Lord; and He is known in his entirety or He is not known at all. There is no existence of God behind or beyond this entirety of His being … there can be no knowledge of God in time or even in eternity which will lead us beyond this entirety of His being … God exists in this entirety of His being and therefore not in any kind of parts" (Barth, CD II/1, 51–2).

[85]Torrance, *Karl Barth, Biblical and Evangelical Theologian*, 151. This problematic assertion is heightened when Torrance claims that there is an "ultimate openness of being and its semantic reference" (*Reality and Scientific Theology*, 47) and that "we find our human being opened up and disclosed to us as there strikes at us through the blank face of the universe a mysterious intelligibility which takes us under its command in such a way that we feel we have to do with an undeniable and irreducibly transcendent reality which becomes intensely meaningful as the inward enlightenment of our own beings" (ibid., 58). This is a far cry from Torrance's often repeated insistence that we have no true knowledge of God except as Father, Son, and Holy Spirit, and it is in conflict with his own assertion that "since there is no likeness between the eternal being of God and the being

as described by Torrance himself, then we may interpret the intelligibility of the universe as pointing to the true God. But an active agency or imperious constraint from beyond cannot really be identified with God as Christians know God through his Word and Spirit. That would mean that one could only think truly about God in faith, by grace, and through revelation, even on Torrance's own understanding. One would then be engaging in a theology of revelation and not a natural theology; and that theology of revelation might include what George Hunsinger described as "natural revelation" as it was made intelligible through revelation alone in its identity with Christ himself.[86] Unfortunately, none of these important issues are addressed by Irving in his article because he did not seem to appreciate the full difficulty that I raised in my original article discussing Torrance's new natural theology in 2005.

This leads to my second point, namely, that it is imperative that this reasoning be seen for what it is because there can be no doubt that here Torrance's thinking is opposed not only to Barth's view as explicated above but also to his own view that human knowledge needs to be reconciled by the actualization of atonement in our minds before we can truly know God.[87] This is the case because, for Torrance, God can only be known by God, that is, from a center in God and not from a center in ourselves.[88] In other words, as Torrance applies the doctrine of justification to human knowledge of God, he really does believe and consistently holds to the fact that the whole person is questioned down to the root of his or her being in that we, as sinners who are justified by grace and thus by Christ alone, are summoned to look away from ourselves and only to Christ. Indeed, he insists in other contexts that this ability to follow Christ itself is enabled only by the Holy Spirit actualizing the atonement in us and thus uniting us with Christ so that we may actually share in the Son's unique knowledge of the Father (Mt. 11:27).[89]

---

of created reality, God may be known only out of himself" (Torrance, *The Trinitarian Faith*, 52). Hence, "when we approach God as Father through the Son, our knowledge of the Father in the Son is grounded in the very being of God and is determined by what he essentially is in his own nature" (ibid., 53).

[86]See Hunsinger's view of how Barth interpreted "natural revelation" in n. 76 above.

[87]A very clear and decisive example of this can be seen in Torrance's book on *Atonement*. He insisted to his students that the gospel must have its way with them so that "you will find the very shape and structure of your mind beginning to change." This will involve "a radical repentant rethinking of everything before the face of Jesus Christ" so that repentant thinking means taking up one's cross and following Christ with the result that "you cannot separate evangelical theology from that profound experience of the radical changing and transforming of your mind that comes through dying and rising with Christ" (*Atonement*, 433). From this Torrance instructively concludes that "divine revelation conflicts sharply with the structure of our natural reason, with the secular patterns of thought that have already become established in our minds through the twist of our ingrained mental alienation from God. We cannot become true theologians without the agonising experience of profound change in the mental structure of our innermost being" (ibid.). See also Paul D. Molnar, "The importance of the doctrine of justification in the theology of Thomas F. Torrance and of Karl Barth," *Scottish Journal of Theology* 70 (2) (2017): 198–226. See also Torrance, *Christian Doctrine of God*, 53, 100; Torrance, *Reality and Scientific Theology*, 150–1; and Torrance, *Theology in Reconstruction*, 29, 134.

[88]Torrance, *The Trinitarian Faith*, 52; Torrance, *Theological Science*, 29; and Torrance, *Theology in Reconstruction*, 9, 48, and 126.

[89]Ibid., 58–9. See also Torrance, *Christian Doctrine of God*, 77–8; and Thomas F. Torrance, "The One Baptism," *Theology in Reconciliation: Essays towards Evangelical and Catholic Unity in East and West* (London: Geoffrey Chapman, 1975), 101–2. See also Molnar, *Torrance: Theologian of the Trinity*, 305–6.

None of these problems are addressed by Irving, and in fact we are only led into further confusion with the idea that as theologians we can and should find a place for natural theology as it functions within revelation. The only problem is that natural theology really does cease to be natural theology when our thinking is actually determined by who God has revealed himself to be in his Word and Spirit. That, I have argued, is precisely why one never sees a word about this "new" natural theology when one reads Torrance's books on the Trinity or when one reads about the fact that grace cannot be separated from the Giver of grace. That is because, in his dogmatics proper, Torrance's thinking is generally quite consistently a theology grounded in grace and understood in faith on the basis of revelation alone just because he really applies the *sola gratia* to the whole realm of human knowledge, as Karl Barth himself did. I say generally because whenever Torrance uses the analogy from geometry as described above, his thinking does not remain consistent with his avowal of a theology of *sola gratia*.

So in his book *Space, Time and Incarnation*, he says that "four-dimensional geometries … involve a profound correlation between abstract conceptual systems and physical processes" and that this "has considerable epistemological implications for theological as well as natural science, if only because it yields the organic concept of space-time as a continuous diversified but unitary field of dynamic structures, in which the theologian as well as the natural scientist is at work." This, Torrance says, "gets rid of the old dualisms between material existence and absolute space and time, or between nature and supernature." Therefore, "it is no longer possible to operate scientifically with a separation between natural theology and revealed theology any more than between geometry and physics" because geometry must be pursued "in indissoluble unity with physics" and not independent of it in a way that is detached from knowledge of "physical processes." It is then seen as "its inner rational structure and as an essential part of empirical and theoretical interpretation of nature."[90]

This leads him to conclude that natural theology, like geometry, must be "undertaken in an integrated unity with positive theology in which it plays an indispensable part in our inquiry and understanding of God. In this fusion 'natural' theology will suffer a dimensional change and will be made natural to the proper subject-matter of theology."[91] Notice what has happened here. Gone is any mention of the fact that we are enemies of grace, that our reason is twisted and distorted and that we need reconciliation and repentant thinking brought about by the Holy Spirit changing the structure of our natural thought. I suggest that the reason for this is that Torrance's analogy from geometry led him to conclude that natural theology, like geometry, could be bracketed from revelation and, like geometry bracketed from physics, it could still make sense but it would be incomplete and need completion beyond itself. However, elsewhere in his thinking, as it is shaped by the grace of revelation, Torrance insists that we need a complete *metanoia*

---

[90]Thomas F. Torrance, *Space, Time and Incarnation* (Edinburgh: T&T Clark, 1997), 69.
[91]Ibid., 70.

and total change in that we must take up our cross and follow Christ if we are going to think rightly as theologians. The analogy from geometry you might say leads to a bloodless death to self and an all too smooth transition to a theology of revelation. This is the "continuity" between nature and grace that both Barth and Torrance opposed on scriptural grounds.[92]

Now, one could dismiss this discussion with the idea that these are rather abstruse ideas being debated by Torrance scholars with little practical relevance for theologians today. That would be a serious mistake, however, because unfortunately whenever it is thought that there must be mutual cooperation between natural theology and a theology based exclusively on revelation, then serious problems arise. We have already noted that in Barth's view such thinking blurs the distinction between Creator and creature, and we have seen that Alister McGrath has been led beyond anything that Torrance would countenance with his portrayal of a supposed trinitarian natural theology. Let me give one further example.

Ray S. Anderson

Let us consider how Ray Anderson employs Torrance's "new" natural theology. He attempts to construct a "new" natural theology as a basis for moral theology following Torrance's approach, and he deliberately attempts to harmonize Barth and Brunner in the process. Hence,

> we have attempted to bring the concerns of Brunner for a viable *theologia naturalis* into closer proximity to Barth's concern for the "single task of theology." We have sought to establish a new direction for natural theology within Barth's trajectory of evangelical theology through closer attention to the structure of Barth's theological anthropology. The natural goodness of humanity continues to be a matter of divine determination, despite the effects of the fall.[93]

In this context, Anderson uses this natural goodness as a common ground for discussing Christian ethics: "One could paraphrase Barth by saying that all persons can be presumed to have moral openness, but not moral readiness. This would seem to allow for a natural theology which takes into account a common ground for moral responsibility which finds its criteria in the natural goodness of humanity."[94] However, this is exactly the thinking that Barth rejected in rejecting natural theology:

---

[92]For a detailed discussion of Torrance's rejection of a continuity between creatures and Creator, see Chapter 4.
[93]Ray S. Anderson, "Barth and New Direction for Natural Theology," in *Theology Beyond Christendom: Essays on the Centenary of the Birth of Karl Barth May 10, 1886*, ed. John Thompson (Allison Park, PA: Pickwick, 1986), 241–66, 261.
[94]Ibid., 260–1.

Calvin did not, any more than St. Paul in his Epistle to the Romans, draw …the systematic conclusion that a "natural" knowledge of the law of God is to be ascribed to us and that this knowledge has to be put to a positive use in theology *either* antecedently *or* subsequently ("in faith"). On the contrary, he plainly denied that knowledge of the ethical good is gained by means of an ability (*facultas*) of man.[95]

For Barth of course this was the case because

the doctrine of the point of contact and the whole of Brunner's teaching on nature and grace … has to be most categorically opposed on the score that it is incompatible with the third article of the creed. The Holy Ghost, who proceeds from the Father and the Son and is therefore revealed and believed to be God, does not stand in need of any point of contact but that which he himself creates. Only retrospectively is it possible to reflect on the way in which he "makes contact" with man, and this retrospect will ever be a retrospect upon a *miracle*.[96]

This is why Barth also insisted that any point of contact within us, such as the continuing existence of our good nature, in spite of the fall

could never signify conformity to God, a point of contact for the Word of God. In this sense, as a possibility which is proper to man *qua* creature, the image of God is not just, as it is said, destroyed apart from a few relics; it is totally annihilated. What remains of the image of God even in sinful man is *recta natura*, to which as such a *rectitudo* cannot be ascribed even *potentialiter*. No matter how it may be with his humanity and personality, man has completely lost the capacity for God.[97]

Barth also believed that one could not speak both theologically and philosophically about this point of contact but only theologically because it can be discussed only in faith and thus through the grace of revelation.[98] Barth insisted that theological ethics must be "on its guard against a retrospective reinterpretation of the fall, as though the presumption of man in wishing to know of himself what is good and evil were only a natural inclination to do the will of God."[99] For this reason Barth would never allow our ethical responsibility to be dictated by criteria found in the "natural goodness of humanity." The divine command, in Barth's understanding, comes to us from God himself

---

[95] Barth, *Natural Theology*, 108.
[96] Ibid., 121. Importantly, at appropriate points in his reflections, Torrance also thought, with Barth, that *how* our knowledge came about was a miracle which could not be explained from the human side but only acknowledged as an act of the Holy Spirit and then understood: "As knowledge of God actually arises, however, we know that we cannot attribute it to ourselves and know that we can only say something of how it arises by referring beyond ourselves to God's acts upon us" (*God and Rationality*, 166).
[97] Barth, CD I/1, 238.
[98] Ibid., 239.
[99] Barth, CD II/2, 523.

in our encounter with Jesus Christ: "Ethics as the doctrine of the divine command, and therefore as the doctrine of the sanctification given to man by God, is grounded in the knowledge of Jesus Christ. It can be attained and developed only as the knowledge of Jesus Christ."[100] Thus,

> it [our sanctification in the form of the divine command that meets us in Christ] does not exist as one of the facts which we seek and can discover because it is we who are searched and discovered in our existence by it. It cannot be grounded because it is itself the basis which is our starting-point for all our demonstrations … It speaks always as the voice from above. That is why we wait in vain for it to speak in any voice from below … It is the voice of the Good Shepherd which speaks to us in this unique way … Jesus Christ is the completed fact of our sanctification, the fulfilled and realised purpose of God in God's judgment, just as He is also its presupposition and its execution.[101]

Importantly, T. F. Torrance also opposed the idea that Christian ethics could find its criteria in any sort of moral responsibility found in the moral law or our natural human goodness. In fact, he argued that all of that was called into question by God's judgment and grace in Jesus Christ in a manner similar to Barth. Torrance argued that "from the point of view of ethics we see that human moral awareness tends to sever its connection with God … to establish itself on an autonomous or semi-autonomous basis."[102] Thus, in ethics people "relate themselves to God, consciously or subconsciously through duty to their neighbour—that is, they relate themselves to God indirectly through the medium of the universal [the idea of the moral law] … and do not relate themselves to God in particular."[103] But Torrance maintains that when this behavior is understood from the vantage point of faith, what we see here is that sin "is seizing the ethical imperative of God, making it an independent authority which is identified with human higher nature, so escaping God and deifying humanity—'you will be like God.' "[104]

Sin, Torrance holds, uses the law of God by falling back on observance of the law (perhaps the moral law) and thus yields formal obedience to the law without actually committing us to responsible action under God. It is in this situation that Jesus himself fulfilled the law for us and justified us, thus setting us "free not only from the bondage of the external law but from [our] own self-imprisonment in the condemnation of [our] own conscience … he made our judgement of ourselves acquiesce in God's complete judgement."[105] Consequently, Torrance says the "act of grace in justification which breaks through to us apart from law is spoken of as 'revelation.' "[106] It is the "revealing

---

[100]Ibid., 777.
[101]Ibid.
[102]Torrance, *Atonement*, 112.
[103]Ibid.
[104]Ibid., 113.
[105]Ibid., 116.
[106]Ibid., 118.

of a righteousness that could not be known otherwise. It is revelation that is grounded upon its own act as a breakthrough in sheer grace."[107] Indeed, and most importantly, this "new righteousness that forgives and justifies the sinner could not be inferred logically from the abstract order of law or ethics. From that point of view forgiveness is impossible—it is legally speaking immoral or amoral. And if it is a fact, it is a stupendous miracle."[108] This is what led Torrance to speak of what Kierkegaard called a " 'teleological suspension' of ethics. Because it entails this suspension, justification or forgiveness is not something that is demonstrable from any ground in the moral order as such. It only can be acknowledged and believed as a real event that has in the amazing grace of God actually overtaken us."[109]

Conclusion

Let me conclude by saying that Irving's argument that Torrance's "reconstructed natural theology as the rational structure of theological cognition, which is determined by God's self-revelation"[110] is thoroughly unconvincing as it stands: first because Torrance himself insists, as we have seen, that "divine revelation conflicts sharply with the structure of our natural reason."[111] Second, when our rational structure does operate within faith and revelation by grace, it is what it is as part of the "new" creation as reconciled in the person and work of the one Mediator. Thus, it is no longer natural theology in any sense since it is a theology shaped from beginning to end by grace alone and thus in faith alone. Even to say, as Torrance does, that it is natural to its object when that object is the God who justifies the ungodly conflicts with Torrance's frequent insistence on the priority of grace. Nature is true to what it is as part of God's "new" creation only by grace and as Barth frequently insisted not at all by nature after the fall. So, when Irving writes that "Torrance's reconstruction of natural theology, therefore, takes its place within his understanding that God's self-revelation is a 'self-contained' *novum*,"[112] that remark opens the door to utter confusion. Why?

Because Torrance's own understanding of revelation to which Irving here refers is taken from CD I/1 and is defined by Torrance as follows: "it has its reality and truth wholly and in every respect within itself and so can be known only through itself and out of itself."[113] If revelation is a self-contained *novum*, then in Torrance's own understanding that rules out any natural knowledge of God just because he also claims there is no analogy in human experience on the basis of which we can know the truth since that

---

[107]Ibid.

[108]Ibid.

[109]Ibid.

[110]Irving, "The Epistemological Relevance of the Holy Spirit," 225.

[111]See n. 87 above.

[112]Irving, "The Epistemological Relevance of the Holy Spirit," 225.

[113]Torrance, *Christian Doctrine of God*, citing CD I/1, 306.

comes to us only from the Father, through the Son, and in the Spirit as a miracle. So, "when we encounter God in Jesus Christ, the truth comes to us in its own authority and self-sufficiency. It comes into our experience and into the midst of our knowledge as a *novum*, a new reality which we cannot assimilate to what we already know."[114] Indeed, in a manner reminiscent of Barth, Torrance insists that "we cannot deduce the fact of Christ from our knowledge of other facts," and it "is a new and unique fact without analogy anywhere in human experience or knowledge."[115]

If that is in any sense true, then Torrance's claim that the knowledge of God given in his self-revelation "is a mystery so utterly strange and so radically different that it cannot be apprehended and substantiated except out of itself"[116] rules out the idea advanced by McGrath and Irving that natural theology provides us with some reliable knowledge of God that then links up with God's revelation to constitute theological science. It rules it out just because, as Torrance himself argues, "in point of fact it actually conflicts sharply with generally accepted beliefs and established ideas in human culture and initiates a seismic reconstruction not only of religious and intellectual belief but of the very foundations of human life and knowledge."[117]

In light of Barth's understanding of sin as an impossible possibility, I think it is appropriate to conclude this discussion by saying, using Barth's terminology, that natural theology is and remains an impossible possibility[118] employed by those who

---

[114]Torrance, *Incarnation*, 1. This thinking of course rules out any attempt to fit what we know from revelation into a Christian worldview and then claim that such a view can be equated with the life of faith since the life of faith requires utter dependence on Christ from beginning to end. Thus, Barth said "in faith we abandon ... our standing upon ourselves (including all moral and religious, even Christian standing), ... for the real standing in which we no longer stand on ourselves [including our faith as such] ... but ... on the ground of the truth of God ... We have to believe; not to believe in ourselves, but in Jesus Christ" (CD II/1, 159). Torrance similarly claimed that our very act of faith was seen to rest "upon Christ and his faith, not upon my faith or my need for this or that answer, and hence the assurance was unshakable, because it was grounded in the solid faithfulness of Christ" (*Theology in Reconstruction*, 160). Contrast these views of faith with McGrath's: "Faith is about the transformation of the human mind to see things in a certain manner, involving the acquisition of certain habits of thinking and perception" (McGrath, *A Fine-Tuned Universe*, 39). While Torrance and Barth insisted that faith meant having the mind of Christ and thus obedience to Christ alone in all things, here we are thrown back on our transformed views of reality and not exclusively upon Christ. That remains the inherent problem in the natural theology offered by both McGrath and Irving. Here it is worth noting that in extended conversations after the original publication of this piece in *Participatio*, Alex Irving and I came to agree that Christ must be at the center of any serious theological discussion of natural theology and that McGrath's view of natural theology is indeed questionable from within Torrance's perspective when grace and the problem of sin are taken into account.

[115]Torrance, *Incarnation*, 1.

[116]Torrance, *Christian Doctrine of God*, 19.

[117]Ibid.

[118]It is impossible because the creature can never really be the Creator. But it is possible because "a creature freed from the possibility of falling away would not really be living as a creature. It could only be a second God" (CD II/1, 503). Sin, Barth says, places us in opposition to God and to our own existence. This is why Barth held that "in face of the cross of Christ it is monstrous to describe the uniqueness of God as an object of 'natural' knowledge. In face of the cross of Christ we are bound to say that knowledge of the one and only God is gained only by the begetting of men anew by the Holy Spirit, an act which is always unmerited and incomprehensible,

are either unwilling or unable to allow their thinking to be exclusively and completely reconstructed in subordination to God's grace and revelation and in faith. It is employed by those who do not allow Jesus Christ himself to be the *first* and *final* Word in our knowledge of God and in our ethical behavior. That is the choice required here. In light of this, I still think, with Elmer Colyer, that Torrance may well have regretted calling what really amounts to a theology of human nature functioning within revelation, a new natural theology, and probably should have called it a theology of nature.[119] Even that, however, cannot resolve all the difficulties, as seen above, since there is definitely a residue of the old natural theology, which Torrance himself theoretically rejected, at work in his thought that comes to expression in his analogy drawn from geometry. That analogy prohibits him from consistently noticing that in light of revelation we are all sinners who stand in utter need of grace in its identity with the Giver of grace in order to speak truly of God and of ourselves.

---

and consists in man's no longer living unto himself, but in the Word of God and in the knowledge of God which comes by faith in that Word" (ibid., 453).

[119]Elmer M. Colyer, *How to Read T. F. Torrance: Understanding His Trinitarian and Scientific Theology* (Downers Grove, IL: InterVarsity Press, 2001), 192.

CHAPTER 4
CONTRASTING VISIONS: COMPARING T. F. TORRANCE AND KARL RAHNER ON NON-CONCEPTUAL KNOWLEDGE OF GOD

Thomas F. Torrance explicitly insisted that theological theology, if I may take a phrase from John Webster,[1] had to be scientific. For Torrance, "science and meta-science are required not because God is a problem but because *we* are ... It is because *our* relations with God have become problematic that we must have a scientific theology."[2] Because our relation with God is damaged, Torrance thought we tended to obstruct knowledge of God by placing ourselves in the center instead of allowing God to be in the center. However, he also believed that God would not let himself be prevented by the disorder of our minds, since his presence "presses unrelentingly" upon us, challenging us and repairing our minds, thus requiring us "to yield [our] thoughts to His healing and controlling revelation."[3] For Torrance then, "scientific theology is active engagement in that cognitive relation to God in obedience to the demands of His reality and self-giving."[4] With this remark Torrance wanted to stress that in his book, *Theological Science*,

---

[1]See John Webster, "Theological Theology," in *Confessing God: Essays in Christian Dogmatics II* (London: T&T Clark, 2005), 11–32. As he understood it, theology's importance in the university is "secured by its being not less theological but *more* theological, by 'exercising theology's right to be exclusively theological'" (ibid., 24). See also R. David Nelson, Darren Sarisky, and Justin Stratis, eds., *Theological Theology: Essays in Honour of John Webster* (London: T&T Clark, 2015).

[2]Torrance, *Theological Science*, v. This book was based on the Hewett lectures for 1959.

[3]Ibid.

[4]Ibid. Torrance later expressed this clearly in connection with the doctrine of the Trinity: "it is through personal dwelling in Christ and interiorising his Word within us that we enter into a cognitive union with him as God incarnate, and are thereby admitted to an intimate knowledge of God's self-revelation in its intrinsic wholeness and are enabled to discern the truth of his self-revelation as we could not do otherwise" (*Christian Doctrine of God*, 38). Torrance goes on to say that by "indwelling the Scriptures of the New Testament and interiorising their message we become drawn into the circle of God's revelation of himself through himself. Spiritually and theologically regarded, this kind of indwelling, in Christ and his Word, involves faith, devotion, meditation, prayer and worship in and through which we are given discerning access to God in his inner Communion as Father, Son and Holy Spirit" (ibid.). However, because Jesus himself as the incarnate Word is the "epistemic bridge ... between man and God that is grounded in the Being of God and anchored in the being of man ... the incarnation of the Son or Word constitutes the epistemological centre, as well as the ontological centre, in all our knowledge of God, with a centre in our world of space and time and a centre in God himself" (ibid., 100-11). And this self-revelation in Christ to us occurs through the Holy Spirit since "the Holy Spirit is the creative Agent in mediating knowledge of God to us in himself and the creative Agent in our reception and understanding of that revelation, although he is not himself the Word ... or the Form ... which that revelation assumes in Jesus Christ as it comes from the Father and is appropriated by us" (ibid.).

he intended to present a "philosophy of the science of God" and most definitely not "a Philosophy of Religion." He took this position because, as he saw it, in a philosophy of religion, "religion is substituted in the place of God" while in a philosophy of theology he wanted to be "directly engaged with knowledge of the Reality of God and not just with religious phenomenality."[5] In his view, since religion is concerned with "the behaviour of *religious people*, sooner or later" that will mean "the substitution of humanity in the place of religion—the point at which our 'secularizing' philosophers of religion appear to have arrived."[6]

What really is going on here? The answer is to be found in the heart of Torrance's theological epistemology in which he argued that, because of human sin, our minds are damaged, and we need God's reconciling action so that, with the mind of Christ, we may know God in truth.[7] This is why he explicitly maintained two crucial insights: (1) "We cannot know God against His will, but only as He wills to reveal Himself" and (2) we cannot know God "apart from His claim upon the whole of our existence, or apart from His will to redeem and reconcile it to Himself."[8] Thus, for Torrance, "we cannot truly know God without being reconciled and renewed in Jesus Christ" such that our

---

[5]Torrance, *Theological Science*, iv.

[6]Ibid., v. While these ideas were expressed in 1959 and 1969, I hope to show that they are as applicable today as they were some sixty to seventy years ago.

[7]With St. Paul, Torrance believed that "we are alienated or estranged in our minds, and indeed are hostile in mind to God" (*Atonement: The Person and Work of Christ*, 437). Insightfully, he claimed that this basic New Testament view was "deeply resented by the rational culture of the ancient classical world of Greece and Rome" and that this is something that our modern world also finds "difficult to accept" (ibid., 438). He noted that even "evangelical Christianity" today "does not seem to have thought through sufficiently the transformation of human reason in the light of the Word made flesh in Jesus Christ" (ibid.). To that extent people's minds both in the church and in society are still, he thought, basically "unevangelised" because we have not taken seriously enough the fact that "the mind of man is alienated at its very root. It is in the human mind that sin is entrenched, and so it is right there, the gospel tells us, that we require to be cleansed by the blood of Christ and to be healed and reconciled to God" (ibid.). Since our behavior is governed by our minds, Torrance held that includes our free will so that "although we may have freewill, we are not at all free to escape from our self-will" so that it is "in the depths of the human mind … which governs and controls all our thinking and culture that we have become estranged from the truth and hostile to God. And it is right there, in the ontological depths of the human mind, that we desperately need to be redeemed and healed" (ibid., 438–9). Torrance thus insisted that it was only in the incarnation that our minds could be healed because by assuming our fallen nature Jesus Christ "converted it, healed it, and sanctified it in himself" (ibid., 440). Indeed, "he descended into the hell of the utmost wickedness and dereliction of the human mind under the judgement of God, in order to lay hold upon the very root of our sin and to redeem us from its stranglehold upon us. Yes, it was not only our actual sins, but it was original sin and original guilt that the Son of God took upon himself in incarnation and atonement, in order to heal, convert, and sanctify the human mind in himself and reconcile it to God" (ibid.). Following Athanasius, Torrance insisted that "our *mind* is sanctified and renewed *in* Christ," and for that reason he opposed the teaching of Apollinaris (*Theology in Reconciliation*, 230). While some might claim to find an inconsistency in Torrance's thought on this matter by suggesting that if our humanity is healed in the incarnation, then Torrance's insistence, that it is our sinful humanity he assumed in order to convert us back to God, is in conflict with the idea that he lived his human life as the incarnate Word in a "healed" humanity, that claim is mistaken. Such a view is possible only if one ignores Torrance's frequent assertions that the healing of our humanity in the life of the incarnate Word took place from his birth and throughout his entire human life and ministry and was completed in his death and through his resurrection and ascension.

[8]Torrance, *Theological Science*, 41.

knowledge is always directed to God as the object of our knowledge. Consequently, "far from being able to bend the object to our will, or to fashion knowledge of it to our liking, we cannot know it without being drawn into its redeeming and reconciling activity, without being renewed and re-ordered in accordance with its saving will."[9]

Torrance explained these crucial insights in a number of contexts. But, at the beginning of his book *Theological Science*, it is already in evidence since he claimed that "in knowing God I am deeply aware that my relation to Him has been damaged, that disorder has resulted in my mind, and that it is I who obstruct knowledge of God by getting in between Him and myself, as it were."[10] This statement illustrates that in Torrance's philosophy of theology and in his dogmatic theology, he consistently wanted to engage in "scientific knowledge" which "was held to result from inquiry strictly in accordance with the nature (κατά φύσιν) of the reality being investigated, that is knowledge of it reached under the constraint of what it actually and essentially is in itself."[11] With the

---

[9]Ibid. Hence, "the objectivity of our theological knowledge is immutably soteriological in nature" (ibid.). Importantly, Torrance frequently cited Mt. 11:27, with Athanasius, because the mutual relation of knowing between the Father and Son in which "no man knows the Son except the Father, and no man knows the Father except the Son" is "a mutual and exclusive relation between the knowledge of the Father and the knowledge of the Son" (*Theology in Reconciliation*, 240). However, it is through the Spirit that that very relation "has been inserted, as it were, into human flesh, in the Incarnation so that we through the same Spirit may participate in the relation of the Son to the Father and of the Father to the Son, and know and love the triune God as he is in himself, even though he infinitely transcends our conceiving and speaking of him" (ibid., 241). The result of this situation is that "scientific theology" refers to the fact that "we are forced to adapt our common language to the nature and reality of God who is disclosed to us in Jesus Christ, and even where necessary to coin new terms, to express what we thus apprehend" in order that "theological terms" must be stretched beyond their natural reference so that they terminate "on God himself at one end and upon the world or man at the other end" (ibid.). See also, ibid., 223.

[10]Torrance, *Theological Science*, v.

[11]Torrance, *The Trinitarian Faith*, 51. For Torrance this meant that "faith was not regarded in Nicene theology as some form of non-cognitive or non-conceptual relation to God, but was held to involve acts of recognition, apprehension and conception, of a very basic intuitive kind, in the responsible assent of the mind to truth inherent in God's self-revelation to mankind" (ibid., 20). Importantly, for Torrance, intuitive knowledge does not ground knowledge in our intuitions but rather is understood to refer to "the direct knowledge of an actually present object caused naturally by that object and not by another" *Theology in Reconstruction*, 79. This is contrasted with "abstractive knowledge" in which "we do not have to do with immediate experience but with ideas detached from experience and related to one another logically through the discursive reason" (ibid.). Following Calvin, Torrance rejected nominalism and realism in order to hold that language "is subordinated to the objective realities it serves." And those realities were "supplied by the doctrines of justification by grace or election" and "the mighty living Word of God which sounds through the Scriptures enabling us to hear and apprehend God speaking to us in person" (ibid., 84). Thus, "intuitive knowledge of God arises ... under the direct impact or causality of his divine Being. This involved the rejection both of Thomism and Ockhamism" because for the former, our knowledge of God is taken from sense-experience of "created realities" and thus never rises above those but construes God "in accordance with them" (ibid.). For the latter, "abstractive knowledge abstracts from actual existence," and it thus "prevents us from knowing God in accordance with his own personal mode of Being. We know God, Calvin insisted, through his works or effects, but in his works or effects we meet God speaking to us personally through his Word" (ibid., 85). See also *Theological Science*, 165, where Torrance astutely held that while we must describe our intuition to others, we cannot thereby "induce them to have a similar experience, for no act of knowledge is explainable from the side of the knowing subject (i.e., psychologically) but only from the side of the object known, for true knowledge arises in proportion as the subject allows his knowing to be determined by the nature of the object before him." For that reason, our

early church Fathers, Torrance wanted to know God in a manner that was "strictly in accordance with the nature of God as he has revealed himself to us."[12] This, for Torrance, who followed Athanasius, was "godly" thinking as opposed to ungodly or false thinking which consisted in a rationalizing and mythologizing "perversion of the Gospel."[13]

Karl Rahner

In this chapter, I will compare and contrast Torrance's "scientific theology" with Karl Rahner's transcendental theology with a view toward seeing exactly why Torrance was critical of Rahner's attempt to bring "St Thomas and Kant together, instead of overcoming Kantian phenomenalism" such that his thinking could be said to represent a "retreat from the truth of being."[14] This is no small issue, and dealing adequately with the problem Torrance identifies in the transcendental Thomist position will, in the end, bring Roman Catholic and Protestant theology closer together in the form of a truly theological theology, that is, a theology that arises from and remains based upon the "truth of being" and not the supposed truth which is thought to arise from our subjective responses to being, in this case, the being of God himself. Let me contrast their views briefly to show what I mean.

There is no doubt that Rahner did not want to be a "subjectivist" in his consideration of God, Christ, and revelation since he asserted that "God himself through his own act of self-communication upholds" our human act "of hearing" his Word "as an intrinsic principle" which "we are accustomed to call the supernatural grace of faith."[15] But while Rahner intended to uphold the truth of God's being and the truth of revelation, his method inhibits this because he believed that revelation "has its existence in man's own conscious thought and hence is subject to the *a priori* structure of human knowledge."[16] That very assertion separates Rahner's approach from Torrance's as one side of the Grand Canyon is separated from the other simply because Torrance would never, under any circumstances, admit that revelation is subject to any a priori at all. That is why Torrance held, following Karl Barth, that

> knowledge of God is thus not the relationship of an already existing subject to an object that enters into his sphere and is therefore obedient to the laws of this

---

intuitions are entirely dependent "upon the nature of the object" (ibid., 166). See also Thomas F. Torrance, *The Hermeneutics of John Calvin* (Edinburgh: Scottish Academic Press, 1988), 4–5, 86–7, 129.

[12] Torrance, *The Trinitarian Faith*, 38.

[13] Ibid., 29.

[14] Thomas F. Torrance, "Truth and Authority: Theses on Truth," *Irish Theological Quarterly* (hereafter *ITQ*), 39 (3) (September 1972): 215–42, 226. This article was reprinted in *Transformation & Convergence in the Frame of Knowledge: Explorations in the Interrelations of Scientific and Theological Enterprise* (Grand Rapids, MI: Eerdmans, 1984), chapter 10, "Truth and Authority in the Church," 303–32.

[15] Rahner, TI 11, 92.

[16] Ibid., 91.

sphere. On the contrary, this knowledge first of all creates the subject of this knowledge by coming into the picture … Only because God posits Himself as the Object is man posited as the knower of God. And so man can only have God as the self-posited object.[17]

Torrance was very clear here arguing that God does not set aside our subjectivity in enabling us to know him. Instead, God makes us free and fully responsible by himself establishing

the possibility of man's knowledge of Him. In this approach to man God engages man in active responsibility toward Him, and it is therein that man is established in his being a free and responsible person. That is the ground of his knowledge of God … it is in this responsible act in which man steps out of his self-isolation and returns to God that he comes to find and know himself.[18]

Transcendentality and a priori Knowledge

Rahner's assumption here then leads to a number of claims that Torrance would clearly identify as making it impossible to allow the "truth of being" to shape his thought. He held that "it is from the limitless *a priori* transcendentality of knowledge and freedom in themselves that we come to know what is really meant when we speak of God as absolute being or absolute good."[19] This thinking follows from Rahner's belief that "the absolute goal of this transcendentality is not something additional to, or external to itself, but rather something that is present all along and in its very origins, albeit without being recognized as a conscious theme of thought."[20] A crucial question, however, arises in connection with these remarks. Does knowledge of the Christian God, based on the revelation of God in his Word and through his Holy Spirit, really arise *from* "the limitless *a priori* transcendentality of knowledge and freedom in themselves" such that one could then claim to speak truly of the Christian God by speaking of "absolute being or absolute good"? Rahner clearly believed the answer is yes, since he also thought that natural theology and revealed theology mutually condition each other.[21]

---

[17]Torrance, *Theological Science*, 47, cited from CD II/1, 21-2. Because for Torrance, "in giving Himself to us as the object of our knowing and thinking the Gift is not detached from the Giver, so that God retains His own Majesty in our knowing and thinking of Him" therefore "genuinely objective knowledge of Him" is possible by God's own act which resists "all objectifying attempts to subject Him to our natural habits of thought and forms of knowledge" (ibid., 300). Torrance mentions that "it is difficult to understand how so many contemporary thinkers can hold the silly notion that for us to have objective knowledge of God compromises His being and jeopardizes His independent Reality!" (ibid.).
[18]Ibid., 47–8.
[19]Rahner, TI 11, 92.
[20]Ibid.
[21]Accordingly, Rahner wrote, "The revealed Word and natural knowledge of God mutually condition each other" (TI 1, 98).

Thus, he also claimed that "in any act of cognition it is not only the object known but also the subject knowing that is involved."[22] Certainly, no one would disagree with this, not least Torrance himself.[23] But Rahner continued by saying that "it [cognition] is dependent not only upon the distinctive characteristics of the object, but also upon the essential structure of the knowing subject."[24] Indeed, he further declared that

the *a priori* transcendental subjectivity of the knower on the one hand and the object of knowledge (and of freedom) on the other are related to one another in such a way that they mutually condition one another, and they do this in such a way that knowledge of the *a priori* conditions which make knowledge possible in the subject necessarily constitutes also an element in the actual knowledge of the object itself.[25]

---

[22]Rahner, TI 11, 87.

[23]See Torrance, *ITQ*, 226–7 where he insists that while our knowledge of the "truth of being" is grounded only in the "the objective intelligibility of reality," nonetheless it also incorporates "a subjective counterpart, since it is after all we who conceive, think, formulate and our knowledge of God grounded upon his own self evidence is not cut off from the fact that it is, *deo dante et deo illuminante, our* knowledge of him."

[24]Rahner, TI 11, 87.

[25]Ibid. Rahner can even say that "knowledge on the part of the knowing subject in himself is always at the same time a knowledge of the metaphysical (and in an objective sense transcendental) structure of the object in itself" (ibid.). That is an amazing remark because, taken at face value, it certainly seems to suggest that self-knowledge *is* knowledge of objects independent of oneself when in reality that is not necessarily so, unless one equates self-knowledge with knowledge of God. It certainly appears that Rahner did that when he claimed that "the personal history of experience of the self is the personal history of the experience of God" (TI 13, 125). Rahner clearly did not want to confuse Creator and creature since he did claim that our self-experience "is finite, even though, precisely as such, and in its sheer transcendentality, it contains an absolute orientation towards the infinite and the inconceivable through which it is this without being identified with it" (ibid.). Nonetheless, other questions arise in connection with these ideas since it is entirely possible to speak of the infinite and inconceivable without actually speaking of the one triune God whose being and act cannot be equated with a generally knowable infinite and inconceivable or with what Rahner frequently referred to as the "the silent incomprehensibility" (TI 6, 249). And the clearest proof that the two simply cannot be equated, as Rahner did, lies in the fact that, as Torrance rightly recognized, from revelation we know that we are not oriented toward God but at enmity with God and in need of reconciliation to know God truly. That is why Torrance emphasized that "face to face with Christ our humanity is revealed to be diseased and in-turned, and our subjectivities to be rooted in self-will. It is we who require to be adapted to Him, so that we have to renounce ourselves and take up the Cross if we are to follow Him and know the Father through Him. It is in this way that the estranged self is restored, and the damaged person of man is healed and recreated in communion with God, and thus that the disjunction in the subject—object relationship gives place to a cognitive union with God in love" (*Theological Science*, 310). Moreover, when Rahner claimed that "all conceptual expressions about God, necessary though they are, always stem from the unobjectivated experience of transcendence as such: the concept from the pre-conception [*Vorgriff*], the name from the experience of the nameless" (TI 4, 50), his thinking was not at all in harmony with revelation as Torrance understands revelation since, for Torrance, all knowledge of God springs in reality from union with Christ, as enabled by the Holy Spirit in faith. And because this God does have a name, any claim to know the Christian God as the "nameless" really places knowledge of God in our hands once more since that claim led Rahner to say that "the pre-conception given in transcendence is directed to the nameless: the condition which makes the names of God possible must itself be essentially unnamed" (ibid., 50–1). Rahner argued that his view of God as "holy mystery" means that "the name of God is the nameless infinity" (TI 4, 60), and "revelation cannot be confined to words, but must be also the giving of grace, as an inner, objectless though conscious dynamism directed to the beatific vision" (TI 4, 61). On the one hand, Torrance would never ascribe grace to us in the form of an "objectless though conscious

But this is exactly the thinking Torrance rejects as the substitution of religion for theology because it cannot clearly distinguish between the object as the sole determinant of true knowledge and the subject who is enabled to know that object through that object making itself known. I will explain this further as the chapter proceeds. Suffice it to say here that for Torrance, following Calvin, the "*analogia fidei*" is "a movement of thought in which we test the fidelity of our knowledge by tracing our thought back to its ground in the reality known, in which we refer everything to God and not to ourselves."[26]

Experience of Self/Experience of God

Before proceeding to my next point, however, it is worth mentioning here that Rahner's view that "the personal history of experience of the self is the personal history of the experience of God" has led one prominent theologian to claim, following Rahner, that

---

dynamism" because grace, for Torrance, could never be detached from Christ, the Giver of grace, since grace is God's self-giving "in his *incarnate* Son in whom the Gift and the Giver are indivisibly one" (*The Trinitarian Faith*, 140). On the other hand, Torrance would question whether any of our "objectless" dynamisms could be equated in any sense with our movement toward the God of Christian faith since to know the Christian God one would have to have faith in Jesus Christ and faith for Torrance meant knowledge, in the form of concepts, of who God actually is as the eternal Father, Son, and Holy Spirit. Part of the problem here is that for Rahner "ontology is not a science distinct from natural theology" (TI 4, 52) while for Torrance, what we reach with natural theology "cannot be equated with the living God, and can only distort knowledge of God if it is" (*Theological Science*, 104). This, because "there is no other God than this God who has revealed himself in this way [in Christ], and there is no other way for us to conceive of the one being of God in accordance with his divine nature except as Father, Son and Holy Spirit" (Thomas F. Torrance, "The Christian Apprehension of God the Father," *Speaking the Christian God: The Holy Trinity and the Challenge of Feminism*, ed. Alvin F. Kimel Jr. [Grand Rapids, MI: Eerdmans, 1992], 121). Torrance helpfully and clearly asserts that both for Judaism and Greek philosophy and for every religion other than Christianity, "God remains ultimately incomprehensible to men and women in the bare and unfigured simplicity of his Being—he is the Nameless One who cannot be apprehended in himself or be conceived in the personal relations of his inner life as a Communion of Love" (*Christian Doctrine of God*, 3). For that reason, he says that any statement made about God apart from God's own active "personal self-revelation," as occurs in ancient and modern philosophy, "are non-cognitive—they are at best of no more than tangential borderline significance. It is quite otherwise in the Gospel when we say that the Father, the Son, and the Holy Spirit are God, the One God whom we know" (ibid.). See also Torrance, *Theology in Reconciliation*, 217.

[26]Torrance, *Theological Science*, x. That is why Torrance insistently maintained that the key problem of modern theology is that "statements about God are reduced to anthropological statements" so that "whenever we try to transcend a subject-subject relation or replace it by a 'pure' subject-subject relation, we are unable to distinguish God from ourselves, and lapse into irrationality" (ibid., xi). With Barth, Torrance maintained that "we can never look for the truth in ourselves but must look for it beyond ourselves in God ... we can never claim the truth of our own statements, but must rather think of our statements as pointing away to Christ who alone is the Truth. Theological statements do not carry their truth in themselves ... That is why justification remains the most powerful statement of objectivity in theology" (Torrance, *God and Rationality*, 68). It is in light of our justification by faith that Torrance opposed those "who deliberately make self-understanding the criterion of their interpretation of the Gospel, or who insist upon an anthropocentric starting-point for theological inquiry" (ibid.). As this applies to a philosophy of religion, it is vital to see that for Torrance "justification reveals in fact that religion can be the supreme form taken by human sin, and be, as it were, an inverted form of atheism. That applies no less to the Christian religion" (ibid., 69).

in the experience of oneself at these depths [in the experiences of love, fidelity, loneliness, and death], at this *prethematic* [nonconceptual] level whence our own mystery arises, we also experience and are grasped by the holy mystery of God as the very context of our own self-presence. In fact the silent, *nonverbal* encounter with infinite mystery constitutes the enabling condition of any experience of self at all.[27]

These assumptions finally led to the conclusion that "the experience of God which is never directly available is mediated, among other ways but primordially so, through the changing history of oneself."[28] This is the fruit of Rahner's "anthropological analysis" which discloses to us that "a human being is primordially 'spirit in the world,' that is, an embodied subject whose capacity for radical questioning and free and responsible action reveals that the person is structured to an ever-receding horizon."[29] Ignoring the problem of sin which is in fact disclosed to us in Christ, and the need for the reconciliation of our minds which, as we have seen, was objectively enacted for us in him and through him, this thinking is built on the erroneous ideas that "human beings are dynamically oriented toward fathomless mystery as the very condition for the possibility of acting in characteristic human ways" and that "human beings are dynamically structured toward God."[30] All of this is what Torrance wished to avoid in arguing against nonconceptual knowledge of God; such knowledge he maintained always meant redefining God *from* our experiences of the nameless, or infinite or perhaps, with Rahner, apprehending God as the "whither of transcendence."[31]

Nonconceptual Knowledge

We already know that Torrance flatly rejected nonconceptual knowledge of God because we simply cannot experience or know the Christian God without conceptual forms of understanding. Nonconceptual understanding, in Torrance's view, snaps the connection

---

[27]Johnson, *She Who Is*, 65, emphasis mine.
[28]Ibid.
[29]Ibid.
[30]Ibid. Inasmuch as we are sinners who need God's reconciling action here and now, it is impossible to claim that we are "dynamically structured toward God," that is, toward the God revealed in Jesus Christ. That would indeed be a form of Pelagianism. We may well be structured toward some idea of "fathomless mystery," but the triune God cannot be equated with that idea since, as Torrance rightly claimed, religion is the ultimate form of our enmity against God. Karl Barth captured this problem perfectly when he wrote that "the religious relationship of man to God which is the inevitable consequence of his sin is a degenerate form of the covenant-relationship, the relationship between the Creator and the creature. It is the empty and deeply problematical shell of that relationship. But as such it is a confirmation that that relationship has not been destroyed by God, that God will not be mocked, that even forgetful man will not be able to forget Him. Man may escape faith and obedience, but he cannot escape—and this is what reveals the judgment under which he stands—this their surrogate" (Barth, CD IV/1, 483).
[31]Rahner, TI 4, 50.

between us and the objective act of God giving himself to us to be known in his Word and Spirit. Since God's Word and Spirit are *homoousios*, "knowledge of God in the Spirit is profoundly conceptual, rational knowledge in its own right, knowledge in which we are carried right over to what transcends us, yet which is apposite to the nature of God as *Spirit*."[32] But since the Spirit unites us conceptually and ontologically to Christ himself in faith, we are enabled to think on the ground of our having been reconciled to God in Christ and thus our "theological statements take their rise from a centre in God and not in ourselves."[33] Torrance therefore insisted that "apart from this impact of the Spirit upon us, the forms of our thought and speech become quite obscure and indeed may even become a form of obstruction to the divine revelation or a means of suppressing the truth through the transmutation of knowledge into our own constructs."[34]

Any idea of nonconceptual knowledge of God then cuts that connection between God giving himself to us in his Word and Spirit and our actual knowledge of God that comes through conceptual union with Christ and thus with God himself. And because that connection is thereby cut, Torrance also criticized the idea of infused grace because he claimed that idea was substituted by Thomas Aquinas for the objective fact that God himself encounters us directly in Christ so that assent to the truth of faith must mean acceptance of Jesus Christ himself as the truth.[35] However, Torrance held that for Thomas, since the "object is not sufficiently compelling of itself to our understanding, we require some kind of *lumen infusum* or some kind of *gratia infusa* or indeed *fides infusa*, which then comes, as it were, from behind in order to enable us to assent to the truth in spite of its non-evidence."[36] It is in this way that truth comes to be determined by us either in the

---

[32]Torrance, *God and Rationality*, 188. Torrance powerfully and rightly insisted that because we must "face the hard fact of man's estrangement from God and his enmity to Him," which also affects our knowledge of God, it is imperative to realize that "our knowing God's Being is exclusively God's act. That means that knowledge of God is possible only on the ground of reconciliation" (ibid., 179). And since in God's eternal being and act God is "articulate Being—Word," God communicates himself to us precisely as the Holy Spirit unites us to the Word so that we have communion with God and can hear that Word through the words of the scriptural witness (ibid., 179–80).

[33]Ibid., 189.

[34]Ibid., 187.

[35]Hence, "since the truth of God is known in its own self-light and in its own self-evidence, by the act of God in the Word and Spirit of his own being, and therefore on the ground of its own authority, we do not need to posit a special illumination or a special infusion of grace, independent of the truth, for its right reception and expression" (Torrance, *ITQ*, 218). While authority in the church is necessary, it is secondary to the "actual disclosure of the truth in its own right," and it is that act of God disclosing the truth to us that "makes us free to know it finally out of itself and by grace alone, and demands of us obedience that transcends our respect for the authoritative institutions of the Church, necessary though they are in the historical mediation of the truth to mankind" (ibid.).

[36]Torrance, *ITQ*, 227. Torrance maintained that Thomas held "that to which the understanding gives assent does not move the understanding by its own power but by the influence of the will," and then Thomas claimed that "the intellect assents to something, not through being sufficiently moved to this assent by its proper object, but through an act of choice, i.e. because it is enough to move the will but not enough to move understanding" (*ITQ*, 225). Torrance said that "this detachment of the understanding, even in the assent of faith, from the self-evidence of God in his own being and truth, means that in the last resort faith has to rest upon moral grounds and operate only with an indirect relation to the *autousia* and *autexousia* of God. In the nature of the case this opens up a gap between faith and its object which is occupied by an *authority other than the truth of being*"

form of authoritative pronouncements by the Church or by our understanding of God based on a supposed nonconceptual awareness of God within us, rather than by "the truth of being" as God's own act of incarnation. Let me rely on Torrance's understanding of love of God and neighbor to explain the profound differences between Rahner and Torrance here in a way that will demonstrate with precision the difference it makes if one conceptually allows the unique love of God which meets us in Christ and through his Holy Spirit to shape our view of these matters.[37]

Torrance claimed that "the Incarnation means that GOD loves, and loves us; but God cannot therefore be resolved into Love."[38] The implications of this remark might go unnoticed except for the fact that Torrance drew the following conclusion, namely, that "we may not construe the Incarnation simply in terms of love; rather must we construe our idea of love in terms of the Incarnation!"[39] This is the case, Torrance claimed, because "Christianity reverses all our values." What Torrance argued here was that God's love and

---

(*ITQ*, 225). This situation, Torrance thought, created what he called a "refraction in its conceptual relation to the self-evidence of God" which meant that, in his view, Thomas retreated "from the truth of being in the full sense" and in a way embraced a type of voluntarist position which opened the door to a kind of nominalism. Torrance's view of refraction meant that instead of allowing the being of God in his actions in his Word and Spirit to directly shape his thought, Thomas opened the door to the idea that the will was necessary to assist in knowledge of God, so that there was a shift in knowing the truth away from "the truth of being," toward the truth present in our understanding. That, Torrance claimed, meant that in the end we could "control and manipulate what we know, and as Kant used to say, make it the object of our thought" (*ITQ*, 226). This is what allowed the transcendental Thomists to convert theology "into some form of theological anthropology" which meant a retreat once more from the "truth of being" with its introduction of "a *non-conceptual element* in our basic knowledge of God," which Anselm would never allow (*ITQ*, 226).

[37]Torrance insists that when Scripture says "God is love," that statement must be one "which God Himself addresses to us in the act of His own self-revelation" so that the "'is' is determined by the nature of its subject 'God,' and is only therefore the kind of 'is' that God is" (*Theological Science*, 233). When love is understood as issuing from God himself, in accord with his nature as Father, Son, and Holy Spirit who is love, then we know that the statement that God is love "is defined in terms of God's activity in the incarnation of His Son and in His atoning work for us" (ibid.). However, when the word love is detached from the love of God who sent his only Son that we might "have life through Him" (1 Jn 4:8), then love becomes a "statement which we have thought up on our own and projected descriptively into God" (ibid.). If it is to be a true statement of God's actual love in himself and for us, then its truth must lie "in God Himself who makes it" so that it "is true as His Word and Act for what He speaks as God and His speaking of it to us are inseparable" (ibid.). The moment God's love for us in Christ is "detached from its ontological source and considered abstractly and timelessly as a general statement in relation to other general statements ... its basic nature and meaning would change" and one could then reverse the statement to imply that "love is God." That would turn the biblical statement of truth "into a lie, in which we would be absolutizing and divinizing our human love ... in terms of [a] hypostatized love of ours" (ibid., 234). For Torrance, "that God is love is certainly universally true, but it is not a necessary truth, for He does not have to love us, nor does He owe it to himself or to us to love us. He loves us out of His love, in the transcendent freedom of His Grace, but we know it because He has come among us in Jesus Christ and revealed that what He is toward us in Christ He is eternally and antecedently in Himself" (ibid., 234). However, that means that the statement "God is love" cannot be known in advance but only *a posteriori* in light of God's self-revelation to Israel and in the incarnation (ibid., 234–5).

[38]Torrance, *The Doctrine of Jesus Christ*, 86. Torrance's understanding of God's love is firmly grounded in the Trinity, and because he holds God's being and act together, he also held that in Christ it is the very love of God that meets us in his sacrifice for us on the cross and in the power of his resurrection from the dead. See Torrance, *Christian Doctrine of God*, 133–4 and 165–6.

[39]Ibid.

our human acts of love cannot under any circumstances be properly conceptualized in a mutually conditioning manner as Rahner in fact understood them. To do so would obliterate the true meaning of the incarnation itself. It would also make it impossible to distinguish divine and human love. That would in turn make it impossible to grasp God's free love which meets us in his Word and Spirit, and which liberates us from sin and self-will and thus from our own attempts to get to God without actually relying on the true God in faith. This is no small issue to be sure. And it can easily be encapsulated in Torrance's own remark that "we cannot relate our knowing to the Being of God, or the actuality of our knowledge to the Truth of God *by thinking our own way into God*—that would be tantamount to substituting the movement of our own spirit for that of the Spirit of God and to erecting our own word into the Word of God."[40] Torrance insisted that "theology does not know God by virtue of its own ideas and concepts or by the inner power of its own dialectic and spirituality, but only in response to God's Word, only in the recognition of His truth, and only under the leading of His Spirit."[41] Torrance's position thus is shaped by his belief that "the co-ordinating principle of theological knowledge does not lie in theological activity itself but in the speaking of the Word by the Spirit and in our participation in the Word through the Spirit."[42]

Let us consider some of the implications of these insights. First, Torrance insisted that because the incarnation is an act of the eternal God, that act originates from "outside time altogether, quite apart from our world."[43] To grasp this meant to grasp "half of Christianity" because it meant ability to grasp the meaning of God's grace. Importantly, this implies that the incarnation cannot in any sense be understood to have arisen from within history but must be understood as "an invasion of history" because it comes from outside and thus from "Eternity," that is from the eternal God himself, entering into history. This assertion is directly in conflict with Rahner's idea that a phenomenology of love would show that there is an "unfinished and eternal quality inherent in love"[44] since for Torrance we simply cannot understand the unique action of God's eternal love in the incarnation by exploring human love or some notion of love in general.

Second, Torrance insisted that this act of God is an act of revelation precisely as an act of reconciliation since in Christ, God was reconciling the world to himself. Inasmuch as the incarnation began with God himself and God alone, that is precisely what makes the incarnation what it is and that is what gives us the kind of faith that can depend on this act of God completely. Third, in the incarnation, God who comes to us does not wait for us to seek him. God has come to seek us. God "does not wait for us to be good; he does not wait even for us to try! God's love is not a calculated love, it is not prompted or 'caused' by anything in us."[45] The initiative lies "absolutely" with God alone. Therefore, "God's love does not take on its colour and value from the nature of its object. Our Love to God may and does.

---

[40]Torrance, *God and Rationality*, 181, emphasis mine.
[41]Ibid.
[42]Ibid.
[43]Torrance, *The Doctrine of Jesus Christ*, 86.
[44]Rahner, TI 6, 242.
[45]Torrance, *The Doctrine of Jesus Christ*, 86–7.

We love him for what he is and love him only because he first loved us. Our love is thus quite different from his love."[46]

Notice here that Torrance's conception of incarnation and of grace, which he frequently asserted could not be separated from Christ, the Giver of grace,[47] led him to recognize that there is no mutual conditioning between human love and God's love. Torrance insisted that the Holy Spirit is the sovereign God acting from God's side creatively within history and from the human side to realize the purpose of his love to establish us in proper relationship with him. Thus, the "special function" of the Spirit "is to bring to completion the creative purpose of God."[48] But, since this is a sovereign action of God's love, Torrance maintained that "the creature does not have a continuity in relation to God that belongs to the creature in itself, for this is continuously given and sustained by the presence of the Spirit within the creation … This makes impossible for us any notion of a mutual correlation between the creature and the Creator."[49] God's love is not only uncreated, but it is grounded in the Trinity and "does not depend on our being fit or good or having value." Unless this is the case, Torrance insisted, there would be no salvation at all for us. Any suggestion that God had to love us because he is love simply misunderstands the nature of God's love according to Torrance. Such an idea of love "starts out from human love and … is then foisted upon the Almighty."[50] Any notion that God's love is forced upon him by our infinite value or in some other way simply misses the fact that God loves "freely, royally and sovereignly." The idea that God must love us is, according to Torrance, simply a "cheap view of the Love of God." God's eternal love, which comes to us in the incarnation, is his unconditional bestowal of himself upon us. The other kind of love is "a refined form of egoism, a deep-seated self-centredness." Indeed, "its loud insistence upon external social relations can well be a sign that it is internally ruptured in its connection with the Creative Love of God."[51] God's love is a free and "spontaneous overflow, the uninhibited outflow of the Divine Nature." This led Torrance to conclude that to "think of there being a Law in the Divine nature which makes God love, is to misunderstand it quite as much as to think of something in man which demands that God love him."[52]

---

[46]Ibid., 87.

[47]See n. 25 above.

[48]Torrance, *God and Rationality*, 171.

[49]Ibid.

[50]Torrance, *The Doctrine of Jesus Christ*, 87.

[51]Ibid.

[52]Ibid. The similarity between this crucial insight and the thinking of Karl Barth should not be overlooked. Barth maintained that "God is He who, without having to do so, seeks and creates fellowship between Himself and us. He does not have to do it, because in Himself without us, and therefore without this, He has that which He seeks and creates between Himself and us. It implies so to speak an overflow of His essence that He turns to us … it is an overflow which is not demanded or presupposed by any necessity, constraint, or obligation, least of all from outside, from our side, or by *any law by which God Himself is bound and obliged*" (CD II/1, 273, emphasis mine). Further, like Torrance, Barth forcefully opposed notions of mutual conditioning between us and God: "The right understanding of God's will excludes all those views which seek to represent the relation between God and the reality distinct from Himself as a relation of mutual limitation and necessity. In the first

Fourth, these insights finally led Torrance to an important point that is exactly opposite to the views espoused by Rahner. He claimed that just because God's love is free, it is an ultimate fact that cannot be explained from the human side at all. This is what makes Christianity different from anything else, Torrance said, with its simultaneous theocentric and Christocentric emphasis. So, the question is simply not the question that Rahner posed and answered. It is not "How can man come to God?"[53] And it cannot be that question because a focus on God that is truly Christocentric will already realize that we only know God and God's love because, while we were still sinners, God came to us of his own accord to save us from sin and death. The real coming of God to us in the incarnation, because it is such a decisive act of God, means at once that the door is firmly shut against any idea that we either can or must attempt to move toward God by loving our neighbors or by relying on any other human effort to reach God. The fact that God in Christ has come in person to the human race means that it is in Christ himself and in him alone that we are actually confronted by God's "self-grounded Love, God's giving of himself to men. He, as coming from the Father, is Love. We have to do with him alone." From this it follows that because it is in Christ that God has established an utterly new relation with the human race, we must recognize that this love of God itself and this alone transforms us because it "generates a surrender and love on our part."[54] But that surrender in love on our part is both conceptually and really tied to our response to Jesus Christ and not to some nameless mystery which could go by many other names.

Incarnation

We are in fact bound to the incarnation to know this truth which cannot be known from any other source. That is why, in contrast to Rahner's attempt to speak of God as absolute being, as the nameless whither of our experiences of self-transcendence or as "holy mystery," instead of starting and therefore ending with faith in Jesus Christ, and thus with knowledge of the eternal Father, Son, and Holy Spirit, Torrance's view is firmly tied to the incarnation from the outset because it is simultaneously theocentric and Christocentric.[55] Importantly, however, it is just because Torrance takes revelation

---

instance this includes all pantheistic and panentheistic systems according to which the existence of this other reality belongs in some way to the essence and existence of God Himself. The reason why God gives them real being and why from eternity they are objects of His knowledge is not that God would not be God without their actual or even possible existence, but because He wills to know them and to permit them to be actuality … He is not conditioned by them. They are conditioned by Him. They have not proceeded from His essence" (ibid., 562). This is the case of course because he created them from nothing, and thus they "have not proceeded from His essence … He was not obliged to do this. *He did not do it to satisfy some need in His own being and life*" (ibid., emphasis mine).

[53]Torrance, *The Doctrine of Jesus Christ*, 87.

[54]Ibid., 88.

[55]It is no accident that in Torrance's approach to knowledge of God and love of God and love of neighbor he always begins and ends with Christ himself while Rahner does not. By the time Rahner introduces Christology into his reflections on love of God and neighbor, it is already too late to mean anything decisive

in its identity with Jesus himself seriously as the only avenue to knowledge of God the Father that he then is led to assert, against Rahner's view, that

> I cannot love God through loving my neighbour. I can love my neighbour truly and only through loving God. To love God through loving my neighbor is to assert that the Incarnation is not a reality, the reality it is, that relation to God is still a mediated one. To love God through my love to my neighbour is to move toward God. It does not know a movement of God toward man.[56]

True love of neighbor then can only result from one's love of Christ and one's devotion to Christ. To begin with the idea that love of neighbor is the way to love God and that, as Rahner said, "the categorised explicit love of neighbour is the primary act of the love of God"[57] so that "the primary basic act of man who is always already 'in the world' is always an act of the love of his neighbour and *in this* the original love of God is realized in so far as in this basic act are also accepted the conditions of its possibility, one of which is the reference of man to God when supernaturally elevated by grace,"[58] is from Torrance's perspective the ultimate form of self-justification.[59] This, because for Torrance, true love of God "flows spontaneously from an immediate vision of God in Christ. Unless God in Christ be everything, everything else will be nothing!"[60] This means then that "true love of others is generated in the heart of the believer by the Holy Spirit; but the Holy Spirit

---

because he has previously argued that it is "*by* loving one's visible brother lovingly" that one "can love God whom one does not see" (TI 6, 247). So instead of allowing the love of God revealed in Christ to completely reshape his view of love, he claims that "the unity of the love of God and of neighbour on which we have been reflecting becomes even more radical from a Christological and eschatological point of view and thus reaches its climax; thus the man Jesus takes on and continues to have an eternal significance for our relationship to God right into the 'direct' vision of God" (ibid.). For Torrance, however, the incarnation is not a more radical view of anything we can discover apart from Christ. It is a *novum*, something without analogy anywhere in human experience, precisely because it is an act of the eternal God coming into history from outside; it is not something arising from history as its climax. For Torrance, the eternal significance of the man Jesus rests solely on the fact that his humanity is the humanity of the Word and that as such, he is the only one who can and does reveal God to us and reconcile us to God. And he is the one Mediator even now as the risen, ascended, and coming Lord who, through his Holy Spirit, enables true knowledge of God as well as true love of neighbor.

[56]Torrance, *The Doctrine of Jesus Christ*, 88–9.

[57]Rahner, TI 6, 247.

[58]Ibid., 246.

[59]This is why Torrance insisted that "the Christian religion has its justification either in the name of Jesus Christ or not at all. It is certainly abolished when everything is made to pivot upon man's own self-understanding. However we think of it, then, justification calls for a radical self-renunciation, a displacement of the self by Jesus Christ, and therefore for a relentless objectivity in which you do not love your neighbor because love is a form of your self-fulfilment, in which you do not think out of your own self-centredness but out of a centre in the incarnate Word who summons you to leave all and follow Him, and in which you do not pray or worship God in your own name or in your own significance but only in the name and significance of Jesus Christ, in which therefore you do not baptize yourself but are baptized out of yourself into Christ, and in which you do not feed upon yourself but feed only upon the Body and Blood of the Lord" (*God and Rationality*, 70).

[60]Torrance, *The Doctrine of Jesus Christ*, 89.

operates in that way in and through us only as our eyes are fixed unselfishly on the Lord Jesus Christ."[61]

But that implies that Christian faith is not Christian faith without a conceptual and ontological relation with the man Jesus himself as revealer and reconciler. And that itself suggests that such recognition comes through the Holy Spirit and not anonymously by us attempting to love our neighbors with the idea that that very act in and of itself is already love of God even if we do not explicitly know God and God's unconditional love revealed in Christ himself. That is why Torrance insisted that whatever good we do toward others is not what counts, because it is only if we do those things in and through Christ himself whose love enables those actions, that makes us Christians in the first place. And for that to happen, specific conceptual knowledge of God as the Father of Jesus Christ is necessary at the outset and not as a conclusion to a phenomenology of love understood from our loving others. So, for Torrance, "the Incarnation of God in one man, a Man who has no existence apart from the Incarnation, means that to this one Man we must turn and nowhere else. It is another way of asserting the absolute Theocentricity, and the Christocentricity, which uniquely characterises the Christian Gospel and Christian Faith."[62]

Love of God and Love of Neighbor

To illustrate exactly where Rahner's anthropologically based thinking leads, it will be helpful to see in more detail how Rahner and Torrance understand love of God and love of neighbor. This is extremely important because those theologians today who think that one can discover the truth only by first fighting against oppression and for liberation miss the all-important point that such activities follow from being freed from our self-will and sin by Christ to do so. Ignoring that fact always leads to new forms of self-justification and alienation from God and neighbor with the idea that just loving one's neighbor is in fact the locus for finding the Holy Spirit.[63] Because Rahner conceives

---

[61] Ibid.

[62] Ibid., 91.

[63] Such a mistaken idea ignores the important point that one simply cannot understand the Holy Spirit by starting with "manifestations or operations of the Spirit in creaturely existence, in man or in the world, but from the propriety of the Spirit to the being of God on the divine side of the line of demarcation between the Creator and the creature … because the Holy Spirit is the Spirit of the Father and the Son." Torrance followed Athanasius and held that understanding the Spirit must develop "from his essential relation to the one God and his one undivided activity as God, and specifically from his inherence in the being of the eternal Son" (*Theology in Reconciliation*, 231). It is just because the operations of the Spirit are not to be understood as being on a "lower level than the operations of the Son, as if they were limited to the many spiritual manifestations within us" that "a proper understanding of the gifts and diverse operations of the Spirit is reached from the perspective of their source and ground in the divine Trinity, from the Father, through the Son and in the Spirit … controlled knowledge of the Spirit is taken from our knowledge of the Son and of the Father through the Son" (ibid., 232). One such misguided approach to understanding the Spirit can be seen in Rubén Rosario Rodríguez, *Dogmatics after Babel: Beyond the Theologies of Word and Culture* (Louisville, KY: Westminster John Knox Press, 2018),

the "unity between the experience of God and the experience of self" as "the condition which makes it possible to achieve that unity which theological tradition recognizes as existing between love of God and love of neighbor,"[64] he proceeded to reflect on the unity of love of God and love of neighbor within that perspective. His conclusion is astonishing when compared to Torrance's approach. He argued that since for Christians "the fact that on the one hand the experience of God and the experience of the self are one, and on the other that the experience of self and the encounter with our neighbour are one, that all these three experiences ultimately constitute a single reality with three aspects *mutually conditioning* one another."[65]

Since Rahner believed that these three relationships mutually condition each other, he then argued that we can say that "man discovers himself or loses himself in his neighbour; that man has already discovered God, even though he may not have any explicit knowledge of it, if only he has truly reached out to his neighbour in an act of unconditional love, and in that neighbor reached out also to his own self."[66] This coheres with Rahner's further claim that "love of God and love of neighbor stand in a relationship of mutual conditioning. Love of neighbor is not only a love that is demanded by the love of God, an achievement flowing from it; *it is also in a certain sense its antecedent condition*."[67] Consequently,

> love for God only comes to its own identity through its fulfillment in a love for neighbor. Only one who loves his or her neighbor can know who God actually is. And only one who ultimately loves God (whether he or she is reflexively aware of this or not is another matter) can manage unconditionally to abandon himself or herself to another person.[68]

From this it follows that it is only when people genuinely open themselves to their neighbors that they "receive the possibility of going forth from themselves, coming out of themselves and loving God."[69]

---

when he argues that one can find the "the presence of the Holy Spirit in liberating work—especially when such work is located outside the church" so that truth claims for Christian doctrine must not be tested exclusively by their correspondence with who God is for us in Jesus Christ, but rather by "comparative theological analysis" grounded in acts of liberation and humility (143, 176). Accordingly, he believes that "to participate in the process of liberation is already, in a certain sense, a salvific work" so that one can locate "divine revelation in the work of historical and political liberation" (142). We will discuss this issue in detail in Chapter 5.

[64]Rahner, TI 13, 126.

[65]Ibid., 128, emphasis mine.

[66]Ibid., 128–9.

[67]Karl Rahner, *The Love of Jesus and the Love of Neighbor*, trans. Robert Barr (New York: Crossroad, 1983), 71, emphasis mine.

[68]Ibid.

[69]Ibid., 72. It is vitally important to note here the difference between Torrance and Rahner on this point. For Torrance, the Holy Spirit acting in union with the Word and directing us toward God the Father is the one who personally is present to us and freely actualizes within us a true knowledge of God. The Spirit thus creates within us the "capacity for God" and thus fulfills knowledge of God within us (Torrance, *God and Rationality*,

Rahner did not stop at that. Since he based his understanding of God on a nonconceptual or unthematic set of experiences, he argued that

> God is always given as the subjectively and objectively all-bearing *ground* of experience, a ground which is beyond this world; he is therefore given indirectly in a kind of boundary experience as the origin and destination of an act which is objectively directed towards the world and which ... is a loving communication with (or "no") to the Thou in the world.[70]

Thus, God is given to us "primarily and originally ... in (or as) the transcendental, unclassified horizon of the knowing and acting intentionality of man and not as an 'object' represented by an idea within this horizon."[71] And within this outlook, Rahner daringly advanced his idea that "the love of God and the love of neighbour are one and the same thing,"[72] even though he clearly did not wish to reduce love of God to our love of neighbors. However, it is his stress on the mutually conditioned nature of the two that drives his thought toward claiming that we should espouse the "radical identity of the two loves"[73] such that he then argued that our love of neighbor brings us closer to them and also "brings us to God and his love *by* the love of our neighbour."[74]

Because Rahner considered this act of love an "infused" virtue, he also contended that "the love of neighbor is not merely the preparation, effect, fruit and touchstone of the love of God but is itself an act of this love of God itself" since he held that it is supported by God's self-communication and the Holy Spirit.[75] Importantly, Rahner realized that

> most theologians today would still shrink from the proposition which gives [his] fundamental thesis its ultimate meaning, its real clarity and inescapable character, viz. that wherever a genuine love of man attains its proper nature and its moral absoluteness and depth, it is in addition always so underpinned and heightened by God's saving grace that it is also love of God, *whether it be explicitly considered to be such a love by the subject or not.*[76]

Rahner pondered "whether all interhuman love, provided only that it has its own moral radicality, is also *caritas* (i.e. love also of God), since it is orientated towards God, not

---

171). For Torrance, "this lordly freedom of the Spirit means that the creature does not have a continuity in relation to God that belongs to the creature in itself, for this is continuously given and sustained by the presence of the Spirit within the creation bringing creaturely relations to their *telos* in God" (ibid.). That is why Torrance insisted that we cannot think "our own way into God—that would be tantamount to substituting the movement of our own spirit for that of the Spirit of God and to erecting our own word into the Word of God" (ibid., 181).

[70] Rahner, TI 6, 244–5.
[71] Ibid., 245.
[72] Ibid., 233.
[73] Ibid., 236.
[74] Ibid., 235, emphasis mine.
[75] Ibid., 236.
[76] Ibid., 237, emphasis mine.

indeed by an explicitly categorised motive but (and this is the question) by its inescapably given transcendental horizon which is given gratuitously by God's always prevenient saving grace."[77]

For Rahner, the answer was a definite yes because he maintained that "wherever man posits a positively moral act in the full exercise of his free self-disposal, this act is a positive supernatural salvific act in the actual economy of salvation even when its *a posteriori* object and the explicitly given *a posteriori* motive do not spring tangibly from the positive revelation of God's Word but are in this sense 'natural.' "[78] One might reasonably ask how could Rahner equate such a moral act with a supernatural act of salvation without confusing nature and grace? His answer is that "the thereby already given, supernaturally transcendental even though unconscious horizon of the spirit (its *a priori* orientation towards the triune God of eternal life) includes an element of (transcendental) revelation and possibility of faith which also gives such an act that sufficient character of 'faith' necessary for a moral act being a saving act."[79] This thinking rests on Rahner's assumption that there is a "strict mutual identity of the love of God and the love of neighbour."[80]

Several familiar themes are at play here. Rahner consistently maintained that some sort of nonconceptual knowledge is at work when we love our neighbors. Therefore, when we do so, we are already loving God whether we know that or not. Furthermore, he then claimed that it is precisely and only through loving our neighbor that we can know God and experience saving grace. And by supposing that love of God and love of neighbor mutually condition each other, he really had unwittingly reduced knowledge of God to loving others, even though that clearly was not his intention from the outset.

---

[77]Ibid., 238.

[78]Ibid., 239.

[79]Ibid. Interestingly, Torrance would flatly reject the idea that a moral act is a "saving act" on the grounds that the only saving act is that act of God's having justified and sanctified us in the life, death, and resurrection of Jesus Christ himself and God alone actualizes that in us through the action of the Holy Spirit. Nonetheless, he did note that history has shown that the fathers at Trent, who accused the Lutherans of turning faith into a justifying work, were shrewder than was realized at the time since that frequently occurred in Lutheran and Reformed theology (Torrance, *God and Rationality*, 57). That is why Torrance so strongly rejected any notion of *conditional grace* or conditional salvation, with the idea that people are saved and thus justified by grace only "*if* they repent and believe" (ibid.). It is in this context that he again rejected the Roman Catholic idea of infused grace because that idea led to the notion that once grace is received then "we may co-operate with divine grace in living the Christian life, meriting more grace through repentance and obedience and receiving it through the sacraments" (ibid.). Torrance maintained that the Reformers rightly rejected this thinking with its "quantitative notion of grace," and they also "exposed the Pelagian heresy latent in the Roman notion of merit, for it obscured the Gospel of free forgiveness of sins granted on the merits of Christ alone," (ibid.). Torrance held that any idea of *conditional salvation* meant a "new legalizing of the Gospel" since it made " 'justifying faith' into a saving work" (ibid.). He followed James Fraser of Brea, an eighteenth-century theologian, and argued that faith must be grounded "upon the active obedience of Christ and His complete sufficiency for our justification, which gave rise to an unconditionally free proclamation of the Gospel" (ibid., 57–8). For Torrance, while the Gospel calls for repentance and obedient faith, it never says "this is what God in Christ has done for you, and you can be saved on condition that you repent and believe" because it "is not faith that justifies us, but Christ in whom we have faith" (ibid. 58).

[80]Rahner, TI 6, 239.

However, it is this very thinking, based on a notion of "infused" grace, that finally led Rahner to claim that self-acceptance is the same as accepting God and Christ.[81] It isn't of course. And Torrance's more precise thinking about these matters will illustrate the point.

Placing this discussion in the context of the commands to love God and one's neighbor illustrates once more the differences that emerge from a "philosophy of theology" and a "philosophy of religion." The problems that emerge in this contrast between the views of Torrance and Rahner concern the fact that it is just Rahner's assertion that the absolute goal of our transcendentality is "not something additional to, or external to itself" that makes it impossible for him to ground knowledge of God consistently in the very being of God as he certainly wished to do. That very assertion impels Rahner to look within *us* and thus to trace the origin of human knowledge of God to our own transcendental dynamisms, instead of consistently pointing us away from ourselves to the need for obedience to revelation in its identity with Jesus Christ. Moreover, Rahner clearly embraces, here and elsewhere, a kind of nonconceptual knowledge of God in the form of a supposed unthematic awareness of God present in all human beings reflecting on themselves.[82] There is no doubt that Rahner embraces what Torrance identifies as nonconceptual or nonobjective knowledge of God and that this affects not only his theological method but everything he says about God, Christ, and salvation.

In the first instance he claims that "the transcendence in which God is already known, although unthematically and nonconceptually, may not be understood as an active mastering of the knowledge of God by one's own power."[83] Read in the most charitable light, this statement could be interpreted to be an attempt to recognize and maintain God's freedom. Indeed, Rahner goes on to assert that "in biblical language" such transcendental experience of God is "from the very beginning the experience of *being known* by God."[84] However, while Torrance also insists that knowledge of God is based on our being known by God,[85] Torrance's concept of God is always conceptually shaped by his understanding

---

[81]Thus, "if a man freely accepts himself as he is, even with regard to his own inner being whose basic constitution he inevitably has not fully grasped, then it is God he is accepting" (TI 16, 67). Indeed, for Rahner, "a man may accept his existence and his humanity … in silent patience and perhaps without any verbal formulation which explicitly refers to the Christian revelation … The man who accepts his life in this way is in fact assenting to something to which he entrusts himself as to what is immeasurable, because God has filled it with the immeasurable, in other words with himself, in letting his Word become flesh. Even if he does not know it, that man is giving assent to Christ" (Karl Rahner and Wilhelm Thüsing, *A New Christology* [New York: Seabury Press/Crossroad, 1980], 16–17).

[82]For instance, in his *Foundations*, Rahner says our human knowledge of God is "a *transcendental* knowledge because man's basic and original orientation towards absolute mystery, which constitutes his fundamental experience of God, is a permanent existential of man as a spiritual subject" (52). Consequently, knowledge of God or any proof of God's existence "is a reflection upon man's transcendental orientation towards mystery," and thus, following Blondel, Rahner maintains "that *speaking* of God is the reflection which points to a more original, unthematic and unreflexive knowledge of God" (ibid.).

[83]Rahner, *Foundations*, 58.

[84]Ibid.

[85]Thus, for Torrance, "it is in and through this encounter with Jesus Christ in His implacable objectivity in which we become crucified to the world and to ourselves that we are enabled to know objectively *as we are*

of God in light of the incarnation and outpouring of the Holy Spirit, while Rahner's view of God is shaped by a view of mystery formed from our unthematic experiences of transcendence. What I just illustrated and will demonstrate further as this chapter proceeds is that this led Rahner to ascribe the power to know God to us, initially in our supposed obediential potency for revelation, and then in the form of what he called our supernatural existential. While he did claim that all human experience is permeated by grace and thought he thereby avoided any sort of Pelagianism, the fact is that these ideas finally led him to confuse nature and grace by detaching grace from Christ, the Giver of grace and locating it in our transcendental experiences of mystery.[86] It further led him to marginalize the problem of sin and the need for reconciliation *in order* to know God in truth. And finally, it led him to confuse knowledge of the Christian God, which can only take place in faith through union with Christ, with our knowledge of absolute being. This is why he says that the "term" or "source" of our experience of transcendence can be "called 'God' " because in this experience "we can also speak of being, of ground, of ultimate cause, of illuminating, revealing logos, and we can appeal to what is meant by a thousand other names."[87] Knowledge of God then occurs as human explication in reflection of "what is already present in [our] transcendentality."[88]

This thinking is antithetical to Torrance's view that only God can name God to us and that is what he means when he asserts that our knowledge of God is grounded in God's knowing us.[89] For Rahner, God's knowing us is equated with our knowing ourselves just as our loving God is equated with our loving our neighbors. That is the problem here. Rahner thinks knowledge of God comes from what we call God based on our unthematic experiences of ourselves in our self-transcendence toward absolute being. Rahner also thinks we can really love God *by* loving our neighbors. Further, Rahner claimed that "when we call God 'Father' with the Bible and with Jesus himself, and notice the criticism which this name provokes today, we can understand how a word like this, a word in which Jesus dared to express his ultimate understanding of God and his relationship to God, can be misunderstood or not understood at all."[90] Notice what is missing here. There is no mention of the fact that Jesus did not just express his understanding of God.

---

known by Him and so to think appropriately of God in accordance with His nature, and not out of a centre in ourselves in which we impose our own patterns of thought upon Him and then fail to distinguish Him in His reality from our own subjective states and conditions" (*God and Rationality*, 54, emphasis mine).

[86]Thus, for Rahner, "the universality of the factuality of grace from the outset [is] … an existential of man's transcendentality as such" (Rahner, TI 18, 182).

[87]Rahner, *Foundations*, 60.

[88]Ibid., 44.

[89]See Torrance, *Christian Doctrine of God*, 105, where he maintained that "within the sphere of divine revelation an *epistemological inversion* takes place in our knowing of God, for what is primary is his knowing of us, not our knowing of him." For Torrance, God's "self-revealing and self-naming as *I am* proclaimed in the Old Testament … was appropriated by Jesus Christ and identified with his own *I am* proclaimed to us in the Gospel of the saving love and grace of God the Father … his own 'I am' is grounded in the indwelling of the Father and the Son in one another, in the eternal Communion which belongs to the inner Life of God as Father, Son and Holy Spirit" (ibid., 124).

[90]Rahner, *Foundations*, 60.

He was God the Son revealing God the Father such that he was not just expressing his human relationship to God, but he was God acting as our reconciler and revealer. He was, according to Torrance, acting from the divine and human side to heal our minds which, because of sin, are at enmity with God who alone names himself to us. His revealing God as Father therefore was, as Torrance claimed, grounded in his eternal relation to the Father within the inner Trinity. Thus, it did not just express his understanding of God as Father but his unique relation of being with the Father.

Most importantly, the truth of the matter here is that we really have no knowledge of this God, the Christian God, without conceptual awareness of who God was and is in Jesus Christ. So, while Rahner proceeded to ask "what name we should give to the term and the source of our original experience of transcendence,"[91] Torrance insisted that such a move illustrates the fact that we are prone to self-justification by relying on ourselves to name God and to love God, instead of allowing God to name himself as he has and still does in Jesus Christ. It is not out of our original experience of transcendence that we know the Christian God because the God who meets us in Christ reveals to us who he is by including us in the Son's knowledge of the Father through union with the human Jesus himself. And that knowledge can only occur, in Torrance's view, when we live our justification and sanctification in and from Christ himself and thus in faith and by grace. But of course, none of this would be at all possible unless we are conceptually and thus ontologically united with Christ through the miraculous action of the Holy Spirit.

Because Rahner grounds his theology in his philosophy of religion, he can say that the goal of our transcendentality is "present all along and in its very origins, albeit without being recognized as a conscious theme of thought."[92] Because Torrance thinks that we can only know God truly when God comes to us in Christ and opens us in his reconciling grace through the Holy Spirit to a true knowledge of himself, he would once more flatly reject the idea that the Christian God actually can be recognized in truth without a precise conceptual awareness of who God is. And that conceptual awareness does not come from an analysis of *our transcendentality*, but only from God himself coming into history from outside, as noted above. Put simply, Torrance followed Anselm to insist that "even though God transcends all that we can think and say of Him, it still holds good that we cannot have experience of Him or believe in Him without conceptual forms of understanding—as Anselm used to say: *fides esse nequit sine conceptione*."[93]

This is why Torrance unambiguously claimed that "in Jesus Christ God has come to reconcile man to Himself so that man may be delivered from his self-enclosure and be restored to true objectivity in God and true subjectivity in himself."[94] What this means to Torrance is that God's making himself an object of our knowledge occurs

---

91 Ibid.
92 Rahner, TI 11, 92.
93 Torrance, *God and Rationality*, 170. See also Torrance, *ITQ*, 215–16.
94 Torrance, *Theological Science*, 48.

within the sphere of our alienation from Him … where we are actively engaged in subjugating the external world to the processes of our thought in order to give us power and control over them so that we may use them to reassure and establish ourselves in the world, and also where in the midst of all that we have even sought to be independent of God, and so have estranged ourselves from Him by resisting His will and taking the way of self-will.[95]

So, for Torrance, the incarnation reveals our hostility to God and discloses our need for reconciliation so that we might become "adapted to that object" in order to have "true knowledge of it."[96]

Here we approach the heart of the issue we are considering in this chapter. Torrance unequivocally insisted that theologians such as Rahner and Schillebeeckx, in spite of their proper desire to get beyond "some of the more difficult pronouncements of the Curia," problematically introduced "a *non-conceptual element*" into "our basic knowledge of God."[97] By doing this they inadvertently opened the door to the very subjectivism they intended to overcome precisely because they presented a mutually conditioned view of God and our knowledge of God. This, I believe, is what led Rahner himself to confuse revelation and grace with our experience of ourselves with far-reaching problematical results. We have already seen how this affected Rahner's understanding of love of God and love of neighbor and how and why Rahner never even considered the problem of sin and the need for reconciliation in explicating his philosophy of religion. At this point I would like to illustrate exactly how Torrance's scientific approach to knowledge of God can offer a satisfying resolution to the difficulties inherent in Rahner's approach. This might lead to closer relations between Catholics and Protestants in connection with the doctrine of God and Christology.

Rahner and Torrance on Knowledge of God

By promoting nonconceptual knowledge of God, I have been contending that Rahner stands in conflict with his own idea of God's freedom implied in his belief that we only know God based on God's knowing us. This is because he begins thinking about God from our experience of ourselves; he thinks he is beginning with God's self-revelation because for him that self-revelation is embedded in our experience of ourselves in the form of a supernatural existential. Hence, "God's self-revelation in the depths of the spiritual person is an a priori determination coming from grace and is in itself unreflexive … it is not something known objectively, but something within the realm of consciousness."[98] However, once it is suggested that God's self-revelation is part of

---

[95]Ibid.
[96]Ibid.
[97]Torrance, *ITQ*, 226.
[98]Rahner, *Foundations*, 172. Rahner's nonconceptual approach here leads to what I claim is a confusion of nature and grace. In the words of Stephen Duffy, for Rahner, "grace, therefore, is experienced, though not as grace, for

one's spiritual experience as an a priori determination of our existence that cannot be known objectively, we are left in a position that encourages the idea that since we cannot know God's grace objectively, therefore it can be described by describing our religious experiences. As we have seen, this approach unfortunately causes Rahner to detach God's self-revelation from Christ himself by locating it within us at the outset. Let us hear what he says based on his philosophy and theology.

First, Rahner assumes that because there is an "interlocking of philosophy and theology" with the result that "when the reality of man is understood correctly, there exists an inescapable circle between his horizons of understanding and what is said, heard and understood."[99] Based on this thesis Rahner maintained that "Christianity assumes that these presuppositions which it makes are inescapably and necessarily present in the ultimate depths of human existence."[100] Therefore philosophy is understood by Rahner to refer to any theoretical reflection on human existence thus understood. In one sense, he also explicitly holds that philosophy is already a kind of theology.[101] That is why he asserted that "we can never philosophize as though man has not had that experience which is the experience of Christianity."[102] And the experience to which he here refers is "the experience of what we call grace."[103] From this it follows that "theology itself implies a philosophical anthropology which enables this message of grace to be accepted in a really philosophical and reasonable way, and which gives an account of it in a humanly responsible way."[104] For Rahner, philosophy "reflects upon its historical origins and asks whether it sees itself as still bound to these origins in history and in grace as something valid."[105]

In connection with Rahner's view of philosophy and theology, some have argued that Rahner should not be seen as a "foundationalist" and if he is not, then his theology might be read independently of his philosophical presuppositions. On that basis, it is then presumed that his concept of the *Vorgriff* could be seen within a strictly theological context, and it would thus make theological sense. The question I am raising, however,

---

it is psychologically indistinguishable from the stirrings of human transcendentality" ("Experience of Grace," in *The Cambridge Companion to Karl Rahner*, 48). This coheres with Rahner's own assertions that "God's offer of himself belongs to all men and is a characteristic of man's transcendence and his transcendentality … God's self-communication in grace, as a modification of transcendence … cannot by simple and individual acts of reflection … be differentiated from those basic structures of human transcendence" (*Foundations*, 129). In reality, to experience Jesus Christ is to experience God's grace which, as stated above, cannot be detached from the actions of Christ himself at any time or place. And grace certainly cannot be equated with any psychological stirrings within us without confusing nature and grace.

[99]Rahner, *Foundations*, 24.
[100]Ibid.
[101]Thus, for Rahner, "a philosophy that is absolutely free of theology is not even possible in our historical situation" (*Foundations*, 25). Indeed, Rahner claimed that, in light of his theory of anonymous Christians, "it is correct to say that in every philosophy men already engage inevitably and unthematically in theology, since no one has any choice in the matter" (TI 9, 79).
[102]Rahner, *Foundations*, 25.
[103]Ibid.
[104]Ibid.
[105]Ibid.

is whether or not the very attempt to speak of Christian revelation in its identity with Jesus Christ the revealer can bring in any idea of a preapprehension of being (*Vorgriff auf esse*), which is assumed to be the being of the Christian God at all, without detaching revelation from Christ and locating it within general human experience which is simply thought to be "graced." There is no question that Rahner thinks that is possible.

But, as we have seen, Torrance explicitly opposed such thinking because he refused to detach grace and revelation from God's Word and Spirit at any point in his reflections. This will explain why I think their methods are fundamentally irreconcilable as they stand.[106] Karen Kilby, for instance, thinks that the tensions in Rahner's early and later theology and between his embrace of "pluralism" together with his "transcendental theology" can be overcome if his theology is just seen as one possible approach in "a certain set of circumstances."[107] This can be accomplished, she thinks, only if "it does in fact decouple Rahner's theology from his early philosophical works," that is, "if Rahner is not read as grounding his theology on an independently known universal experience of God … but is rather read as grounding his understanding of the nature of universal human experience in a particular theology."[108] However, given that Rahner's own view that philosophy is already theology, I do not think one actually can decouple his philosophy from his theology without completely abandoning his transcendental method, his a priori attempts to understand God, Christ, and revelation and, perhaps most importantly, his idea that we all have some sort of nonconceptual knowledge of God, Christ, and revelation itself. In my view, Kilby's suggestion does not solve the problems created by Rahner's transcendental method. This is the case because the question posed to Rahner's thinking by Torrance's simultaneous theocentric and Christocentric understanding of God concerns whether or not Rahner's theology, which all agree begins with transcendental experience, allows Jesus Christ in his uniqueness to be the sole starting point, criterion, and conclusion for what he says theologically about God, revelation, faith, and grace.

It is evident from the texts presented in this chapter that he does not and cannot do that because for him transcendental revelation is part of universal human experience while categorical revelation identifies certain events within history as instances of that revelation embedded unthematically (nonconceptually) in everyone's experience of themselves. However, as Torrance rightly insisted, since revelation cannot in fact be detached from the revealer (Christ himself), Rahner's view of transcendental revelation undercuts both the need for Christ himself and the fact that because he really is the Way, the Truth, and the Life, there is no other way to the Father than through him. Therefore, Rahner's turn to the human experience of the nameless as the basis of our knowledge of God in and of itself undercuts a truly theological theology all along the line.

---

[106]For the nonfoundational reading of Rahner, see Karen Kilby, "Philosophy, theology and foundationalism in the thought of Karl Rahner," *Scottish Journal of Theology* 55 (2) (2002): 127–40.
[107]Ibid., 139.
[108]Ibid.

The questions that I have raised in this discussion illustrate the differences between a theological method such as Rahner's which claims that natural theology and revealed theology mutually condition each other and Torrance's, which claims an unequivocal priority for revelation and grace such that neither of these realities can be ascribed to people's experiences without detaching revelation and grace from the Giver of grace and the revealer himself, namely, Jesus Christ. That, to me, is the central issue that at present divides Rahner's thinking from Torrance's. And, as I have been arguing, the problem is to be found in Rahner's embrace of nonconceptual knowledge of God. In the end, Kilby thinks that "Rahner's conception of the human being is best judged, then, not by the questionable arguments he offers for it, or not mainly by these, but by its fruit in the whole of his thought."[109] Even if that is so, the fact is that a theology that leads to the idea that self-acceptance is identical with accepting Christ is one that has gone wrong because it methodologically undercuts the *need* for Christ as the starting point and exclusive criterion for its reflections with that very idea.

Second, for Rahner, as persons and subjects, we transcend ourselves when we ask analytical questions about ourselves, and so we affirm ourselves "as more than the sum of such analyzable components of [our] reality."[110] In this way we demonstrate, perhaps without acknowledging it or even realizing it, that "man is a transcendent being."[111] As such all of our knowledge and conscious activity "is grounded in a pre-apprehension (*Vorgriff*) of 'being' as such, in an unthematic but ever-present knowledge of the infinity of reality."[112]

Third, Rahner's entire philosophy of religion as expressed, for instance, in his *Hearer of the Word* is driven by his assumption that an "authentic philosophy of religion" is itself a "theological anthropology, insofar as we understood ourselves as the beings who, in freedom have to listen to the possible message of the free God."[113] From this he concluded that "all empirical observable 'religions' are religions only insofar as they succeed in … connecting us existentially to the real, living God."[114] Consequently, "the philosophy of religion, as it establishes our existential bond with God, not only has to know about God, but also us, who have to have this bond with God." Moreover, Rahner claims that he has shown his readers "in a purely philosophical way … to be the beings who stand necessarily in freedom before the God of a possible revelation."[115] Finally, Rahner argued that philosophy of religion, as natural theology, and thus as a "fundamental theological anthropology," expresses "the ready openness and the open readiness for theology"

[109]Karen Kilby, *Karl Rahner*, Fount of Christian Thinkers, Series, ed. Peter Vardy (London: Fount Paperbacks, an imprint of HarperCollins, 1997), 14.
[110]Rahner, *Foundations*, 29.
[111]Ibid., 31.
[112]Ibid., 33.
[113]Karl Rahner, *Hearer of the Word: Laying the Foundation for a Philosophy of Religion*, trans. Joseph Donceel, ed. and intro. Andrew Tallon (New York: Continuum, 1994), 147.
[114]Ibid., 148.
[115]Ibid., 149.

which clearly indicates that it has the capacity to "prepare" us for theology and thus "establishes the obediential potency for revelation."[116]

With this last remark Rahner presented a recurrent theme of this theology, namely, that all persons, especially in light of their unthematic and nonconceptual grasp of revelation in grasping absolute being philosophically, have the freedom to hear and accept the revelation of the living God. He did of course want to stress God's free grace, and he did so by asserting that God himself brings about our readiness at least to listen to and perceive God's silence. He maintained that "since God brings about the readiness for listening *as* a condition for hearing God's own word, theology is wholly based upon itself: the word of the living God." However, this claim is undercut by his further assertion that "the philosophy of religion is previous to it [theology] only as a condition" which itself supposedly "comes from the self-revealing God" such that "it is a condition of receptive theology only insofar as it is conditioned by God's word."[117]

This, however, is *the* problem which I will explore in a moment by discussing Torrance's important view of philosophy and faith. In sum, a theology conditioned by God's Word in its identity with the incarnate Word demonstrates that we have no capacity for God in ourselves and are at enmity with God because of original sin. Furthermore, from God's Word, according to Torrance, we know that our capacity for knowing God comes from the Holy Spirit enabling our faith in Jesus Christ himself through union with him, so that knowing God could never be equated with our self-knowledge. And, since our free will is our self-will from which only Christ can extricate us, we could never suppose, with Rahner, that knowledge of God is the result of any knowledge or freedom which is our own. This is the case because when genuine knowledge of God occurs, it does so as a result of the Spirit actualizing Christ's objective justification and sanctification of our human knowledge and freedom within us through our union with Christ by faith which, as I have been arguing necessarily involves conceptual union with Christ since faith means knowledge of the truth.

In these reflections then one can see very clearly some of the stark differences between a "philosophy of theology" as offered by Torrance and a "philosophy of religion" as offered by Rahner. As noted above, it is striking that in Rahner's move from his philosophy of religion to a theology of revelation he rarely mentioned Jesus Christ and never consistently allowed Jesus Christ to be the pivotal determining factor in his conception of revelation. I say this because for Torrance, as noted, Jesus himself must be the starting point and criterion of revelation as God's self-communication so that Torrance never argued for a "possible revelation" of God as Rahner himself did. He insisted that theology must always begin with the fact that Jesus Christ himself *is* the revelation of God in history precisely as the Way, the Truth, and the Life (Jn 14: 6); he is the very Word of God incarnate in history and given his utter uniqueness, there is no way to the Father except through him. As such, revelation is never a *possibility*

---

[116]Ibid., 150–1.
[117]Ibid., 151.

we can work up to in our philosophy or in our anthropology because "we cannot earn knowledge of Christ, we cannot achieve it, or build up to it … in the very act of knowing him we ascribe all the possibility of our knowing him to Christ alone, and none of it to ourselves."[118] Torrance therefore believed that "it is only when we actually know Christ, know him as our personal savior and Lord, that we know that we have not chosen him but that he has chosen us; that it is not in our own capacity to give ourselves the power to know him."[119] This is because he believed, as discussed above, that revelation itself, as God's personal act of self-disclosure in Jesus Christ himself, shows us that we are at enmity with God's grace and need Christ's forgiveness before we can know God in truth.

Since he himself is the very Word of the living God, Torrance insisted that we have no true knowledge of the Christian God unless we are thinking in faith, of the Father through his Son as enlightened by the Holy Spirit. But there is an important, even a decisive, proviso that separates the two theologians. That concerns the easy *continuity* Rahner presumes to exist between his demonstration that since all human beings are spirit, therefore they have an obediential potency for hearing and accepting the revelation of the living God.[120] In his own discussion of the relationship between philosophy and faith, it is noticeable that Torrance stresses a point which is completely absent from Rahner's reflections. That point concerns the problem of sin and evil, as noted above. Rahner repeatedly assumes that "because we are the openness for being as such" therefore "we face the real possibility of a revelation, at least insofar as it is the free personal self-manifestation of a divine *Thou*."[121] But *a* divine Thou is not necessarily identical with Jesus Christ who *is* God present in history, actively enabling our knowledge of the one true God. With his idea of an obediential potency, Rahner claimed that metaphysics itself can perceive a word of God and that word is God's silence.[122] Such metaphysics, he believed, "sets up someone who can hear God's message, insofar as such a power of hearing derives from human nature."[123]

Therein lies a major difficulty. Torrance claimed that there is nothing more needed in philosophy today than a critique of the idea that one could rely on one's natural beliefs to know the truth about God and ourselves.[124] And he immediately introduced the dogma of original sin to make his point. He argued that the "Schoolmen" of medieval philosophy "carried over from Greek thought the idea that at bottom man is at one

---

[118]Torrance, *Incarnation*, 2.

[119]Ibid.

[120]As seen above, Rahner's belief that "grace, therefore, is experienced, though not as grace, for it is psychologically indistinguishable from the stirrings of human transcendentality," rested on his belief in nonconceptual knowledge of God, revelation, and grace itself. And from this it followed, according to Stephen Duffy, who interpreted Rahner accurately on this, that "nature is in continuity with and positively open to grace" ("Experience of Grace," *Cambridge Companion to Rahner*, 51).

[121]Rahner, *Hearer of the Word*, 152.

[122]Ibid., 153.

[123]Ibid.

[124]Thomas F. Torrance, "Faith and Philosophy," *Hibbert Journal* 47 (3) (October 1948–July 1949), 237–46, 238.

with God," and so they "posited a doctrine of continuity in the human consciousness to God."[125] This, Torrance claimed, tended toward an "underlying monism" which meant that they failed to take the "doctrine of original sin" seriously due to the fact that they accepted "the Platonic conception of evil as essentially negation of the good."[126] While modern philosophy "knocked the bottom out of medieval thought as a system by calling in question its first principles," such philosophy also "repudiated the religious attitude which dominated the thought of the Middle Ages." Thus, modern philosophy uncritically advanced a humanist mindset that was "characterised by a greater failure than there was in medieval philosophy, in spite of the Reformation, to realise the dogma of original sin and its corollary of a radical discontinuity in the world."[127] While Kant did indeed recognize a radical discontinuity in the world, along with radical evil "as a positive resistance of the will to the good," nonetheless he also "posited once again a continuity in our consciousness with the Divine." This led him to claim it was possible to offer a unified view of reality "which resolves all contradiction."[128] Once again, Torrance maintained that this approach did not take the problem of sin and evil seriously enough. Torrance argued, as noted above in other contexts, that Christian faith within which any serious theology of revelation develops not only must take sin and evil seriously but that it does so precisely in light of revelation itself. For him that meant that it is the cross of Christ that shows us the evil in the human heart that led to the crucifixion in the first place. So, Torrance maintained that

> Christian faith insists that no matter how much a philosopher thinks about it, he cannot bridge the contradiction between man and God in guilt. This contradiction can be resolved only by a desperate act on the part of God, called atonement, in which man in contradiction to God is reconciled and yet in such a way that the discontinuities of evil are not glossed over but are taken honestly and seriously.[129]

Continuity and Discontinuity

Torrance offered some important reflections on this issue. He argued that modern thought, following Hegel, adopted "the basic principle that in the depths of his self, in the so-called ideal self of every man, he is divine, is in *continuity* with the divine. The real is the rational, the ideal, and so far as man partakes of that he is one with the divine."[130] In this thinking Torrance stressed that there is "a secret identity of man with God" and

---

[125]Ibid., 239.
[126]Ibid.
[127]Ibid.
[128]Ibid.
[129]Ibid., 240–1.
[130]Torrance, *The Doctrine of Jesus Christ*, 67, emphasis mine.

then asked, "What place does Jesus occupy in this process?"[131] His answer is instructive. Referring to Heinrich Weinel and Albrecht Ritschl, Torrance noted that for the former "Jesus only brought to completion what the best of men before him had desired," and referring to the latter, he noted that "as the author of the perfectly spiritual and ethical religion Jesus is above all other men."[132] As the perfection of the moral and religious ideal Jesus simply intensifies "the movement which is already present in humanity towards the ideal."[133] Torrance opposed all such thinking because he believed that there is an extreme *discontinuity* between us and God caused by sin. And, importantly, this belief was not some arbitrarily conceived notion. It was based on what was actually disclosed by Jesus himself in his obedience to the Father even to the point of dying on the cross. In that event the revelation itself in its identity with the revealer disclosed the depths of evil in the human heart. In response to God's love and forgiveness, humanity in the persons of both Jews and Gentiles rejected God himself. Even now one might ignore Jesus, make him over into an ideal ethical model, or construe him as the perfect image of what it means to be human. But in each of these ways, by evading or denying his deity as God directly present to us in history as the one who alone atoned for our sins and sanctified our humanity in his life of obedience, we today also express the depth of our enmity with God. In other words, God is not just the good we construed as the origin and goal of our lives or of our moral behavior. That very construction represents a projection from our alienated lives onto reality and thus keeps us from seeing the true meaning of the incarnation, of revelation, and of sin and salvation.

Thus, Torrance argued that it is "the Incarnation of the very Son of God himself, that reveals the depth of the breach, or of what is called the 'fall' of the world, and of man, from God."[134] Hence, for Torrance, "the purpose of the Incarnation relates rather to sinful fallen humanity; not therefore to humanity as such, but to *fallen* humanity. The Incarnation is not to be understood as the perfection but the restoration of the creation."[135] It is only because Christ himself has borne away our sins "that our desperate condition as sinners becomes revealed."[136] However, if this is the case, then any idea that we possess an obediential potency for a possible revelation of the "living God" is exposed as a contrivance of an approach to revelation that bypasses not only the cross but also Christ himself as the one in whom we are disclosed as sinners in need of the reconciliation, which he accomplished for us. It is in this context that Torrance powerfully maintained that the incarnation should not be understood as "the flowering of the race, the height of civilisation and all that!"[137] Opposing what he termed a view of the incarnation that "is little short of a humanistic paganism," with its idea that the incarnation simply brought

---

[131]Ibid.
[132]Ibid.
[133]Ibid.
[134]Ibid., 76.
[135]Ibid.
[136]Ibid., 77.
[137]Ibid., 78.

new life to a weary world, Torrance insisted that the incarnation meant "the end of all that."[138]

In fact, it meant "the end of all *human* thought, the end of *human* hopes, but the coming of a really *new* Order, to which no continuity in history may be drawn."[139] And because this order is truly *new* and "wholly other, it does not mean, and cannot mean an historical extension in the time of our world, but rather its final and complete transformation" in the kingdom of God. That very kingdom is not "an historical extension of time" but the "bringing in what is radically new and which cannot be construed in terms of the world that waits for its final transformation and renewal at the return of the incarnate and resurrected Lord Jesus Christ."[140] Therefore, the philosophical principle of continuity for Torrance must be denied because the "Christian message is one of repentance, rebirth and renewal, and calls for the confession of sin, of failure, and the recognition of original sin."[141]

In this vein, Torrance's view of philosophy is such that it needs faith to understand that no continuity we can discover can actually disclose how desperate our discontinuity caused by evil and sin actually is. That is why he held that "continuity cannot throw any light on discontinuity."[142] Indeed he asserted that "faith insists on taking the discontinuities and contradictions in human life seriously and honestly and challenges the superficiality of the philosopher who thinks that by dialectic he can reach a coherent interpretation of existence in which the gaps of evil and sin and pain are healed by the activity of reason alone."[143] Torrance argued that philosophers need to be more critical and to him that meant that they should not adopt a worldview that does not seriously confront the problem of sin and evil. But this they will never do, he thought, until "there is a fundamental change in their mental make-up, *i.e.* until in faith they are able to stand outside of themselves on the ground of a Word which reaches them from without and not from within."[144]

A truly serious philosophy for Torrance is one in which a person will not accede to the powerful urge to unify all thought but will in faith avoid "the original sin of the mind" and acknowledge that, in light of the "Cross of Jesus Christ," the problem is so serious that it could only be solved by an act of God. He said that faith does not require of philosophers a "Christian attitude" or a "new dogmatic philosophy" but a philosophy that is "truly critical and undogmatic." That, he held, could happen only when someone "is brought to stand outside his naturalistic presuppositions and to view them from another standpoint."[145] Importantly, because Torrance envisioned the Word coming to us from outside ourselves as something completely new, he insisted that it is really "autonomous reason" that will "only admit what is transcendent to it, if it supposes a

138 Ibid.
139 Ibid.
140 Ibid., 78–9.
141 Ibid., 79.
142 Torrance, *Hibbert Journal*, 240.
143 Ibid. 240–1.
144 Ibid., 241.
145 Ibid.

secret identification of that transcendent with the ground of its own being."[146] In that approach he claimed, "Revelation is never taken seriously and is reduced to the last stages of a conscious recollection of what was already there."[147] Or one may attempt to subdue the unknown by translating it "into terms of what is already known" because it "cannot conceive an absolute unlikeness except in terms of itself." In this way "autonomous reason can only truly try to understand God in terms of itself, presupposing an ontic continuity between itself and God." But this, he said, amounts to worshipping "the creature instead of the Creator."[148] Against this, Torrance insisted that "faith is the capacity of reason to behave in terms of a unique object that is also subject. It is of the nature of God always to be Subject." Thus, for reason to function properly it must allow God to be who he is and not attempt to envision God as "a mere object" or as a "conclusion of a philosophical argument."[149]

But here is the catch. While people, as sinners, attempt to find some continuity in their thought and experience with God, genuine knowledge of God, grounded in revelation will never commit this sin which is "the sin of idealism, which for Christian faith must be regarded as the sin of all philosophical sins."[150] For reason to be truly rational, it must genuinely confront "a unique Object to which there is no analogy ... it is the huge boulder of a *Thou* blocking the path which cannot honestly be subdued to an *it*." This is why human reason "cannot bring forward any category or capacity of its own with which to apprehend the Other. Only in the act of acknowledgment can it receive the capacity to behave in terms of the Object, but must therefore be prepared to transformation in obedience to its unique Subject-object."[151] This finally led Torrance to conclude that faith, which is "the capacity of reason to behave in terms of a unique object that is also subject,"[152] allows one to realize that we do not possess the truth in ourselves but that we can only receive it from outside of us. And this reception will always mean that one will know "that he is actually in the wrong and needs to be put right with the Truth before he can know. That is why the New Testament thinks of faith always in terms of [*metanoia*] (change of mind), and justification, *i.e.* being put in the right with God or the Truth."[153]

Conclusion

We have discussed Torrance's "scientific theology" which led him to present his "philosophy of the science of God" rather than a "philosophy of religion." His reason was that in the former, one's thinking would be engaged with the reality of God from

---

[146]Ibid., 243.
[147]Ibid.
[148]Ibid.
[149]Ibid.
[150]Ibid., 244.
[151]Ibid.
[152]Ibid., 243.
[153]Ibid., 244.

start to finish, while in the latter one could easily substitute the content of one's religious experience for the mystery of God revealed in his Word and Spirit. This led Torrance to take revelation seriously as it meets us in the Old and New Testaments and in particular in the person and work of Jesus Christ and the outpouring of his Holy Spirit. Because of this he took sin seriously just because, in light of the cross and resurrection, he understood that our minds needed to be reconciled to God through union with Christ and thus in faith and through the action of the Holy Spirit before we could know the Christian God in truth. His theology was not only Christological, but for that very reason it was trinitarian as well. Without having the "mind of Christ," Torrance argued that we would bend the object of our reflection, namely, God himself to our own choices and agenda. And that, we saw, was another indication that we cannot know God without actually relying on God's reconciling grace and judgment as they meet us in our encounter with Christ himself. In other words, for Torrance, God could only be known through God.

After discussing Torrance's views, we contrasted his thinking with Karl Rahner's approach to knowledge of God. The main difference between the two theologians we saw concerned the fact that Rahner embraced what he called an unthematic or nonconceptual knowledge of God supposedly grounded in an experience of God present in everyone as the basis for understanding all aspects of Christian theology. We noted that Torrance's scientific theology implicitly and explicitly disallowed any such thinking precisely because it was unscientific in the sense that it did not allow the unique object of Christian faith to determine the truth of its understanding from start to finish. This, in Torrance's view, opened the door to all forms of subjectivism which always end in distorting the truth of the Christian faith. While Rahner, like Torrance, accepted the traditional Christologies and the importance of the doctrine of the Trinity, his philosophy of religion led him to ground his understanding of God in the experience of the "nameless" instead of exclusively in our encounter with the incarnate Word, Jesus Christ. This very move was based on the idea that everyone experiences God unthematically (nonconceptually) and thus without reflection, so that knowledge of God really meant making explicit what is always already present in everyone's experience of themselves. The point of this comparison between Torrance and Rahner then was to illustrate exactly what happens when one embraces any form of nonconceptual knowledge of God.[154] We saw that Rahner was unable to consistently distinguish without separating nature

---

[154]It is worth noting that, while Rahner himself rejected Bultmann's approach to theology, his espousal of nonconceptual knowledge of God, from Torrance's perspective, places him in exactly the same problematic position as Bultmann. Consider the following interesting remarks by Torrance: "Quite consistently, therefore, Rudolf Bultmann used to claim 'The question of God and the question of myself are identical'. However, since knowledge of God alleged to arise in this way is essentially symbolic and indirect, or metaphorical and oblique, and *non-conceptual*, it must be rationalised through borrowing conceptuality from elsewhere if it is to have any acceptable place in human culture at all. Scientifically regarded, this way of thinking by retreat into the realm of the indeterminate, the mythical or the poetic, is particularly reactionary and obscurantist, for it detaches the basic knowledge of faith from the given fabric of empirical reality and disjoins it from all other objective rational structures of knowledge with reference to which it may be tested and purged of pseudo-scientific as well as pseudo-theological ideas and constructs" (Thomas F. Torrance, *Christian Theology and Scientific Culture* [Eugene, OR: Wipf and Stock, 1998], 140).

and grace, reason and revelation and that in the end Rahner held that natural theology and revealed theology mutually conditioned each other. The main point of this chapter was to show that while such an assumption might easily follow from a philosophy of religion, it could never follow from a theology grounded in the object of Christian faith, namely, the God confessed in the Nicene Creed.[155] The importance of this chapter is wide-ranging, with prospects for significant ecumenical agreement, once theological thinking is consistently grounded in a properly Christological and trinitarian view of the Christian faith.

---

[155]It is no accident that Torrance held that it was precisely to the extent that the Nicene Council understood the evangelical faith of the Church as a "saving faith" that it made a "radical shift" under the impact of their having been enlightened by the living God and "freed from imprisonment in the darkness of their own prejudices, baseless conjectures and fantasies, that is, a shift away from a centre of thinking in the in-turned human reason (ἐπίνοια) alienated from its intelligible ground in God, to a centre in God's revealing and reconciling activity in the incarnation of his Mind and Word (*Logos*) in Jesus Christ" (*The Trinitarian Faith*, 19).

CHAPTER 5
LIBERATION AND THEOLOGY: A THEOLOGICAL ANALYSIS

It has become customary for contemporary theologians who embrace the method of liberation theology to argue *from* experiences of liberation to a knowledge of God. Thus, in a recent attempt to move beyond Barth's theology of the Word and Tillich's correlation theology as that is grounded in experience, it has been argued by Rubén Rosario Rodríguez, following Moltmann, that while "the continuity between human spirit and divine Spirit originates in and is preserved by divine initiative, this indwelling by the Spirit of God makes human knowledge and action possible despite our epistemological uncertainty because of the Christlike praxis it engenders."[1] From this it follows that one can therefore recognize "the presence of the Holy Spirit in liberating work—especially when such work is located outside the church" so that truth claims for Christian doctrine must not be tested exclusively by their correspondence with who God is for us in Jesus Christ and who we are in him as the incarnate Word who is the Way, the Truth, and the Life but rather by "comparative theological analysis" grounded in acts of liberation and humility.[2] Rosario Rodríguez thinks that today there is a "false dichotomy" which is "characteristic of both anthropological and revelational theologies—which favor either experience or revelation but are unable to bring both together."[3] His proposal therefore is to bring both of these together in a "doctrine of revelation grounded in the ongoing work of the Holy Spirit." He thus aims to build "on Jürgen Moltmann's attempts at bridging this gap" by working on the assumption that "we cannot recognize God's self-communication as revelation without first experiencing the Spirit of God."[4] But, as noted above, for him one can speak of the continuity between the human spirit and the Holy Spirit by considering "Christlike praxis" with the assumption that one can recognize "the presence of the Holy Spirit in liberating work." Because of this Rosario Rodríguez thinks that when liberative praxis is joined to a humility that affirms the hiddenness of God in his revelation, then we would have a theology "in which no tradition speaks with absolute certainty or universal application." That leads him to conclude that "multiple doctrinal formulations are not only tolerated but encouraged, and theological truth claims are tested in comparative theological analysis."[5]

---

[1]Rosario Rodríguez, *Dogmatics after Babel*, 143.
[2]Ibid..
[3]Ibid.
[4]Ibid.
[5]Ibid.

What I will show in this chapter is that, on the one hand there is no continuity between the human spirit and the Holy Spirit that can be found directly within our experiences of liberation because when we actually experience the Holy Spirit who is *homoousios* with the Father and the Son, then we are directed by the Holy Spirit to Jesus himself as our only Liberator and our only source of truth precisely because he is the Way, the Truth, and the Life (Jn 14:6). What we discover in this encounter is that, in ourselves we are sinners at enmity with God and thus with the truth.[6] But, in faith, we also discover that God himself has put us in the truth through his Holy Spirit from whom, "as the moving and unity of the Father and of the Son from eternity and in eternity," we know that in eternity God himself as Father and Son and in the power of the Holy Spirit is not against us but for us.[7] This is because

> the Holy Spirit is the temporal presence of the Jesus Christ who intercedes for us eternally in full truth. Therefore for us life in the Holy Spirit means "already," even in the midst of the "not yet," to stand in the full truth of what, considered from our "not yet," is pure future, but on the strength of this "already" pure present.[8]

In other words, we really know the truth only as we live from our reconciliation in Christ in whom our enmity against the truth is already overcome.

---

[6]This issue of continuity is discussed in detail in Chapter 4. This is a crucial issue, for the question really concerns whether in the end we are automatically at one with God, so that we possess some sort of innate continuity with God in our human consciousness of God. Such thinking ignores the problem of sin and displays an underlying monism. Torrance expresses these ideas beautifully in his fine chapter "Questioning in Christ," in *Theology in Reconstruction*, 117–27. In *Theological Science*, Torrance properly claims that "face to face with Christ our humanity is revealed to be diseased and in-turned, and our subjectivities to be rooted in self-will. It is we who require to be adapted to Him, so that we have to renounce ourselves and take up the Cross if we are to follow Him and know the Father through Him. It is in this way that the estranged human self is restored, and the damaged person of man is healed and recreated in communion with God, and thus that the disjunction in the subject—object relationship gives place to a cognitive union with God in love" (*Theological Science*, 310). What Torrance is referring to here is the fact that he thinks the "epistemological significance of the Incarnation" is such that "we are summoned to know God strictly in accordance with the way in which He has actually objectified Himself for us in our human existence, in Jesus Christ" (ibid.). But that means that we cannot "read back our own humanity into God," and we cannot "confine knowledge of Him within our human subjectivities" (ibid.) since in knowing God in and from Jesus, the incarnate Word, we are thinking from a center in God and not from a center in ourselves. For Torrance, "the doctrine of the lordly freedom of the Spirit to be present to the creation and bring its creaturely relations to their proper *telos* in the Creator, means that the creature does not have a continuity in relation to God that belongs to the creature in itself, for this is continuously given and sustained by the presence of the Spirit" (*Theology in Reconstruction*, 223). Holding the Spirit together with Christ, the Word enables theologians to avoid the subjectivism that has plagued modern theology from Descartes on through Schleiermacher, Tillich, and beyond. That is why Torrance always insisted, with Barth, that "unless we know the Holy Spirit through the objectivity of the *homoousion* of the Son in whom and by whom our minds are directed away from ourselves to the one Fountain and Principle of Godhead, then we inevitably become engrossed with ourselves, confusing the Holy Spirit with our own spirits" (*Theology in Reconstruction*, 227).
[7]Barth, CD II/1, 157.
[8]Ibid., 158.

That is why Barth claims that "our truth is our being in the Son of God, in whom we are not enemies but friends of God, in whom we do not hate grace but cling to grace alone, in whom therefore God is knowable to us."[9] It is in light of this fact that Jesus Christ is and must be, according to Karl Barth, "the first and the last word of Christian faith."[10] Hence, it is in him that we are truly free for God and thus free for our neighbors since in him our enmity to God and neighbor have been overcome

> because in eternity He intercedes for us; and because in the Holy Spirit the unity of the Father and the Son becomes effectual among and in us too in the twofold form of faith and the Church … we have then only to look to Jesus Christ—and it is indeed the work of the Holy Spirit, it is indeed the nature of true faith and of the true Church that this happens—to see the man to whom God is knowable, to see and understand ourselves as those to whom God is knowable.[11]

This is why Barth insists that

> the instruction of the Holy Spirit awakens and calls us, with that authority, precision and sovereignty, to use and exercise our freedom in Jesus, to the good work which we specifically are to do here and now in unqualified obedience to Him, which I must do because "I am not my own, but belong to my faithful Saviour Jesus Christ." This is the gloriously positive element in His instruction, which is distinguished from all fanatical self-instruction by the fact that it shows itself to be the instruction of the living Jesus Himself, obviously awakening and summoning us to participation in His exaltation.[12]

On the other hand, Rodríguez's claim that theological truth claims can and should be tested through comparative analysis actually undermines any possibility of recognizing the truth of the Christian faith at the outset since, as we have just argued, truth is and remains identical with Jesus himself who is the truth of God enabling our understanding of the truth in the first place. The point to be stressed here is that since Jesus, the crucified and risen Lord, is himself the very Word of God, the eternal Son of the Father, both Jesus himself and what he teaches us simply cannot be compared with anyone or anything else if we hope to attain any correct theological analysis. We must be clear about this at the outset. Karl Barth has claimed that in Jesus Christ "the statement that God is knowable to man can and must be made with the strictest possible certainty, with an apodictic certainty, with a certainty freed from any dialectic and ambiguity."[13] Barth could make this statement for at least two important reasons. First, he equates

---

[9]Ibid.
[10]Ibid., 162.
[11]Ibid., 161.
[12]Barth, CD IV/2, 374.
[13]Barth, CD II/1, 162.

this certainty with "the statement that 'the Word became flesh,'" so that all statements about God must be made only by those who realize that they have been "reconciled in Jesus Christ." Second, Barth insists that if we look in any direction but toward Christ himself we will not see the truth about humanity, namely, our sin, the law against which we have sinned, and the fact that in Christ our sins have been forgiven because in him all human beings have been "judged and removed, really removed, i.e., moved and taken up into fellowship with the life of the Son of God."[14] However, for Barth, all of this happens for us only as the Holy Spirit unites us to Christ and thus enables our reconciled fellowship with God, and thus with the truth. That is why a proper liberation theology would have to be one that begins by acknowledging that Jesus Christ is the one who frees humanity to love God and to live in the freedom from the sin and self-will that is ours only in him.

In this chapter, I will focus in part on the thinking of Rubén Rosario Rodríguez in order to illustrate that whenever it is thought that the truth of the Christian faith can be recognized and understood in the struggle for liberation, important as that is, rather than exclusively from Christ the Liberator, the danger of self-justification looms large. While Rosario Rodríguez argues that theology today must move *beyond* the "impasse" that supposedly exists between theologies grounded in the Word of God and theologies of culture which clearly correspond with the kinds of correlation theology found in Tillich and David Tracy, I will argue that a proper liberation theology would be one in which the theologian first recognizes our actual liberation from sin, which took place in the life, ministry, death, and resurrection of Jesus Christ, and on that basis one is freed to love one's neighbor by fighting against oppression.[15]

Therefore, I will argue that the ultimate question raised by Rosario Rodríguez's book concerns whether theologians can move beyond a proper theology of the Word and still know the God of Christian faith confessed in the Nicene Creed. Put bluntly, the issue is this: Can a theology, such as the one proposed by Rosario Rodríguez, that moves beyond the Word of God incarnate, that is, the God who was in Christ reconciling the world to himself, ever present a proper view of liberation? Can such a theology ever present a proper theological view of the Holy Spirit? Does not such an approach to theology end in some form of modalism by undermining a properly functioning doctrine of

---

[14]Ibid.

[15]George Hunsinger gets this point exactly right when he notes the danger of monism "when love of God collapses into neighbor-love" and thus "when it becomes increasingly difficult to differentiate liberation from salvation" (*Disruptive Grace: Studies in the Theology of Karl Barth* [Grand Rapids, MI: William B. Eerdmans, 2000], 56). As we shall see below, Thomas F. Torrance captures the issue perfectly when he claims that any attempt to love God by loving one's neighbor is a form of "egoism" because it fails to recognize that our proper love for neighbor can only occur when we love Christ who frees us or liberates us from the sin of self-reliance. Hunsinger rightly claims that "the precedence given to God's praxis [by Barth] serves to mobilize rather than detract from human praxis" such that this approach might suggest "how a theology of liberation might be anchored more securely in a theology of grace" (ibid., 57). What I am arguing in this chapter is that whenever liberation theology is grounded in acts of liberation, then the Holy Spirit has already been confused with the human spirit and what is presented is not yet or no longer a theology grounded in the grace of God which cannot be detached from Christ, the Giver of grace.

the Trinity, separating Christ's atoning act of reconciliation from his incarnation and finally undermining the fact that the Spirit who was poured out upon the Church and the world at Pentecost acts within history precisely by actualizing reconciliation within believers by uniting them to Christ through faith? Does not such a theology run the risk of confusing the Holy Spirit with the human spirit? Methodologically, then I will argue that whenever fighting against oppression comes first; whenever that fight against oppression is the starting point or locus for theological reflection, then theology becomes an ideology employed to advance whatever agenda is considered necessary to attain that end. And that approach simply represents another instance of self-justification that distorts the Christian faith by pointing Christians to themselves and their efforts at liberation instead of to Christ as the only one who can truly free us from the sin which is the self-will that puts us at enmity with God and divides us from each other here and now.[16]

Paul F. Knitter's View of Liberation Theology

An extreme example of the kind of thinking that I regard as overwhelmingly problematic and which I will discuss once again at the conclusion of this chapter should illustrate my argument. Paul F. Knitter claims to be presenting a version of liberation theology when he writes,

> For liberation theology, the one thing necessary to be a Christian and to carry on the job of theology is commitment to the kingdom vision of liberating, redemptive action. What Christians *do* know, on the basis of their praxis, is that the vision and power of Jesus of Nazareth *is* a means for liberation from injustice and oppression, that it *is* an effective, hope-filled, universally meaningful way of bringing about God's kingdom. Not knowing whether Jesus is unique, whether he is inclusive or normative for all others, does not interfere with commitment to the praxis of following him ... liberation Christology allows, even requires, that Christians recognize the possibility of other liberators, or saviors, other incarnations. If

---

[16]This is why T. F. Torrance can say that "justification by grace alone remains the sole ground of the Christian life; we never advance beyond it, as if justification were only the beginning of a new self-righteousness, the beginning of a life of sanctification which is what we do in response to justification" (*Theology in Reconstruction*, 161). Torrance insists that sanctification is not something we do in addition to what God has done for us in justification; any such idea would mean that "in the last resort our salvation depends upon our own personal or existential decision" instead of upon grace, that is, upon what Christ himself has done objectively and subjectively for us in making us free to live from him alone as the Way, the Truth, and the Life (ibid., 162). Interestingly, Torrance was critical of the World Council of Churches in its efforts to combat racism because he said their use of economic and political pressure employed to oppose "oppression" played into the hands "of the secular will to power so evident in the widespread violence of our times" (*Theology in Reconciliation*, 79). While he said that the leaders were likely sincere in refusing to support violence, he then claimed that "when as a matter of fact they use political theology as a basic hermeneutic to interpret the Gospel and mission of the Church ... they nevertheless become trapped in an ecclesiastical will to power" (ibid.)

liberating praxis is the foundation and norm for authentic divine revelation and truth then Christians must be open to the possibility that in their dialogue with other believers they may encounter religious figures whose vision offers a liberating praxis and promise of the kingdom equal to that of Jesus.[17]

Knitter thus maintains that normative claims for Jesus are both unnecessary and impossible today. Has he really understood what Christocentrism actually means for Barth and for all those Christians who hold to the Nicene faith? The answer must be a clear No because in his own comments he substitutes our *vision* of liberating action for Christ himself who alone liberates us for service of God and neighbor as already discussed above. He thus leaves out at least three crucial facts that would never be left out if revelation had been properly recognized, acknowledged, and understood at the outset. First, revelation for Christians is identical with Christ himself as the revealer. That is why Barth held that

> revelation denotes the Word of God itself in the act of its being spoken in time
> ... it is the condition which conditions all things without itself being conditioned
> ... [it] means the unveiling of what is veiled ... Revelation as such is not relative.
> Revelation in fact does not differ from the person of Jesus Christ nor from the
> reconciliation accomplished in him. To say revelation is to say "The Word became
> flesh."[18]

Since this is the case, therefore it is a mistake to claim, as Knitter does, that "liberating praxis" is or could ever become the norm for revelation because that would have to mean that our human actions of fighting against oppression or loving our neighbors could be a norm for judging the actions of God himself in his Word and Spirit. This would be an overt reversal of the roles of Creator and creature which would obliterate the truth about us that is revealed only in Christ. And that truth is the fact that, apart from grace (apart from the revelation of God in Christ), we are in reality at enmity with grace and in need of reconciliation *before* we can speak rightly about God and about theological and ethical truth itself.

---

[17]Paul F. Knitter, *No Other Name?: A Critical Survey of Christian Attitudes toward the World Religions* (Maryknoll, NY: Orbis, 1985), 196–7.

[18]Barth, CD I/1, 118–19. Later on, Barth carries this insight through that our faith in Christ "is not a product or work of faith" because "the believer lives by the fact that Jesus Christ lives, and not *vice versa*" (CD IV/3.1, 45). Hence, "this knowledge does not add anything at all to the fact that He really and truly lives" since "in the fact that He lives it has not merely its object and content, but its origin. If we thought that knowledge could even strengthen, let alone condition or produce, the reality and truth of what is known, it would not be the knowledge which is the basis of faith. In this knowledge we for our part are absolutely conditioned and produced. We are first known by the One whom we may know, and it is only then that we may know and believe and confess. The fact that Jesus lives is true and real in itself. It precedes with sovereign majesty all knowledge and therefore all faith and confession that it is so" (ibid.).

That leads to a second difficulty. Knitter seems unaware of the problem of sin in his analysis since he thinks that just by being faithful to our *vision* of liberating action we would be faithful disciples of Jesus himself. However, to be a faithful disciple of Jesus himself we would have to take up the cross and follow him.[19] But to do that would require that we would have to abandon at once any idea that we could substitute our *vision* of liberating action for Jesus himself as our only Liberator. In this way, Knitter claims that Jesus is *a* means of liberation but that he cannot be the exclusive enabling condition of our liberation which we experience as the Spirit unites us to him as his disciples. He thus not only equates discipleship with our commitment to *our vision* of liberating action but also equates redemption with our action of working with others for a better world. Finally, that leads him to conclude that liberation Christology not only allows but also requires the possibility of other liberators and saviors as well as other incarnations. This thinking, which is essentially polytheistic since it opens the possibility that there might be more than one true God and thus more than one true action of salvation in history, is quite obviously as far from any reasonable Christian understanding of liberation as it possibly could be. And it is so precisely because Knitter ignores and undermines not only who Jesus was and is in his uniqueness as the incarnate Word, but he plainly argues

---

[19]This is why T. F. Torrance repeatedly argues that justification means that we are made righteous objectively through Jesus Christ's own active and passive obedience for us so that "throughout the whole course of his life he bent the will of man in perfect submission to the will of God, bowing under the divine judgment against our unrighteousness, and offered a perfect obedience to the Father, that we might be redeemed and reconciled to him" (*Theology in Reconstruction*, 132). Thus, revelation which took place in the incarnate life of Christ in the midst of our sinful humanity achieves its goal in atonement. But that is objectively effected in Christ's own life, death, and resurrection for us. In his humanity there was in fact an obedient "reception of revelation" which involved "communion through the reconciliation of the estranged parties, as reconciliation of the will and mind of man with the will and mind of God" (ibid., 132–3). Hence, discipleship means for us that our union with Christ in faith through the act of the Holy Spirit issues in discipleship "including all theological *disciplina*" which means that, as Jesus himself said, "if any man will come after me, let him deny himself and take up the cross and follow me" (ibid., 133). It is in this regard that Torrance speaks of costly grace over against those theologies which move from a center in human experience instead of from a center in God that comes to us in the incarnation. The former "are out for *cheap grace*, i.e. the 'God' *they* want, one to suit themselves and modern 'secular' man, rather than the God of *costly grace* who calls for the renewing of our minds in which we are not schematized to the patterns of this world but are transformed in conformity with His own self-revelation in Jesus Christ. They balk at Jesus Christ at the crucial point in His message, where He asks them to renounce themselves, take up the cross and follow Him unreservedly all along the road to crucifixion and resurrection" (*God and Rationality*, 82). Finally, this is why Torrance can speak properly of liberation insisting that in our encounter with the crucified and risen Christ "God does not override man but recreates, reaffirms him and stands him up before himself as his dear child, and man does not seek to use or manipulate knowledge of God for the fulfilment of his own ends in self-will and self-understanding, but loves him objectively for his own sake and is so liberated from himself that he can love his neighbour objectively also" (*Theology in Reconstruction*, 237). This thinking is fully in line with Barth's insistence that "the freedom of the children of God begins only where the freedom, which we think we experience in our humanity, ends" (CD I/2, 405). Indeed, Barth rightly claims that it is only in Christ that a person is "a new creation by the Holy Spirit. In the Holy Spirit he actually hears and believes the Word of God, and the Word of God is the eternal Word, which assumed flesh and in that flesh raised up our flesh and the flesh of all those who hear and believe that Word to the glory of the Father" (ibid., 370, translation slightly amended).

for a version of self-justification that fails to understand that the true meaning of sin and salvation can only be perceived in light of the unique, once for all mediation of Christ himself or as Barth put it, by the eternal mediation of Christ himself in union with the Father and through his Holy Spirit.[20]

Because Knitter's approach to Christology is an approach he characterizes as "doing before knowing," he completely fails to see that for Christians our love of neighbor and our working against oppression spring from the fact that we and all people have been already liberated from sin and self-will by Jesus Christ alone so that in loving him we love God truly in freedom because through his Spirit here and now he frees us to do so and on that basis we love our neighbors and work against oppression. Knitter thinks that who Jesus is depends upon the community's choices and responses to various savior figures. That would be a version of what Barth called Ebionite Christology which unfortunately grounds the truth of Christianity in us and our reactions to Jesus rather that in Christ himself as God who has come to us in order to liberate us.[21] However, if Jesus really is the Way, the Truth, and the Life (Jn 14:6), then this whole line of reasoning ends up separating us from the God revealed in Christ and throws us back upon ourselves in such a way that we are completely cut off from God's own liberating action for us in history precisely because and insofar as it is thought that Jesus is only one savior among others and thus is only *a* means that we use toward an end that we seek to achieve.

---

[20]This kind of self-justification is in evidence in every hermeneutic applied to Christology that assumes that "we must judge the truth of any christological statement by its ethical fruits" (Knitter, *No Other Name?*, 163). Such a hermeneutic places our ethical behavior over Christ himself as the one who frees us to love God for his own sake and thus to love our neighbors. This makes love of neighbor the criterion even for the truth of who Jesus himself was and is. That is the reversal of Creator and creature both Barth and Torrance recognize and avoid in their theology and in their considerations of ethics. Following his line of reasoning, Knitter concludes that Christology should be located within ethics and not prior to it (ibid., 164). He then cites Rosemary Ruether claiming that traditional Christology which affirms the normativity of Jesus is immoral and was responsible for anti-Semitism, without realizing that it is not the traditional affirmations of Jesus' uniqueness that cause immoral behavior, but Christians who are sinners and who are thus in conflict with the truth and freedom that is theirs in Christ alone, who do that. St. Paul was hardly anti-Semitic when he preached that salvation was by grace through faith in Christ alone! Once again, T. F. Torrance gets this right when he says that it is Christ alone who sets us free from "the obscuring of God through our own subjectivity" so that through him "we become emancipated from imprisonment in ourselves and learn to distinguish the reality of God from our own subjective states and conditions" (*God and Rationality*, 54). He argues that it is Christ alone who "can put to us the true questions that make us free for the truth. Through His forgiveness He sets us free from ourselves; through taking our place where we are questioned by God, He enables us to renounce ourselves and take up the Cross in following Him; by making us share in His life and what He has done with our human nature in Himself, He … transforms us through a renewal of mind that enables us to look away from ourselves to love God with all our heart and mind, and our neighbour as ourselves. But it is only through this encounter with Jesus Christ in His implacable objectivity in which we become crucified to the world and to ourselves that we are enabled to know objectively as we are known by Him and so to think appropriately of God in accordance with His nature, and not out of a centre in ourselves" (ibid.).

[21]For more on this see Molnar, *Incarnation and Resurrection*, 17–20 and 171–90 and *Divine Freedom*, chapter 2.

Rosario Rodríguez, Gutiérrez, and Barth

Returning to the reasoning offered by Rosario Rodríguez, we may note that his understanding of liberation theology is based on the thesis that " 'to participate in the process of liberation is already, in a certain sense, a salvific work' " so that, following Rahner's "anonymous Christianity," along with Gustavo Gutiérrez, Rosario Rodríguez thinks he can locate "divine revelation in the work of historical and political liberation."[22] This leads to the "underlying thesis" of his book *Dogmatics after Babel*, namely,

> that God desires that all humankind live peaceably together guided by God's compassionate justice. By exploring scriptural views of the work of the Spirit in each of the three Abrahamic religions *before* these conceptions calcified into exclusivist doctrines, it is argued that the work of the Spirit serves as a theological locus for pluralistic dialogue and cooperation because the sacred Scriptures of all three faiths share an ethical norm grounded in the themes of liberation, justice and compassion.[23]

Here it must be stressed as clearly and decisively as possible that even the slightest idea that what unites all three Abrahamic religions is an *ethical norm* which is grounded in the themes of liberation, justice, and compassion represents an overt reversal of the roles of Creator and creature once again and avoids the fact that what actually unites all three religions is the fact that God really was in Christ reconciling the world to himself. How did Rosario Rodríguez come to this view?

There can be little doubt that Rosario Rodríguez was led to this thinking by Gustavo Gutiérrez. Gustavo Gutiérrez's theological approach is diametrically opposed to Barth's approach. While some of their political views may coincide, as George Hunsinger has suggested, their theological views are quite at variance.[24] That is why Hunsinger stresses that "what separates the Barthian and liberation theologies are two very different controlling passions."[25] Barth, he notes, gave "unqualified precedence to the sovereign Word of God, whereas by contrast the controlling passion of liberation theology is most certainly to bring liberation to the oppressed."[26] He also notes that this does not mean that the liberation theologians "give no precedence to God's Word" or that Barth

---

[22]Rosario Rodríguez, *Dogmatics after Babel*, 142.

[23]Ibid., 167.

[24]According to Hunsinger, Gutiérrez and Segundo share with Barth "a belief that theological integrity is subject to certain practical and basic political tests" (*Disruptive Grace*, 44). Lest anyone conclude from this that Hunsinger is arguing that political agendas and actions are normative for theological claims, it is important for me to add here that he also says that for Barth "it was precisely because the Word of God as the central criterion was concrete that political criteria—in a relative and *strictly subordinate*, but still operative sense— were necessary. Failures in political judgment were characteristically traced by Barth as being related to failures in theological judgment" (ibid., 44–5, emphasis mine).

[25]Hunsinger, *Disruptive Grace*, 48.

[26]Ibid.

"cared nothing about the oppressed and their needs."[27] Still, Hunsinger maintains that for the Word of God to be a controlling passion for theology, it has to give "not just precedence but unqualified precedence to God's Word."[28] This insight is surely in keeping what Barth's remark, cited above, that Jesus himself must be the *first* and *final* word in theology. Hunsinger says, for instance, that "if for no other reason than a recognition of sinful humanity's proclivity for self-deception, theology will attach itself fervently and exclusively to God's Word" since that is the "event by which God shatters our self-deceptions and reveals to us what only God can reveal—God's true identity."[29] And that identity for Hunsinger, as for Barth, can be found "nowhere else than in Jesus Christ, as witnessed in all of Scripture, for he alone is the one Word of God and the only source for our knowledge of God."[30]

The differences here are not merely semantic. They are very real. Listen to the words of Barth:

> The great gulf between the believer and the One in whom he believes carries with it the fact that he cannot receive that pardon and experience his liberation from unrighteousness and to righteousness without having to become aware and recognise and confess that in himself he is altogether unworthy of it, that although he is liberated in very truth by Jesus Christ, yet in himself, in his daily and even hourly thoughts and words and works, he is not liberated at all. His own being contradicts his being in Jesus Christ. Confronted with that being, in the clear light of that being, he finds that in his own being the old man is not yet dead or the new created. In his own being—contrary to divine judgment—he will again and again find that he is a covenant-breaker, a sinner, a transgressor. In his own being—contrary to the divine verdict—he will never find the faithful servant and friend and dear child of God. In his own being he will never with his own eyes see himself as in any respect justified, but always in supreme need of justification by God. And all this in faith itself and as such.[31]

The crucial fact is that Rahner, Gutiérrez, and Rodríguez all undermine our actual justification by faith because and to the extent that they do not *begin* and *end* their

---

[27]Ibid.
[28]Ibid., 48.
[29]Ibid., 49.
[30]Ibid.
[31]Barth, CD IV/1, 97. What does Barth mean when he speaks here of our pardon? He means that there is a twofold pardon that comes to humanity only in Christ, namely, that in him the "destruction of the unrighteous and creation of the righteous" took place so that faith must be "in the One to whom man can only cling as to the high-priest who officiates and speaks and acts for him, that is to say, in faith in Him. Not in faith in himself" (ibid.). It is only when we turn to ourselves then that we act sinfully in the ethical realm; it is only when we rely on ourselves that we could even dream of becoming anti-Semitic. So, as noted above, it is not the confession of Christ's uniqueness as the Word of truth enacted and spoken to both Jews and Gentiles that leads to immorality and anti-Semitism, it is we as the sinners we are apart from Christ who engage in that sort of behavior.

reflections on liberation with Jesus Christ the one in whom we really live in freedom for God and others. We shall return to this below when we consider the actions of the Holy Spirit in union with Jesus, the incarnate Son.

But, for now, it is clear that what separates many contemporary liberation theologies from a properly *theological* theology is the fact that all too many liberation theologians more often than not argue *from* the human struggle for freedom or *from* some notion of humanity's innate capacities for freedom and on that basis for knowledge of and relationship with God himself. And it is assumed that such freedom can be seen by them and described by them by appealing to some sort of nonconceptual knowledge of God and Christ. As I have already explained in Chapter 4, there really is no such thing as nonconceptual knowledge of God. Yet Rahner's theology is grounded precisely in that idea so that as he thinks in that way he is led to the notion that everyone has some innate knowledge of the true God (as absolute being, as nameless mystery or as holy mystery), that self-acceptance is the same as accepting God and Christ, and that anyone who experiences genuine love, especially love of neighbor is an "anonymous Christian."[32] All of these ideas, however, betray the fact that for Rahner and those who follow his thinking, Jesus Christ in his true humanity and true deity was not and is not the *first* and *final* Word for his understanding of God, Christ, truth, and freedom. This is no small issue as it concerns the fact that our only proper liberation can only come *to* us from Christ himself as our liberator and not from anything we think, say, and do on our own, whether it be religious or not. As seen above, Paul Knitter not only marginalizes the core truth that Barth and Hunsinger wished to uphold, namely, that Christ alone is the source of our knowledge of God and of salvation, but he had to, given the fact that he believed the truth could come *from us* working with others for the betterment of humanity. That led him to directly reject Jesus' uniqueness and therefore the very reality of the Word of God as the source of a truth which can only come *to us* as grace from God himself through his unique incarnation in the man Jesus.

All of this explains a key difference that I am stressing in this chapter. Barth insisted that our creation of worldviews is a sign of the fact that, as sinners, we avoid the reality of our reconciliation in Christ by turning to ourselves for our knowledge of God and thus also our knowledge of liberation in the Christian sense.[33] By contrast, Gutiérrez argues that in a secularized world such as the one we now live in "we perceive ourselves as a creative subject … we become aware … that we are agents of history, responsible for our own destiny. Our mind discovers not only the laws of nature, but also penetrates those of society, history and psychology. This new self-understanding of humankind necessarily

---

[32]For a comparison of Rahner and Barth on love of God and love of neighbor, see Paul D. Molnar, "Love of God and Love of Neighbor in the Theology of Karl Rahner and Karl Barth," *Modern Theology* 20 (4) (2004): 567–98.
[33]Thus, in his doctrine of reconciliation Barth insisted that the creation of worldviews represented one's human attempt to incorporate God's act of grace in Jesus Christ, the reconciler into a view of reality which would then become the criterion for understanding grace itself. This certainly happens to Rahner as he says that grace is "an inner objectless though conscious dynamism directed to the beatific vision" (TI 4, 61. See Molnar, *Divine Freedom*, 220–61) for a discussion of this issue.

brings in its wake a different way of conceiving our relationship with God."[34] Notice that there is no indication here that knowledge of God can *only* come from God himself as he meets us in his incarnate Word. Consequently, that very assertion methodologically bypasses God himself (since Jesus is the very Word of God present in history) in order to know God. Thus, Gutiérrez says that secularization "is a process which not only coincides perfectly with a Christian vision of human nature, of history, and of the cosmos; it also favors a more complete fulfillment of the Christian life insofar as it offers human beings the possibility of being more fully human."[35]

Gutiérrez and Rahner

From these reflections Gutiérrez notes that Rahner "proposed the idea of a 'supernatural existential,' that is, the universal salvific will of God creates in the human being a deep affinity which becomes a gratuitous ontologico-real determinant of human nature" which can be understood as "the central and enduring existential condition of man in the concrete."[36] He eventually concludes that within our historical perspective today we can affirm "the possibility of the presence of grace—that is, of the acceptance of a personal relationship with the Lord—in all persons, *be they conscious of it or not*."[37] And from this assumption of a nonconceptual relationship with God,[38] Gutiérrez then claims that we are led "to the consideration of an anonymous Christianity, in other words, of a Christianity beyond the visible frontiers of the Church. The advent of a 'Christendom without the name' has been proclaimed."[39] Gutiérrez asserts that these concepts need to be refined so that "they will point with greater precision to a reality which is itself indisputable: all persons are in Christ efficaciously called to communion with God. To accept the historical viewpoint of the meaning of human existence is to rediscover the Pauline theme of the universal lordship of Christ, in whom all things exist and have been saved."[40] This is precisely the reasoning that Hunsinger was criticizing when he said of Gutiérrez that, while he gave some precedence to God's Word, he did not give "unqualified precedence to God's Word."

So the question raised here by Gutiérrez's analysis is, where exactly do we find the universal lordship of Jesus Christ when we are told to look to human existence in its secularity? How can anyone equate "the historical viewpoint of the meaning of human existence" with the ability to lead us to Christ's universal lordship since what is disclosed in the cross and resurrection of Christ is that we are sinners and enemies of grace in

---

[34]Gustavo Gutiérrez, *A Theology of Liberation: History, Politics, and Salvation*, trans. and ed. Sister Caridad Inda and John Eagleson (Maryknoll, NY: Orbis Books, 1996), 42.
[35]Ibid.
[36]Ibid.
[37]Ibid., 45, emphasis mine.
[38]See Chapter 4 for a discussion of the problems embedded in theories of nonconceptual knowledge of God.
[39]Gutiérrez, *A Theology of Liberation*, 45.
[40]Ibid.

ourselves as fallen creatures? What is further disclosed in him is that we need God's personal act of reconciliation to see and acknowledge that fact, and thus to recognize the universal Lordship of Christ in its identity with his Person and Work as he speaks his Word now as the risen, ascended, and coming Lord. Isn't it the case then that only Christ himself, speaking his Word through the power of his Holy Spirit, can enable such knowledge? And isn't it the case that we could not possibly know the Lordship of Jesus Christ without some *concept* of who Jesus was and is as the one who was crucified and now is present as the risen, ascended, and coming Lord? The fact that Gutiérrez, like Rahner, thinks all people are capable of a personal relationship with the Lord without being conscious of it is actually in complete conflict with Paul's conception of Christ's universal Lordship.[41] It is also in conflict with Barth's firm and instructive insistence that

> it is not the case that we have only to extend our idea of lord and lordship into the infinite and absolute and we will finally arrive at God the Lord and His lordship. The decisive distinguishing mark of the lordship of God is this fact that He is really the Lord over all things and therefore supremely over ourselves, the Lord over our bodies and souls, the Lord over life and death. No idea that we can have of "lord" or "lordship" will ever lead us to this idea, even though we extend it infinitely.[42]

Christ's Lordship is universal in the sense that he died for the sins of all and rose from the dead for the salvation of all because he is indeed God acting as man for us. But because Gutiérrez and Rahner are looking for God's grace within our human historical experience instead of looking directly to Jesus himself who is the grace of God present among us, they both end up universalizing grace as an existential of human existence, instead of realizing that grace literally cannot be detached from the Giver of grace, namely, Christ himself. It is this universalizing of grace that Barth would utterly reject, along with any idea of nonobjective or nonconceptual knowledge of Christ's Lordship, as a form of Idealism. He would most certainly reject Rahner's idea of anonymous Christianity because for him to be a Christian means to confess Jesus Christ himself. And since faith for Barth means knowledge of the truth, that confession cannot occur without knowing him conceptually from the biblical witness! I believe the difficulties

---

[41]It is not surprising that Gutiérrez could ascribe this secularized version of Christianity to St. Paul given the fact that he claims in a note that the "writings of Teilhard de Chardin, among others, have greatly influenced the trend toward reaffirmation of Christ as Lord of history and the cosmos" (ibid., 194). Gutiérrez thinks Teilhard's influence can be seen in the conclusions of the first section of *Gaudium et Spes*. To say that there is a contrast between Gutiérrez's views and Barth's views would be an enormous understatement since Barth thought Teilhard undermined Christ's actual Lordship rather than affirming it. After reading the *Divine Milieu*, Barth not only said that he had no desire to read further but also asserted that "it seems unmistakable to me that in T. de C. we have a classic case of Gnosis, in the context of which the gospel cannot possibly thrive. The reality that is supposedly manifest there, and that we are supposed to believe, is the deity of evolution—naturally decked out with the name of Jesus Christ, as always happened and still happens in Gnostic systems" (Karl Barth, *Letters 1961–1968*, trans. and ed. Geoffrey W. Bromiley, ed. Jürgen Fangmeier and Hinrich Stoevesandt [Grand Rapids, MI: Eerdmans, 1981], 119–20).

[42]Barth, CD II/1, 75–6.

that I have highlighted here illustrate the differences between a theology that gives unqualified precedence to God's Word in its identity with Jesus Christ and one that simply identifies Jesus' Lordship with evolution or with a set of secularized ideas that clearly do not allow him to be the *first* and *final* Word in their reflections. Anonymous Christianity, in whatever form, represents a vision of Christianity without Christ. In that way it represents what in Barth's view would be an extreme version of self-justification which equates Christian discipleship with what we do by way of loving our neighbors or by way of working for a better world.

In any case, Gutiérrez makes the fatal theological mistake here of concluding from this analysis that there is a "religious value ... to human action in history, Christian and non-Christian alike. The building of a just society has worth in terms of the Kingdom, or in more current phraseology, to participate in the process of liberation is already, in a certain sense, a salvific work."[43] Once again, this approach to liberation is far from Christian simply because it equates salvation with our human efforts at liberation, when in fact, salvation was and is a completed event in the history of Jesus of Nazareth on the basis of which we may, in faith, acknowledge that particular truth and live the liberation from sin that is ours only in him. Because it is ours only in him, this whole method espoused by Gutiérrez would have to be reversed to become a truly Christian perspective. In other words, it is because Christ has liberated us from sin as self-will that we are now free to love him above all things and *thus* to love our neighbors and fight against all that would oppress them and us.

Gutiérrez and Rosario Rodríguez put the cart before the horse and claim that salvation can be equated with our human efforts at liberation. In this chapter, I am contending that this cannot be done without implying some form of Pelagian self-justification and without thus obviating the true theological meaning of liberation.[44] Barth makes the point very succinctly when he says, "If we know the truth, it can happen only by the liberation which comes from the truth itself (Jn. 8:32)."[45] Further, he diagnoses the problem when he says,

[43]Ibid., 46.
[44]In case anyone might suppose that my claims about Pelagianism and self-justification might be unfounded, consider the following remarks made by Gutiérrez: "The liberation of our continent means more than overcoming economic, social and political dependence. It means, in a deeper sense, to see the becoming of humankind as a process of human emancipation in history. It is to see humanity in search of a qualitatively different society in which it will be free from all servitude, in which it will be the artisan of its own destiny. It is to seek the building up of *a new humanity*" (Gutiérrez, *A Theology of Liberation*, 56). The very notion that we could possibly be the artisans of our own destiny so that one could equate a society we might build with a "new humanity" is to miss the whole point of the Gospel. It misses the fact that our new humanity is already a reality in Jesus Christ alone so that it is only in obedience to him in faith that we could build up the kingdom of God on earth as he empowers us to do so through his Holy Spirit.
[45]Barth, CD II/1, 208. Thus, Barth can also say that "God is wise in so far as His whole activity, as willed by Him, is also thought out by Him, and thought out by Him from the very outset with correctness and completeness, so that it is an intelligent and to that extent reliable and liberating activity" (ibid., 425).

When we describe both the conformity of man to God that takes place in faith and also the point of contact for the Word of God posited in this conformity, *not as an inborn or acquired property of man but only as the work of the actual grace of God*, our only final word at this point can be that God acts on man in His Word. Because man's work in faith is that on which God's work is done, man can know the Word of God. He knows as he is known by God.[46]

Even more to the point Barth asserts that "the instruction of the Holy Spirit awakens and calls us, with that authority, precision and sovereignty, to use and exercise our freedom in Jesus, to the good work which we specifically are to do here and now in unqualified obedience to Him."[47]

The Holy Spirit and the Abrahamic Religions

Here we return to the underlying thesis of Rosario Rodríguez's book, namely, that he will explore the work of the Spirit in the three Abrahamic religions before their conceptions became "calcified into exclusivist doctrines" so that the work of the Spirit might be seen as a "theological locus for pluralistic dialogue and cooperation" among the three faiths. Let me say here that I also would want to argue that all three religions should stand in solidarity and work in mutual cooperation as I do in Chapter 8, but not because of any common ethical norms, as suggested by Rosario Rodríguez, since that would only imply some version of religious or ethical self-justification. My argument is that because the God of the Gospel has freed all of humanity in Christ and through his Spirit to live as his covenant partners, our love of God and neighbor can only be truly seen and understood in faith and by grace through the unique and exclusive revelation of God in history and not through any common religious or ethical activities of humanity. While Rosario Rodríguez thinks "all three faiths share a conception of Spirit as the *historical* manifestation of God in the world *through* acts of liberation that preserve human dignity,"[48] I wish to argue that this very idea separates the Spirit from the Word and undermines the Christian understanding of the Holy Spirit as the Spirit of Jesus Christ guiding the community in the truth as this was revealed and established by Jesus himself who is the incarnate Word and thus is the exclusive mediator of our reconciliation and redemption.

It is a mistake to assume that there was a time before the Christian community held that Jesus was the exclusive savior of the world as the risen and ascended Lord who sent his Spirit into the world after his death and resurrection. Indeed, the very notion that the conception of the Holy Spirit referred to in the Nicene Creed might have represented a calcification of a concept of the Spirit that could be active outside the Church as a Spirit who could be conceptualized without acknowledging the *homoousial* relation

---

[46]Barth, CD I/1, 244, emphasis mine.
[47]Barth, CD IV/2, 374.
[48]Rosario Rodríguez, *Dogmatics after Babel*, 167.

between the Spirit and the Father and Son would undermine the truth of the Christian understanding of God at root. Since God himself is the source of any authentic liberation, it really matters whether or not one's thinking is grounded in who God really is *in se* and *ad extra*. As already noted, Rosario Rodríguez believes he can find the presence of God in "divinely inspired acts of justice, compassion, and liberation."[49]

Pneumatology and Christology

Here it is important to note that his perspective is shaped by the methodological assumption that one can start theology "with pneumatology *rather than* with christology."[50] However, there is a major theological problem that immediately surfaces at this point by starting with pneumatology *rather than* with Christology. Such a presupposition makes an assumption that, practically speaking, separates the Spirit from the Word once again. Yet, in any properly Christian approach to liberation, a theologian would necessarily recognize that it is precisely the Holy Spirit who directs us to Christ himself as the Liberator. Consequently, one cannot recognize the Holy Spirit or true Christian liberation if one separates the Spirit from the Word even momentarily. It is precisely because Rosario Rodríguez makes this mistake that he then feels free to explore human acts of justice, compassion, and liberation to identify the working of the Holy Spirit. Yet, as we have already seen, all that one can see when one explores human actions apart from faith in Christ are actions of sinners who stand in need of reconciliation before they can grasp the true meaning of liberation and of Christian action. From what has already been said about the approach that begins with human acts of justice and compassion, it would appear that many who follow such a liberationist perspective might assume that it is perfectly appropriate to separate the Spirit from the Word in this way. But I believe that Karl Barth was right when he insisted that our justification by faith means that we must cling obediently to God's sovereign act of judgment and grace in Jesus Christ himself by which God, acting in his own cause, destroyed the old "man" and created the "new man."[51]

Hence our new being cannot be found by looking at ourselves and our own faith or even our confidence that what took place in Jesus Christ for all also applies to us.[52] That is why Barth insisted that a Christian "is referred, not to himself but to the God who points him to his neighbour, and to his neighbour who points him toward God."[53] However, a

---

[49]Ibid., 168.
[50]Ibid., 145, citing Amos Young, emphasis mine.
[51]Barth, CD IV/1, 96–7.
[52]This is why George Hunsinger can say that "we believe in Christ ... not in our experience of Christ; in the gospel, not in our experience of the gospel; in salvation, not in our experience of salvation. Jesus Christ is not an experience but an event, the gospel is not an experience but the news of an event, and the presence of salvation is 'not an experience, precisely because and as it is the divine decision concerning us'" (*How to Read Karl Barth: The Shape of His Theology* (New York: Oxford University Press, 1991), 121.
[53]Barth, CD IV/3.2, 652.

Christian "does not look into himself, but in the most pregnant sense outwards, i.e., to the fact that Jesus lives, rules, and conquers, and to all that this fact includes."[54] Our new being in Christ is the reality that is ours because of our conversion to God which took place for us only in Jesus Christ in his life of perfect obedience to his Father. Thus, we can only "cling" to Jesus himself as the "high-priest who officiates and speaks and acts" for us. That is what it means to have faith; it is faith in Christ and not faith in ourselves.[55] This point is captured nicely by Jane A. Barter who maintains that Barth offers "a thoroughly theological exploration of human freedom: it is only within humanity's true horizon, which is the reconciling work of God through Jesus Christ, that the true justification can be experienced and pursued."[56]

In this chapter, I am arguing that the method, advocated by Rosario Rodríguez in particular, is inherently problematic from the perspective of our justification by grace and through faith. One cannot begin, as he proposes, with pneumatology *rather than* Christology simply because a properly formulated Christology and trinitarian theology require that the Holy Spirit can never be separated either theoretically or practically from Christ himself since all three persons of the Trinity are *homoousia* and their actions *ad extra* must never be divided. When they are divided by locating knowledge of God in experiences of liberation instead of in our knowledge of the Father that results from the Spirit uniting us to the incarnate Son through faith and by grace, then theology becomes, perhaps inadvertently, and sometimes quite deliberately, unitarian rather than trinitarian, with disastrous results.[57]

The most problematic result of this I believe is that one's theological method then *becomes* grounded in human experience. Or to put this another way, when this happens then our belief is in our experience of the Holy Spirit rather than in the Holy Spirit himself. As a result, theology is no longer pursued within faith as that faith is based on the grace of revelation in its identity with Christ the revealer seeking understanding but instead becomes a type of self-justification which ascribes salvation to works of righteousness on our part.[58] Such works can then be pursued as avenues of true knowledge of God

---

[54]Ibid.
[55]Barth, CD IV/1, 97.
[56]Jane A. Barter, "A Theology of Liberation in Barth's *Church Dogmatics* IV/3," *Scottish Journal of Theology* 53 (2) (2000): 154–76, 155.
[57]See, e.g., Paul D. Molnar, "Some Dogmatic Consequences of Paul F. Knitter's Unitarian Theocentrism," *The Thomist* 55 (3) (July 1992), 449–95.
[58]Karl Barth argued that the solution to religious differences could not be solved by analysis of religion even in its particularity but could only be solved by God's revelation attested in the Old and New Testament Scriptures. If he is right, and I believe he is, then Rosario Rodríguez's claim that because the three Abrahamic religions are united in their ethical concerns for liberation, one can therefore say that it is no longer necessary to make exclusivist claims for one religion in relation to the other is misguided in the extreme. Why? Because that position ends with a unitarian view of God and God's relations with us and undermines the very meaning of Christian revelation in its identity with the Word who became flesh in Jesus Christ and whose Spirit guides the community in truth. More will be said about this below. For now, it is enough to note that for Barth "in face of the cross of Christ we are bound to say that knowledge of the one and only God is gained only by the begetting of men anew by the Holy Spirit, an act which is always unmerited and incomprehensible, and consists in man's no longer living unto himself, but in the Word of God and in the knowledge of God which comes by faith in that Word" (CD II/1, 453). This leads to the following decisive conclusion Barth reaches regarding natural

precisely by avoiding the necessity of knowing God as the Father of Jesus Christ since, according to Jn 14:6, there is no way to the Father except through the Son. Thomas F. Torrance saw this issue very clearly as he insisted that "if we turn our attention to the Spirit independently instead of turning our attention with the Spirit to Christ, or try to make the Spirit visible through perfecting his operation by our own works, then we violate the holiness of the Spirit by resisting him in his self-effacing office and confusing him with our own spirits."[59] For Torrance, a proper concept of the Holy Spirit "snaps the notion of mutual correlation between the Spirit and the created world, and therefore snaps at the same time any connection of mutuality between divine revelation and creaturely understanding."[60] In our knowledge of God within the economy then

> the doctrine of the Spirit requires the doctrine of the Son. It is only by the Spirit that we know that Jesus is Lord and can assert the *homoousion* of him, but apart from the Son, and the inseparable relation of the Spirit to the Son, the Spirit is unknowable, and the content of the doctrine of the Spirit cannot be articulated.[61]

These are important statements for they demonstrate that the Spirit simply cannot be known by exploring anything within the world since the Spirit can only be known, as Torrance suggests following Athanasius, by "moving from the knowledge of the Son, and the affirmation of him as *homoousios* to the Father, to the knowledge of the Spirit, and the affirmation of him as *homoousios* to the Son and the Father."[62] For that reason, together with Karl Barth as well, Torrance asserts that "the Spirit does not utter himself but the Word and is known only as he enlightens us to understand the Word."[63] This is why Barth insisted that the Holy Spirit who enables our participation in revelation is the Spirit of Jesus Christ and thus "is not to be regarded … as a revelation of independent content, as a new instruction … that goes beyond Christ; beyond the Word."[64] And

---

theology and the monotheism of Islam and Judaism: "It is strange but true that confession of the one and only God and denial of Him are to be found exactly conjoined but radically separated in what appears to be the one identical statement that there is only one God. This one sentence can actually mean what it says, and it can actually not mean this, but its opposite. What distinguishes these two possibilities, raising the one to reality and invalidating the other, is the resurrection of Jesus Christ, the outpouring of the Holy Spirit and faith" (ibid., 454). Jane Barter captures this point nicely saying that "the liberation of the Christian is the 'image and analogy of the total and material liberating act of God in the resurrection of Jesus Christ'" ("A Theology of Liberation in Barth's *Church Dogmatics* IV/3," *Scottish Journal of Theology*, 172).

[59]Torrance, *Theology in Reconstruction*, 258. Barth also insists that "the Spirit gives man instruction and guidance he cannot give himself … the Spirit is not identical, and does not become identical with ourselves … As our Teacher and Leader He is in us, but not as a power of which we might become lords. He remains the Lord" (CD I/1, 454).

[60]Torrance, *Theology in Reconstruction*, 212.

[61]Ibid., 213.

[62]Ibid., 214.

[63]Ibid. In a similar manner Barth insists that "the Holy Spirit is the authorisation to speak about Christ; He is the equipment of the prophet and apostle; He is the summons to the Church to minister the Word" (CD I/1, 455).

[64]Barth, CD I/1, 452–3.

importantly, he also maintained that "the fact that Jesus Christ lives is true and real in itself. It precedes with sovereign majesty all knowledge and therefore all faith and confession that it is so."[65] Because the Spirit is antecedently God in himself with the Father and Son, so that one could say that "it is *in himself* that the Spirit fulfils [the] work of Christ, of revelation and salvation, upon us … If he were not essentially and intrinsically holy and divine in himself, he would not be able to fulfil this work in making us participate in the Son and in the Father. He is thus, coordinate with the Son and the Father, himself creative source of our life and sanctification and recreation."[66]

From this perspective, it is important to note that to become righteous in Christ means to be liberated by Christ himself here and now through the power of his Holy Spirit to love God precisely by loving him (Jesus Christ). Thus, through the Holy Spirit our reconciliation with God the Father becomes our experience of freedom in a miraculous way through union with Christ. Consequently, the Christian is free or, in Karl Barth's categories, receives a permission to obey God and thus to love his or her neighbor with a freedom that is given and received in faith and is not innate in human experiences of freedom or liberation as Gutiérrez, Rosario Rodríguez, and many others assume.[67] Two

---

[65]Barth, CD IV/3.1, 45.

[66]Torrance, *Theology in Reconstruction*, 222. Barth also holds that the Holy Spirit as God himself acting for us in history "is 'antecedently in Himself' the act of communion, the act of impartation, love, gift. For this reason and in this way and on this basis He is so in His revelation. Not *vice versa*! We know Him thus in His revelation. But He is not this because He is it in His revelation; because He is it antecedently in Himself, He is it also in His revelation" (CD I/1, 470–1).

[67]The idea that this freedom is innate to human beings is the nub of the difficulty in both Rahner's theology and the theology of Gutiérrez. Following the thinking of Yves de Montcheuil and Henri de Lubac, Gutiérrez explains that Blondel followed their thinking and described the "human state as 'transnatural.' Devoid of supernatural life, human beings are nevertheless oriented to it by necessity. They are 'highly stimulated in relation to this vocation; after the loss of the initial gift, [they] do not fall back into an undifferentiated nature. Rather [they retain] the mark of the point of insertion ready and as it were in potency to receive the restitution [they need] to attain [their] real and obligatory destiny'" (Gutiérrez, *A Theology of Liberation*," 44–5). This reasoning circumvents one of Karl Barth's most decisive and important insights, namely, that in light of the revelation of God disclosed in the cross and resurrection of Jesus Christ, humanity is understood to have completely lost any inherent "potency" for revelation because the exclusive point of contact for the restoration of that connection is Jesus Christ himself. This is why Barth maintains that "to know and declare the truth, to establish the truth as such, to live by the truth and in the truth, does not lie in man's capacity and existence" (CD II/1, 207). Hence, we can know the truth only as it "is imparted to [us] by the speaking and acting of God. With him is the truth: it is His truth; He Himself is the truth … If we know the truth, it can happen only by the liberation which comes from the truth itself (Jn. 8:32)" (ibid., 298). Barth also astutely claimed that when we do experience God through the Spirit and in faith, we "become rich in Him and poor in ourselves. Both become our experience; that we are rich in God and that then and only then we truly become poor in ourselves. But we do not have the divine and spiritual riches and the divine and spiritual poverty in our experience. What we have in our experience … what can be the theme of the anthropology, psychology or biography of the believer, is a human sign of the fact that God has given Himself to us by His revelation in faith, and as such it is certainly not to be treated lightly … [still] The impregnable basis of faith, the assurance of faith by God's revelation, depends on whether this basis, not just at the beginning but in the middle and at the end too, is sought in God alone and not anywhere else, not in ourselves. Grace is the Holy Spirit received, but we ourselves are sinners. This is true. If we say anything else we do not know the deity of the Holy Spirit in God's revelation" (CD I/1, 464–6). Thus, we cannot understand theological truth by looking at ourselves and our supposed innate capacities but only at Christ in whom our relationship with God and others has been restored once and for all. Torrance maintained these same insights insisting that "we ourselves are rightly related to God only as we serve his divine majesty,

extremely important statements from Barth will make my point clear. First, he insisted that our knowledge of God always comes from God himself awakening and sustaining our faith, which therefore never begins with us or our experiences of liberation. Thus,

> in love we are set on the circular course in which there is no break, in which we can and shall only go further—from faith to faith, from knowledge to knowledge— never beginning with ourselves (and that means, with our own ability for faith and knowledge) but therefore also never ending with ourselves (and that means, with our own inability for faith and knowledge).[68]

Indeed, Barth maintains, "To have the Holy Spirit is to be set with Christ in that transition from death to life"; thus a person's "freedom, ability and capacity for God can be understood only as the power of the resurrection of Christ not as an immanent freedom of his own."[69] Barth contends that only God can make us certain of our freedom in Christ so that all "statements about the Holy Spirit, like all statements about the Son of God, can relate only to this divine fact [the fact that "God makes us sure of Him and makes Himself sure of us"]."[70]

Second, that is why for Barth the Gospel is not something we choose but instead it is God's choice of us as his covenant partners in Christ and through his Holy Spirit; it is thus recognizable and lived only in faith, a faith "which derives from a mode of being of God, from a mode of being which is in essential unity with Him who in the New Testament is described as Father and Son."[71] For that reason, Barth also insisted that knowledge of God is a "gift of God" and so could not be construed as "an element in our own real existence, and therefore, in a larger content, in the life of the people, the community, the family or society generally."[72] Further, Barth consistently held that

---

freedom and authority, in the absolute prerogative of his own truth ... in such a way as never to transfer the centre of authority from the objective revelation of God to ourselves, and never to mask the authoritative majesty of God by an authoritarian exercise of our calling to serve him in the Church" (Torrance, "Truth and Authority: Theses on Truth," *ITQ*, 240). Further, he held that it is only when we recognize the "ultimate authority of the Supreme Truth over all other authorities" that there is "freedom for the faithful, for it makes us to know the truth finally out of itself and by its grace alone, and demands of us an obedience that transcends our respect for the authoritative institutions of the Church ... it is only as these institutional authorities in the Church are rigorously sub-ordinated to the majesty and authority of the Supreme Truth ... that they are not authoritarian tyrants ... but instruments of the Truth that makes us free ... the Spirit of Truth ... speaks only what he hears from another. That is the Spirit of Truth who informs all authentic magisterium in the Church, directing it away from itself to the one Truth of God revealed and incarnate in Jesus Christ, in order that it may serve that Truth in such a way that it is allowed to retain its absolute priority over all the Church's teaching" (ibid., 242).

[68]Barth, CD II/1, 37–8.
[69]Barth, CD I/1, 458.
[70]Ibid.
[71]Ibid., 461.
[72]Barth, CD II/1, 141. Such a view Barth held represented the attempt to make "the Gospel respectable" by making it something we can choose along with other things we can choose and to that extent control. Here it is worth mentioning once again Barth's aversion to "world-views" because they only are able to "find room for an abstract God and an abstract man, but not for Him, the God-man ... They offer plenty of pictures, panoramas,

our human being as reconciled sinners "is thus enclosed in the act of God. Confessing this faith in the Holy Ghost, we cannot as it were look back and try to contemplate and establish abstractly this being of ours as God's redeemed and liberated children as it is enclosed in the act of God."[73] Additionally, Barth argued that beginning theology with our own experience of the Gospel always places us in control in place of God; this always will occur, Barth claimed, "when from an object of faith the Gospel becomes the object of our own experience of faith."[74] Barth certainly did not reject the fact that we really do experience God in the freedom of his Word which comes to us in the Holy Spirit; nonetheless, he affirms the fact that because we are really free for God only because God in Christ actually has freed us from all self-reliance to live from him alone, therefore we can live as God's children precisely as liberated sinners in obedience to Christ and thus as those who love God in that act and consequently love our neighbors and work for liberation from all forms of oppression.

Liberation and the Holy Spirit

Hence, from Barth's perspective "we cannot try specifically to make ourselves strong and sure again by contemplating ourselves as the strong and sure. To have the Holy Spirit is to let God rather than our having God be our confidence."[75] This, because real experience of God's Word does not rest on anything we think, say, or do (including acts of justice, compassion, and liberation) but rather "on God's making Himself present in the life of man" such that we "yield" to God's Word which does not break us but bends us with all our experiences including conscience, feeling, and will so that it brings us "into conformity with itself."[76] This means finally that "the life of man, without ceasing to be the self-determining life of this man, has now its centre, its whence, the meaning of its attitude, and the criterion whether this attitude really has the corresponding meaning—it has all this outside itself, in the thing or person acknowledged."[77] Barth therefore insists that

> in faith we abandon … our standing upon ourselves (including our moral and religious, even Christian standing) … for the real standing in which we no longer stand on ourselves (on our moral and religious, or even our Christian state) … but … on the ground of the truth of God … We have to believe: not to believe in ourselves, but in Jesus Christ.[78]

---

generalities, doctrines, human attempts at self-understanding. But His voice … is not heard in any of them" (CD IV/3.1, 257).

[73]Barth, CD I/1, 462.

[74]Barth, CD II/1, 141.

[75]Barth, CD I/1, 462.

[76]Ibid., 206.

[77]Ibid., 207–8.

[78]Barth, CD II/1, 159. It is worth noting the radical difference between Barth's view of grace and Karl Rahner's view in relation to this view of faith in Christ in whom the reconciliation of the world is an accomplished

Indeed, when our knowledge of God is grounded in Christ as it must be, once the Holy Spirit enables us to acknowledge Jesus as Lord, then Barth powerfully contends that our knowledge of God is not and does not remain epistemologically uncertain, in the manner suggested by Rosario Rodríguez, but is and becomes "apodictically certain" just because and to the extent that it is grounded in God's own act of revelation and reconciliation in the person and work of Christ himself.

This is why Barth argues that "about man as such, about autonomous man, existing otherwise than in Jesus Christ, the only thing we need to know is that he has brought Jesus Christ to the cross and that in this same cross his sins are forgiven."[79] Consequently, "all sound doctrine," including our knowledge of God in truth, must be asserted "with the strictest possible certainty, with an apodictic certainty, with a certainty freed from any dialectic and ambiguity, with all the certainty of the statement 'the Word was made flesh.' "[80] Inasmuch as Jesus Christ is God himself acting in the power of his Holy Spirit to enable our knowledge of the truth, we can have apodictically certain knowledge of God and ourselves only as we allow Jesus Christ himself to be the *first* and *last* Word of

---

fact. Barth insists that God's Word of grace given in Christ the reconciler which judges us and sets us in right relation to God and our neighbors says "the most radical, warm and unconditional Yes that could ever be conceived. Hence it does not forbid him [the person of faith] to say Yes to himself in his own place … It allows him, however, to say to himself only the Yes which is an answer to the Yes said to him. This is its dangerous force. This is why it is an offence to him. A world-view is the glorious possibility of evading this offence, of fleeing from it. So long as man, viewing the world is observer, constructor and manager, he is safe, or at any rate thinks he is safe from this offence" (CD IV/3.1, 257). That Yes is said to him by the risen, ascended, and coming Lord as he himself speaks his Word here and now so that the speaker is Christ and the response is a response of faith, enabled by the Holy Spirit, to the Jesus who lived, died, and rose from the dead for all. Contrast this with Rahner's idea that "anyone therefore, no matter how remote from any revelation formulated in words [clearly an espousal of nonconceptual knowledge of revelation], who accepts his existence, that is, his humanity … in quiet patience, or better, in faith, hope and love—no matter what he calls them, and accepts it *as* the mystery which hides itself in the mystery of eternal love and bears life in the womb of death: such a one says yes to something which really is such as his boundless confidence hopes it to be, because God has in fact filled it with the infinite, that is, with himself, since the Word was made flesh. He says yes to Christ, even when he does not know that he does … Anyone who accepts his own humanity in full … has accepted the Son of Man." (TI 4, 119). Equating self-acceptance with acceptance of Christ undercuts the need to rely on Christ himself as the present enabling condition of our yes to ourselves in the power of his resurrection and through the action of the Holy Spirit.

[79]Barth, CD II/1, 162.

[80]Ibid. This thinking echoes Barth's view of revelation cited above as "the condition which conditions all things without itself being conditioned … [it] means the unveiling of what is veiled … Revelation as such is not relative. Revelation in fact does not differ from the person of Jesus Christ nor from the reconciliation accomplished in him. To say revelation is to say 'The Word became flesh' " (CD I/I, 118–19). When Rosario Rodríguez claims that Barth and Tillich are closer than is usually thought, he overlooks the fact that even he noted that for Tillich objective revelation and its subjective reception by us are interdependent. Nothing could be further from the truth for Barth since that would have to mean that objective revelation (the incarnation of the Word) was somehow dependent upon our reception of that Word, which it most definitely is not. That is why, contra Tillich, Barth insisted that the kingdom of God "must be known as a unique reality and truth with its own nature and power. It is thus independent of human will and act and different from all the human works and achievements into whose sphere it enters. It is God's own independent action which limits all human history from outside, which is sovereign in relation to it, and which thus determines and controls it. Man can and may attempt many things, but he cannot bring in the kingdom of God" (CD IV/4, *Lecture Fragments*, 240).

God to us; Christ cannot just be "at best an additional word."[81] This positive knowledge of God takes place then as we participate "in the person and work of Jesus Christ" and thus as "we are in the Church" and indeed as we "are the Church." Barth maintains that this is "like the receiving of the Holy Spirit, or faith" since it rules out any autonomous "way or means of salvation."

Hence, "The Church is not the Church when it tries to be this" since it

> does not live in and from itself … It lives literally and really only in Jesus Christ as its Head to which it is the body … This is just as literally and really the case as the Holy Spirit in us is only the temporal presence of Jesus Christ Himself, or faith is only our relationship to Him. The Church is the historical form of the work of the Holy Spirit and therefore the historical form of faith.[82]

Barth consistently holds that the Church in its ministry and sacraments lives only because Christ, the risen Lord, lives and intercedes for us in eternity, "because in the Holy Spirit the unity of the Father and the Son becomes effectual among and in us too in the twofold form of faith and the Church."[83] In this context, it should now be easy to see why Barth argued that "starting from man as such [the sinner in need of reconciliation] we can arrive only at the domestication of the Gospel that takes place continually in natural theology."[84]

Separating Spirit from the Word

If Barth is correct in his claim that true knowledge of God is an event enclosed in the mystery of the Trinity,[85] then any attempt to ground the truth of the Christian faith in a view of the Spirit that separates the Spirit from the Word in the manner suggested

---

[81] Barth, CD II/1, 163.

[82] Ibid., 160.

[83] Ibid., 161.

[84] Ibid., 163. Note well that for Barth "in face of the cross of Christ it is monstrous to describe the uniqueness of God as an object of 'natural' knowledge" (CD II/1, 453). This, because it is precisely in the name of Jewish monotheism that Israel's Messiah was handed over "to the Gentiles and nailed by them to the cross with Israel's approval. Could there be a better proof that this monotheism is not a final achievement and expression of Israel's obedience to the first commandment?" (CD II/1, 453). This is why, in contrast to Rosario Rodríguez's approach which simply assumes that Judaism, Islam, and Christianity are at one in their affirmation of monotheism, Barth insists not only that Jesus was rejected in the name of Israel's monotheism as an expression of its disobedience to God himself, but also says "That which men can divine or construct as well as believe, that which, as an object of human divining or constructing, is as dialectical as the absolutised idea of uniqueness, may be anything we like to call it—and we certainly cannot deny that it is something—but it is not God. It is, therefore, unthinking to set Islam and Christianity side by side, as if in monotheism at least they have something in common. In reality, nothing separates them so radically as the different ways in which they appear to say the same thing—that there is only one God" (ibid., 449). This issue is explored in detail in Chapter 8.

[85] Barth, CD II/1, 181, 205, and CD I/2, 247.

by Rosario Rodríguez will necessarily lead away from liberation in the Christian sense just described. In order to present this issue here in an extreme form, once again let me return to the view of liberation theology offered by Paul F. Knitter, who relies in part on the thinking of Rosemary Ruether. After that I will consider Rosario Rodríguez's view that "the work of the Holy Spirit is what enables us to recognize 'God's action in the world *wherever* we find the work of liberation."[86]

Knitter contends that if we make "praxis" or "orthopraxis" primary in relation to dogmatic concerns, then we might say, with Rosemary Ruether, that "the subject of liberation theology is not theology but liberation."[87] She writes, "Gustavo Gutiérrez constantly reminds Christians of the First World that the subject of liberation theology is not theology, but liberation. Christ calls us to be about the task of liberation, not about the task of theology, unless that theology is a servant of liberation."[88] Here the problem I have identified in this chapter is writ large. With her claim that "theology is a servant of liberation," Ruether has unmistakably substituted liberation for Jesus Christ the Liberator, and it is precisely this substitution that enables her, along with Knitter, Rosario Rodríguez, and many others, to separate the kingdom from Jesus and locate it in acts of human liberation. The problem with this is that it opens the door not only to a Pelagian view of human action but to rather blatant forms of self-justification that place the weight of liberation from sin (whether social or individual) back on us, thus leaving us lost, rather than truly free to love the God who has definitively freed us from sin in Christ himself and only on that basis, through the power of the Holy Spirit, to love our neighbors and fight effectively against oppression.

This is why Ruether can argue that "Christian faith, as resurrection faith, arises through a refusal to take these facts of the victory of evil as the last word. In the face of the assassination of prophets, Christian faith reaffirms that life and liberation are possible and God will win in the end."[89] Instead of affirming that Christ is our Liberator as the very Word of God who acted from the divine and human side to reconcile us to God the Father once and for all in his own life history, Ruether reduces him to a human figure, a prophet who himself needs liberation. Accordingly, she claims,

> Jesus, the crucified prophet, thus becomes the name in which we continue to reaffirm this faith, his own faith, that the kingdom is at hand. But we affirm this faith not simply by verbal affirmations, but by following his liberating praxis and putting ourselves, as much as possible, in the place where he put himself, as ones who make themselves the last and servant of all.[90]

---

[86]Rosario Rodríguez, *Dogmatics after Babel*, 142.
[87]Knitter, *No Other Name?*, 194. This quotation is taken from Rosemary Radford Ruether, *To Change the World: Christology and Cultural Criticism* (New York: Crossroad, 1981), 27.
[88]Ruether, *To Change the World*, 27.
[89]Ibid., 23.
[90]Ibid., 24.

Unfortunately, this analysis misses the very foundation of Christian faith which, as noted above, Barth forcefully stated is that resurrection faith arises from an encounter with the risen Lord himself who alone is faith's enabling condition here and now as he speaks to us in the present through the power of his Holy Spirit and as he thus personally empowers us to be the servants of all. That is why he insisted that "the fact that Jesus Christ lives is true and real in itself. It precedes with sovereign majesty all knowledge and therefore all faith and confession that it is so."[91] Faith does not arise from our refusal to allow evil the last word. Of course, Christians do refuse to allow evil to be the last word. But that refusal arises from the fact that Christians recognize and live on the basis of the fact that Christ himself has overcome evil, sin, and death itself in his own life history as the crucified and risen Lord and empowers us to live in and from him as part of the new creation.

It is his personal resurrection from the dead that is the basis of true Christian liberation, and it is the basis of any proper view of liberation theology itself, when liberation theology is understood in a truly *theological* way. Jesus Christ himself is the center and that center cannot be ceded to a *vision* of the kingdom or a *view* of *liberation* without obviating our true justification and sanctification as these were realized in the history of Jesus himself for us and as these are actualized in us even now through his Holy Spirit.[92] Therefore, we do not follow Jesus' "liberating praxis" as Rosemary Ruether argued, since that would imply that we are his equal because he only humanly lived by faith and praxis as we must do now. By contrast, we become free to follow *him* in faith and through the power of his Holy Spirit since his human action was itself the action of God reconciling us to God inasmuch as his human action was hypostatically united with his being and act as the Word. To be united to him in faith here and now thus means to participate in his new humanity as the risen, ascended, and coming Lord; it means to live as those who have died to sin as self-will and as those who have risen with Christ to participate in the freedom which is ours in him. He is the only true liberator because of who he was and is as the Lord himself forgiving our sins and liberating us for service of God and neighbor! Following anyone and anything else than him will mean a failure

---

[91]Barth, CD IV/3.1, 45. See above, n. 18.

[92]In this regard Torrance astutely argues that "when we speak of the Holy Spirit as pouring out the love of God in our hearts, we are to think of his activity in strict correlativity to the atoning substitution in the life, death and resurrection of Jesus Christ—that is to say, we are to think of the work of the Spirit not simply as the actualizing within us of what God has already wrought for us in Jesus Christ once and for all, but as opening us up within our subjectivities for Christ in such a radical way that we find our life *not in ourselves but out of ourselves, objectively in him* … This is the objectivity that will not allow us to confuse the Holy Spirit with our own spirits, or to confound his objective activity with our subjective states, for it turns us inside out. It is an objectivity that demands the renunciation of ourselves, with all their pre-understanding, and requires of us the readiness to hear and learn what contradicts our preconceived self-understanding in order that we may develop a way of understanding appropriate to the nature of God's redeeming love and therefore genuinely objective. It is precisely by taking in all its terrible seriousness the objection of God to our sin, and the fulfilment of that objection in the Incarnation and Atonement, and therefore the opening up of a way of true love in objective relations with God, that we are healed of the mental and spiritual disease in which we fail to distinguish our own subjective conditions from objective realities" (*Theology in Reconstruction*, 238–9).

to recognize the true meaning of Christian service of God and neighbor; it will mean a genuine failure to live in freedom.

The Subject of Liberation Theology

In any case, Paul Knitter takes Ruether's initial remark that the subject of liberation theology is liberation and not theology to mean that the "ultimate arbiter of truth" can neither be dogma nor tradition but "the transformative response of Christian praxis,"[93] and he is certainly not alone in this. Thus, he claims "not only that orthodoxy must be adjusted under the pressure of orthopraxis but that one can more comfortably bear with uncertainty about what is orthodox as long as one is able to make the responsible effort to bring about transformation and liberation in the world."[94] From this it follows for Knitter that making praxis primary protects us "against the persistent danger of the decay of doctrine into ideology." One such ideological belief, according to Knitter, is "the exclusivity of salvation in Christ." He thinks such a belief is "possibly nurtured more by the desire to maintain power and privilege than by the desire to promote truth and freedom." Accordingly, such ideology must be unmasked so that liberation theology can "clear the ground for a more fertile dialogue."[95] Citing Leonardo Boff, Knitter argues that "many ecclesiastical traditions and ecclesial institutions were functional at one time but today have become obsolete" because they inhibit dialogue "between faith and the world, the church and society."[96]

In order to begin such a dialogue Knitter insists that "it is not necessary that all partners agree on certain universal truths—for instance whether there is one savior/incarnation or many. The mutual starting point will be how Christians and others can struggle, together, against those things that threaten their common humanity. Only in the praxis of such struggle can clarity on universal truth emerge."[97] Applying this method, which he ascribes to Sobrino, Boff, and Ruether, to Christology, Knitter says, "We cannot begin to know who this Jesus is unless we are following him, no matter what that demands. That is the starting point."[98] This assertion certainly makes it appear that knowing Jesus can only occur as Jesus himself makes himself known to his followers just as Barth and Torrance have claimed. Knitter even claims that "everything we know or say about him [Jesus] must be repossessed and reclarified in the praxis of following him through the changing contexts of history. That is a never ending process."[99] If he really means that truth can only be perceived in genuinely following the Jesus proclaimed

---

[93] Knitter, *No Other Name?*, 194.
[94] Ibid.
[95] Ibid.
[96] Ibid.
[97] Ibid.
[98] Ibid., 194–5.
[99] Ibid., 195.

in the New Testament and witnessed in the church's teaching at Nicaea, Ephesus, and Chalcedon, then truth would be acknowledged to be identical with Jesus himself as the Way, the Truth, and the Life (Jn 14:6). Such truth would not be the possession of the church in its orthodoxy *or* in its orthopraxis because it would have to be given and received in specific encounters with the living Christ through faith and by revelation anew each day, even each moment of each day.

However, it quickly becomes evident that his claim that it is the praxis of following Jesus that is the criterion of truth represents little more than the truth of a practice of liberation that is not at all inspired by who Jesus really was and is as the Lord who alone can free us from ideology and self-will. This, because Knitter argues that since Jesus preached about the kingdom and not himself, therefore building the kingdom must be our main concern and then "the nature of God and Jesus himself, will follow." It is most instructive to notice that once Christology has been clarified by praxis, we are told, following the thinking of Boff, that "no title conferred on Christ can be absolutized" because each one "must be understood in all its limitations and reexamined under the lens of praxis."[100] Here is what Knitter discovered: (1) when the kingdom is restored to the center then we will see that "liberation theology also throws into question much of the language of finality that the Christian church has been wont to use of Jesus. We cannot speak of Jesus as having 'fulfilled' the hopes of Israel, for these were hopes for the kingdom of God."[101] Therefore, (2) since that kingdom "has not been established on earth in any final or unambiguous form," Knitter contends that Christian praxis does not permit us to "establish any kind of absolute finality for Jesus" because we would have to study other religions and be sure that there are no others like Jesus and that is presently impossible. From this he reaches the following decisive conclusions which were noted above:

> For liberation theology, the one thing necessary to be a Christian and to carry on the job of theology is commitment to the kingdom vision of liberating, redemptive action … Jesus of Nazareth is a means for liberation … Not knowing whether Jesus is unique, whether he is inclusive or normative for all others, does not interfere with commitment to the praxis of following … liberation Christology allows, even requires, that Christians recognize the possibility of other liberators, or saviors, other incarnations.[102]

It is not difficult to see how this thinking subverts the meaning of faith as faith in Christ from start to finish. First, Knitter claims the one thing necessary to be a Christian is faithfulness to one's own *vision* of liberating action. Thus, true faith quite literally cannot find its basis and meaning outside its own *view* of liberation; it cannot find its true basis in Jesus Christ as the one who frees us for faithfulness to himself as the Liberator.

---

[100]Ibid.
[101]Ibid., 196.
[102]Ibid.

Second, because Knitter will not allow Christ in his uniqueness as God incarnate to be the sole starting point and enabling condition of acts of love toward others in the form of liberating actions, he resists the Christian view that the justification and sanctification of the entire human race has already been accomplished once and for all in the life history of Jesus of Nazareth and thus is uniquely actual in Christ himself. Thus, he contends that one need not recognize Jesus in his uniqueness. All one needs to do, to act faithfully, is to act unquestioningly in relation to one's own *vision* of liberating action. Such an approach Knitter assures us will mean that liberation Christology will not only allow but will require that Christians recognize "the possibility of other liberators, or saviors, other incarnations."

The point of this chapter, however, is to suggest that when Christ is marginalized, as he certainly is in this perspective and as he also is in the perspective of Rosemary Ruether, then the true meaning of Christian liberation is lost in an unconcealed form of self-justification which places the weight of salvation and liberation back on us by equating salvation with our working for a better world in accordance with a worldview shaped by one's vision of liberation. This conclusion illustrates exactly why Christian theology cannot look for the truth of revelation, the truth of religion, or true knowledge of God by exploring acts of justice, liberation, or compassion, important as those actions may be as signs of faith in Christ himself. Knitter's mistake was to assume that it is our praxis of following Jesus instead of Jesus himself enabling our discipleship that then would allow us to either view him as one savior or one incarnate figure among others depending upon how we choose to respond to him. That is his basic argument for his nonnormative Christology which claims that Jesus is normative for Christians because they believe in him but not for others who do not.

However, it is just this thinking that both Karl Barth and T. F. Torrance flatly and rightly rejected as a form of Ebionite Christology that all too easily can be and often is transposed into some form of Docetic Christology. The former, in their understanding, refers to a type of adoptionism in which Jesus' significance for faith is grounded in the impression he made on the community. The latter view, according to Barth and Torrance, sees Jesus as the embodiment of what people think is divine or the divine idea gleaned from elsewhere than from Jesus who revealed the Father to us.[103] In both instances, however, the power of one's perception of truth and the power of discipleship would come from us in our experiences or ideas or visions of the kingdom, instead of from Jesus himself who is the Way, the Truth, and the Life. Here it is extremely important to stress that while Knitter and many others claim that Jesus preached about the kingdom and not about himself, theologians such as Torrance and Barth insist repeatedly and correctly that Jesus himself was the incarnate presence of God's kingdom on earth.

Listen to the words of T. F. Torrance regarding Jesus in his uniqueness:

---

[103]See Molnar, *Incarnation and Resurrection*; and *Divine Freedom* for a detailed discussion of these issues.

His work and action lie in the fact that *he* as very God is present in the world of humanity, present vicariously and in identification of himself with the world in its condition. He does not proclaim the action of God or of another; he points to himself and acts in his own Person: *he himself is the Kingdom of God and the King.* In him is God present with the World, and in him takes place the battle of God with the World of darkness. His Person is the arena of the Great Struggle and by bearing sin in himself he defeats it by carrying it to death on the Cross where sin and evil are vanquished and slain.[104]

Since Jesus, in his uniqueness as God and man and as the sole savior of the world, is himself the very presence of God's kingdom on earth and of the kingdom which is to come, therefore all human attempts to bring in the kingdom or to be faithful Christian disciples without actually relying on this King are doomed to failure. That is one reason why Torrance astutely claims that any idea that we are free in ourselves and can free others is thoroughly mistaken because such a view fails to notice that "fallen men are really not free even in an ethical sense because our natures are not free from evil desire."[105] But that means that he thinks for us to be truly free and to work for the freedom of others, "our very natures must be changed." So he says, "To cultivate human personality and goodness is thus apparently to come very near the Kingdom of God in form, but in reality to get farther way from it."[106] Why would Torrance say this?

The answer is simple but with profound implications. He said this because even in our goodness we need Christ's own reconciling grace to be truly good in relation to God and others. Any idea that we can put ourselves into right relation with God by our good works simply continues to express our sin; it is only through union with Christ in faith therefore that we are free and can live as the children of God reconciled to God by God himself. This is why Torrance goes on to say that, understood in light of Christ, "real freedom is freedom which cannot sin. Christ had such freedom." And Torrance thinks, in agreement with John's Gospel, that "when he says that he that is born of God cannot sin" that means that this particular freedom is a freedom from sin that "the Christian receives from Christ, and [this] is only obtainable in Christ."[107] This freedom, in Torrance's view, is a freedom "that is from behind the law and the ethical imperative,"[108] because it comes freely from God in Christ and can be recognized only in faith and lived in true discipleship in obedience to Christ alone and not to any worldview or vision that we may set up and then impose on ourselves and others! In other words, the freedom that is ours in Christ cannot be achieved through the law or through any ethical behavior.

---

[104]Torrance, *The Doctrine of Jesus Christ*, 153, some emphasis mine.
[105]Ibid., 128.
[106]Ibid.
[107]Ibid., 129.
[108]Ibid.

Without presenting a detailed development of ideas here, I simply note that for Barth too the kingdom of God was identical with Jesus himself as when he said about Jesus as the Son of God incarnate that

> in His being and activity, in His suffering and dying as this obedient One, He is quite different from all other men. He is a man, but quite unlike all other men. He is among men, yet in contrast to all other men He is at the side of God. In His human person He is the kingdom of God come down from heaven to earth. This kingdom (the power of God exercised by Him as Lord, His glory as King) is incorporated and truly present and active in Him. It has truly and actually become flesh in Him.[109]

In identifying the kingdom that has come in him and that is coming again in him, Barth is faithful in recognizing exactly what makes Jesus unique, namely, that he alone of all other human beings is God himself and is thus able to reconcile the world to God in his human obedience just because he is the unique Son of God acting *as* man in precisely that way for our benefit. That is why Barth can also say that the fulfilment of the covenant consists

> in the historical proclamation attested in the Old Testament, and the historical existence attested in the New, of the Mediator, that is, of the eternal Word of God and therefore of God Himself in His historical identity with the man Jesus of Nazareth: in the coming of His kingdom on earth, that is, in the coming and being and living and speaking and acting of this man, in the establishing and maintaining and revealing in Him of the sole supremacy of His grace in the world of men, and of the subordination of that world to this supremacy.[110]

With these examples my intent was to demonstrate that by separating the kingdom of God from Jesus both Knitter and Ruether undermine a properly theological theology of liberation just because they fail to understand Jesus' uniqueness as the one Mediator between us and God the Father.

At this point, it is worth calling attention to the fact that Paul Knitter accepts John Hick's belief that in the early church it was understandable that those Christians spoke of the Father/Son relation and of Jesus' consubstantiality with the Father. However, Knitter notes that for Hick this view is no longer tenable today because he says it leads to all the "uncomfortable 'onlys'" in Christian self-consciousness: Christ is the 'only Savior' or the 'only final norm' for all other religions."[111] From this, Hick concludes that "the real point and value of the incarnational doctrine is not indicative but expressive, not to assert a metaphysical fact but to express a valuation and evoke an attitude."[112] Therefore for Hick

---

[109]Barth, CD IV/1, 208.
[110]Ibid., 67.
[111]Knitter, *No Other Name?*, 150.
[112]Ibid., 151.

we are told by Knitter, "Christians can declare that God is *truly* to be encountered in Jesus, but not *only* in Jesus … Such a Christology lays the foundation not only for the possibility but the necessity of interreligious dialogue."[113] While this viewpoint may sound very open, honest, and forthright, it really is quite authoritarian in the worst sense precisely because while Knitter and Hick say they want to overcome any exclusivist position about religion so that Christianity would not be perceived as truer than any other religion since that vision, in their view has to demean other religions, the fact is that Knitter and Hick are both unwilling to acknowledge the truth of the Christian religion as it is actually grounded in Jesus' uniqueness. That is their false authoritarianism at work. They will accept any view of Jesus except the one espoused from within the Nicene Creed and the Creed of Chalcedon because they disallow belief in his utter uniqueness as God become man without ceasing to be God for the salvation of creation. The position for which I am arguing here is that any exclusivist position that is not grounded solely in Jesus himself as the true liberator will always lead to oppression, authoritarianism, and perhaps even to the denigration of one religion by another. That is why Barth insisted that the Church is the locus of true religion only as by grace it lives by grace. That means that the Church's truth is not grounded in itself—either in its orthodoxy or any of its practices—but only in Christ as the Holy Spirit enables Christians to live as part of the new creation in and from the risen, ascended, and coming Lord. Since what makes Christianity unique is Christ himself, confessing him as Lord in no way denigrates others because such confession acknowledges the fact that he is there precisely for all—no one is excluded. Such confession therefore is not a statement about others but about who Christ simply is as the Lord and savior of the world.

Loving God by Loving One's Neighbor

The position for which I am arguing can perhaps be more clearly seen by considering what at first glance may seem to be a rather perplexing remark made by Thomas F. Torrance. In his Auburn Lectures, Torrance argued that "I cannot love God through loving my neighbour. I can love my neighbour truly and only through loving God."[114] To understand what he means here, it is important to realize that Torrance, like Barth, holds incarnation and reconciliation together by insisting that the incarnation "does not arise out of history, nor is it presupposed by history; but it is rather an invasion of history … It upsets history!"[115] As such this is an act of revelation and thus an act of "*God* in Christ reconciling the world unto himself." Hence,

> the Incarnation means … that God does not wait for men to seek him but that he has and does come seeking them, his lost children! God does not wait! He

---

[113]Ibid., 152.
[114]Torrance, *The Doctrine of Jesus Christ*, 88–9.
[115]Ibid., 86.

does not wait for us to be good; he does not wait even for us to try! God's love is not a calculated love, it is not prompted or "caused" by anything in us. God does not love us because we are of value or because we are worth loving! The initiative lies absolutely with God, and not even a passive stimulation is to be attributed to mankind.[116]

The most important point to be made here is that Torrance argues that while our love of God takes its shape and importance from the nature of God as the one who loves us unconditionally, the reverse is not the case. In other words, God's love does not take its shape from human love. "We love him for what he is and love him only because he first loved us. Our love is thus quite different from his love; ours is a responsive love, created, creaturely love. His is uncreated, and itself creative!"[117] Thus, for Torrance, God's love is self-grounded within the Holy Trinity and if that were not the case "there would be no salvation for any of us."[118]

Interestingly, Torrance describes the kind of love that we tend to project upon God with the idea that God must love us because of "the infinite value of the human soul" as expressing our human pride because such a view implies that we could compel God to love us. Further, this thinking also could lead people to "deride" God if he did not love us. Torrance strongly opposes any notion that God would not be love *unless* he loved us and banished punishment and hell as well.[119] This kind of love Torrance says is "created by fear! That kind of love is the kind that starts out from human love and which is then foisted upon the Almighty." By contrast, the love of God that meets us in Christ is a love that "casts out fear! … We cannot think of God's love as forced love, even if the force be that 'we are of infinite value'" because any such view negates the fact that God's love is "spontaneous … free, overflowing, abundant, luxurious love" which, as an act of God, is royally free and sovereign.[120]

The point here is that not only is there no law in the divine nature which causes God to love us but also it is at least equally wrong to assume that there is something in us which causes or forces God to love us. Thus, the incarnation is a free and sovereign movement of God's unconditional love toward us that is thoroughly effective in overcoming pride, fear, sin, suffering, evil, and death itself just because it arises in eternity as a free "spontaneous overflow" of God's own nature as one who loves. To take this seriously means that a

---

[116]Ibid., 86–7.
[117]Ibid., 87.
[118]Ibid.
[119]For more on the issue of universalism, see Chapter 7 below.
[120]Torrance, *The Doctrine of Jesus Christ*, 87. This thinking echoes Barth's thinking as noted above in Chapter 1 when he argued that "it does not follow either from creation, in the sense that God was in duty bound to it or to Himself to command a halt to its destruction through sin by a fresh creation. If He has actually done this, we have to recognize His free good will in doing so, and nothing else" (CD I/2, 135). Importantly, Barth adds that he did not think Athanasius and Anselm had thought this through consistently since Athanasius believed that God became incarnate in Jesus because it would have been unseemly and incompatible with God's goodness to allow the destruction of the human race, while Anselm claimed that God would not allow his finest work to be destroyed.

theocentric theology must simultaneously be Christocentric because in Christ we really encounter God himself. This means that in the incarnation, a completely new relation between God and the human race that is unconditioned by ethical standards and even by religion itself has been established. And it is that which transforms us just because that transformation is grounded in a sovereign act of God's own love for us. It is this divine action in the incarnation that "generates a surrender and love on our part."[121] But to whom or what do we surrender? Here Torrance makes a subtle but monumentally important point, namely, that it is not just to love that we surrender, but to this specific divine act of love which alone enables proper human love. That is precisely why Torrance makes the bold assertion that "I cannot love God through loving my neighbour. I can love my neighbour truly and only through loving God."[122]

It is this point that finally and completely dislodges the approach to liberation advocated by those who think that we can put the struggle for human liberation first and then come to a knowledge of who God is and who we are. Let us consider the view of Rubén Rosario Rodríguez from this final angle since he argues for a knowledge of God through comparative analysis of different religious perspectives in our pluralistic world that he thinks is compatible with Christian knowledge of God. Throughout this chapter I have argued against such a view because true knowledge of God can only come from God and not from our making comparisons among the religions. It is clear that many want to argue that we should speak about "human struggles for liberation *as* the

---

[121]Torrance, *The Doctrine of Jesus Christ*, 88.

[122]Ibid. For how this thinking relates to the moral law and our use of the moral law to avoid relying on God himself, see Torrance, *Atonement*, 110–20 and chapter 7, 367–400. See also Torrance, *God and Rationality*, 62–3, where Torrance criticizes Bultmann's "disastrous … ethic" because it subverts the fact that "in Jesus Christ God has already taken a decision about our existence and destiny in which He has set us upon the ground of His pure grace where we are really free for spontaneous ethical decisions toward God and toward men" (62). For this reason, our ethical decisions and actions repose "upon the prior and objective decision that He has taken on our behalf and which He announces to us freely and unconditionally" (ibid.). What is disastrous about Bultmann's ethic is that "it rejects the objective decision, the actualized election of grace, upon which the whole of the Christian Gospel rests" with the result that his ethic, though it may be radical, "is only a prolongation of man's already existing experience and a reduction of it to what his previous knowledge includes, or at any rate could acquire through philosophical analysis" (ibid.). This thinking Torrance powerfully and rightly maintains only incarcerates us "quite cruelly in [our] own existentialized self-understanding, for there is no divinely provided fulcrum whereby [we] may be lifted out of the prison-house of [ourselves] and [our] own naturalistic existence, no really objective Christ, no vicarious Saviour" (ibid.). But that's not the end of it. Torrance then makes the all-important point that morality has an entirely different look in light of our justification by Christ himself since he intervened in our ethical predicament in relation to good and evil. In him alone our free will, which in fact is our self-will, which we are utterly unable to escape from and which leaves us in a "vicious moral circle created by our self-will," is in fact overcome for us in Christ since in him God has intervened to enable us "to be selflessly free for God and for our neighbour in love" (ibid.). What difference does that make? It makes all the difference in the world because Christ himself has freed us from the "curse of the law" so that in him "we are now free to engage in obedience to His will without *secondary motives,* but also so free from concern for ourselves and our own self-understanding that we may love both God and our neighbour objectively for their own sakes. It is thus that justification involves us in a profound moral revolution and sets all our ethical relations on a new basis, but it happens only when Christ occupies the objective centre of human existence and all things are mediated through His grace" (ibid., 63, emphasis mine).

historical experience of God" today.[123] Indeed, in the case of Rubén Rosario Rodríguez, he thinks that spirit language in popular culture and specifically in the social action found therein can and should be understood as a "spiritual dimension" encompassing what he calls "liminality, integrative vision, and emancipatory desire" such that these "describe the work of the Spirit and provide a theological framework for 'tracking spirit' in culture *without* adhering to any one confessional or ideological tradition."[124] Thus he believes that "these 'confession-less' yet profoundly spiritual movements of liberation have become the new *loci theologici* ('places of theology') for understanding and encountering the work of the Spirit in history."[125]

I am arguing here that this approach to Christian doctrine leaves us with a kind of agnosticism with regard to who God really is as the eternal Father, Son, and Holy Spirit. Just because of that, it functions in a way that marginalizes the true liberation that liberation theologians ostensibly seek but fail to recognize when they begin their theologies contextually by claiming to speak of the Holy Spirit quite apart from faith in Christ who is in essential union with the Spirit. Let me explain. Rosario Rodríguez argues, with Christine Helmer, that since "doctrine has lost its referential point of contact with the divine" he will stress that "dogmatic certainty is not an epistemological possibility and that seeking such certainty only steers us toward theological totalitarianism."[126] This may sound good to pluralists who refuse to acknowledge consistently that Jesus himself and Jesus *alone* is the Way, the Truth, and the Life (Jn 14:6). But it is precisely this kind of thinking that is truly totalitarian. Why? Because, in the name of liberation, it leaves us without any apodictically certain knowledge of the true God who alone can liberate us from the human attempt to establish the kingdom of God on earth by being faithful to our worldviews or to our kingdom vision of liberating action as Paul Knitter put it. In other words, the totalitarian aspect of their position is that only one view is unequivocally rejected and that is the view that Jesus Christ in his utter uniqueness must be the *only* starting point and norm for a proper theology of liberation because it is *his* Holy Spirit that always directs us to him as the one true Word of God.

---

[123]Rosario Rodríguez, *Dogmatics after Babel*, 169.

[124]Ibid., 170.

[125]Ibid., 172. Within this perspective, Rosario Rodríguez follows David Tracy and argues that in dealing with "limit questions" what Jaspers called "boundary situations," we can affirm "the objective reality of liminal experiences 'through some personal sense of the uncanny' that we recognize in a 'power not one's own'" (*Dogmatics after Babel*, 172). Rosario Rodríguez goes on to explain that since "the Spirit inhabits, and is very often encountered, in these interstitial spaces" therefore we must recognize that "'spirit' is not always connected to specific beliefs or convictions" with the result that "a shared revolutionary practice [might be] a manifestation of the Spirit when the liminal experience gives way to a *liberative* holistic vision" (ibid., 173). Of course, all of this is extremely problematic because this thinking locates the truth of Christian liberation not in the one who liberates us for service of God in Christ but in a unifying *vision* of liberation which then becomes the source and norm for relevant Christian action. This thinking actually displaces Christ, the true Liberator, from the picture and ends with a form of self-justification which places the weight of salvation back on us once again, thus undermining our true human freedom which is life in the Spirit through union with Christ as Barth so eloquently described this in CD IV/3 and elsewhere.

[126]Rosario Rodríguez, *Dogmatics after Babel*, 168.

Rosario Rodríguez claims his work, which focuses on

> the work of the Spirit in human history—especially through works of compassion and liberation—indicates a possible strategy for moving past the impasse between *theologies of the Word* that take a fideistic stance on Scripture as God's self-revelation without subjecting their dogmatic claims to external criticism, and the *theologies of culture* that contend God can only be known through the medium of culture but lack criteria for differentiating revelation from the cultural status quo.[127]

Since Barth's theology is indeed a theology of the Word, as is Torrance's theology, one would have to ask whether or not those theologies are fideistic as Rosario Rodríguez implies here. The answer is rather simple. Neither of their theologies is fideistic because both theologians consistently and frequently insist that faith means knowledge of the truth and their theologies bear out that fact both in their epistemological and ontological conclusions regarding God, Christ, and liberation. Fideism espouses the idea that faith displaces reason. Neither Barth nor Torrance does that. They both insist that, as knowledge of the truth, faith leads to a knowledge of God that can only be had by relying on the grace of God revealed and active in history in his Word and Spirit.

This entire chapter was intended to illustrate that any theology that moves beyond a properly understood theology of the Word has lost the truth of the Christian faith and also the ability to present a truly *theological* theology of liberation. There is in fact no criterion beyond or other than the Word of God that is or can be the criterion of theological truth for the Christian. Dogmatic claims are subject only to the Word of God. My point here is that this chapter has demonstrated exactly why Rosario Rodríguez and those who follow his methodology are profoundly mistaken in espousing the idea that because doctrine has lost its contact with God, therefore any attempt at a proper view of doctrine must end in totalitarianism. I believe I have shown that it is precisely his approach, along with that of Knitter, Ruether, and others, that is in fact totalitarian since all of these theologians can only view Christ as *a means* for liberation such that liberation and not Christ, the very Word of God in incarnate, is their true starting point, criterion, and goal for their reflections. Rosario Rodríguez is certainly wrong to imply that Barth was a fideist. While he is right to note that theologies of culture cannot properly distinguish revelation from culture, he himself is just as unable to do so as I shall illustrate in a moment. First, however, with respect to doctrine let me introduce a statement from Barth:

> What gives faith its seriousness and power is not that man makes a decision, nor even the way in which he makes it … On the contrary, faith lives by its object. It lives by the call to which it responds … The seriousness and the power of faith are

---

[127]Ibid., 175–6.

the seriousness and power of the truth, which is identical with God Himself, and which the believer has heard and received in the form of definite truths, in the form of articles of faith … In believing, man obeys by his decision the decision of God.[128]

While it is unquestionably true that Barth would never equate truth with doctrine or orthodoxy,[129] it is just as certainly the case that he believed we could not understand the truth of the Christian faith without the articles of faith asserted in those Christian doctrines inasmuch as these were and are grounded in revelation and not in anyone's religious consciousness. This is why Barth held that in conceptualizing our union with Christ, which is reciprocal but not at all dependent upon our response since in it our faith in Christ, our obedience and our confession of him are all "undertaken through the Spirit" as Christians are "called to do so by the risen One … Believing in Jesus Christ and obeying and confessing him, he simply does the natural thing proper to him as the man he is in Christ and therefore in truth."[130] Karl Barth's theology is a theology of freedom grounded in God's freedom for us enacted in the incarnation of his Word and the outpouring of his Spirit at Pentecost. Hence, it is a theology of freedom grounded in the knowledge of the truth that God, the triune God of the Nicene faith, was in Christ reconciling the world to himself.

That is exactly why he could never agree with a theologian like Paul Tillich who argued that if you do not like the traditional meaning of the word God, you should translate it and speak of the depths of your own life experience or of what you take seriously as of ultimate concern.[131] It is just that thinking that always marginalizes the truth question

---

[128]Barth, *Credo*, 2.

[129]For instance, Barth asserted that zeal for "ecclesiastical and doctrinal orthodoxy in every age" and concern for the content of Christian witness to the truth of who God is and who we are in Christ is in itself "a good thing." But when it is indifferent to or depreciates "the existential determination of the Christian by the content of its witness" it becomes a "lifeless idol" (CD IV/3.2, 655). Barth wrote, "Even the trinitarian God of Nicene dogma, or the Christ of Chalcedonian definition, if seen and proclaimed in exclusive objectivity and with no regard for this accompanying phenomenon, necessarily becomes an idol like all others" (ibid.). This kind of orthodoxy Barth believed is both menacing and dangerous because it then prompts "relatively justified" reactions which eventually lead to the wrong answer as to the meaning of Christian witness to the truth. Thus, to "the fatal orthodox picture of Christ without living Christians there is almost always opposed the no less fatal mystical, liberal or existential picture of Christians without Christ" (ibid.). Barth goes on to note that within these circumstances one might be tempted to argue that Christ and Christians are somehow mutually dependent in this relationship. But he quickly and correctly debunks any such supposition arguing that the "liberation of all creation which God has undertaken and accomplished in Jesus Christ" and the "majesty, holiness and power of this cause, its superiority to all other powers and in face of all contradiction or resistance, its victory already won in Jesus Christ and to be definitively and universally demonstrated in His final revelation, *do not depend on your or my personal Christianity. The love of God does not await my response to love to become eternal and omnipotently saving love*" (ibid., 656, emphasis mine). This is the crucial point that liberation theologians overlook or disregard when they begin with liberating experiences in order to identify God and claim that those experiences give knowledge of the Spirit when in fact the only one who can give that knowledge is the very Word of God himself as he gives his Spirit to those who believe in him.

[130]Barth, CD IV/3.2, 544.

[131]See Paul D. Molnar, "'Thy Word Is Truth': The Role of Faith in Reading Scripture Theologically with Karl Barth," *Scottish Journal of Theology* 63 (1) (2010): 70–92, 84–6. Exploring experiences of depth to understand

in theology. If, however, only the truth can set us free from pride, self-will and thus from sin which enslaves all of us then the only one who actually can do that and has in fact done it is Jesus himself according to John 8.[132] But that has to mean that Torrance, following Barth, is profoundly correct in insisting that those theologies that advocate trying to love God through loving one's neighbor always attempt to move toward God without first recognizing God's decisive movement toward us in the incarnation as the true liberator of the human race who alone enables us to love God and on that basis alone to love our neighbors.

Encountering God in Works of Justice

Rubén Rosario Rodríguez claims that "God is encountered in history *in* works of justice, compassion, and liberation, even when the locus of this spiritual work is a body politic not historically associated with any religion whose members describe their emancipatory work without appealing to explicitly theological language."[133] From this he concludes that, after doing a critical reading of the Scriptures of all three Abrahamic faiths, there exists within all three "a theological affirmation … that *wherever* the work of establishing justice, extending compassion, and facilitating human liberation occurs, *there* is the true Spirit of God."[134] What I have demonstrated in this chapter is that this very view is completely antithetical to a proper understanding of the Old and New Testaments because it is impossible to speak of the Spirit of God without referring to the covenant that God made with Abraham and fulfilled in Christ himself as the Messiah of Israel. In other words, any claim that the true Spirit of God can be identified without believing in his Word undermines not only pneumatology but Christology and the doctrine of the Trinity. What we have in Rosario Rodríguez's book is a universalism that

---

God, Tillich claims, "The name of this infinite and inexhaustible depth and ground of all being is God. That depth is what the word God means. And if that word has not much meaning for you, translate it, and speak of the depths of your life, of the source of your being, of your ultimate concern, of what you take seriously without any reservation. Perhaps, in order to do so, you must forget everything traditional that you have learned about God … For if you know that God means depth, you know much about Him" (Paul Tillich, *The Shaking of the Foundations* [New York: Charles Scribner's Sons, 1948], 57). Needless to say, Barth thinks we cannot know God without acknowledging the truth properly witnessed to in the Nicene doctrine which refers to the Trinity as the one true God in whom Christians believe. This God cannot be known by speaking of our own depth experiences but only through revelation as the Holy Spirit unites believers to Christ and thus to the Father. Tillich's assumption clearly is that true knowledge of God comes from us and to that extent once again reverses the roles of Creator and creature.

[132]See above nn. 18, 67 and 129. The fact that this has occurred means that the truth of our liberation and salvation is not "conditioned by the fact or manner of its expression in your or my existence. It is the truth even though all its human witnesses fail. It does not live by Christians, but Christians live by it" (CD IV/3.2, 656). Still, Barth also argues that "it is also not the case that God wills to tread without us, as He might so well have done, the path which He has entered in prosecution of His cause in the world." This, because "Jesus Christ, who is both the reality of this cause and its truth, its Prophet and Revealer, does not will as such to be alone, to be without His own, His disciples, Christians as His witnesses" (ibid.).

[133]Rosario Rodríguez, *Dogmatics after Babel*, 176.

[134]Ibid.

reduces the truth of the Christian faith to an idea of the Spirit which can be recognized, understood, and presented as a new form of works-righteousness. Rosario Rodríguez maintains that various emancipatory movements in history "embody the divine will for all humankind regardless of confessional or creedal origin. In other words, focusing on the work of the Spirit opens the door to the notion of history as sacrament" so that this will provide "a phenomenological vocabulary for describing divine agency in human history but also affirming the work of the Spirit in the religious and cultural 'other.' "[135] There is only one major problem in evidence here and throughout Rosario Rodríguez's argument: in a properly functioning pneumatology, the Spirit directs us not to a universally recognizable "divine agency" which can be directly read off people's practices of liberation or compassion but to Christ himself as the very Word of God speaking to us here and now as the Liberator and as the one who overcomes all our attempts to ground a theology of the Spirit in universal human experiences.

Rubén Rosario Rodríguez and S. Mark Heim

One gets a hint of the kind of solution that Rosario Rodríguez thinks he has found when he speaks of S. Mark Heim's attempt to embrace religious pluralism with his view of the doctrine of the Trinity. According to Rosario Rodríguez, "Heim's proposal embraces religious pluralism by means of the Trinity, emphasizing the work of the Holy Spirit in such a way that he preserves Christ's unique saving role *while* valuing the contribution of other faiths to this very thick and complex understanding of divinity."[136] He says that Heim

> argues that "Trinity provides a particular ground for affirming the truth and reality of what is different" by ruling out narrowly exclusivist conceptions of God as inauthentic since there "is an irreducible variety in what is true or of greatest significance. Christians can find validity in other religions because of the conviction that the Trinity represents a universal truth about the way the world and God actually are."[137]

First, did Heim preserve Christ's saving role in his consideration of the Trinity and pluralism? Heim says that "the Trinity teaches us that Jesus Christ cannot be an exhaustive or exclusive source for knowledge of God nor the exhaustive and exclusive act of God to save us."[138] In light of this remark, I think the answer to our question must be a resounding NO. Why? Because the doctrine of the Trinity teaches that Jesus is the

---

[135]Ibid.
[136]Ibid., 141.
[137]Ibid.
[138]S. Mark Heim, *The Depth of Riches: A Trinitarian Theology of Religious Ends* (Grand Rapids, MI: Eerdmans, 2001), 134.

only begotten Son of God the Father and as such it teaches that he is indeed the exclusive savior of the world since no other human being was, is, or will be hypostatically united with the eternal Son incarnate in history as Jesus of Nazareth was and is. So it is obvious that in his approach to pluralism Heim has completely undercut Christ's saving role. He has not preserved it at all. He hasn't even recognized it. If there is another act of God saving the world then there must be another God. And that idea would open the door to polytheism which is directly opposed to the doctrine of the Trinity. Heim's thinking and Rosario Rodríguez's thinking which is based on the views of Heim are mistaken because Jesus really is the exclusive savior of the world since he is the eternal Son of the Father. That is why Barth insisted that

> the true and essential distinction of the Christian religion from the non-Christian, and with it its character as the religion of truth over against the religions of error, can be demonstrated only in the fact, or event, that taught by Holy Scripture the Church listens to Jesus Christ and no one else as grace and truth, not being slack but always cheerful to proclaim and believe in Him.[139]

Since the truth of the Christian religion is grounded exclusively in Christ, the truth that Christians are free to live by grace is what is there asserted. "It is of grace that the Church and the children of God live by His grace." But this means for Barth that the Church lives "through the name of Jesus Christ."[140] However, this exclusivity is not meant in any way to exclude other religions by way of competition since it is an action of the one, true, and ever living God on behalf of all people, whatever their religious commitments might be. That is why Barth claimed that God's will is often done better outside the Church rather than in it.[141] And that is why Barth insisted that the judgment of God's grace must be applied firmly to ourselves and to others and that we must also see ourselves in solidarity with others as we anticipate them in repentance and hope and live by faith and by grace.[142]

Second, because Heim, like Rosario Rodríguez, does not begin his theology of religions with Jesus Christ himself and faith in him as the incarnate Word and unique savior of the world, he argues that "the communion Christ came to instigate is itself the fundamental instrument for understanding who Christ is."[143] However, if the communion we experience is the instrument for understanding who Christ is, then Christology has been undermined at the outset because the only person who can make himself known to us in his uniqueness as the incarnate Word is Jesus himself. That is why T. F. Torrance rightly insists that

---

[139]Barth, CD I/2, 344. Both Barth and Torrance base their knowledge of the Trinity in Jesus Christ because they really acknowledge that he is the Way, the Truth, and the Life and that no one comes to the Father except through him (Jn 14:6). See, e.g., CD II/1, 320; and Torrance, *Christian Doctrine of God*, 22–6, 124–35.
[140]Barth, CD I/2, 345.
[141]See Barth, CD II/2, 569.
[142]Barth, CD I/2, 327–8.
[143]Heim, *The Depth of Riches*, 137.

Jesus Christ gives himself to be known as the object of our experience and knowledge, within our history and within our human existence—but when we know him there, we know him in terms of *himself*. We know him out of pure grace as one who gives himself to us and freely discloses himself to us. We cannot earn knowledge of Christ, we cannot achieve it, or build up to it. We have no capacity or power in ourselves giving us the ability to have mastery over this fact. In the very act of our knowing Christ he is the master, we are the mastered. He manifests himself and gives himself to us by his own power and agency, by his Holy Spirit, and in the very act of knowing him we ascribe all the possibility of our knowing him to Christ alone, and none of it to ourselves.[144]

Take away the fact that only Christ himself can disclose to us who he is in himself and in his relation to the Father, and theology becomes another work of ours. Once that occurs, we are no longer thinking from a center in God but from a center in ourselves. Theology becomes mythology. It is no longer shaped by the truth of who God is as the eternal Trinity. We have already seen throughout this chapter the difference it makes when Jesus himself is allowed to be the starting point and criterion for theological reflection on liberation theology.

What happens to Heim in his assumption that it is communion and not Christ which is the instrument for understanding here is that religion and the study of religious ends become that instrument so that it is communion experienced within the community that becomes the criterion of truth. Thus, on the one hand Barth rightly insisted that all religion, including the Christian religion, is inherently unbelief. He held that religion is our human attempt to reach God on our own without recognizing that God has already come to us to enable us to know him in the incarnation and outpouring of the Holy Spirit. That is why Barth insisted that human religion was our capricious and arbitrary attempt to reach God. In that regard no religion per se will allow Christ himself to be the sole starting point and norm for what is said about the truth of God and revelation. On the other hand, Heim claims that religions

> demonstrate that every moment of human response to God's "Yes" to creation is met by God's further "Yes" as well … Religions represent real relations to aspects of the triune life and aspects of God's economic activity … God will in crucial measure conform God's relation with the person to the person's choice of terms on which to relate to God.[145]

---

[144]Torrance, *Incarnation*, 1–2.
[145]Heim, *Depth of Riches*, 268. Torrance's strong opposition to this kind of viewpoint is grounded in his view of the doctrine of election and wonderfully expressed in the following remarks: "The doctrine of election is to be appreciated as a way of expressing the unqualified objectivity of God's Love and Grace toward us, and the ultimate invariant ground in God himself on which all our faith and trust in him for our salvation in life and death repose. It represents a strictly theonomous way of thinking, from a centre in God and not from a centre in ourselves. As such the doctrine of election rejects any idea that we may establish contact with God or know or worship him through acting upon him, and certainly any idea that we can induce God to act in accordance with what we think or claim or want, for all our relations with God derive from his activity in Grace upon us

This reasoning is about the clearest statement anyone will ever see suggesting that our choices somehow determine how God will relate with us and even who God is. That idea represents an overt reversal of the relationship between Creator and creature which undermines the sovereignty of God's grace and love. And this reversal makes all the difference in the world because in faith Christians recognize that God's grace meets all people in judgment just as the revelation which meets all of humanity in Christ is offensive because as a free act of God, that act of love comes to us in a form that is clearly not of our choosing. It is because God has chosen us in his Son that we may live in the freedom and love that is ours in him. It is because "God so loved the world that he gave his only Son, so that everyone who believes in him might not perish but might have eternal life" (Jn 3:16). God's love for the world is very specific and cannot be universalized using trinitarian terminology without undermining the very meaning of faith, grace, and revelation as these categories are defined by God's actions in history in his Word and Spirit. For Barth, it is because "we understand His life as His existence" that

> it is a matter of His existence under a specific name which characterises Him, which marks Him off from all others, and by which He is to be called and addressed. This name is not accidental or capricious. It had not merely been conferred or appended. He Himself pronounces it. In so doing He expresses His inward self … All real acquaintance with Him rests on the fact that He makes Himself known … No other can do this for Him. He does not need the help of any other.[146]

It is for this reason that his history is itself "the history of salvation."[147]

When Barth speaks of God's grace, he speaks of the fact that all of us are justified according to this choice on the part of God. God is the one who is righteousness itself and for this reason God exercises his righteous action for us as grace since "the grace of God as such is the outworking and fulfilment of the right of God, God's righteous judgment."[148] For Paul this meant that such righteousness did not come from the law (Gal. 3:21; Rom. 10:5) and was not just any sort of righteousness, because all attempts at righteousness by us "are opposed to the grace of Jesus Christ" in such a way that they are in fact opposed to the very righteousness of God himself. So, even though they may appear to be righteous, they are not, because what is actually revealed in Christ in the first instance is "not the justification of the believer in Jesus Christ but the basis of it—that God shows Himself to be just"[149] and as such to be the one who justifies by

---

whereby he freely establishes reciprocity between himself and us, within which he makes room for us and establishes us in an authentic creaturely freedom grounded and secured in his own unlimited Freedom as God" (*Christian Theology and Scientific Culture*, 132).

[146]Barth, CD IV/3.1, 46.
[147]Ibid.
[148]Barth, CD IV/1, 531.
[149]Ibid., 532.

faith. That is why "the *freedom* of grace is revealed in the fact that it is always manifest in judgment. But it is the freedom of *grace* which is revealed in this way."[150]

But this means that when God meets us in his grace that he is always in opposition to us as we are because in ourselves and as such we are sinners at enmity with grace. The power of Barth's position in following Paul is that since Paul based our justification on the faithfulness of God himself, that faithfulness could not "be destroyed by any unfaithfulness of man (Rom. 3:3)." Barth asks how Paul knows that God is true to himself and answers that 2 Cor. 1:19 "tells us that it is by the fact that in Jesus Christ, the Son of God, proclaimed by him [Paul] what is revealed and active is not a Yes and No by the plain Yes of God."[151] Our justification in Christ therefore is no act of caprice or arbitrariness but instead it is an act of majesty "which gives the knowledge of faith an infallible certainty" which is the certainty that "God affirms Himself in this action, that in it He lives His own divine life in His unity as Father, Son and Holy Spirit. But in it He also maintains Himself as the God of man, as the One who has bound Himself to man from all eternity ... who has elected Himself for man and man for Himself."[152] Because this is an act of God himself for us, it is in no way based on a "mere value-judgment of religion, dependent for its truth upon the power of the human religiosity expressed in it."[153] Because this is the specific action of the triune God for us, it is therefore in his own Son and through the Holy Spirit that God

> shows Himself to be the One who as the gracious God is righteous and as the righteous God gracious. It is not at the expense but in the exercise of His Godhead that for the sake of all flesh His Word becomes flesh (Jn. 1:14). It is not a denial but a confirmation of His Godhead that He causes His Holy Spirit to dwell and work as the witness of His grace in those who are still threatened by sin and the flesh and death.[154]

These remarks are powerful and crucial in connection with our discussion of the Holy Spirit because I have been contending that one cannot simply know the Holy Spirit of the triune God by referring to human experiences of compassion and liberation or any other experience for that matter. Barth makes this connection perfectly when he asserts that no doctrine as a human work has the power to communicate truth to us. He says that

> in the mouth of human teachers and the ears of human listeners it [the truth] is always threatened by some measure of misunderstanding, deception, falsification and corruption ... [because, like human knowledge itself] no doctrine has of

---

[150]Barth, CD II/1, 367.
[151]Barth, CD IV/1, 532.
[152]Ibid.
[153]Ibid.
[154]Ibid., 532–3.

itself the power to unmask the sinner, i.e., the power of the event in which he is irresistibly detected and exposed as a liar.[155]

But that situation does not leave us to ourselves to decide what the truth is because "the truth alone has the power" to summon us out of our falsehood "to a knowledge and confession of the truth, to obedience and service."[156] Since the criterion of truth is Jesus Christ himself "in the promise of his Spirit" therefore "doctrine participates or does not participate in the truth to the extent and in the measure that directly or indirectly it teaches Him or fails to do so."[157] Since, however, he is the Lord "He is not conditioned by nor bound to it [doctrine], as it is conditioned by and bound to Him." So what then is truth? The answer here is what has concerned us throughout this chapter. Barth says,

It certainly cannot be expected … to encounter man as a phenomenon which is immediately and directly illuminating, pleasing, acceptable and welcome to him. He would not be who he is if the promise of the Spirit came to him easily and smoothly. The gate through which it comes to him, if at all, is not wide but strait, and its way to him is not broad but narrow.[158]

Barth goes on to say that the Spirit does indeed speak to our "innermost self" by telling us "about the reconciliation of the world to God which has taken place in Jesus Christ" and about our own "justification and sanctification" as well as "the freedom and peace" of our true being as new creatures in Jesus Christ.[159] But, to do this, Barth insists that the Spirit contradicts us precisely because we need to become new creatures in Christ to hear, see, and understand this. We need to have our sinful selves changed in and through our relation to our new life in Christ to experience the Holy Spirit. Otherwise, if the truth was just "served up … on a platter, if it disclosed itself to us cheaply and otherwise than in a desperate conflict of decision," this certainly would not be the truth of God.[160]

Everything said here points to the fact that Barth was right in his analysis of religion in relation to revelation. Thus, the truth of religion can only be recognized in faith which means faith in God himself as our righteous judge and savior in Christ. However, if that is true, then the idea that we might incorporate revelation into the context of a conception of communion dictated by anyone or anything other than who God is for us in Christ would have to mean that such a move was in reality a denial of the truth of Christian revelation in its particularity and specificity in Christ as an act of judgment and grace. It is just because Heim makes this move that he asserts that "trinitarian conviction rules out the view that among all the possible claimed manifestations of God, one narrow

[155]Barth, CD IV/3.1, 376.
[156]Ibid.
[157]Ibid.
[158]Ibid.
[159]Ibid., 376–7.
[160]Ibid., 377.

strand alone is authentic.”[161] This very assertion damages the heart of both Christology and trinitarian doctrine precisely because it opens the door to the idea, espoused by Heim, that there is a plurality of valid religious ends. And the main problem here is that trinitarian conviction for Heim merely expresses a value-judgment about various religious ends whereas a proper trinitarian theology linked with a proper Christology will always be determined only by one simple fact, namely, that God was in Christ reconciling the world to himself. That is the narrow strand set up by God himself and for that very reason it is not simply a claimed manifestation of God by one community among others as Heim assumes.

Thinking in these universalist terms, Heim maintains that other religions with their very different ends actually place their members in contact with dimensions of the triune God. But, of course, the only way that could be true is if the triune God is understood to refer to a reality accessible to people without specific faith in Jesus Christ as the Lord and therefore without belief in him enabled by the power of the Holy Spirit. Having broken free conceptually from the revelation of God in Christ, Heim thus argues that Islam finds the Christian doctrine of the Trinity to be offensive since Muslims believe it introduces division into God.[162] This is not surprising in itself. But Heim then claims that “the Muslim religious end focuses on the personal ‘I’ of the Trinity.”[163] However, if that were in any sense true then the Muslim idea thus asserted would be bound to affirm the oneness in being between the Father and the Son. Yet, that is the one thing that the Muslim idea of God’s oneness will not acknowledge. And to the extent that this is the case, it is more than a little inaccurate to claim that the Muslim religious end focuses on the “I” of the Trinity. Focusing on the deity of oneness is not to focus on the Trinity at all since the gateway to an acknowledgment and understanding of the oneness of the God of Christian faith is Jesus himself as the revealer and reconciler. But no one can actually say Jesus is Lord except through the power of the Holy Spirit. So, whatever “I” it is that Muslims have conceptualized with their concept of God, as long as the *homoousion* between the Father and the Son is neither recognized nor acknowledged, it definitely could not refer to the Trinity.

---

[161]Heim, *Depth of Riches*, 127.

[162]In Chapter 8, I discuss how a well-informed Muslim theologian attempts to reconcile Muslim belief in God’s oneness with Christian belief. It is suggested by that particular theologian that if we espouse what, in my judgment, amounts to a modalist position with regard to God’s oneness, then Christians and Muslims could be said to believe in God’s oneness without worrying about the doctrines of the incarnation and the Trinity which Muslims could never accept at face value. However, the real problem is this: Who determines the nature of God’s oneness? Is it Christians or is it Muslims? And the answer is that such a question will only lead to conflict if one attempts to answer it by placing Christianity and Islam side by side as expressions of human religious consciousness. However, if God’s oneness is in fact the oneness of who God actually is from and to all eternity as the eternal Father, Son, and Holy Spirit, then the answer to that question is not under the control either of Muslims or Christians. It is determined by who God actually is in himself and for us. And that is something we can only know for sure when we rely exclusively upon the grace and freedom of God who has reconciled sinners to himself in his Son and through his Spirit.

[163]Heim, *Depth of Riches*, 233.

It turns out then that Heim's description of dimensions of the triune God is a description of the content of religious value-judgments made by religious people who attempt to reach true knowledge of God without actually relying on grace, faith, and revelation as these categories receive their meaning from the revelation of God in Christ. Thus, as noted above, Paul Tillich claimed that if someone does not like the traditional name for God, that person could simply translate the word God by speaking of the depth of their own lives or of what they take seriously as of ultimate concern. Yet, the depth of my life and whatever may be of ultimate concern for me could never be the source of true knowledge of God since it led Tillich to claim that experiencing "depth" is experiencing God. It isn't, since our depth is a human experience and we are not divine! According to Barth's analysis just presented, Tillich's approach is just a cheap and easy way of assigning knowledge of God to everyone who has an experience of depth without regard to the fact that we are sinners who really need to have our minds reconciled to God before we can actually know who God truly is.

Finally, Heim's trinitarian theology of religious ends clearly does not allow who God is in Jesus Christ to determine his own view of God. For Heim, God is a "communion-nature."[164] While it is certainly true that as three persons, one being God is in communion. It is just as true that communion is not God. Heim clearly does not make this distinction since he argues that "the very fact that our being is constituted in relation to others, relation with what is unlike (and this includes most basically of all the fact that we are different from God who made us), is the most fundamental way that we are like God. It is the deepest thing we have in common."[165] Does this assertion suggest that we can discover that we have a life in common with God directly within our human experiences of others without faith in Christ? The answer apparently is yes for Heim as he says that "I as a Christian do not deny that a Hindu may actually realize identity with the divine, with absolute *Brahman*. I regard this as in fact identity with the underlying immanence of the triune God."[166]

But the only way this identification can be true is if somehow there is an identity between divine and human being so that our relations or communion with others gives us something in common with God. Indeed, since the *Brahman* is seen as an ultimate cosmic principle that operates within everyone, at most such a view would leave us with a unitarian or modalist view of God which appears to be pantheistic in identifying the divine with us in some sense. But the most important point to be made here is that Heim considers this Hindu concept descriptive of an aspect of the Trinity when it is not. To refer to the Trinity one would have to refer to the eternal Father, Son, and Holy Spirit. But that cannot happen outside the context of the Nicene faith. And since faith itself

---

[164]Heim, *Depth of Riches*, 180. He writes, "The doctrine's primary benefit for us is to sensitize us to the communion-nature of God, and hence to the various dimensions or frequencies through which God can simultaneously connect with us." Understood in this way, Heim can identify dimensions of the trinitarian life of God with the Muslim "personal 'I'" and with the Hindu experience of *Brahman*.

[165]Heim, *Depth of Riches*, 126–7.

[166]Ibid., 229.

comes from the Holy Spirit, in union with the Father and Son, one could never equate an experience of any ultimate cosmic principle with the triune God of Christian faith unless one had transformed the Trinity itself into a religious principle used to describe everyone's religious experiences. One of the key reasons why Heim does not notice this problem is because he really believes that "trinitarian conviction rules out the view that among all the possible claimed manifestations of God, one narrow strand alone is authentic"[167] and so he honestly believes that "religious ends are co-determined by persons themselves in their relational activity."[168] If that is in any sense true, then once again, Barth was right in claiming that in religion we seek to construct our own arbitrary and capricious concept of God. And thus, what is lost here in Heim's analysis is the fact that in Christ and through his Holy Spirit we really have true knowledge of God and of our reconciliation with God because that truth is not even slightly co-determined by us! Listen to Barth's words. They are packed with meaning.

> The revelation of God in the outpouring of the Holy Spirit is the judging but also reconciling presence of God in the world of human religion, that is, in the realm of man's attempts to justify and to sanctify himself before a capricious and arbitrary picture of God. The Church is the locus of true religion, so far as through grace it lives by grace.[169]

This is a loaded set of remarks because Barth draws several definitive conclusions from them. First, not only does revelation mean reconciliation, but through the Holy Spirit our justification and sanctification in Christ is actualized for and in us in union with Christ himself. Second, that is why Barth asserts that "both the reality and the possibility of this event [of revelation as reconciliation] are the being and action only of God, and especially God the Holy Spirit."[170] Third, that means that any attempt to find a possibility for revelation in us, in humanity, is impossible because "we could not ascribe the event to God, and yet attribute to man the instrument and point of contact for it."[171] This, because that point of contact, as is well known, is to be found only in the incarnation and outpouring of the Holy Spirit.

The power of Barth's argument is that since it is only by grace, and thus by what God has done for us in Christ and actualized in us by the Spirit that one can know the truth, therefore the truth of religion cannot be directly equated with any religion, including the Christian religion. One knows and lives by participating in that truth only in faith and by grace, only by relying on Christ and not ourselves. It is this specificity that rules out Heim's idea that "one might 'anonymously' move toward the pursuit of the Christian end" as a Muslim or as a Christian "one might 'anonymously' move toward pursuit of

---

[167]Ibid., 127.
[168]Ibid., 76.
[169]Barth, CD I/2, 280.
[170]Ibid.
[171]Ibid.

the Muslim end."[172] The problem here is that since faith in Christ means knowledge of the truth, and therefore knowledge of God's grace and revelation, there is nothing anonymous about that. To make knowledge of God (the Christian end) anonymous is to render it impossible because by definition it would have to be knowledge of something other than Jesus as the crucified and risen Lord.

Conclusion

We have now come full circle. In this chapter, I have argued that a properly theological theology of liberation would begin and end with the fact that we are liberated from enmity against God by God himself and thus freed to love God in Christ and on that basis to love our neighbors and therefore to fight against oppression. I have demonstrated what happens when theologians do not take that properly theological approach seriously and attempt to construct their theologies of liberation from communities working against oppression. Among other things this problematic approach of much liberation theology simply uses Jesus as a means toward a political, social, or religious end instead of opposing oppression in solidarity with all members of society, whatever their religious convictions might be, on the basis of God's having freed us to do so in his Word and Spirit. Thus, instead of redefining Christian faith in a way that moves beyond the Word of God in the manner suggested by Rubén Rosario Rodríguez, Paul Knitter, and others, a properly theological theology of liberation would base its political and social judgments on the freedom that comes to the world by God's grace in reconciling the world to himself and freeing us to realize that all attempts to oppress others or to misuse others or to use them at all are simply excluded by the fact that the sin that leads to that kind of behavior has already been overcome for humanity in and by Christ himself. All are free to live from and in Christ who is the savior of the world.

To live as part of that new creation then is to live in a freedom that we do not have to and indeed cannot create for ourselves. It is simply there for us. All we need to do is to live from it. The key point then of this chapter has been that it is a serious mistake to think that simply to participate in the process of liberation is already in a certain sense a salvific work. No, it is not. And it is not, because to be saved means to find our liberation in Christ alone where it is a reality and, on that basis, to then work for the betterment of society. The moment this is reversed as it is by Rosario Rodríguez, for instance, then one can detach the Holy Spirit from the Word of reconciliation and locate "divine revelation in the work of historical and political liberation" instead of in Christ himself. Then the kingdom of God comes to be equated with a new version of salvation by works which places the weight of salvation on us and undermines its truth and reality. Then, also it is thought that we could speak properly of the Holy Spirit simply by describing our experiences of compassion and liberation in society. Then, as

[172]Heim, *Depth of Riches*, 237.

Rosario Rodríguez himself states, "focusing on the work of the Spirit opens the door to the notion of history as sacrament, not only providing a phenomenological vocabulary for describing divine agency in human history but also affirming the work of the Spirit in the religious and cultural 'other.' "[173] That viewpoint not only changes the meaning of sacraments by detaching them from the direct action of Jesus and the Holy Spirit and universalizing them within history, but such an approach fails to recognize that the Spirit actually opposes any such approaches by specifically uniting us to the crucified, risen, ascended, and coming Lord here and now. To my knowledge, no Christian has ever been baptized into the "nameless" or into "holy mystery" but rather into the name of the Father, Son, and Holy Spirit. At the Lord's Supper the celebration of the Eucharist is in memory of Jesus himself at his own instruction until he comes again.

What I have shown here is that there is a serious problem with Rubén Rosario Rodríguez's assertion that "it follows from recognizing the presence of the Holy Spirit in liberating work—especially when such work is located outside the church—that, as in Heim's Trinitarian pluralism, God desires and values doctrinal diversity and theological pluralism" because "theological truth claims are tested in comparative theological analysis."[174] For Rosario Rodríguez, that assertion clearly means that whenever Christ-like praxis is engendered, there we have a proper liberation theology. Nothing could be further from the truth for Christian faith because all truth claims are judged only by God himself in and through his own forgiving grace as actualized in Christ and enacted in each new present by the Holy Spirit in union with the Father and Son. So, the very idea that theological truth claims grounded in the truth itself, as it is identical with Jesus as the very Word of God and his Spirit as the Spirit of the Father and Son, need to be tested in comparative theological analysis, would have to mean that there is a superior or at least another vantage point equal to this God by which the truth claims of Jesus can be judged. However, if Jesus really is God from God and the Spirit really is one in being with the Father and Son, then there is no such viewpoint and can be no such comparison! Hence, a properly *theological* theology of liberation will always allow Jesus himself as the true Liberator and as the light of the world to be the *first* and *final* Word that gives meaning to all human efforts at liberation of others from oppression.

---

[173]Rosario Rodríguez, *Dogmatics after Babel*, 176.
[174]Ibid., 143.

CHAPTER 6
LANGUAGE FOR GOD: CONSIDERING THE DIFFERENCE BETWEEN "DISCLOSURE MODELS" AND "PICTURING MODELS" IN KNOWING THE TRINITY WITH T. F. TORRANCE

One of the truly burning issues in trinitarian theology over the last two decades at least has been the question of how to name God in a way that would not undermine the full equality of men and women. It has been argued that for women to have equality in the Church, the exclusive language for God used in worship and doctrine to name God Father and Son must be either changed or augmented to avoid patriarchalism. In this chapter, I would like to explore this difficult issue with the help of Thomas F. Torrance who understood this matter better than most. Ultimately, it really is a matter of where the truth of our knowledge of the Trinity comes from. Torrance is very careful not to dismiss the idea that our knowledge of God is certainly related to our experience of the reality of God. So he will speak of the fact that our main concern is "not in any conceptual system as such, but [with] the immanent relations in God himself as Father, Son and Holy Spirit."[1] He therefore stresses that "what we must never allow ourselves to do is to forget the constitutive elements in God's self-communication to us and in our experience and apprehension of him which gave rise to those concepts."[2] Our concepts of course are necessarily related to our experience of God and thus to what Torrance calls our intuitive knowledge of God. For Torrance, "*intuitive knowledge* is the direct knowledge of an actually present object caused naturally by that object and not by another."[3] And the knowledge that he has in mind here is "*direct intuitive knowledge of God in his Word … in which the centre of gravity [is]* shifted from the subjective to the objective pole of intuitive knowledge" such that language "is subordinated to the objective realities it serves."[4] The realities Torrance has in mind are, as he says, "supplied by the doctrines of justification by grace or election, and of the mighty living Word

---

[1] Torrance, *Reality and Scientific Theology*, 161.
[2] Ibid., 161–2.
[3] Torrance, *Theology in Reconstruction*, 79.
[4] Ibid., 84.

of God which sounds through the Scriptures enabling us to hear and apprehend God speaking to us in person."[5]

The important point here is this: Torrance wanted to avoid thinking developed in abstraction from actual experience of and knowledge of God through God's self-revelation in his Word and Spirit and he also wanted to eschew any idea that knowledge of God comes from us and not from God alone. Therefore, he consistently followed both Athanasius and Hilary because he thought they "realised quickly that terms applied to the Deity involve a real shift in meaning from that which they have in ordinary use … It is the teaching of Hilary in particular that he mentions, to the effect that thing is not subjected to speech but speech to thing (*quia non sermoni res sed rei est sermo subiectus*)."[6] Torrance also frequently cited Athanasius's statement that it is "more godly and true to signify God from the Son and call him Father, than to name God from his works alone and call him Unoriginate."[7] For Torrance, this meant that when thinking about God in faith and thus from a center in God who meets us directly in his incarnate Word and not from a center in ourselves, our thinking would begin with the Son who himself enables our knowledge of the Father through the power of his Holy Spirit.[8] Therefore, our thinking would not begin by reflecting on ourselves or on the world in an attempt to know God by inference from the things God has made.

If Torrance's remarks about experience of God are not understood with precision, one might mistakenly draw the conclusion that for Torrance knowledge of God is grounded in our experience. But he is not saying that here. He is saying that in our experience of the reality of God in revelation, we know that our focus is not only on our conceptual system in and through which we know God, or upon ourselves, but on God as he has made himself known to us in faith and through revelation and thus *through* our concepts.

---

[5]Ibid.

[6]Torrance, *The Hermeneutics of John Calvin*, 50.

[7]Torrance, *The Trinitarian Faith*, 49, and *Christian Doctrine of God*, 117.

[8]That is one reason why he asserts that our minds need to be reconciled with God through Christ in order to know God truly. For Torrance, "that takes place in the Christian *metanoia*, when the believer, transformed by the renewing of his mind, knows that he has not chosen Christ, but that Christ has chosen him; that his knowing of God is grounded on his being known of God; and that every analogy of men, such as fatherhood, is grounded reflexively upon the action and love of the heavenly Father, after whom every fatherhood in heaven and earth is named" (*Theology in Reconstruction*, 116). Importantly, Torrance frequently insists that the creaturely content of the terms "father" and "son" "may not be read back into the inner relations of God's own Being." However, they are not just "conventionally related to God as detachable, imaginary imitations of divine Reality and therefore quite changeable." As they point beyond themselves to the real relations within the Trinity as revealed by God himself in Christ and through the Spirit they were understood at Nicaea to refer to God himself. The fathers at Nicaea were thus convinced that "the relation of the Father to the Son and of the Son to the Father constitutes the basic ontological relationship or reciprocity in the Godhead in which all the language of the gospel is finally rooted and shaped" (Torrance, *Reality and Evangelical Theology*], 111).

Conceptual Knowledge of God

Torrance is not always as clear as he might be about this. But his intentions are always very clear. So, for instance, he insists that the terms "father" and "son" used within the doctrine of the Trinity are valid only to the extent that they remain "correlated with our fundamental experience of God and *controlled by his self-revelation* to us in Jesus Christ the incarnate Son of the Father."[9] Here Torrance is crystal clear that while our concepts for God must be correlated with our actual experience of God, they are nonetheless controlled by God's self-revelation in Christ. That is in keeping with his view of intuitive knowledge as knowledge that is controlled by the object known. That insight was also in harmony with his understanding of scientific theology as reflection that allows the unique nature of the object being considered to determine the truth of what is said.

These are crucial points that are often missed in contemporary discussions of the Trinity. Inasmuch as those statements are true, their truth is and always remains grounded in God and not at all in us and certainly not in our concepts as such. So Torrance maintains, correctly in my view, that "we can no more get away from using the expressions 'father' and 'son' than we can do without God's self-revelation as Father through the Son and in the Spirit." From this he concludes that

> the concepts and expressions we employ can be of genuine theological significance for us if they direct us away from themselves to the ineffable Reality of God himself … for they fulfil their God-given function in revelation when they enable us to grasp something of the inner relations of God which are the fundamental relations in and behind our experience of him and are independent of our concepts and expressions referring to them.[10]

Because his thought is shaped by the doctrine of justification by faith, Torrance forcefully holds that our concepts must point away from themselves toward God because, as he says elsewhere, none of our concepts in theology are true in themselves but only as they are grounded in revelation and thus ultimately within the eternal Trinity.[11] But he might

---

[9]Torrance, *Reality and Scientific Theology*, 162, emphasis mine.
[10]Ibid.
[11]Thus, Torrance writes that "justification by grace alone tells us that verification of our faith or knowledge on any other ground, or out of any other source, than Jesus Christ, is to be set aside. Justification has an *epistemological* as well as an ethical reference—epistemologically it insists that the only legitimate demonstration of Christian truth is that which is in accordance with its nature, which is grace, and that to seek justification of it on any other ground is not only fundamentally false in itself but to falsify the Gospel at its very basis" (*Theology in Reconstruction*, 163). From this he concludes that all our theological statements must allow themselves to be "called into question by the very Christ toward which they point, for he alone is the Truth." And that is not the end of it. He then asserts that "justification means that our theological statements are of such kind that *they do not claim to have truth in themselves*" (ibid., emphasis mine). They must, instead, point away from themselves to Christ who is himself the "truth of God." Moreover, he insists that to claim our statements are true in themselves is a form of "self-justification" (ibid.). See also Torrance, *Reality and Evangelical Theology*, 123–5, where he follows Calvin and argues that "the doctrine of justification by Grace, which means that in all our

have been clearer than when he went on to say that our concepts and expressions for God "enable us to grasp something of the inner relations of God." The problem with that assertion is that Torrance himself knows and stresses the fact that it is not our concepts and expressions which enable our knowledge of God but only God through the power of his Holy Spirit who does that *through* our concepts. He himself clarifies this matter on the very same page when he makes a decisive distinction between what he calls a *"disclosure model"* and a *"picturing model"* of God.

Torrance rightly claims that all our formulations of the doctrine of the Trinity are inadequate. Consequently, he firmly rejects the idea that in knowing the Trinity there is "some kind of point to point correspondence between [our model] and God."[12] That, he says, is the *"picturing model,"* which he firmly rejects because such a model clearly does not allow for the fact that the truth of what is said must be shaped exclusively by who God has revealed himself to be in Christ and through the Spirit. Therefore, he maintains that we should use *"a disclosure model* through which God's self-revelation impresses itself upon us, while discriminating itself from the creaturely representations necessarily employed by the model, and so bears upon our minds that its own inner relations are set up within them as the laws of our faithful understanding of God."[13] Here Torrance makes it very clear that the truth of our knowledge of the triune God is enabled neither by our knowledge nor by the model we employ but only by God himself in his self-revelation. Torrance himself clarifies this matter further by explaining that "the terms 'father' and 'son' can only be interpreted in a 'sexist' sense if they are used as picturing models rather than as disclosure models. Used as disclosure models they function in divine revelation

---

relations with God as moral or religious beings, we can never claim to have right or truth in ourselves, but may find our right and truth only in Christ ... we may never claim the truth for our own statements ... Theological statements do not carry their truth in themselves, but ... direct us away from themselves to the one Truth of God" (ibid., 123).

[12]Torrance, *Reality and Scientific Theology*, 162.

[13]Ibid. This is why, as seen in our chapter discussing nonconceptual knowledge of God, Torrance insisted that "within the sphere of divine revelation an *epistemological inversion* takes place in our knowing God, for what is primary is his knowing us, not our knowing of him" (*Christian Doctrine of God*, 105). This is also why he maintains that "to know God we must know him in accordance with the form or structure of his own Being—that is, in terms of God's inner divine relations. And that means we must know him as the Triune God who within himself has relations between Father, Son and Holy Spirit" (Torrance, *Ground and Grammar*, 148). In that sense there must be a trinitarian structure in our mind "corresponding to the trinity of relations in God himself" (ibid.). However, Torrance rejects Augustine's attempt, and any other attempt, "to operate with a trinitarian structure that we have in our minds, independent of or apart from our actual knowledge of God, as he claimed, for example in the statement that there is an image of God in the mind of man even apart from its participation in God" (ibid., 149). This is also why Torrance invariably insists, in harmony with Martin Buber, that there can be no conceptual letting go of God in his inner relations as happened, for example, in the thinking of Paul Tillich who he said "operates with what is called a nonconceptual relation to God ... meaning, of course, that the cognitive content in what is called knowledge of God derives, not from faith in God, but from some aspect of human culture" (ibid., 150). That, as we shall see below, is the major problem that is still evident in the thought of Elizabeth Johnson and others who approach knowledge of God from experience instead of from revelation through our experience of faith in the triune God. It is *the* major problem that plagues contextual theology today.

through 'imageless' reference to God, in accordance with the second Commandment, Exodus 20.4."[14]

What does he mean by this? He means that to know God truly we must know God the Father through his Son in faith and thus by the power of the Holy Spirit. That sounds simple enough. But it needs some explanation. Torrance is affirming the fact that all true knowledge of the Trinity is grounded in the reality of God the Father, Son, and Holy Spirit and thus occurs when our thinking takes place from a "centre in God as he reveals himself to us through his Word incarnate in Jesus Christ," as already noted. Hence, "we know him [God] as Father in himself *in an utterly unique and incomparable way,* which then becomes the controlling standard by reference to which all notions of creaturely fatherhood and sonship are to be understood."[15] This manner of phrasing our knowledge

---

[14]Torrance, *Reality and Scientific Theology*, 201, n. 4. Torrance also made this important point in the context of Christology where he argued against trying to understand Jesus "within the patterns of our own various cultures" since that would end by our conceptualizing Jesus apart from his own Jewish context and thus misunderstanding him. In Torrance's view, if we plaster "upon the face of Jesus a mask of different gentile features" that will prevent us "from seeing him and understanding him as he really is, as a Jew" and that will prevent "our brethren the Jews from recognising in this stylised Christ which we equate with the 'historical Jesus' the Messiah whom they are still expecting" (Thomas F. Torrance, *The Mediation of Christ* [Colorado Springs: Helmers & Howard, 1992], 19–20). Torrance thus rightly rejects any schematizing of the Old and New Testament picture of Jesus "to our own culture, a western culture, a black culture, an oriental culture, as the case may be" (ibid., 19). From this he argued that Christians should "enlist the aid of the Jews in helping us to interpret Jesus as he is actually presented to us in the Jewish Scriptures" since he says we "desperately need Jewish eyes to help us see what we cannot see because of our gentile lenses, that is, the culture-conditioned habits of thought and interpretation which we bring to Jesus and which make us read into him the kind of observational images which have played such a dominant role in our literary culture and, until recent decades, in our scientific culture as well" (ibid., 20). After then claiming that in reality, against common assumptions of the late date assigned to the fourth Gospel because of the Greek ideas found in it, John's Gospel "is probably the most 'Hebraic' book in the New Testament," Torrance gives an example to support his thinking. He says the "Jewish mind can help us" think about God in a way in which "we do not project our creaturely images into God" (ibid.). That applies in this instance to the terms "'father' and 'son'" which in Israel "were not projected into God, far less the creaturely sex-content of those images. The Hebrew language is replete with vivid dramatic images, for example, in which feminine feelings are applied to God, but the relation between those images and God is an *imageless* relation. The images used are referred to the invisible God imagelessly" (ibid.). That means that God is not defined by the projection of those images into God, but through those images, God is allowed to reveal himself to us as the eternal Father, Son, and Holy Spirit.

[15]Torrance, *The Trinitarian Faith*, 69, emphasis mine. Torrance repeats this extremely important point many times. Thus, he asks, "What then does it mean to think of the three divine Persons specifically as 'Father,' 'Son' and 'Holy Spirit'? This was a question that had kept cropping up in the Church since the Arian controversy when attempts were made to speak of divine Fatherhood and Sonship on the analogy of human fatherhood and sonship" (Torrance, *Christian Doctrine of God*, 157). Importantly, here and elsewhere, Torrance rightly insists that the Fatherhood and Sonship of the trinitarian Persons must be understood "in ways that point utterly beyond what we mean by 'father' and 'son' among ourselves and thus utterly beyond all sexist connotations and implications" because the generation of the Son and procession of the Spirit are "incomprehensible mysteries which are not explicable through recourse to human modes of thought" (ibid.). Thus, he says that both Athanasius and Gregory Nazianzen insisted that all analogies "drawn from the visible world" must be set aside "in speaking of God, helpful as they may be up to a point, for they are theologically unsatisfactory and even objectionable, and [we] must think of 'Father' and 'Son' when used of God as *imageless relations*" (ibid.). And that means that we cannot "read the creaturely content of our human expressions of 'father' and 'son' analogically into what God discloses of his inner divine relations" (ibid., 158). So, to think imagelessly means to think in a "'see through' way, to the Father and the Son without the intrusion of creaturely forms or sensual

of the Trinity is important because it means that Torrance has barred the door to reading sex or gender back into the Trinity since all proper knowledge of God has God the Father as its controlling standard. He does this because, in his mind, "unique Fatherhood and unique Sonship in God mutually define one another in an absolute and singular way. As Athanasius pithily expressed it in rejection of Arian anthropocentric mythologising: 'Just as we cannot ascribe a father to the Father, so we cannot ascribe a brother to the Son.'"[16]

There are at least three important factors at work here that must be mentioned. First, and importantly, Torrance contrasted Hellenic thinking which prioritized the visual over other senses and so tended to think in images that were "projected by human beings beyond themselves in the form of myths."[17] Second, this approach to knowledge of God was exactly what led to the Arian crisis because the moment it was thought that the terms "father" and "son" should be understood "as visual, sensual images taken from our human relations and then projected mythologically into God," then one could hardly avoid the idea that by using these categories one had to be "projecting creaturely gender into God, and thinking of him as grandfather as well as father, for the only kind of father we know is one who is son of another father."[18] Third, Torrance then contrasted this Hellenic approach to what he called a Hebraic approach which required that "all images properly used in speech and thought of God refer to him away from themselves *without imaging him*."[19]

Of course, this did not mean that we were supposed to think about God without using any images. That would be impossible. Instead, it meant that we must not use images in a "mimetic" way by which one might assume that our images have a way of describing God based on our own experiences. Torrance instead insisted that we should allow our images to function as "transparent media or open analogies through which the truth of God may disclose itself to us and through which the Word of God himself may sound through to us and be heard by us, and not some word of ours that we project into God's mouth."[20] In other words this approach is the picturing model noted above while the properly theological model is one that recognizes that all genuine knowledge of the

---

images into God" (ibid.). The importance of this thinking cannot be overstressed because if Torrance is right, and I think he is, then what is known of God from the revelation of the Father through the Son in the Spirit has and can have no gender whatsoever attached to it. Therefore, even the slightest suggestion that we might need to change the name for God based on the notion that such a change might be required in the interest of gender equality when speaking of God is trapped within the very same anthropocentric and subjectivist framework of thought that characterized the Arian crisis in the first place. Consequently, the crucial question posed in these circumstances is this: from where does the truth of our knowledge of God come? Does it come from God alone or from us? Torrance makes this same point powerfully when he insists that when the words Father, Son, or Spirit in Greek are used to speak of God they cannot be shaped by "the gender which by linguistic convention they have in Greek, for gender belongs only to creatures and may not be read back into the Nature of God as Father, Son and Holy Spirit" (*Trinitarian Perspectives: Toward Doctrinal Agreement* [Edinburgh: T&T Clark, 1994], 129–30). Thus, Torrance insists that "human fatherhood may not be used as a standard by which to judge divine Fatherhood" (ibid.).

[16]Ibid., 70.
[17]Ibid.
[18]Ibid., 69. See also Torrance, "The Christian Apprehension of God the Father," 137.
[19]Torrance, "The Christian Apprehension of God the Father," 129. See also Torrance, *The Trinitarian Faith*, 71.
[20]Ibid.

Christian God occurs as God personally enables us to know him *through* our images without projecting them back into God. This is crucial, because unless God himself enables this knowledge through our images which in and of themselves can only refer to creaturely realities, we will never know God as he is in himself.[21] But one might ask why can we not think of God as mother and father under certain circumstances? This is indeed the position taken by Paul Fiddes and by many others, including Elizabeth Johnson, Sallie McFague, and Catherine LaCugna.

Picture Model/Disclosure Model

Following Torrance's thinking from a center in God, he would reckon that Fiddes, Johnson, McFague, and LaCugna are using "picture models" instead of "disclosure models" with the result that they do not allow their thinking to be controlled by the revelation of God the Father through the incarnate Son. Instead, they project knowledge of God from their own experiences. This is an exceptionally important point. The difference between the two approaches to God really is the difference between accurate scientific theology that allows the reality of God to determine the truth of what is said, and Arian theology that mythologically projects models of God from those experiences that matter most to us. Let me illustrate the point.

Because Fiddes thinks abstractly about the Holy Trinity, that is, his thinking is not consistently grounded in the very being of the immanent Trinity as God meets us in the economy, he claims that "God is a name for an event or happening of relationships in which we are engaged" so that " 'life-in-relationship' is our best way into a vision of God as Trinity."[22] From this it follows that his view "makes relation the final available

---

[21] Here it is important to note that Torrance placed a priority on "auditive apprehension" both in natural science and in theological science since this manner of knowing allows objective reality rather than our subjective apprehension of it to shape what is heard and understood. Thus, in knowing objective reality, our minds function "under the pressure of objective reality upon them" (Torrance, *Christian Frame of Mind*, 79). But Torrance says there is more to it. He says that, "like the fundamental religious beliefs to which they are akin, ultimate scientific beliefs arise in us as we *listen* to what is said from a source beyond ourselves. In the emergence of these ultimate beliefs there takes place a subliminal hearing of a 'speech' embedded in reality, which precedes, accompanies and shapes specific acts of scientific understanding" (ibid.). He noted that Clerk Maxwell, Einstein, and Polanyi spoke of their scientific intuition or intuitive contact with reality. But he then stressed that "intuitive apprehension of this kind is *auditive* rather than perceptive in nature, akin to the mode of hearing rather than of seeing or observing, and that what results in this way is an intuitive correlate of the creative address of God" (ibid., 79–80). Torrance says this is crucial because (1) "in seeing or observing, the natural emphasis is on the observer himself, or the subjective pole of the knowing relation" and (2) "in seeing, the observer is thrown back upon himself or herself to authenticate and give meaning to what he or she sees, especially if the object of observation is a thing or an inanimate body" (ibid., 80). When this thinking is applied to theology, Torrance argues that our hearing and God's speaking implies always that "the weight of emphasis is upon God" (ibid., 80–1). God's authoritative Word questions us and "penetrates our self-centredness and tells us what we are utterly incapable of learning by ourselves or telling to ourselves," and that means that the modality and "*inherent force*" of our ultimate beliefs "are due to the commanding Voice or Word of God" (ibid., 81). Thus, true knowledge of God can only come from God *to* us and not *from* us at all.

[22] Paul S. Fiddes, *Two Views on the Doctrine of the Trinity*, 160.

concept we have for thinking about God and so [he] is taking relationality to a radical conclusion."[23] This approach is problematic exactly because it expresses what Torrance identified as a "picturing model" of God based on human experiences of relationship which are presumed to be experiences of God since for Fiddes relation is the final concept we have for God. That is precisely why Fiddes can claim that God is a name for a "happening of relationships in which we are engaged." Of course, that is untrue since God is the name the incarnate Son reveals to us here and now through the Holy Spirit enabling us to know God the Father through union with Jesus Christ himself in faith. Importantly, Fiddes misses the point that both Torrance and Barth consistently made, each in their own way. For Barth,

> we cannot say anything higher or better of the "inwardness of God" than that God is Father, Son and Holy Spirit, and therefore that He is love in Himself without and before loving us, and without being forced to love us. And we can say this only in the light of the "outwardness" of God to us, the occurrence of His revelation.[24]

Torrance holds this very same position when he regularly asserts, with Barth, that only God can reveal God or name himself to us and that what is revealed is that the Father/Son relation always has unequivocal priority over Creator/creature relations. In Torrance's words,

---

[23]Ibid., 161.

[24]Barth, CD I/2, 377. Both Barth and Torrance acknowledge that the God who meets us in Christ and through the Holy Spirit is the God who is self-sufficient as the eternal Father, Son, and Holy Spirit. This God preexisted creation and did not need us to be who he eternally was and is. As Barth succinctly put it, "if God comes to man in His divine Word, He does not do so because He needs man. God does not flee to man for refuge. He is not obliged to be the Creator, nor to be gracious to man. He is glorious in Himself. He could be content with that inner glory. The fact that He is the Creator of man and is gracious to man is a free overflowing of His glory" (CD III/2, 187). Hence, it is the God who is free in himself who loves us and acts for us as Creator, Reconciler, and Redeemer. That is why Torrance asserts, with Athanasius, that while God was always Father, he was not always Creator, and while God was always Son, he was not always incarnate (*Christian Doctrine of God*, 108). That is why Barth frequently insists that God would have been the eternal triune God even if he never had decided to be God with us, as he indeed did (*The Humanity of God*, trans. Thomas Wieser and John Newton Thomas [Richmond, VA: John Knox Press, 1968], 50). See also CD I/2, 135, where Barth writes, "His Word will still be His Word apart from this becoming [the incarnation], just as Father, Son and Holy Spirit would be none the less eternal God if no world had been created". Fiddes uncritically reads the economy back into the immanent Trinity by projecting relationality as we experience this into God and then mistakenly claiming that we are "necessarily included" in God's inner relations because the "'for us' is included in whatever is meant by the eternal begetting of the Son by the Father. There can be no self-sufficient, self-contained society of the Trinity, for God has not chosen to be in that way" (Paul Fiddes, *The Creative Suffering of God* [Oxford: Clarendon Press, 1988], 123). It is just this thinking that clearly reduces the immanent to the economic Trinity because it is an instance of projection which is not grounded in the trinitarian self-revelation. Simply put, we are not included in the eternal begetting of the Son by the Father. If we were, we too would be God from God. While God has in fact chosen to be God for us in his incarnate Son, that was in reality a choice of God, who eternally begets the Son and chooses to love us from all eternity. The inability to distinguish the eternally begotten Son from God's free action of grace in electing to be in covenant relation with us is the hallmark of a confused understanding of the Trinity.

God reveals *himself* through *himself,* in a triadic movement of self-communication whereby he announces himself to us and names himself as *Father, Son and Holy Spirit.* This is not a revelation simply of different modes of being that God transiently assumes in his activity toward us, but a revelation of what he really is in his own eternal nature apart from us. God *is* Father, Son and Holy Spirit.[25]

Relationality and God

The result is that one could never say that the final concept for the Christian God is relation because, while God is certainly relational within his own eternal life and in relating with us, he is so precisely and only as the eternal Father, Son, and Holy Spirit who loves in freedom and is free in his loving us.[26] Because Fiddes's knowledge of God is not in fact governed exclusively by this Father/Son relation, he thinks it is appropriate and necessary to critique patriarchy convincingly "when 'Mother' becomes a name to be invoked in prayer as well as (but not replacing) 'Father.'"[27] He maintains that "if divine persons are relations … we use mother-language specifically on those occasions when we are involved in relationships in God that make it apt for us to call on God as mother."[28] What then is the basis for calling upon God as mother? Since Fiddes envisions the triune God "as a perichoresis of relationships,"[29] he thinks "that wherever there are movements of empathy between human persons, these are leaning upon perfect empathetic movements which are there already before them" so that he can use "trinitarian symbols" to describe "these movements as being like the entering of a father into the feelings of a son, or of a daughter into the feelings of a mother."[30] In case

---

[25]Torrance, "The Christian Apprehension of God the Father," 121, 123, 140. See also Torrance, *Christian Doctrine of God*, 99. For a discussion of the priority of the Father/Son relation see Molnar, Introduction to *Christian Doctrine of God*, Cornerstones edition, xvii–xx; and Molnar, *Torrance: Theologian of the Trinity*, 40–72. It was Origen's failure "to give clear-cut ontological priority to the Father/Son relation in God over the Creator/cosmos relation" that was the culprit leading him to blur "the difference between the internal and external relations of God" (Torrance, *The Trinitarian Faith*, 85). Torrance insists that "we may not … bypass God's self-naming. The one way that God has thus chosen in making himself known to us as Father, Son, and Holy Spirit and addressing us in human language specifically adapted to his self-revelation as the Father, Son and the Holy Spirit sets aside any ways of speaking about him that we may devise and choose for ourselves" (Torrance, "The Christian Apprehension of God the Father," 140). See also Torrance, *The Trinitarian Faith*, 110–25.

[26]This is why Torrance regularly insists that since our knowing God is grounded first in God's knowing us, "when we speak of God as Father, therefore, we are not using the term 'Father' in a transferred, improper, or inadequate sense; we are using it in its completely proper sense, which is determined by the intrinsic Fatherhood of God himself … And when we say 'God is love,' the love that God is is different from any other kind of love. As St. John says, 'Herein is love, not that we loved God, but that he loved us, and sent his Son to be a propitiation for our sins, and not for our sins only, but for the sins of the whole world' (1 John 4:10)" ("The Christian Apprehension of God the Father," 137).

[27]Paul S. Fiddes, *Participating in God: A Pastoral Doctrine of the Trinity* (Louisville, KY: Westminster John Knox Press, 2000), 94.

[28]Ibid.

[29]Ibid.

[30]Ibid., 208.

one might wonder here whether Fiddes had confused the immanent and economic Trinity with his notion that we can know and experience God by experiencing human relationships of love, consider his view that

> the projection of the immanent Trinity as a self-sufficient divine grouping from which man is or even might be, absent is sheer speculation; this is not actually how God has manifested himself ... There can be no self-sufficient, self-contained society of the Trinity, for God has not chosen to be in that way. His relationships within himself are open to the world.[31]

On the one hand, a properly formulated doctrine of the immanent Trinity is not a projection at all since that would represent what Torrance identified for us as a "picture model," but a statement of who God eternally *is* as Father, Son, and Holy Spirit who loves in freedom. On the other hand, God cannot love in freedom if God is not self-sufficient; such a God as conceived by Fiddes is in fact dependent upon the world to be who he is.[32] Barth and Torrance reject both of these viewpoints because, as just noted, while God was always Father, he was not always Creator. And while God was always Son, he was not always incarnate. Further, God did not need to create and did not need to become incarnate. Inasmuch as Fiddes thinks that we human beings could never be absent from within the Trinity, his thinking not only illustrates the fact that by his making relationality the subject and the triune God the predicate, he could arbitrarily change the name for God to mother depending upon our experiences but also that, in his view, there never could have been a time when "man" was absent from the inner trinitarian relations. That assertion in itself is an overt confusion of the immanent and economic Trinity. The point here is that such confusion results whenever knowledge of God is grounded in our experiences of relationality instead of in Christ himself as the revelation of God in history. Such an approach projects knowledge of God *from* us rather than presenting knowledge of God from a center in God himself as the eternal, and indeed, the eternal self-sufficient Trinity. In Fiddes's thinking, the

---

[31]Fiddes, *The Creative Suffering of God*, 122–3.

[32]While Fiddes rightly and theoretically claims that "creation does not determine the meaning of fatherhood; the truth is quite the opposite" (*Participating in God*, 95), his claim that man could never be absent from the relations of the immanent Trinity is in conflict with that assertion. His problem is that he does not understand perichoresis as referring exclusively to the Persons of the eternal Trinity but to God's relations with us: "The perichoresis of the divine persons with each other cannot be torn apart from the perichoresis of God with creation" (ibid.). If God's relations with creation were "perichoretic" then the relation of Creator and creatures would have to be construed as a mutually conditioning relationship. Such thinking comes from confusing the begetting of the Son with creation as Origen did. Thus, for Fiddes explaining perichoresis with the image of a divine dance, "if God desires to include created persons within the communion of divine life, the dance will not be complete until this has been achieved. The moment of begetting and creating is thus one of humility, and an opening of the divine life to pain and suffering" (ibid. 95–6). Indeed, "all human creatures are held within the divine intention for fellowship, at the eternal moment of the begetting of the Son" (ibid., 95). This thinking undercuts the freedom of God's grace with the idea that the perichoretic relations within the Trinity will not be complete until salvation is complete and then equates the moment of begetting with the moment of creating. That thinking obliterates the freedom of grace. Perichoresis will be discussed more later in the chapter.

Father/Son relation cannot have priority over the Creator/creature relation because there never was a time when human beings were absent from the immanent Trinity.

The most important point to be made here, however, is that while Fiddes attempts to critique patriarchy by speaking of God as mother, the truth is that he missed the point that I am making in this chapter with the help of Torrance's insights. Patriarchy is the result of sinful men attempting to claim superiority over women instead of recognizing that in Christ's having reconciled the world to himself, such sinful attempts by men to suppose that women are or should be subordinate to them have already been overcome.[33] The result is that living by grace, that is, by the reconciliation of the world that has already taken place for humanity in Jesus himself, through union with Christ in the Spirit, men and women can both perceive and live the equality that is already theirs in Christ, without one dominating or attempting to dominate the other.

One does not therefore need to change the name for God to achieve such equality. Indeed, that very attempt would be a form of self-justification at variance with the fact that we have already been justified and sanctified by God's grace in the life, death, and resurrection of Jesus himself. In the end, the very idea that we could or should change the name of God from Father to mother represents mythological projection rather than true knowledge of God. There are immense implications here. Let me briefly give three more examples of thinking that employs a picture model rather than a disclosure model of understanding and thereby undercuts two critical facts: (1) We not only do not

---

[33]Torrance makes this point sharply by claiming that "the fact that the Son of God became man through being conceived by the Holy Spirit and being born of the Virgin Mary, that is, not of the will of the flesh nor of the will of a human father, but of God (Jn 1:13), means that at this decisive point in the incarnation the distinctive place and function of man as male human being was set aside" T. F. Torrance, *The Ministry of Women* (Edinburgh: Handsel Press, 1992), 5. On this basis, Torrance flatly rejects Augustine's idea that while a man on his own might be in the image of God, a woman on her own "considered apart from her character as a helpmeet for man, is not in the image of God." Torrance insists that "if that were the case, the mother of Jesus considered in herself as a virgin could not have been said to be in the image of God!" He concludes that this "is a quite offensive notion of womankind that conflicts directly with the truth that in Christ there is neither male nor female; it even contradicts Augustine's own statement in the same passage that 'human nature is complete only in both sexes.' " This also conflicts, Torrance says, "with the biblical and orthodox teaching that woman as well as man was made in the image of God" and may therefore be considered an "*ikon* of God as well as man" (ibid., 4-5). Indeed, Torrance concludes that Augustine's position "also conflicts with the orthodox understanding of the incarnation as the saving assumption of the whole human being, male and female, and as the healing of our complete human nature. This must surely be understood as involving the healing of any divisive relation between male and female due to the curse imposed upon them at the fall (Gen 3:16), while sanctifying the distinction between them. It thus rejects any manichaeistic denigration of the female sex" (ibid., 5). Torrance goes further to make a decisive point crucial to my argument in this chapter, namely, that the virgin birth signified a judgment on "the sinful, not the natural, element in sexual life" as well as "upon any claim that human nature has an innate capacity for God … Moreover, the sovereign act of God in the virgin birth of Jesus carries with it not only a rejection of the sovereignty of man over his own life, but a rescinding of the domination of man over woman that resulted from the fall (Gen. 3:16). Thus any preeminence of the male sex or any vaunted superiority of man over woman was decisively set aside at the very inauguration of the new creation brought about by the incarnation. In Jesus Christ the order of redemption has intersected the order of creation and set it upon a new basis altogether. Henceforth the full equality of man and woman is a divine ordinance that applies to all the behaviour and activity of 'the new man' in Christ, and so to the entire life and mission of the Church as the body of Christ in the world", (ibid., 5).

need to change the name for God from Father to mother for women to have equality in the church, since God has named himself to us in his Word and Spirit and has, in the person of the Mediator, overcome the sin that leads to patriarchalism in the first place. Furthermore, since there really is no gender in God, there is no need to change the name for God to eliminate the false idea that God is male. (2) The very idea that we could rename God places the power of revelation, which is God's alone, in our hands such that we then are merely projecting who we think God is from our own human experiences, including gender, back into God in a mythological or symbolic way. If there really is no gender in God as all theoretically believe, then the terms "father" and "son" do not and never did or could carry that meaning in any sense at all, when properly understood. Therefore, there would be no reason to change them in order to affirm gender equality. That equality is already achieved for humanity in the incarnation itself, as Torrance so helpfully explained.

Sallie McFague

While we have seen that Torrance firmly excludes all sexual connotations when referring to God as Father since his criterion for understanding God's fatherhood was not any experience of human fatherhood but God's revelation in Christ, McFague insists that "to speak of God as father has obvious sexual connotations (as is evident in the trinitarian language of the 'generation' of the Son from the Father)."[34] It will be recalled that Torrance's approach was exactly opposite to this. Since the generation of the Son from the Father was an ineffable mystery within the eternal Trinity, therefore it could have no sexual connotations at all. That was one of the key errors of Arius who projected sensual images into God and did not acknowledge the uniqueness of the revelation of God in Christ himself. In a similar way, McFague's concept of God is not at all dictated by who God *is* in Jesus Christ because for her Jesus is not ontologically unique as she says and can be no more than a paradigmatic model of God's love comparable to other people who love. Indeed, in her view of God as lover she mistakenly claims that Jesus is special to Christians not because of who he is but because Christians chose him as the paradigm of God's love.[35] Important as that mistake is since it directly discards the heart

---

[34]Sallie McFague, *Models of God*, 98.

[35]Thus, McFague writes, "One can, in our model of God as lover, understand the incarnation of God in Jesus of Nazareth in this way. Jesus' response as beloved to God as lover was so open and thorough that his life and death were revelatory of God's great love for the world. His illumination of that love as inclusive of the last and the least, as embracing and valuing the outcast, is paradigmatic of God the lover but is not unique. This means that Jesus is not ontologically different from other paradigmatic figures either in our tradition or in other religious traditions who manifest in word and deed the love of God for the world. He is special to us as our foundational figure: he is our historical choice as the premier paradigm of God's love" (*Models*, 136). She concludes that all human beings "have potential as the beloved of God to reflect or respond to their lover. That many, most, human beings do not is in our model the definition of sin ... Those who do respond are called the disciples, and they, like the paradigmatic life and death they follow, are signs or incarnations of divine love" (ibid.).

of the Nicene faith by eliminating the truth that Jesus' ontological uniqueness resides in the fact that his humanity is the humanity of the eternal Word of God by virtue of the hypostatic union, it simply underscores the fact that her pictorial model of God is based on human experience and never even approaches a serious knowledge of the immanent Trinity because she sees no way that we can speak of the immanent Trinity at all.[36] Hence, she begins her metaphorical reconstruction of who God is as mother by asserting that "there is no gender-neutral language if we take ourselves as the model for talk of God, because we are sexual beings."[37] But, of course, that illustrates my point. McFague thinks that because we, as male and female, are in the image of God, therefore God can and should be imagined in female as well as male metaphors.[38]

McFague's basic point then is that she will image God "on analogy with human beings, and so far as that is all that [she is] doing: God is she and he and neither."[39] What if one were to ask McFague if her naming God as mother, lover, and friend as she does is arbitrary, given the fact that God revealed himself to us as Father and Son in an utterly unique sense, as Torrance has claimed? She herself poses that question. And her answer is instructive. She says, "The most direct answer to that question is that they are not arbitrary, because, along with the father model, they are the deepest and most important expressions of love known to us, rather than because they are necessarily descriptive of the nature of God."[40] Notice that McFague will not allow for the fact that in the incarnation, God's love was revealed in Christ himself in a unique way through an act of God who came into history from outside. In him, God so loved the world that he

---

[36]Thus, for McFague, the Trinity is "a summation of … ontology or of the Christian experience of God" (*Models*, 223, n. 2), so that her models of mother, lover, and friend can replace the name of the Father, Son, and Spirit (ibid., 181), and she can thus focus exclusively on God's relation to the world since she asserts that she can make "no claims about the so-called immanent or intrinsic trinity" because she sees "no way that assumptions concerning the inner nature of God are possible" (ibid., 224). Importantly, however, any theology that is not actually grounded in the inner being and act of God is no longer theologically relevant at all. No wonder McFague says she does not actually know who God is but that her models describe her projection of who she thinks God is just the same, from her experiences of motherhood, love, and friendship.
[37]McFague, *Models*, 98.
[38]Here again Torrance's view of the image of God is not only more accurate than McFague's but also it helpfully avoids confusing divine and human being and action as she does not. For Torrance, the image of God must be understood relationally to mean that, as male and female, we were created for fellowship with God. Thus, to be in God's image cannot mean "that the image of God inheres in man's nature, far less in male or female nature, as such, but that it is a *donum superadditum*, a gift wholly contingent upon the free grace of God … hence we are not to think that men and women through creaturely human nature, by virtue of some intrinsic analogy of being, reflect God's uncreated Nature, but that they are specifically destined by grace to live in faithful response to the purpose and movement of God's love toward them as his creaturely partners" (Torrance, *The Ministry of Women*, 7). For Torrance then, "we cannot, therefore, set forth a doctrine of the image of God or of analogy already lodged in the being of man, as Augustine taught, before men are partakers of God," and that means that true analogies "will be grounded entirely upon the hypostatic union as its true and only valid analogy; that is, upon the central relation and union of God and Man of which every other relation must partake" (Torrance, *Theology in Reconstruction*, 114).
[39]McFague, *Models*, 99.
[40]Ibid., 192.

gave his only begotten Son "so that everyone who believes in him might not perish but might have eternal life" (Jn 3:16).

Because the basis for her modeling God is human experience in the form of motherhood and love in particular, she claims that the deepest love known to us can only come from us and not from beyond us as an act of God in Christ. Thus, she can assert that in principle "we image God according to what we find most desirable in ourselves and what we find constitutive of our world."[41] Her reasoning misses the all-important fact that knowledge of God comes *to* us as an act of God himself in Christ and not from us. Hence, according to the Gospel of John, "to those who did accept him [Jesus] he gave power to become children of God, to those who believe in his name" (Jn 1:8). That, however, involves not only revelation but reconciliation since it is through Jesus Christ that our minds and hearts are reconciled to God the Father through the Holy Spirit actualizing the reconciliation that took place objectively on the cross and was revealed in and by the risen Lord.

That is not the end of it. Utilizing her model of God the lover, she not only claims that God needs us "to help save the world." She also claims that salvation cannot be understood as a vertical act of God coming into history from outside to act within history to overcome our enmity toward God and others. Rather, for her, salvation refers to our horizontal relations with the world which is thought by her to be God's body[42] since in her model of God as mother, the "universe, from God's being, is properly body (as well as spirit), because in some sense God is physical (as well as beyond physical). This shocking idea—that God is physical—is one of the most important implications of the model of creation by God the mother."[43] From this it follows that "God will therefore need the world … as offspring, beloved, and companion." Indeed, "as a physical event: the universe is bodied forth from God, it is expressive of God's very being. It is not something alien to or other than God but is from the 'womb' of God, formed through 'gestation.' "[44] While McFague claims to be espousing panentheism in distinction from pantheism, there is little doubt that her model of God as mother is at the very least emanationist but also pantheist because a god who needs the world has lost his sovereignty and freedom as Creator and thus his primacy in relation to the world as Creator and reconciler as well.

Having projected images of God as mother and lover from her own experiences, McFague has completely lost any possibility of grounding her theology in the objective reality of God of the Nicene confession. That is why she explicitly maintains that her functional trinitarian view is "focused on God's activity in relationship to the world and talk about that activity. It makes no claims about the so-called immanent or intrinsic

---

[41]Ibid., 134.

[42]Ibid., 139. Thus, "from our perspective of our model of God as lover of the world … sin is the turning-away not from a transcendent power but from interdependence with all other beings, including the matrix of being from whom all life comes … It is a horizontal refusal to be part of the body of God rather than a vertical refusal to be inferior to God" (ibid., 139–40).

[43]Ibid., 112.

[44]Ibid., 110.

trinity" because she sees "no way that assumptions concerning the inner nature of God are possible."[45] Without any way of knowing God in himself, the eternal Trinity, namely, God as Father, Son, and Holy Spirit, her thinking illustrates exactly what happens when one refuses to allow the transcendent God who meets us directly and personally in his incarnate Word, to determine the truth of who God is and who we are. That is why, in defense of her claim that her models are not arbitrary, she explains that instead of knowing God's nature, she is "persuaded that there is a personal, gracious power who is on the side of life and its fulfillment, a power whom the paradigmatic figure of Jesus of Nazareth expresses and illuminates." However, to say any more than that, she says, we must turn not to the revelation of God in Jesus Christ but to

> the "loves" we know (unless one is a Barthian and believes that God defines love and that all human love only conforms to the divine pattern). That is to say, I do not know whether God (the inner being of God) can be described by the models of mother, lover, and friend; but the only kind of love I know anything about and that matters most to me is the love of these basic relationships, so I have to use these loves to speak of divine love ... I do not *know* who God is, but I find some models better than others for constructing an image of God commensurate with my trust in a God as on the side of life.[46]

The only problem is that one does not have to be a Barthian to realize that she has not said one word about God, as God truly exists antecedently in himself and for us in history as the eternal Father, Son, and Holy Spirit as confessed in the Nicene Creed by all Christians since the fourth century. And she literally cannot do so because, like Arius himself, she honestly thinks that Jesus is not the very incarnation of God in history. For her, incarnation refers not to Jesus as God become man without ceasing to be God. Rather it refers to "creation as a whole (God's body)" which she thinks of as "a sacrament or sign of the presence of God" and also to human beings, "especially those human beings ... open and responsive to God" who are "sacraments or signs of God the lover."[47] In case anyone might suppose that my reference to her position as akin to that of Arius might be a bit harsh, consider once again her specific view of Jesus in light of her model of God the lover. She says that in light of that model one can

> understand the incarnation of God in Jesus of Nazareth in this way. Jesus' response as beloved to God as lover was so open and thorough that his life and death were revelatory of God's great love for the world. His illumination of that love as inclusive of the last and the least, as embracing and valuing the outcast, is paradigmatic of God the lover but is not unique. This means that Jesus is not ontologically different from other paradigmatic figures either in our tradition or in

---

[45] Ibid., 224.
[46] Ibid., 192.
[47] Ibid., 136.

other religious traditions who manifest in word and deed the love of God for the world. He is special to us as our foundational figure: he is our historical choice as the premier paradigm of God's love.[48]

With these views McFague has undercut the main point of the Bible and the tradition by claiming that Jesus revealed God because he was open to God. That, however, is not what made Jesus the revealer of God. It is the fact that he himself *is* the very Word of God, the incarnate Son of the Father, apart from whom we simply cannot know God in his internal relations as Father, Son, and Holy Spirit. He is the revealer as he is the reconciler and redeemer because he is *homoousios* with the Father and the Holy Spirit within the eternal Trinity and with us as God incarnate in history encountering us directly in the man Jesus and in the outpouring of the Holy Spirit after his death and resurrection.

The Homoousion

That is why T. F. Torrance calls the *homoousion* "the ontological and epistemological linchpin of Christian theology."[49] It is because there is a hypostatic union "of God and man in the one Person of Christ, that the epistemic reference we make can have any substantiation in reality, for it is through that *hypostatic* union in Christ that such a reference is firmly anchored in the reality of God and of man."[50] Indeed, Torrance helpfully insists that through our union with Christ in faith our own understanding of God "is an actual sharing on our part—through the Communion of the Spirit, who dwells immanently both in the Father and in the Son—in the unique and closed mutuality not only of knowing and loving but also of being between the Father and the Son."[51] This thinking eliminates any possibility of basing one's thinking about God on a "preconceived idea of God" because

if we know Christ only as the Son of the Father, and only as in and through him we know God, then our knowledge of Christ the Son and our knowledge of God the Father coincide. In this event any prior knowledge of God which we may claim to have is reconstructed through our sharing in the mutual knowing of the Father and the Son.[52]

Thus, the *homoousion*

crystalizes the conviction [expressed at the Council of Nicaea] that while the incarnation falls within the structures of our spatio-temporal humanity in this

---

[48]Ibid.
[49]Torrance, *Ground and Grammar*, 160–1.
[50]Ibid., 160.
[51]Ibid.
[52]Torrance, *The Trinitarian Faith*, 60.

world, it also falls within the Life and Being of God. Jesus Christ is thus not a mere symbol, some representation of God detached from God, but God in his own Being and Act come among us, expressing in our human form the Word which he is eternally in himself, so that in our relations with Jesus Christ we have to do directly with the ultimate Reality of God.[53]

In these remarks, Torrance has said all that needs to be said here. Jesus is not simply another person illuminating God's love by caring for others; he is the incarnation of God himself acting for us in history. He is one in being with God by nature and with us as the incarnate Word (by grace). He is therefore not just a typical example of God's love, as McFague asserts with her "picturing model" of God. He is the very love of God present in history as the man Jesus was present in hypostatic union with the Word or Son who is God from God. For that reason, he is not a paradigmatic model of God's love. He is uniquely God incarnate, God acting as the man Jesus acted because he alone of all human beings who have ever lived exists in hypostatic union with God himself. His humanity is *anhypostatic* because it has no existence apart from its grounding in the Person of the Son. And it is *enhypostatic* because it has its genuine human existence in the Person of the Word or Son. However, that means that Jesus is ontologically distinct precisely because he alone was God the Son directly present among us in Jesus' life history and now as the risen, ascended, and coming Lord who is present in the power of his Holy Spirit. Thus, his importance for Christian faith does not rest even remotely on our historical choices; it rests upon who he actually was and is as the eternal Son of the Father.

That is what McFague has misunderstood, and it is the very same error made by Arius in the fourth century. She has damaged and thus undercut Jesus' unique relation with God the Father and so has made knowledge of the Christian God impossible. That is why she felt free to invent models of God based on human experiences of motherhood, love, and friendship, instead of allowing her understanding of God to be shaped by who God eternally was and is as Father, Son, and Holy Spirit. Here then is another example of what happens when theologians attempt to think of God from a center within themselves instead of from a center in God as provided for us in history in the Person and Work of Jesus himself. It led McFague to claim that we could never really know the immanent Trinity but that we could and should name God as mother, lover, and friend from those experiences that matter most to us. But the cost of this naming of God from human experience is enormous; it flatly rejects the central truth of the Christian faith which is that Jesus is himself God for us and it makes theological truth something that we construct for ourselves rather than something that can only

---

[53]Torrance, *Ground and Grammar*, 160. This thinking is expressed frequently by Torrance when he says, "What God the Father is in his self-revelation through the Son and in the Spirit he is in himself, and what he is in himself he is in his revelation. It is impossible for us, therefore, to seek to know God apart from his revelation, or to try to go behind that revelation to what God is in himself, for there is no God apart from his revelation" ("The Christian Apprehension of God the Father," 121).

come to us from God himself. These problems underscore the point of this chapter once more: there is no need for us to change the name of God from Father, Son, and Holy Spirit for women and men to achieve equality, because in reality there is no gender or sex attached to the name of God as Father, Son, and Spirit. Moreover, since God in Christ has already freed us from the sin of patriarchy, the very idea that we can or should change the name of God illustrates the fact that, relying on ourselves, we are still at enmity with God because we think we can have the God we want instead of acknowledging God as he actually exists in himself and for us. That is the epitome of self-justification. Once again, as with the attempt to substitute relation for the Persons of the Trinity as Father, Son, and Holy Spirit, McFague's models of God exemplify the problems with "picturing models" of God as opposed to the "disclosure model" favored by Torrance.

Catherine LaCugna/Elizabeth Johnson

Here I will contrast several key ideas espoused by Catherine LaCugna and Elizabeth Johnson to make my points more precisely. I am including both theologians in this section since I have already discussed Johnson's position at length in Chapter 2, and I have discussed the views of both theologians in detail elsewhere as well.[54] The position for which I am arguing in this chapter is fourfold: (1) since there is in fact no gender in God, it is a mistake to think that the language of "father" and "son" used to refer to the trinitarian persons connotes male gender in any sense at all. (2) Since only God can and does reveal God, our knowledge of God comes from God alone as God actively discloses himself to us in his Word and through his Spirit, and thus as we participate in the mutual knowing and loving of the eternal Father and Son within the eternal Trinity through the Spirit. Consequently any idea that the terms "father" and "son" were merely projections advanced by a patriarchal society that need to be changed is mistaken since the truth advanced in those terms is a truth grounded in the very being and act of God himself in whom there is no gender since that is an aspect of creaturely being and not an aspect of the divine being and act. (3) Inasmuch as all knowledge of God thus comes to us by the grace of God who loves us and establishes and maintains fellowship with us in his incarnate Word, any attempt to understand the Christian God from experience, whether male or female, instead of from God as he meets us in our experiences of him, ends up reversing the positions of Creator and creature and destroying the possibility and reality of knowledge of God. (4) Finally, those who think that patriarchy needs to be overcome by our changing the language for God actually espouse some version of self-justification and mistakenly suppose that we have the power to name God from ourselves in order to achieve our own social, political, or religious agenda. We simply do not have this power in ourselves and never will because "when we know God, we know him only on the free ground of his own being who reveals himself, *names himself*, and proves himself

---

[54]See Molnar, *Divine Freedom*, chapters One and Six.

in his act of revelation, and who confronts us with none other than himself in that act of revelation. This is not a revelation that can be detached from God."[55] It goes without saying here that LaCugna and Johnson employ a "picturing model" of God instead of a "disclosure model."

We begin, then, by noting that in a properly understood doctrine of the Trinity, there is, as I have been arguing in this chapter, no need to even consider changing the name of God from Father, Son, and Holy Spirit in order for women to have equality in the church and in the world at large. The reason, as we have seen, for this is twofold. First, only God can reveal God, and thus only God can name himself to us. For this reason, T. F. Torrance insists that the words and concepts taken from our ordinary experience (which are the only concepts we have to speak of God) have "a natural and primitive sense ... apart altogether from God's self-revelation to us."[56] However, "when they are taken up by God and employed in his self-revelation to us as Father, Son and Holy Spirit, they suffer a fundamental change in being adapted to be vehicles of his Word." That applies specifically to the word "being" as applied to God. Apart from revelation, the word connotes an impersonal sense, especially in the Greek concept of being; but when transformed through "God's *self*-revelation and *self*-naming to Israel as 'I am' which was applied by Christ to himself in his 'I am' (Εγώ είμι) sayings" the personal nature of God's being was disclosed in a deeper way as the Father, Son, and Holy Spirit.[57]

Any other position simply reflects projection or a mythological attempt by us to define God according to our own designs. Hence knowledge of God comes *to* us from God alone and not at all *from* us. Second, since God is Spirit and there is no gender in God, there is no reason to change the name of God in the first place, and the very idea that there might be gender in God represents an illegitimate reading back our human experiences into God either directly or by negating those experiences to achieve knowledge of God. Hence, even the slightest notion that the categories "father" and "son" import or project male gender into God either in order to subordinate women to men, as some have argued, or because those categories, when used in ordinary parlance, always connote the male gender is mistaken.

Gender and God

This idea that there is male gender in God usually stems from some sort of Christological confusion such as that which is evident in the thinking of Elizabeth Johnson. While Johnson certainly recognizes that the traditional doctrine of the Trinity excluded any notion of gender in God,[58] she introduces gender into God via Christology, perhaps

---

[55]Torrance, "The Christian Apprehension of God the Father," 121.

[56]Torrance, *Christian Doctrine of God*, 103.

[57]Ibid., 103–4.

[58]Thus, "while officially it is rightly and consistently said that God is spirit and so beyond identification with either male or female sex, yet the daily language of preaching, worship, catechesis, and instruction conveys a different message: God is male, or at least more like a man than a woman, or at least more fittingly addressed as male than as female" (Johnson, *She Who Is*, 4–5). Note well here that proper preaching, worship, catechesis,

unintentionally, and then constructs her own doctrine of the Trinity based on the idea that the name of God must be changed in order for women to have equality in the Church.[59] Before discussing the Christological problem, let me briefly mention how Johnson herself introduces gender into God. She expressly claims that the daily language for God as Father and Son communicates the message that God is male and is thus "more fittingly addressed as male than as female." In this remark, and in spite of her assertion that there is no gender in God, she has nevertheless introduced gender directly into the divine being with the claim that the Church's language in worship, teaching, and preaching does indeed refer to God as male. My point here, and throughout this chapter, is that it does not and never did do so because it is that very notion that was rejected by the Nicene theologians (especially Athanasius) in the fourth century as mythological projection of ordinary human experience into God. Johnson's mistake therefore is not

---

and instruction never could convey the message that God is male since those activities were grounded in the triune God, who has no gender, acting for us in the economy. However, as we shall see in a moment in more detail, Johnson's mistaken assumption here is that the truth of our language for God comes from us rather than exclusively from the transcendent God who is present to us in the incarnation and outpouring of the Holy Spirit.

[59]Two further problematic errors are in evidence in her thinking: (1) she mistakenly and problematically claims that since Jesus can be understood as "a filter through whom God is made known" (Johnson, *Quest for the Living God*, 217), she can then utilize a "pneumatological inflection" and assert that (2) we never have "one straight-as-an-arrow name" (ibid., 21) for God because God's name "cannot be fixed in a single form of speech nor in a fixed name" (ibid., 221). This thinking is problematic because Jesus is not a "filter through whom God is made known." He is God himself enabling us to know God the Father through the power of the resurrection and the power of the Holy Spirit here and now. As the eternal Son of the Father, the incarnate Son personally takes us up into the exclusive knowledge and love of the Father and Son so that through him we may know God as he truly is. Johnson's thinking is also problematic because her pneumatological inflection is not properly pneumatological at all since she detaches the Spirit from the Word specifically by rejecting the fact that it is the Holy Spirit who enables us to know the Father precisely by uniting us to the Son and actually hearing the Word speak to us through the human Jesus here and now. The whole of Christian theology therefore stands or falls with the fact that God's one straight-as-an-arrow name is the name of Jesus Christ himself! According to Ac. 4:12, "there is no salvation through anyone else, nor is there any other name under heaven given to the human race by which we are to be saved." We are baptized in the name of the Father, Son, and Holy Spirit. That is the name of God which is identical with the name of Jesus Christ himself in and through whom we know the Father by the power of the Holy Spirit. We are not baptized either into the name of the "nameless" or into "holy mystery" as Rahner and Johnson understand these names, which in their understanding, can go by many different names. Contrary to this kind of thinking, Torrance properly maintains, "in our knowing of God we know that it is through God's knowing of us that we are enabled to know him, that our knowing of God is included within the circle of mutual knowing which he freely establishes with us. Thus our knowing of God rests not on a center in ourselves but on a center in God, not on the ground of our own being but on the free ground of God's being" (Torrance, "The Christian Apprehension of God the Father," 123). Hence, Torrance properly insists that "our ability to know him is grounded not in some capacity of our own but in the activity of God in opening himself to our knowing and in actually making himself known to us through his Word," and that knowledge "is realized and sustained in us through the presence of his Spirit" (ibid.). It is no small issue, then, when Johnson undercuts Jesus' uniqueness by thinking of him only as a filter through which we supposedly know God. She also thinks of him only as an envoy or messenger of God and indeed as Sophia incarnate as previously discussed. In each of these ways she obliterates Jesus' uniqueness at great cost—at the cost of cutting us off from any true knowledge of God himself. To sum up then, because Johnson does not begin and end her thinking about the Trinity from Jesus Christ in his uniqueness as the incarnate Word, she honestly thinks that the power of our symbol for God comes from us and not from Christ alone.

only a Christological one, as I will explain in a moment. It is a theological one, or more precisely, it is a methodological mistake affecting all her theology.

Because she thinks "the symbol of God functions," she maintains that this symbol "sums up, unifies, and expresses a faith community's sense of ultimate mystery."[60] No, it does not; at least it does not when the object of reflection is the triune God of Christian faith. The whole point of the doctrine of the Trinity, as I have been arguing, is that our thinking about God expresses the community's faith in Jesus Christ, the only Son of the Father and not it's sense of ultimate mystery, since ultimate mystery could go by many other names than that of the eternal Father, Son, and Spirit! And in any case, if the "symbol" simply expressed the community's sense of mystery, it would not be objectively grounded in the revelation of God and his naming of himself to us in his Word and Spirit. Ultimately, then theological language considered in this way, could do no more than express our human sense of mystery and our ultimate concerns in a Tillichian sense. That explains why Johnson goes on to claim that because women have been excluded "from the realm of public symbol formation and decision making," they have thus been subordinated "to the imagination and needs of a world designed chiefly by men."[61] Consequently, she thinks it is the task of theology to overcome women's subordination to this world designed mainly by men precisely by making this symbol function in a way that will emancipate women from this subordination. This will be accomplished, she thinks, as women become "engaged in creative 'naming toward God' ... from the matrix of their own experience."[62]

There is, however, a very serious problem evident in this approach. It is a form of self-justification to suppose that the community can actually emancipate women from subordination to men by creatively naming God in a new way from its own experiences whether they be male or female. Had Johnson allowed Jesus in his uniqueness to shape her view of God, she would have recognized that women have already been emancipated from subordination to men because Christ has already justified and sanctified all humanity in himself.[63] Therefore, she would have realized that this is not something

---

[60]Johnson, *She Who Is*, 4.

[61]Ibid.

[62]Ibid., 5.

[63]Torrance explains this by noting that Christ assumed our sinful human nature without himself sinning, and thus "it is only through this union of the human nature with his divine nature that Jesus Christ gives us not only the negative righteousness of the remission of sins but makes us share in the positive righteousness of his obedient and loving life lived in perfect filial relation to the Father from the cradle to the grave ... it is that saving and sanctifying union in which we are given to share that belongs to the very substance of our faith and life in Christ" (Torrance, *Theology in Reconstruction*, 156). Jesus was "the Word of God brought to bear upon man, but he was also man hearing that Word, answering it, trusting it, living by it—by faith. He was the great Believer—vicariously believing in our place and in our name ... In becoming one with us he laid hold upon our wayward human will, made it his very own, and bent it back into obedience to, and oneness with, the holy will of God" (ibid., 157). That is why "it is only through union with Christ that we partake of the blessings of Christ, that is through union with him in his holy and obedient life ... we share in his judgment and in his exaltation, in his passive and active obedience ... in his Death and also in his Resurrection and Ascension" (ibid., 158). Importantly, however, this means that Christ "has already received from God all his blessings and has sealed that reception of it for us in his own life and death. Faith is thus a polar concept that reposes upon and derives

we either need to do or even could do because the problem of sin which gives rise to such subordination of women is not a problem we can overcome at all. However, it is a problem which God, in Christ, actually did overcome for us because in Christ, as Torrance frequently points out, our self-will has been bent back into harmony with God's will through Christ's vicarious obedience to the Father. So, to live as part of the new creation in and from Christ alone, and thus on the basis of grace alone, would have to mean that we look toward Jesus, the risen, ascended, and coming Lord as the true source of community relations in which women are not subordinated to men. And we live as part of that new creation in faith and hope through union with Christ who himself enables our faith and hope in the first place. I will explain this, along with some further implications, when later in this chapter I compare Torrance's view of conversion to Johnson's view of this important theological concept.

It is enough to note here that Johnson's theological method is not at all dictated by the revelation of God in Jesus Christ, but by how the community of faith constructs its symbols from a male or a female perspective based on the assumption that the power of the symbol comes from us and not exclusively from the transforming power of God in Christ, as it must if it is to be truly theological. So, while T. F. Torrance, following Athanasius, insists that our knowledge of God comes exclusively from God himself in the incarnation and outpouring of the Holy Spirit, Johnson argues that "women, long considered less than adequate as human persons, claim themselves as active subjects of history and name toward God out of this emerging identity, to practical and critical effect."[64] Johnson's mistake here is not that she opposes traditional characterizations of women as inferior to men such as the view of Augustine which we have already seen Torrance firmly reject. Her mistake is to try to correct that erroneous view with the claim that she can actually know the one true God, namely, the eternal Father, Son, and Holy Spirit by naming God out of women's emerging identity as created in the image of God. She does this by repeatedly claiming that "the symbol God functions"[65] and that we must make it function so as to emancipate women from being oppressed by being subordinated to the imaginations of men. She thus argues that, as long as that symbol receives its meaning chiefly from men, then and to that extent, women will remain subordinate to men. Moreover, she also thinks that language for God in female images will challenge "the literal mindedness that has clung to male images in inherited God-talk."[66]

Two problems will have to be discussed in connection with these assumptions. First, can we literally know who God is or not? Her answer is no, while the answer of the early church, as expressed at the Councils of Nicaea and Chalcedon in particular, was yes. Torrance and Barth follow this tradition and argue that unless we have true and certain knowledge of God

---

from the prior faithfulness of God which has been translated permanently into our actual human existence in Jesus Christ. We do not rely, then, upon our act of faith, but upon the faith of Christ which undergirds and upholds our faith" (ibid., 159).

[64]Johnson, *She Who Is*, 5.

[65]Ibid.

[66]Ibid.

that comes from God alone through Christ, we do not know God at all. Second, the very idea that the terms "father" and "son" express male imagery when applied to the Trinity means that she has not yet conceptualized the Trinity as understood at Nicaea and by both Karl Barth and T. F. Torrance. That is because her reasoning is not actually grounded in the incarnation and outpouring of the Holy Spirit at the outset. Since knowledge of God for Johnson comes from our making our symbols function to liberate women from subordination, her thinking is grounded in the way women and men use their symbols to signify "divine liberating action or self-involving love for the world" with the result that the "present ferment about naming, imaging, and conceptualizing God from perspectives of women's experience repristinates the truth that the idea of God, incomprehensible mystery, implies an open-ended history of understanding that is not yet finished."[67]

However, nothing could be further from the truth because the one liberating action on the basis of which women's subordination to men has already been overcome by God himself is the action of God in the life history of Jesus Christ, which includes his life, ministry, death, resurrection and ascension. It was and is Jesus Christ himself who decisively reconciled the world to God in his own vicarious life of obedience to the Father, as we have already seen. So, while God certainly remains an incomprehensible mystery, that mystery is in fact a mystery with a very definite name, that is, the name of the Father, Son, and Holy Spirit. Johnson's view of God certainly does not begin or end with that specific being of God precisely because it does not begin with faith in Jesus Christ which would have to include an acknowledgment that we all have been justified and sanctified by the free grace of God himself. And since we have been justified and sanctified objectively in Christ, then it is in and from him that we are truly liberated subjectively from all attempts by men to subordinate women, as the Holy Spirit actualizes that atoning reconciliation in our minds and hearts, thus enabling proper relations between men and women in the Church and in the world at large.

That is why she can make three astounding remarks about God that no properly functioning doctrine of the Trinity would allow. First, she claims we never have "one straight-as-an-arrow name" for God because God's name "cannot be fixed in a single form of speech nor in a fixed name."[68] These remarks undercut the simple fact that there really is salvation in no other name than that of Jesus Christ himself because he alone is the grace of God through whom true liberation from sin has already occurred. Our freedom therefore is the freedom to live from him alone as those who are in fact reconciled to God and thus to each other. Second, she repeatedly insists that we can have no "literal" knowledge of God. So, she can say that "even when used almost exclusively, the paternal symbol never signifies theologically that God is a father in a literal or ontological sense."[69] We have already seen more than once that God really is our Father, but in an utterly unique sense that is not at all shaped by our human experiences of

---

[67] Ibid., 7.
[68] Johnson, *Quest for the Living God*, 21 and 221. See n. 59 above. See also, *She Who Is*, 117–18.
[69] Johnson, *She Who Is*, 173.

fatherhood, not even by ideas of fatherhood constructed by negating our best experience of human fathers. By contrast, as we shall see in a moment, she thinks our knowledge of God's "fatherhood" comes by negating our experiences of human fatherhood. It does not. Third, because she clearly does not think from a center in God provided for us in the incarnation, but rather from a center in herself, she claims that "the symbol of the Trinity is not a blueprint of the inner workings of the godhead … In no sense is it a literal description of God's being *in se*. As the outcome of theological reflection on the Christian experience of relationship to God, it is a symbol that indirectly points to God's relationality … Our speech about God as three and persons is a human construction that means to say that God is *like* a Trinity, *like* a threefoldness of relation."[70]

While it is certainly true that our speech about God is a human construction, the truth of that human construction is not at all grounded in our experience but only in the eternal relations of God as Father, Son, and Holy Spirit. Thus, God is not *like* a Trinity. God *IS* the Trinity precisely because God is none other than the eternal Father, Son, and Holy Spirit. For Johnson then language for God must, in a manner similar to approaches of contemporary liberation theology, "serve a discourse about divine mystery that would further the emancipation of women."[71] Enough has been said here to make my point. For Johnson, since the truth of theological concepts comes from men and women it can provide no literal knowledge of God. Its truth is shaped by the extent to which such language can emancipate women from male domination in all its forms, including the form of conceptualizing God as Father and Son. Let me now present the specific Christological errors in Johnson's approach that lead her to undercut a properly functioning doctrine of the Trinity and also cause much of the mischief associated with the idea that we are somehow obliged to rename God today for women to achieve equality in the Church and society.

Instead of thinking of Jesus in his uniqueness as recognized at Chalcedon, Johnson claims that "if Jesus as a man is the revelation of God … this points to maleness as an essential characteristic of divine being itself."[72] No it does not. Any such idea represents just the confusion of natures in Jesus Christ that Chalcedon sought to avoid with its assertions that Christ existed

> in two natures without confusion or change, without division or separation. The distinction between the natures was never abolished by their union but rather the character proper to each of the two natures was preserved as they came together in one Person and one hypostasis. He is not split or divided into two Persons, but he is one and the same only begotten Son, God the Word, the Lord Jesus Christ, as formerly the prophets and later Jesus Christ himself have taught us.[73]

---

[70]Ibid., 204–5.

[71]Ibid., 9.

[72]Elizabeth A. Johnson, "Redeeming the Name of Christ," *Freeing Theology: The Essentials of Theology in Feminist Perspective*, ed. Catherine Mowry LaCugna (San Francisco: Harper Collins, 1993), 119.

[73]Heinrich Denzinger, *Compendium of Creeds, Definitions, and Declarations on Matters of Faith and Morals*, ed. Peter Hünermann, Robert Fastiggi, and Anne Englund Nash, 43rd edition (San Francisco: Ignatius Press, 2012), 109–10.

If the two natures are not confused or changed, then it is impossible to conclude, with Johnson, that the fact that the man Jesus is the revelation of God points to maleness as a characteristic of God. That idea confuses the two natures in Christ instead of seeing them united in the Person of the Son. Also, as Torrance repeatedly and rightly stresses, in the incarnation God assumed human nature into *union* with his divine being to reconcile all humanity to himself as he did in the man Jesus. Thus, he did not assume maleness as an essential characteristic of the divine being.

Rosemary Radford Ruether

Johnson here follows the thinking of Rosemary Radford Ruether who claims that "the unwarranted idea develops that there is a necessary ontological connection between the maleness of Jesus' historical person and the maleness of *Logos* as male offspring and disclosure of a male God."[74] Here it must be said that the only way that this unwarranted idea could develop is if one confuses the two natures in Christ and then mistakenly projects maleness into God instead of recognizing that in the incarnate Word, God in the Person of the Logos (who never had a gender in the first place), assumed human nature into union with the divine being without taking into the eternal Godhead human characteristics such as Jesus' maleness.[75] Such an idea represents an illegitimate reading back into the immanent Trinity of human gender which fails to acknowledge the uniqueness of God revealed in the incarnate Son. The only way this could happen is if it is assumed that the terms "father" and "son" receive their meaning from within human experience. They do not. However, when that occurs, then and there, the relationship

---

[74]Johnson, "Redeeming the Name of Christ," 119.

[75]Torrance repeatedly and rightly makes this point: "As the one and only Form and Image of God given to us, Jesus Christ constitutes the crucial point of reference to which we have constantly to appeal in putting all spatial and temporal and creaturely ingredients in our thought to the test, in order to filter away from our conceiving of God all that is inappropriate or foreign to him such as, for example, sexual relations or distinctions in gender which by their nature belong only to creaturely beings" (*Christian Doctrine of God*, 107). This is why Torrance also helpfully insists that since God is Spirit (Jn 4:24), therefore "all the language used of God in biblical revelation and in Christian theology must be interpreted in a wholly spiritual, personal and genderless manner, in accordance with God's intrinsic nature which infinitely transcends all human imaging and imagining" (Torrance, *Ministry of Women*, 7). In light of the fall, Torrance stresses that "justification by grace alone declares in no uncertain terms that fallen man is utterly destitute of *justitia originalis* or *imago dei*. It must be imputed by free grace" such that the image of God in us can only be interpreted in "eschatological terms" since we see this image only in faith and hope "until we see Christ as he is and become like him. In Christ, therefore, we see the *Imago Dei* to be the ground of our existence beyond our existence, but which becomes sacramental event here and now in the hearing of faith, as we are sealed with the Holy Spirit until the redemption of the purchased possession" (Torrance, *Theology in Reconstruction*, 108–9). The *imago dei* then refers to our living by grace and in dependence upon grace rather than arrogating the fact that we were made in God's image to our own being. The image of God is a dynamic image "corresponding to grace" but sin blots that out, although it cannot change "God's gracious intention by which man is still grasped in the hand of God" (ibid., 108).

between Creator and creature is reversed so that God is then "conceived in the image of man" instead of man being "conceived as formed after the image of God."[76]

But such an assumption, as we have already argued, grounds knowledge of God in us and thus represents an attempt to define God from a center in human experience rather than from a center in God. This problem will never be eliminated as long as it is supposed that our analogies for speaking about God can be constructed in the way Johnson, claiming to follow Thomas Aquinas, thinks we should. She claims that "analogy … means that while it [human naming of God] starts from the relationship of paternity experienced at its best in this world, its inner dynamism negates the creaturely mode to assert that God is more unlike than like even the best human fathers."[77] From the theological perspective I am advancing here, this is exactly wrong. Both Torrance and Barth rightly insist that the only proper analogies for speaking truly about the eternal Father, Son, and Holy Spirit are those which arise from our encounter with Jesus Christ. I agree with them both because Jesus himself is the very Word of God who alone can and does name God to us as he speaks to us even now through the power of the Holy Spirit and as his message reaches us through the witness of Scripture.[78] Since true knowledge of God arises from this encounter with Christ himself, human speaking of God never starts from our experiences of human fatherhood but only from our experience of God the Father, as we know him through union with his incarnate Son in faith.[79]

This reversal by Johnson makes all the difference in the world. If the analogy of faith starts from Jesus Christ because he really is the Way, the Truth, and the Life and because no one comes to the Father except through him, then we really need Christ's reconciling and healing action to touch our minds which, without his healing grace, cannot recognize God for who he truly is. We need to be liberated from the attempt to name God from our own experiences and freed from our self-will and self-reliance to think of God on the basis of God's own revealing and reconciling action in his Word and Spirit. This, because we really are saved by grace through faith in Christ himself. When this occurs, as seen above, then we acknowledge that God is Father in an utterly unique sense, that is, in the sense in which the Father/Son relation exists uniquely within God

---

[76]Torrance, "The Christian Apprehension of God the Father," 125.

[77]Johnson, *She Who Is*, 173.

[78]Torrance, for instance, gets this just right when the writes, "The Being of God was not understood in terms of any preconceived idea or definition of divine Being, but exclusively in the light of God's naming of himself as 'I am who I am' in the Old Testament revelation and as the Father, the Son and the Holy Spirit in the New Testament revelation, as in the dominical formula for Holy Baptism" (*Christian Doctrine of God*, 104).

[79]In connection with the doctrine of Providence, Karl Barth maintained that God is over us as our Creator precisely as, in his grace he is for us in his Son, Jesus Christ. Then he says that God is gracious "as a Father to His children. And in this connexion we have to remember that the truth of this relationship is not to be found in what might take place between a human father and his children, but in what has taken place from all eternity, and then in time, between the Father and the Son. He is our heavenly Father, in a way which surpasses all that we can see or think. We are thus warned in advance that we cannot make what we think we know as fatherly or any other kindness, friendliness and love the measure and criterion of His. It is a matter of the eternal fatherly fidelity which we can only try to see and grasp where it is revealed to us. 'He that hath seen me hath see the Father' (Jn. 14:9). It is here that Christian belief in Providence sees the Father, and therefore God over us, and therefore the Lord of the world-process" (CD III/3, 29–30).

himself as depicted in Mt. 11:27. But that means that all human fatherhood can only be rightly understood in light of this divine Fatherhood which can only be known through Christ himself as we are drawn into that relationship of knowledge and love within the eternal Trinity. In Torrance's words,

> In addressing his Word to us in our human words God uses the notions of "father" and "son" taken from us to reveal something of himself to us in the interrelations of his own inner Communion, yet in such a sway as to reject any mythological projection by us into God of the creaturely relations and images latent in the natural and pre-theological significance of these concepts. Within the sphere of divine revelation an *epistemological inversion* takes place in our knowing of God, for what is primary is his knowing of us, not our knowing of him. This is precisely how we are to understand God's Fatherhood, for all other fatherhood is properly to be understood from its relation to his Fatherhood and not the other way round.[80]

On this basis Karl Barth insistently and rightly argued that

> it is not true that in some hidden depth of His essence God is something other than Father and Son. It is not true that these names are just freely chosen and in the last analysis meaningless symbols, symbols whose original and proper non-symbolical content lies in that creaturely reality. On the contrary, it is in God that the father-son relation, like all creaturely relations, has its original and proper reality.[81]

Torrance certainly agrees with Barth here asserting that analogies must be governed by God's self-revelation in Christ and thus cannot be read back into God from our experiences of faith. That is why, as seen above, he insisted that our references to God the Father and Son take place in an "imageless way," that is

> in a diaphanous or "see through" way, to the Father and the Son without the intrusion of creaturely forms or sensual images into God. Thus we may not think of God as having gender nor think of the Father as begetting the Son or of the Son as begotten after the analogy of generation or giving birth with which we are familiar among creaturely beings.[82]

Catherine LaCugna

Let us briefly consider the views of Catherine LaCugna before I conclude the chapter with a discussion of two crucial theological ideas that will illustrate exactly how

---

[80]Torrance, *Christian Doctrine of God*, 105.
[81]Barth, CD I/1, 432.
[82]Torrance, *Christian Doctrine of God*, 158.

some theologians either ignore or simply refuse to acknowledge the sovereignty of grace. My argument is that those who do not acknowledge the sovereignty of grace for whatever reason invariably do so exactly because they begin and end their theologies with the assumption that God is a symbol that society and the church invest with meaning such that the divine names are indeed considered the products of the church and society. Within that perspective, they naturally could never admit that we have literally true knowledge of God because they generally take God's incomprehensibility to mean that we never really or literally know who God is in himself. In other words, they take an agnostic position with respect to the immanent Trinity. Here, I begin by agreeing with Colin Gunton, who believed that Catherine LaCugna's position in *God for Us* really was not only a polemic against the doctrine of the immanent Trinity but also a position that espoused views that verged on pantheism.[83]

Those are crucial criticisms because if T. F. Torrance is right in his belief that unless our knowledge of God is finally grounded in the eternal being of God as Father, Son, and Holy Spirit (the immanent Trinity), then failure to take the doctrine of the immanent Trinity seriously by wittingly or unwittingly ignoring or marginalizing God's actual freedom *in se* and *ad extra* always leads to a reversal of the roles of Creator and creature. The result is mythology rather than scientific theology because then models of God are used to symbolically reflect peoples' religious experiences instead of referring to the very nature of God himself. As seen above, that indeed was the position for which Sallie McFague argued. And Elizabeth Johnson followed McFague with the idea that the symbol God functions, and it is up to us to make it function to overcome patriarchalism. Both theologians did not seem to recognize that in changing the name of God as they did, they ended up denying who God really is as confessed in the Nicene Creed. Instead, they substituted their own ideas for the revelation of God in Jesus Christ. In his own way, we also saw that Paul Fiddes had a similar difficulty because he substituted "relations" for the eternal Father, Son, and Holy Spirit.

As I have argued elsewhere, it is the immanent Trinity that we encounter in the economic Trinity so that while there must be a distinction without separation of the immanent and economic Trinity, the key difficulty that plagues many contemporary expositions of the doctrine and all attempts to rename God using female as well as male categories is either the separation of the former from the latter or the collapse of the former into the latter or a combination of both. Either of those options leads to an inability to think accurately about the triune God and our relations with God. However, those two options are the only ones that seem to follow the attempt to know God apart from faith in Jesus Christ as the Word of God who alone can disclose to us who God truly is. LaCugna makes a number of statements that smack rather heavily of pantheism. First, she writes that "the God who does not need nor care for the creature, or who is

---

[83]See Colin Gunton, "Review of Catherine LaCugna," *God for Us*, *Scottish Journal of Theology* 47 (1) (1994): 136–7.

immune to our suffering, does not exist."[84] Second, she maintains that "the doctrine of the Trinity is not ultimately a teaching about 'God' but a teaching about *God's life with us and our life with each other*."[85] This statement overtly collapses the immanent into the economic Trinity because the whole point of the doctrine of the Trinity is to teach about God himself as the eternal Father, Son, and Holy Spirit. It is only when God is acknowledged in faith and known through union with Christ and by the power of his Holy Spirit that we can begin to recognize who God for us really is. To simply claim that trinitarian life is our life as LaCugna does, and that the doctrine of the Trinity only teaches us about God's life with us and our life with each other, represents a blatant confusion of divine and human being and action.

Thus, LaCugna can say that "an immanent trinitarian theology … cannot be an analysis of what is 'inside' God, but a way of thinking and speaking about the structure and pattern of God's self-expression in salvation history."[86] This confused and confusing

---

[84]Catherine Mowry LaCugna, *God for Us: The Trinity and Christian Life* (San Francisco, CA: HarperSanFrancisco, 1991), 397. While LaCugna certainly wishes to avoid a pantheistic perspective, statements such as this suggest she cannot. This is not the only such remark. She appears to espouse an emanationist view of God's relations with the world when she writes that "the centrifugal movement of divine love does not terminate 'within' God but explodes outward; God gives rise to the world just as God gives rise to God" (ibid., 354–5). There are a number of problems embedded in these remarks. If God's love does not terminate within the divine Trinity, then God could not be God without loving us. The fact that LaCugna seems to believe this is confirmed by her statements that "love by its nature is outgoing and self-giving … Divine self-sufficiency is exposed as a philosophical myth … [Thus God's love] spills over into what is other than God, giving birth to creation and history" (ibid., 353). God's love of course is self-giving. But God is indeed self-sufficient and perfect love in himself so that his love of us is a free act of grace; it is a new act even for God. Thus, for Torrance as for Barth, both of whom follow Athanasius, while God was always Father, he was not always Creator. And God could have remained who he is as the one who loves without us and would have suffered no lack. LaCugna explicitly rejects these notions. So, her idea that God's love not only spills over "into what is other than God" (a strange notion since this idea implies that the world already coexists eternally with God in the first place), coupled with the notion that in that way God gives birth to creation and history, is a rather overt form of emanationism that cannot really distinguish God in his self-sufficiency from the world. God does not give birth to the world; that would imply that the world arose out of God's being instead of coming into existence from nothing by a free act of God's will. The fact that LaCugna tends to reduce God to his creative function is illustrated in her remark that "to be God is to be the Creator of the world" (ibid., 355). One is here reminded of the sharp remarks of Etienne Gilson who once rejected the natural theology of Descartes claiming that while the Christian God is free to create because he is eternally self-sufficient, "a God whose very essence is to be a creator is not a Christian God at all" but the free Christian God reduced to a philosophical principle since this view of God embodies the notion that God's "creative function had integrally absorbed his essence" (Gilson, *God and Philosophy*, 88–9). This is further illustrated in her statement that seems to echo the view of Origen, namely, that "the exodus of all persons from God and the return of all to God is the divine dance in which God and we are eternal partners" (ibid., 304). The idea that divine self-sufficiency is a philosophical myth is the ultimate myth that most definitely needs to be demythologized. If the triune God is not self-sufficient, then God needs the world and us. This very view obliterates any notion of God's free grace and once again opens the door to the idea that it is we who in some sense determine who God is by the way we think about God. The ultimate confusion of divine and human persons is illustrated in her statements that "*the life of God does not belong to God alone*" (ibid., 354) and that "the mystery of existence is the mystery of the *commingling* of persons, divine and human, in a common life" (ibid., 383, emphasis mine). All of these problematic concepts underscore the fact that Gunton's worry that LaCugna's view tended to be pantheistic was well founded indeed.
[85]LaCugna, *God for Us*, 228.
[86]Ibid., 225.

remark coheres with her view that "the immanent Trinity is not transhistorical, transempirical, or transeconomic … to speak about God in immanent trinitarian terms is nothing more than to speak about God's life with us in the economy of Christ and the Spirit."[87] This wording once again overtly collapses the immanent into the economic Trinity because it fails to recognize, as Torrance consistently does, that our encounter with God in Christ and the Spirit in the economy leads us to a knowledge of the eternal Father, Son, and Holy Spirit who transcends the economy and lives his own eternal life into which we are drawn through faith, by grace and thus through union with Jesus himself, the incarnate Son of the Father. LaCugna is right to look to the economy to know God but wrong to suppose that referring to the immanent Trinity can actually occur by restricting who God is to the economy.

I mention LaCugna's views here because it is precisely her inability to recognize the freedom of God as the one who loves that then allows her, like Fiddes, McFague, and Johnson (each in their own ways of course), to claim that we not only can but that we must name God Mother as well as Father in order to overcome the idea that God is male. LaCugna alleges that there is no consensus "on whether God's name as Father, Son, Spirit is revealed and therefore cannot be changed, or whether it can be changed, on what basis, in what contexts, or by whom."[88] When I first read this statement, my immediate reaction was that it is more than obvious that LaCugna did not spend much time reading Athanasius's anti-Arian writings. Indeed, she did not read Scripture very carefully either since, for instance, it is as clear as can be that the name of God into which we are baptized is the name revealed by Jesus himself who is the very Word of God.

Thus, Barth could rightly assert that God the Father remains unknown to us unless Jesus himself personally reveals that name to us. That is why Barth insisted that the content of revelation could not be separated from the form of revelation. Hence, "the form here is essential to the content, i.e., God is unknown as our Father, as the Creator, to the degree that He is not made known by Jesus."[89] And, as we have already seen, on the basis of that revelation, Barth maintains that there is nothing higher or better to God than that God is the Father, Son, and Holy Spirit. That makes sense and Torrance clearly agreed with Barth's thinking because he also espoused the importance of the baptismal formula referring to our baptism in the name of the Father, Son, and Holy Spirit. That is who God is. That is the God of the Nicene confession. That is who God has named himself to be, Torrance repeatedly stresses throughout his works. So, to suggest that God's name might not be revealed and thus could be changed by us is once more to argue that it is we who determine who God is and not God alone! That, according to Torrance, is precisely the self-will of fallen creatures that was overcome by Christ himself in his vicarious life of obedience in relation to the Father. We thus find ourselves once again at

---

[87]Ibid., 229.
[88]Catherine Mowry LaCugna, "God in Communion with Us," in *Freeing Theology: The Essentials of Theology in Feminist Perspective*, ed. Catherine Mowry LaCugna (New York: HarperCollins, 1993), 83–114, 99.
[89]Barth, CD I/1, 390.

the heart of the problem regarding language for God. Who is it who determines the truth of that language? As we have been seeing, the answer to that question for Torrance and Barth, who follow Athanasius and the Nicene Creed, is that the truth of our language for God is and must be grounded in God alone. It must also be anchored in history in the witness of Israel when God revealed his name to Moses and the prophets, and finally in Jesus himself who is the bridge between us and the eternal Trinity as Torrance repeatedly stresses. The truth of revelation is grounded in the one who is the Way, the Truth, and the Life, that is, Jesus himself. There really is no way to the Father, except through him.

Karl Barth made that point in a way that obviated any possible subjectivist reduction of revelation to something that comes *from* us when he wrote that

> revelation denotes the Word of God itself in the act of its being spoken in time
> … it is the condition which conditions all things without itself being conditioned
> … [it] means the unveiling of what is veiled … Revelation as such is not relative.
> Revelation in fact does not differ from the person of Jesus Christ nor from the
> reconciliation accomplished in Him. To say revelation is to say "The Word became
> flesh."[90]

Revelation then is the act of God speaking to us through the witness of Scripture and through proclamation such that "they continually become God's Word." However, Barth says we must say the very opposite concerning revelation itself because "revelation becomes God's Word, i.e., in the Bible and proclamation, because it is this Word in itself."[91] Thus, in his view of revelation in its identity with the incarnate Word, Barth intended to say that "the reference here is not to a possibility still to be realised but to the reality of the Word of God as the basis of all possible self-realisations."[92] From this Barth draws two decisive conclusions. First, God's revealed Word which had been veiled is the mystery now made known in Christ. "But this means that no other reason is to be sought or suggested for its disclosure than the actual disclosing itself."[93] He then cites Luther to make a second important point, namely, that "no creature can come to this knowledge. Christ alone revealeth it to it in the heart. There all merit falleth to the ground, all the powers and abilities of reason, and count for nought with God. Christ alone must give it."[94] From this Barth concludes that when we use the word revelation to say

> "the Word was made flesh and dwelt among us," then we are saying something
> which can have only an intertrinitarian basis in the will of the Father and the

---

[90]Barth, CD I/1, 118–19.
[91]Ibid., 118.
[92]Ibid.
[93]Ibid., 119.
[94]Ibid.

sending of the Son and the Holy Spirit, in the eternal decree of the triune God, so that it can be established only as knowledge of God from God, of light in light.[95]

With these statements in mind then it is easy to understand why Barth could also say

"God" is not a magnitude, with which the believer is already acquainted before he is a believer, so that as believer he merely experiences an improvement and enrichment of knowledge that he already had ... we have to begin with the admission that of ourselves we do *not* know what we say when we say "God," i.e. that all that we think we know when we say "God" does not reach and comprehend Him Who is called "God" in the symbol [the Nicene Creed] ... Only God's revelation, not our reason despairing of itself, can carry us over from God's incomprehensibility.[96]

Illustrating the decisive point that revelation is in fact the act of the Father, Son, and Holy Spirit from start to finish, Barth concludes that when the Nicene Creed tells us this it

expresses absolutely for the first and only time *Who* God is and *What* God is. God is God precisely and only in that being and action which are here, in a new and peculiar way, designated as those of the Father, the Son and the Holy Spirit. Only in this reality of His that bears on us is God God. All our preconceived representations and ideas of what from our own consciousness we think we are compelled to take for "God," have, when we confess "I believe in God," not indeed to disappear—for they cannot do that; that would mean that we should have to remain speechless—but to give way before the utterance of revelation, to subordinate themselves to it completely and absolutely.[97]

In Barth's view then, all our preconceived ideas about God are really "turned upside down" before God's revelation of himself in Christ and through the Spirit because, like Torrance after him, he maintained that

it is not because we have already sought Him that we find Him in faith, but, it is because He has first of all found us that we seek Him—now really *Him*—in faith. Truly and only as Father, Son and Holy Spirit, as Who He has revealed and will reveal Himself to us, is God God—He is not also God in addition in the thoughts of our hearts and in the works of our hands.[98]

Barth's position never changed when he referred to revelation in the *Church Dogmatics*. His thinking was shaped by the doctrine of justification by faith and by grace so that he would never ascribe true knowledge of God to us directly but would only speak of our

---

[95]Ibid.
[96]Barth, *Credo*, 11–12.
[97]Ibid., 12–13.
[98]Ibid., 13.

true knowledge of God taking place in obedience to God's Word in faith and by grace. So even here he concluded that "it is just the man who has received God's revelation, who will ascribe God's being present as God to him, entirely to His revelation and not at all to himself, entirely to grace and not at all to nature."[99]

One can easily recognize here that all our references to the triune God of Christian revelation are true only as they are grounded in the eternal Father, Son, and Holy Spirit. These are not simply optional metaphors developed from our human experiences and then projected symbolically onto some nameless mystery by us.[100] They are the words through which God has spoken and will again speak his Word to us as it comes from the Father, through the Son and is recognized through the faith given and received from the Holy Spirit. If Barth is right in what he says here about revelation, then in truth the name of God cannot be changed. And indeed, if I am right in what I have been arguing, there is no need to change it because that name of God does not in any way import gender or sex into the divine being. Therefore, since the use of the terms "father" and "son" is meant to be understood "imagelessly" as discussed above, they cannot in any sense suggest the superiority of men over women. But neither can they suggest that the proper meaning of those "names" as applied to God came from us men and women at all. Because of that and because in Christ himself the sin (self-will) that has led and would again lead men to subordinate women has already been overcome through our justification and sanctification in him there is no need to think we have to change the name of God for women to have equality in the Church and elsewhere. For to really hear the reconciling Word of God here and now means that no gender-neutral language or gender equalizing language is necessary for women to recognize and live the freedom which is fully theirs in Jesus Christ himself.

All of these important positive insights are undercut and lost then when LaCugna, like Fiddes, Johnson, and McFague in their own ways, speaks about "the far-reaching negative consequences of exclusively masculine imagery for God."[101] Yes, the imagery is "masculine." But the moment it is assumed that that imagery can be projected directly into the divine being, then and there one has ceased speaking of the eternal Trinity confessed in the Nicene Creed simply because the truth of what is thereby recognized is a truth grounded in God that comes *to us through* our "imagery" in a way that transforms its ordinary meaning. In Barth's words, it turns all our preconceived ideas upside down. Because LaCugna has not understood revelation in its identity with Jesus himself in his utter uniqueness, she claims, with many modern theologians that "there is no doubt that the use of only masculine images and metaphors in worship and in theology creates

---

[99]Ibid.

[100]T. F. Torrance fully agrees with Barth on this point. Since "our knowing of God is grounded in his knowing of us, and our understanding of the Fatherhood of God, who is who he is as Father of the Son, is of the one Fatherhood from which all other fatherhood is named" ("The Christian Apprehension of God the Father," 137), therefore "'Father,' 'Son,' and 'Holy Spirit' are essential to the informational content of revelation and are not just metaphorical ways of speaking of God derived from Jewish culture; for they are rooted in and determined by what God is inherently in himself" (ibid., 140).

[101]LaCugna, "God in Communion with Us," 99.

the impression that God is male."[102] Indeed, she maintains that "the one-sided way of imaging and referring to God contributes to the religious legitimization of patriarchy in the sense that the male and masculinity are the center, assumed to be normative for all human beings."[103] When weighed against the truth of who God has actually revealed himself to be, these statements are exposed as so wide of the mark that it is unimaginable that anyone would take them seriously. Yet, anyone who is even moderately aware of present-day theology will know that the majority of theologians might agree with LaCugna on this point.

They are wrong, however, because even in her understanding, which is representative of much feminist and liberation theology today, she mistakenly is claiming that when the terms "father" and "son" are used, then this represents "legitimization of patriarchy" because it places the male and masculinity at the center. Yet, that is exactly and completely wrong because in light of revelation, those terms must unequivocally refer away from men and from women and their concepts and experiences. Thus, those terms must refer away from us and exclusively to God himself if they are to speak of the Trinity confessed in the Nicene Creed. Males are not normative for human beings at all since the only norm for what it means to be truly human is God himself who meets us in the Person and Work of the one Mediator, who alone justifies and sanctifies sinners. This is where Christology is crucial. Fiddes, Johnson, McFague, and LaCugna, each in their own way, marginalize Jesus' uniqueness by ignoring, redefining, or evading the fact that he is utterly unique as God become man and that he is the one who not only names God to us but also enables us to live in freedom and equality as men and women who are reconciled with God by grace. We know what it means to be truly human therefore from Jesus himself and no one and nothing else. Failure to acknowledge this point means failure to acknowledge God himself as he meets us in the historical Jesus.

Language for God

LaCugna sees the basic problem of language for God this way: "The exclusive use of masculine images in worship or theology contributes to an overwhelming sense of God as male."[104] Hence, following Sallie McFague's notion that "the problem with the Father image is 'its expansion, its inclusiveness, its hegemony, its elevation to an idol,' "[105] LaCugna suggests that Christian feminism is concerned not only about the equality of men and women but "to overturn the idolatry of worshiping a male God."[106] She then outlines six strategies for dealing with God's name. I will not develop all six of these here. For our purposes, I will note the first and then summarize LaCugna's proposed solution.

---

[102]Ibid., 100.
[103]Ibid.
[104]Ibid., 100–1.
[105]Ibid., 101.
[106]Ibid.

The first is that since God revealed his name, therefore it cannot be changed. With respect to this strategy she refers to Karl Barth and the Orthodox theologian Deborah Belonick, who argued that "the revealed status of these names makes them immune from conditioning effects of history and culture" so that they were not "products of a particular structure, male theology, or a hierarchical church."[107] LaCugna claims that "this kind of argumentation is directed against the view, enunciated by Thomas Aquinas and given special prominence by Sallie McFague," namely, that "all biblical names and forms of address to God are metaphors."[108] She praises McFague's approach as "freeing the Christian imagination from the stranglehold of a deadly literalism" while noting that her theology has been criticized for being unitarian and not actually addressing "the central issues raised by the doctrine of the Trinity."[109]

She concludes by noting that Joseph DiNoia believes that because "God names Godself," one cannot substitute the name mother for the first divine person of the Trinity. To this she responds that the idea that the biblical terms cannot be changed because "they express 'God's naming of Godself,' and thus to change them would be idolatry, is at odds with contemporary biblical scholarship, which recognizes the conditioned character of biblical testimony and the patriarchal context of biblical writings."[110] The "biblical" scholars cited are feminist theologians who clearly subscribe to the kind of contextual theology that functions on the presupposition that in some sense the terms "father" and "son" are historically and culturally conditioned with the implication that they can be changed. However, that assumption is more than a little problematic because it marginalizes the fact that revelation is a free new act of God coming into history from outside in the incarnation so that revelation is not something that arises *from* history and culture but *from* a miraculous act of God himself. Therefore, God's naming himself is not the product of an historically conditioned community in the first place.

God's revelation to Moses as "I am," and in Jesus Christ, God's naming himself as Father, Son, and Holy Spirit is, as Torrance has said, a sovereign act of God's grace, judgment, love, and mercy. And, since revelation is, as Barth put it, the condition which conditions all things without itself being conditioned, it cannot be changed because God simply *is* the eternal Father, Son, and Holy Spirit. Thus, God is not a metaphor in McFague's sense because, as mentioned above, she herself claimed her metaphors could not say anything about the nature of God at all. In any case, LaCugna clearly has a view which is, if one attempts to defend God's freedom from creatures with the idea that his name cannot be changed, then that person has dissociated God "from us and from human language, however partial and imperfect it may be. This strategy violates the intention of the doctrine of the Trinity to affirm God's real relation to us in creation and exposes the absence of a truly relational ontology that can affirm God's

---

107Ibid.
108Ibid.
109Ibid., 102.
110Ibid.

self-determination and sovereign freedom without creating an unbridgeable chasm between God and us."[111]

LaCugna thinks the "Fatherhood of God is susceptible to grave misunderstanding" and can be used to support sexism and patriarchalism. So, she directs our attention to Christ which on the surface would seem to be exactly the right thing to do. She says, "The self-revelation of God in Christ remains the only sure source for overcoming distortions in theology and church practice, because it is only by living *in Christ* that we meet the living God whom Jesus proclaimed and through Christ are faithful to the true, living God."[112] However, a question arises here: is it our living in Christ that enables us to meet the living God or is it because Jesus Christ himself *is* God the Son directly confronting us in our sin and estrangement from God the Father who, as our reconciler, thus enables our knowledge of the true God?[113]

I ask this question because in her book *God for Us*, LaCugna claims that "our relationship to others, which is indistinguishable from our relationship to Jesus Christ, determines whether we are or are not finally incorporated into God's household."[114] This statement is more than a little problematic because if our relationship to others is indistinguishable from our relation to Christ, then, in her thinking, Christ is little more than an idea she is using to speak of our relations with others! In other words, her appeal here is not to a properly functioning Christology which would begin by acknowledging Christ's uniqueness as the revelation of God which, as Barth rightly noted, is the condition which conditions all things without itself being conditioned and involves his reconciling us to God the Father. Rather, for her, we do not need Christ's forgiving grace to know God; we do not need the action of the Holy Spirit uniting us to Christ himself so that he can enable our knowledge of God the Father. Instead, our relations to Christ supposedly are determined by our relationships with others. Her appeal to Christ therefore is illusory.

So, how finally does she solve this problem of language and knowledge of God? She maintains that the problem of sexism in the church and society is so deep that we must realize that "the basic problem goes much deeper than language." Thus, "we must change

---

[111]Ibid.

[112]Ibid., 105.

[113]Torrance helpfully puts this matter this way: "By the very nature of its object, the creating, revealing, reconciling and regenerating Word of God, theology is committed to a movement of transformation in which material modes of thought and speech are created in appropriate adaptation to the material truth they have to express. Thus instead of suppressing the personal and social coefficients of human knowledge, theology is evangelically concerned for their conversion and regeneration in accordance with the Truth of God as it is in Christ Jesus, and instead of using logically abstracted and perfected forms as empty moulds into which to pour its subject-matter, it opens up the way for the subject-matter to transform the modes of our thought and speech that they may be suitable and apposite in the service of our knowledge of God" (Torrance, *Theological Science*, 278). This kind of knowledge Torrance says is not easy for those who think "only in pictorial images or plastic ideas" because they will not admit that "it is in Jesus Christ where the Word of God has become man that man is restored to union and knowledge with God," and "it is by reference to Jesus Christ, critically and constructively, that we must develop appropriate forms of thought and speech about God" (ibid., 279).

[114]LaCugna, *God for Us*, 384.

the pattern of relationships in the Christian community as well as depatriarchalize the concept of God."[115] She then speaks of being baptized into the name of God and opening ourselves to the Spirit of God "who restores in us the blemished image of God, male and female."[116] Again, those sound like promising insights, except for the fact that she does not seem to recognize that since the Spirit and the Word are *homoousios*, it is the Spirit who unites us to Christ and thus to the Father. But then one could not claim the Spirit of God restores the image of God in us without obviating the fact that Christ himself is the true image of God and we must therefore refrain from claiming that God's image is in us and not in our relationship with God in Christ. In any case, LaCugna argues that theology and church practices that denigrate women "will impoverish and falsify how we name and address God." That is indeed a strange assertion since the truth of who God is cannot be said to be determined by church practices because they are judged by their relationship to Christ himself and not by the way people treat women. In other words, language for God is true or false to the extent that it allows the very Word of God incarnate in Jesus Christ to be the sole determining reality in what is said.

LaCugna goes on to say that since "language shapes worlds of meaning and creates social systems, it requires ongoing revision."[117] Of course it does. But the key question is, what exactly is the criterion for a proper revision of language for God? Or to put it in terms we have been developing in this chapter, where does the truth of our language for God come from? Does it come exclusively from the Father through the Son and in the Spirit or does it come from us as individuals or in community? These questions are never really answered because LaCugna simply asserts that we are all united in desiring to praise God and that there are many ways to do so which cannot be dictated by the church or by theology. Indeed, she maintains that "ways of praising God should not become a source of division among persons, nor should we overinvest a particular way of praising God." She advises against trying to control God or "settle into a rut in our praise of God." None of this actually addresses the issue of course. Her final conclusion is that "a variety of images for God is appropriate because God is incomprehensible, inexpressible mystery"; also, "no one image or name for God may be turned into an idol, and no one image or name expresses the totality of God's sacred mystery."[118] In the end she claims that "the doctrine of the Trinity affirms that the God into whose name we are baptized is neither the patriarchal Father-God nor a God who created women 'less' than men. Rather, it affirms, like Rublev's icon, that true communion among persons is the deepest meaning of life."[119]

Enough has been said here to illustrate that LaCugna never solves the difficulty in naming God at all. She espouses an agnostic view of God similar to the view of Elizabeth Johnson, namely, that since God is incomprehensible mystery, no one name for God

---

[115]LaCugna, "God in Communion with Us," 106.
[116]Ibid.
[117]Ibid., 107.
[118]Ibid., 108.
[119]Ibid.

is appropriate. This corresponds with the agnostic position she espoused in her book *God for Us* when she wrote that "it is impossible to say exactly and definitively what this personal *ousia* of God is, because this would entail explaining both what it means for God to be the Unoriginate Origin ... and what it means for divine persons *to be* in communion with every creature. What God *is* remains unspeakable."[120] But in fact there is only one name for God into whom we are baptized, that is, the Father, the Son, and the Holy Spirit. So, the idea that we can use a variety of images for the triune God begs the question of where the truth of our knowledge of God comes from.

In a proper doctrine of the Trinity, we would have to say that only God reveals God and that since Jesus himself is the Way, the Truth, and the Life, no one comes to the Father except through him. This is not what LaCugna finally maintains. She claims that our prayer and giving praise to God should "create an inclusive community of persons who in their communal life are the icon of the Trinity."[121] Hence, the doctrine of the Trinity, as noted, affirms that "true communion among persons is the deepest meaning of life." Actually, this misses the point of trinitarian doctrine completely, especially since LaCugna claims that the mystery of God is "the mystery of persons in communion who embrace death, sin, and all forms of alienation for the sake of life [while the Spirit transforms us so] 'we become by grace what God is by nature,' namely, persons in full communion with God and with every creature ... The life of God—precisely *because* God is triune—does not belong to God alone."[122] Coupled with her views that trinitarian life is also our life and that "the mystery of existence is the mystery of the *commingling* of persons, divine and human in a common life,"[123] it is easy to see that her thinking substitutes communion between God and us and even the commingling of God and us, for the eternal communion of the Father, Son, and Holy Spirit.[124] There is finally no

---

[120]LaCugna, *God for Us*, 334.

[121]LaCugna, "God in Communion with Us," 108.

[122]LaCugna, *God for Us*, 1, 354, emphasis mine.

[123]See n. 84 above.

[124]LaCugna claims that "there is a practical reason to resist equating 'immanent Trinity' with 'inner life of God.' The life of God is not something that belongs to God alone. *Trinitarian life is also our life* ... To conceive trinitarian life as something belonging *only* to God, or belonging to God apart from the creature, is to miss the point entirely. To analyze the 'immanent Trinity' as a purely intradivine reality also misses the point. The doctrine of the Trinity is not ultimately a teaching about 'God' but a teaching about *God's life with us and our life with each other*" (*God for Us*, 228). With these remarks it is easy to see not only that LaCugna has obliterated the reality of God in himself such that God no longer can be conceived as having his own independent existence even as he relates with us in his Word and Spirit. She also confuses trinitarian life with our life since she really believes we become what God is by nature through grace. Of course, we can never become what God is, but we do participate in God's eternal life through union with his Son and the power of the Holy Spirit by grace which remains identical with Christ's own giving of himself to us—nevertheless, trinitarian life remains God's life; that life does not become our life. Further, the idea that the doctrine of the Trinity is not a teaching about God misses the entire point about the doctrine of the immanent Trinity and once again repeats the error of Origen. As Torrance rightly argues, "we must be careful, as Gregory Nazianzen warned, not to understand 'God always was' in a time-related way. 'God always was and always *is*; or rather God always *is*. For was and will be are fragments of our time, and are of changeable nature, but he *is* eternal being.' The point at issue is that God is who he is in himself, entirely unconditioned by any reality other than himself, and thus totally independent of his creation and infinitely exalted over all time and space" (*The Trinitarian Faith*, 89). Torrance goes on to

way to distinguish God's life from ours in her thinking and she assumes that it is our prayer and praise and not the Holy Spirit who creates and sustains the community as the body of Christ on earth. Before concluding this chapter, I would like to discuss two important concepts that will shed additional light on this matter, namely, *perichoresis* and conversion.

Perichoresis

Thomas F. Torrance is particularly helpful in understanding the importance of this concept for trinitarian theology. He links together the *homoousion* with the concept of *perichoresis* to make several important points. First, he argues that the *homoousion* "stands for the basic insight deriving from God's self-communication to us, that what God is toward us in his saving economic activity in space and time through Christ and the Holy Spirit, he is antecedently and inherently in himself."[125] The basis of this knowledge is found in Jesus Christ himself. Because he is God acting *as* man and not just God present in a man, our knowledge of God that comes to us in the incarnation, and therefore in our encounter with Jesus Christ, is factually grounded in God himself.[126] However, Torrance

---

say correctly exactly what LaCugna cannot and does not say because she confuses divine and human being, namely, that "God has become our Father, not by nature but by grace, after he had become our Creator" (ibid., 90). But this means God "is known by us within the creation only in accordance with what he is eternally, intrinsically and antecedently in himself as Father, and indeed as Father, Son and Holy Spirit, apart from the creation. There is, therefore, no necessary relation between God and the created cosmos, as if God needed relation to what is not himself in order to be what he eternally is in himself as God the Father Almighty" (ibid.). [125]Torrance, *Christian Doctrine of God*, 99. Torrance frequently makes this statement. But its implication here is that, since God really has made himself known personally in his self-revelation in Jesus Christ, we cannot simply choose an alternative formula for the Trinity such as "Creator, Redeemer, and Sustainer" because while that expression refers to God's actions *ad extra*, it "does not express what God eternally and personally is in himself—three persons who mutually contain and indwell one another—but only something of what he is toward us" ("The Christian Apprehension of God the Father," 141). Thus, to detach that formula from the eternal (immanent) Trinity would mean that those terms "primarily correlate with what we are, so their meaning for us is reduced to little more than symbolic expressions of an in-turned religious consciousness" (ibid.). Torrance rightly claims that such a formula functioning in that way would do "no more than give expression to a unitarian conception of God characterized by three different names, modes, or operations" (ibid.). Indeed, he says, if one were to substitute the expression "Creator, Redeemer, and Sustainer" for Father, Son, and Holy Spirit, that would imply that "God creates, redeems and sustains himself!" and that would then "identify God's functional relations toward the creaturely world with the intrinsic interrelations of his divine being, which would amount to a very gross form of anthropomorphism" (ibid.). Torrance insists that any trinitarian formula that is detached from who God is in himself as the eternal Father, Son, and Holy Spirit undercuts the fact that God is personal in the relations of the three persons in the one being of God. The result would be a conception of God as impersonal or as a "nonpersonal one" which would merely become "the personification and deification of our own desires and ideals" (ibid., 142). And that is not the end of it. Such a view would also undercut the singularity and finality of God's self-revelation in Jesus Christ himself and put in question "any claim to be authentically Christian" (ibid.). This, because it would suggest that Jesus was mistaken and even wrong to teach that we should "hallow the name of the 'Father and to believe in himself as the 'Son' of the Father" (ibid.). [126]Torrance, *The Trinitarian Faith*, 150–1; and Torrance, "The Christian Apprehension of God the Father," 135.

insists that the *homoousion* is precisely what prevents us from indiscriminately reading back into God "our own subjective notions or fantasies."[127] He asserts that scientific theology will help us develop ways to prevent any sort of "mythological projection of ideas of our own devising into God" and thus "confounding God known by us with our deficient knowing of him." In all knowledge of course it is important to distinguish objective reality from our subjective knowing of it. But, especially in theology this is not all that easy because, as Torrance points out, "in our self-centredness we constantly tend to eclipse the object which we seek to know from ourselves by getting ourselves in the way."[128]

The problem here is the problem of sin and therefore our self-will as already noted above. Here, in Torrance's understanding, we are up against a crucial point that was missing almost entirely from the presentations of Fiddes, McFague, Johnson, and LaCugna. Torrance insists that we need to be reconciled to God in order to know him properly. And this, he says, was made clear by Jesus himself when "he insisted that [the disciples] must renounce themselves and take up their cross in following him."[129] The important point to note here is that the center from which our knowledge of God takes place is Jesus Christ himself and thus the *hypostatic union*. That means that in him alone humanity and divinity are united, and we are one with God in him and thus not directly in ourselves.

Next, Torrance speaks of the actions of the Holy Spirit who is *homoousios* with the Father and with the Son. This is really important because while "the Son is, as the Word, the distinctive *hypostasis* or Person in whom God utters or expresses himself" such that "an epistemic bridge is established in Christ between man and God that is grounded in the Being of God and anchored in the being of man," the Spirit can only be known by referring to the incarnate Son who himself "constitutes the epistemological centre, as well as the ontological centre, in all our knowledge of God."[130] It will be immediately evident here that Torrance's explicit starting point and criterion for proper knowledge of God is quite different from the four theologians considered above. He begins and ends his thinking with Jesus Christ himself as the only place in history where true knowledge of the Trinity occurs precisely because of who Jesus was and is. McFague, for instance, could only think of Jesus as a human instance of one who loved God and others and thus herself said she could not know who God is in himself. She was right. For all her talk about God as mother, lover, and friend, she never once spoke accurately about who God actually is according to the Nicene Creed.

Let us not get sidetracked here, however. The important point here is that Torrance claims that it is only by reference to the incarnate Son or Word that we can clarify our understanding of the Spirit. The Spirit, he says, "is not knowable in his own distinctive Person or *hypostasis* in the same way [as the Son], for he is not embodied, like the

---

[127]Torrance, *Christian Doctrine of God*, 99.
[128]Ibid.
[129]Ibid., 100.
[130]Ibid., 100–1.

incarnate Son, in … our world of space-time, or, like him, therefore brought within the range of our human knowing at our lowly creaturely level." This, because "the Holy Spirit is God of God but not man of man."[131] This implies therefore not only that our knowledge of the Spirit rests directly upon God himself and thus on nothing within history per se but also that it is mediated to us in history and thus in space and time "through relation to the Son with whom he is of one being as he is with the Father."[132] This is an exceptionally important insight which is missing from most contemporary presentations of the doctrine of the Trinity. From this Torrance concludes that it is the Holy Spirit who creatively mediates our knowledge of God in himself and also enables our reception of and understanding of revelation as it meets us in the incarnate Son within history.

Hence, and this is a key point for this chapter, the knowledge of God as he is in himself that is mediated to us through Christ and the Spirit is knowledge of "the Father through the Son and the Son from the Father" so that "we know the Spirit in himself as Lord God no less than the Father and the Son, who therefore with the Father and the Son together is worshipped and glorified." These are not just throwaway phrases for Torrance because here he insists that "it is through holding constantly in our thought the inseparable unity between the economic activity of God in the Spirit and the economic activity of God in the Son that we may be prevented from reading back into God himself the material creaturely images (e.g. latent in human father-son relations)" because "the creaturely images naturally latent in the forms of thought and speech employed by divine revelation to us are made to refer transparently or in a diaphanous way to God without being projected into his divine Nature."[133] This thinking was discussed above in relation to knowing God in a spiritual way and thus imagelessly.[134]

Now we can briefly explain what Torrance means by *perichoresis*. It is a theological term that helps us explain the "mutual indwelling of the Father and the Son and the Spirit," and thus it helps explain "the Communion of the Spirit."[135] Torrance explains that the word itself derives from two Greek words, that is, from *chora* (χώρα), which is the Greek word for " 'space' or 'room', or from *chorein* (χώρειν), meaning 'to contain', 'to make room for', or 'to go forward'. It indicates a sort of mutual containing or enveloping of realities, which we also speak of as *coinherence* or *coindwelling*." But the key point here is that the term *perichoresis* when used with respect to the Trinity refers to the "complete

---

[131]Ibid., 101. See also Torrance, *Ground and Grammar*, 165–6.

[132]Torrance, *Christian Doctrine of* God, 101. See also *The Trinitarian Faith*, where Torrance notes that because Jesus Christ is *homoousios* with the Father and with us that it is only in him that we "really know God as he is in himself and in accordance with his nature" (203). Then he maintains that it is on that same basis that we know the Spirit "for it is in the Spirit sent to us by the Father through the Son that knowledge of God is mediated and actualised within us. Thus knowledge of the Spirit as well as of the Father is taken from and is controlled by knowledge of the Son" (ibid.). See also ibid., 306.

[133]Torrance, *Christian Doctrine of God*, 101.

[134]See also Torrance, "The Christian Apprehension of God the Father," 138–9; and Torrance, *The Trinitarian Faith*, 194–5.

[135]Torrance, *Christian Doctrine of God*, 103.

mutual containing or interpenetration of the three divine Persons, Father, Son and Holy Spirit, in one God."[136] Torrance asserts that *perichoresis* was first used by Gregory Nazianzen to refer to the divine and human natures in Christ to maintain the integrity of the two natures in the one Person of Christ. However, when the term was used to refer to the Persons within the eternal Trinity as just described, Torrance maintains that it could no longer be applied to the hypostatic union of natures in Christ "without serious damage to the doctrine of Christ" since whenever that was done it always led to some kind of "docetic rationalising and depreciating of the humanity of Christ."[137]

The crucial point to be made here is that a proper understanding of the term *perichoresis* requires that it refer to the "intra-trinitarian relations in God," so that the "three divine Persons in the one God" would be understood in such a way that "the ontic relations between them belong to what they essentially are in themselves in their distinctive *hypostases*." This, Torrance says, led to a

> new *concept of person*, unknown in human thought until then, according to which the relations between persons belong to what persons are. Just as the differentiating relations between the Father, the Son and the Holy Spirit belong to what they are as Father, Son and Holy Spirit, so the *homoousial* relations between the three divine Persons belong to what they are in themselves as Persons and in their Communion with one another.[138]

From this Torrance concludes that "this onto-relational concept of 'person', generated through the doctrines of Christ and the Holy Trinity, is one that is also applicable to inter-human relations, but in a created way reflecting the uncreated way in which it applies to the Trinitarian relations in God."[139]

Among the many important implications of the term *perichoresis* is that it "reinforces the fact that the Holy Trinity may be known only as a whole, for it is as a whole that God makes himself known to us through himself and in himself as Father, Son and Holy Spirit."[140] This implies that one cannot focus on one person of the Trinity to the exclusion of the others.[141] From this it follows that

---

[136]Ibid., 102.
[137]Ibid. See also Torrance, *Ground and Grammar*, 172–3.
[138]Torrance, *Christian Doctrine of God*, 102–3.
[139]Ibid., 103.
[140]Ibid., 180–1.
[141]We saw this problem above in Elizabeth Johnson's supposed "pneumatological inflection" which led her to claim we do not have "one straight-as-an-arrow name" for God. If her thinking had been truly pneumatological, she would have been led to assert that it is through the Spirit that we hear God's Word and come to know God precisely as Father, Son, and Spirit since, in virtue of the perichoretic character of the immanent trinitarian relations in God, we cannot focus on one person to the exclusion of the others. That is another problem that arises when theologians think they can change the name for God by renaming God from experience instead of thinking about God based on God's own self-revelation. See n. 59 above.

the self-revelation of God as triune is a self-enclosed *novum* which may be known and interpreted only on its own ground and out of itself. Hence our knowing of God engages in a perichoretic circular movement from Unity to Trinity and from Trinity to Unity, for God is God only as he is Father, Son and Holy Spirit, and cannot be conceived by us truly otherwise.[142]

Quite obviously then, Torrance believes that who God is as Father, Son, and Holy Spirit is disclosed to us by God himself such that the terms "father," "son," and "spirit" really are ultimate terms denoting the ineffable reality of God in his inner divine relations and actions. Since God makes himself known to us in the incarnate Son who is the one Mediator, there "is no separate activity of the Holy Spirit in revelation or salvation in addition to or independent of the activity of Christ."[143] Consequently, Torrance regularly stresses that

the Father, the Son and the Holy Spirit always act together in every divine operation whether in creation or redemption, yet in such a way that the distinctive activities of the Father, the Son and the Holy Spirit, are always maintained, in accordance with the propriety and otherness of their Persons as the Father, the Son and the Holy Spirit. This may be called the "perichoretic coactivity of the Holy Trinity."[144]

My reason for discussing this view of *perichoresis* here is to illustrate that for Torrance while the terms "father," "son," "spirit," and "being" are all taken from our human thought and speech, they do not receive their meaning from us but only from the eternal Trinity who comes to us in the incarnation and outpouring of the Holy Spirit. Therefore, we cannot use them as they normally function in human language and experience to speak properly of God and God's relations with us unless and until they "suffer a fundamental change in being adapted to be vehicles of his Word."[145] Once this is understood, then one can see the real reason why any attempt to change our language for the triune God from Father, Son, and Spirit to mother, lover, and friend, for instance, or simply to "relation," is so terribly problematic. It is problematic, as we have seen, because every attempt to change language for the Christian God in this or in other ways actually rests on a preconceived notion of the divine being that comes from us. It thus rests on a notion of the divine being constructed by us and then projected into God. As such, it cannot and does not speak of the Trinity at all. It simply employs trinitarian language to speak of relationality or motherhood, love, and friendship.

To speak properly of the Trinity, our human language must be used "exclusively in the light of God's naming of himself as 'I am who I am' in the Old Testament revelation and as the Father, the Son and the Holy Spirit in the New Testament revelation."[146] It

---

[142]Torrance, *Christian Doctrine of God*, 181.
[143]Ibid., 196.
[144]Ibid., 198.
[145]Ibid., 103.
[146]Ibid., 104.

is because God is this God objectively and because God is neither a metaphor we use to speak of our experience of mystery nor can God be known apart from faith in Jesus Christ and the outpouring of the Holy Spirit, that we simply cannot name God from our experiences of mystery, love, motherhood, relationality, or friendship as we understand those terms metaphorically. The Christian God is not only intrinsically personal as Torrance says but is "intrinsically triune" precisely as the eternal Father, Son, and Holy Spirit. All of this presupposes that because we are all in fact sinners, we need God's reconciling grace actualized in us by the Holy Spirit to recognize who God is as he meets us in his incarnate Son and who we are as those reconciled to God in Christ.[147] As seen above, all of this is undercut by the approaches to the doctrine of the Trinity offered by Fiddes, McFague, Johnson, and LaCugna.

Let me briefly illustrate how different LaCugna's view of *perichoresis* is and why her understanding of that term not only distorts who God is but also functions in a way that allows her to do what Torrance would never do, that is, to rename God from our experiences of fatherhood or motherhood in order to achieve something that was already achieved for the human race in Christ's own vicarious life of atoning obedience to the Father for our benefit. That something is the overcoming of the sin that leads to inequality between men and women. She claims that it "remains disputed for many whether calling God 'Mother' is ever appropriate."[148] Then she says, "It think it is," even though many feminist scholars now recognize that "the problems with the Father-metaphor are more complex than previously realized, and substituting 'Mother' for 'Father' does not resolve the deep-seated problems of a unitarian theism."[149] Consequently, her view is that "the heavy masculine imagery for God has deadened the Christian imagination, and the ubiquitous references to God as Father in trinitarian literature can be very distracting, to

---

[147]That is why Torrance insists upon two significant insights: (1) The Spirit of God is freely present to us and also freely "brings to completion the creative purpose of God for the creature … from the side of the Creator to the creature [and] from the side of the creature toward the Creator" (*Christian Doctrine of God*, 152). (2) It is in this way that the Spirit establishes "an enduring ontological relation to God. While the creature does not have any continuity in relation to God that belongs to the creature in itself, it does have a relation to God which is continuously given and unceasingly sustained by the presence of the Holy Spirit. This two-way activity of the Holy Spirit is particularly evident in reconciliation and recreation" (ibid.). That is why Torrance also holds that "we must think of the Spirit as participating in the vicarious and intercessory activity of Christ. Thus we must think of the presence of the Spirit as actualising within us the intervening and reconciling work of Christ when as the Son of God he assumed our wayward and disobedient humanity and through his own obedient life and atoning sacrifice offered himself to the Father in our place and in our stead, and thereby restored it in obedient sonship to the Father as our Father as well as his Father" (ibid., 153–4). Hence, our union with Christ is actualized by the Spirit, and in that way, we become open and free toward God and others. For Torrance the Holy Spirit "realizes in us the recreative power of the risen and glorified Humanity of Christ" so that it is through Christ's atonement that we are renewed. Hence, it is through the risen Lord's "self-presentation before the Father and the pouring out of the Holy Spirit upon us, that the Atonement became effective for the remission of our sins and the cleansing of our conscience … He [the Spirit] renews us by drawing us within the self-consecration of Christ made on our behalf and by assimilating us into his holiness" (Torrance, *Theology in Reconstruction*, 250).
[148]LaCugna, *God for Us*, 18.
[149]Ibid., 18.

say the least."[150] While she says this would not lead her to "excise every single reference to God as Father in biblical and theological literature," she would use "'God' instead of 'Father' where there would be no loss of meaning." LaCugna then explains that her agenda is to engage the tradition "on its own terms" in order to "come to a fresh and more adequate doctrine of the Trinity." She says,

> The fact that the issue of God's Fatherhood has become so confused and divisive points all the more to the need for a radically revised and revitalized trinitarian theology of God. I have used the construction "God in Godself" instead of "God in Him/Herself" though ultimately, if what I am suggesting in this book has merit, we could eliminate these awkward pronouns by focusing on "God with us" instead of probing an intradivine realm ("God *in se*").[151]

We have already discussed LaCugna's revised and revitalized view of the Trinity above. Even here one can see that her book is indeed, as Colin Gunton noted, a polemic against the doctrine of the immanent Trinity since in eliminating the pronouns for God by focusing on the economic Trinity instead of the immanent Trinity she is led to collapse the latter into the former. And what I wish to stress in this chapter is that, unless and until one's theology of the Trinity is actually governed by who God truly and objectively is in his eternal being and act as none other than the Father, Son, and Spirit confessed in the Nicene Creed, there will be no accurate objective knowledge of God and it will be mistakenly supposed that our speaking of God takes place in "picture models" or as metaphors drawn from human experience instead of through "disclosure models" as discussed above. As long as that is the case, such a view will always begin and end as projection of terms into God instead of understanding God from a center in God provided for us in the incarnation. To put matters bluntly, each of the four theologians discussed above did not begin and end their thinking by acknowledging that the truth of who God is comes to us only from the incarnate Word and thus only through the power of the Holy Spirit.

Given these issues then I would just like to explain here very briefly how LaCugna's perspective on these matters shapes her mistaken view of *perichoresis*. She says that "*theologia* is not the Trinity *in se* but, much more modestly and simply, the mystery of

---

[150]Ibid.

[151]Ibid. While the expression "Godself" has now become almost a received tradition, it is worth noting that both Robert Jenson and Colin Gunton objected to this term because it has modalist connotations and tends to understand the divine being in an impersonal way that undercuts a proper understanding of the Trinity. I think Jenson and Gunton were right. However, for those who think the pronouns used for God as Father and Son carry with them some sort of gender or sexual connotations, I can only ask them to consider the fact that, when the meaning of these terms is transformed in light of revelation and God's reconciling actions in his Word and Spirit, then they do not have this connotation and indeed must not have this connotation because the personal God who is the eternal Father, Son, and Spirit names himself to us as one who exists eternally in his own uniquely transcendent being and action as the one who loves in freedom precisely as the God he is. See my discussion of this issue in the *T&T Clark Handbook of Colin Gunton*, ed. Andrew Picard, Murray Rae, and Myk Habets (London: T&T Clark, 2021), chapter 3.

God ... *an 'immanent' trinitarian theology of God is nothing more than a theology of the economy of salvation.*"[152] Within this perspective, LaCugna then presents her view of *perichoresis* which she thinks should be understood as the "divine dance" that signifies not "intradivine communion" but rather signifies

> divine life as all creatures partake and literally exist in it ... Everything comes from God, and everything returns to God, through Christ in the Spirit. This *exitus* and *reditus* is the choreography of the divine dance which takes place from all eternity and is manifest at every moment in creation. There are not two sets of communion—one among the divine persons, the other among human persons ... the one *perichoresis*, the one mystery of communion includes God and humanity as beloved partners in the dance.[153]

She finally concludes that "the exodus of all persons from God and the return of all to God is the divine dance in which God and we are eternal partners."[154]

The first thing to notice here is that LaCugna has misunderstood the actual meaning of the term *perichoresis* because in fact it refers to the relations of the Persons of the Trinity within the immanent Trinity and then to their homoousial actions in history. But, since she refuses to ground her thinking solely in Christ himself and thus in a center in God, and because she focuses exclusively on the economy in abstraction from the immanent Trinity, she ends up confusing God and creatures. She does that with the claim that God and we are eternal partners in a divine dance. That thinking replicates the error of Origen who could not distinguish the eternal generation of the Son from God's creation of the world and so thought of the world and God as coeternal.[155] This, as Torrance has noted, was roundly refuted by Athanasius and for good reason. If we are from all eternity exiting God and returning to God and that is indeed "the divine dance" which is supposedly signified by the term *perichoresis*, then in her view God really cannot exist either prior to our existence or without our existence. This thinking is indicative of the pantheism discussed above and leads to LaCugna's problematic conclusion that God's life does not belong to himself and that God's life is our life.

Moreover, as Torrance stressed, the term *perichoresis* is linked with a proper understanding of the hypostatic union and of the *homoousion* with reference to Jesus Christ as the sole point within history where we meet directly with God himself. For her, there is no such need to focus on the incarnation for knowledge of the Trinity because she thinks that the choreography of the divine dance not only takes place from all eternity

---

[152]Ibid., 223–4.

[153]Ibid., 274.

[154]Ibid., 304. It is worth noting here that the very concept of a divine dance was problematic in Torrance's view because it confused two Greek words "χωρέω" with "χορεύω." The former referred to the mutual containing of one another in which the persons of the Trinity eternally exist. The latter referred to dance and could lend itself to the use LaCugna mistakenly makes of it.

[155]See Torrance, *The Trinitarian Faith*, 85; and Torrance, *Divine Meaning: Studies in Patristic Hermeneutics* (Edinburgh: T&T Clark, 1995), 184–95.

but that it is "manifest at every moment in creation." However, if Torrance is correct, and I think he is, then one could not speak of God's manifestation in history unless one is referring to the God who revealed his name as "I am" in the Old Testament and as the Father, Son, and Holy Spirit in the New. And indeed, one could not recognize the New Testament revelation apart from the specific manifestation of God in the incarnate Word, that is, in Jesus himself. In other words, from a Christian standpoint, one could not interpret creation properly except in light of the incarnation.

LaCugna's understanding of God then, in terms of the "divine dance," misses both the particularity of Christian revelation and its connection with Christ himself. And it is my contention that it does so because she refuses to acknowledge the freedom of God within the immanent Trinity and the fact that our knowledge must indeed be grounded within the immanent Trinity to be truly theological. This is not some abstruse debate, however, because it is precisely LaCugna's failure to see the importance of grounding theology in the eternal being of God as God has named himself to us that stems from her idea that our naming God is a metaphor for incomprehensible mystery which can be understood without faith in Jesus Christ and without the action of the Holy Spirit uniting us to Christ and thus to the Father. This illustrates the point of this chapter. On the one hand, the truth of our language for God does not come from us but to us from God alone. On the other hand, whenever it is thought that truth of our language comes from us (as one must if one fails to recognize the freedom of God), then we are left only with the possibility of projecting our metaphors mythologically into God, and thus, we are in reality left without any true and certain objective knowledge of the Trinity, no matter how trinitarian our language might be.

That is where the thinking of McFague and LaCugna leaves us. In that perspective, we might then assume that we need to rename God mother and perhaps also lover and friend in an effort to heal the minds of those who think women are subordinate to men. Yet, this assumption is thoroughly unhelpful because if it is in any sense true, then the healing of our minds must be done by us. Since, however, we are sinners who need God's forgiveness and thus God's healing and reconciling action through the Spirit before we can speak rightly of God and in order to realize that the sin that leads to men attempting to dominate women has already been overcome in Christ's atoning death for all of us, the very idea that we can accomplish any of this by the way we use language is just another form of self-justification. It places the burden of salvation back on us who cannot in fact save ourselves!

Conversion

I would like to make one final comparison to illustrate the point of this chapter from another angle. As we end this chapter, I would like to show where Elizabeth Johnson's mistaken approach to analogous language for God leads by very briefly considering her view of conversion. Then, I will end by briefly contrasting that view with the views offered by T. F. Torrance. Remember, however, that I am not pitting one theologian here against others. I am claiming that Torrance is offering a view of who God truly is as Karl Barth also did based on God's own self-revelation in his Word and Spirit, while the others discussed above do not do so, because the thinking of Torrance and Barth is objectively grounded in God and not subjectively grounded in us. And it is on that basis that I have argued that the whole issue of language for God can only be rightly understood and resolved when it is understood from within a properly functioning doctrine of the Trinity.

We have seen that Elizabeth Johnson thinks that new language for God must be generated from women's experience in order to overcome the marginalizing of women or the domination of women by men. Her basic argument for knowledge of God then rests on her assumption that we can know God as "holy mystery" through the changing history of ourselves.[156] Thus for her, God cannot be experienced directly but only "as the ultimate depth and radical essence of every personal experience such as love, fidelity, loneliness, and death" so that we can pre-thematically experience God and know God as the very content of our own presence to ourselves. She therefore believes that "the silent, nonverbal encounter with infinite mystery constitutes the enabling condition of any experience of self at all."[157] This connects with her idea, following Rahner, that "the personal history of the experience of the self is in its total extent the history of the ultimate experience of God also."[158] It goes without saying that her approach to God through experience in this way leads to an abstract idea of God as holy mystery who can go by many names. That explains why she thinks it is not only possible to name God from our own experiences of ourselves, but necessary to do so. Her basic position, as noted above, is that women can and should name God from themselves because they, like men, were created in the image of God. And naming God from women's experience, she thinks, will heal our imaginations and lead to a community that advances beyond patriarchalism.

Much misunderstanding here stems from problematic views of human beings created in the image of God. Torrance helpfully understands this relationally arguing that "God has created man for fellowship with himself in such a way that despite the utter *difference* between them, man—by which term I mean both male and female human beings—is made after the likeness and the image of God."[159] That, however, does not mean

> that the image of God inheres in man's nature, but that it is a *donum superadditum*, a gift wholly contingent upon the free grace of God. Hence it does not mean that man is the offspring of the divine nature or that through his own human nature he can somehow reflect God's nature; it means only that man is specifically destined

---

[156]Johnson, *She Who Is*, 65.
[157]Ibid., 65. For a discussion of why supposed silent nonverbal encounters with God are impossible, see my discussion of Torrance and Rahner on nonconceptual knowledge of God in Chapter 4.
[158]Ibid., 66.
[159]Torrance, "The Christian Apprehension of God the Father," 124.

by grace to live in faithful response to the movement and purpose of God's love toward him as his creaturely partner.[160]

Clearly, Johnson and many others conceptualize the image of God as something that inheres in our human nature so that we can rely on our pre-thematic or "nonverbal" experiences of what we conceptualize as holy mystery to know the Christian God and indeed to name the Christian God from our own experiences. Given what was said above, it hardly needs to be repeated that a proper view of the Christian God can only be attained in faith through union with Christ and through the action of the Holy Spirit enabling us to know God the Father through his Son. It is within this context that Johnson explains that as women have new experiences of being liberated from male domination that they experience God in new ways.[161] This leads to her view of conversion. She writes,

> Through women's encounter with the holy mystery of their own selves as blessed comes commensurate language about holy mystery in female metaphor and symbol, gracefully, powerfully, necessarily … speaking about God and self-interpretation cannot be separated. To give but one example, conversion experienced not as giving up oneself but as tapping into the power of oneself simultaneously releases understanding of divine power not as dominating power-over but as the passionate

---

[160]Ibid., 125. See also n. 75 above.

[161]Johnson thus argues that "feminist reflection is … not alone in its use of human experience as a resource for doing theology. What is distinctive, however, is its specific identification of the lived experience of women … as an essential element in the theological task" (*She Who Is*, 61). Therefore, experiences such as suffering along with "typical patterns of coping and victoriously resisting, strategies … enable women to survive" (ibid.). Out of many such experiences Johnson says there is "one strand that is fundamental to emancipatory speech about God in feminist liberation theology, namely, the experience of conversion. A central resource for naming toward God, the very matrix that energizes it, is the breakthrough of power occurring in women's struggle to reject the sexism of inherited constructions of female identity and risk new interpretations that affirm their own human worth. This foundational experience can be suitably described in the classic language of conversion, a turning around of heart and mind that sets life in a new direction" (ibid., 61–2). This experience, she claims, is simultaneously "a new experience of God" so that conversion then suggests that in their positive assessments of themselves women who awaken to their own worth discover "new contours" for "what is fitting for the mystery of God to be and to do" (ibid., 62). From this she claims pride can only be applied to the "ruling male" and not to women since they have already been "relegated to the margins" (ibid., 64). We are thus told that "women's primordial temptation is not to pride and self-assertion but rather to the lack of it" so that to apply any idea that they must lose themselves in experiencing God's grace "functions in an ideological way to rob them of power" (ibid.). It will be noticed that in this discussion there is not one word about Christ or about the fact that taking up one's cross and following him is necessary to be a disciple. It is really a question of humans exercising power and which ideas of power lead women to have the power they consider to be rightly theirs. The question I am raising in this chapter is this: where does the power to name God come from? For Johnson, the answer is clear and simple: it comes from women who experience God in their experiences of liberation from sexism. All agree that sexism should be overcome. But I am claiming that it was indeed overcome in the reconciliation accomplished for all humanity in the life of Jesus himself so that the power of revelation and the power of liberation for men and women, when rightly understood in a theological way, can only come from him and from the power of the Holy Spirit uniting us to Christ and through him to the Father. The idea that such power can come from us at all suggests that the problem of sin for both women and men still is pride, that is, the unwillingness to surrender ourselves to Christ alone as the sole savior of the world.

ability to empower oneself and others … in the ontological naming and affirming of ourselves we are engaged in a dynamic reaching out to the mystery of God.[162]

It hardly needs to be said that Johnson's view of conversion is defined by reference to women's experiences of themselves and therefore not by reference to Jesus Christ who is the very image of God and who, as the incarnate Word, is the only point of contact in history through which we may know God the Father through his Son and by the power of the Holy Spirit.

It is no accident that Johnson's view of God is abstract and understood without reference to the revelation of God in Jesus Christ. That allows her to pursue her idea that God, as holy mystery, can go by many names. But the important point here is that her approach to knowledge of God and to understanding conversion is by referring women to themselves such that they become the source of knowledge of God and the meaning of conversion. The result is what can only be described as a rather transparent form of self-justification. If women can tap into the power of themselves not only to know God and thus to conceptualize divine power with the idea that they actually can reach out to God by naming and affirming themselves, then that approach is nothing less than one of self-reliance instead of reliance on the grace of God disclosed in Christ. However, if what I have argued in this chapter is correct, then the very idea that women or men can tap into their own power to reach the mystery of God and to understand God's power represents just the kind of self-reliance that is ruled out by the grace of God revealed in Christ. This is the case because, as we have seen, Christ insisted that the disciples renounce themselves and take up their cross and follow him.

There are four notable facts here that are clearly missing from Johnson's analysis. First, she refers women to themselves and not to Christ. Second, she thinks that women should tap into the power of themselves when in reality they need to give that up and turn to Christ and rely exclusively upon his forgiving grace to be the creatures of God that they were created to be. That is the very nature of Christian discipleship. And the reason for this is that grace cannot be separated from the Giver of grace, namely, Christ himself. It cannot be located directly in the experiences of women or of men. Third, she thinks that women, and presumably men as well, have within themselves, in their experiences of depth, the power to reach out to God and to know God without having to rely conceptually and existentially on Christ who alone can enable such knowledge in the first place. Fourth, there is no recognition in Johnson's reflections of the need for the Holy Spirit to actualize the reconciliation accomplished for the human race in Christ's life, death, and resurrection in us before we can know who God truly is as he meets us in his Word and Spirit.

In these four ways one can see why she would have no problem arguing that for women to have equality in the church, the symbol God must be reconstructed by the meaning that women give to that symbol, because unless that happens, its meaning

---

[162]Johnson, *She Who Is*, 66–7.

would be determined only by men. However, she is wrong on both counts because the truth of who God is actually can only be revealed personally in Jesus Christ himself and through union with him in the Spirit through faith. Therefore, the truth of who God is can be determined only by God and neither by women nor by men. And, since we are all sinners who need God's healing grace *before* we can know God truly, it is imperative that any sort of self-reliance is abandoned because to be disciples, we are called to take up our cross and follow Christ alone as the Way, the Truth, and the Life since no one comes to the Father except through him (Jn 14:6). It will be noticed here that my references to God all focused on Jesus Christ as the revelation of God in history and upon the fact that as we live by his forgiving grace through union with him by faith we are drawn into relation with God the Father and not to some abstract notion of holy mystery. Thus, all of this does not occur pre-thematically or nonverbally but conceptually and really as we hear the Word of God in our encounter with Jesus Christ himself through the witness of the Old and New Testaments and the preaching and teaching of the church.

The reason for this is that I am thinking specifically of the Trinity on the basis of the Nicene Creed and not of a mystery that can be named and renamed by me or anyone else. That once again confirms the argument of this chapter. I have argued that we do not need to rename God for women to have equality in the church because the sin and our enmity in relation to God that led and still might lead men to subordinate women to their agenda have been overcome already for our benefit in the life, ministry, death, and resurrection of Jesus Christ. God has already established the freedom of humanity from the sin that might lead men to subordinate women. All that needs to be done then is to live that freedom which applies to everyone and is theirs in Christ alone. However, since Johnson and many others turn to themselves with the idea that the image of God inheres within them, they end in Pelagian fashion with some version of self-reliance even in their description of conversion, which should mean taking up our cross and following Christ.

Consider how very different Torrance's view of conversion is when compared with the view offered by Johnson.

As fallen human beings, we are quite unable through our own free-will to escape from our self-will for our free-will is our self-will. Likewise sin has been so ingrained into our minds that we are unable to repent and have to repent even of the kind of repentance we bring before God. But Jesus Christ laid hold of us even there in our sinful repentance and turned everything round through his holy vicarious repentance, when he bore not just upon his body but upon his human mind and soul the righteous judgments of God and resurrected our human nature in the integrity of his body, mind and soul from the grave … the Gospel speaks of regeneration as wholly bound up with Jesus Christ himself … our new birth, our regeneration, our conversion, are what has taken place in Jesus Christ himself, so that when we speak of our conversion or our regeneration we are referring to our sharing in the conversion or regeneration of our humanity brought about by Jesus in and through himself for our sake. In a profound and proper sense, therefore, we must speak of Jesus Christ as constituting in himself the very substance of our conversion … without him all so-called repentance and conversion are empty… conversion in that truly evangelical sense is a turning away from ourselves to Christ, it calls for a conversion from our in-turned notions of conversion to one grounded and sustained in Christ Jesus himself.[163]

Several crucial points will be noticed here. First, while Johnson's view of conversion never mentioned the problem of self-will and sin (since she thinks pride and self-will apply only to those with power), Torrance begins by noting that as fallen creatures our very free will itself is our self-will and we (both women and men) cannot escape that. That means that if we attempt to know God and to know ourselves as God's creatures by relying on ourselves in any way, we are bound to fail because we are in fact at enmity with God as fallen creatures and cannot escape that by relying on ourselves. Second, Torrance claims that sin is so ingrained in our minds that we are completely incapable even of repentance. Third, Torrance further presupposes that we know all of this not from ourselves and certainly not by tapping into our own power in any sense, but from our encounter with Jesus Christ who comes to us as the one who has acted vicariously for all of us as the Judge judged in our place. All of this applies to both women and men just as Christ's saving grace applies to both women and men. In him, our minds, which are sinful and alienated from God, are healed and bent back to right relation with God. He converted us sinners back to God in a life of perfect filial obedience to God the Father. The result, Torrance claims, is that our conversion is completely bound up with Jesus Christ himself who, though he never sinned, experienced God's judgment on sin by going to the cross for us from within the sinful humanity he took from us. Fourth, Torrance insists that since Christ himself constitutes our conversion, our conversion is a turning away from ourselves toward Christ in whom we are a new creation. Insofar as we turn inward toward ourselves then, in Torrance's view, we turn away from Christ and thus away from God himself. None of this is to be understood statically but only dynamically so that even now in worship and prayer it is precisely as we are united to Christ himself as the risen, ascended, and coming Lord that we share in his new humanity in relation to God the Father and thus live in fellowship with God through faith and in hope. In that way we participate in the knowledge of God the Father through his Son and in the power of his resurrection and of the Holy Spirit.

These rather clear and stark differences between the thinking of Elizabeth Johnson and Thomas F. Torrance concerning conversion illustrate the profound implications involved in thinking through the question of which language for God is the correct language and why. When one compares the statements by Torrance with those of Johnson on the nature of conversion, perhaps the most glaring difference between them is that Johnson never even mentions Jesus Christ. So, it is not surprising that she would claim that we could know God by relying on our own experience of ourselves. From this, it might follow that one could envision God as a symbol we invest with meaning so that

---

[163]Torrance, *The Mediation of Christ*, 85–6.

we could and should change that symbol to overcome the sin of sexism. However, if one were to think about the Christian God in faith, then that faith would be tied to Jesus Christ himself at the outset as its enabling condition. Then one would realize that there is salvation in no other name, because Jesus himself is the one who came to overcome and did in fact overcome all that separates us from the love of God revealed in him.

Thus, it is not only unnecessary to rename God for women to have equality with men, since God has already overcome the sin that leads to any such inequality, and any disciple of Christ would in fact live in that freedom by supporting the full equality of men and women in the church and outside the church as well. It is also impossible to rename God since, in light of the revelation of God in Jesus Christ, we know with certainty that only the eternal Father, Son, and Holy Spirit can name himself to us in such a way that we are prevented by that very revelation from reading back preconceived notions of fatherhood and sonship into God instead of thinking from a center in God. This very same reasoning then would apply to any attempt to rename God as mother, lover, and friend or as relation from those experiences that matter most to us.

Conclusion

What I have shown in this chapter is that whenever that is attempted, there and then we are presented with a distorted picture of who God is as the eternal Father, Son, and Holy Spirit confessed in the Nicene Creed. And perhaps most importantly, whenever that is attempted, people then become unsure of how to speak about God because the certainty that comes from the revelation of God alone in his Son Jesus Christ is marginalized, ignored, or simply rejected. Unfortunately for Johnson the meaning of sin, salvation, and naming God are seen in light of her version of liberation theology which constructs the meaning of these theological categories in terms of human power and who wields that power. Since that power has been traditionally wielded by men, she reckons that sin can no longer be described as pride for women who are dominated by men and salvation must be described as women tapping into their own power to become free and to know God in new ways. However, the problem with that very approach is that it misconstrues the true meaning of sin, salvation, and who God is, precisely because from start to finish it is not even remotely informed by revelation in its identity with Jesus Christ himself.

Conclusion

CHAPTER 7
THOMAS F. TORRANCE AND DAVID BENTLEY HART IN CONVERSATION ABOUT UNIVERSALISM

Knowing that Karl Barth often has been accused of "universalism" even though he believed only in its possibility and directly rejected the idea that we could make a final determination with regard to the issue this side of the *parousia*,[1] you can imagine my surprise when I read Jürgen Moltmann's book *Sun of Righteousness, Arise! God's Future for Humanity and the Earth*, only to find him confidently and directly asserting a version of universal reconciliation. He even claimed that hell itself would be destroyed.[2] Then I turned to another book entitled *"All Shall Be Well": Explorations in Universalism and Christian Theology, from Origen to Moltmann* only to learn that various versions of belief in universal salvation now seem to be very widely held. In the introduction to that volume, we are told that Christian universalism should be located somewhere between heresy and dogma.[3] Christians do not need to adhere to it as they do to the doctrine of the Trinity or "the union of deity and humanity in the one person of Christ."[4] Rather it should be seen as a *theologoumenon*, that is, a teaching about which orthodox Christians may disagree within the bounds of orthodoxy. In this context, the author concludes that one may not preach universalism as "*the* Christian view"; nonetheless, one "*may* believe in it and one may also develop a universalist version of Christian theology."[5] At one and the same time, the author proposes that we should not claim universalism as a straightforward orthodox Christian teaching though he himself is "a convinced universalist," and therefore he thinks those who do not accept the proposition that "God

---

[1] For an excellent summary of four ancient and modern views of hell and damnation, see George Hunsinger, "Hellfire and Damnation: Four Ancient and Modern Views," *Scottish Journal of Theology* 51 (4) (2009): 406–34; reprinted in his *Disruptive Grace*, chapter ten. Hunsinger offers an insightful, accurate, and helpful understanding of Barth's view of universal redemption concluding that for Barth "although universal salvation cannot be deduced as a necessity, it cannot be excluded as a possibility" since these alternatives (logical deduction and definite exclusion) would not respect God's freedom (429). For a very interesting discussion of how the second coming (*parousia*) of Jesus shapes and should shape our view of Christian action and of the church in light of Christ's resurrection, ascension, and impending return, see Barth, CD III/2, 506–11.

[2] Jürgen Moltmann, *Sun of Righteousness, Arise!: God's Future for Humanity and the Earth*, trans. Margaret Kohl (Minneapolis: Fortress Press, 2010), 142.

[3] *"All Shall Be Well": Explorations in Universalism and Christian Theology, from Origen to Moltmann*, ed. Gregory MacDonald (Eugene, OR: Cascade Books, 2011), 4, 11.

[4] Ibid., 11.

[5] Ibid., 12.

will save everyone through Christ" are mistaken.[6] It did seem a bit odd to me that this same author went on to stress that he never taught or preached universalism "in a church context" and that if he did, he never would claim this was "the Christian teaching" while simultaneously offering the book with the intention of gaining respect for universalism as "an authentically Christian attempt at faith seeking understanding."[7]

In a more recent work, David Bentley Hart boldly insists that "if Christianity taken as a whole is indeed an entirely coherent and credible system of belief, then the universalist understanding of its message is the only one possible."[8] Does he mean by universalist simply that Christ died and rose from the dead for everyone so that there is no such thing as limited atonement? Or does he mean to affirm, with Moltmann and others, that universalism, that is, the doctrine that in the end all must necessarily be saved since God willed the salvation of all, is the only possible way to understand the Christian Gospel? While Hart does say that he believes in a hell of our creation in the sense that it refers to "the hatred within each of us that turns the love of others—of God and neighbor—into torment," and thus is a "state we impose on ourselves," he also maintains that God could not really be the ultimate "Good" if God allowed "the eternal loss of any soul to endless sorrow."[9] He thus opposes the idea of an "eternal hell" claiming that "most putative believers in an eternal hell do not really believe in it at all, but rather merely believe in their belief in it."[10] Hart then makes a rather revealing remark claiming that "the whole question of hell is one whose answer should be immediately obvious to a properly functioning moral intelligence."[11] As we will discuss in more detail later in this

---

[6]Ibid., 13.
[7]Ibid., 24.
[8]David Bentley Hart, *That All Shall Be Saved: Heaven, Hell, and Universal Salvation* (New Haven: Yale University Press, 2019), 3. In line with this thinking, Hart insists that "the question of whether a soul could freely and eternally reject God … is not even worth the trouble of asking" (ibid., 181). This, because he believes that "if God is God and spirit is spirit, and if there really is an inextinguishable rational freedom in every soul, evil itself must disappear in every intellect and will, and hell must be no more. Only then will God, both as end of history and as that eternal source and end of beings who transcends history, be all in all" (ibid., 195). Hence, "the doctrine of eternal hell is *prima facie* nonsensical" (ibid., 202). In a sense, like John Robinson, whose views Torrance rightly questioned, Hart believes an eternal hell would mean a failure on God's part to save the world from sin and death. Indeed, Hart writes, "Any rational will that does not surrender to God as the true end of desire and knowledge is a whole world from which God is absent, and so is God's defeat" (ibid., 194). The problem with this idea is twofold: first, it functions on the assumption that every human soul has an inbuilt drive toward God, understood as the Good; second, it concludes that God is absent from us when we are not truly rational by realizing that God is the transcendental horizon in which our rationality functions. As we shall see, Torrance rejects both of these ideas because he rejects natural theology and would consider any notion of an inbuilt drive toward God Pelagian in origin and outcome. Furthermore, he claims that God is not absent even from those who are in hell but loves us even in the depths of hell and he understands evil as that aspect of human free will that in fact does not choose God, the God who reconciled the world to himself in Christ, but always chooses an idol and cannot do otherwise unless the reconciling grace enacted once for all in Christ is enacted in that person's own understanding and life of obedience through the Holy Spirit. Moreover, for Torrance, it is precisely God's nearness to us in Christ that exposes our sinfulness in the first place.
[9]Ibid., 27–8, 62, and 208.
[10]Ibid., 29, 204.
[11]Ibid.

chapter, this remark certainly suggests that we can not only discern the true meaning of sin and evil but also grasp the proper meaning of hell from our "properly functioning moral intelligence." It is that very assumption that flies in the face of the thinking advocated not only by Torrance but also by Karl Barth, since both theologians rightly held that we cannot attain a proper view of sin, evil, hell, or salvation by means of our "properly functioning moral intelligence." That is because a proper view of sin, evil, hell, and salvation can only come from revelation in its identity with Jesus Christ himself. More on that later.

Torrance's Disapproval of Universalism

In relation to what has been presented so far, I must now mention that these views appear rather problematic, to say the least, in comparison with the views of Thomas F. Torrance, initially expressed in his response to John A. T. Robinson on this subject in a 1949 article in the *Scottish Journal of Theology*. In that article, Torrance roundly condemned universalism saying that "the voice of the Catholic Church … throughout all ages has consistently judged universalism a heresy for faith and a menace to the Gospel."[12] These are indeed sharp words, and it is my task in this chapter to try to explain exactly why Torrance so forcefully opposed what he called the doctrine of universalism,[13] before putting Torrance into conversation with the position advanced by David Bentley Hart. It is important to make a distinction at the outset between the doctrine of universalism and the possibility that God might save all humanity, a possibility that both Barth and Torrance affirmed even though Hart, for example, unequivocally rejects that idea as avoiding the issue entirely.[14] In typed notes of an address he was preparing on "Karl

---

[12]The Rev. T. F. Torrance, "Universalism or Election?," in the *Scottish Journal of Theology* 2 (1949): 310–18, 310.
[13]Ibid., 313. Torrance held that "at the very best universalism could only be concerned with a hope, with a possibility, and could only be expressed apocalyptically" so that if it is made into a "dogmatic statement, which is what the doctrine of universalism does," then that destroys "the possibility in the necessity."
[14]Thus, in opposition to the view of Hans Urs von Balthasar, Hart rejects the view that "Christians *may* be allowed to *dare* to hope for the salvation of all." Hart writes that he has "very small patience for this kind of 'hopeful universalism'" (*That All Shall Be Saved*, 66, also 103). This, because he thinks that anyone with such a view must already "believe that this would be the best possible ending to the Christian story" (ibid.). His conclusion is very revealing as he then claims that such a person really would have "no excuse for imagining that God could bring any but the best possible ending to pass *without thereby being in some sense a failed creator*" (ibid., emphasis mine). That line of reasoning suggests first that we can prescribe the best possible ending to the "Christian story" without actually awaiting God's own eschatological act which has not yet occurred and will not occur until Christ's second coming. Second, this reasoning fails to approach the matter with the proper "eschatological reserve" advocated by Torrance precisely by substituting our own view that God has failed as Creator because somehow human beings refused to live by grace alone. Third, this line of reasoning overtly presumes that we can know God and God's true purposes for us *from* moral reasoning instead of exclusively from God's soteriological actions within history in his Word and Spirit. Hence, Hart claims that God "is the ground and substance and end of every moral action" and that since "we have some very real knowledge of what moral action is, we know something also of who God therefore is" (ibid., 61). That claim, as we shall see in more detail later, is the nub of the difference between Hart's overt espousal of universalism and the views of Torrance and Barth, since the latter theologians would flatly reject the idea that

Barth and Universalism," Torrance opened his remarks noting that "Karl Barth believed in the universality of Christ's saving work, but did not subscribe either to universalism or to limited atonement."[15] Here we get a hint of what it is that bothered Torrance so deeply about universalism; in his mind, it is a form of rationalism that ignores the need for eschatological reserve and reads logical necessities back into the Gospel of free grace. It thereby undercuts the true meaning of election as the ground of hope and leads to ideas of both limited atonement and determinism. It also opens the door to versions of conditional salvation. The ultimate problem with this notion from Torrance's perspective can be traced to some form of Nestorian thinking with respect to Christology and to a theoretical and practical separation of the Person of Christ from his atoning work for us. In the end, those who embrace a doctrine of universalism as opposed to its possibility also have an inadequate understanding of the Trinity, as I hope to show.

The Doctrine of God

Let me begin by pointing out why I think that the problem of universalism ultimately is a problem grounded in the doctrine of God. In the article that elicited Torrance's response, John A. T. Robinson connected eschatology with the doctrine of God precisely in order to refute Emil Brunner's view that "a doctrine of universal restoration is wholly incompatible with a truly *Biblical* theology."[16] Problems immediately arise, however, because Robinson claimed that for the Bible "God's nature is to be known and studied, not as He is in Himself, but always as He reveals and vindicates Himself in relation to the purposes He has to achieve and the powers He has to conquer."[17] A comparable statement already concerned Torrance when, in his famous book *Jesus Christ and Mythology*, Rudolf Bultmann wrote that "we cannot speak of what God is in Himself but only what He is doing to us and with us."[18] In Torrance's estimation, Bultmann had confused mythological statements about God

we can know the God who is the Father of Jesus Christ via moral reasoning; at best, moral reasoning could lead to an idea of God projected from our understanding of morality. However, it is that very notion that could encourage some form of self-justification with the idea that we can rely on our own moral goodness to come to a proper view of God's goodness. This is an idea Barth and Torrance emphatically rejected because the goodness of God can only be known from that fact that God was in Christ reconciling the world to himself. As we shall shortly see, Torrance rightly insisted that it is impossible to grasp the nature of atonement "in terms of a moral or legal framework external to the incarnation" because it is precisely our morality and the law that "needs to be set right" according to Paul's doctrine of justification (Torrance, "The Atonement: The Singularity of Christ and the Finality of the Cross," 225–56, 250–1).

[15]Unpublished typescript of notes from an address dated October 31, 1994, taken from the Princeton Seminary archives, 1. For Torrance's defense of Barth against the charge of universalism or "universal salvation," see Thomas F. Torrance, *Karl Barth: Biblical and Evangelical Theologian*, 236–40.
[16]The Rev. Dr. J. A. T. Robinson, "Universalism—Is It Heretical?," *Scottish Journal of Theology* 2 (1949): 139–55, 139. See also John A. T. Robinson, *In the End, God … A Study of the Christian Doctrine of the Last Things*, ed. Robin Parry, foreword by Gregory MacDonald, intro. Trevor Hart (Eugene, OR: Cascade Books, 2011), 125.
[17]Robinson, "Universalism—Is It Heretical?, 139. Also Robinson, *In the End, God*, 125–6.
[18]Rudolf Bultmann, *Jesus Christ and Mythology* (New York: Charles Scribner's Sons, 1958), 73.

with analogical statements, and thus he rejected the idea that statements about God as Creator could be understood as objective. Since they were mythological, they had to be understood "as existential statements."[19] And to this Torrance reacted with the following question: "But if we can say nothing about God in himself or about what he does objectively, can we still give any content to his actions in relation to ourselves, and can we really say anything at all of God, even in analogical language?"[20] This excellent question becomes even more significant, if that is possible, when the results of such analysis are seen in Bultmann's view of the resurrection as "purely mythical"[21] and thus only as something that takes place in us and not objectively in the history of Jesus himself. No wonder Torrance accused Bultmann of embracing a docetic Christology and a Christology that denied Christ's true divinity.[22] In Torrance's view, such Christology resulted from an attenuated concept of God such that God is thought to be "present and active in the death of Jesus Christ in no other way than he is present and active in a fatal accident in the street."[23]

It is worth adding here that for Torrance, as for Barth, "the only valid analogy we have" for understanding God's love for us in Christ and the proper meaning of sin and salvation "is in the life and death of Jesus Christ."[24] For it is there that we know God as he is in himself and thus as he is for us. And what is it that we learn in this way? First, we discover that we cannot know God's love for us from any analysis of human love. Second, what we learn from the love of God disclosed in Jesus Christ is that it is exactly at that point where "divine love was poured out to the utmost that men in unbelievable hardening of heart rejected it to the very last."[25] Third, therefore any attempt to go behind what happened on Calvary to argue from logic for a doctrine of universalism would "make the Cross meaningless." Thus, in Torrance's view, based on his analogical reasoning grounded in the life, death, and resurrection of Christ and not in any logical necessity, "if universalism is true, is a necessity, then every road whether it had the Cross planted on it or not would lead to salvation."[26] The problem that is circumvented here concerns the fact that one simply cannot explain evil in any logical way and thus one simply cannot explain why Judas "who had the priceless privilege of enjoying to the full the love of the Son of God should not have found that love irresistible" since he finally

---

[19] Torrance, *Incarnation*, 288.
[20] Ibid.
[21] Ibid., 287.
[22] Ibid., 289. He thought Bultmann's Christology was docetic because he held that "Bultmann would say that the Son of God never assumed our flesh [sinful flesh] at all, and that it is precisely this which is the mythology" so that in his reinterpretation of the *kērygma* the *Logos* could only be interpreted in "some scientifically purified and rarified speech of the flesh" rather than in "the speech of our fallen flesh" (ibid.). Hence, for Torrance, "there can be no doubt that ultimately it is on Christological grounds like these that we have to repudiate Bultmann's position as involving a docetic Christology, as well as Socinianism (denial of the divinity of Christ)" (ibid.).
[23] See Torrance, *Theology in Reconstruction*, 277.
[24] Torrance, "Universalism or Election?," 312. See also Thomas F. Torrance, "Predestination in Christ," *Evangelical Quarterly* 13 (1941): 108–41, 127, and n. 79, 140–1.
[25] Ibid.
[26] Ibid.

betrayed that love "with a dastardly kiss."[27] Torrance's reasoning here is crucial because it displays his belief that there is no God behind the back of Jesus Christ. Hence, to know Jesus Christ in his atoning and revealing actions within history is to know God himself and God's purposes for us. This thinking is grounded in a knowledge of who God is in himself as the eternal Father, Son, and Holy Spirit.

By conceptually marginalizing the immanent Trinity in relation to the economic, Robinson himself was led to embrace a view of eternity that is more than a little doubtful because he made God's eternity dependent on what God will do in relation to history as when he wrote,

> *How* He maintains Himself as God and the *nature* of his final lordship is therefore at the same time the answer to *what* He essentially is. The truth or falsity of the universalistic assertion, that in the end He is Lord entirely of a world *wanting* His lordship, is consequently determinative of the whole Christian doctrine of the nature of God.[28]

What happens at the end of history therefore determines the nature of God. God is not who God is prior to and even without creation; God is God rather as one who is eternal in the sense that he "outstays the assault of the final enemy and yet abides."[29] By confusing God's being with his actions in history, Robinson makes God's nature dependent on what happens in history, whereas in a proper Christian doctrine of God, what happens in history at the end must be understood with what Torrance called an "eschatological reserve" because God is not determined by historical events but acts in history as one who is both loving and free. It is no accident that by thinking of God and of salvation in mythological terms Robinson reduced God to his will and thus to his purposes in history.[30] By confusing God's nature and will, Robinson was led to espouse the idea that because God wills the salvation of all, all must be saved. And, if they are not, then that is a failure of his omnipotent love. Hence, because God is both loving and omnipotent Robinson argued that if God's love "cannot draw out men's wills to free response, then it has no other resource: it is finished."[31]

This is exactly what Torrance found objectionable, since it introduces a logical necessity into the picture where God's free actions of love should be recognized, by

---

[27]Ibid.

[28]Robinson, "Universalism—Is It Heretical?," 139–40; and Robinson, *In the End, God*, 126.

[29]Robinson, "Universalism—Is It Heretical?, 139.

[30]For Robinson's understanding of myth, see *In the End, God*, 26–8, 55–63, 83–92. Since myth for Robinson is "not free speculation" but "a picture designed to bring out the true depths of the present awareness" (56), his very understanding suffers from the same existentializing difficulty that Torrance objected to in Bultmann's thinking. One can offer a mythological view of the resurrection, for example, without actually allowing the risen Lord himself to dictate the meaning of what is said; not a word about Christ's bodily resurrection determines Robinson's analysis of what bodily resurrection means for us because for him "the doctrine of bodily resurrection is not forecast but myth" (84).

[31]Robinson, "Universalism—Is It Heretical?," 147; and Robinson, *In the End, God*, 134.

attempting to get behind God's self-manifestation in Jesus Christ to construct an idea of God's love abstractly by taking "omnipotence and love as logical counters" and thus setting up the problem in a way that requires a "logical answer."[32] In that scenario, Torrance insisted that Robinson's "desired conclusion, universalism, follows easily"[33] since Robinson introduced a "logical-causal relation between the atoning death of Christ and the forgiveness of our sins" so that "if that atoning death applies to all men then logically and causally all men must of necessity be saved: but if some men actually go to hell then logically and causally the efficacy of that atoning death does not and cannot apply to them."[34]

Universal Salvation and Limited Atonement: Twin Errors

Here the twin errors of universal salvation and limited atonement arise as a result of a failure to properly acknowledge God's free love in himself and in God's acts of incarnation and atonement in the history of Jesus of Nazareth. Limited atonement, in Torrance's view, arises as a possibility only in the thought of those who introduce "a limitation of the very being of God as love." In other words, it rests upon what Torrance unambiguously called "a schizoid notion of the incarnation, *i.e.* upon a basic Nestorian heresy."[35] In his book on atonement, Torrance explained that it is vitally important that we recognize the impossibility of separating Christ's deity from his humanity or Christ from the Father. While he rejected patripassianism, he nonetheless insisted that "God the judge made himself also the one judged in our place."[36] But this means that what Torrance labeled the "hyper-Calvinist" view that "he suffered only in his humanity" and that what Christ did on the cross was efficacious "only for those whom the Father had given him"[37] will never do. Torrance unequivocally rejected this view because it keeps God in heaven and thus utterly apart from what Christ did on the cross for us. And that would have to mean that all that Christ did for us humanly was not necessarily what God did. Hence Christ's sacrifice may just be seen "as satisfaction only for the number of the elect that God has previously chosen or determined."[38]

Torrance adamantly rejected this thinking as arbitrary because it conflicts with the fact that in the incarnation God assumed our burden of guilt and judgment. Consequently, he held the view that since God stands with humanity under judgment in the incarnate

---

[32]Torrance, "Universalism or Election?," 311; and Robinson, *In the End, God*, 144.

[33]Ibid.

[34]Torrance, "The Atonement: The Singularity of Christ and the Finality of the Cross," 246.

[35]Ibid.

[36]Torrance, *Atonement*, 184.

[37]Ibid.

[38]Ibid. For more on this problematic thinking and how it stems from an improper view of God as the eternal Trinity, see Thomas F. Torrance, *Scottish Theology: From John Knox to John McLeod Campbell* (Edinburgh: T&T Clark, 1996), 131–45.

Word by becoming "himself the man judged and bearing his own judgement upon the sin of humanity," therefore, "we cannot divorce the action of Christ on the cross from the action of God."[39] In his mind, this would amount to a view of limited atonement which only becomes possible by separating Christ's divinity and humanity. In that sense such thinking is based upon "a basic Nestorian heresy."[40] Limited atonement in the end would mean that God had not uttered a *final* No against sin; Christ's substitutionary act then would have only been partial, and this would in reality detach final judgment from the cross and open the door to the idea that sinners still must face their final judgment instead of realizing that this is what Christ experienced on our behalf. Dividing God from Christ in this way would have to lead to the idea that God will still judge humanity apart from the cross and eliminate the idea that all judgment was committed to the Son.[41] This thinking originates in a type of thinking that presumes there really is a God "behind the back of Jesus Christ."[42]

Several other questionable ideas are at work here as well. First, there are the notions of irresistible grace and absolute divine causality based on a "philosophical or metaphysical conception" that must be rejected.[43] On the one hand, it must be the case that "all for whom Christ died efficaciously must necessarily be saved."[44] On the other hand, a doctrine of "absolute predestination" seems to offer a notion of causal efficacy to Christ's death that makes it applicable only to the elect; "otherwise all would be saved."[45] If, however, divine causality is conceptualized this way, then the crucial question arises as to exactly how we can "preserve the freedom and transcendence of God." Some theologians attempted to preserve God's freedom by grounding atonement in God's free will as an arbitrary act in order to avoid suggesting that atonement flows from God's nature. Others claimed that atonement does indeed flow from God's nature. But, according to Torrance, "if the nature of God is only to love some and not to love others … then the nature of God is attacked."[46]

In any case it is just such thinking that logically leads to the idea of universal salvation because "if the nature of God is absolute causality and if atonement flows out of that divine nature, then an atoning death for all means the necessary salvation of all."[47] This leads to two more problematic ideas that Torrance rightly rejected. The first one is that what God provided was only the possibility of salvation on the cross of Christ so that every person must "translate that general possibility into actuality in their own

---

[39]Torrance, *Atonement*, 185. Torrance reiterated this point frequently and never wavered from this position. See, e.g., *The Trinitarian Faith*, 185 and *Christian Doctrine of God*, 249.
[40]Torrance, *Atonement*, 185.
[41]Ibid. See also Torrance, "The Atonement the Singularity of Christ," 245.
[42]For a concise presentation of this see Torrance, *Karl Barth: Biblical and Evangelical Theologian*, 239–40.
[43]Torrance, *Atonement*, 186–7. Torrance traced the fatuous idea that "while the death of Christ was sufficient for all people it was efficient only for some" to Alexander of Hales ("The Atonement: The Singularity of Christ," 245).
[44]Torrance, *Atonement*, 186.
[45]Ibid.
[46]Ibid., 186–7.
[47]Ibid., 187.

case."[48] But that thinking opens the door to Arminianism which makes salvation contingent on people's responses of faith. That unfortunately advances the distasteful idea of conditional salvation which, in Torrance's view, ultimately teaches that "everyone is their own saviour, in so far as they have to co-operate with Christ for their salvation."[49] Regarding salvation only as a possibility, and not as a completed reality, creates uncertainty regarding our salvation and transfers the weight of salvation itself to those who are powerless to save themselves. The "hyper-Calvinists" resolved this problem by claiming that atonement was "efficacious" only for those "for whom it was intentionally undertaken, and for them alone."[50] But this was to separate the cross from God's love and ultimately to separate Christ's person from his work and thus "to destroy the atonement as well as the incarnation."[51] Not a small issue! Here Torrance claimed that both universalism and limited atonement are ideas put forward by those who have yet to bow their reason to the cross of Christ. In other words, these logical explanations of atonement are rationalistic attempts to explain Christ's atoning action that do not do justice to the mystery of salvation that actually took place on the cross and was revealed in the resurrection and ascension.

Christ's Atoning Death on the Cross

Torrance's own argument runs like this. Since we have access to God both ontologically and epistemologically only through Christ's atoning death on the cross, this must mean that what God does as God for us in the incarnation and atonement is anchored in the eternal triune being of God himself as the one who loves. So, following St. Paul (Eph. 2:13-22), when Torrance says that both Jews and Gentiles have access "by one Spirit to the Father"[52] because of Christ's atoning propitiation, he certainly does not mean that God needed a propitiating act to be placated in order to reconcile us to himself. Rather, he meant that, in that act of Jesus on the cross, God had drawn near to us and "draws us near to himself through the blood of Christ"—in other words "God acts from both sides of the barrier of enmity between us, from the side of God toward us sinners, and from our side toward himself, thereby effecting reconciliation between us."[53] But this act of God for us must mean that "Christ died for all humanity—that is a fact that cannot be undone."[54] Because the person and work of Christ are one, God

---

[48]Ibid. This is an extremely important point which is illustrated in David Bentley Hart's observation that Eleanor Stump and Alvin Plantinga "have argued that it does not lie in God's power to assure that all will be saved, for the salvation of each person is contingent on his or her free choice, and God cannot compel a free act and yet preserve it in its freedom" (*That All Shall Be Saved*, 182). That is the Arminian thinking Torrance here has rejected because it ends in a view of conditional salvation with the idea that a person's salvation is contingent on one's free choice.
[49]Torrance, *Atonement*, 187.
[50]Ibid.
[51]Ibid.
[52]Torrance, "The Atonement: The Singularity of Christ," 242.
[53]Ibid.
[54]Torrance, *Atonement*, 188.

has loved us unconditionally in the incarnation and in Christ's death on the cross and that cannot be undone. It is a fact "that God has taken the great positive decision for man."[55] For that reason, we must acknowledge that "God does not withhold himself from any one, but he gives himself to all whether they will or not—even if they will not have him."[56]

The Holy Spirit Is Mediated through Christ's Atoning Death

It was Torrance's view that the New Testament stresses that the Holy Spirit is mediated to us only through Christ's atoning death on the cross so that through the Spirit we are united to Christ in his "vicarious humanity" and we participate in his saving work. That means that it is only through Jesus himself, and thus through the Spirit uniting us to him, that we are given access "to knowledge of [God] as he is in himself as Father, Son and Holy Spirit."[57] Apart from his death on the cross and his resurrection then, we never really know God in himself in his internal relations and to that extent we do not know the love of God that was and is revealed in Jesus Christ. Indeed, apart from these events Torrance said that "we may not know God in the inner relations of his triune being, but only in the undifferentiated oneness of his unnameable being as is claimed in Judaism."[58] It is crucial to ground what Christ did on the cross in the eternal being of the Trinity. Without this, one might reasonably claim that what Jesus did on the cross was immoral because one human being cannot really stand in for another before God; Christ can do this, Torrance insisted, only because he is God himself acting both from the divine and from the human side simultaneously as our representative and savior. It is in this context that Torrance unequivocally rejected any sort of limited atonement because by conceptually limiting the range of atoning redemption to some, we also would be limiting "the range of the nature, being and love of the Father, the Son and the Holy Spirit."[59] But it is also in this context that he insisted that a doctrine of universalism destroys the possibility of universal salvation as an object of eschatological hope by transforming it into a necessity, thereby undermining the need for the free decision of faith and obscuring the seriousness of sin and evil as realities that cannot be explained logically, if at all.[60]

---

[55]Ibid.

[56]Ibid., 189. Importantly, Torrance consistently stressed, following Calvin, that "God does not love us because of what Christ has done, but it is because he *first* loved us that he came in Christ in order through atoning sacrifice in which God himself does not hold himself aloof but suffers in and with Christ to reconcile us to himself" (*Scottish Theology*, 19, 213).

[57]Torrance, "The Atonement: The Singularity of Christ," 243.

[58]Ibid.

[59]Ibid., 244.

[60]Torrance, "Universalism or Election?," 313–14; and Robinson, *In the End, God*, 147–8. See also Thomas F. Torrance, *Kingdom and Church: A Study in the Theology of the Reformation* (Eugene, OR: Wipf & Stock, 1996), 104–8 where Torrance insisted on the need to hold Predestination and Eschatology together, as Calvin did.

Universalism and Election

It is in his understanding of election or predestination that Torrance offered a proper view of God's omnipotence that avoids determinism and preserves both divine and human freedom. "Omnipotence is not causality absolutised, potence raised to the *n*th degree" because that is not the power of God that meets us in revelation.[61] As opposed to the God we might imagine in a natural theology that "causes all the mischief"[62] *with regard to predestination*, a proper view of the doctrine, which is often overlooked, sees that it primarily has to do with Christ. "Just because Christ is, therefore, the author and the instrument of election, we may not think of it in any deterministic sense."[63] Predestination, according to Torrance, "has nothing whatsoever to do with it [determinism]."[64] Rather, he insisted, it has to do with the love of God "as related to the divine aseity" and thus with God's grace. While Torrance freely admitted that Scripture tells us that some people are elected and others are apparently damned, this cannot be understood to mean that "there can be no election without damnation."[65] It cannot mean that one person is damned and the other elected "simpliciter." Such a view would introduce "the element of necessity." Nonetheless, Torrance opposed any idea of free will that might be neutral, because it is this false idea that leads people to reject belief that some actually are elect and some damned. In a manner intended to be more consistent than the Reformers, Torrance wanted to stress that the grace of God must be understood both "extensively" and "intensively."[66] It must never be understood in an impersonal way that could lead to an extreme Augustinianism where theologians could assume cause and effect when viewing one who is taken and one who is left. Torrance insisted that no such thought occurs to Paul, especially in Romans 9–11. For Paul, "Christ died for all," and "Grace extends freely to every man."[67] Because grace is grounded in the divine aseity, it must be seen as wholly grounded in itself and therefore as free in the sense that God's freedom is not bounded by any other. Torrance thus unequivocally rejected the idea that God's freedom is in any sense "bounded by ours."

Predestination (Election)

The "pre" in predestination then neither refers to a temporal nor a logical *prius*, "but simply to God Himself, the Eternal."[68] Predestination could only be falsely interpreted in terms of cause and effect if our understanding of it became a projection of our view

---

[61]Torrance, "Predestination in Christ," 114.
[62]Ibid.
[63]Ibid., 109.
[64]Ibid., 115.
[65]Ibid.
[66]Ibid.
[67]Ibid.
[68]Ibid., 116.

from within time, that is, from within our fallen world. Yet, for Torrance, the "pre" in predestination is "the most vigorous protest against" such a view available in Christian theology. Election, Torrance insisted, must be seen to be an act of the "Eternal" which is "'per se' or 'a se.'" That means it is grounded "in the personal relations of the Trinity. Just because we know God to be Father, Son and Holy Spirit, we know the Will of God to be supremely Personal—and it is to that Will that predestination tells us our salvation is to be referred."[69] But this is possible only if God himself has come among us and made himself personally known, as he did in the incarnation, so that in Jesus Christ "the act of predestination is seen to be the act of creative Grace in the communion of the Holy Spirit."[70] Because election is God's sovereign act of grace, his omnipotence can never be conceived as an arbitrary act, a necessity or some "immanent force acting under the compulsion of some *prius* or unknown law within His being. A doctrine of election that involves the element of necessity at the human end cannot escape asserting the element of necessity at the divine end."[71] Because election means that God acts personally from the divine side and from the human side to overcome our bondage to sin, this view of the matter utterly negates equating predestination with determinism. For Torrance, "the divine freedom is independent, 'a se' freedom; the freedom of the Creator as distinguished from the freedom of the creature"[72] and as such is an act of love. God has chosen us because he loves us. But he simply loves us because he loves us. There is a danger in this. To give any other reason for God's love than his love itself, even if that reason is grounded in some divine *prius* that is thought to precede grace, or in human experience itself, is "to deny love, to disrupt the Christian apprehension of God and to condemn the world to chaos!"[73]

Because God's omnipotent love is his electing love, it is true before we know it to be true. Consequently, "we are not free to make it true—we can only acknowledge its truth in obedience, or of course deny it by our disobedience."[74] Those who know they are chosen by God will never claim that they chose God of themselves. They will always recognize that their choices can add nothing to the fact that God has already chosen us in Christ. This was a crucial insight for Torrance with wide-ranging effect. Because election is grace as just described, the love of God cannot be known by exploring human love. Rather, this decision of God for us is "absolutely decisive."[75] And this means that it literally cannot be understood in terms of anything else. Its character does not come from us but from God alone. If its meaning came from us in any sense at all, then it could be understood as "an event in a series, a worldly event, part of the causal continuum."[76]

[69] Ibid.
[70] Ibid.
[71] Ibid., 117.
[72] Ibid.
[73] Ibid.
[74] Ibid.
[75] Ibid., 118.
[76] Ibid.

Yet, Torrance insightfully noted that this very idea that we have some choice with regard to our salvation is precisely the idea that opens the door to determinism.

In electing us in Christ, God does something new, new even for himself. This has become a somewhat controversial point today. But it was crucial for Torrance because with this idea he could stress that God was always Father and always Son but not always Creator and not always incarnate, thus avoiding projecting necessities back into the immanent Trinity. Like Karl Barth, Torrance wanted to think in terms of *wholes* with subsidiary relations to parts in their essential relations to wholes and therefore "never of wholes as the sum of their parts."[77] In this way, he could say at one and the same time that these new acts are new even for God and "yet they are indivisibly one with what he eternally is and does."[78] Hence, as new actions even for God, creation and incarnation imply "staggeringly, that even in the life of God there is change: God was not eternally Creator … Nor was God eternally incarnate, for in Jesus Christ he became what he never was eternally, a creature, without of course ceasing to be the eternal God."[79] Yet precisely as these new actions, they belong to "the dynamic wholeness of God's perfect work"[80] and as such God can be understood to bring about new actions and yet remains "what he ever was and is and ever will be, in his eternal being and activity." This does not detract from what is really new, and so, with Barth, Torrance could speak of "the history of God"[81] in a way similar to the way he could speak of God's time and our time.[82]

Free Will and Sin

In reality, deterministic thinking is based on a false idea of free will. Torrance often characterized our free will as our self-will just because he took sin seriously claiming that in the history of human thought the ambiguous concept of free will "is the correlative of determinism."[83] Freedom, Torrance contended, must not be seen as something that is neutral. That is a "pure figment" and the cause of a good deal of mischief with regard to this and other doctrines. The "question is Freedom for what?"[84]

---

[77]See the Torrance typescript on "Barth and Universalism," 1. Thus he could say that "the Trinity is a whole with differentiations such that while remaining distinct each Person is *whole God*, while *whole God* is *three distinct Persons*" (1).

[78]Ibid., 2.

[79]Torrance, *The Ground and Grammar of Theology*, 66.

[80]Torrance typescript on "Barth and Universalism," 2.

[81]Ibid. See also Torrance, *Christian Doctrine of God*, 242.

[82]For how Torrance understood God's time and ours, see Molnar, *Thomas F. Torrance: Theologian of the Trinity*, 253–9. See also Thomas F. Torrance, *Preaching Christ Today: The Gospel and Scientific Thinking* (Grand Rapids, MI: Eerdmans, 1994), 69–71, where he speaks of a "before" and "after" in God's life because in some sense, without being limited as we are, God's uncreated life is marked by time inasmuch as for God there is a before and after creation and incarnation. Cf. also Torrance, *Christian Doctrine of God*, 241–2; and Thomas F. Torrance, *The Apocalypse Today: Sermons on Revelation* (London: James Clarke, 1960), 162–7.

[83]Torrance, "Predestination in Christ," 120. See also Thomas F. Torrance, *A Passion for Christ: The Vision that Ignites Ministry*, ed. Gerrit Dawson and Jock Stein (Edinburgh: Handsel Press, 1999), 30–2.

[84]Torrance, "Predestination in Christ," 120.

Torrance certainly admitted, with Luther, that we have freedom with respect to things in this world, even though that is "impaired." But we have none in relation to God and thus with regard to our salvation. While we may direct ourselves toward God, even that will be empty unless God himself wills to give himself to us. Strictly speaking, in Luther's view, "only God has free-will,"[85] for "He alone 'doth (as the Psalm sings) what He will in Heaven and earth.' "[86] Because of sin, however, when we do direct ourselves toward God we are met by the criticism of the divine judgment because our wills are neither neutral nor objectless but wills that have only ourselves for an object! In other words, "the will of the sinner is free, but it is determined by a usurped freedom which is itself sin."[87]

Here, in a deeper way, we may see why Torrance was so opposed to universalism. Its thinking actually becomes possible only where there is a "shallow view of sin."[88] Torrance had no shallow view of sin because he understood sin in light of the revelation of God in Jesus Christ. Thus, he claimed that because sin takes place *before* God there are two sides to it. First, there is "the holy resistance of God to sin" which must take place since if God did not resist evil "there would be no distinction between good and evil," and that would have to mean that "God's nature was such that He did not care whether a man committed murder, for example, or not."[89] Second, there is God's wrath which we experience as guilt. God's wrath refers to the fact that God does indeed resist and oppose our sin; and sin is real to God—so real, Torrance said, "that it meant the Cross."[90] It is real in the sense that it does not just refer to something that is defective in creation but to an opposition to God and to God's opposition to this rebellion in such a way that we have no freedom whatsoever to overcome this situation. In Torrance's words, "Sin is utter separation from God, alienation from God."[91] It really is rebellion against God in the sense that we utterly depend on God—"The creature requires relation to the creator in order to be a creature."[92] But that relation is given in the Spirit of God and requires his Spirit; thus sin, seen in light of the biblical witness, presupposes our unity with God given in the Spirit and actualized by the Spirit in the community at Pentecost.

We are literally in bondage to sin. This cannot be described in terms of a metaphysical distance between creatures and God the Creator. Rather, our distance from God is due "precisely to the nearness of God" to us and thus to "the antagonism between God's holy will of love and our sin." This is why "the nearer God comes, the more intense the conflict and we are forced to cry, 'Depart from me, for I am a sinful man, O Lord.' "[93]

---

[85]Ibid.
[86]Ibid., 136, n. 45. Torrance here is quoting from Luther.
[87]Ibid., 121.
[88]Ibid., 122.
[89]Ibid.
[90]Ibid.
[91]Torrance, *Incarnation*, 247.
[92]Ibid.
[93]Ibid.

Because of this, any attempt by us to extricate ourselves from sin will only alienate us from God all the more. Sin is both objective and subjective and means something to God and to us; and we have no ability to control it. Into this picture Torrance inserted the fact that in spite of all this, God judges our sin by taking our place and experiencing hell and damnation for us on the cross of Christ. He justifies the ungodly apart from the law so as to fulfill the law. This is why Torrance characterized the wrath of God as the *"wrath of the lamb"* which is "the wrath of redeeming love."[94] God's wrath then is part of God's atoning act in the person of the mediator in that it brings about the new creation. "It is the rejection of evil, of our evil by the very love that God himself eternally is."[95]

Besides that, Torrance insisted that the Bible nowhere offers a view of sin independent of God's grace and love. Nowhere is there a presentation of sin in an abstract or independent way in order then to show "over against that background the grace and love of God in redemption."[96] We must never forget, Torrance insisted, that the cross has a light and a dark side; the former refers to the resurrection and our affirmation in Christ and the latter refers to our inhumanity. This is why Torrance claimed that the more Jesus went about his ministry, the more he uncovered the depth of evil in the human heart that finally led to the cross and that needed to be overcome and was in fact overcome in the person of the Mediator.[97] The cross was God's supreme judgment on humanity, and it was "pronounced by mankind themselves in this dastardly act of crucifixion, as well as pronounced by God who submits to man's outrage and bears it all in his love."[98] Things are so bad that the only salvation there can be is that which is grounded in the Son's crucifixion for us. Here is our judgment:

> Mankind is so bad that it rose up, spat in the very face of God and slew him on a tree. None of us can dissociate ourselves from that, from those Jews and Gentiles, the representatives of church and state, and the crowd of the common people, who crucified Jesus—to do that would involve us, if possible, in even greater sin by sheer hypocrisy. If Christ came today we would still crucify him, only no doubt with a greater refinement of cruelty than even the Romans were able to think of.[99]

Sin is so utterly destructive to us that it is a "form of suicide," a rebellion against the "innermost relation that constitutes their very being as a creature, as human being. Sin is therefore an 'impossible possibility,' as the medieval schoolmen sometimes called it."[100]

---

[94]Ibid., 249.
[95]Ibid., 250.
[96]Ibid., 245.
[97]See, e.g., ibid., 150–6, 246–56, and 323.
[98]Ibid., 246.
[99]Ibid.
[100]Ibid., 247–8.

Law and Sin

Perhaps one can understand the depth of Torrance's argument here by exploring briefly how he understood the law and sin. Following St. Paul and the thought of Kierkegaard, Torrance argued for what he called the "teleological suspension of ethics"[101] or the "soteriological suspension of ethics"[102] whereby we understand our justification as a miraculous act of God because it refers to God's act of righteousness that forgives our sin and thus justifies sinners. This is an act that literally cannot be understood from within the moral law as it now stands or as a legal transaction, because from the point of view of morality and the law "forgiveness is impossible—it is legally speaking immoral or amoral."[103] Forgiveness as justification thus cannot be understood "from any ground in the moral order as such" but "only can be acknowledged and believed as a real event that has in the amazing grace of God actually overtaken us. It is a *fait accompli.*"[104] This does not mean that the law is put aside any more than God's judgment is put aside. What it means is that Christ brought about our regeneration from within his own personal activity from the divine and the human side so that he lived "an altogether new way of life for us resulting from our being translated out of the bondage of law into the freedom of the children of God."[105]

Torrance maintained that the will of God is not manifest in abstract terms of ethics or law or even goodness but only in love, that is, in God's holy love which brings about peace between us and God. As sinners we use the law to "escape from God's judgement, in order to escape from God."[106] We use the moral law, "seizing the ethical imperative of God, making it an independent authority which is identified with human higher nature" and thus escape God by "deifying humanity—'you will be like God.' "[107] Human moral awareness in other words "tends to sever its connection with God" becoming "autonomous or semi-autonomous" so that our relations with God cease to be direct and become indirect, taking place through the ethical imperative, "by inference from it."[108] People thus attempt to relate themselves to God "through the medium of the universal" by means of "duty to their neighbour" instead of to God in particular.[109] This

---

[101]Torrance, *Atonement*, 118.
[102]Torrance, "The Atonement: The Singularity of Christ," 252.
[103]Torrance, *Atonement*, 118.
[104]Ibid.
[105]Torrance, "The Atonement: The Singularity of Christ," 253.
[106]Torrance, *Atonement*, 112.
[107]Ibid., 112–13. Torrance here referred to Gen. 3:5.
[108]Torrance, *Atonement*, 112.
[109]Ibid. Torrance is here thinking of Kant's universal moral imperative. This is why Torrance astutely maintained that in the incarnation "we are not concerned with goodness or religion or cult; we are concerned with the fact that in Christ Jesus God creates a *new* relation between human people and himself which actually penetrates behind all the other relations and tensions of people and transforms them by God's giving himself to them. It is not just to love that we are called in Christianity, but to *this* divine kind of Love. The fact that God has drawn near means that it is this relation that must come first: everything else, second. I cannot love God through loving my neighbour. I can love my neighbour truly and only through loving God. To love God through loving my neighbour is to assert that the Incarnation is not a reality, the reality it is, that relation to God is still

is why Torrance held that sin always produces a "legal outlook." Sinners fall back upon legal observance of the law to validate their actions. But in that way, they "can yield obedience formally to the law without actually surrendering the citadel of the soul" and thus exchange the "spirit for the deadness of the letter" and "God for an ideal."[110] The cross of Christ discloses "the secret operations of the human heart in holding down the truth in unrighteousness and turning it into a lie"; hence sinners worship idols "be they of gold and silver or of ethics and moral ideals" and thus the "creature rather than the creator." God's atoning action in Christ thus is actualized as "God's truth" in the "teeth of abstract truth" or as God's righteousness "in the teeth of abstract justice" or God's personal presence in Christ "in the teeth of religion, for religion becomes the highest form of sin."[111] God does not destroy this law but fulfills it by personally loving us in the substitutionary action of Christ himself on the cross. God will not let us go even in the exercise of his wrath because God always acts toward us in love. In Christ's perfect obedience, we can see "beyond the law to God himself" so that we now can realize that insofar as the "law has become an end in itself, even relatively, a law in itself, it is suspended … as an intermediary between God and man." It is not set aside or ignored, but here we look beyond the law to God himself who personally loves us in judging us in Christ's very own death. For those who are in Christ, Torrance said, there is no condemnation.[112] In a very real sense, what has been overcome for us in Christ's atoning action is the type of dualistic view that threatens us as sinners, namely, our attempt to separate ourselves theoretically and practically from God by using the law which was given by God.

Sin must be understood here to mean that we do not just sin against love or goodness or even against others. Sin means "it is sin *against God* … As such sin is 'cursed' by God—it comes under his total ban."[113] Even though we *are* sinners because of the fall, and even though we stand under God's wrath or opposition to sin and God's curse or "banishment" to our own denial of our being in God—"into the very darkness upon which God has for ever turned his back in creation and on the cross"[114]—God has "established a new covenant founded upon and ministered by his direct, utterly gracious, and personal

---

a mediated one. To love God through my love to my neighbour is to move toward God. It does not know a movement of God toward man … Until devotion to Christ immediately is absolutely central; the true Christian relation to God is not discerned. True love to my neighbour, goodness, 'religion,' comes only by the way and are properly only by-products of this devotion to Christ" (Torrance, *The Doctrine of Jesus Christ*, 88–9). This all-important issue is at the heart of the problems discussed concerning liberation theology today as considered above in Chapter 5.

[110]Torrance, *Atonement*, 113

[111]Ibid., 114.

[112]Ibid., 117, referring to Rom. 8:1.

[113]Torrance, *Incarnation*, 250.

[114]Ibid., 251. This is the meaning of *sheol* in the Old Testament, i.e., "existence in man's self-chosen perversity and blindness. That curse lies upon all sinners as their destiny in their sin and it already casts its shadow over them … *sheol* is, however, a sort of suspended darkness, a suspended existence behind the back of God" awaiting God's final act of judgment as justification for those who cast themselves upon God's judgment and "banishment for those who choose to remain in their alienation."

dealing with sinners in which he freely grants forgiveness and life."[115] Hence, "the cross of Christ" is an "interruption of the ethical order of the fallen world" and sets "our life on the wholly new basis of grace."[116] This is why all forms of self-justification are so horrible. In those actions we pretend to be something we are not—free for God when in reality, apart from grace, our free will remains our self-will.[117] We are guilty before God in that we are inclined away from God and also because God opposes and must oppose our sin. What is revealed, however, on the cross and in the resurrection is that God will not let us go as sinners. In his amazing love, God maintains relation with us even in our resistance against God. It is into this situation that the Son of God entered "to endure the contradiction of sinners against himself, and to shatter the bond of sin and death."[118]

Torrance and the Meaning of Hell

Here God deals with our sin and our guilt, that is, with the full force of divine resistance against our sin. This is what Torrance meant by hell. Christ descended into the "black abyss" that separates us from God, namely, our self-willed independence of God and resistance to God's will for us. In his incarnate person, he bore our sin and our guilt in order to redeem us. Only Christ the mediator could and did bridge "the chasm of hell in his own incarnate person" in both his bodily suffering and "in the fearful pain and judgement which he bore on his soul."[119] Torrance insisted that God cannot and will not go back "upon the death of his dear Son, for there is perfect oneness between the Son and the Father and he accepts his sacrifice on our behalf as full satisfaction for our sin and guilt, a satisfaction which he accepts because it is offered by himself and borne by himself."[120] The cross then means that God has finally and fully rejected our sin by taking

---

[115]Torrance, *Atonement*, 117.
[116]Ibid.
[117]Torrance, *Incarnation*, 253.
[118]Ibid., 255.
[119]Ibid.
[120]Torrance, *Atonement*, 154–5. Here satisfaction means that "God has fulfilled the will of his love in taking our judgement on himself and in bearing it in our stead." Torrance's thinking here certainly was influenced by John McLeod Campbell's "deeply spiritual" view of Christ's vicarious repentance in our place and on our behalf. Hence, in his view of McLeod Campbell, Torrance explained that "when the sinner confesses his sins, all too unworthily, the Gospel tells him that *Christ has already answered for him*, and that *God in Christ has already accepted him*, so that the sinner does not rest on any repentance of his own, but on what Christ had already offered to the Father not just in his place but on his behalf" (*Scottish Theology*, 308). That is why Torrance also insisted that one could not understand justification in a merely forensic way but as a reality that took place for us in the person and work of the one mediator, Christ himself. This thinking opposed "the rationalist Calvinism of his [McCleod Campbell's] day" which conveyed a legalist and "quantitative view" of Christ's "suffering and substitution" that portrayed the Father as "punishing the Son, rather than in terms of what took place in Christ as God and Man in one incarnate Person" (ibid.). Importantly, Torrance did not believe the New Testament understood Christ's atoning death as a punishment from the Father because it was an act of the Son for us in union with the Father who himself participated "in the atoning sacrifice." Any idea that the Father simply "inflicted" judgment "externally" on the Son in our stead was "a serious lapse into Nestorian heresy" (ibid., 303). This is a view of atonement "which God in his grace freely provides in order to reconcile

it upon himself. God himself experienced his own rejection of sin in the person of Jesus Christ, and that is the positive final act of divine love. That is what free forgiveness is. It does not rest upon our worth but only upon the blood of Christ and thus upon God's "overflowing love."[121]

Hell and Universalism

What then happens to those who do finally resist God's love as manifested on the cross and in the resurrection? Was hell eliminated? Can people actually go to hell? And what does that mean? Because Torrance believed that Christ's death is the expression of God's unceasing love toward the human race, he argued that "if a sinner goes to hell, it is not because God rejected them, for God has only chosen to love them, and has only accepted them in Christ."[122] If indeed anyone does go to hell, "they go to hell, only because, inconceivably, they refuse the positive act of the divine acceptance of them, and refuse to acknowledge that God has taken their rejection of him upon himself … reprobation is the reprobation only of the man who refuses the election of grace."[123] Torrance insisted that "because of the blood of Christ there is no positive decision of God to reject anyone."[124] That statement seems only a hair's breadth away from a universalist position. But it differs from universalism because Torrance wants to stress that what was enacted on the cross and in the resurrection of Jesus was completed objectively and effectively for all; no one is excluded and yet one cannot assume that all are automatically saved because it is the Holy Spirit who actualizes reconciliation in us subjectively.[125] Hence our minds need to be healed through our acceptance of Christ's forgiving grace so that we may know God in truth and know also of our salvation in Christ. It is in our minds that we are alienated from God. And even though there are some people who "strangely and un-understandably reject Christ and bring upon themselves the final judgment of God,"[126] Torrance insisted that even though there is "objective revelation" and "objective forgiveness" as well as "objective reconciliation" and an "objective Christ," the fact is that "we may pass all these by and pass Christ by and not know it, or blind ourselves to it."[127]

---

us to himself, not one which *makes* God gracious" (ibid., 298). This, because in the Bible God's love to us in the incarnate Son is not the effect, with the atonement "as the cause—just the contrary—they [the Scriptures] represent the love of God as the cause, and the atonement as the effect. 'God so loved the world, that he gave his only begotten Son, that whosoever believeth in him, might not perish, but have everlasting life'" (ibid.).
[121]Torrance, *Atonement*, 156.
[122]Ibid., 156–7.
[123]Ibid., 157.
[124]Ibid. Interestingly, Pope John Paul II said something quite similar in his reflections on hell in a general audience on July 28, 1999: "'Eternal damnation,' therefore, is not attributed to God's initiative because in his merciful love he can only desire salvation … it is the creature who closes himself to this love" (https://www.vatican.va/content/john-paul-ii/en/audiences/1999/documents/hf_jp-ii_aud_28071999.html, 4).
[125]See Torrance, *Christian Doctrine of God*, 154; and Torrance, *Atonement*, 189–90, 326–9.
[126]Torrance, *The Doctrine of Jesus Christ*, 95.
[127]Ibid., 96.

Sin of course is not limited to our minds but affects us *in toto* ontologically so that in the depths of our minds, hearts, and being we *are* sinners as those who oppose God and who are thus opposed by God.[128] Into this "black abyss," as we have seen, Christ came to reconcile us to God. But it is that abyss which Torrance calls hell. Christ descended into the "blackness of man's alienation from God" to save us precisely by uniting us to God in his own Person and bearing our guilt by bearing it away.[129] That is what it means to be saved by grace. Apart from any work of ours and apart from any worthiness on our part, God acted as our reconciler in the divine—human person of the mediator. We are included both in his death and in his resurrection. But apart from the Spirit, we neither see that nor are able to live in that freedom that has been wrought for us.

Did Torrance think it is possible for some people to go to hell? His answer was yes. To deny this is to deny both divine and human freedom by failing to allow our understanding of God's actions for us to be the actions of one who has come, is present now in his Spirit, and is coming again to complete the redemption. Those are God's actions. Therefore, to make salvation an ontological necessity is to encroach upon God's free love. With regard to human freedom, Torrance observed that "a universalist 'must' of necessity is a constant denial that the question is open. Ultimately God's will is unendurable: the sinner *must* yield."[130] What is needed is an "eschatological reserve." So naturally Torrance would not believe, with Moltmann and Hart, that hell itself will be done away with. But is hell a place that can be described with the lay preacher in the fictitious "Church of the Quivering Brethren" where there is "endless horrifyin' torment," with people's "poor sinful bodies stretched out on hot gridirons in the nethermost fiery pit of hell, and demons" mocking them while cool jellies are waved in front of them?[131] No, because hell is not a place we can locate on MapQuest any more than heaven can be so located. Hell means godforsakenness. Speaking of Christ's cry of dereliction recorded in Mk 15:34, Torrance writes that it indicated Jesus' "descending into the hell of our darkness and godlessness. He was asking the ultimate question from the point of identification with man in his ultimate need."[132]

The Book of Revelation

In his discussion of the book of Revelation, Torrance directly addressed the issue of God's final judgment. He wrote, "The judged are described apocalyptically as those who are intoxicated with anger against God, but His judgment upon sin so long suspended

---

[128]See esp. Torrance, *Atonement*, 437–47.

[129]Torrance, *The Doctrine of Jesus Christ*, 163–4.

[130]Torrance, "Universalism or Election?," 311.

[131]Hunsinger, "Hellfire and Damnation," 407. This is taken from *Cold Comfort Farm*, a comic novel by Stella Gibbons, first published in 1932.

[132]Torrance, *Theology in Reconstruction*, 117–18. Torrance noted that these words were those of the twenty-second Psalm, which Jesus made his own.

in order to leave room and time for salvation is meted out at long last in fulness."[133] As the result, he said,

> The character of hell is given as that of ceaseless resentment before the face of the Lamb and His holy angels. That is the un-understandable tragedy of it, that in the presence of Jesus Christ come as the Lamb to bear our sin, it is possible to choose evil so finally that even in the presence of forgiveness the only reaction is sullen anger.[134]

Indeed, for Torrance, "before the love of God that will not let the sinner go, hell is the unending revolving of the soul upon its own ultimate decision against the truth."[135] Torrance adds that "there is no judgment but the judgment of one touched with the feeling of all our infirmities! There is no judgment but the judgment of the Cross, the altar of God's love bearing our sin and guilt! That judgment brings no fear to the forgiven or the redeemed, but is rather the day of vindication and justification and peace."[136] While Torrance admitted that "in some mysterious way evil ripens with the good" in history so that the more the Word of God is proclaimed "the more and more organic the forces of evil seem to become," the fact is that "all the Gospels speak of that final moment of reckoning and separation and judgment."[137] He noted that Jesus himself said that "I judge you not, but the Word that I speak unto you, that shall judge you at the last day."[138] Hence, the Word "always acts upon men whether they will or not. To those who receive it, it becomes the seed of eternal life, while to those who spurn it, it maintains its appeal; but unless it is given free course, sooner or later matters come to a head."[139] Finally, Torrance maintained that in relation to history, there would be

> the moment of harvest when at last God will utterly divide the right from the wrong, the truth from the falsehood, the wheat from the tares, when all evil and unrighteousness, all suffering and death, and all that is imperfect and corruptible shall utterly pass away, and the perfect and the holy and all that serves the love of God shall endure.[140]

In Torrance's view, the all-important point here is that, in the hypostatic union, Christ assumed our sinful and damned human existence marked by sin and death and forged a union between divine and human being demonstrating in his life of obedience that death could not control him. Jesus' resurrection indicated that death and sin were not

---

[133]Torrance, *The Apocalypse Today*, 118.
[134]Ibid., 118–19.
[135]Ibid., 119.
[136]Ibid., 120.
[137]Ibid., 120–1.
[138]Ibid., 121.
[139]Ibid.
[140]Ibid., 122.

natural to human life because the hypostatic union itself survived his descent into hell.[141] Torrance will say that in his resurrection with his perfect Amen to the Father, Jesus destroyed the power of hell. But he will also say that there is what he calls the "enigma of Judas," namely, the inexplicable refusal of God's love. Nonetheless, even those who are damned cannot escape the love of God that is active and revealed in Christ. God's love resists the sinner's attempt to isolate himself. That is why a person's being in hell is not the result of God's decision "to damn him" but "the result of his own decision to choose himself against the love of God."[142]

Here, in contrast to Augustine's view that God "consigns sinners to eternal death,"[143] Torrance maintained that hell is a consequence of our own choice of ourselves in place of God who is the only source of life and light. Yet, there is a puzzling aspect to this part of his explanation, because, as we have seen, Torrance also stressed that the wrath of God is an action that God must take in opposition to our sin, or he would cease being righteous himself. In that sense, it would seem that one would have to say that our damned existence which Christ assumed in order to save us from hell and damnation is what it is also by an act of God in response to our rebellion. But the difference in each case is this. While God does indeed vent his wrath as Torrance put it,[144] he does so by vicariously absorbing the divine resistance to sin in the incarnate Son so that it would not fall on us. Torrance of course insisted that the New Testament nowhere refers to this as punishment but rather thinks of it as God's suffering his own active opposition to sin in order to bestow himself upon us.[145] In that sense, Torrance clearly meant that Christ is the one who descended into hell for us. Yet, it is still inexplicably possible for people even to reject that, and that is the hell they inevitably may bring upon themselves.

The Latin Heresy

As is well known, T. F. Torrance consistently opposed what he called the "Latin Heresy." This heresy involved what Torrance often referred to as an epistemological and ontological dualism that led to such heresies as Arianism and Nestorianism historically and to the kinds of theology that would deny Christ's bodily resurrection from the dead as the factor that enables a serious theology of divine and human interaction even today. In this chapter, I have attempted to explain why Torrance rejected universalism and limited atonement, as forms of understanding Christ's saving work in a way that detached that work from his person as the incarnate Word. Any such logical or causal way of understanding atonement was, in Torrance's estimation, just one more example

---

[141]Torrance, *Space, Time and Resurrection*, 54.

[142]Thomas F. Torrance, *The School of Faith: The Catechisms of the Reformed Church* (Eugene, OR: Wipf and Stock, 1996), cxiv–cxv.

[143]Hunsinger, "Hellfire and Damnation," 413.

[144]Torrance, *The Doctrine of Jesus Christ*, 171.

[145]Ibid., 171–2.

of the "Latin Heresy" because it leads only to a moral explanation of our redemption instead of one that sees redemption as an act from the divine and human side that really took place for us in the person of the mediator. Such a view, Torrance held, offers only a juridical and external moral view of Christ's sacrifice on the cross and misses the fact that what Christ did on the cross could only be explained by reference to the internal relations of the Son to the Father with the result that we would then see that God himself had "come down from heaven" and was active in Jesus Christ for our sakes but not for his own sake.[146]

This implies that redemption and creation must be held together and "allowed to interpenetrate each other."[147] When reconciliation is seen as a creative and atoning act of God accomplished "in the ontological depths of human existence" marked by sin, guilt, and misery, then our regeneration and redemption will be understood to mean that in the resurrection, which belongs essentially to the essence of atonement, our human nature was raised into "union with the divine life embodied in Jesus Christ and exhibited in his resurrection from the dead."[148] Moreover, when the incarnation is not understood in some dualistic way, it then can be seen that "Jesus Christ does not mediate a reconciliation, any more than a revelation, other than what he is in himself, as though he were merely the intermediary or instrument of divine reconciliation."[149] This is the living heart of the Gospel, namely, that Jesus Christ as the Word made flesh is the "content and reality of divine reconciliation. He *is* the propitiation for our sins; he *is* our redemption; he *is* our justification."[150] What all of this means is that there is an "intrinsic oneness between Jesus Christ and God" and thus between his person and his work.[151] Any dualistic separation of these affects every doctrine, but here, where universalism is concerned, it is particularly problematic because while we know that Christ died for all without exception, and that God wills the salvation of all, we also know that God is still at work in the risen and ascended Lord and will not complete the redemption until he returns. That calls for "eschatological reserve" when approaching the question of universalism. Hence, Torrance maintained that it is a possibility but that any attempt to make it a necessity means intrusion into the mystery of God's continuing free actions of love in his Word and Spirit.[152] In Torrance's words, "the problem of universalism versus limited atonement is itself a manifestation of 'the Latin heresy' at work within Protestant and evangelical thought."[153] Having said this and having read what I have presented here,

---

[146]Torrance, "Karl Barth and the Latin Heresy," in *Karl Barth: Biblical and Evangelical Theologian*, 228–9.
[147]Ibid., 229.
[148]Ibid.
[149]Ibid., 230.
[150]Ibid.
[151]Ibid.
[152]See Torrance, "Universalism or Election?," 314. Torrance maintained that "true dogmatic procedure at this point is to suspend judgment … for here that is the most rational thing reason can do. Whether all men will *as a matter of fact* be saved or not, in the nature of the case, cannot be known."
[153]Torrance, "Karl Barth and the Latin Heresy," 239.

perhaps one can see a bit more clearly exactly why Torrance would consider a doctrine of universalism a "menace to the Gospel."

Thomas F. Torrance and David Bentley Hart in Conversation

It is important to note that both Torrance and Hart would reject any idea that hell is a creation of God and thus is a place of torment devised by God such that God "consigns sinners to eternal death." That is an extreme Augustinian view that both theologians explicitly and rightly reject. Moreover, both theologians agree that the New Testament does not envision Christ's death on the cross as a form of punishment inflicted by God on Jesus. Rather, the cross is to be understood as God's expression of love and forgiveness for the human race. Additionally, both theologians rely on the theology of St. Paul, especially in Romans 9–11, to insist that God's love extends to everyone; no one is excluded because God's grace is grounded in the divine aseity, that is in the Trinity. While there is broad agreement on these points, there is some clear disagreement on a number of other enormously important issues.

Understanding God from Revelation Rather Than from the Moral Law

Torrance, for instance, was more consistent in thinking about God only as the triune God and not abstractly. Consequently, Torrance insisted that predestination is grounded "in the personal relations of the Trinity" so that we know God's will as supremely personal as the one who has come to us in the incarnation. That means that the continuity between us and God can only be seen and understood in Christ himself as the one in whom God has overcome the discontinuity between Creator and creature brought about by sin. By contrast, Hart does not find the "continuity" for the "meaning of our words" about created reality and God's transcendent reality exclusively in the incarnate Word and thus claims that God "is transcendent moral Agency as such" while we are "moral agents as a result of privation."[154] Additionally, he holds that God "is the ground and substance and end of every moral action" and that since "we have some very real knowledge of what moral action is, we know something also of who God therefore is."[155] Further, he says God is "the Good as such" while we might "gravitate instead toward nothingness." From this he argues that God's acts of love always "terminate in perfect goodness" and that "for Christians this is *frequently* stated in trinitarian terms" and that God "is unlike finite moral agents precisely by being infinitely better than they—by being himself, that is perfect benevolence, an infinite willing and loving of the Good, revealed as such for Christians in Christ."[156] Finally, Hart argues that

---

[154]Hart, *That All Shall Be Saved*, 57.
[155]Ibid., 61.
[156]Ibid., 57–8, emphasis mine.

one principle that absolutely must be deduced from Christian metaphysical tradition, and from the logic of "classical theism" as a whole, is that it is *precisely because* God is not some finite ethical agent … because he is transcendent perfection and simplicity rather than a mutable individual of variable goodness— that one can assume that all his acts must be expressive of his nature's infinite benevolence.[157]

There is a major difference between the two theologians here.

For Torrance, it is not just for Christians that one speaks about the triune God as Father, Son, and Holy Spirit because God is none other than the one who loves and is free as Father, Son, and Spirit. Furthermore, the statement that Christians *frequently* use trinitarian terms to speak of God who is good suggests that we might have other options. That is a problem since the goodness of God is grounded in his eternal being as Father, Son, and Holy Spirit. To speak of God in any way other than as the eternal Trinity is not to speak of the Christian God at all. There is no other God who is love and that is why Torrance can insist that, as God meets us in history in his Son on the cross and in his resurrection, we have in him both God's judgment and God's grace. But, for Torrance none of that is grounded in a "metaphysical" and logical necessity, as it is for Hart. I am arguing that it is because Hart has projected that metaphysical necessity back into an abstract idea of God as moral goodness, instead of grounding it consistently, as Torrance did, in the triune God himself, that he can then insist that God cannot be who God is as absolute goodness if there is any such thing as an eternal hell.[158] It is just at that point where Hart also goes beyond the "eschatological reserve" discussed above and consistently maintains that it is morally and logically impossible to embrace any idea of an eternal hell.[159] That is the main difference between the two theologians. And it is no small issue because it clearly illustrates that it is Hart's natural theology, as blended with

---

[157]Ibid., 58.

[158]The problem here is that Hart focuses on *us* to try to explain evil, sin, salvation, and God himself and not exclusively upon God's having saved us in Christ and in him alone. Thus, Hart maintains that "we are, as it were, doomed to happiness, so long as our natures follow their healthiest impulses unhindered: we cannot *not* will the satisfaction of our beings in our true final end, a transcendent Good lying behind and beyond all the proximate ends we might be moved to pursue. There is no constraint upon the freedom of the will, coherently conceived; it is simply the consequence of possessing a nature produced by and for the transcendent Good" (*That All Shall Be Saved*, 41). Hence, for Hart, we possess an "aboriginal orientation within us toward the one transcendental Good" (ibid., 42). This is the Pelagianism Torrance recognized follows from trying to explain not only our knowledge of God from reflecting on ourselves but also the problem of evil, the meaning of grace, and who God is as well. And it is the logic embedded in Hart's approach that leads to a rationalistic view of sin and salvation and ultimately to the doctrine of universalism espoused by Hart. Torrance's view quite simply is that in all our free actions since the fall, whether good or bad, we are factually estranged from God, the triune God, and can only come to a knowledge of the truth and thus to true freedom through union with Christ who has in fact set us free to love God and neighbor. However, it is only in the cross that this truth is disclosed to us and it is only as we live by faith as part of the new creation in Christ that we grasp this and experience it. None of this can be accomplished by our attempts to rationally be in harmony with what we conceive as the transcendent Good.

[159]See above, n. 8.

his rather abstract view of revelation and grace, that is the problem here. It is exactly why he rejects what he calls "hopeful universalism" in the sense advocated by Balthasar, and he does so because he insists that "anyone who hopes for the universal reconciliation of creatures with God *must* already believe that this would be the best possible ending to the Christian story" and that any other view, such as belief in an eternal hell, would have to mean that God had acted as "a failed creator."[160]

That, however, is precisely the view presented above that is in harmony with the position of John Robinson that Torrance rightly and flatly rejected as a reading of logical necessities back into the being of God, thus ignoring the truth of God as it actually meets us in the incarnate Word himself. The fact that some might actually go to hell in the end does not mean that God's love and reconciliation have not occurred objectively and effectively for the entire human race; it means that because of the surd of evil and sin, some might actually reject that very love of God forever, for reasons that are simply inexplicable. And any claim that God could be a "failed creator" because some might finally reject his love is to adumbrate the love and freedom of the eternal Trinity itself. It is my contention here that Hart's conclusions result directly from the logic he imposes upon God from the outset, namely, that "Christians dare not *doubt* the salvation of all, and that any understanding of what God accomplished in Christ that does not include the assurance of a final *apokatastasis* in which all things created are redeemed and joined to God is ultimately entirely incoherent and unworthy of rational faith."[161] In this position, unfortunately, the objective salvation of all that has in fact occurred in the history of Jesus Christ is collapsed into a universal logical conclusion that it is incoherent and irrational to believe in anything but universal salvation. That is the thinking that does not, according to the position advanced by Torrance and presented above, respect either the freedom of grace in its identity with the Giver of grace (Christ himself) or the simple fact that, in the nature of the case, we cannot know that all will necessarily end in an *apokatastasis*, because the second coming has not yet occurred.

God has not yet acted to consummate the final redemption. Thus, it is an infringement not only upon God's freedom but also upon human freedom to impose that decision on God as a necessity grounded in an abstract view of redemption. However, such thinking by Hart necessarily follows his view that "the moral destiny of creation and the moral nature of God are absolutely inseparable."[162] If that be true, then the freedom of grace,

---

[160]Hart, *That All Shall Be Saved*, 66, emphasis mine.

[161]Ibid. It is Hart's belief that "if God is the good creator of all, he must also be the savior of all, without fail … If he is not the savior of all, the Kingdom is only a dream" (ibid., 90–1). Again, here the logic of Hart's position compels him to confuse the objective act of God to save all in Jesus Christ himself, in his life, death, and resurrection with the idea that, unless all are necessarily saved in the end, no matter how long that takes (even after death), then God himself has failed to act as the ultimate God who is "the Good as such" and as savior of the world. This thinking misses the fact that evil, as the human act which disrupts God's good creation, is not something that can be understood by analyzing human moral behavior because, whether we are morally good or bad or a combination of both, we might still, as Torrance claims "un-understandably," reject the love of God that meets us in Christ. For Hart, Christ's love ultimately cannot be rejected by anyone (ibid., 157-8). That, unfortunately, is the element of determinism that stems from an attempt to grasp election without focusing exclusively on Christ as the one in whom election is established in history and revealed to us.

[162]Hart, *That All Shall Be Saved*, 69

in which God has joined humanity to himself in the incarnation and thus uniquely and inseparably in Jesus Christ *alone*, is dissolved idealistically into an absolutely necessary moral union of God and creation. That is the error here; our union with God is assured in Christ *alone*, by grace *alone*, and therefore by faith *alone*. It is a union grounded in and maintained by the freedom of God, and thus it is not an absolute necessity which must also be imposed upon God at the end of history precisely because the love of God in Jesus Christ is and always remains even now an act of free grace which we can only apprehend as the Holy Spirit enables us to do so through union with Christ.

Predestination in Christ and Free Will

Here Torrance's subtle but profound insistence that because predestination is "the act of Salvation seen to be grounded in the eternal will of God as made known in Jesus Christ"[163] is crucial. This implies that human freedom not only is not repudiated but also is properly established because the God who meets us in Jesus Christ encounters us with our freedom of choice and decision but "in the midst of [our] sin and bondage, and it places [us] under the total claim of God."[164] However this means that "man is brought to book and for the first time made fully responsible to God when face to face with the Cross, and there he is judged. That applies to all men. But God chooses to judge men only in Christ, that is to say, He judges them supremely by His Grace—by bringing them forgiveness."[165] Yet, for Torrance, forgiveness is given "only to those that the forgiver condemns" so that it is precisely on the cross that salvation occurs since we are all in reality elected and rejected in Christ. That means that in confronting humanity in its fallen condition in Christ, "man's will is not overridden. His self-will is certainly judged and forgiven, but it is recreated and determined by love; it is directed in the only path where it can find true freedom—and in all that it is man that wills! God is not elected! Nor is it God that believes!"[166]

For these reasons, Torrance emphatically rejected the idea that free will can be understood apart from the cross as a neutral human action, because whenever human freedom is considered apart from the cross, it becomes correlative with determinism. It also opens the door to a "secret identification of all the operations of will with the all-comprehensive immanent working of Omnipotence" which he said "is to be utterly repudiated."[167] It is important to recognize here that while both Hart and Torrance do argue that human beings must find their meaning only in relation to God, Hart conceptualizes that determination of humanity for God as an intrinsic factor in human

---

[163]Torrance, "Predestination in Christ," 119.
[164]Ibid.
[165]Ibid.
[166]Ibid, 119–20.
[167]Ibid., 120. That is the view that embodies a form of Pelagianism by ascribing grace to us in our choices and supposed inherent freedom.

behavior and in human freedom itself,[168] whereas Torrance insisted that while we must direct our wills toward God, the reason for that is because "God refuses to forgo His claim over man." Moreover, when fallen human beings direct their wills toward God they are in reality "met with a negative on the part of God which really means that the human will instead of finding freedom is hardened in its self-will" because, following St. Paul and Luther's view of the bondage of human will to evil apart from grace (Jesus Christ), Torrance believed that "the Law enslaves man all the more. It is thus impossible for man to dispose of himself from the side of self-will; *it is impossible for him to appropriate redemption. He can only attempt that with a sinful will and that God must judge, else He were not Holy love.*"[169]

This is an extraordinarily critical insight because with it, Torrance maintained that we have usurped our freedom and for that reason we are "imprisoned" within ourselves. Consequently, as a creature who has "fallen from God" one must recognize that

> the very freedom which he usurped is now his very sin. That is why the Law when it comes presents the illusion: You ought, therefore you can! The "I can" provoked by the Law is itself sin—and it is impossible through this "I can" to appropriate redemption, that is to say, to appropriate it by the basic power of sin! That is why legal relation is treated by St. Paul as a sinful one.[170]

Here Torrance insisted that St. Paul's thinking is antithetical to Plato's idea, adopted by Augustine, that evil is privation of the good, because it is that very notion that leads to a "shallow view of sin" which then opens the door to "the doctrine of universalism."[171]

Torrance and Hart: Irreconcilable Conflict

Therefore, I submit that Hart's thinking is in irreconcilable conflict with Torrance's position as presented above for at least four reasons. The first is that a doctrine of universalism as opposed to belief in its possibility infringes not only on God's freedom to continue to act in history and at the end of history as the Lord who will return to judge the living and the dead. It also infringes upon human freedom, rightly understood. It will be recalled that for Torrance "a universalist 'must' of necessity is a constant denial that the question is open. Ultimately God's will is unendurable: the sinner *must* yield."[172] This of course abrogates human free choice. In connection with this first point, we will need to consider the problems of determinism, limited atonement, and conditional salvation.

---

[168]See nn. 8 and 14 above.
[169]Torrance, "Predestination in Christ," 121, emphasis mine.
[170]Ibid.
[171]Ibid., 121–2. Importantly, Hart consistently claims that "evil is a privation of an original goodness" (*That All Shall Be Saved*, 143).
[172]Torrance, "Universalism or Election?," 311.

The second, as just noted, concerns the very difficult issue of natural theology. Torrance clearly held that natural theology is the culprit in making a proper view of election and predestination understandable as the heart of the Gospel. The third issue concerns the nature of sin and salvation. This issue once again also relates to natural theology because it concerns the question of whether and to what extent one can know the true meaning of sin and evil without allowing their nature to be disclosed exclusively by God himself on the cross and in the resurrection of Jesus Christ. A fourth issue concerns whether one can read a logical necessity back into the being and activity of God without compromising divine and human freedom once again. Finally, we shall see that each theologian's view of hell is shaped by the extent to which he allows Jesus Christ himself as the incarnate Word to be his starting point and criterion for understanding the meaning not only of who God is but also of who we are in Christ and thus also the actual meaning of revelation, sin, and salvation itself. Both certainly agree that hell is not a place that can be located on any map! Both also agree that hell is of our own making. And while Hart thinks that hell itself cannot possibly exist eternally, Torrance rejects that view for eschatological reasons.

A Doctrine of Universalism versus Its Possibility/Logical Necessity

In discussing this first issue, it will be important to connect this with the fourth issue just mentioned, namely, the projection of logical necessities into God instead of allowing God in his being and actions within history to be the sole determinant of one's thinking. This of course connects with the fact that, while Hart occasionally appeals to Christology and more frequently to the Bible to advance his position, he also engages in a kind of natural theology all along the line as when he argues that God "is the ground and substance and end of every moral action. And, as we have some very real knowledge of what moral action is, we know something also of who God therefore is."[173] That is why Hart can also argue that it is unacceptable to hold that even one person could be lost to an eternal hell and that "we should probably already know all of this—not for theological reasons, but simply from a sober consideration of any truly coherent account of what it means to be a person."[174] We have already noted that Hart presents an abstract view of

---

[173]Hart, *That All Shall Be Saved*, 61.

[174]Ibid., 144. From a Christian theological standpoint, the problem here is that we really cannot know what it means to be a person apart from Christ himself, the personalizing person, because in ourselves, even in our goodness, we are at enmity with God. In other words, we have here another argument for universalism from natural theology. While Hart does base much of his view later in his book on the views of Gregory of Nyssa whose theology, he thinks, is "thoroughly universalist" (ibid., 164), the fact remains that, throughout his work, Hart builds his argument for universalism on a blending together of natural theology with his version of revelation. The point I am making in this chapter is that because he does not consistently begin and end his thinking about sin and salvation with Christ, he regularly pulls apart the incarnation and atonement and thus fails to see the crucial point that Torrance sees so clearly, namely, that our moral relations with God need to be cleansed by the blood of Christ before we can even know of our sin and the righteousness that is ours in Christ. For Torrance, Christ, as the incarnate Son, personalizes us as he enables us through the Spirit to be obedient to

God that marginalizes the fact that to think theologically in a Christian way one cannot be thinking of anyone other than the eternal Father, Son, and Holy Spirit, and one thus cannot know who God is in himself by analyzing morality. And one cannot really know what it truly means to be human in a Christian sense apart from revelation, that is, apart from Jesus Christ himself in and through whom we come to know the truth about God and about our humanity. That is why, in light of God's revelation in Jesus Christ, Torrance pointedly held that

> the moral relations between man and God that obtain in our fallen world have to do with the unbridgeable rift between what we *are* and what we *ought* to be, for no matter how much we try to be what we ought to be we can never transcend that deep rift in ourselves. It belongs to our fallen humanity and the very root of our sin that we are trapped within that rift—that is why all our free will is finally a form of self-will.[175]

From this it follows that "even what we call morally 'good' in fulfilment of what we ought to do before God, needs to be cleansed by the blood of Christ," and it must be admitted that "the very moral order itself has been compromised and distorted and needs to be put right."[176] That is indeed what happened when Christ actually took our place and was the Judge judged in our place, that is, the just dying for the unjust. From within the moral order as it presently stands, Torrance maintained "the substitutionary death of Christ would be judged morally wrong."[177] That, Torrance held, is what Paul meant when he said that "Christ subjected himself 'under the law' to redeem those that are under the law, nevertheless his act of grace in justifying us freely through redemption was 'apart from the law.'"[178]

Thus, Christ's personal atoning mediation involved what Torrance called "a soteriological suspension of ethics" in the sense that in him our moral life becomes new because in him it now "flows from grace in which external legal relation is replaced by inner filial relation to God the Father." And it is precisely this that can never be properly understood

> in the light of abstract moral or legal principle, nor in terms of the works of the law, but only in light of what Christ has actually done in penetrating into the dark depths of our twisted human existence, where moral obligations and duties conflict with one another, in doing away with the unbridgeable rift with which the moral nature of human being has been bound up since the fall.[179]

---

him and thus to be in right relation with the Father through him. See, e.g., Molnar, *Torrance: Theologian of the Trinity*, 144, 203–4, and 348–9.
[175]Torrance, "The Atonement: The Singularity of Christ," 251.
[176]Ibid., 252.
[177]Ibid.
[178]Ibid.
[179]Ibid., 252–3.

Our new life in Christ then is no longer ruled by any legalistic or moralistic relation with God such that we might claim genuine knowledge of God or of God's justice and grace from the moral law as it now stands. Such a view will always be on the wrong track by missing the fact that our new life in the Holy Spirit and thus in the freedom of the children of God which itself is grounded in Christ's "atoning triumph" over sin "is inwardly ruled by the indicatives of God's love rather than externally governed by the imperatives of the law."[180]

Torrance was not tossing aside morality or the law in this thinking, but arguing that since our new life in Christ is grounded in him and his righteousness, "the moral order in God is no longer a detached imperative bearing down abstractly and externally upon us" because it now

> takes the concrete and creative form of new righteousness that transcends the split between the is and the ought, the righteousness of our Lord's obedient Sonship in which our human relations with our Father in heaven have been healed and reconciled. We are now made through justification by grace to share in the righteousness of God in Christ. Thus we are made to live in union with him and in the communion of his Holy Spirit who sheds the love of God into our hearts, and informs our life with the very mind of Christ, the obedient Son of the Father.[181]

But this means that true knowledge of God's righteousness and goodness can only come from Christ just as true knowledge of God himself also can only come from Christ because what God is toward us in him, he is eternally in himself. This rules out all attempts to know God or God's goodness and justice *from* either the moral law or from analogies within the sphere of human experience. All proper analogies in Torrance's view must be grounded in what God has actually revealed and accomplished for us in the incarnation and in Christ's atoning mediation for us.[182]

Understanding Analogy in Faith

To put this matter even more precisely, Torrance insisted on several key points in relation to our knowledge of God. First, while Jesus himself "puts into our mouths" God's general Fatherhood in the prayer "our Father," Torrance maintained that "this is not a conception

---

[180]Ibid., 253.

[181]Ibid., 254.

[182]Torrance followed Anselm's remark that "because sin is against the infinite majesty of God, it is infinite in guilt" and argued that because of that "no explanation—which proceeds only on the principle of continuity, explaining A in terms of B, B in terms of C, etc.—can cope with sin without explaining it away. Nor do we have any analogy here which can help us out, and so sin presents to the end a surd-like quality. But in regard to election we do have an analogy—in the Person of Jesus Christ. If Grace means the personal presence of God to men, then that means concretely, Jesus Christ. Therefore it is in the relation of the deity to the humanity of Jesus Christ that we are to look for our final answer to this question" ("Predestination in Christ," 127).

of divine Fatherhood analogically built upon the basis of human fatherhood."[183] Second, since according to Eph. 3:15 "it is from God that 'every fatherhood in heaven and on earth is named'" therefore "the meaning of the word 'father' as applied to God derives wholly from God himself."[184] Third, since there is a genuine oneness in being between the eternal Father and the eternal Son within the immanent Trinity and thus quite apart from God's relations with us as Creator, Reconciler, and Redeemer, it is thus the "exclusive unbroken relation between the incarnate Son and God the Father that is absolutely normative for our knowledge of God, for it is precisely in Jesus Christ his Son that God is our Father, and so there is no way for us to come to the Father except through him."[185] Fourth, this led Torrance to assert that "God may be known as God only out of himself and according to his divine nature" so that the Father/Son relation always has priority over the Creator/creature relation. Consequently, any attempt to derive knowledge of God from creaturely experience and not from Christ himself would mean that we would be projecting our creaturely understanding back into God mythologically instead of understanding God scientifically in accordance with his own inner nature as Father, Son, and Holy Spirit.[186] Beyond this, Torrance explicitly insisted that because "evil means discontinuity, such discontinuity as the Cross revealed there was between God and man," therefore "no explanation which proceeds only on the principle of continuity" will deal adequately with sin because it will always just "explain it away."[187] Since, for Torrance, Christ himself was and is the enabling condition for our overcoming this discontinuity, Torrance also maintained that it is only in and through Christ and the Holy Spirit and in faith that we can know this.[188]

Thinking from a Center in God

This thinking clearly makes an enormous difference because for Torrance we do not know God's Fatherhood unless Jesus, the eternal Son of the Father, makes that known to us. This means that true knowledge of God must take place from a center in God provided to us in Jesus Christ himself.[189] Because there is a unique relation of knowledge

---

[183]Torrance, "The Christian Apprehension of God as Father," 131.

[184]Ibid.

[185]Ibid., 131–2.

[186]Ibid., 132–3.

[187]Torrance, "Predestination in Christ," 127.

[188]Torrance thus flatly rejected the *analogia entis* in his Christological view of this matter and insisted that "there is no fusion between the deity and the humanity of Christ in such a way that it would be possible to pass automatically from the one to the other. No one simply by being clever can see God in Jesus Christ. 'No man says Jesus is Lord, but by the Holy Ghost.' The doctrine of *analogia entis* applied to Christology inevitably means the humanisation of God ... Similarly a doctrine of *analogia entis* in Grace and election inevitably means synergism or determinism ... It is only in the God-Man that *we* can get through to God; and we only by becoming conformed to that analogy (*imago Dei!*) in faith" ("Predestination in Christ," 140–1). This, because Christ himself is the "only Anknüpfungspunkt" and thus the "only point ... where God and man come indissolubly together" (ibid.).

[189]Torrance, "The Christian Apprehension of God as Father," 133.

and love between the Father and Son in eternity (Mt. 11:27), that unique relation is really closed to us and only becomes open to us when, through the Holy Spirit, we are united to Christ through faith in knowledge and love. Therefore, all true knowledge of God cannot move from the moral law to knowledge of the Trinity. And, as just noted, for Torrance, it cannot move from human analogies of fatherly love to knowledge of the unique love of the Father of Jesus Christ either. Torrance repeatedly insisted on this point. I will just give one more brief example as it relates to revelation. Torrance rightly insisted that "the self-revelation of God as Father, Son, and Holy Spirit made exclusively through Jesus Christ is one in which content and form are inseparable."[190] Therefore, God himself is the content of his revelation, and the form of that revelation cannot be separated from Jesus himself. As a result, "'Father,' 'Son,' and 'Holy Spirit' are essential to the informational content of revelation and are not just metaphorical ways of speaking of God derived from Jewish culture; for they are rooted in and determined by what God is inherently in himself, and are thus not detachable or changeable representations or images of God."[191] For this reason, our talk about God based on revelation cannot be construed as our own freely chosen imagery grounded in our religious or moral experiences of the good. Our talk about God in faith is and must always be "grounded in the mutual and coinherent relations immanent in the eternal being of God and arising out of God's unique triadic revelation of himself through himself, as Father, Son and Holy Spirit."[192]

This thinking follows the pattern of revelation in the sense that it never reverses our knowledge of God that comes to us from God in Christ and through the Holy Spirit and thus in faith, with knowledge that comes from our own experiences, whether they be religious or not. It is, as seen in Chapter 6, what Torrance called "imageless" thinking about God or thinking that does not project theological knowledge back into God from our own experiences. Thus he opposed "analogies projected out of our own self-analysis and self-understanding onto God"[193] insisting that "the concepts of fatherhood and sonship do not derive from any analogy or inherent likeness between the creature and the Creator."[194] This is the case because in Torrance's view such concepts "are laid hold of by divine revelation and are made to point back away altogether from their creaturely and human use to their creative source in the transcendent nature of God, who is eternally Father in himself, apart from and altogether antecedent to any relation with us."[195] This means that "God uses the creaturely term for fatherhood to bring us to know him in encounter with his transcendent Fatherhood" so that as Barth himself taught, it is "because we know God's Fatherhood we afterwards understand what human fatherhood truly is. The divine truth precedes and grounds human truth."[196]

---

[190]Torrance, "The Christian Apprehension of God as Father," 140.
[191]Ibid.
[192]Ibid., 141.
[193]Ibid., 128.
[194]Ibid., 129.
[195]Ibid.
[196]Ibid., 130.

Notice how very different this approach to theology and to morality is from the views presented by David Bentley Hart. He argues, for instance, that "Christ instructs his followers to think of God on the analogy of a human father, and to feel safe in assuming that God's actions toward them will display something like—but also something far greater than—paternal love."[197] This is based on Mt. 7:9-11 and Lk. 11:11-13, where Jesus says, "If you, therefore, who are wicked, know to give good gifts to your children, how much more will your Father in the heavens give good things to those who ask him."[198] From this perspective, Hart then says that Eph. 3:14-15 "identifies God's as a universal fatherhood, extending to all the children of the heavens and the earth"[199] and concludes from this that "a father who punishes his child for any purpose other than that child's correction and moral improvement, and who even then fails to do so only reluctantly, is a poor father."[200] On this basis, Hart then insists that any belief in an eternal hell is at variance with this view of "punishment." He makes this argument more than once in the book.[201] But the key point here is that his argument really is unscriptural for all his insistence that he is reading scripture properly. The important point to be made is this: Hart's objection to the idea of an eternal hell stems from his view of morality and his

---

[197]Hart, *That All Shall Be Saved*, 53.

[198]Ibid.

[199]Ibid., 53-4.

[200]Ibid.

[201]Hart asserts that "the very notion of punishment that is not intended ultimately to be remedial is morally dubious" and that in light of the fact that "no rejection of God on the part of a rational soul is possible apart from some quantum of ignorance and misapprehension and personal damage, we would certainly expect divine justice to express itself in a punishment that is properly educative, and therefore conducive of moral reform" (Hart, *That All Shall Be Saved*, 44). In his abstract view of justice, there could be no eternal damnation because "no one could really ... fulfill the requirements of a justice that eventuates in eternal damnation, because no one could actually achieve perfect culpability" (ibid., 45). Of course, the problem with this viewpoint is that it bases its idea of eternal damnation casuistically on whether and to what extent one can sufficiently identify culpability in what we do, instead of acknowledging that, even in our goodness, we *are* sinners because our very free will is our self-will since the fall, as outlined above. Furthermore, this viewpoint fails to deal with the fact that at the final judgment the time for reform will be over! That is what final judgment means. Hart simply ignores or thinks away biblical texts that conflict with his universalist assumptions. I will just mention the following here. First, Jesus describes the kingdom of heaven as follows: "the kingdom of heaven is like a net thrown into the sea, which collects fish of every kind. When it is full they haul it ashore and sit down to put what is good into buckets. What is bad they throw away. Thus it will be at the end of the age. The angels will go out and separate the wicked from the righteous and throw them into the fiery furnace, where there will be wailing and grinding of teeth" (Mt. 14:47-50). Second, while Hart admittedly could not make much of the book of Revelation, there is more than one reference there to the "second death" (Rev. 2:11), that is, to eternal death where it says that "as for cowards, the unfaithful, the depraved, murderers, the unchaste, sorcerers, idol-worshipers, and deceivers of every sort, their lot is in the burning pool of fire and sulfur, which is the second death" (Rev. 21:8). And there is a reference to the fact that the devil, in whom there is no truth since he is the father of lies according to Jn 8:44, will be "thrown into the pool of fire and sulfur, where the beast and the false prophet were. There they will be tormented day and night forever and ever" (Rev. 20:10). Nonetheless, and this is immensely important, given what was presented above as Torrance's view, we *may* hope for universal salvation, because we know in faith, that final judgment cannot be detached from the judgment and grace enacted on the cross of Christ and disclosed in his resurrection from the dead; we know that if Christ is not divided from God conceptually and actually, then we ought not to entertain the idea that God will judge humanity apart from the cross.

understanding of human fatherly love as correction aimed toward moral improvement. It is not exclusively and consistently grounded in the unique love of God the Father disclosed in and by Jesus himself who is one in being with the Father and with us by virtue of the incarnation. But, most importantly, given Torrance's position as just presented, it does not allow Christ's personal atoning mediation between us and the Father to dictate his view of sin and salvation. That view for Hart is in large measure shaped by his view of what is morally acceptable and by what he considers to be logically necessary. This is what leads to several of his key positions throughout his book.

While for Torrance, Christ himself must be both the starting point and norm not only for understanding who God is but also for understanding revelation, faith, sin, and salvation, Hart says that "one need not, incidentally, presume any aspect of Christian doctrine in order to grasp the logical issues involved" in understanding the proper meaning of freedom.[202] He does not stop there but goes on to explain, rightly, that true human freedom means "union with God." However, since he also thinks that what it means to be truly human and truly free can be understood just by analyzing the human experience of knowing of God as the ultimate Good, his thinking is quite at variance with Torrance's. He says that a Christian view of freedom "requires belief not only in the reality of created natures, which must flourish to be free, but also in the transcendent Good toward which rational natures are *necessarily* oriented. To be fully free is to be joined to that end for which our natures were originally framed, and for which, in the *deepest reaches of our souls we ceaselessly yearn.*"[203]

From Torrance's perspective, which focuses first and foremost on the cross and resurrection of Christ as the revelation of who God is and who we are, such thinking would be unequivocally rejected because what we learn from the cross is that humanity is evil in the "deepest reaches of our souls." Therefore, we are not "necessarily" oriented toward God since, as we have already seen, we have lost our continuity with God because of Adam's sin.[204] That is precisely why, in the persons of both Jews and Gentiles, humanity directly rejected God and God's love for us by rejecting Christ himself. That is the crucial point about keeping one's focus on Christ as the revelation of God in history. When that occurs, one cannot simply equate knowledge of the "Good" with knowledge of the Christian God without ignoring the real problem of evil in light of the actual solution of that problem in Christ's own life of atonement for us. The very idea that we could rely in any sense on ourselves is exactly the Pelagianism Torrance would reject. Thus, Torrance

---

[202]Hart, *That All Shall Be Saved*, 172.

[203]Ibid., 172–3, emphasis mine.

[204]For a discussion of this issue, see Chapter 4 above, 138, 153–7. Torrance held that the mistake of the Schoolmen's version of medieval philosophy "posited a doctrine of continuity in the human consciousness of God," and that meant that they failed to take the "doctrine of original sin" seriously. And the reason he gave for this mistake was that they adopted "the Platonic conception of evil as essentially negation of the good" (Torrance, "Faith and Philosophy," 237–46, 238). There can be little doubt that it is that notion of evil that Hart adopts in his book. Torrance's point was that there is a radical discontinuity between creatures and God as a result of original sin and that could only be overcome by God himself in and through the incarnation and atonement actualized in Jesus' own life, death, and resurrection.

would insist that we are truly free when we live as part of the new creation in and from Christ himself who alone can set us free and who does so through the power of his resurrection and the actions of the Holy Spirit.

He would never say then, as Hart does, that we are truly free "only when we have chosen well. And to choose well we must ever more clearly see the 'sun of the Good' (to employ the lovely Platonic metaphor), and to see more clearly we must continue to choose well."[205] In light of what was said above, this thinking is, from Torrance's perspective, an argument for conditional salvation—we are saved and united to God when we choose well. No. This thinking may be in line with the idea advanced by Hart that "there may be within each of us (indeed, there surely is) that divine light or spark of *nous* or spirit or *Atman* that is the abiding presence of God in us."[206] But this is to detach grace from Christ the Giver of grace and ascribe it to our own innate experiences. That ignores the problem of sin which is that we have lost that connection with God and can find it only through union with Christ and not within ourselves. Clearly, while for Hart, as already mentioned, evil is privation of the good,[207] for Torrance, sin as well as evil refer to our loss of the freedom that comes only through our justification by grace through faith. Sin, as original sin, meant for Torrance that all our acts of free will, even the good ones morally speaking, are acts of self-will and as such express our enmity with God which was in fact overcome in Christ and thus can be lived now only through union with Christ.

Human Freedom and Sin Reassessed

This thinking directly relates to Hart's understanding of freedom. His model of freedom does not begin and end with the freedom we have from Christ alone who has freed us from our self-will to obey him and thus to love God and neighbor. Hart argues instead that it is

impossible to speak of freedom in any meaningful sense at all unless one begins from the assumption that, for a rational spirit, to see the good and know it truly is to desire it insatiably and to obey it unconditionally, while not to desire it is not to have known it truly, and so never to have been free to choose it.[208]

When one compares this thinking to Torrance's view of freedom, one can see a world of difference.

For Torrance, we know that our free will is our self-will and we have no way of escaping this, no matter how rational we may be. So, we may indeed seek God, but unless

[205]Hart, *That All Shall Be Saved*, 173.
[206]Ibid., 155.
[207]Ibid., 175. Thus "the ontological status of evil must be a pure 'privation of the good.'"
[208]Ibid., 79–80.

God opens us to himself, we cannot in fact know God truly. Hart claims that scripture supports his view by citing Jn 8:32: "And you will know the truth and the truth will make you free."[209] But, unlike Torrance, he employs it quite differently. For Torrance, Jesus *is* the Truth, as he is the Way and the Life. And that means that there really is no way to the truth of who God is or who we are in him, except through him. Furthermore, while Hart is formally correct to say that freedom and truth are one and thus not to know the truth is to be enslaved, he mistakenly thinks of truth according to his view of rationality instead of consistently holding freedom and truth together in their identity with the person and work of Christ. And while he is also correct to point out that everyone who commits a sin is "a slave to sin," he nonetheless overlooks the fact that in John's Gospel the chief sin under discussion in John 8 is indeed the self-will of those who refuse to acknowledge Jesus as the Truth who alone can set them free from that self-will which led Jesus to claim that those who opposed him were in fact being faithful to their father, the devil, that is, the father of lies. In other words, really to know the truth in this context is to think with the mind of Christ. What difference does this make with respect of one's understanding of sin?

Let us explore this for a moment. Torrance claimed that since sin takes place *before* God, it therefore has two sides to it. The first, as noted above, is God's "holy resistance" to sin. The second is God's "wrath," which is another way of stating God's opposition to our sin. And Torrance held that because God really is good and because there is thus a distinction between good and evil, consequently God cares about whether or not someone commits a murder. Indeed, sin is so real that it "meant the Cross." Notice that for Torrance the essence of sin could be seen in the fact that sin meant the rejection of God's truth as it was in fact incarnate in Jesus himself. That meant a rejection of true freedom which can only be obedience to Christ as the one who sets us free to love God and neighbor. Thus, for Torrance sin always meant opposition to God and could not be understood from within the moral law, which itself needs to be understood from the grace of reconciliation to avoid moralism and legalism when discussing this matter.[210] Important implications follow from this thinking. First, Torrance followed St. Paul to argue that, in light of Christ, there must be a soteriological suspension of ethics in the

---

[209]Ibid., 80.

[210]An especially clear statement of this is made by Torrance in connection with his critique of the *Westminster Confession of Faith* for making room for "a moralistic notion of sin and the 'total depravity' of human nature which has often been considered rather pessimistic" (*Scottish Theology*, 142). He then said, "When seen from the perspective of the *saving grace* of God in the Incarnation, atoning death and resurrection of Christ, sin is exposed in its ultimate nature as sin against God. When understood from the substitutionary death of Christ, a person's being is seen to come under the *total* judgment of Christ. Sin is then regarded in a much more radical way than in the Westminster Theology, but it yields a doctrine of sin which is formulated as a corollary of grace alone, not as a lapse from original righteousness permitted by God 'who was pleased, according to his wise and holy will, to permit, having purposed to order it to his own glory.' If Christ died for us, not in a partial but in a total way, such that the whole of our being comes under the judgment of the Cross, our good as well as our evil, then it is in that light that a proper understanding of what the Confession calls 'total depravity' is to be understood, not on moralistic grounds" (ibid., 142–3). Torrance's view here also opposes a legalistic view of justification as already noted.

sense that we can use the law (the ten commandments) and the moral law to avoid surrendering to Christ as the only proper source of our freedom for God. Torrance claimed that we are not at all free to overcome this situation. Second, Torrance thus understood sin as opposition to God and rebellion against God. But Hart understands sin based on our moral behavior and freedom as determined by the amount of rationality we employ when living our lives in relation to others. While both theologians do say that we, as creatures, require our relation to God the Creator to be who we are supposed to be, Torrance insisted that this relation is given in the Spirit who unites us to Christ since the Spirit and the Word are *homoousios*. Thus, sin itself can only be understood in light of the fact that God has established that unity with us in the Spirit at Pentecost. So, for Torrance any attempt on our part to extricate ourselves from this situation will only alienate us more and more from God. Ultimately, then his point was that we really don't know the true meaning of sin unless we understand it in light of the cross of Christ and his resurrection because on the cross God judged humanity by being the Judge judged in our place. This judgment took place precisely by humanity crucifying Jesus and by God actually submitting to that "outrage" by bearing it in his love. So, the essence of sin disclosed in this way is that humanity is so bad that "it rose up, spat in the very face of God and slew him on a tree." Indeed, as noted above, "if Christ came today we would still crucify him." Sin is indeed destructive precisely as a form of rebellion against "the innermost relation that constitutes" our "very being as a creature."

Here then is the key issue. For Hart, "true freedom is contingent upon true knowledge and true sanity of mind. To the very degree that either of these is deficient, freedom is absent."[211] Notice what is missing here. There is no mention of the fact that our true freedom comes precisely from the Holy Spirit uniting us to Christ and thus to the Father in faith. Because Hart does not allow Jesus himself to define the meaning of sin and freedom in this and other contexts, he is led to a moralistic view of sin and salvation. And he is finally led to claim that if anyone finally were to end up in hell for all eternity, then that would mean in some sense that God is responsible for evil in the world. This sort of analysis utterly misses the problem of sin and its real solution. The fact that some people might reject God to the very end does not result because God wills that. It results from the fact that humanity really can oppose God's positive will for us. That is not God's failure, as Hart claims, but our human failure which God took upon himself in the incarnation to overcome. However, even that can be rejected because it is not a logical necessity that automatically shapes humanity. Indeed, the fact that it can be rejected, according to Torrance, points to the truth that sin and evil are finally inexplicable. Why would anyone reject the love of God for us in Christ? No one can explain why that might happen. But it did happen in Jesus' own lifetime and still can happen today and thus it might happen even into eternity.

Listen to how different Hart's analysis of these issues is. On the one hand, he claims that willing happiness is an "intrinsically sane" action, while willing what can make one

[211]Hart, *That All Shall Be Saved*, 177.

unhappy, "if not for some greater good—is intrinsically the result of some disorder of the mind."[212] To undergird this argument, Hart maintains that Christians must believe "that the Good is not merely a matter of personal evaluation, but an objective verity: God himself, in fact, the very ground of reality, who is not simply one truth among others, but Truth as such."[213] Hence, "the mind conformed to him is the very definition of mental sanity: a purely rational act united to its only true occasion and end."[214] In these remarks, the problem of natural theology, which Torrance claimed is the culprit in any attempt to come to a proper view of election or predestination, is fully on display. While Hart consistently presumes that he can equate "the Good" as generally understood with the God of Christian revelation, that equation is a kind of natural theology which Torrance rightly and consistently rejected.

Understanding God's Goodness and Determinism

Certainly, the Christian God *is* good. But the good as generally understood is not God. When one understands the good without explicitly recognizing and acknowledging that the truth, which is identical with God himself as the God who is good, and that this is the truth which comes to us in the person and work of Christ, then that is far from a Christian view of reality. This allows Hart to argue that sin mainly has to do with our rationality and ethical behavior when in fact sin really is our direct refusal either by way of sloth or active impulse to accept the truth of our new being as it meets us in Christ himself. So Hart argues that if "there is such a thing as eternal perdition as the result of an eternal refusal of repentance, it must also be the result of an eternal ignorance."[215] Therefore he says it would have nothing "to do with freedom at all."[216] Consequently, he rejects this possibility because he says, "Not only is an eternal free rejection of God unlikely: it is logically a vacuous idea."[217]

Final Implications for Universalism

Here the real issue involved in his position comes to the fore. He says that if one were to worry that this amounts to a kind of "metaphysical determinism of the will," then he (Hart) might not "be able to provide perfect comfort." However, since any Christian would be looking to Christ alone for that perfect comfort, Hart need not worry about that. But what really is worrisome is the fact that Hart admits that his view of this matter

---

212 Ibid., 178.
213 Ibid.
214 Ibid.
215 Ibid.
216 Ibid.
217 Ibid.

is a "kind of determinism."[218] That is extremely instructive because Torrance claimed that "universalism" as a doctrine never takes sin and evil seriously and always ends in a kind of determinism that undercuts both divine and human freedom.

It will be recalled that Torrance claimed that predestination has nothing at all to do with determinism because it really has to do with God's grace and love as God has freely acted in choosing us to be his covenant partners in Jesus Christ. So, he claimed that because predestination refers to God's actions in Christ as our God, one cannot equate the fact that some are elected and others damned with the idea that there could be no election without damnation. That kind of thinking led to false and deterministic ideas of double predestination which both theologians rightly reject. Torrance's main reason for saying this of course is that Christ himself, as our election, has already experienced God's final judgment on sin in our place! In other words, Torrance insisted "that Christ is also the full ground of election, *causa et materie*," and therefore election could not precede grace as Calvin thought.[219] This means that there is no secret plan of God which cannot be known that might be the ground of election. Since God's grace is identical with Christ himself, God's grace extends to everyone, and one cannot go behind the back of Jesus Christ to speculate on predestination. Torrance firmly asserted that any notion that one person is damned and another is elected "simpliciter" would introduce the "element of necessity."

Notice how different Hart's argument is. He claims that his version of determinism is one that occurs "only at the transcendental level, and only because rational volition must be determinate to be anything at all … Freedom is a relation to reality, which means liberty from delusion. This divine determinism toward the transcendent Good, then, is precisely what freedom is for a rational nature."[220] The problem here is that "the transcendent Good" that Hart has in mind is not consistently identified with the grace of God in its identity with Jesus Christ. That is why, on the one hand, he can insist that God would not be the ultimate good if he allowed even one person to be damned. And on the other hand, he argues that one can indeed know what it means to be truly human and truly free without actually knowing God the Father through his Son Jesus Christ who alone can enable such knowledge in the first place through the power of his Holy Spirit. Hart finally argues that "there is an original and ultimate divine determinism of the creature's intellect and will, and for just this reason there is such a thing as true freedom in the created realm. As on the cross (John 12:32), so in the whole of being: God frees souls by dragging them to himself."[221] But, his thinking is not consistently shaped by the revelation of God in Jesus Christ. He claims that "if we lived like gods above the sphere of the fixed stars, and saw all things in their eternal aspects in the light of the 'Good beyond beings,' then perhaps it would be meaningful to speak of our capacity freely to affirm or freely to reject the God who made us in any absolute sense."[222] But, since we have no such

---

[218]Ibid.
[219]Torrance, "Predestination in Christ," 109.
[220]Hart, *That All Shall Be Saved*, 178–9.
[221]Ibid., 179.
[222]Ibid., 180.

power in this life, "what little we can do may earn us some small reward or penalty; but heaven and hell, according to the received views, are absolute destinies, and we have in this life no capacity for the absolute." It is for that reason that "the question of whether a soul could freely and eternally reject God … is not even worth the trouble of asking."[223]

Then he argues that God "is … the fullness of Being and the transcendental horizon of all reality that animates every single stirring of reason and desire, the always more remote end present within every more immediate end. Insofar as we are able freely to will anything at all, therefore, it is precisely because he is *making* us to do so."[224] Indeed, Hart maintains that "inasmuch as he [God] acts upon the mind and will both as their final cause and also as the deepest source of their movements, he is already intrinsic to the very structure of reason and desire within the soul."[225] First, the claim that God makes us do what we do does not allow for the kind of thinking that sees our free actions as permission and freedom to live as God wills us to live in and from Christ as part of the new creation. Second, the claim that God acts within us as the first and final cause and thus is "already intrinsic to the very structure of reason and desire" is a rather overt confusion of divine and human activity.[226]

No wonder Hart can claim that if anyone were to be able to eternally reject God that would be evil and then would imply that God is also the author of evil! That is the problem with his attempt to combine his natural theology which sees God as first and final cause with revelation which understands God as our eternal Father through his incarnate Son in the power of the Holy Spirit. If God is understood simply as a first and final cause, then one clearly does not need faith in Jesus Christ to know who God truly is and what salvation really is. One does not need to speak of heaven and hell in light of the grace of God revealed exclusively in Jesus Christ. But then one also misses the real nature of sin and evil as well as the true meaning of salvation. In light of the cross and resurrection of Jesus, sin really is the explicit rejection of God himself to the extent that one rejects or even just ignores Jesus as the one he is. Sin means that there is in fact within creation no *continuity* between us and God that can be found within us in our moral or

---

[223]Ibid., 180–1.

[224]Ibid., 183.

[225]Ibid.

[226]This is in harmony with his peculiar belief that heaven and hell do indeed really exist but that they exist within all of us, every day (Hart, *That All Shall Be Saved*, 62). So he says, "Redemption, if there is such a thing, must consist ultimately in a conversion of the heart so complete that one comes to see heaven for what it is—and thus also comes to see, precisely where one formerly had perceived only the fires of hell, the transfiguring glory of infinite love" (ibid.). The problem here is that for Hart, on the one hand, hell refers only to our "imprisoning misery that we impose upon ourselves by rejecting the love that alone can set us free." This is a good and proper statement as far as it goes; he even acknowledges that we cannot free ourselves from this and need God's grace. On the other hand, however, he says, "We walk in hell every day" but there is "another and greater secret too: We also walk in heaven, also every day" (ibid.). The problem once again is that he misses the crucial point that redemption is not an open issue for Christians because it is an assured reality in the living Christ. Because his thinking is so focused on our experiences of hell and what he calls heaven, he here misses the fact that grace is identical with our union with Christ through the action of the Holy Spirit. Hence, heaven and hell cannot simply be explained as human experiences of alienation and possible redemption; they can only be properly understood Christologically, as I have been arguing.

religious behavior. That is what was disclosed to us on the cross. The *continuity* between us and God and thus the restoration of the image of God within history occurred for us in Jesus himself and can be lived only in and from him. It cannot be found directly within us without blurring the distinction between Creator and creature which is vital to all Christian theology.

CHAPTER 8
DO CHRISTIANS WORSHIP THE SAME GOD AS THOSE FROM OTHER ABRAHAMIC FAITHS?

In this chapter, I will argue that when Jews, Christians, and Muslims are said to worship the same God on the basis of their common monotheism, they are not able to address the pressing issue that ultimately unites and divides them. This pressing issue is not under their control, but provides the controlling factors that make possible the recognition of the truth that alone can and does unite Jews, Christians, and Muslims. I also want to argue that, while eschatology is important, this matter should not simply be postponed to the future but should be answered at least provisionally now in a way that supports the solidarity and mutual cooperation of all three Abrahamic faiths. I will construct my argument by way of a comparative analysis of the thinking of Reza Shah-Kazemi, Research Fellow, The Institute of Ismaili Studies, Alon Goshen-Gottstein, Executive Director, The Elijah Interfaith Institute, and Christoph Schwöbel, Professor of Systematic Theology, University of St. Andrews, Scotland, UK. I will employ the insights of Karl Barth and Thomas F. Torrance in addressing the subject of worship and monotheism.

Karl Barth on Religion and Revelation

There has been much discussion about whether and to what extent one should hold an exclusive, inclusive, or pluralist position with respect to the truth of religion. It has been argued that religions need other religions in order to be properly what they themselves were intended to be and that therefore no religion can realistically claim to be the true religion. Yet this very argument is in danger of giving up the truth question because in the end such a view cannot allow for the fact that any religion actually could be true. This is a difficult issue because in reality Christianity would not and cannot exist without its necessary relation with Judaism. And that relation itself is based on the fact that it is the Lord of the covenant himself who fulfilled that covenant in the history of Jesus Christ. Indeed, that covenant was fulfilled, according to St. Paul, not just for the chosen people (the Jews) but for all others as well. It is just for this reason that theologians such as Karl Barth and Thomas F. Torrance argued that, in connection with ecumenical dialogue, Christians' first responsibility is toward their fellow Jews with whom they should be united and actually are united because of who Jesus Christ was and is, but in fact are not. It has also been argued that any exclusivist position must lead one to denigrate the religion of others in order to answer the question of truth with respect to religion. Such a position in reality would be possible only if the truth of religion could be established by focusing on religion rather than revelation as the source of religious truth. What is the best way to deal with this situation today as this relates to the question of whether or not Jews, Christians, and Muslims worship the same God?

Religion and Revelation

I want to argue that this issue cannot be solved coherently or realistically by focusing on religion but only on revelation as that which makes religion true. Of course, that raises the question of exactly what revelation is and who decides which revelation is true. My position is that since revelation is the act of God alone and since it is the Jewish/Christian God who is incarnate and revealed in the history of Jesus of Nazareth, therefore, from a Christian standpoint, any claim that revelation is true must be based in God's own act of revealing himself as the God of Abraham, Isaac, and Jacob (Exod. 3:14). This means, needless to say, that there is an intrinsic connection between Jesus' claim that before Abraham was "I am" and God's revealing himself to Moses as "I am," where, according to Jn 8:53, Jesus is asked,

> "Are you greater than our father Abraham? He died, and so did the prophets. Who do you think you are?" Jesus replied, "If I glorify myself, my glory means nothing. My Father, whom you claim as your God, is the one who glorifies me." Though you do not know him, I know him. If I said I did not, I would be a liar like you, but I do know him and obey his word. Your father Abraham rejoiced at the thought of seeing my day; he saw it and was glad." "You are not yet fifty years old," they said to him, "and you have seen Abraham!" "Very truly I tell you," Jesus answered, "before Abraham was born, I am!"[1]

In this exchange, it is clear that, as a Jew, Jesus is making a monumental claim, that is, a claim that he is equal to God the Father of Abraham in that he existed and exists eternally as Son of the Father or as the Word of the Father as indicated in the opening verses of John's Gospel.

When coupled with Mt. 11:27 and its parallel Lk. 10:22, where Jesus is presented as saying that "all things have been committed to me by my Father. No one knows the Son except the Father, and no one knows the Father except the Son and those to whom the Son chooses to reveal him,"[2] it seems clear that while both sides in the discussion claim to know the one true God of Israel, the truth of their claims is presented in such a way that it is decided not by the strength of their beliefs but by the revelation of God as it meets them in Jesus himself who is presented in the New Testament as the unique revealer of their Father. No wonder Thomas F. Torrance could say that the distinction between Christians and Jews is to be seen in the fact that so many Jews refused to acknowledge

---

[1] *The New International Version* (2011) (Jn 8:53-58) (Grand Rapids, MI: Zondervan).
[2] *The New International Version* (2011) (Mt. 11:27) (Grand Rapids, MI: Zondervan).

Christ's resurrection from the dead and to move forward together with Gentiles on the basis of that particular truth of revelation. For Torrance, as for Barth,

> the resurrection of Jesus Christ in the full non-dualist sense [which does not separate the bodily from the spiritual], in which it was proclaimed by the apostles from the very start, meant that he who was of the seed of David was declared to be the Son of God with power (Rom. 1: 3f.); it meant … that God himself was directly present and personally active in the resurrection of Jesus, and that implied that he was equally present and personally active in the passion of Jesus.[3]

From this Torrance concluded:

> That Jesus the crucified, now proclaimed to be risen from the dead, should grant forgiveness of sins and judge the quick and the dead, and thus share the ultimate prerogatives of God Almighty, that he the Son of Man should be standing on the right hand of God (Acts 7: 55f.), was the great stone of stumbling, which gave such offence to recalcitrant Judaism, for it was unwilling to go forward with the Christian Church in accepting the full implication of the resurrection of Christ. This meant that the fundamental understanding of God, which had more and more assumed a fixed pattern in later Judaism, had to undergo change: far from being namelessly and transcendentally remote or detached, operating only through intermediaries, God himself must be thought of as having visited his people, to take upon himself their nature and their destiny, so that the whole doctrine of God, his relation … to all mankind, and therefore even the ancient covenant of God with Israel, had to be reconstructed in face of the crucifixion and resurrection of Jesus.[4]

---

[3]Torrance, *Space, Time and Resurrection*, 42.

[4]Torrance, *Space, Time and Resurrection*, 42–3. Compare this to Barth: "It is strange but true that confession of the one and only God and denial of Him are to be found exactly conjoined but radically separated in what appears to be the one identical statement that there is only one God. This one sentence can actually mean what it says, and it can actually not mean this, but its opposite. What distinguishes these two possibilities, raising the one to reality and invalidating the other, is the resurrection of Jesus Christ, the outpouring of the Holy Spirit and faith" (Barth, CD II/1, 454) (hereafter referred to in text). See also Torrance, *The Mediation of Christ*, 44–6. Torrance maintains that the covenant gave Israel "a unique function in history, a vicarious role to fulfil on behalf of mankind in teaching us all about the living God" so that in connection with the holocaust he could say that the only answer to their suffering "is the Cross of Jesus which tells us that God has not held himself aloof from us in our wicked, abominable inhumanity, or from its violence and sin and guilt, but has come into the midst of its unappeasable hurt and agony and shame, and taken it all upon himself in order to forgive, and redeem and heal mankind at the very point where we human beings are at our worst, thus making our sins the bond by which in atoning sacrifice we are for ever tied to God" (*The Mediation of Christ*, 44–5). Torrance believed that there are "profound lessons" which "Christians and Jews must learn together, each serving the insight of the other before the self-disclosure of God" (ibid., 39). One crucial lesson, as just described, "is that the Incarnation was the coming of God to save us in the heart of our *fallen* and *depraved* humanity, where humanity is at its wickedest in its enmity and violence against the reconciling love of God" (ibid.). In this light, Torrance insists that God has laid hold of humanity in its "incalculable crime" against Israel in the holocaust "and through Israel against God." In correspondence with this, "God in his immeasurable love has laid hold of it in order to absorb it in his own passion in the crucifixion of Jesus and make it through atoning sacrifice for sin to serve the bond of union he has for ever forged with mankind in Jesus" (ibid., 42). In this way the

Having said all of this, it should be clear that by solving this problem coherently I mean that it must be solved in a way that avoids two problematic possibilities, namely, (1) the idea that all religions basically point to the same God or (2) any claim that one's religion is true must mean that such a claimant has to denigrate other religions in order to reach that view of truth. Here I follow the thinking of Karl Barth, which as we have just seen has much in common with the views of Thomas F. Torrance, because I think his position might help us achieve a view of truth which neither denigrates other religions nor undermines the nature of truth in its identity with God in his self-revelation. His position was simply this: all religion represents our human attempt to reach God. But, since we are disclosed as sinners who need God's reconciling (forgiving) grace as it meets us in the outpouring of the Holy Spirit in the revelation of God attested in the Old and New Testaments, Barth argues that no religion is true in itself. This is, he rightly claims, an insight that can only be achieved on the basis of revelation and not by analyzing human religion, including human religious experience, which, left to itself, only represents the expression of godless human beings who need to repent and believe *before* they can speak accurately about the truth of the Christian religion in particular. It is extremely important to realize that for Barth, as well as Torrance, the Christian religion in itself and as such is just as much in need of justification and sanctification as the other two religions in question. Indeed, in Barth's view in particular, all religions are included in this judgment. But undeniably, for Barth, God's judgment or God's no to human sin always and only takes place as grace and forgiveness.

What Is the Locus of True Religion? Religion as Unbelief

What that means is that for Barth it is not the case that some people are vindicated as *opposed* to others or that one part of humanity is vindicated in relation to some other part of humanity. Rather it means that "God Himself is vindicated as opposed to and on behalf of all men and all humanity" (CD I/2, 356–7). It is thus crucial to realize two important points implied in this thinking: (1) while Barth contends that the church is "the *locus* of true religion" because, as Christ's earthly-historical form of existence between his resurrection, ascension, and return, it is in communion with Jesus Christ

---

holocaust, as drawn into God's loving embrace in the incarnation, "can be made the means of Christians and Jews being reconciled to one another in the one mission of mediating divine reconciliation to mankind" with the result that he thinks "Jews and Christians need to help each other in hitherto unthought of ways" (ibid.). From this he concludes not only that Christians who are separated from each other could never really be united or "reconciled with one another" without their fellow Jews, but also that Israel retains a central role in the mediation of God's reconciling grace "and that the Christian Church will not be able to fulfil its own mission in proclaiming that God was in Christ reconciling the world to himself, except in so far as it is incorporated with Israel in the one mission of God's love for all his creatures. That is what the fullness of the mediation of reconciliation in Jesus Christ means" (ibid., 46).

who is the Word of God, "this does not mean that the Christian religion *as such* is the fulfilled nature of human religion" (CD I/2, 298, emphasis mine). Therefore, the Christian religion cannot be understood to be "fundamentally superior to all other religions" (CD I/2, 298). Since it is the grace of revelation, namely, God's free act of binding himself to the world in his Word and Spirit which makes religion true (because he is the one who justifies and sanctifies *all humanity* according to his own free love), therefore it is only as the church lives by *grace alone* that it is the sphere of true religion.

Above all, that means to Barth that the Christian Church never has its truth in itself even when it lives by grace and faith united to its heavenly Head through the power of the Holy Spirit. Consequently, "we cannot differentiate and separate the Church from other religions on the basis of a general concept of the nature of religion" (CD I/2, 298). From this it follows that no religion can be said to be true based on some neutral, impartial concept of "perfect religion" thought to be "evolving in history" in some Hegelian sense (CD I/2, 299). Hence, all religion, including the Christian religion, Barth maintains, is "unbelief" (CD I/2, 299). How did Barth come to this position? The answer is simple, but with profound implications. For Barth religion is construed as our human behavior. But, for him, all human behavior, as noted above, is marked by the sin of unbelief, that is, the unwillingness to accept God as God truly is and as God has acted for us in establishing his covenant with Israel and fulfilling that covenant in the incarnation of his Word and the outpouring of his Holy Spirit. To put the matter bluntly, Barth believes that because Jesus Christ himself is the very Word of God who has assumed our sinful humanity into union with himself and reconciled the world to himself, therefore, we can speak relevantly about the truth of the Christian religion only on the basis of the doctrine of justification by faith. Let me develop this set of ideas briefly.

Some Implications of the Doctrine of Justification

Karl Barth consistently avoided the difficulties noted above by insisting that one can neither establish nor discern the truth of the Christian religion by analyzing it religiously, that is, as one religion among others. This, because religion, in his view, "is the one great concern, of godless man" (CD I/2, 300). This is not a value judgment, however, based on an assessment of Christianity in relation to Judaism, Islam, or any other religion. Thus, it does not "affect only other men with their religion. Above all it affects ourselves also as adherents of the Christian religion," Barth maintains (CD I/2, 300). Inasmuch as it acknowledges the divine judgment upon *all* religion, it can only "repeat the judgment of God," and thus "it does not involve any renunciation of human values, any contesting of the true and the good and beautiful which a closer inspection will reveal in almost all religions" (CD I/2, 300). Without getting into the full details of Barth's argument, which is extremely interesting to say the least, it is important to note here that for Barth the only thing that distinguishes Christianity from all the other religions is the name of Jesus Christ. And this name, he says, "stands in free creative power at the beginning of the Christian religion and its vital utterances" and therefore cannot be introduced by us or anyone else at the end of our religious reflections as a choice that might be made to enhance our understanding of religion! (CD I/2, 348).

Consequently, Barth's thinking is at once thoroughly Christological and trinitarian—not because he chose to think that way, but because for him "the Christian religion is simply the earthly-historical life of the Church and the children of God" (CD I/2, 348). Following Jn 1:14, then Barth argues that "there never was a man Jesus as such apart from the eternal reality of the Son of God" (CD I/2, 348). In other words, the human Jesus had and has no historical existence apart from the "creative act in which the eternal Son of God assumed the human possibility into His reality" (CD I/2, 348). Therefore, just as Christ's humanity had and has no reality apart from its existence in the eternal being of God the Son, so the Church has no real existence in itself apart from Christ's creative enabling its existence in union with him. Because of this, the basis of true religion is thus God's election, grace, and faithfulness demonstrated in the revelation and reconciliation of the world to himself in Christ and through his Holy Spirit. For this reason, the name of Jesus Christ and the Christian religion must, in Barth's eyes, never be reversed (CD I/2, 350). Who he is and his relevance for the truth of religion are not based on any choice of ours. These are based not on our election of God but of God's election of all humanity in Christ.[5]

Barth's thinking eliminates a huge problem. It means that if we think we have to decide who Jesus is and what his relevance is for religion, then in that very assumption we have substituted our choice for God's choice. And that once more reflects how true it is to say that all human religion is unbelief, and this always leads to idolatry. To be very direct, Barth rightly claims that the church of the eighteenth through the twentieth centuries thought it could establish the truth of the Christian religion based on its own "Christian experience and morality and universal order as such" (CD I/2, 350). To that extent it missed the fact that the truth of the Christian religion is based only on Jesus Christ himself as the grace of God who justifies and sanctifies all of humanity in himself. Hence it is only because God in Jesus Christ has justified and sanctified sinners that the Christian religion which is "absolutely unworthy to be the true religion" actually becomes the true religion as it lives from and in Christ and points *away from itself* toward him (CD I/2, 352–3). Thus, to look at our "redeemedness" to understand the truth of the Christian religion is to miss the fact that because of Christ "we are clean in our uncleanness and in all [our] unredemedness redeemed" (CD I/2, 353). By itself

---

[5]In light of these remarks, one can see how truly problematic a statement like that of Sallie McFague's really is when she writes that Jesus "is special to us as our foundational figure: he is our historical choice as the premier paradigm of God's love" (*Models of God*, 136). Thus, for her, in contrast to those like Barth, who embrace the Nicene faith, Jesus is "*paradigmatic of God the lover but is not unique. This means that Jesus is not ontologically different from other paradigmatic figures* either in our tradition or in other religious traditions [who manifest God's love]" (*Models*, 136, emphasis mine).

therefore all religion is and remains unbelief and untrue so that if the Christian religion is true, the reason for this "does not reside in facts which might point to itself or its own adherents, but in the fact which as the righteousness and the judgment of God confronts it as it does all other religions" (CD I/2, 353).

Barth's View of Monotheism: Implications for Judaism, Islam, and Christianity

Having said all of this, we can now perhaps understand better why Barth would say some of the things that he said about Judaism and Islam. For one thing, he believed that just as Christianity "is not justified in itself" and is "sinful both in form and also in its human origin," so also he believed that "it is no less so [sinful] than can be said of the story of Buddhism or of Islam" (CD I/2, 352–3). From this Barth reckoned that "a kind of monotheism is represented not only by Judaism and Islam but in some form, whether in the background or as the culminating superstructure of its pantheon or pandemonium, by almost every religion right back to the animisms of the so-called nature religions of Africa" (CD I/1, 353). As a result, he concluded that "one need not expect that the dogma and dogmatics of the Church will simply confirm *any* *monotheism* or let itself be *measured* by *any* *monotheism*. The antitrinitarian heresies arose and will continually arise on this false presupposition" (CD I/1, 354, emphases mine). Furthermore, because Barth refused to reverse religion and revelation, he also maintained that while the triune God is simple as one who is also differentiated and multiple as Father, Son, and Holy Spirit, that can never mean that the simple is God, since any such notion would be a product of idolatrous human projection and not an obedient response to the God who revealed himself in Jesus Christ (CD II/1, 449). Additionally, he claimed

> That which men can divine or construct as well as believe, that which, as an object of human divining or constructing, is as dialectical as the absolutised idea of uniqueness, may be anything we like to call it—and we certainly cannot deny that it is something—but it is not God. It is, therefore, unthinking to set Islam and Christianity side by side, as if in monotheism at least they have something in common. In reality, nothing separates them so radically as the different ways in which they appear to say the same thing—that there is only one God. (CD II/1, 449)

What is more, regarding Jewish monotheism Barth pointedly indicated that historically when Jewish monotheism had seemingly eliminated polytheism and idolatry that "it was just then, under the sway of this victorious monotheism, that Israel's Messiah was handed over by Israel to the Gentiles and nailed by them to the cross with Israel's approval" (CD II/1, 453). Regarding this monotheism Barth asks, is this "not a proof that, like the monotheism of Islam (its later caricature), it is simply the supreme example, the culmination and completion of the disobedience which from the beginning constituted the human side of the dealings of the one and only God with His chosen people?" since this very monotheism led them into disobedience with respect to the first commandment (CD II/1, 453).

This is the point I would like to focus on in this chapter. Many Jews, Christians, and Muslims think that they can unite in the love of God and their neighbors based on the idea that since all three religions are monotheistic, therefore we may say, with certain reservations and distinctions, that all three religions believe in and worship the same God. This assertion in my view is more than a little problematic because it then allows Jews, Christians, and Muslims to understand God's oneness apart from who God eternally is as Father, Son, and Spirit. It also encourages people in all three religions to redescribe who God is in ways that undermine the truth of the Christian faith and thus the truth of the Christian religion. If this issue can be addressed on the basis of the revelation of God's forgiving grace, however, then Jews, Christians, and Muslims would see themselves in solidarity with each other and no one would even dream of denigrating the other. Let us explore this issue further by explicating some specific Islamic, Jewish, and Christian perspectives.

An Islamic View

In a scholarly and very interesting discussion, Reza Shah-Kazemi addressed the question of whether or not Muslims and Christians believe in the same God and he reached conclusions that, I believe, support Barth's view of religion and revelation. Shah-Kazemi is well aware of the fact that the Christian doctrines of incarnation and the Trinity pose a problem for the view he supports, namely, that Christians and Muslims "do indeed believe in the same God, insofar as the ultimate referent of their belief is That to which the word 'God' metaphysically refers: the transcendent Absolute, ultimate Reality, the unique source of Being."[6] He believes this problem can be solved if we realize that the fundamental differences between Christianity and Islam appear only on the level of theology when each "belief system" refers to "the attributes and acts of this Reality" (Shah-Kazemi, 78). Therefore, he contends that as long as "we remain conceptually bound by the limits of theology" these differences "will remain" and argues that these theological differences can be overcome "on the higher plane of metaphysics and the deeper plane of mysticism" because neither of these "planes" is controlled "by the limitations of theology" (Shah-Kazemi, 78).

---

[6]Reza Shah-Kazemi, "Do Christians and Muslims Believe in the Same God?," in *Do We Worship the Same God?: Jews, Christians, and Muslims in Dialogue*, ed. Miroslav Volf (Grand Rapids, MI: Eerdmans, 2012), 76–147, 78. Further references to this work will appear in the text.

Theology and Mysticism

With this set of presuppositions Shah-Kazemi proceeds to develop his conclusions following the thinking of an Islamic and a Christian mystic. And his conclusions manifest what happens when the truth of theology is ignored or detached from the object of Christian faith. He reasons that if we direct our attention away from "Allah" and away from the Trinity as theologically defined, then our focus will be on the "supratheological or metaphysical referent" so that "we shall be in a position to affirm that, despite the different names by which the ultimate Reality is denoted in the two traditions, the Reality thus alluded to is indeed one and the same" (Shah-Kazemi, 79). That, however, is *the* question. Is the reality so denoted one and the same? And is it possible for Christians to detach the object of faith from knowledge of the truth which can only occur when God is understood in his internal relations (as Father, Son, and Holy Spirit) on the basis of his revelation in the history of Israel and finally in Jesus Christ and the outpouring of the Holy Spirit?

Shah-Kazemi analyzes texts from the Qur'ān and from Christian theologians to explain that while for all Muslim theologians "distinction implies relativity, while divinity implies absolute unity," one still can make an argument based on verses from the Qur'ān that "the Christians do indeed believe in and worship the selfsame God as the Muslims" (Shah-Kazemi, 102). Without going into the many references that Shah-Kazemi has compiled from Muslim and Christian figures historically, including popes and other luminaries from both religions, indicating that Christians and Muslims do indeed believe in the same God, let me present his major thesis and conclusions. Shah-Kazemi sums up the view of a Sufi mystic (Al-Ghazzālī) to note that theology "was a weapon, essential for defending the truths of faith, but not an instrument by which the truth itself could be found … it demolishes but it does not build" (Shah-Kazemi, 82). Consequently, he maintains that the "'divinity' believed in" and that unites Jews, Christians, and Muslims "is one and the same" (Shah-Kazemi, 83). What is more, "just as in Islamic theology, the one God has ninety-nine 'Names,' without thereby becoming anything other than one, so the different 'names' given to God in the different revelations do not make the object named anything but one" (Shah-Kazemi, 84).

In Shah-Kazemi's thinking, this obviates any charge of polytheism or idolatry. But, of course, the question that I am raising in this chapter concerns the truth of revelation, the truth of faith, and the truth of theology with the result that if theology, as knowledge of faith, also means knowledge of the truth, then one simply cannot detach faith from the object of belief, as must be done according to this particular mystical approach to what is thought to be "Ultimate Reality." And since God is one and his revelation is one, there cannot be many different revelations that would place them in conflict with the one revelation of the one God confessed by Christians in the Nicene Creed. By detaching theology from its object theoretically via his mystical approach, Shah-Kazemi is able to claim that all three religions believe in the same ultimate reality. But in order to depict this ultimate reality, Shah-Kazemi has to deal with the Muslim theological objection to the Christian doctrines of the incarnation and of the Trinity. He cites a number of

Muslim theologians with conflicting views as to whether or not the doctrine of the Trinity is compatible with Muslim belief in God's oneness and concludes that there are conflicting Muslim views concerning this matter and claims that is no different from the conflicting views about God himself within the Christian tradition since there also are conflicts between Orthodox and Catholics over how to understand the Trinity (Shah-Kazemi, 97).

Islam, Incarnation, and the Trinity

The real question that Karl Barth asks us to wrestle with, however, concerns whether or not this thinking genuinely points to the reality of God affirmed by Christians? According to Shah-Kazemi, it does so only if "the oneness of the divinity in whom the Christians affirm belief takes priority over the fact that their description of this God entails a Trinity within the Unity" (Shah-Kazemi, 103). He attempts to press forward on the basis of the 2007 interfaith initiative advanced in an open letter entitled "A Common Word Between Us and You" which was signed by 138 Muslim leaders and scholars and sent to Christian leaders. It was an invitation "to engage in dialogue on the basis of love of God and love of the neighbor" which of course is central to both faiths (Shah-Kazemi, 131). Shah-Kazemi says that "the overwhelmingly positive Christian responses ... implied that the basic, albeit unspoken, premise of the text—belief in the same God—was accepted" (Shah-Kazemi, 132). Indeed, Rowan Williams, the Archbishop of Canterbury at the time, not only affirmed that Christians and Muslims believed in the same God but went "to great pains to point out that the Trinitarian God is in essence not other than the One God believed in and worshiped by Muslims" (Shah-Kazemi, 132).

Here we must ask whether or not this thinking is accurate and helpful. According to Shah-Kazemi, Muslims and Christians can be said to worship the same God only as long as the oneness of the divine essence has *priority* over any belief in the Trinity. But this very assertion eliminates the central Christian belief and thus also Christian knowledge of God as one being, three persons. As I see it, the fundamental question here is the one raised by Karl Barth, as noted above. Can or should Christian thinking be measured by a monotheism that disallows the full eternal reality of Father, Son, and Holy Spirit with the notion that it is possible to believe in God's unity and simplicity without believing in the three persons of the Trinity? Once that particular knowledge of God is precluded or forestalled, so also is any belief in and knowledge of Jesus Christ as *homoousios* with the Father and the Holy Spirit. That of course solves the problem for Muslims concerning the nature and role of Jesus Christ as the incarnation of God himself. But it solves the problem in a way that, for Christians, detaches revelation from the revealer (Jesus Christ) and leads to a unitarian view of God, a view that is not in harmony with who God truly is in his internal relations as Father, Son, and Holy Spirit, that is, within the immanent Trinity. These difficulties illustrate exactly why it was and is so important for Christian theology to recognize that the Nicene faith of the church is controlled by genuine knowledge of God in his internal relations (as Father, Son, and Holy Spirit) as these have been revealed in Christ and through his Holy Spirit.

Trinity and Modalism

Here, ironically, Shah-Kazemi is able to cite Christian theologians in support of his position—a position which, from a Christian standpoint, is essentially modalistic. He follows John of Damascus and argues that Christians are able to affirm that God exists but not what God is in his essence (Shah-Kazemi, 105–6). This might seem to be a properly apophatic view of the matter. But, given the position stated above, it affirms that theologians simply cannot know who God is in his inner essence other than the fact that this essence is essentially one. So, Shah-Kazemi reasons that each person "sticks to a particular creed concerning his Lord" (Shah-Kazemi, 108) and concludes that "a believer who sticks to his particular creed believes only in a god that he has subjectively posited in his own mind. God in all particular creeds is dependent upon the subjective act of positing on the part of the believers" (Shah-Kazemi, 108).

Unfortunately, however, it was just this thinking that Karl Barth rightly and consistently rejected since it makes knowledge of God dependent on us. And any such view not only obviates the question of truth in theology but also leads to subjectivism, that is, to the idea that somehow truth is dependent upon our point of view or our personal belief. Shah-Kazemi asserts that "God not only creates man, but in a sense allows man to create Him, which he does by conceiving of Him and believing in Him and worshiping Him according to the modes determined by the form assumed by his belief" (Shah-Kazemi, 109). This is a startling remark because all three religions claim to believe in the God of Israel, the God whose existence is in no way the creation of any of our beliefs, but the one who alone enables such belief in the first place as the sovereign and free God who revealed his name to Moses and actually became incarnate in Jesus of Nazareth in his free love for the world in order to fulfil his covenant with Israel and thus reconcile the entire world to himself.

At any rate, here Shah-Kazemi follows Meister Eckhart and explains how his position can be stated metaphysically: "The One, the Ground, the Godhead is 'beyond Being,' while the Persons of the Trinity are 'suspended' at the level of Being, there where God is definable as God in relation to creatures" (Shah-Kazemi, 134). This, once again, regrettably is an essentially modalist position which all Christian theologians with a proper knowledge of trinitarian doctrine would reject, just as they would reject any subordinationist view as it relates to Jesus himself. It is modalistic because it claims that, as understood in relation to creatures, God may be referred to as three persons but that God in himself in eternity is ultimately one. Such thinking does not take seriously the *homoousia* of the persons of the Trinity and undercuts the meaning of Christology and Pneumatology as well as the doctrines of reconciliation and redemption. These are not insignificant issues! At this point in his argument Shah-Kazemi takes Thomas Aquinas's rejection of partialism to imply that Thomas wanted to say what Muslim theologians might say, namely, that there are multiple ways in which we conceive God's oneness such that this might suggest that "the subjective nature of the doctrine of the Trinity" might imply that such a doctrine "is but a mode of 'plurality' subsisting in the mind of the creature, not in the objective reality of the Creator, who is 'one in reality' and only 'multiple in idea' " (Shah-Kazemi, 136).

Of course, if that really was Thomas Aquinas's view, then his view of the doctrine of the Trinity would have been more than a little problematic. In reality, however, Thomas held that God was eternally one and three and that as such he could and did relate with us effectively in history in the incarnation and the outpouring of his Holy Spirit. But here another major problem surfaces, namely, the fact that Thomas Aquinas believed it was indeed possible to speak of God's oneness apart from his threeness since he thought we could know God's oneness through reason and God as triune only through revelation. Christian theologians, following Karl Rahner, have been properly critical of Thomas for apparently separating his two treatises on God in this way. This is something that Karl Barth and Thomas F. Torrance in particular absolutely refused to do. And that explains Barth's opposition to natural theology.

Neglecting this problem, Shah-Kazemi finally turns to Thomas Aquinas to argue that philosophers, including Muslims and Greeks, can come to a knowledge of God's goodness, wisdom, power, and attributes "that are undifferentiated in the simplicity of the divine Essence" through reason but can only know the persons of the Trinity through faith. Given Shah-Kazemi's subjectivist view of faith, however, this means that Christians and Muslims agree regarding the one, simple, and unique divine essence while disagreeing theologically about the divine attributes as they relate to the divine persons believed in by Christians. Hence, in his view "the agreement on the plane of the Essence can prevail over the disagreement on the plane of the Persons" (Shah-Kazemi, 138–9). From this he concludes that "it would appear that the Christian can believe in God, therefore, without this belief being predicated on the Trinity" (Shah-Kazemi, 140). This, because "belief in the one divine Essence—takes priority over what differentiates them ... (whether attributes or Persons) ascribed to that Essence within the two theologies" (Shah-Kazemi, 140).

Conceptualizing God's Oneness

That, however, is *the* question. Can Christians truly believe in the one divine essence or the divine unity unless that belief is grounded in Christ and enabled by the Holy Spirit? The answer to that question from within a properly functioning doctrine of the Trinity as this was understood by Karl Barth and Thomas F. Torrance is clearly *no* because any attempt to do so would have to result in a God produced by religious Christians rather than one that is grounded exclusively in revelation and thus understood in faith as shaped by who God eternally is as Father, Son, and Holy Spirit. Once again therefore Shah-Kazemi is led to conclude that what unites Christians and Muslims "even in the absence of any reference to the Trinity" is belief in "God as such" or "God *qua* Essence, Substance, or Nature" (Shah-Kazemi, 140). But that assertion only highlights the problem involved in asserting that Christians and Muslims believe in the same God because they are monotheists. That, I believe, is why Barth said it was unthinking to claim that Christians and Muslims believe in the same God on the basis of their monotheistic affirmations. If God is eternally the Father, Son, and Holy Spirit confessed at Nicaea and this God is indivisible *in se* and *ad extra*, then nothing divides Christians and Muslims more than their particular monotheistic beliefs. While I agree with Shah-Kazemi that Jews, Christians, and Muslims *intend* to speak of the same God in that they all appeal to the God who revealed himself to Moses as the God of Abraham, Isaac, and Jacob, what they say about that God inevitably demonstrates that they do not in fact have the same reality in view when they do speak of God theologically and in faith. We would all agree that this difference between us should not mean that we cannot stand in solidarity with each other in our joint realization that only the grace of God can and will unite us even in our interreligious dialogue. But, given the twin facts that (1) grace cannot be detached from the Giver of grace (Jesus Christ) and (2) Jesus himself is utterly unique precisely because he was and is God acting *as* man for the entire human race, it would in the end be an enormous mistake to conclude that we both believe in the same God because God is ultimately one and that oneness can be described and presented without acknowledging the Trinity of persons. Any belief in God's oneness that excludes the eternal divinity of the Son and Spirit necessarily means that we do not yet or no longer believe in revelation as attested in the New Testament. Moreover, it means that we no longer believe in the God affirmed in the Nicene Creed which has united all Christians since the fourth century.

Monotheism and Modalism Revisited

Let me conclude this discussion of Reza Shah-Kazemi's position with a brief analysis of his claim that the "unique Essence" of God is the essence that is "the common ground upon which all monotheists can come together and assert with unanimity that they believe in the same God" (Shah-Kazemi, 142). If Barth is right, and I believe he is, that the Christian doctrine of the Trinity disallows any monotheism that asserts belief in and knowledge of God's oneness apart from or in conflict with the eternal act and being of God as Father, Son, and Holy Spirit, then to assert unanimity of faith based on the monotheism presented by Shah-Kazemi would mean that Christians had surrendered their belief in God as he truly is in himself and as he acts for us within history. This is clearly no small issue! In any case, Shah-Kazemi finalizes his argument by asserting that Thomas Aquinas's "statement that it is possible to abstract the Trinity from one's conception of God, without ruining one's conception of this Essence" (Shah-Kazemi, 142) was also implied in a declaration made by the Fourth Lateran Council in 1215. The Council opposed any idea of a quaternity within the eternal being of the Trinity and thus stated,

We ... confess with Peter the Lombard that there is one highest, incomprehensible, ineffable reality, which is truly Father, Son, and Holy Spirit; the three Persons together, and each Person distinctly; therefore in God there is only Trinity, not a quaternity, because each of the Persons is that reality, that is, the divine substance, essence, or nature which alone is the beginning of all things, apart from which nothing else can be found. This reality is neither generating nor proceeding, but it is the Father who generates, the Son who is generated, and the Holy Spirit who proceeds, so that there be distinctions between the Persons but unity in nature. Hence, though 'the Father is one Person, the Son another Person and the Holy Spirit another Person,' yet there is not another reality but what the Father is, this very same reality is also the Son, this the Holy Spirit, so that in the orthodox and Catholic faith we believe them to be of one substance.[7]

Shah-Kazemi argues that this text clearly indicates "the possibility of distinguishing It [the divine Essence] from the Persons, and thus, inversely, the possibility of abstracting the Persons from the Essence without detriment to one's conception of the intrinsic nature of the Essence; this essential nature being defined in this conciliar text by the fact that it 'neither begets nor is begotten nor proceeds' " (Shah-Kazemi, 143). From this he conjectures that,

for Aquinas the unity of the divine Essence is the philosophical 'infrastructure' of the dogma of the Trinity: one has to understand first what the essence or nature of God is, and on this basis proceed to discussion of God qua Trinity. And this indeed is why the *Summa* starts with a treatise on the unity of God and then proceeds to the Trinity. This, together with the fact that he accepts that the unitarian conception of God remains valid on its own level, even if the Trinitarian conception be abstracted from, means that it is entirely legitimate for Christians to invoke Aquinas's perspectives outlined here as justification for positing the unique Essence of God as that in which Christians, Muslims, and Jews believe, irrespective of the fact that both Muslims and Jews disbelieve in the Trinity. (Shah-Kazemi, 143–4)

In the end therefore, Shah-Kazemi contends that we can say that Christians and Muslims believe in the same God because of the Christian view "of a transcendent Essence which 'neither begets nor is begotten' " (Shah-Kazemi, 144). But here he misunderstands the position of the Fourth Lateran Council which was that it was not the essence that begets or is begotten, but the essence which is the Father and Son who are each fully divine within that essence. If it were the essence and not the Persons who begot and were begotten, then there would indeed be a fourth within the Trinity and that would be a

---

[7]Denzinger, *Enchiridion symbolorum, Compendium of Creeds, Definitions, and Declarations on Matters of Faith and Morals*, 268.

form of modalism and thus an improper view of God's triunity. On this basis, Shah-Kazemi claims that Muslims would have to reject the doctrines of the incarnation and of the Trinity "which Christians deem the ultimate fulfillment of monotheism" saying that "this incompatibility can be accepted on one level, without compromising the compatibility achieved at another: each can recognize the other as a fellow-believer in the one true God" (Shah-Kazemi, 144). Indeed, "the agreement can take priority over the disagreement, for the agreement is situated on the universal ground of monotheism, and in relation to the transcendent Essence of the one God which defines the very terms of that monotheism" (Shah-Kazemi, 144).

That, however, is the problem that I have identified in this chapter: can we know God's oneness apart from the fact that the one God is eternally Father, Son, and Holy Spirit? Can we know the one true God without knowing the Father through the Son as enabled by the Holy Spirit in faith? When God's unity is not separated from God's trinity, the Christian answer to that question is and has been a very definite *no*, at least since the Council of Nicaea in the fourth century. Here we can see where disagreements even among Christians arise since one of the great difficulties in evidence throughout this discussion concerns the problem of natural theology, as Karl Barth clearly saw. If one separates the treatise on the one God from the treatise on the triune God with the idea that philosophers and others can know God's oneness apart from faith in Jesus Christ and without relying specifically on the Holy Spirit in his union with the Word, then an impermissible division in the concept of God has occurred.[8] That is the question we face here. If we all agree that we can accept a monotheism which excludes belief in the incarnation and the Trinity, then the entire Christian faith falls to the ground because the central point of those two doctrines rests upon the fact that Jesus was not just another Jew claiming to forgive sins and claiming to have an eternal relation with his Father in heaven. And the Holy Spirit is not simply an aspect of the human spirit. Unless Jesus himself has his being in the very being and action of the eternal Word or Son of the Father as portrayed above, he is nothing more than a blasphemer in his claim to forgive sins, and the New Testament claim that we are reconciled to God in his death on the cross is vacuous. Indeed, his resurrection and ascension could also be dismissed as

---

[8]This is why Barth insisted that (1) "the reality of revelation is in no sense an answer to all kinds of questions originating elsewhere than in itself … The reality insists upon being understood in its own light"; (2) how then does God's revelation reach us? Barth says: "Man is free for God by the Holy Spirit of the Father and the Son"; (3) thus, "it is real in the Holy Spirit that we are free for God"; (4) that means that "the work of the Holy Spirit itself cuts away from us the thought of any other possibility of our freedom for God. It encloses this possibility within itself"; (5) finally, "as God, the Holy Spirit is a unique person. But He is not an independent divinity side by side with the unique Word of God. He is simply the Teacher of the Word: of that Word which is never without its Teacher … for the Word is never apart from the Holy Spirit … It is God Himself who opens our eyes and ears for Himself. And in so doing He tells us that we could not do it of ourselves, that of ourselves we are blind and deaf. To receive the Holy Spirit means an exposure of our spiritual helplessness, a recognition that we do not possess the Holy Spirit. For that reason the subjective reality of revelation has the distinctive character of a miracle, i.e., it is a reality to be grounded only in itself . . . apart from it there is no other possibility of being free for God" (CD I/2, 243–4). See also CD II/1, 79 for Barth's rejection of any division in our concept of God.

decisive events that enable us to understand who God eternally was and is as the Father, Son, and Holy Spirit.

Not Any Monotheism

Here we return to the point of this chapter, which is that we do not need to posit a monotheism on the basis of which we can say that Jews, Christians, and Muslims believe in the same God in order to argue that members of all three religions should love God and love their neighbors. We do not need to construct a view of God which eliminates the very meaning and basis of Christian monotheism to argue that Christians are free to live in solidarity with Jews and Muslims. This is not a problem that can be solved *religiously* by relying on analysis of various conceptions of divine unity. It is a problem that is solved only to the extent that religious people actually are willing to rely on God's grace and revelation in its identity with Jesus Christ. And that is under no one's control as Barth so clearly recognized. That is why he rightly insisted that our understanding of religion and religions "and therefore man" must be taken seriously and not patronized with a tolerance based on a kind of moderation grounded in one's "own religion or religiosity" for which we are "secretly zealous," but because we have been told that fanaticism is bad and that "[ours] is not the only faith," and "that love must always have the first and the last word," therefore we can exercise "self-control" in relation to others (CD I/2, 299). Moreover, such tolerance should not be confused with "the clever aloofness of the rationalistic Know-All—the typical Hegelian belongs to the same category—who thinks that he can deal comfortably and in the end successfully with all religions in the light of a concept of a perfect religion which is gradually evolving in history" (CD I/2, 299). Nor should it be confused with any sort of "relativism and impartiality" in the form of "an historical scepticism which does not ask about truth" (CD I/2, 299). Barth says that tolerance in the "form of moderation, or superior knowledge, or scepticism is actually the worst form of intolerance" (CD I/2, 299). The answer thus lies in fact that religion and religions should "be treated with a tolerance which is informed by the forbearance of Christ, which derives therefore from a knowledge that by grace God has reconciled to Himself godless man and his religion" (CD I/2, 299).

What Makes Religion True? Grace, Faith, and Revelation

Barth spells out what this means when he explains that Christianity, like all religions, is not true in itself and as such; it is the true religion only as Christians live by the forgiving grace of Christ who is the justification and salvation of sinful human beings. Thus,

> if the Christian religion is the right and true religion, the reason for it does not reside in facts which might point to itself or its own adherents, but in the fact which as the righteousness and the judgment of God confronts it as it does all

other religions, characterising and differentiating it and not one of the others as the right and true religion. (CD I/2, 353–4)

Once Christianity is seen and understood as the religion that finds its truth only in Christ himself as it lives by his forgiving grace, his forbearance, then every possibility of denigrating other religions is completely eliminated. Then all inclination to refuse to work in solidarity with Muslims and Jews would be seen as a refusal to acknowledge that Christ's forgiving grace applies to all people and not just to Christians. Such refusal would amount to a refusal of the freedom that comes to all people as permission to obey God himself by loving God just because God has freed us to do so in Christ and through his Holy Spirit. Love of neighbor follows this love of God because it is itself spontaneously enabled by God himself as he meets us in Christ and liberates us for that service of God and others.[9] This is why Barth quite rightly insisted that

> as a human faith it [Christianity] needs the divine forgiveness just as much as the faith of other religions. But it does actually receive and enjoy this forgiveness … [which in the first instance] is made only to Jesus Christ, the only man who has maintained and demonstrated the obedience of faith. But for the sake of Jesus Christ, i.e., for the sake of fellowship and participation guaranteed to men by Jesus Christ, for the sake of the solidarity of our humanity with His bestowed by Him, for the sake of the faith in Him of discipleship, those whom He calls His brethren, and who in that faith in Him recognise and honour their first-born brother, are also (with their religion) the objects of the righteous award of God. (CD I/2, 355)

This is the case because the Christian religion "has its justification either in the name of Jesus Christ, or not at all" (CD I/2, 356).

A Jewish View

Alon Goshen-Gottstein begins his answer to the question of whether or not Christians and Jews believe in the same God by noting that in reality there is "no single Jewish understanding of God."[10] Because God has been understood differently in different periods and by varied schools of thought, Goshen-Gottstein argues that such diversity will help in developing a Jewish approach to the Christian God. Like the Islamic scholar discussed above, Goshen-Gottstein insists that "differing views of God can coexist" and that this implies that "it is the same God to which the various approaches point, despite their obvious differences" (Goshen-Gottstein, 50). Goshen-Gottstein mentions a

---

[9]For a discussion of how this thinking relates to Liberation Theology, see Chapter 5.
[10]Alon Goshen-Gottstein, "God Between Christians and Jews: Is It the Same God?," in *Do We Worship the Same God?: Jews, Christians and Muslims in Dialogue*, ed. Miroslav Volf (Grand Rapids, MI: Eerdmans, 2012), 50–75, 50. Further references to this work will appear in the text.

statement on Christianity published by a team of Jewish scholars in 2000 entitled *Dabru Emet* in which they state that "Jews and Christians worship the same God" (Goshen-Gottstein, 51). Noting that throughout most of Jewish history it was thought that theirs was the only God and all others were to be rejected, Goshen-Gottstein says that today we can approach this question differently. He then reviews the rabbinic tradition in relation to what they termed *Avoda Zara* (foreign religions) which were considered to be somewhere "between idolatry and false worship" (Goshen-Gottstein, 52). During the Middle Ages, the question of whether or not Christianity was considered such a foreign religion became a problem since Jews were forbidden to engage in commerce with idolaters. So this was not just a theological issue but an issue of survival Goshen-Gottstein declared. Without an understanding of Christianity that allowed for such commerce, Jewish survival was imperiled. Goshen-Gottstein claims that Maimonides's position that Christianity, with its doctrine of the Trinity, is indeed a foreign religion could be read differently and thus, in spite of Maimonides's reading, the sameness of the Jewish and Christian God could be upheld since, "even if it is not deemed 'clear' or 'clean' of *Avoda Zara*, it may nevertheless appeal to the same God" (Goshen-Gottstein, 55).

According to Goshen-Gottstein, the renowned Jewish philosopher and theologian Maimonides was more deferential to Christians than to Muslims because he believed that Christians believed in the same revelation as Jews while Muslims did not show the same respect to the Jewish Scriptures since they claim they had been falsified. Goshen-Gottstein takes this position by Maimonides to be a virtual approval of the fact that Christians and Jews recognize the same God. Goshen-Gottstein cites an interesting passage from a famous seventeeth-century Rabbi to make his point that in relation to some non-Jews, the Jewish people were obligated to pray for the welfare of those who believed "in the creation of the world and the Exodus from Egypt and in the principles of faith" and whose intention is focused on "the maker of heaven and earth." He noted that "David's prayer for God to pour His wrath on the nations who do not know Him (Ps. 79:6) refers to the non-Jews who do not believe in the creation of the world" and the Exodus or the giving of the Torah (Goshen-Gottstein, 58–9). Still, "the nations in whose shadow we live and dwell under their wings, they believe in all these, and we continually pray for the[ir] peace" (Goshen-Gottstein, 59).

Trinity and the God of Israel

Goshen-Gottstein proceeds to argue that the best way to understand Christianity and Judaism today is to consider them in light of their stories and forms of worship rather than by focusing on their theologies. He therefore claims that "Judaism and Christianity did not divide over the appropriate understanding of God" but rather because of their different definitions of Israel and "the continued relevance of the commandments" (Goshen-Gottstein, 62). He even says that he is convinced that if Judaism and Christianity had not parted ways as they did, then "a particular understanding of God, such as the Trinitarian understanding, could have been recognized as part of a wide range of acceptable Jewish understandings of and approaches to God" (Goshen-Gottstein, 63). Now this is surely an amazing statement since the trinitarian understanding of God arose only insofar as it was a faithful expression of who Jesus Christ was as the eternal Son of the Father; it arose on the ground of God's revelation to and in Israel as an act of God fulfilling his covenant promises to Israel. T. F. Torrance therefore was right, as noted above, to observe that the difference between Christians and Jews is based on the fact that Christians were willing to move forward in their understanding of God based on Christ's resurrection from the dead while recalcitrant Jews refused to do so. Nonetheless, Goshen-Gottstein argues that had the faith of Christianity "remained true to classical Jewish ritual expression" then even if their thinking about God differed, there would have been "little question as to the identity of God being worshipped through this ritual" (Goshen-Gottstein, 63). Indeed, "Christian understanding could have conceivably developed as one form of Jewish understanding" (Goshen-Gottstein, 63). What all of this is meant to suggest is that Goshen-Gottstein believes there is a new way to establish God's identity in both religions based on a "common text," as found for example in the Psalms (Goshen-Gottstein, 64–5). Goshen-Gottstein thus wishes to stress our common story and to avoid the division embodied in our theologies. He rightly notes that Christianity and Islam presented unique challenges in relation to the history of Judaism because they both claimed to be worshipping the same God (Goshen-Gottstein, 68).

Here we must call attention to Karl Barth's astute analysis mentioned above, namely, that nothing separates Christians and Jews more radically than their apparent agreement about monotheism; what in fact separates them is precisely their understanding of God. Therefore, Goshen-Gottstein's proposed solution sidesteps the real issue by suggesting that theological division can be brushed aside by emphasizing our common story. This, because the truth of our common story is that, left to our own devices (moral, theological, or religious), we will always be disobedient to the one God of Israel who became incarnate in Jesus Christ; one might say that even today we together would hand Jesus over to be crucified rather than accepting him as our savior, helper, and friend![11]

What is the best way to deal with this today from this particular Jewish perspective? Goshen-Gottstein suggests, that in view of the thinking once offered by a fourteenth-century Rabbi, Menachem HaMeiri, one can suppose "a theory of religious progress" so that *Avoda Zara* can be considered a matter of the past since religions have progressed from earlier and primitive understanding to a "higher understanding of God" (Goshen-Gottstein, 70). Today people of differing religious views work together and realize that they are persons of high moral character and are thus not "base idolaters" as described in the Talmud. That, he says, applies today especially to Christians and Muslims. So, he bases his idea that all three religions may be said to believe in and worship the same God

---

[11]T. F. Torrance puts it this way: "Let no one man draw up his hypocritical skirts and disassociate himself from the race of men who slew Christ; for we are all part of it; and if Christ came today, we would do the same, only no doubt with a greater refinement of cruelty than even the Romans were able to devise and adopt" (Torrance, *The Doctrine of Jesus Christ*, 158). The crucifixion of Christ, Torrance insists, shows us the "stark reality of sin." See also Torrance, *Incarnation*, 246; and above, Chapter 7.

on what might be called a moral argument which shifts the ground from theology to moral behavior. Hence, "rather than focus upon the nature of the understanding of the Divine espoused by a given religion, Meiri claims the relevant consideration is the moral life enabled by the religion" (Goshen-Gottstein, 70).

From this position, Goshen-Gottstein reaches the following conclusions: (1) "the life of the believers rather than the theological statements of the religion, is the ultimate proof of identity of its God" (Goshen-Gottstein, 71); (2) "a religion that teaches and upholds a moral way of living is proof of the God who is worshiped through that religion"; (3) the means by which we come to know this God "is through an examination of the moral quality of their lives"; (4) "religion is about transforming the human person towards a higher spiritual vision associated with God. Details of theology are secondary to the approach to God" (Goshen-Gottstein, 71); (5) "There is no God of this and God of that religion. There is only God. Therefore, a religion, a lifestyle, or a set of practices either does bring one into relationship with God, or it doesn't … Once it is recognized that a given religion provides access to God, all other details are secondary" (Goshen-Gottstein, 71); and finally, (6) "God is known through the ethical lives of believers" (Goshen-Gottstein, 71).

Goshen-Gottstein extends this approach to understanding God from moral behavior to peoples' "overall spiritual lives" as a way of "advancing our discussion of the same-God question" and reasons that "recognizing God through the traces of contact left in His human relationship partners may serve as an alternative to theological formulations that attempt to define or proclaim the nature of God" (Goshen-Gottstein, 71–2). Equipped with this set of insights, Goshen-Gottstein finally determines that "true and false knowledge of God are no longer the demarcating lines distinguishing between my religion and the religion of the other. Instead, true and false knowledge, true worship, and idolatrous appeal to religion are inherent in all religions" (Goshen-Gottstein, 72). Thus, "validity and value are not givens of any religion" but rather are "a function of the degree to which any religion forms a true attachment to God" (Goshen-Gottstein, 72). Indeed, if we shift "the testing ground for religious authenticity and for the identity of God from theology to human behavior and experience" then "Testimony and listening would replace philosophical argument and interreligious debate" (Goshen-Gottstein, 73). Consequently, if we recognize that "God's presence and reality in the life and religion of the other constitutes a testimony to God that transcends differences in names of God and in forms of religious life" then, instead of having to assume that one religion might or might not appeal to God, that is, to the "correct God," we should instead "seek traces of the one living God where these are found" (Goshen-Gottstein, 73).

God, Morality, Religion, and Truth

How might these suggestions relate to Karl Barth's view that, in light of revelation, *all religions* stand under God's judgment and grace? First, it is important to realize that

Goshen-Gottstein comes very close to saying what Barth says when he claims that validity and value are not givens of any religion. Second, it is also important to realize that Jews and Christians do indeed believe in the same God but that they are in reality divided precisely by their understanding of who that God is in light of the appearance of Jesus Christ himself. Here, what was said above must be stressed, namely, that Jews, Christians, and Muslims all *intend* to speak of the God of Abraham, Isaac, and Jacob. Nevertheless, when they explicate their understanding of that God, their thinking illustrates the fact that they do not have the same reality in view precisely to the extent that they do not allow God's forgiving grace alone disclosed in and through the risen Lord to shape their views. This shows, once again, that what divides the three religious traditions is precisely the fact that the truth which binds them together cannot be recognized apart from the name of Jesus Christ, as Barth held.

Consequently, there can be little doubt that Barth would certainly oppose the attempt to shift the discussion concerning the truth of religion away from God and our understanding of God and thus away from theology and toward a focus on people's spiritual lives and moral behavior. This, because the spiritual lives and moral behavior of all people, including Jews, Christians, and Muslims are precisely the lives of those who in themselves are unbelievers and idolaters and therefore sinners who stand in need of justification. And that justification simply cannot be achieved by and through our ethical behavior as Goshen-Gottstein supposes. Indeed, such an idea, in Barth's thinking, betrays once again the fact that self-justification is what separates us from the true God and divides us from each other. In reality, for Barth, such separation and division and the fact that these have been overcome through God's having reconciled the world to himself in Christ are exactly what can only be learned from revelation by relying on the forgiving grace of Christ through faith. Since God actively and definitively judged such human behavior in the life, death, and resurrection of his Son Jesus Christ, Barth's argument is that any religion that attempts to guarantee its truth by reference to its own ethical behavior does so at its own peril because, apart from God's own reconciling action which includes *all humanity*, there can be no true religion.

The truth of religion, as seen above, becomes a human possibility only by way of judgment and by way of forgiveness, with the result that one can neither know the righteousness of God nor the truth of religion by focusing on the spiritual or ethical lives of those practicing that religion. Such a focus would in reality place the burden of overcoming sin and of relating to God on us, and that would make it impossible to speak properly of the truth of religion. Such a perspective would only leave us with religions in conflict which simply cannot be solved religiously—either theologically or ethically. This, because, as Barth argued, that truth can only be found outside of us and in Christ alone and thus through grace alone. Failing to do this would only mean conflict with God and with each other over which religion is true. These difficulties seem to me to undercut the very basis of Goshen-Gottstein's argument. In the end, I think Barth might say that the Christian religion is indeed the true religion only because and to the extent that Jews and Gentiles live by faith, relying on the free grace of God by which they have been forgiven and by and through which they are free to live as reconciled sinners. That means they are free to live their lives in and from Christ who did what he did in his own life history for everyone and not just for Jews or Christians. Let us now consider a Christian perspective before concluding our discussion.

A Christian Perspective

After discussing and commenting on the declaration of Vatican II, *Nostra Aetate*, Christoph Schwöbel remarks that the question of whether or not Jews, Christians, and Muslims believe in and worship the same God is a complicated question indeed. In answer to this question, Schwöbel mentions that *Nostra Aetate* states that "Christians and Muslims worship the one and only God because there is only one God who is the origin and goal of the whole of humankind. There is thus an identity of reference, more precisely an identity of the referent (the object of reference) in the way Christians and Muslims understand God."[12] Noting that this common referent offers a partial "consensus" and partial "dissensus" requiring further dialogue, Schwöbel then asks who is to decide whether Christians and Muslims believe in and worship the same God? Such a question, Schwöbel says, presumes there is a position above the differing religious perspectives. But such a position, he maintains, cannot be attained until the *visio beatifica* since "there is no view from nowhere" (Schwöbel, 6). Where then does this leave the discussion with respect of the question of truth we have been considering?

The first important point Schwöbel makes is that all statements about the sameness or difference among the religions are themselves made from within certain perspectives. The second point therefore is that "the grounds that can be offered for either stating sameness or difference will therefore depend on the way they appear from a particular perspective" (Schwöbel, 7). This, because there are no abstract criteria for determining "sameness" or "difference" since "even logical criteria of sameness have to be applied from some perspective to a particular problem as it appears from that perspective" (Schwöbel, 7). While this thinking might appear to open the door to a kind of "subjectivism" with respect to the question of truth, Schwöbel flatly rejects any sort of "relativistic perspectivism" since that would mean the "demise of all truth claims" and "the end of all communication, which depends on the law of noncontradiction" (Schwöbel, 7). Such relativism can be avoided, Schwöbel thinks, only if an epistemic perspective does not present another *reality* but rather "*another* perspective on the *same* reality" (Schwöbel, 7). Hence, "only if particular perspectives can be understood as being constituted by the subjective certainty concerning the objective truth of a view of reality can they avoid the twofold pitfalls of perspectivistic relativism or a general skepticism," Schwöbel thinks (Schwöbel, 7).

In line with this approach, Schwöbel maintains that if God is the "creator of heaven and earth, the ground of all reality, as both Muslims and Christians believe, then the

---

[12]Christoph Schwöbel "The Same God? The Perspective of Faith, the Identity of God, Tolerance, and Dialogue," in *Do We Worship the Same God: Jews, Christians, and Muslims in Dialogue*, ed. Miroslav Volf (Grand Rapids, MI: Eerdmans, 2012), 1–17, 6. Further references to this work will appear in the text.

concept of God guarantees the unity of reality" (Schwöbel, 8). This would mean that it would be extremely problematic for Christians and Muslims to "agree that they worship and believe in different gods" since that would either mean that "Christians and Muslims live in different realities or that there is no unitary ground of all reality" (Schwöbel, 8). Any such view would end the possibility of debate between Christians and Muslims because it would undercut the possibility of any sort of mutual understanding; it would also end the possibility of mutual cooperation "for common goals" (Schwöbel, 8). At this point Schwöbel raises what appears to be an insurmountable difficulty. He notes that if we claim "that Christians and Muslims worship and believe in the same God while they continue to claim either the Qurʾān or Jesus Christ as the ultimate revelation of truth respectively, and both hold that these beliefs are incompatible," this would undermine "any truth claim that could be associated with God or any meaningful use of the notion of 'sameness' and 'otherness'" (Schwöbel, 8).

Facing the Truth Question

In connection with this issue, Schwöbel asks who is to decide which perspective is true and concludes that the "obvious answer is: only Christians and Muslims can decide from their different respective perspectives of faith" (Schwöbel, 8). What I want to argue here is that neither Christians nor Muslims decide this issue at all since it is already decided by the truth of revelation itself and not by anyone's perspective. Here we are up against a genuine difficulty. On the one hand, Schwöbel rightly claims that for Christians it is the Holy Spirit alone who enables faith such that it is not constituted *by* humans but only by the Spirit. On the other hand, following Luther, he then says that this faith is "commonly summarized by the technical concept of 'revelation'" (Schwöbel, 9) and that this concept of revelation "expresses the mode of knowledge that is constituted for us by a disclosure experience that constitutes personal certainty of faith" (Schwöbel, 9). However, in my view, these statements are at war with themselves because if it is the Holy Spirit who enables faith, then that faith is true only as it is faith in Jesus Christ himself since the Spirit, as noted above, unites us to Christ and enables our knowledge of God in and through him as he actively speaks his Word to us through the scriptural witness. But if that is true, then it is not a mode of knowledge that is *constituted* by any sort of *disclosure experience*—it is instead constituted and enabled by God himself in our experience of the Word through the Spirit in faith. So, it is problematic to assume that the concept of revelation describes a disclosure experience since that concept should refer to revelation in its identity with Jesus the revealer, as I will indicate below.

Understanding Revelation

This is not a small issue because Schwöbel goes on to say that "the concept of revelation only makes sense if we do not restrict it to a specific religious realm but see it as denoting the general way in which the foundations of our active knowing are constituted for us" (Schwöbel, 9). Consequently, Schwöbel argues "for a general theory of revelation, and not necessarily for a theory of general revelation" (Schwöbel, 9) and claims that it is a "decisive characteristic of religions as opposed to ideologies that they claim that their insight is disclosed to them and cannot be actively achieved by human beings" (Schwöbel, 9). Thus, Schwöbel contends that since Christian faith and the faith of others is "passively constituted" and not produced by anyone in other religions who claim a relationship "to God or the ultimate" (Schwöbel, 9), therefore God is the ultimate unifying factor for all three religions. Nevertheless, in my view, these assertions are not especially helpful inasmuch as someone might still claim to know "God or the ultimate focus of meaning" as "passively constituted," that is, as a reality disclosed to them and not actively achieved by them. That particular knowledge, however, is no assurance that what they know really is the true God who alone can justify and sanctify their belief. A person can easily conjure the God he or she wants instead of thinking of God as he truly is while claiming that his or her knowledge was passively constituted by God. That is no guarantee that one has actually relied on the God of Christian faith. While I completely agree with Schwöbel that because Christian faith is constituted by God therefore Christians are empowered by this to grant religious freedom to others, I disagree that such a position must mean that "what they [non-Christians] claim as revelation has been disclosed to them in just the same way—although it has not become a revelation for me as a Christian" (Schwöbel, 10).

The difficulty here is ingredient in the attempt to resolve the question of truth regarding revelation with a general theory of revelation. This, because no general theory will necessarily begin and end with revelation in its identity with Christ since no general theory of revelation will acknowledge that only the Holy Spirit is the miraculous enabling power who empowers genuine knowledge of the true God.[13] If, as Barth held, the truth of religion can only be known in faith and by grace through the particular revelation of God in Jesus Christ, then it is problematic to assert that what non-Christians claim as revelation is disclosed to them in just the same way as it is for Christians. This, because acknowledgment of the truth from a Christian theological perspective means acknowledging Jesus himself as the very self-disclosure of God for us and for all humanity since according to Jn 14:6 he alone is the Way, the Truth, and the Life and no one comes to the Father except through him. He is the truth which sets all people free (Jn 8:32).

Reconsidering Religion and Revelation

These considerations point to the problem of religion in relation to revelation in a very sharp way. Hence, if a Muslim begins and ends his or her thinking exclusively with

---

[13]See, e.g., n. 8 above.

revelation in its identity with what is supposed to be the final revelation in the Qur'ān as Shah-Kazemi indeed does, then that theologian will find himself or herself in conflict with Christian revelation in its identity with Christ and the Spirit. This is exactly what happens in the thinking of Shah-Kazemi when he writes that

> from the Muslim point of view, the Christian conception of a transcendent Essence which "neither begets nor is begotten nor proceeds," in the words of the Fourth Lateran Council, can form the basis upon which the affirmation can be made that Christians and Muslims do indeed believe in the same God; but added to this affirmation will come a rejection of the very doctrines—The Trinity and the Incarnation—which the Christians deem to be the ultimate fulfillment of monotheism. (Shah-Kazemi, 144)

Shah-Kazemi claims that the incompatibility between these two views can be accepted on one level while compatibility can be achieved at another level. Each, he says, "can recognize the other as a fellow-believer in the one true God" since each believes that "God is one and transcends all things" (Shah-Kazemi, 144). Still, each will disagree "over the claim that God is also three and is uniquely immanent in Jesus Christ" (Shah-Kazemi, 144). Nonetheless, Shah-Kazemi argues that "agreement can take priority over the disagreement, for the agreement is situated on the universal ground of monotheism, and in relation to the transcendent Essence of the one God which defines the very terms of that monotheism" (Shah-Kazemi, 144).

This ostensibly helpful suggestion, however, completely demolishes the truth of Christian revelation and the truth of who God eternally is as one being, three persons. One can claim unity of belief in this context only to the extent that one marginalizes Jesus Christ in his identity with God himself as the eternal Son of the Father and only to the extent that one holds to what is essentially a unitarian view of the divine being. Here is where I think Barth's position on the relation of religion and revelation might be of some assistance. He maintains that the truth of the Christian religion or of any religion (and he does admit that there is truth in other religions as noted above) cannot be recognized or accurately described if it is seen apart from the name of Jesus Christ who is not only God's judgment but also the one who justifies and sanctifies human beings in relation to God himself. If Barth is right in his analysis, then the disagreements between Muslims and Christians cannot be solved simply by claiming that they are monotheists. This is the case because, as I have argued, the Christian faith simply does not affirm and indeed cannot affirm *any* monotheism and cannot be judged in relation to any monotheism, as Barth rightly claimed. Christian understanding of God must begin and end with faith in Jesus Christ and not in a perspective which allows for a unity other than the unity of God disclosed in Jesus Christ to bind Christians and others (Muslims) together. Christian monotheism either is trinitarian from the outset because it is faithful to the revelation of God in Jesus Christ or it is not. That is what it means to live by grace and by faith. For Barth, the truth of revelation is the truth of God acting for all humanity in Jesus Christ. It is not an abstract truth that can be identified simply by referring to something that cannot be actively achieved by human action as Schwöbel supposes. This is why Barth argues that

> revelation denotes the Word of God itself in the act of its being spoken in time … It is the condition which conditions all things without itself being conditioned … [It] means the unveiling of what is veiled … Revelation as such is not relative. Revelation in fact does not differ from the person of Jesus Christ nor from the reconciliation accomplished in him. To say revelation is to say "The Word became flesh." (CD 118–19)

Inasmuch as revelation is identical with Christ the revealer, any idea of revelation that is based on the abstract or general notion that it is something that must come *to us* instead of from us simply circumvents the meaning of Christian revelation. Christian revelation is the act of God incarnate in Jesus Christ which comes *to us* as a miracle or it is not revelation at all. As such, this revelation simply cannot be abstractly or generally conceived but can only be acknowledged in faith and by grace in its identity with Jesus Christ himself through the present action of his Holy Spirit.

Consequently, any attempt to unite or separate Christianity and Islam using the "idea of God" as Creator, first cause or as a transcendent "Essence" simply means that we Christians and Muslims have redefined God's oneness in a way that damages the oneness in being of the Father, the Son, and the Holy Spirit. Any such thinking therefore undercuts the truth of the Christian faith and misses the truth of who God is as the savior of the world. So, while Shah-Kazemi's solution to the problem of whether or not Christians and Muslims believe in the same God may seem to be a viable solution, it can only work theologically, as Shah-Kazemi himself notes, if the "Persons of a Trinity … can be abstracted from belief in God, without this abstraction negating or undermining the essential postulate of monotheism: belief in one God" (Shah-Kazemi, 144). From a Christian perspective, that is faithful to revelation in its identity with Jesus Christ and which is empowered by an act of the Holy Spirit in union with the Word incarnate in Jesus Christ, this is a solution that once again proves that Barth was right in his assessment of religion.

This is a monotheistic religious construct which allows Christians and Muslims to claim that they believe in the same God. But the cost of this belief is that that which actually makes the Christian religion true is lost because only Jesus Christ himself in his essential unity with the Father and the Holy Spirit, as the one God who has already reconciled us to the Father, is the one who alone makes Christianity true! He is not only the revealer but the reconciler who has overcome all human attempts to understand God's oneness without actually relying on the judgment and grace actualized in his history for the salvation of the entire world. Shah-Kazemi ends his essay claiming that

> the Muslim theologian can embrace Christians as fellow-monotheists, while inviting them to consider the crystalline consummation of the defining principle of the monotheism they share in common: *lā ilāha illa'Llāh*, "no divinity but God,"

such as it is expressed in a myriad of ways by God's ultimate revelation to man, the Glorious Qur'ān. Once it is accepted that the Qur'ān completes the cycle of prophetic revelation ... and that it restores not just the pristine purity of the faith of Abraham, but also the primordial nature of man as such ... then it is entirely logical to take the next step: follow in the footsteps of the last Messenger who was sent by God as the "seal of the Prophets." (Shah-Kazemi, 146–7)

This finally will mean that belief in "no divinity but God" would have to entail the Islamic appeal to God and "not to God become man" but rather to the "Perfect Man" as expressed "by the second testimony: 'Muhammad is the Messenger of God'" (Shah-Kazemi, 147).

This thinking poses a major problem. From this Muslim perspective, Christians and Muslims can be said to believe in the same God only if and to the extent that that belief excludes Christian reliance on Jesus Christ himself from beginning to end. Yet, according to Karl Barth, that is both the strength and the weakness of the Christian religion—Christians have no other truth because there is no other truth than the truth of God revealed in and by Jesus himself as the only human being who was and is one in being with God himself and with us by virtue of the incarnation. This is the foundation of unity, and it was laid by God and cannot be laid by anyone else (cf. CD I/2, 868).[14] So, it seems that leaving aside the incarnation and the doctrine of the Trinity means that Christian monotheism will no longer be a monotheism dictated by the God attested in the Old Testament and in the New Testament as long as it begins and ends with a view of God that marginalizes Jesus Christ and the Holy Spirit.

Where does this leave us? Should Christians then stand opposed to Muslims? Or should Christians see themselves in solidarity with Muslims as they are in fact in solidarity with Jews as well, since all of us depend upon God's love and grace as attested in the Old and New Testaments in order to perceive the truth that actually unites us. It is interesting but true that in the document *A Common Word*, addressed by Muslims to Christians, appeal is made both to the book of Deuteronomy and to passages from the New Testament to assert the importance of not only the first commandment, which is to love God, but also the commandment to love our neighbors. To that extent it seems true that Jews, Christians, and Muslims do indeed appeal to the one God who is the God of Abraham, Isaac, and Jacob. And that appeal is based on God's revelation as attested in the Old and New Testaments so that in fact we are all united in our total dependence on

---

[14]This is why Barth argues that it is "only the Word of God which presupposes itself and proves itself by the power of its content" that is the proper foundation and center of dogmatics. Thus, "in dogmatics, laying the foundation means recollection that the foundation is already laid, and expectation that it will continually be laid ... The laying of this foundation means the shaking of all and any systematic certainties that may arise ... The best and most significant thing that is done in this matter is that again and again we are directed to look back to the centre and foundation of it all" which is "the Word of God, which is the event of God's work and activity" (Barth, CD I/2, 868–9).

grace, that is, God's forgiving grace both to recognize God as he truly is and to love and serve him by loving and serving our neighbors.

Therefore, as Christians we cannot suppose that solving this issue can be done by pitting one religion against another. That would be an attempt at self-justification using our religion which, in and of itself, is prone to idolatry and is born of unbelief, to define its truth when in fact only God can and will do that according to his promise. Christians who acknowledge the grace of revelation in its identity with Christ himself will find themselves moving toward others in the knowledge of the truth based on the revelation that God has in fact reconciled the world to himself. This is why I have argued in this chapter that if revelation and not religion is the criterion for the truth of religion itself, then it is a mistake to think that we must construct an idea of God's oneness as the basis for what is common to all three religions. Here I agree with Christoph Schwöbel who mentions that "Luther says that non-Christians *have* the same God as Christians, because there is only one God and this God is the triune God who revealed himself in his threefold divine self-giving as 'pure unutterable love'" (Schwöbel, 13). Schwöbel asks how Christians should approach other religions based on this idea that all *have* the same God but that they do not necessarily know that. He maintains that "Christians cannot claim that God is the almighty creator of heaven and earth who is everywhere present to his creation and deny God's presence in the religions" (Schwöbel, 14). This God is present precisely in his actions in Christ and the Holy Spirit. But it is a hidden presence because this God who is encountered both in other religions and in the Christian religion is hidden and obscured "through sin and unbelief," and "only God knows who the true believers are" (Schwöbel, 14). Accordingly, this same God is encountered by all. Thus, Schwöbel argues that "Christians will expect to experience the same God in new ways also in the religions" (Schwöbel, 14).

Interpreting the Trinity

The question raised in this chapter then is this: can we Christians use this set of ideas to argue that Muslims who clearly do not recognize or accept the oneness of God as he truly is as Father, Son, and Holy Spirit genuinely recognize aspects of the triune God? As seen in Chapter 5, this is what is argued by S. Mark Heim when he asserts that other religions, with their very different religious ends, place their members in contact with dimensions of the triune God. Thus he says that, even though Muslims are offended at the doctrine of the Trinity, still "the Muslim religious end focuses on the personal I of the Trinity."[15] Yet, if the triune God is one, then, as we saw above, the focus of Muslim reflection is on a unity of God that is not the unity of being of the Father, Son, and Holy

---

[15]S. Mark Heim, *The Depth of Riches*, 233. Further references to this work will appear in the text. For an assessment of Heim's trinitarian theology of religions, see Molnar, "'Thy Word is Truth,'" 70–92; and Chapter 5 above.

Spirit and to that extent cannot be said to be the "I" of the Holy Trinity. The problem that I have highlighted then concerns the fact that S. Mark Heim believes that "the Trinity teaches us that Jesus Christ cannot be an exhaustive or exclusive source for knowledge of God nor the exhaustive and exclusive act of God to save us" (Heim, 134). This assertion stands in stark contrast with Barth's view that

> the true and essential distinction of the Christian religion from the non-Christian, and with it its character as the religion of truth over against the religions of error, can be demonstrated only in the fact, or event, that taught by Holy Scripture the Church listens to Jesus Christ and no one else as grace and truth, not being slack but always cheerful to proclaim and believe Him … it all amounts to this: that the Church has to be weak in order to be strong. That there is a true religion is an event in the act of the grace of God in Jesus Christ … it is an event in the outpouring of the Holy Spirit … it is an event in the existence of the Church and the children of God. (CD I/2, 344)

Hence, for Barth, "the Church must … see that it expects everything from *Jesus Christ* and from Jesus Christ *everything*; that He is unceasingly recognized as the way, the truth and the life (Jn. 14.6)" (CD II/1, 320).

Connecting the dots with what was said above, we recall that Barth argued that any claim that monotheism should be seen as that which unites us in truth is unhelpful since the monotheism of Israel led to the rejection of their own Messiah while the monotheism of Islam Barth labeled as a caricature of the God of Israel since he believed that Islam had absolutized the idea of uniqueness instead of recognizing God's uniqueness as disclosed to Israel and as fulfilled in Jesus' own life, death, and resurrection for the sake of all people, including Jews, Christians, and Muslims. Barth rightly discouraged the idea that Christians should or could proclaim the one true God to Jews since "as the people of the covenant, they already worship and serve the one true God."[16] And he thought it was inappropriate to attempt to find a common ground with Islam on the basis of monotheism since he regarded their monotheism as more than a little problematic as we shall see below.

With regard to Christian/Jewish relations, Thomas F. Torrance had some important things to say. For instance, he maintained that "the fulfilment of God's revealing and saving purpose in Jesus Christ did not mean that the ancient covenant of God with Israel was abolished, but rather that it retained its force in the divine election of Israel as the people to whom were committed the oracles of God."[17] Israel was indeed the "appointed ground upon which and from which the mission and expansion of divine salvation to all mankind broke forth from Israel into the world and became established among the

---

[16]George Hunsinger, "After Barth: A Christian Appreciation of Jews and Judaism," in *Conversational Theology: Essays on Ecumenical, Postliberal, and Political Themes, with Special Reference to Karl Barth* (London: T&T Clark, 2015), 93–107, 98.
[17]Torrance, *The Mediation of Christ*, 102.

gentile nations."[18] Torrance thus believed that since the Church is a "new dispensation" of the "one covenant of grace forged by God with Israel," therefore the promises made by God to Israel are in no way abrogated so that "the roles and destinies of Israel and the Church were locked into each other. With the accomplishment of reconciliation in Jesus Christ in the midst of Israel, reconciliation was no longer just a promise announced through divine revelation to Israel." As that promise was actualized in the incarnate Son, Jesus Christ, we know that "reconciliation constitutes the inner dynamic content of revelation … Hence Jews and Christians need and complement each other both in their service of divine revelation and in their service of reconciliation, and cannot but frustrate their dual mission from God to mankind when they are estranged from one another."[19]

Finally, Torrance insisted that "by his cross Christ has reconciled both Jews and gentiles in one body to God, putting an end in himself to all enmity between them."[20] It is in this context that Torrance asked what this interlocking of Israel and the Church might mean with respect to the "doctrine of the one God advocated by Judaism and the doctrine of the Triune God advocated by Christianity?" His answer was that on the one hand "the Christian understanding of God is grounded in and inseparable from the revelation of the one Lord God Almighty given to Israel and mediated through the Old Testament Scriptures." On the other hand, for Torrance, "there is no access to knowledge of God as he is in himself apart from the reconciliation with God brought about by the cross of Christ. In their understanding of God Christians and Jews need to be reconciled to God and to each other."[21] In this light, Torrance also held that the Christian understanding of God as the Trinity "must not be, and cannot really be, divorced from Jewish understanding of God as One, otherwise it also becomes distorted through alien patterns of thought which our gentile minds and cultures impose upon it" which might lead to tritheism.[22] However, apart from the reconciliation accomplished for us in Christ, Torrance claimed that "the people of Israel can know God only in his undifferentiated oneness and not as he in his intrinsic trinitarian relations" with the result that "Jesus Christ and his death on the Cross are a bewildering enigma."[23]

Conclusion

Following Barth and Torrance as well, I have argued that Christian faith does not confirm just any monotheism and is not confirmed by just any monotheism; rather it is monotheistic precisely in a unique way as embodied in God's trinitarian self-revelation. Thus, "God's triunity does not imply any threat to but is rather the basis of the Christian

---

[18]Ibid.
[19]Ibid., 102–3.
[20]Ibid., 105.
[21]Ibid.
[22]Ibid., 106–7.
[23]Ibid., 107–8.

concept of the unity of God" (CD I/1, 348). Because of that, any idea that Christianity is simply the radicalization of monotheism, as Schwöbel believes it is, could open the door, against his own intentions, to a conception of God's unity that is not dictated by his triunity. That is the door that must be closed more tightly at this point since even perception of God's unity (monotheism) cannot be rightly asserted apart from this particular divine revelation. In this context, Barth appealed to the fact that "Yahweh-Kyrios," who is the one God revealed according to the Old Testament witness, is the one God whose Lordship is revealed in Jesus, the Son of the Father. Accordingly, for Barth, "the triunity of God does not mean threefold deity either in the sense of a plurality of Gods or in the sense of the existence of a plurality of individuals or parts within the one Godhead" (CD I/1, 350). Barth therefore insists, with the eleventh Council of Toledo, that "we distinguish the persons, but we do not divide the divinity" (CD I/1, 348). The deity of course would be divided by any idea that God is composed of parts and is not fully divine as Father, Son, and Holy Spirit.

Here, in sum, I suggest that Barth's diagnosis of the problem of religion and revelation and his proposed solution would mean that (1) Shah-Kazemi's solution is unworkable because it advances a notion of monotheism that is in conflict with the heart of Christian faith since in the end he insists on God's oneness at the expense of the incarnation and of God's triunity; (2) Goshen-Gottstein's solution will not work because it appeals to our ethical behavior as that which indicates truth; but even good people need to live by God's forgiving grace and cannot know the truth apart from actually relying on that grace in its identity with the Giver of grace—Jesus Christ himself. Any attempt to transfer the question of truth in theology from genuine knowledge of the truth, as that truth is grounded in itself, to our ethical behavior amounts simply to an espousal of a kind of subjectivist self-justification based on our human behavior;[24] (3) Schwöbel's proposal, while helpful in certain respects, is weakened by his suggestion that the certainty of faith is constituted by a disclosure experience. This, because the truth of revelation and the truth of our concept of revelation can neither be constituted by nor recognized by our supposed disclosure experiences but must be acknowledged as truth that positively comes to meet us in a specific action of God's trinitarian self-revelation. Certainty here is guaranteed therefore only by the Holy Spirit acting in the event of faith which acknowledges that Jesus is the Way, the Truth, and the Life. What is more, if that is the true revelation of God in history as Christians believe it is, then no general theory of revelation will ever compel us to acknowledge that particular truth since that compulsion either comes from the grace of God's own self-impartation through his Holy Spirit or it does not come at all. From this I conclude that all attempts to harmonize Jewish, Christian, and Muslim beliefs that appeal to their supposed common monotheistic view of God falter precisely because all religions, including the Christian religion, can only recognize and live in solidarity

---

[24]This is precisely what I opposed in Chapter 5 as a form of self-justification when I argued against the idea that we can love God through loving our neighbors and fighting against oppression instead of because God in Christ has freed us to do this precisely by his loving us and thus reconciling us to himself while we were still sinners.

as they actually rely on God's forgiving grace (justification by grace). That, however, means that all three religions can recognize and live in and from the truth only as they point away from their practices, religious or ethical, toward the truth of God himself as attested in the Old and New Testaments and as recognized at Nicaea and Chalcedon.

From a Christian theological perspective then, I propose that the only way forward in this difficult matter is not to deny to Jesus his unique function as the only one who justifies and sanctifies Jews and Gentiles but to cheerfully proclaim the fact that in him all religions may find the truth without which they would be nothing more than human attempts to construct the God they want. This means that it is an enormous mistake to think that Christians should allow their thinking about God to be shaped by a natural theology that posits a oneness recognizable to philosophers and others without faith engendered by the Holy Spirit which, as true faith, unites them to Christ and thus to God the Father.

Moreover, it is a serious mistake on the part of Christians to think that they can affirm God's oneness without affirming that oneness through the incarnate Word and in reliance upon the Holy Spirit. Such an approach would allow those of other religions whose thinking about God's oneness clearly is not shaped by the oneness of the triune God to hold sway. This remark must not be construed as an attempt to pit one religion against another. Rather, it is an attempt to firmly assert that no concept of monotheism (Christian, Jewish, Muslim, or other) can be considered true in itself as a religious construct since truth is determined exclusively by God's gracious love for all as the revealer, reconciler, and redeemer in his Word and Spirit. As we saw above, while Barth certainly held that since the Jews have the covenant and they already know, serve and worship the one true God, he also argued that any claim that monotheism should be seen as that which unites us in truth is unhelpful since the monotheism of Israel at the time of Jesus' ministry finally led to the rejection of their own Messiah. Barth also believed that it was inappropriate to attempt to find a common ground with Islam on the basis of monotheism since he regarded their monotheism as more than a little problematic saying:

> The artifice adopted by Islam consists in its developing to a supreme degree what is at the heart of all paganism, revealing and setting at the very centre its esoteric essence, i.e., so-called "monotheism." In this way it was able to become a deadly danger to all other forms of paganism and to a Christianity with a pagan conception of the oneness of God. The fact should not be overlooked that this danger, its seductive profundity, consists in what is (compared with other forms of paganism) simply the greater primitiveness with which it proclaims the unique as God instead of God as the One who is unique. (CD II/1, 448)

As stated above, this leaves all of us (Jews, Christians, and Muslims) in a position that should be informed by the forbearance of Christ. That means we should freely admit that our unity cannot and should not be sought and found in ethical practice no matter how important that may be; it should not be sought and found in religious practice no matter how important that may be, and it certainly should not be sought and found in a supposed common concept of monotheism no matter how important that also may be. My argument has been that since all of humanity can live in freedom by grace alone, therefore Jews, Christians, and Muslims should indeed recognize their solidarity as those who God has in fact bound together in union with himself by his own act of revelation and reconciliation as this has occurred historically in the history of his incarnate Son and continues to be effective even today in the present actions of his Holy Spirit within and outside the church. In this context, I hope we can all agree that love of God and love of neighbor finally do unite all three religions since when Jesus was asked about which was the greatest commandment his response was, "You shall love the Lord, your God, with all your heart, with all your soul, and with all your mind. This is the greatest and the first commandment. The second is like it: You shall love your neighbor as yourself. The whole law and the prophets depend on these two commandments" (Mt. 22:37-40).

SELECT BIBLIOGRAPHY

Anderson, Ray S. "Barth and New Direction for Natural Theology," in *Theology beyond Christendom: Essays on the Centenary of the Birth of Karl Barth May 10, 1886*. Edited by John Thompson. Allison Park, PA: Pickwick, 1986, 241–66.

Barr, James. *Biblical Faith and Natural Theology: The Gifford Lectures for 1991 Delivered in the University of Edinburgh*. Oxford: Clarendon Press, 1993.

Barter, Jane A. "A Theology of Liberation in Barth's Church Dogmatics IV/3," *Scottish Journal of Theology* 53 (2) (2000): 154–76.

Barth, Karl. *Ad Limina Apostolorum: An Appraisal of Vatican II*. Translated by Keith R. Crim. Richmond, VA: John Knox Press, 1967.

Barth, Karl. *Church Dogmatics*. 4 vols. in 13 pts.

Vol. I, pt. 1: *The Doctrine of the Word of God*. Edited by G. W. Bromiley and T. F. Torrance. Translated by G. W. Bromiley. Edinburgh: T&T Clark, 1975.

Vol. I, pt. 2: *The Doctrine of the Word of God*. Edited by G. W. Bromiley and T. F. Torrance. Translated by G. T. Thomson and Harold Knight. Edinburgh: T&T Clark, 1970.

Vol. II, pt. 1: *The Doctrine of God*. Edited by G. W. Bromiley and T. F. Torrance. Translated by T. H. L. Parker, W. B. Johnston, H. Knight, and J. L. M. Harie. Edinburgh: T&T Clark, 1964.

Vol. II, pt. 2: *The Doctrine of God*. Edited by G. W. Bromiley and T. F. Torrance. Translated by G. W. Bromiley, J. C. Campbell, Iain Wilson, J. Strathearn McNab, Harold Knight, and R. A. Stewart. Edinbugh: T&T Clark, 1967.

Vol. III, pt. 1: *The Doctrine of Creation*. Edited by G. W. Bromiley and T. F. Torrance. Translated by J. W. Edwards, O. Bussey, and Harold Knight. Edinburgh: T&T Clark, 1970.

Vol. III, pt. 2: *The Doctrine of Creation*. Edited by G. W. Bromiley and T. F. Torrance. Translated by Harold Knight, G. W. Bromiley, J. K. S. Reid, and R. H. Fuller. Edinburgh: T&T Clark, 1968.

Vol. III, pt. 3: *The Doctrine of Creation*. Edited by G. W. Bromiley and T. F. Torrance. Translated by G. W. Bromiley and R. J. Ehrlich. Edinburgh: T&T Clark, 1976.

Vol. IV, pt. 1: *The Doctrine of Reconciliation*. Edited by G. W. Bromiley and T. F. Torrance. Translated by G. W. Bromiley. Edinburgh: T&T Clark, 1974.

Vol. IV, pt. 2: *The Doctrine of Reconciliation*. Edited by G. W. Bromiley and T. F. Torrance. Translated by G. W. Bromiley. Edinburgh: T&T Clark, 1967.

Vol. IV, pt. 3: *The Doctrine of Reconciliation*. First half. Edited by G. W. Bromiley and T. F. Torrance. Translated by G. W. Bromiley. Edinburgh: T&T Clark, 1976.

Vol. IV, pt. 3: *The Doctrine of Reconciliation*. Second half. Edited by G. W. Bromiley and T. F. Torrance. Translated by G. W. Bromiley. Edinburgh: T&T Clark, 1969.

Vol. IV, pt. 4: *The Christian Life*. Lecture fragments. Translated by G. W. Bromiley. Grand Rapids, MI: William B. Eerdmans, 1981.

Barth, Karl. *Credo: A Presentation of the Chief Problems of Dogmatics with Reference to the Apostles' Creed* (Sixteen lectures delivered at the University of Utrecht in February and March, 1935). Translated by J. Strathearn McNab. London: Hodder & Stoughton, 1936.

Barth, Karl. *Letters 1961–1968*. Edited by Jürgen Fangemeier and Hinrich Stoevesandt. Translated and edited by G. W. Bromiley. Grand Rapids, MI: William B. Eerdmans, 1981.

Barth, Karl. *Natural Theology: Comprising "Nature and Grace" by Professor Dr. Emil Brunner and the Reply "No!" by Dr. Karl Barth*. Translated by Peter Fraenkel. Introduction by John Baillie. Eugene, OR: Wipf and Stock, 2002.

Barth, Karl. *The Göttingen Dogmatics: Instruction in the Christian Religion Volume One*. Edited by Hannelotte Reiffen. Translated by Geoffrey W. Bromiley. Grand Rapids, MI: William B. Eerdmans, 1991.

Barth, Karl. *The Humanity of God*. Translated by Thomas Wieser and John Newton Thomas. Richmond, VA: John Knox Press, 1968.

Barth, Karl. *Theology and Church: Shorter Writings 1920–1928*. Translated by Louise Pettibone Smith. Introduction by Thomas F. Torrance. New York: Harper & Row, 1962.

Bruce, Matthew J. Aragon. "Election" in *The Oxford Handbook of Karl Barth*. Edited by Paul Dafydd Jones and Paul T. Nimmo. Oxford: Oxford University Press, 2019.

Bultmann, Rudolf. *Jesus Christ and Mythology*. New York: Charles Scribner's Sons, 1958.

Busch, Eberhard, ed. *Barth in Conversation: Volume 1, 1959–1962*. Translated by The Translation Fellows of the Center for Barth Studies Princeton Theological Seminary, Karlfried Froehlich, German editor, Darrell L. Guder, English editor, David C. Chao, project manager. Louisville, KY: Westminster John Knox Press, 2017.

Catechism of the Catholic Church. Mahwah, NJ: Paulist Press, 1994.

Colyer, Elmer M. *How to Read T. F. Torrance: Understanding His Trinitarian and Scientific Theology*. Downers Grove, IL: InterVarsity Press, 2001.

Couenhoven, Jesse. "The Necessities of Perfect Freedom," *International Journal of Systematic Theology* 14 (4) (October 2012): 398–419.

Dempsey, Michael T., ed. *Trinity and Election in Contemporary Theology*. Grand Rapids, MI: William B. Eerdmans, 2011.

Denzinger, Heinrich, *Compendium of Creeds, Definitions, and Declarations on Matters of Faith and Morals*. Edited by Peter Hünermann, Robert Fastiggi, and Anne Englund Nash, 43rd edition. San Francisco: Ignatius Press, 2012.

Duffy, Stephen J. "Experience of Grace," in *The Cambridge Companion to Karl Rahner*. Edited by Declan Marmion and Mary E. Hines. Cambridge: Cambridge University Press, 2005, 43–62.

Fangmeier, Jürgen, and Stoevesandt, Hinrich, eds. *Karl Barth Letters 1961–1968*. Translated and edited by Geoffrey Bromiley. Grand Rapids, MI: Eerdmans, 1981.

Fee, Gordon D. *Pauline Christology: An Exegetical-Theological Study*. Peabody, MA: Hendrickson, 2007.

Fee Nordling, Cherith. *Knowing God by Name: A Conversation between Elizabeth A. Johnson and Karl Barth*. New York: Peter Lang, 2010.

Fiddes, Paul S. *The Creative Suffering of God*. Oxford: Clarendon Press, 1988.

Fiddes, Paul S. *Participating in God: A Pastoral Doctrine of the Trinity*. Louisville, KY: Westminster John Knox Press, 2000.

Fiddes, Paul S. *Two Views on the Doctrine of the Trinity*. Edited by Jason S. Sexton and Stanley N. Gundry. Grand Rapids, MI: Zondervan, 2014.

Florovsky, Georges. "St Athanasius' Concept of Creation," *Studia Patristica*, vol. VI, edited by F. L. Cross (Berlin: *Akademie Verlag; Texte und Untersuchungen zur Geschichte der altchristlichen Literatur, Band* 8, 1962), 36–57. Reprinted at https://afkimel.wordpress.com/2014/11/07/florovsky-on-st-athanasius-and-the-doctrine-of-creation/, 1-13, 1-6.

Gallaher, Brandon. *Freedom and Necessity in Modern Trinitarian Theology*. Oxford: Oxford University Press, 2016.

Galvin, John P. *The Invitation of Grace, 64-75. A World of Grace: An Introduction to the Themes and Foundations of Karl Rahner's Theology*. Edited by Leo J. O'Donovan, S.J. New York: Crossroad, 1981.

Gilson, Etienne. *God and Philosophy*. New Haven: Yale University Press, 1979.

Godsey, John, ed. *Karl Barth's Table Talk*. Richmond, VA: John Knox Press, 1962.

Goshen-Gottstein, Alon "God between Christians and Jews: Is It the Same God?," in *Do We Worship the Same God?: Jews, Christians and Muslims in Dialogue*. Edited by Miroslav Volf. Grand Rapids, MI: Eerdmans, 2012, 50–75.

Gunton, Colin E. *A Brief Theology of Revelation*. Edinburgh: T&T Clark, 1995.

Gunton, Colin E. "Review of Catherine LaCugna," *God for Us, Scottish Journal of Theology* 47 (1) (1994).

Gutiérrez, Gustavo. *A Theology of Liberation: History, Politics, and Salvation*. Translated and edited by Sister Caridad Inda and John Eagleson. Maryknoll, NY: Orbis Books, 1996.

Habets, Myk, and Tolliday, Phillip, eds. *Trinitarian Theology after Barth*. Eugene, OR: Pickwick, 2011.

Habets, Myk, ed. *Ecumenical Perspectives on the* Filioque *for the Twenty-First Century*. London: T&T Clark Bloomsbury, 2015.

Hart, David Bentley. *That All Shall Be Saved: Heaven, Hell, and Universal Salvation*. New Haven: Yale University Press, 2019.

Haught, John. *What Is God? How to Think about the Divine*. New York: Paulist Press, 1986.

Hector, Kevin. "Immutability, Necessity and Triunity: Towards a Resolution of the Trinity and Election Controversy," *Scottish Journal of Theology* 65 (1) (2012): 64–81.

Heim, S. Mark. *The Depth of Riches: A Trinitarian Theology of Religious Ends*. Grand Rapids, MI: Eerdmans, 2001.

Hilary, St. of Poitiers. *On the Trinity*, Church Fathers. Translated by E. W. Watson, L. Pullan and others. Edited by W. Sanday. A Select Library of Nicene and Post-nicene Fathers of the Christian Church. Second series. Edited by Philip Schaff and Henry Wace. Volume IX. Grand Rapids, MI: William B. Eerdmans, 1997.

Hunsinger, George. "After Barth: A Christian Appreciation of Jews and Judaism," in *Conversational Theology: Essays on Ecumenical, Postliberal, and Political Themes, with Special Reference to Karl Barth*. London: T&T Clark, 2015, 93–107.

Hunsinger, George. *Disruptive Grace: Studies in the Theology of Karl Barth*. Grand Rapids, MI: William B. Eerdmans, 2000.

Hunsinger, George. "Election and the Trinity: Twenty-Five Theses on the Theology of Karl Barth," *Modern Theology* 24 (2) (April 2008), 179–98.

Hunsinger, George. "Election and the Trinity: Twenty-Five Theses on the Theology of Karl Barth," in *Trinity and Election in Contemporary Theology*. Edited by Michael T. Dempsey. Grand Rapids, MI: William B. Eerdmans, 2011.

Hunsinger, George. *Evangelical, Catholic and Reformed: Doctrinal Essays on Barth and Related Themes*. Grand Rapids, MI: Eerdmans, 2015.

Hunsinger, George. "Hellfire and Damnation: Four Ancient and Modern Views," *Scottish Journal of Theology* 51 (4) (2009): 406–34.

Hunsinger, George. *How to Read Karl Barth: The Shape of His Theology*. New York: Oxford University Press, 1991.

Hunsinger, George. "Karl Barth's Doctrine of the Trinity, and Some Protestant Doctrines after Barth," in *The Oxford Handbook of The Trinity*. Edited by Gilles Emery OP and Matthew Levering. New York: Oxford University Press, 2011.

Hunsinger, George. "The Mediator of Communion: Karl Barth's Doctrine of the Holy Spirit," in *Cambridge Companion to Karl Barth*. Edited by John Webster. Cambridge: Cambridge University Press, 2000, 177–94.

Hunsinger, George. *Reading Barth with Charity: A Hermeneutical Proposal*. Grand Rapids, MI: Baker Academic, 2015.

Hunsinger, George. "Review of *Trinity and Kingdom*," *The Thomist* 47 (1983): 129–39.

Select Bibliography

Irving, Alexander J. D. "Does the Epistemological Relevance of the Holy Spirit Mean the End for Natural Theology? A Response to Paul Molnar with Reference to Thomas F. Torrance's Reconstruction of Natural Theology," in *Trinity Journal* (2017): 225–45.

Irving, Alexander J. D. "Natural Theology as the Intra-structure of Theological Science: T. F. Torrance's Proposals for Natural Theology in the Context of the Synthesis of Rational Structure and Material Content," *Participatio, The Journal of the Thomas F. Torrance Theological Fellowship* 7 (December 2017): 99–124.

Jenson, Robert W. *The Triune Identity: God according to the Gospel*. Philadelphia: Fortress Press, 1982.

Johnson, Elizabeth A. *Quest for the Living God: Mapping Frontiers in the Theology of God*. New York: Continuum: 2008.

Johnson, Elizabeth A. "Redeeming the Name of Christ," in *Freeing Theology: The Essentials of Theology in Feminist Perspective*. Edited by Catherine Mowry LaCugna. San Francisco: HarperCollins, 1993.

Johnson, Elizabeth A. *She Who Is: The Mystery of God in Feminist Theological Discourse*. New York: Crossroad, 1992; reissued in 2002 as a tenth anniversary edition and in 2017 as a twenty-fifth anniversary edition.

Karl Rahner in Dialogue: Conversations and Interviews 1965–1982. Translated by Harvey D. Egan. Edited by Paul Imhof and Hubert Biallowons. New York: Crossroad, 1986.

Kasper, Walter. *The God of Jesus Christ*. Translated by Matthew J. O'Connell. New York: Crossroad, 1986.

Kaufman, Gordon. *In Face of Mystery: A Constructive Theology*. Cambridge, MA: Harvard University Press, 1993.

Kaufman, Gordon. *Theology for a Nuclear Age*. Philadelphia: Westminster Press, 1985.

Kilby, Karen. "Philosophy, Theology and Foundationalism in the Thought of Karl Rahner," *Scottish Journal of Theology* 55 (2) (2002): 127–40.

Kilby, Karen. *Karl Rahner*. Edited by Peter Vardy. Fount of Christian Thinkers, Series. London: Fount Paperbacks an Imprint of HarperCollins, 1997.

Knitter, Paul F. *No Other Name? A Critical Survey of Christian Attitudes toward the World Religions*. Maryknoll, NY: Orbis, 1985.

LaCugna, Catherine Mowry. *God for Us: The Trinity and Christian Life*. San Francisco: Harper San Francisco, 1991.

LaCugna, Catherine Mowry, ed. "God in Communion with Us," in *Freeing Theology: The Essentials of Theology in Feminist Perspective*. New York: HarperCollins, 1993.

Lewis, Alan E. *Between Cross and Resurrection: A Theology of Holy Saturday*. Grand Rapids, MI: William B. Eerdmans, 2001.

Long, D. Stephen. *Saving Karl Barth: Hans Urs von Balthasar's Preoccupation*. Minneapolis, MN: Fortress Press, 2014.

MacDonald, Gregory, ed. *"All Shall Be Well": Explorations in Universalism and Christian Theology, from Origen to Moltmann*. Eugene, OR: Cascade Books, 2011.

Marshall, Bruce D. "Christ the End of Analogy," in *The Analogy of Being: Invention of the Antichrist or the Wisdom of God?* Edited by Thomas Joseph White OP (Grand Rapids, MI: Eerdmans, 2011), 280–313.

Marshall, Bruce D. *Christology in Conflict: The Identity of a Saviour in Rahner and Barth*. Oxford: Basil Blackwell, 1987.

McCormack, Bruce L., and Alexandra Pârvan. "Immutability, (Im)passibility and Suffering: Steps Towards a 'Psychological' Ontology of God," in *Neue Zeitschrift für Systematische Theologie und Religionsphilosophie* 59 (1) (March 2017): 1–25.

McCormack, Bruce L., ed. "The Actuality of God: Karl Barth in Conversation with Open Theism," in *Engaging the Doctrine of God: Contemporary Protestant Perspectives*. Grand Rapids, MI, Baker Academic, 2008, 185–242.

McCormack, Bruce L. "The Doctrine of the Trinity after Barth: An Attempt to Reconstruct Barth's Doctrine in the Light of His Later Christology," in *Trinitarian Theology after Barth*. Edited by Myk Habets and Phillip Tolliday. Eugene, OR: Pickwick, 2011.

McCormack, Bruce L. "Election and the Trinity: Theses in Response to George Hunsinger," in *Trinity and Election in Contemporary Theology*. Edited by Michael T. Dempsey. Grand Rapids, MI: Eerdmans, 2011, 115–37.

McCormack, Bruce L., ed. *Engaging the Doctrine of God*: *Contemporary Protestant Perspectives*. Grand Rapids, MI: Baker Academic, 2008.

McCormack, Bruce L. "Grace and Being: The Role of God's Gracious Election in Karl Barth's Theological Ontology," in *The Cambridge Companion to Karl Barth*. Edited by John Webster. Cambridge: Cambridge University Press, 2000, 92–110.

McCormack, Bruce L. "The Passion of God Himself: Barth on Jesus's Cry of Dereliction," in *Reading the Gospels with Karl Barth*. Edited by Daniel L. Migliore. Grand Rapids, MI: Eerdmans, 2017, 155–72.

McFague, Sallie. *Models of God*: *Theology for an Ecological, Nuclear Age*. Philadelphia: Fortress Press, 1987.

McGrath, Alister E. *Scientific Theology: Volume I Nature*. Grand Rapids, MI: Eerdmans, 2001.

McGrath, Alister E. *A Fine-Tuned Universe: The Quest for God in Science and Theology: The 2009 Gifford Lectures*. Louisville, KY: Westminster John Knox Press, 2009.

McGrath, Alister E. *The Open Secret: A New Vision for Natural Theology*. Oxford: Blackwell, 2008.

Migliore, Daniel L. *Faith Seeking Understanding: An Introduction to Christian Theology*. 3rd edition. Grand Rapids, MI: Eerdmans, 2014.

Molnar, Paul D. "Can Theology Be Contemporary and True? A Review Discussion," of Joseph Cardinal Ratzinger's *Principles of Catholic Theology*, *The Thomist* 52 (3) (July 1988): 513–37.

Molnar, Paul D. *Divine Freedom and the Doctrine of the Immanent Trinity*: *In Dialogue with Karl Barth and Contemporary Theology*. 2nd edition. New York: T&T Clark, 2017.

Molnar, Paul D. *Faith, Freedom and the Spirit: The Economic Trinity in Barth, Torrance and Contemporary Theology*. Downers Grove, IL: IVP Academic, 2015.

Molnar, Paul D. "Gunton on the Trinity," in *T&T Clark Handbook of Colin Gunton*. Edited by Andrew Picard, Murray Rae, and Myk Habets. London: T&T Clark, 2021, chapter 3, 41–58.

Molnar, Paul D. "The Importance of the Doctrine of Justification in the Theology of Thomas F. Torrance and of Karl Barth," *Scottish Journal of Theology* 70 (2) (2017): 198–226.

Molnar, Paul D. *Incarnation and Resurrection*: *Toward a Contemporary Understanding*. Grand Rapids, MI: Eerdmans, 2007.

Molnar, Paul D. "Love of God and Love of Neighbor in the Theology of Karl Rahner and Karl Barth," *Modern Theology* 20 (4) (2004): 567–98.

Molnar, Paul D. "Natural Theology Revisited: A Comparison of T. F. Torrance and Karl Barth," *Zeitshrift Für Dialektische Theologie* 20 (1) (December 2005): 53–83.

Molnar, Paul D. "The Obedience of the Son in the Theology of Karl Barth and of Thomas F. Torrance," *Scottish Journal of Theology* 67 (1) (2014): 50–69.

Molnar, Paul D. "Some Dogmatic Consequences of Paul F. Knitter's Unitarian Theocentrism," *The Thomist* 55 (3) (July, 1992): 449–95.

Molnar, Paul D. "Theological Issues Involved in the Filioque," chapter three, in *Ecumenical Perspectives on the* Filioque *for the Twenty-first Century*. Edited by Myk Habets. London: T&T Clark, 2015.

Molnar, Paul D. *Thomas F. Torrance*: *Theologian of the Trinity*. Aldershot: Ashgate, 2009.

Molnar, Paul D. "'Thy Word Is Truth': The Role of Faith in Reading Scripture Theologically with Karl Barth," *Scottish Journal of Theology* 63 (1) (2010): 70–92.

Molnar, Paul D. "The Trinity, Election and God's Ontological Freedom: A Response to Kevin W. Hector," *Trinity and Election in Contemporary Theology*. Edited by Michael T. Dempsey. Grand Rapids, MI: William B. Eerdmans, 2011.

Molnar, Paul D. "What Difference Does One's View of God Make in Understanding Sin and Salvation? Some Suggestions from Karl Barth," forthcoming in the *Scottish Journal of Theology*.

Moltmann, Jürgen. *God in Creation: A New Theology of Creation and the Spirit of God*. Translated by Margaret Kohl. New York: Harper & Row, 1985.

Moltmann, Jürgen. *Sun of Righteousness, Arise!: God's Future for Humanity and the Earth*. Translated by Margaret Kohl. Minneapolis, MN: Fortress Press, 2010.

Moltmann, Jürgen. *The Trinity and the Kingdom, The Doctrine of God*. Translated by Margaret Kohl. New York: Harper & Row, 1981.

Nelson, R. David, Sarisky, Darren, and Stratis, Justin, eds. *Theological Theology: Essays in Honour of John Webster*. London: T&T Clark, 2015.

Rahner, Karl, and Vorgrimler, Herbert. *Theological Dictionary*. Edited by Cornelius Ernst OP. Translated by Richard Strachan. New York: Herder and Herder, 1965.

Rahner, Karl, and Weger, Karl–Heinz. *Our Christian Faith: Answers for the Future*. Translated by Francis McDonagh. New York: Crossroad, 1981.

Rahner, Karl. *Foundations of Christian Faith: An Introduction to the Idea of Christianity*. Translated by William V. Dych. New York: Seabury, 1978.

Rahner, Karl. *Hearer of the Word: Laying the Foundation for a Philosophy of Religion*. Translated by Joseph Donceel. Edited with an introduction by Andrew Tallon. New York: Continuum, 1994.

Rahner, Karl. *The Love of Jesus and the Love of Neighbor*. Translated by Robert Barr. New York: Crossroad, 1983.

Rahner, Karl. *Theological Investigations*. 23 vols.
   Vol. 1: *God, Christ, Mary and Grace*. Translated by Cornelius Ernst OP. Baltimore: Helicon Press, 1961.
   Vol. 4: *More Recent Writings*. Translated by Kevin Smyth. Baltimore: Helicon Press, 1966.
   Vol. 6: *Concerning Vatican Council II*. Translated by Karl–H. and Boniface Kruger. Baltimore: Helicon Press, 1969.
   Vol. 9: *Writings of 1965–1967*. Translated by Graham Harrison. New York: Herder and Herder, 1972.
   Vol. 11: *Confrontations 1*. Translated by David Bourke. New York: Seabury Press, 1974.
   Vol. 13: *Theology, Anthropology, Christology*. Translated by David Bourke. London: Darton, Longman & Todd, 1975.
   Vol. 16: *Experience of the Spirit: Source of Theology*. Translated by David Morland. New York: Seabury Press, 1976.

Radford Ruether, Rosemary. *To Change the World: Christology and Cultural Criticism*. New York: Crossroad, 1981.

Ratzinger, Joseph Cardinal. *Principles of Catholic Theology: Building Stones for a Fundamental Theology*. Translated by Sister Mary Frances McCarthy, S.N.D. San Francisco: Ignatius Press, 1987.

Robinson, Dominic. *Understanding the "Imago Dei" the Thought of Barth, von Balthasar and Moltmann*. Farnham: Ashgate, 2011.

Robinson, John A. T. *Honest to God*. Philadelphia: Westminster Press, 1963.

Robinson, John A. T. "Universalism—Is It Heretical?," *Scottish Journal of Theology* 2 (1949): 139–55.

Robinson, John A. T. *In the End, God … a Study of the Christian Doctrine of the Last Things*. Edited by Robin Parry. Foreword by Gregory MacDonald. Introduction by Trevor Hart. Eugene, OR: Cascade Books, 2011.

Rosario Rodríguez, Rubén. *Dogmatics after Babel: Beyond the Theologies of Word and Culture*. Louisville, KY: Westminster John Knox Press, 2018.

Schwöbel, Christoph. "The Same God? The Perspective of Faith, the Identity of God, Tolerance, and Dialogue," in *Do We Worship the Same God?: Jews, Christians, and Muslims in Dialogue*. Edited by Miroslav Volf. Grand Rapids, MI: Eerdmans, 2012, 1–17.

Shah-Kazemi, Reza. "Do Christians and Muslims Believe in the Same God?," in *Do We Worship the Same God?: Jews, Christians, and Muslims in Dialogue*. Edited by Miroslav Volf. Grand Rapids, MI: Eerdmans, 2012, 76–147.

Tillich, Paul. *The Shaking of the Foundations*. New York: Charles Scribner's Sons, 1948.

Torrance, Thomas F. *The Apocalypse Today: Sermons on Revelation*. London: James Clarke, 1960.

Torrance, Thomas F. *Atonement: The Person and Work of Christ*. Edited by Robert T. Walker. Milton Keynes, UK: Paternoster; Downers Grove, IL: IVP Academic, 2009.

Torrance, Thomas F. "The Atonement: The Singularity of Christ and the Finality of the Cross: The Atonement and the Moral Order," in *Universalism and the Doctrine of Hell: Papers Presented at the Fourth Edinburgh Conference in Christian Dogmatics, 1991*. Edited by Nigel M. de S. Cameron. Carlisle, UK: Paternoster Press; Grand Rapids, MI: Baker Book House, 1992, 225–56.

Torrance, Thomas F. *A Passion for Christ: The Vision that Ignites Ministry*. Edited by Gerrit Dawson and Jock Stein. Edinburgh: Handsel Press, 1999.

Torrance, Thomas F. "The Christian Apprehension of God the Father," In *Speaking the Christian God: The Holy Trinity and the Challenge of Feminism*. Edited by Alvin F. Kimel Jr. Grand Rapids: Eerdmans, 1992, 120–43.

Torrance, Thomas F. *The Christian Doctrine of God, One Being Three Persons*. Edinburgh: T&T Clark, 1996; reissued in Cornerstones Series with an Introduction by Paul D. Molnar, 2016.

Torrance, Thomas F. *The Christian Frame of Mind: Reason, Order, and Openness in Theology and Natural Science*. Colorado Springs: Helmers & Howard, 1989.

Torrance, Thomas F. *Christian Theology and Scientific Culture*. Comprising the Theological Lectures at The Queen's University, Belfast for 1980. Eugene, OR: Wipf and Stock, 1998.

Torrance, Thomas F. *Divine and Contingent Order*. Edinburgh: T&T Clark, 1998.

Torrance, Thomas F. *Divine Meaning: Studies in Patristic Hermeneutics*. Edinburgh: T&T Clark, 1995.

Torrance, Thomas F. *The Doctrine of Jesus Christ*. Eugene, Oregon: Wipf and Stock, 2002.

Torrance, Thomas F. "Faith and Philosophy," *Hibbert Journal* xlvii (3) (October, 1948–July, 1949): 237–46.

Torrance, Thomas F. *God and Rationality*. London: Oxford University Press, 1971; reissued Edinburgh: T& TClark, 1997.

Torrance, Thomas F. *The Ground and Grammar of Theology*. Charlottesville: University Press of Virginia, 1980.

Torrance, Thomas F. *The Hermeneutics of John Calvin*. Edinburgh: Scottish Academic Press, 1988.

Torrance, Thomas F. *Incarnation: The Person and Life of Christ*. Edited by Robert T. Walker. Milton Keynes, UK: IVP Academic, 2008.

Torrance, Thomas F. *Karl Barth, Biblical and Evangelical Theologian*. Edinburgh: T&T Clark, 1990.

Torrance, Thomas F. *Kingdom and Church: A Study in the Theology of the Reformation*. Eugene, OR: Wipf & Stock, 1996.

Torrance, Thomas F. *The Mediation of Christ*. Colorado Springs: Helmers & Howard, 1992.

Torrance, Thomas F. *The Ministry of Women*. Edinburgh: Handsel Press, 1992.

Select Bibliography

Torrance, Thomas F. "Predestination in Christ," *Evangelical Quarterly*, 13 (1941), 108–44.

Torrance, Thomas F. *Preaching Christ Today: The Gospel and Scientific Thinking*. Grand Rapids, MI: Eerdmans, 1994.

Torrance, Thomas F. *Reality and Evangelical Theology*. Philadelphia: Westminster Press, 1982.

Torrance, Thomas F. *Reality and Scientific Theology*. Eugene, OR: Wipf and Stock, 2001.

Torrance, Thomas F. *The School of Faith: The Catechisms of the Reformed Church*. Translated and edited with an introduction by Thomas F. Torrance. Eugene, OR: Wipf and Stock, 1996.

Torrance, Thomas F. *Scottish Theology: From John Knox to John McLeod Campbell*. Edinburgh: T&T Clark, 1996.

Torrance, Thomas F. *Space, Time and Incarnation*. London: Oxford University Press, 1969; reissued Edinburgh: T&T Clark, 1997.

Torrance, Thomas F. *Space, Time and Resurrection*. Edinburgh: T&T Clark, 1998; reissued in Cornerstones Series with an Introduction by Paul D. Molnar, 2019.

Torrance, Thomas F. *Theology in Reconciliation: Essays towards Evangelical and Catholic Unity in East and West*. London: Geoffrey Chapman, 1975.

Torrance, Thomas F. *Theology in Reconstruction*. London: SCM Press, 1965.

Torrance, Thomas F. *Theological Science*. Oxford: Oxford University Press, 1978.

Torrance, Thomas F. *Transformation and Convergence in the Frame of Knowledge: Explorations in the Interrelations of Scientific and Theological Enterprise*. Grand Rapids, MI: Eerdmans, 1984.

Torrance, Thomas F. *The Trinitarian Faith: The Evangelical Theology of the Ancient Catholic Church*. Edinburgh: T&T Clark, 1988; reissued in a Second Edition in the Cornerstone Series with a New Critical Introduction by Myk Habets, 2016.

Torrance, Thomas F. *Trinitarian Perspectives: Toward Doctrinal Agreement*. Edinburgh: T&T Clark, 1994.

Torrance, Thomas F. "Truth and Authority: Theses on Truth," *Irish Theological Quarterly* 39 (3) (September 1972): 215–42.

Torrance, Thomas F. "Universalism or Election?," *Scottish Journal of Theology* 2 (1949): 310–18.

Webster, John. "Theological Theology," in *Confessing God: Essays in Christian Dogmatics II* (London: T&T Clark, 2005), 11–32.

NAME INDEX

Name Index

Lewis, Alan E. 20–6, 28–9, 52
Lombard, Peter 318
Long, D. Stephen 57, 60
Luther, Martin 239, 276, 290, 327, 332

Maimonides 332
Marcellus of Ancyra 20
Marshall, Bruce D. 57–9
McCormack, Bruce L. 4, 6–7, 9–11, 17–18, 30,
    33, 36, 44
McFague, Sallie 85–7, 215, 220–22, 224–6, 236, 238,
    241–3, 248, 252, 255, 310
McGrath, Alister E. 110–14, 116, 120, 124
McLeod Campbell, John 280
Migliore, Daniel 97
Molnar, Paul D. 3, 6, 14, 19, 29, 40, 55, 57–8, 83, 95,
    118, 171, 177, 196, 217, 332
Moltmann, Jürgen 15–18, 20, 22, 26–9, 35–7, 39,
    47–9, 52–3, 55, 63, 67, 110, 161, 263–4, 282
Montcheuil, Yves de 179

Nazianzen, Gregory 213, 246, 250
Nyssen (Nyssa), Gregory 41, 291

Origen 1, 4, 10, 217–18, 237, 246, 254, 263

Pârvan, Alexandra 10
Plantinga, Alvin 271
Przywara, Erich 7–8

Radford Ruether, Rosemary 168, 184–6, 188, 190,
    195, 233
Rahner, Karl viii, ix, 16, 19, 57–9, 67–70, 72–80,
    83, 89–90, 97, 106, 127, 129–37, 139–53, 158–9,
    169–73, 179, 181–2, 228, 256, 316
Ratzinger, Joseph Cardinal 57–9

Rilke, Rainer Maria, 41–2
Ritschl, Albrecht 155
Robinson, Dominic 57
Robinson, John A. T. 264–6, 268–9, 272, 288
Rosario Rodríguez, Rubén xiii, 141, 161, 164, 169,
    174–7, 179, 182–4, 193–5, 197–9, 207–8
Rosenzweig, Franz 29

Schillebeeckx, Edward 148
Schleiermacher, Friedrich 162
Schwöbel, Christoph 305, 326–8, 330, 332, 335
Shah-Kazemi, Reza 305, 312–19, 330–1, 335
Silesius, Angelus 14, 34, 41–3, 48
Sobrino, Jon 186
Stump, Eleanor 271

Teilhard de Chardin, Pierre 173
Tillich, Paul ix, 17, 161–2, 164, 182, 196–7, 205,
    212, 229
Torrance, Thomas F. viii, ix, xi, xiii, 1, 6, 14, 23–5,
    27–9, 31, 33–4, 37, 41, 53–5, 61, 92–3, 95–125,
    127–58, 162, 164–5, 167–8, 178–80, 185–6,
    188–9, 191–3, 195, 197, 199–200, 209–21, 224–31,
    233–41, 243–4, 246–56, 259–60, 263–302, 305–8,
    316, 323, 333–4
Tracy, David 32, 164, 194

Vorgrimler, Herbert 11

Webster, John B. 4, 127
Weinel, Heinrich 155
Williams, Rowan 314
Wobbermin, Georg 7
Winckler, Robert 7

Young, Amos 176

SUBJECT INDEX

Subject Index

Eternal Cosmos 1

cross vii, 20, 23, 26–30, 32, 35–7, 43, 84, 96, 98, 101, 103, 107–8, 115, 118, 120, 124, 132, 136, 154–6, 158, 162, 167–8, 172, 177, 179, 182–3, 189, 222, 248, 257–60, 267, 269–72, 276–7, 279–81, 283, 285–7, 289, 291, 294, 296–7, 299–300, 302–4, 307, 311, 319, 334

deity 6, 23, 25, 27, 42, 88, 90, 98, 155, 171, 173, 179, 204, 210, 263, 269, 293–4, 335
    dependent deity 6, 25, 42
determinism 2, 266, 273–5, 288–90, 294, 301–2
Deus pro nobis (God for us) 8
dialectical identity 19, 63
dialectic of freedom and necessity vii, 30–3, 36, 39, 46, 48–50, 54
divine
    causation 42, 55
    freedom vii, xi, 2–3, 6–10, 12–17, 19, 22, 26–7, 29–33, 35–6, 39–44, 47–51, 53–5, 63, 74, 89, 93, 98, 138, 179–80, 192, 202, 217–18, 236, 243, 250, 253, 255, 270, 273–4, 282, 286, 291, 294, 302–3
    impassibility (impassible) viii, 10, 23–4, 27, 39
    incomprehensibility 13, 314
    name (naming) xi, 13, 49, 66–7, 69, 72, 80, 89–90, 93, 98, 133, 146–7, 228–9, 231–7, 241, 243, 246–7, 250, 253, 255–8, 272, 294, 321, 329
    passibility (passible) viii, 10, 23–5, 27, 39
    self-sufficiency 13, 20, 26, 47, 124, 144, 237
    subject 14, 22, 33, 38, 42–4, 50, 74, 129, 133
    wrath 276–7, 279, 284, 299, 322
divinization 41
dogmatics 119, 311, 331
dualism 21, 76, 119, 284

Easter Saturday 28
election 4, 6–7, 9–10, 14, 22, 30, 33, 39, 40, 44, 48, 53–4, 74, 107, 129, 193, 200, 209, 265–7, 269, 272–4, 281–2, 285, 288, 291, 293–4, 301–2, 310, 333
emanationism (emanationist, emanation) 12, 47–8, 92, 222, 237
Emmanuel (God with us) 35, 65
eschatological 140, 233, 265–6, 268, 272, 282, 285, 287, 291
eschatological reserve 265–6, 268, 282, 285, 287
Eschatology 266, 272, 305
eternity vii–viii, x, 4–5, 10, 13–14, 16, 18–22, 33, 42, 44, 48, 52–3, 55, 63–5, 67, 76, 89, 117, 137, 139, 162–3, 183, 192, 202, 204, 216, 234, 254, 268, 294, 300, 315
Eucharist 54, 208
event 4, 10, 28–9, 34, 46, 57, 69, 74, 89, 97, 123, 150, 155, 170, 174, 176, 183, 199, 203, 206, 215, 222, 224, 233, 268, 272, 274, 278, 320, 331, 333, 335
extrinsicism 57, 67, 77

faith viii–xii, 39, 52, 59–61, 68, 70–1, 73–84, 87, 89, 91, 93, 95–100, 103–5, 107–9, 111, 113–15, 117–19, 121–5, 127, 129–30, 132–5, 137, 139, 141, 144, 146–7, 150, 152–4, 156–9, 162–70, 173–89, 194–208, 210–13, 216, 221, 224–5, 229–31, 233–8, 240–1, 252, 255, 257, 259–61, 264–5, 271–2, 287–9, 293–300, 303, 305, 307, 309–10, 312–14, 316–23, 325–31, 334–6
Father (God as Father) vii, ix–xii, 1–6, 8–14, 16, 18–22, 27–9, 31–3, 35–6, 38–43, 49, 51–5, 60–2, 65–7, 77–80, 82–4, 86–94, 96, 98, 101, 103–4, 106–7, 112–13, 115–18, 121, 124, 127, 129–30, 132–3, 136, 139–42, 146–7, 150, 152–3, 155, 162–3, 167–8, 176–80, 183, 184, 188, 190, 194, 197, 199–200, 202, 204–6, 208–53, 255, 257–61, 266, 268–9, 271–2, 274–5, 280, 284–5, 287, 292, 294–7, 299–300, 303, 306, 311–20, 323, 328–30, 332, 335–6
fellowship 13–14, 16, 20, 31, 33, 54, 64, 84, 138, 164, 218, 221, 226, 256, 260, 321
feminism (feminist) 59, 94, 242–3, 252, 257
freedom vii, x–xi, 1–5, 8–15, 17–18, 20–3, 25–7, 29–37, 39, 41–6, 48–55, 61, 63–5, 74–5, 77–84, 89, 92–4, 98, 104–5, 112, 131–2, 136, 143, 145, 148, 151–2, 162–4, 167–8, 171, 175, 177, 179–81, 185–6, 189, 194, 196, 201–4, 207, 217–18, 222, 231, 236, 238, 241–4, 253, 255, 259, 261, 263–4, 270–1, 273–6, 278, 287–91, 293, 297–303, 319, 321, 328, 337
fundamental theological anthropology 151

gender and language for God x–xi, 66–7, 89, 214, 220–1, 226–8, 233, 235, 241, 253
geometry *see* analogy
Gnosticism (gnostic) 12–13, 89, 173
Godself 243, 253
gospel xi, 71, 80–2, 98, 111, 118, 128, 133, 141, 144, 146, 165, 173–6, 180–1, 183, 189, 193, 210–11, 213, 222, 259, 264–6, 280, 283, 285–6, 291, 299, 306
    legalizing of the gospel 144
grace vii, viii–xii, 2, 5–11, 13, 21–2, 25–6, 28–31, 34–7, 39, 44, 47, 52–5, 59–60, 68–74, 76–9, 84–7, 89, 91–3, 95–109, 111–15, 117–25, 129–30, 132–3, 135–40, 143–53, 158–9, 163–8, 171–3, 175–7, 179–82, 189–91, 193, 195, 199, 200–9, 211, 216, 218–19, 221, 225–6, 230–1, 233–4, 236–8, 240–4, 246–7, 252, 256–60, 264–6, 270, 274, 277–8, 280–2, 286–90, 292–4, 296, 298–9, 302–3, 308–10, 312, 317, 321, 324–5, 328–9, 330–7

Subject Index

liberating work 22, 78, 142, 161, 166–8, 178, 184–5, 188, 194, 208

liberalism 7

literal knowledge of God 62, 66–7, 70, 89, 92–3, 173, 183, 187, 230–2, 236, 243

living Lord 23, 38, 73, 78, 101, 153, 163, 187, 190, 285, 290

Logos 3, 51, 76, 82, 102, 110, 146, 159, 233, 267

logos asarkos 8–9

lordship 5, 20, 26, 64, 74, 172–4, 268, 335

love of God/love of neighbor x–xii, 86, 136, 140–6, 148, 163–4, 166, 168, 171, 174–5, 181–2, 184–6, 191, 193, 197, 207, 264, 287, 298–9, 312, 314, 320–1, 331–2, 335, 337

luminosity 69, 77

matrix 86, 110, 222, 229, 257

Messiah 74, 183, 197, 213, 311, 333, 336

metaphor 65–7, 85, 87–8, 92–3, 241, 243, 252–3, 255, 257, 295, 298

metaphorical 158, 221, 241, 252, 295

metaphysical 97, 132, 190, 270, 276, 287, 301, 312–13, 315

miracle 2, 46–7, 49, 51, 86, 105, 121, 123–4, 319, 330

modalism *see* Trinity

mode of being *see* Trinity

models of God 85, 220, 222–3, 226, 236

modernism 63

monotheism xii, 178, 183, 305, 311–12, 314, 317, 319–20, 323, 329–31, 333–7

Mother (God as Mother) 85–6, 90, 93, 215, 217–23, 225, 238, 243, 248, 251–2, 255, 261

Muslim/Muslims xi–xii, 204–7, 305–6, 312–23, 325, 327–33, 335–7

mutual conditioning 19, 33–4, 38, 42, 45, 47, 50, 55, 72, 137–8, 142, 218, 243

mystery 2, 4–5, 27, 66–9, 75, 77–80, 83, 86–7, 89–91, 110, 124, 132, 134, 139, 145–6, 158, 171, 182–3, 208, 220, 228–9, 231–2, 237, 239, 241, 245–6, 252–9, 272, 285

mystical/mysticism 91, 196, 312–13

myth/mythical 158, 237

mythology/mythologizing/mythological 130, 200, 215, 219–20, 227–8, 235–6, 248, 267–8, 294

nameless 50–2, 88–9, 93–4, 99–100, 102, 105, 110, 116, 149, 156, 186, 193, 256–7, 261

natural theology/ "new" natural theology viii, xi, xiii, 59, 61–2, 69, 72–3, 77, 79, 81–3, 85–6, 95–103, 105–21, 123–5, 131, 133, 144, 151, 159, 184, 237, 264, 273, 287, 301, 303, 316, 319, 336

nature viii, 7, 10, 12, 14–16, 18–20, 22–3, 27–8, 30, 35, 38–40, 44–7, 49, 52–4, 57–61, 65–6, 69–70, 72–3, 79–81, 84–5, 87–8, 92, 95, 97–100, 102–5, 107, 109–13, 115–16, 118–23, 125, 128–30, 133, 135, 137–8, 143–4, 146, 148–50, 153, 157–8, 163, 168, 171–2, 179, 182, 185, 187, 189, 192, 204–5, 211, 214–15, 217, 219, 221, 223, 225, 227, 229, 232, 233, 236–7, 241, 243–4, 246–7, 249–50, 256–7, 259, 266, 270, 272, 276, 278, 285, 287, 291–2, 294–5, 297, 299, 302, 307, 311, 314, 317–18, 331

necessity vii, 2, 4, 8, 11–19, 25, 28–39, 41, 43–6, 48–55, 73–5, 138, 178–9, 191, 263, 269, 272–4, 282, 285, 288–90, 302

   factual necessity 48

   logical necessity 7, 53, 267–9, 287, 291, 300

   volitional necessity 14

neo-scholasticism 77

Nestorianism (Nestorian) viii, 266, 269–70, 280, 284

new creation 71, 96, 109, 123, 167, 170, 185, 191, 207, 219, 230, 260, 277, 287, 298, 303

Nicene Creed (faith) 67, 86, 97, 129, 159, 164, 166, 175, 191, 196–7, 205, 221–3, 228, 236, 238–42, 248, 253, 259, 261, 310, 313–14, 317

nineteenth-century theology 34

nominalism (nominalist) 49, 51, 129, 136

obedience ix, 5–6, 39, 74–5, 82, 93–4, 105, 107, 122, 124, 127, 134–5, 144–5, 155, 157, 163, 167, 174–5, 177, 180–1, 183, 189–90, 193, 196, 203, 229–31, 238, 241, 252, 260, 264, 274, 279, 283, 299, 321

obediential potency 69, 84, 146, 152–3, 155

omnicausality 10

omnipotence 10, 27, 36, 269, 273–4, 289

One Mediator 8, 24, 35, 65, 123, 140, 175, 190, 220, 242, 251, 277, 280, 282, 285

ontological (ontologically) 1, 8, 42, 75, 86, 110, 127–8, 135–6, 141, 147, 195, 210, 217, 220–1, 223–5, 231, 233, 248, 252, 258, 271, 282, 284–5, 298, 310

onto-relations 250

ontology 4, 10, 97, 133, 221, 242

orthodoxy 186–7, 191, 196, 263

orthopraxis 184, 186–7

ousia 20, 135, 246

Panentheism 16–17, 46, 52, 55, 63, 91, 222

Pantheism 38, 43, 52, 55, 63, 76, 91, 222, 236, 254

parousia 263

passibility/impassibility viii, 10, 23–5, 27, 39

Patripassianism viii, 269

Patriarchalism (patriarchy) x, 86, 93, 209, 217, 219–20, 226, 236, 242, 244, 256

Pelagianism (Pelagian) 134, 144, 146, 174, 184, 259, 264, 287, 289, 297

Subject Index

fallen humanity (nature) 112, 128 155, 173, 189, 233, 238, 259, 260–7, 274, 280, 289–90, 292, 307
    guilt 128, 154, 269, 276, 280, 282–3, 285, 293, 307
    original sin 128, 152–4, 156, 297–8
    radical evil 154, 156, 297
sonship 213–14, 252, 261, 293, 295
Sophia 35, 86, 88–90, 92–3, 228
Soteriology (soteriological) vii, 24 58, 74, 76, 107, 129, 265
soteriological suspension of ethics 278, 292, 299
sovereignty 50, 163, 175, 201, 219, 222, 236
subordinationism 5, 55
supernatural existential 69, 146, 148, 172
symbol (symbolic) 65–7, 80, 86, 93, 158, 217, 220, 225, 228–32, 235, 240–1, 247, 257–8, 260–1

term of transcendence 68, 146–7
theological anthropology *see* anthropology
theological theology 127, 130, 171, 185, 190, 195, 207, 255
thinking
    from a center in God 106, 115, 118, 162, 200, 210, 215, 218, 225, 228, 232, 234, 248, 253–4, 261, 294
    repentant thinking 118–19
    totalitarian 194–5
    trinitarian 3, 8, 10, 13–14, 30, 35–6, 38, 52, 68, 76, 78, 83, 87, 93–4, 101, 110, 112, 120, 158–9, 177, 196, 201, 203–6, 208–9, 212–14, 216–18, 220, 222, 237–9, 246–7, 250, 253–5, 286–7, 310–11, 318, 322–3, 329, 332, 334
time 4, 18–21, 25, 29, 39–40, 47, 63, 71, 82, 87, 89, 101, 103, 117, 127, 136–7, 149, 156, 166, 175, 218–19, 234, 239–40, 246–7, 249, 274–5
transcendental consciousness 69, 71–2, 76
transcendental experience ix, 58, 68–73, 144–5
transcendental revelation *see* revelation
transcendental method viii, 71, 130, 145, 150
Trinity
    coinherence 91, 249
    doctrine of appropriation 62
    economic Trinity 6, 10, 15–16, 19–21, 26, 32–3, 35–6, 41, 44, 52–5, 61, 64–5, 68, 76, 80, 200, 216, 218, 236–8, 247, 249, 253, 268
    generation of the Son vii, 1, 3–4, 6, 10–12, 30, 41, 54–5, 213, 220, 235, 254, 318
    immanent Trinity vii, 7, 9–10, 14–23, 26, 29, 32–3, 35–6, 44, 52–5, 61, 64–5, 68, 80, 85, 87–8, 209, 215–16, 218–19, 221, 224–5, 233, 236–8, 246–7, 250, 253–5, 268, 274–5, 294–5, 314, 329

modalism (modalist) 5, 88–9, 164, 204–5, 253, 315, 317, 319
mode of being 5, 8, 13, 45, 76, 129, 180, 217, 247
perichoresis 91, 217–18, 247, 249–54
procession (processions) 10, 17, 38, 41, 213
social doctrine 63, 83
trinitarian theology 30, 52, 94, 158, 177, 205, 209, 237, 247, 253–4, 332
tritheism 63, 334
triune God 2–4, 6, 9–10, 12, 14–15, 20, 30–1, 33–4, 36, 38, 40, 43–5, 47–8, 50, 57, 61–3, 75, 77, 79, 85, 87, 90, 93, 98, 101–2, 110, 114, 129, 132, 134, 144, 196, 200, 202, 204–6, 212, 216–18, 228–9, 236–7, 240–1, 246, 251–2, 271–2, 286–7, 311, 316, 319, 332, 334, 336
tritheism (tritheistic) 63, 76, 334
unitarian 177, 205, 243, 247, 252, 314, 318, 329
truth ix–xii, 13, 23, 27, 34, 39, 44, 60, 62, 64, 70–1, 73, 75, 79, 82–4, 87, 90, 93, 96–9, 102, 104–9, 112–13, 115–17, 123–4, 127–33, 135–7, 139, 141–2, 146–7, 150, 152–3, 157–8, 161–6, 168, 170–1, 173–7, 179–83, 187–8, 191, 194–200, 202–3, 206–9, 211–12, 214–15, 218–19, 221, 223, 225–6, 228, 231–2, 234, 239, 241–2, 244–6, 253, 255, 259, 268, 274, 279, 281, 283, 287–8, 292, 295–6, 299–301, 305–10, 310, 312–13, 315, 320–1, 323–33, 335–6

Universalism (universalist) v, vii, xi, xiii, 103, 192, 197, 204, 263–9, 271–3, 275–6, 281–2, 284–8, 290–1, 296, 301
Unoriginate 88–9, 98, 210, 246
unoriginate origin 246
unthematic experience ix, 143, 146, 150, 158

value-judgment 202, 204–5
Vatican I 58, 83–4
Vatican II 58, 60, 67, 84–5, 94, 326
vicarious humanity (human actions) 24, 27, 189, 193, 229, 230–1, 238, 252, 259–60, 272, 280, 284, 307
virgin birth *see* Christology
Vorgriff 132, 149–51

whither of transcendence (experience) 134, 139
Wisdom 22, 59, 88, 96, 316
world-process 49, 234
world-views 111, 116, 171, 180, 194
worship xi–xiii, 107, 110, 127, 140, 157, 200, 209, 227–8, 241–2, 249, 260, 279, 296, 305–6, 312–15, 322–4, 326–7, 333, 336

354